UNIVERSITY OF MINNESOTA
STUDIES IN ECONOMICS AND BUSINESS

Taxation in Minnesota

BY

ROY G. BLAKEY
Professor of Economics
University of Minnesota

AND

ASSOCIATES

NUMBER 4 NOVEMBER, 1932

THE UNIVERSITY OF MINNESOTA PRESS
MINNEAPOLIS

Second Printing, February, 1933

PRINTED IN THE U. S. A.

FOREWORD

Some years ago a group of scholars in the University of Minnesota in the fields of economics, sociology, history, geography, government, forestry, and farm management formed what they called the Northwest Regional Survey. They felt that problems of this region had a certain unity that permitted the study of the area as a distinct economic unit which had also other common factors due to racial, educational, and institutional backgrounds. It was a region that reached from Minnesota into eastern Montana and included North Dakota and much of South Dakota and even the northern counties of Iowa. It was roughly the area for which the metropolitan district of the Twin Cities was the commercial, financial, and transportation center. In another sense it was the spring wheat area. It was also a Federal Reserve Bank district.

Within this area the University of Minnesota was at the time in the front line in staff, resources, and library. That pre-eminence carried with it certain responsibilities for leadership in the study of the social and economic problems of the area. The challenge to apply dispassionate scholarship to constructive investigation of these problems stirred this University group to attempt cooperative studies.

An extended program was mapped out and a beginning was made. But with almost no funds it was a kind of Barmecide feast. The group looked with hungry eyes at the things to be done and then at the limited resources and free time available to do worthily those kinds of things that would be basic to enlightened programs of social action.

Nevertheless they began. Then, suddenly, what democracy has not yet learned to do for itself in the support of research on matters political and social was made possible by outside aid. A grant of moneys to support research in any way the University chose was made by the Rockefeller Foundation. A part of this fund was put at the disposal of the group mentioned above, now called the Social Science Council of the University of Minnesota.

In the program formed earlier certain problems such as taxation, land utilization, transportation, commodity distribution, and local government had stood out. They were both state and regional in their importance. Something along a number of these lines was set going at once through studies headed by members of our staff and supported by the grant from the Rockefeller Foundation.

Studies in distribution directed by Professor Vaile and Dean Stevenson have already reached the publication stage and several are published. Now comes this volume on the all-important and thorny subject of taxation. The council was fortunate in having among its members Professor Roy G. Blakey, who had already been called by other states to conduct studies of state taxation. With such leadership and the cooperation of a very considerable body of associated scholars, it was possible to complete this long overdue survey of the state's taxation system, if system be the proper word to apply to what is here described.

I speak for the Social Science Council of the University and I hope also for the intelligent citizens of the state in expressing appreciation to Professor Blakey and his associates for the labor and the time they have spent in the preparation and presentation of a complex public question.

We need more such work done if we are to have any sound basis for public policy. The riches of a new and undeveloped country have permitted our democracy to ignore facts in their relation to the future just about as long as is safe. If we are to dodge the day of reckoning it will be because we learn to look some unpleasant facts in the face and turn the dial so as to tune out the demagogue and tune in the scholar and the social statesman.

This volume on a controversial public matter was not written to please anybody except those who want to know what *is* as a basis for determining what ought to be. It was not prepared to promote anything but intelligence in dealing with a matter of great social significance. To those ends it is, I believe, a worthy contribution.

GUY STANTON FORD

University of Minnesota
November, 1932

PREFACE

A system of taxation that is equitable, that can be economically and effectively administered, and that promotes to the fullest extent the public welfare is not the product of a day but is built up through long years of intelligent, public-spirited, persevering effort. This survey does not, therefore, purport to offer a magic formula for a perfect tax system, nor does it point out a royal road to financial order and plenty. A good tax system can be secured and maintained in a democracy only when basic facts and principles are widely understood and appreciated. The aim of this study is to contribute toward such an understanding rather than to propose a complete and rigid schedule of taxes and then to urge its adoption without modification.

Scope and Methods

Minnesota tax problems are so numerous and complex that not all can be treated exhaustively within the means available for this study. It has seemed best, therefore, to devote available resources and energies to those phases of taxation and related problems that promise the greatest results for the time and effort expended. Taxes on real estate are very burdensome and of most general concern; hence most field investigations and a large part of the work of this survey have been devoted to such taxes. Consideration has been given to both agricultural and urban realty taxes, as well as to tax delinquency, cut-over lands, and forest taxation. Surveys have been made also of the taxation of iron mines, railroads, public utilities, banks, incomes, and other important subjects listed in the Table of Contents, but it has not been feasible to make the thorough accounting and engineering investigations that an exhaustive study of some of these would require.

In order to make economical use of available space, most of the chapters have been condensed from their original form, and it has been thought best to omit much pertinent material easily available in Professor M. B. Lambie's *Minnesota Yearbook,* in Professor William Anderson's forthcoming monograph on *Local Government and Finance,* and in various official reports. Some chapters for which room could not be found herein may be published later as separate monographs. A few extracts from some of these are included in the Appendix. Some very valuable data have been obtained from many unpublished official records and from numerous unpublished theses and other studies prepared at the University of Minnesota and other universities.

ACKNOWLEDGMENTS

The obligations for aid in preparing this survey are more numerous and substantial than can be stated here, particularly in view of the fact that the laborious work of nearly all the writers of the several chapters and of many of the assistants has been in addition to other heavy regular duties and without additional remuneration. Besides the chief obligations merely indicated in the staff roster following, there are substantial obligations to many consultants, advisers, and others not named there. Much aid has been received also from the criticisms and suggestions of outside and independent specialists, administrators, and professional and business men familiar with the respective subjects under consideration. Their criticisms and suggestions are much appreciated; all of them have been carefully weighed, but obviously not all of them can be incorporated.

The assistance of the United States Lake States Forest Experiment Station, the Minnesota Tax Commission, and other state and local officials of Minnesota — particularly auditors, clerks, and assessors — has been indispensable, as has been the information furnished by tax commissioners and other officials in practically every state in the Union.

We regret that we cannot mention personally all who have assisted and even more than we cannot express adequately our appreciation of the help of all, both named and unnamed. We cannot refrain, however, from mentioning the unusual amount and character of the aid given by Professors F. B. Garver, Henry Rottschaefer, R. S. Vaile, and Warren C. Waite, Deans G. S. Ford and R. A. Stevenson, Mr. H. B. Bacon, chief clerk of the Tax Commission, Mrs. Margaret S. Harding, managing editor of the University of Minnesota Press, and Miss Livia Appel, assistant editor, all of whom have given much greater assistance than would normally be inferred from the staff roster and the text.

ROY G. BLAKEY

University of Minnesota
November, 1932

MINNESOTA TAX SURVEY *

DIRECTOR

Roy G. Blakey, Professor of Economics, University of Minnesota

RESEARCH ASSOCIATES AND WRITERS

J. H. Allison, Forest Economist
Don S. Anderson, Agricultural Economist
Gladys C. Blakey, Research and Editorial Assistant
Arthur Borak, Economist
R. N. Cunningham, Forest Economist
Fred Engelhardt, Professor of Educational Administration
Bernard Frank, Forest Economist
Violet Johnson, Research Assistant
Walter R. Myers, Economist
C. H. Nelson, Engineer
George A. Pond, Agricultural Economist and Director, Agricultural Field Staff
Emerson P. Schmidt, Economist
Glen R. Treanor, Economist
Warren C. Waite, Agricultural Economist
Raphael Zon, Director, Lake States Forest Experiment Station

FIELD STAFF

W. L. Cavert
Joseph B. Day
W. T. Ferrier
D. W. Frear
H. F. Hollands
J. R. McFadyen
John McNamara
George A. Sallee
C. Z. Smith

RESEARCH ASSISTANTS

J. O. Burnett
James W. Copeland
Charles N. Graham
Harold Groven
Jeanne Hague
Kenneth Heggenhaugen
E. E. Hilpert
Clark R. Hopper
Robert Lynn
Stanley Manske
Carl L. Nelson
Oswald Nielsen
Daniel N. Rice
John Thurston

* With some exceptions, staff members and consultants are, or were at the time they assisted in this tax survey, members of the University of Minnesota faculty. Several of the field staff were graduate students of agricultural economics and most of the research assistants were graduate students of public finance.

EDITORIAL COMMITTEE

F. B. GARVER, Professor of Economics
R. A. STEVENSON, Dean, School of Business Administration
R. S. VAILE, Professor of Marketing

LEGAL ADVISER

HENRY ROTTSCHAEFER, Professor of Law

CONSULTANTS

WILLIAM ANDERSON, Chairman, Department of Political Science
W. R. APPLEBY, Dean, School of Mines
E. W. DAVIS, Superintendent, Mines Experiment Station
B. H. HIBBARD, Agricultural Economist, University of Wisconsin
O. B. JESNESS, Chief, Division of Agricultural Economics
E. M. LAMBERT, Professor of Mining Engineering
M. B. LAMBIE, Chief, Municipal Reference Bureau
C. K. LEITH, Geologist, University of Wisconsin
MINNESOTA TAX COMMISSION, Members and Staff
B. D. MUDGETT, Professor of Economics and Statistics
HENRY SCHMITZ, Chief, Division of Forestry
J. A. SCOTT, City Assessor, Duluth
WISCONSIN TAX COMMISSION, Members and Staff

TABLE OF CONTENTS

CHAPTER 1

THE TAX SITUATION IN MINNESOTA
A SUMMARY OF MAJOR PROBLEMS

GENERAL TRENDS

We are still living in the aftermath of the most destructive war the world has ever seen. During that war prices, taxes, and debts vaulted to unprecedented heights. Though the increases were due largely to the inflationary methods that the belligerents adopted for financing the war, nevertheless the price revolution was worldwide and worked enormous changes in the economies of all peoples. The incomes and expenditures of private individuals and enterprises, as well as those of governments, were suddenly and violently shaken as if by an earthquake, and the world has been tossed from trough to crest and from crest to trough of the tidal waves ever since.

The most sudden and violent changes naturally came in the finances of the belligerent national governments. Indeed the requirements of our federal government were so overwhelming that it pressed the state and local governments to reduce expenditures, especially capital outlays, during the period of the war. This was possible in part and for a time by postponing construction of school buildings, highways, and public works generally and by holding down salaries of public officials despite rapidly mounting prices. But with the war over, state and local governments proceeded to make up their deficits in construction, though at enormously inflated prices.

Moreover, both public and private expenditures were encouraged in order to give employment to the demobilizing army at the high wages then prevailing. The automobile was coming into its own, and the movement for expensive improved highways took on new impetus. High-pressure sales and huge flotations of Liberty Bonds, plus the sense of accomplishment and success in big undertakings that the war occasioned, plus high levels of money incomes, all furnished the setting and the means for state and local governments to meet long-delayed requests for more public services, even at high costs and with much borrowing. In many cases this borrowing was on top of old debts and substantial issues of bonds for soldiers' bonuses.

As indicated above, the greatest increases in state and local taxes came immediately following the war, from 1918 to 1921. Since then there have been further substantial increases in most states, though in a few cases taxes have remained relatively stable during the last decade. They have nevertheless been burdensome to those receiving falling prices and reduced incomes. The present tax situation cannot be appreciated or solved without consideration of the war upheaval and its aftermath, including the violent price inflation and deflation, the booms and the depressions, and other important economic, political, and social factors involved.

TABLE 1.— GOVERNMENTAL EXPENDITURES AND OUTSTANDING DEBTS, 1913, 1924, AND 1930

(000,000 omitted)

UNIT	EXPENDITURES			DEBTS		
	1913	1924	1930	1913	1924	1930
Federal	$700	$4,100	$4,200	$1,000	$21,300	$16,200
State	400	1,400	2,300	300	1,100	1,800
Local	1,800	5,400	7,500	3,500	8,000	12,600
Total	$2,900	$10,900	$14,000	$4,800	$30,400	$30,600

At the conference of governors held in Richmond in the spring of 1932 President Hoover quoted the approximate figures given in Table 1 and made this comment: "Today the American works 61 days a year to support governmental activities. Continued progress on this road is the way to national impoverishment." [1] These figures would be startling if we had not already become so accustomed to talk of high taxes, mounting expenditures, enormous debts, and the even worse things accompanying the severest depression of the generation. But they are challenging in any case, indeed too portentous to be ignored by one who knows anything about public finance and the economies of states.

MINNESOTA STATE AND LOCAL TAXES

Bird's-eye views of changes in Minnesota taxes during the past two decades are given in Tables 2 and 3. It will be seen that the total increase has been 286.9 per cent in twenty years, though only

[1] *State Government,* August, 1932, p. 13.

24.2 per cent in the last decade. Per capita increases are appreciably less. Due allowances should be made for differences in purchasing power as well as for population changes, especially when making comparisons with 1921. County taxes have increased most during the two decades, though in the last decade state tax collections have gone far ahead. Recent state increases are due in

TABLE 2. — SUMMARY OF STATE AND LOCAL TAXES IN MINNESOTA BY GOVERNMENTAL UNITS, 1911, 1921, AND 1931 [a]

Unit	1911	1921	1931	Per Cent of Increase: 1921 over 1911	1931 over 1911	1931 over 1921
A. TOTAL TAXES						
State	$10,808,242 [b]	$24,562,688	$44,952,052	127.3	315.9	83.0
County	6,423,660	22,052,001	27,213,716	243.3	323.6	23.4
Local units [c]	10,942,402	38,054,803	41,412,126	247.8	278.5	8.8
School district	10,500,813	39,646,426	40,818,748	277.6	288.7	3.0
Total	$39,914,793 [b]	$124,315,918	$154,411,496 [d]			
Average				211.5	286.9	24.2
B. PER CAPITA TAXES						
State	$5.21	$10.29	$17.53	97.5	236.5	70.4
County	2.70	9.24	10.61	242.2	293.0	14.8
Local units [c]	5.27	15.94	16.15	202.5	206.5	1.3
School district	5.06	16.61	15.92	228.3	214.6	—4.2
Total	$19.23 [b]	$52.08	$60.22			
Average				170.8	213.2	15.6

[a] Compiled from data of the Minnesota Tax Commission. See also page 580.
[b] Some adjustments have been made here because of conflicting official reports.
[c] Includes city, village, and township levies.
[d] Includes a small amount of gross earnings taxes for which actual figures of distribution to each locality are not available.

large part to state collections of motor vehicle, gasoline, and mining occupation taxes, as well as to other revenues, part of which are turned over to local governments. Taxes on general property, money and credits, inheritances, and insurance and telephone companies show approximately average or larger increases, while those on railroads and telegraph companies and mortgages fall far below this average or show actual declines.

If to the $60.22 per capita for state and local purposes (Table 2) the federal per capita of $22.63 is added, the total is $82.85 for Minnesota citizens in 1931. Comparable figures for all states are

TABLE 3. — SUMMARY OF STATE AND LOCAL TAXES IN MINNESOTA, 1911, 1921, AND 1931 [a]

KIND OF TAX	TOTAL			PER CENT OF INCREASE		
	1911	1921	1931	1921 over 1911	1931 over 1911	1931 over 1921
General property [b]	$33,782,020	$106,742,432	$119,044,062	215.97	252.39	11.52
Money and credits	347,025	1,277,242	1,258,865	268.05	262.76	— 1.44
Mortgage registry	522,108	461,407	275,000[c]	—11.63	—47.33	—40.40
Grain (bushel tax)	34,431	67,663	80,066	96.52	132.54	18.33
Gross earnings:						
Railroad companies	3,933,310	7,300,568	4,838,353	85.61	23.01	—33.73
Telephone companies	155,708	471,590	867,500	202.87	457.13	83.95
Express companies	37,290	115,382	38,778	209.42	3.99	—66.39
Sleeping car companies	9,372	52,426	38,270	459.39	308.34	—27.00
Freight line companies	4,058	28,446	98,452	600.99	2,326.12	246.10
Trust companies	....	....	5,355	.....	.....	....
Inheritance	459,406	966,539	2,000,000[c]	110.39	335.34	106.92
Insurance	411,752	1,105,539	1,900,000[c]	168.50	361.44	71.86
Telegraph	125,222	35,887	42,400[c]	—71.34	—66.14	18.15
Vessel tonnage	19,572	28,571	27,000[c]	45.98	37.95	— 5.50
Fire marshal	18,904	46,113	55,000[c]	143.93	190.94	19.27
Motor vehicle	....	5,616,114	10,721,972	.....	.....	90.91
Gasoline	....	....	11,070,423	.....	.....	....
Liquor license	54,615	....	....	.....	.....	....
Occupation tax (mining)	....	....	1,400,000[c]	.....	.....	....
Royalty tax (iron ore)	....	....	650,000[c]	.....	.....	....
All taxes	$39,914,793	$124,315,918	$154,411,496	211.45	286.85	24.21
Average				170.83	213.16	15.63
Per capita	$19.23	$52.08	$60.22			

[a] Compiled from data of the Minnesota Tax Commission. See also pages 576–582 for a brief description of the tax system in Minnesota and additional data.

[b] Exclusive of special assessments.

[c] Estimated by the Minnesota Tax Commission.

not available for 1931, but they may be had for 1930. In that year total per capita state and local taxes were $62.81 in Minnesota. Fourteen states had higher and 33 had lower per capitas. Minnesota's per capita was somewhat higher than the average for the two north-central groups of states but lower than the average for any other group except those in the South.

TABLE 4.—PER CAPITA AVERAGES FOR STATE AND LOCAL TAXES IN VARIOUS SECTIONS OF THE UNITED STATES AND IN FIVE NORTHWESTERN STATES, 1930

SECTION OF COUNTRY	PER CAPITA AVERAGE	MINNESOTA AND STATES ADJOINING	PER CAPITA AVERAGE
New England states	$64.16	Iowa	$57.48
Middle Atlantic states	74.80	Minnesota	62.81
South Atlantic states	43.67	North Dakota	52.00
East North Central states	59.94	South Dakota	75.27
West North Central states	56.91	Wisconsin	62.50
East South Central states	25.21		
West South Central states	37.53		
Mountain states	68.27		
Pacific states	68.07		

EXPENDITURES

Expenditure trends parallel tax trends approximately, of course, though they outrun taxes for two reasons: (1) revenues include fees, earnings, and other receipts besides taxes; (2) but these receipts plus taxes have been insufficient to keep up with expenditures, hence governments have resorted to more and more borrowing. These debts will be mentioned later.

Increases in state expenditures during the last two decades are shown in Tables 5 and 6. By far the greatest increase has been in expenditures for highways. Not only have new and special highway taxes yielded enormous sums but bonds have been floated in addition, so that highway disbursements for 1931 reached nearly $36,000,000. They have continued heavy in 1932 also. The next greatest percentage increase has been in expenditures for debt service, due largely to increases in highway bonds and even more to rural credit indebtedness, which exceeded $61,000,000 by the first of 1932. Increased expenditures for education, including state aid, have been very heavy in the aggregate but less than the average percentage of increase for all state expenditures. Of course allowances should be made in all cases for changes in population and purchasing power of money. (See pages 6 and 583–586.)

TABLE 5.—COMPARISON OF GOVERNMENTAL EXPENDITURES IN MINNESOTA IN 1911 AND 1930

ITEM	1911 [a]	1930 [b]	PER CENT OF INCREASE
General government	$1,046,323	$2,087,710	99.53
Protection of persons and property	663,993	2,310,138	247.92
Health and sanitation	206,952	891,289	330.67
Conservation of natural resources	550,059	1,614,002	193.42
Highways	31,001	16,478,024	53,052.35
Charities and corrections	3,353,352	5,799,104	72.93
Education (exclusive of aids)	2,492,280	10,600,519	325.33
Recreation	22,300	127,012	469.57
Miscellaneous	85,576	85,313	—0.31
Total governmental activities	$8,451,836	$39,993,111	373.19
Prison Revolving Fund (prison industries)	$1,105,893	....	......
Rural Credit Department	....	$4,031,026	......
Total state's direct services	$9,557,729	$44,024,138	360.61
Aids, subventions, grants, etc.	$3,107,875	$13,595,987	337.47
Debt and interest payments	1,153,521	10,773,229	833.94
Total state government costs	$13,819,126	$68,393,354	394.92

[a] Derived from the state auditor's report for 1911–1912.
[b] Derived from the auditor's report for 1929–1930 and the biennial budget of 1931–1932.

TABLE 6.—COMPARISON OF PER CAPITA GOVERNMENTAL EXPENDITURES IN MINNESOTA IN 1911 AND 1931 [a]

UNIT	1911	1931	PER CENT OF INCREASE
State government			
Direct services	$4.60	$17.17	273.26
Aids to local units	1.50	5.30	253.33
Debt and interest	.56	4.20	650
Total state expenditures	$6.66	$26.67	300.45
County government (maintenance only)	$2.33	$12.72 [b]	445.92
Municipalities (maintenance only)			
Under 500 }	$5.67 (Under 500 and 500–1,000)	$5.50 [b] }	16.75 (Under 500 and 500–1,000)
500–1,000 }		6.62 }	
1,000–2,500	7.26	7.00	— 3.58
2,500–5,000	4.69	8.75	86.57
5,000–10,000 }	7.06 (5,000–10,000 and 10,000–25,000)	13.50 }	62.89 (5,000–10,000 and 10,000–25,000)
10,000–25,000 }		11.50 }	
First class cities			
Duluth }	8.98 (Duluth, St. Paul and Minneapolis)	18.99	
St. Paul }		18.40	
Minneapolis }		21.18	
Township (per capita levy)	2.86	7.79	172.38
School district	7.37	21.30	189.01

[a] Data for state government derived from the state auditor's reports; for county government from analysis of audits made by the public examiner; for municipalities from a questionnaire. The data are not complete. See pages 583–600.
[b] The county figures are mostly for 1930, a few for 1929; for municipalities, for 1930.

Unfortunately, accounts of local expenditures are not kept uniformly or completely, nor are they reported regularly to any central agency. Therefore it is not possible to present complete and accurate comparisons of these expenditures over a long period. There are available, however, data for certain municipalities for 1911, and for 421 cities and villages of the state for 1930. Part of these data are summarized in Tables 6 and 7. It should be noted that the state expenditures discussed above include capital outlays, debt service, and aid to school districts and other local units, whereas the figures for municipalities include current costs only.

TABLE 7. — COMPARISON OF AVERAGE PER CAPITA COSTS OF MINNESOTA MUNICIPAL GOVERNMENTS, 1911 AND 1930 [a]

ITEM	CITIES OF 5,000–25,000		FIRST CLASS CITIES	
	1911	1930	1911	1930
Total current cost	$7.06	$19.19	$8.98	$19.22
General administration	1.93	2.96	.81	2.21
Police and fire protection	2.48	4.91	4.38	6.35
Health and sanitation (including sewers)	.55	1.92	1.34	1.48
Streets, sidewalks, and street lights	1.35	5.42	1.11	4.01
Charities	.15	.85	.40	1.33
Recreation	.08	1.87	.54	1.52

[a] The data are not complete. For fuller data see pages 595–600.

In 1911 per capita current costs for counties averaged $2.33 ($2.78 if debt service and improvements are included) as compared with $12.72 in 1929. Total county taxes levied for roads and bridges increased sevenfold in the twenty years from 1911 to 1931, per capita taxes sixfold.

The differences in costs for similar services between different municipalities and counties are as significant as the increases. They indicate where economies might be made; at any rate they raise questions of public policy and suggest more thorough investigation. Inasmuch as this is primarily a study of taxation rather than of expenditure, lack of space and funds have made it necessary to concentrate on taxes and to eliminate most of the expenditure data that were collected. Brief summaries of a few outstanding facts have been put in the Appendix, however. See pages 587–600.

PUBLIC DEBTS

The great increase in expenditures and taxes caused by increased debts has been mentioned above. The trend in indebtedness is

TABLE 8.—NET STATE AND LOCAL INDEBTEDNESS IN MINNESOTA, 1902–1931 [a]

UNIT	1902 [b]	1912 [b]	1922 [b] (000 omitted)	1927 [c]	1931 [c]	1931 Indebtedness: Per Cent of Total	1931 Indebtedness: Per Cent of Increase over 1912
County	$6,137	$14,013	$81,262	$92,573	$67,926	20.7	385
Township	19	7	4,445	4,307	3,497	1.1	49,857
City and village	28,466	46,461	103,834	112,365	97,961	29.9	111
School	4,307 [d]	8,537 [d]	59,759	72,695	75,547	23.0	785
Total local	38,929	69,018	249,300	281,940	244,931	74.7	255
State	1,755	1,345	20,308	54,320	82,971	25.3	6,069
Grand total	$40,684	$70,363	$269,608	$336,260	$327,902	100	366

[a] Compiled by Mr. Harold Groven. See also pages 601–606.
[b] *United States Census,* 1922.
[c] Reports of the Minnesota Tax Commission.
[d] The township and school figures are combined in the census report. In order to separate these the school figures as reported by the State Department of Education were used, although the figures are not entirely comparable because the Department of Education and the Bureau of the Census have different fiscal years.

TABLE 9.—PER CAPITA FEDERAL, STATE, AND LOCAL DEBTS IN MINNESOTA, 1931

LOCAL DEBTS		ALL DEBTS	
City and village	$38.01	State	$32.19
County	26.36	Local	95.05
Township	1.36		
School	29.32	State and local	$127.24
		Federal	135.41
Total	$95.05		
		Total	$262.65

shown in Table 8. As a result of rural credit and highway loans, unemployment relief, declining taxes, and federal and other deficits these debts have increased rapidly in 1932.

The sudden increases in indebtedness in all units of government immediately following the war were direct and indirect results of that conflict. As mentioned above, construction had been postponed while prices and wages had mounted skyward. The new construction was costly, but the demand for highways, schools, and other buildings was greater than ever. Public school and county debts increased enormously. Soldiers' bonus bonds swelled the state debt thirteenfold. From 1922 to 1931, however, county debts and city and village debts declined; the school debt increased

FIGURE 1.—TRENDS OF MINNESOTA TAXES AND INCOME[a]

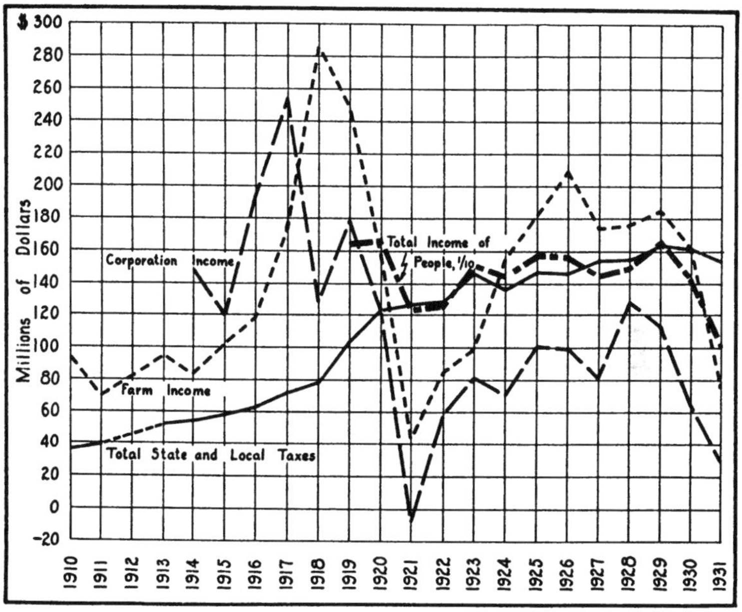

[a] Total state and local taxes are from the reports of the Minnesota Tax Commission. Total net farm cash income is estimated by Professor Warren C. Waite of the Division of Agricultural Economics, University of Minnesota. Corporation income is from the federal *Statistics of Income.* It includes net incomes of Minnesota corporations reporting such incomes, less deficits of Minnesota corporations reporting deficits. The amounts for 1914, 1915, 1930, and 1931 are rough estimates; exact data for these years are not available now. The "income of the people" is estimated by the Brookmire Economic Service, Special Report, June 7, 1932. This estimate is used partly because it is well known but chiefly because it covers a longer period than that of Professor Waite (pages 545 and 555). The curve in the chart represents one-tenth of the total estimated income of the people of Minnesota, rather than 100 per cent, because it would require a much larger diagram, or a diagram on a much smaller scale, to represent the total. It will be observed how closely state and local taxes approximated one-tenth of the estimated total income of the people for several years and how far different the situation becomes in a period of depression.

over 25 and the state debt over 300 per cent, the latter increase being due chiefly to rural credits, though partly to highway bonds. The state's indebtedness now exceeds the sum total of its trust funds. Its endowment for education has been more than counterbalanced by its borrowings.[2]

Income Trends

The unprecedented increases in expenditures and debts naturally resulted in increases in taxes. Whether taxes are burdensome or not depends largely upon their relation to incomes. Data regarding Minnesota incomes are far from complete, but Figure 1 shows the approximate trends of total state and local taxes and the incomes and estimated incomes of Minnesota farms and Minnesota corporations. It is in such depressions as those of the early twenties and thirties, when prices drop precipitously, that taxes become confiscatory and unbearable. Every individual and every enterprise has been seriously affected, but the weight upon real estate has been the most crushing and widespread. (See Figure 1.)

A SURVEY OF MINNESOTA TAXES[3]

Taxes on Real Estate

In order to get a more definite measure of the extent and severity of tax burdens on real estate a special survey has been made of several thousand farms and urban properties throughout the state. (See page 38.) Most of these data are for the year ending June 30, 1931, or December 31, 1930, though some later data have been obtained, and supplementary data have been secured for several series of years. Obviously this summary can cover only a few points and these without explanations, which must be sought for in the chapters treating the respective subjects if all are to be clear.

Farmers' Taxes

Real estate taxes took an average of 45.8 per cent of the net income of rented farm land and 34.5 per cent of the income of land operated by the owner. If the net income of the farmer operating his own land is thought of as consisting of the income that should be credited to land, plus the income that should be credited to equipment, plus the income that should be credited to his and his family's labor, then real estate taxes took an average of 10.4 per

[2] See pages 601–606 for a further analysis of debts and later data.
[3] For an outline of Minnesota's tax system see pages 576–580.

cent of the farmer's net income. Taxes on real estate averaged 1.52 per cent of the appraised value of owner-operated farms and 1.65 per cent of the value of rented farms.

Of the owner-operated farms 60 per cent were mortgaged for an average of 52 per cent of their appraised values; of rented farms, 39 per cent were mortgaged for an average of 63 per cent of their values. For mortgaged farms that were owner-operated it took 11.4 per cent of the farmer's net income, as defined above, to pay the taxes and 19 per cent to pay mortgage interest — 30.4 per cent for both; in the case of rented farms it took 45.5 per cent of net income to real estate to pay taxes and 99.3 per cent of such income to pay mortgage interest, or 144.8 per cent for both taxes and interest. (See page 97.)

Total taxes on township (rural) real estate increased rapidly in the decade prior to 1921, but in the last decade they have decreased somewhat. (See page 109.) From the figures given above it will be noted that interest on mortgage debt required twice as much as taxes in the case of mortgaged farms (to say nothing of payments on the principal of these debts and on the principal and interest of other debts). Moreover, it is obvious that the great deflation in prices is the major cause of farmers' difficulties. Entire

TABLE 10. — ASSESSED VALUES OF LAND AND IMPROVEMENTS IN PERCENTAGES OF APPRAISED VALUES

VALUE PER ACRE IN DOLLARS	PERCENTAGE OF APPRAISED VALUE				
	District I	District II	District III	District IV	District V
$5–$15	....	....	....	171.6	210.7
15– 25	225.0	....	219.3	142.9	156.8
25– 35	183.3	250.0	159.5	115.0	130.8
35– 45	156.5	193.3	135.8	104.1	119.4
45– 55	138.3	155.8	117.8	92.8	102.6
55– 65	133.4	138.4	104.3	76.5	
65– 75	135.8	122.8	100.0		
75– 85	116.8	114.2			84.0
85– 95	101.4	108.1			
95–105	96.5	98.6			
105–115	88.2			68.0	
115–125	83.8				
125–135	79.6		88.2		
135–145	73.3	99.2			
145–155					
155–165	72.0				
Over 165					
Average	106.27	129.25	125.93	105.71	130.88

exemption from taxes would not solve their difficulties. This does not mean, however, that farmers are not concerned about the reduction of their taxes.

Investigation shows that some of the tax difficulties of farmers are due to the very faulty assessment made by nearly 2,800 different local assessors. The general tendency since the great drop in prices is to over-assess farm and other real estate. In a period of rising prices the reverse is true. But assessments on different farmers in the same district, different districts, and different counties show wide and erratic disparities; some farmers pay two, three, four, and five times more in taxes in proportion to the actual value of their property than do others. This situation is fairly common. (See page 60.) Moreover, the tendency to greatly over-assess land of low value as compared with land of high value is characteristic of every section of the state. (See Table 10 and Figure 2.)

Cut-over Lands and Forests

The United States Lake States Forest Experiment Station cooperated in this tax survey by conducting a special study of tax delinquency in the sixteen northeastern counties of Minnesota. It was found that on January 1, 1931, 44 per cent of the total taxable area in this region was tax delinquent. Unpaid taxes in January, 1932, amounted to $21,874,033, as compared with $22,829,111 for the other seventy-one counties of the state. Assessments in these sixteen counties tended to be very unequal and very much higher for cut-over than for other land. Present indications are that the state will be in the possession of about 8,500,000 acres in this region by 1936. Taxes would not be very heavy if the land were accurately valued by assessors and if rates were similar to those in the wealthier areas. But many of these cut-over areas have insufficient wealth and income to support the roads, schools, local governments, and debts that load them down. Proper assessments cannot be secured under the Minnesota system of local assessors, and the present law for the taxation of forests, partly on a yield basis, has so far proved unworkable. (See page 164.)

Taxes on Urban Real Estate

The data for urban real estate practically repeat the story of erratic assessments and high taxes told by the agricultural data, though the two sets of data are not wholly comparable. For example, the most striking facts with reference to inequalities in farm

FIGURE 2. — RELATIONSHIP OF ASSESSMENTS TO SALES VALUES IN THE SEVERAL DISTRICTS

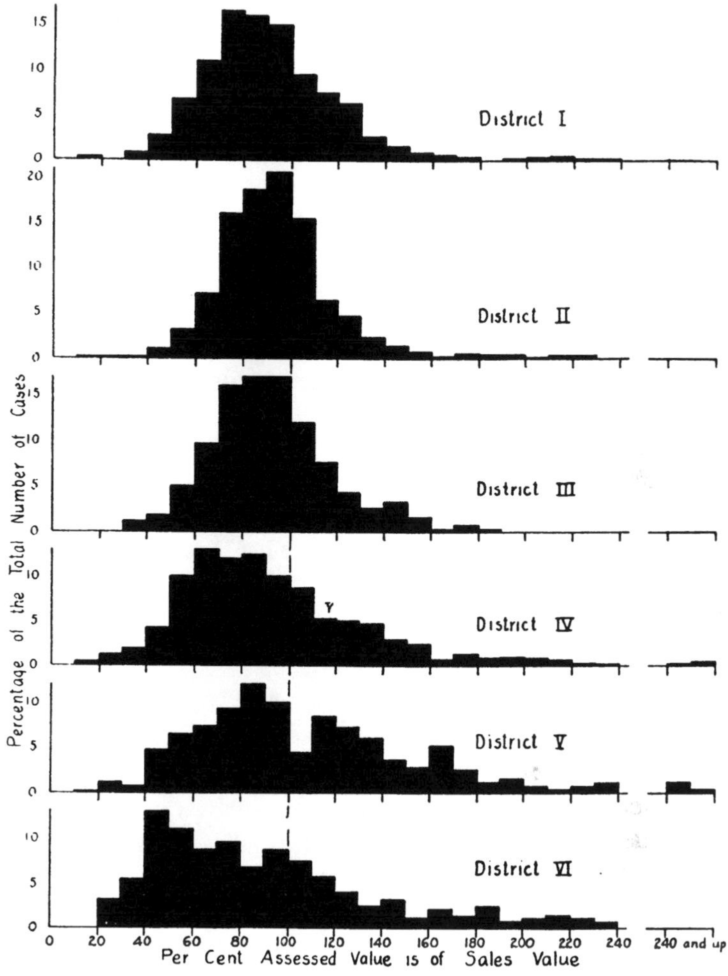

The inequality of assessments in the several districts of the state (see the map on page 38) is shown graphically in this chart, which is based on Table 4 on page 44. Consider the diagram for District VI at the bottom of the chart. The first black bar represents 13 farms (3.2 per cent of the total number of farms examined in this district) which were assessed at between 20 and 30 per cent of sales prices. The second bar represents 22 farms (5.5 per cent of the total) which were assessed between 30 and 40 per cent of sales prices. The third bar represents 53 farms (13.2 per cent of the total) which were assessed between 40 and 50 per cent of sales prices; and so on.

District II shows the most uniform assessments and also assessments nearest the full value required by law. This is indicated by the way the diagram for this district forms a peak with a narrow base nearly centered over 100 per cent at the base. District VI shows the least uniform valuations and most of those much below 100 per cent. A perfect assessment would be represented by one long bar equal to the sum of all the short bars in any one diagram, centered over "100 per cent" at the base. That is, such a bar would represent 100 per cent of the farms (scale at the left) assessed at 100 per cent of full value (scale at the bottom). See the figures and explanations on pages 174 and 175.

land assessments were brought out in the comparisons made on an acreage basis. Similar comparisons are not practicable in the case of urban real estate.

In general, a somewhat smaller proportion of the urban real estate than of agricultural real estate examined was over-assessed, but the taxes took a somewhat larger proportion of net income and they formed a much larger percentage of average appraised value. Except for a few cities, however, assessments of urban real estate are very unequal within the particular municipality as well as between different municipalities. Only a few cities have well-qualified full-time assessors, though the need for such assessors is even greater in the cities than in the country because of the greater difficulties of assessing much urban property.

The proportion of total state and local property taxes paid by Minnesota urban real estate has increased, whereas the proportion paid by agricultural real estate has declined in the last decade. Urban real estate paid 51 per cent of such taxes in 1921 and 59 per cent in 1931; township real estate paid 34 per cent in 1921 and 29 per cent in 1931. (See pages 108 and 581.)

Personal Property

The assessment of personal property is apparently even more inefficient and inequitable than that of real estate. Investigation was made of a random sample of over 1,800 cases of household goods, nearly all of which were independently appraised at over $1,000 each and some of which ran to $10,000, $25,000, and even as high as $60,000 each. The assessors had entirely missed almost exactly half of the cases and those that were assessed showed most erratic valuations. (See page 220.)

In order to check the assessment of moneys and credits a study was made of the inventories of 805 estates of deceased persons; these cases are from eighteen counties of the state, though most of them are from the three largest cities. Of the total value of moneys and credits listed in these inventories for inheritance tax purposes, 34.78 per cent was legally subject to the tax on moneys and credits, but only 17.3 per cent of that taxable, or 6.07 per cent of the total, was listed by the assessors.

Possible remedies for the deplorable situation with respect to assessment in Minnesota are discussed in Chapter 8. Some of these will be mentioned briefly below (page 24), and there will also be brief discussion of other methods of meeting the realty tax problem after other taxes have been discussed.

Iron Ore and Mining

The present system of taxing iron ore and mining in this state[4] does not promise well for the future development of one of the state's greatest natural resources. The Tax Commission's valuations of iron ore appear to be more accurate than the local assessors' valuations of most classes of property. Moreover, the iron industry is taxed more heavily than any other important industry in the state. This class of property, particularly the deeper mines, is difficult to evaluate with accuracy, however, not only because of the difficulty of ascertaining the quantity and quality of the ore but also because of the uncertainty surrounding future prices, interest rates, and other factors that determine current as well as future values of ore bodies. Moreover, the ad valorem system of taxation and the extraordinary expenditures of iron range municipalities (see page 600), threaten to hinder the most economical utilization of low-grade ores and even to check their development in the future after the richer ores are removed. The substitution of a graduated tonnage tax for the ad valorem tax on ores containing less than 35 or 40 per cent iron is suggested for consideration. (See page 268.)

Bank Taxation

The situation with respect to bank taxation in Minnesota has been particularly acute for several years. Three legislatures have failed to solve the problems involved. The main difficulty is due on the one hand to the requirements of Section 5219 of the United States Revised Statutes, as interpreted by the United States Supreme Court in recent years, and on the other hand to our low rate taxation of moneys and credits. There are, of course, economic troubles at the bottom of these difficulties, but the immediate obstacle has been chiefly legal. A series of relatively recent court decisions and information regarding corporation incomes collected by the Minnesota Tax Commission indicate that national banks could be taxed legally and equitably, and perhaps most satisfactorily from the standpoint of revenue, by an excise tax measured by net income, if the pending amendment to the state constitution is approved. (See Chapter 10.) This would, however, probably necessitate a rather radical revamping of the system of taxing cor-

[4] See pages 235, 576–580.

porations with which national banks are to be compared and would encounter a good many difficulties. There are several other possible remedies for the present situation but none that appears both satisfactory and practicable within the near future. In fact, it seems probable that Minnesota and other states will be greatly hampered in applying equitable and adequate taxation to national banks and other financial corporations until Section 5219 is revised.

Railroad Taxes

In 1912 the gross earnings tax on railroads was changed from 4 to 5 per cent to make the levy on such property more nearly equivalent to that on general property. Despite the large increases in general property taxes since 1912, the gross earnings tax rate on railroads has remained the same. On the basis of available data it appears that to put railroads on a parity with other property in the state would require an increase of about 50 per cent. The situation of the railroads is, however, unusually problematical. The recent shrinkage in their capital values may never be recouped. A thorough study of their future is suggested, therefore, in order that a proper tax policy may be determined. (See Chapter 11.)

Public Utility Taxes

Minnesota has a very heterogeneous system of taxing public utilities. Some pay gross earnings taxes and some general property taxes; some are assessed by local assessors and others by the Tax Commission. Some of the revenues go to the state treasury and some to the local units of government. The definitions of real and personal property and the taxation of each are more or less arbitrary and unreasonable. The piecemeal local assessment of various parts of physical properties is often not in accord with best usage or with economic realities. Unit or system assessment by the Tax Commission of practically all these utilities subject to property taxes would make possible a great improvement over present practice. Centralization of assessment is needed especially in the case of electric and pipe line companies.

For some time the Tax Commission has recommended an increase in the tax rate applied to the gross earnings of telephone companies. An independent check indicates that it would require an increase from the present rate of 4 per cent to about 7.4 per cent to equalize tax burdens in normal times. In times of depression telephone business falls off, of course, but probably much less than most business. (See Chapter 12.)

Highway Finance

Minnesota has a higher percentage of surfaced roads than the average state but a smaller percentage of pavement than most states with which it is usually compared. Bond issues for highway construction have been smaller than in many other states, and special taxes on motor vehicles and gasoline are among the lowest in the United States. Present registration taxes, however, do not make proper adjustments between different cars for differences in damages to highways.

It would be entirely feasible to increase automobile taxes, especially those on gasoline, to replace both the state one-mill road levy and also a larger part of the local property taxes levied for roads and bridges. There is good reason for not increasing the rate of the gasoline tax, however, until a better system of allocation is worked out, and it does not appear wise to distribute state aid or the proceeds of gasoline taxes unless they are administered, or at least strictly supervised, by the State Highway Department. Extension of the state highway system is preferable to unsupervised distribution. The apparent fact that administrative and miscellaneous expenses for the local units are many times as large as those for the State Highway Department is significant in this connection. (See page 375.)

Public School Finance

Problems of school finance are most general and most serious in the common school districts of Minnesota. The decline of population and the depression of agriculture in many parts of the state, the shifts of population, industry, and wealth in other parts, and the establishment of schools in sparsely settled, poor areas that cannot adequately support a school have brought about a situation that is serious for the children and burdensome to the taxpayers.

Common school costs per pupil are lowest in those districts where the average daily attendance is about forty. They run much higher where the attendance is very small. In 1930 there were 740 districts with fewer than ten pupils enrolled and 150 that had from 10 to 19. There are also many grade and high schools that are too small to be run economically and efficiently.

Lake and Koochiching counties have made notable contributions to the state by demonstrating how to make great economies and at the same time improve schools. Other counties are considering similar plans; still other suggestions are offered in Chapter 14. The great differences in ability to support schools is one of the chief weaknesses of Minnesota's school district organization. While the Minnesota system of state aid to schools (see page 426), has many merits, it nevertheless discourages more economical and efficient arrangements in numerous cases. (See page 430.) Moreover, most local school officials appear to economize only in the matter of local levies and not in state aid. A plan that lessens local taxes by $10,000 is thought of as that much saved even though it involves $20,000 additional aid from the state.

Sales Taxes

In an effort to keep down property taxes numerous states have adopted sales taxes in recent years. West Virginia and Mississippi are the only ones having general sales taxes, but thirty states have sales taxes in one form or another, besides taxes on gasoline. These taxes seem to flourish best in the South. Sales taxes on articles of mass consumption yield the most revenue, but because they are generally shifted to consumers they are considered most inequitable. The objection is lessened somewhat where such taxes apply to luxuries only, though most sales taxes raise difficult problems of administration. Thirteen states have tobacco and cigarette taxes, the yields in five running from $1,000,000 to $2,000,000 and in Tennessee to $2,300,000 in 1930. It is estimated that a tax of one cent a package in Minnesota would have yielded $1,055,000 in 1929 and $850,000 in 1932. Estimates of yields of other possible sales taxes are given on page 567.

Inheritance Taxes

In the 1931 session the legislature of Minnesota adopted an estate tax to take full advantage of the credit permitted by the federal estate tax law. This was not expected to increase revenues by very much. A series of United States Supreme Court decisions beginning with Farmers Loan and Trust Co. v. Minnesota (1930, 280 U.S. 204) prohibiting the taxing of intangibles in the hands of nonresidents will reduce receipts appreciably, perhaps by $240,000 annually. (See pages 556–563.)

With respect to tax rates and exemptions Minnesota is in the middle rank of states. For example, in the case of a net estate of $50,000 going equally to a widow and one minor child, Minnesota ranks twenty-fourth. The tax here is $300, as compared with a range from $660 to $1,700 in the five states at the top and as compared with no tax in the five states at the bottom. In the case of a net estate of $1,000,000 divided equally between a widow and an adult child, Minnesota ranks nineteenth with a tax of $36,700, as compared with taxes from $63,750 to $72,660 in the five top states and from no tax to $29,400 in the five lowest states. (See page 563.)

INCOME TAXES

The number of states having income taxes has increased relatively rapidly during the last four years. Twenty-three[5] states now have such taxes, though some call them franchise or excise taxes measured by income. Moreover, several states that already had income taxes have revised them upward in the last year or two to give unemployment or other relief without adding unduly to property taxes or bond issues. The states in which income taxes are most successful are those that have provided a good centralized administration.

It is estimated that an income tax like the one introduced into the last session of the legislature would have raised about $5,700,000 in 1921 (a depression year), $9,200,000 in 1924 (a normal year), and $13,600,000 in 1929 (a boom year), assuming that the administration of it had been developed to the stage of efficiency it had reached in Wisconsin in those years. Wisconsin income tax provisions applied in this state would have raised about 50 per cent more than the above-named amounts.

In the present extreme depression, incomes are so greatly reduced that an income tax with reasonable rates and exemptions is likely to yield less than most of its advocates expect and much less than is needed to afford adequate relief to property taxpayers. If an income tax law is enacted the great danger is that both its friends and its enemies will so overload and complicate it that it will break down before there is time to develop efficient administrative machinery and experience. Greatest progress in the long run will be achieved by starting with moderate rates and exemptions and with simple provisions generally. Later the tax can be developed soundly as experience dictates. Under such a program

[5] See the footnote to Table 3, Chapter 15, on page 478.

the income tax offers great possibilities for correcting some of the worst inequities of the present tax system.

GENERAL CONSIDERATIONS

The worsening condition of Minnesota state and local finances has been indicated in the preceding pages. Instead of following the sound policy of paying off debts in times of prosperity our governments have gone in deeper and deeper. To make matters worse, it appears that private individuals and businesses have managed their finances fully as recklessly as these governments, and the bad management of each has reacted adversely upon the others. Now with precipitate drops in prices and incomes, taxpayers cannot meet their fixed charges and also make their accustomed private and public expenditures. Curtailment is absolutely necessary. The difficult immediate question is, where can curtailment be made with least harm to present and future welfare?

All expenditures, private and public, must come out of current income and previous accumulations thereof. Whether the necessary curtailment shall be divided equally between private and public expenditures depends largely upon which of three policies is followed. Probably a combination will prove more feasible than any one alone.

1. Government expenditures may be cut equally with private expenditures, proportionately to the fall in incomes, or they may be cut more or less. Whether they should be cut more or less depends upon the relative importance to society of the respective private and public services involved. The public need for more and better paved highways, nine-months school terms, parks, public nurses, and county agents is to be compared with the private need for more and better food, clothing, housing, radios, automobiles, and trips to Europe. Public economy or public welfare requires the retention of the most useful that can be afforded, but when resources are insufficient to satisfy all needs, the least essential must be eliminated in order that the most essential may be retained.

As is well known, it is often possible to reduce expenditures and at the same time retain or improve essential services by various economies of organization and in other ways. As mentioned earlier, this survey has dealt chiefly with taxes and has been able to investigate the expenditures of state and local departments to a limited extent only. One of the most pressing needs is a thorough investigation of the actual and necessary costs of different public services.

At present we have almost no satisfactory standards by which to measure the costs of different governmental departments. For example, in the cases of fifty-two Minnesota municipalities with populations of from 1,000 to 2,500 for which data were obtained the average current per capita expenditure for streets and sidewalks in 1930 was $3.20 and the median (middle) cost was $1.79, while the range was from 0 to $27.26. Now who can say how much each unit of pavement or maintenance should have cost and to what extent, if any, each of these cities failed to use efficient methods and get value paid for? Or to take another example, in nine municipalities with populations between 10,000 and 25,000, the average current per capita expenditure reported for police was $2.35, the median was $1.62, and the range was from $.79 to $7.55. (See page 598.) Similar disparities were found with respect to costs of other functions in these and other cities, as well as in county and township governments. These figures indicate that there are great possibilities for economies; everybody who is familiar with various governmental organizations is aware of this fact, but it takes specific investigations to show exactly what economies are wise. Indiscriminate horizontal slashes without investigation are certainly not truly economical. The chief difficulties are political. It will be unfortunate if the present economic stress does not result in substantial real economies.

Chapter 14 of this study is devoted largely to discussing possible economies in public school finance, and Chapter 13 makes some suggestions with reference to highway finance. In view of the amount of pavement and other improved roads already established and in view of the depression and the state of public finances, it seems well that the state highway program contemplates an early let-up in construction and expenditure. How far this reduction should be carried may depend somewhat upon plans for unemployment relief and other questions involved. To the extent that expenditures for highways can be afforded and are more productive of values than the same amount spent in any other way they are, of course, justifiable, but to the extent that they increase already unbearable tax burdens and cause the curtailment of services that are more valuable they are not justifiable. It appears doubtful if all the highway construction and maintenance of the present year is more vital to the people of the state than some other services that are threatened with curtailment or elimination.

As a matter of fact, a study made a few years ago estimated that the amounts spent privately in this state for passenger automobiles, outlays and upkeep, far exceeded the total state and local taxes for roads, schools, and all other purposes. One may admit the value of automobile services without admitting that they are so much more valuable than the services of all the schools, libraries, parks, firemen, policemen, and other officials of state and local governments.

The state budget commissioner is advocating other economies, among them proper accounting, central purchasing, possible consolidation of townships and other units, better organization of schools, elementary, secondary, and collegiate, the establishment of a sinking fund commission similar to that of West Virginia to assist the local units with respect to their debts, the reorganization of certain departments, and the curtailment or abolition of certain appropriations.[6] These few are cited as indicative of possibilities rather than as an exhaustive list of economies.

2. A second plan that governments may follow to meet the present emergency in cases where curtailment sufficient to balance the budget is not possible or not wise is to borrow more. For example, unemployment and poor relief must be given even at increased expense. There are limits below which it is unwise to reduce police, fire, school, and other services, even if borrowing is necessary to maintain them, though ordinary current expenditures should be met by current taxes except under extraordinary conditions. Unfortunately too much public borrowing in the past has curtailed the power to borrow now when funds are needed most. In general, most governments as well as individuals need no urging to borrow. The extent to which it is wise to go into debt for necessities in times like these depends upon future price levels and incomes and upon the relative needs of today and tomorrow. If price levels are to fall much lower and remain permanently at these low levels, it would be more disastrous for the future to borrow more now than if price trends are to pursue the opposite course. It requires a nice balancing of many considerations to determine the wise policy in each particular case, but the actual market for bonds puts very

[6] Jean W. Wittich, "An Equitable Program for Minnesota," *Minnesota Municipalities*, 17:246–49 (May, 1932).

definite limits to the practicability of further increases in public debts.

3. A third method of meeting the present financial situation, at least in part, is to improve the organization and administration of the tax system. It is with this method that this survey has been chiefly concerned. The other methods may be just as important, but means and space have required concentration upon this one, that is, upon taxation.

The difficulty of carrying a knapsack depends partly upon its weight but largely upon how it is adjusted to one's back. A thousand persons of all degrees of health and strength might not carry a large aggregate weight of stone if an equal number of pounds were put upon the shoulders of each. An even smaller aggregate could be carried if the weakest were given the heaviest loads and the strongest the smallest loads. The group could carry the maximum aggregate and with the least difficulty if the load of each was adjusted to his ability. So it is with taxes. When it is decided what private and public needs are most important and how much of the total income should be allotted to each, then it is necessary to decide how the part allotted for government services shall be distributed among the different beneficiaries of these services. In general it should be done in the way that is the most equitable and at the same time permits the maximum of services. Many adjustments and compromises are necessary to achieve the best practical results. The general principles that should be followed are discussed in the next and succeeding chapters.

In these chapters the attempt is made to indicate where tax burdens are heaviest, and in the cases of owners of real estate and some other taxpayers some indication has been given of the relation of taxes to incomes and values of property. It has been suggested how property taxes could be lightened by supporting more of the highways by special highway taxes and by making use of income, inheritance, sales, and other taxes to the extent necessary. Take, for example, sales taxes, some of which are the most objectionable of those mentioned. If it is necessary to resort to sales taxes, the least objectionable should be chosen first, and the most objectionable ones discarded or used only as a last resort. Whether these or increased inheritance taxes or other taxes should be used at all should depend upon the balancing of alternatives. Objectionable though sales taxes may be, failure to provide poor relief may be worse; if all better tax and other resources have been exhausted, it may be more justifiable to levy the hated sales taxes than to permit people to starve. This principle applies, of course, to the levying of other taxes also. Great care and social wisdom should be exercised, however, in the application of all these principles. Inasmuch as social prejudices and ignorance play as much part in decisions as social wisdom, it is much easier to lay down principles than to put them into practice.

The greatest possibilities of improvement lie in the field of administration, particularly in the field of assessment. Property taxes are more important than all others combined. They are based upon assessments, many of which are difficult to make with accuracy. Equality between taxpayers and between districts rests upon uniform assessments, yet the greatest inequalities exist. It is important to correct most of these inequalities or, better, to see that they are never made. If once made, ordinary equalization will remedy relatively few cases.

Without more funds, more supervisors, more guidance and instruction of assessors, and, most important of all, more sympathetic public opinion, it is impossible for the Tax Commission to get the results that might be obtained even with the 2,800 mostly unqualified assessors who now list property. In fact most assessing is little more than listing, the copying of the previous year's lists. All assessors should be experienced and many should have technical training along special lines, often along several lines. Districts should be large enough to afford specialists; indeed, districts should be large enough and financially able to maintain a well-qualified full-time chief assessor or supervisor who should have tenure as long as he is efficient. Petty politics and favoritism should be entirely eliminated. Minnesota taxes cannot be even reasonably satisfactory so long as the present system of assessment continues.

The desirability of unifying and otherwise improving the assessment of public utilities by putting all under the Tax Commission has already been suggested. As a matter of fact, the state tax department should have supervision of the administration of all taxes, particularly of all state taxes. It may be desirable to utilize the services of the attorney-general, the secretary of state, the public examiner, the oil inspector, the insurance commissioner, the fire marshal, and other officials and departments, but supervision of all administration of taxes should center in one department instead of being divided among several. The Tax Commission has made commendable use of mining and hydraulic engineers and of other technically qualified assistants. It would be economy in the long run to furnish the commission with sufficient funds for additional qualified assistants and supervisors. A number could be used to good advantage to assist local assessors with classes of property that are particularly difficult to assess. If an income tax is adopted the need for trained personnel will be greatly increased.

As mentioned in Chapter 2 (page 33), it is important that taxes and finances be planned so as to encourage agriculture, industry, and production generally and thereby increase the people's income, and consequently government income, as it is that budgets be balanced when resources are small. This study has attempted to make suggestions along this line, particularly with respect to taxes on farm lands, mines, forests, cut-over lands, and railroads. In fact, this has been the point of view throughout this survey. Further and special studies have been suggested in several cases; a special study of land utilization is already under way at the University of Minnesota, and the governor has appointed a special committee to go into the matter more exhaustively.

As was suggested in the beginning, Minnesota's tax troubles are not merely or chiefly of local origin, though they have been greatly affected by local management. They are in large part the result of world price fluctuations, money and credit policies, debt and reparation policies, tariff and other restrictive policies, and all the dislocations and evils that accompany and follow a destructive world war. When the delicate and complicated economic and political organizations of the world fail to articulate and hence fail to function, the finances of all, private and public, are thrown into confusion and the welfare of all is imperiled. The greatest possible relief for Minnesota taxpayers, indeed the greatest remedy for most of the world's financial ills, can be found only in restoring the world's economic mechanism to good running order. Only stopgap devices are possible until this is done. If this cannot be done, we shall be forced to exist permanently upon a much lower level than is desirable or than seems necessary.

While one state or section may not be able to solve the world's problems alone and though it may have to adjust its finances to conditions as they are until they can be bettered, it can take its part with others in refraining from the narrow sectional activities that are largely responsible for the present situation and it can, moreover, take positive steps in cooperation with others to restore industry and society to normal equilibrium and even to lift them to a level and a stability heretofore unknown. Only on such broad lines and with such an outlook can Minnesota finances be put upon a reasonably stable and permanently sound basis.

CHAPTER 2

WHAT CONSTITUTES A GOOD TAX SYSTEM

What are the requirements of a good tax system? What characteristics should it have? What things should it avoid? When are taxes too high? When are they too low? When does a state or other unit of government spend too much? When does its spend too little? What are the most serious defects in Minnesota's taxes? How may these defects be eliminated or remedied? It is to help answer such questions as these and particularly the last two that this survey has been undertaken. This brief chapter attempts to state or suggest some of the general principles upon which a good tax system must rest. Following chapters discuss in detail various important taxes that go to make up the system.

Many of us would be led astray much less frequently if we always kept in mind certain fundamental principles. Most of them are easily understood, yet we are prone to forget them and hence we often get off the track of sound public finance.

Taxation belongs to the two related fields of economics and public administration. Its watchwords are practicability and economy. Obviously, no tax, or system of taxes, however beautiful or equitable in theory, can meet the requirements of a workaday world unless it is practicable of administration. The essence of economy is the best utilization of available capacities and resources to the end that man's needs may be served as adequately as possible. Perhaps this idea of economy and its relation to taxation should be explained briefly.

The Essence of Economy

Throughout his entire life man devotes all his thoughts and efforts to satisfying his wants. Wants include mental and spiritual as well as material needs, of course. Because wants grow in number and extent and because capacities and resources are limited, man has never yet been able to satisfy more than a part of his wants. Inasmuch as they cannot all be satisfied, and inasmuch as they are of varying importance, economy consists in applying available resources to the satisfaction of different wants in proportion to their importance. This may mean that such primary needs as those for simple food and clothing may be met adequately but that many secondary needs must remain unsatisfied. For example, the desire for an airplane trip around the world may have to go unmet, or met only partially—by a railroad trip to New York, let us say, or by an auto ride to a near-by lake or town. It is true that man has made great advances in satisfying his wants by discovering and adapting to his uses hidden resources and powerful natural forces. His accomplishments have been due mostly to experience, education, discovery, and invention. We marvel at his inventions of tools and machines, at his discoveries in chemistry, electricity, and other fields.

Many of us overlook, however, that some of man's most productive and important discoveries or inventions are in the field of cooperation, or of organization and management. Henry Ford can take a hundred thousand men, certain amounts of steel, and other materials and machines, and with them turn out automobiles so efficiently and cheaply that almost everybody can afford one. By his superior organization and management, by his extraordinary development of the division of labor, he increases man's ability to utilize his capacities and resources and thus to satisfy more and more wants. Obviously, poor and ineffective organization of the same capacities and resources results in lower standards of living, less opportunity for ministering to the mental and spiritual as well as to the material needs of man.

We cannot overstress the importance of the organizations that men devise to bring about the most effective cooperation in satisfying their many and growing wants. Various groups of individuals everywhere and in all times have formed new organizations and revamped old ones to carry out certain purposes; those we now have are the results of thousands of years of experimentation in living together, in promoting what we call civilization.

These organizations are multitudinous, and they vary greatly in character and function. For example, we have many varieties of corporations, partnerships, families, tribes, churches, fraternities, clubs, schools, villages, cities, and states; all are forms of cooperative association and each is organized to meet certain needs better than they can be met in any other practicable way, better, at least, in the eyes of the organizers.

The central truth to which we have been leading is that a state or city or other unit of government is a form of cooperative organization and is justified in so far as it can help to satisfy legitimate human needs better than they can be satisfied in some other way. But such an organization is not justified if some other organization, private or public, can perform its services more economically and satisfactorily.

Under some conditions a certain service — water supply or light supply, let us say — can be furnished best by each individual or family; under other circumstances it can be supplied most satisfactorily by a private corporation; under still other conditions, municipal supply may be best. The transfer of a service from private to public hands or vice versa does not necessarily mean greater or smaller cost to consumers, but mainly a transfer of agencies and costs. The transfer should not be made unless it means better service or lower costs.

There are other services that might be furnished to individuals directly by themselves, or by private corporations, or by their governmental units, *if the people can afford them,* but not otherwise. To take an extreme illustration, we might name airplane service around the city, or the state, or the world. But no individual or government can afford to provide such service if the cost of it prevents the meeting of more essential needs. We have reached the economic stage where some can now afford it; in the future we may reach the stage where most people can. Probably at that time it should be furnished by private corporations, but if it were to be shown that it was in the public interest for the state or city to furnish it, we ought not let prejudice or tradition or vested interest prevent the transfer. Obviously, if the government takes on more functions it will require more revenues, but if it never takes on services that the people cannot afford or that it cannot perform as economically and as well as some other agency, then it will never spend too much nor levy taxes that are too high. On the other hand, the government may spend too little and collect too little revenue by taxation if it fails to perform for its citizens services that they can afford and that it can perform more economically and satisfactorily than anyone else.

How to Share Costs of Public Service

In these illustrations we have indicated fundamental principles governing sound expenditure, public and private; we have even suggested the proper scope of governmental activity and the dividing line between it and private enterprise. Obviously, the amount of public expenditure determines the amount of taxes needed, but it determines nothing about the proper distribution among individuals of the costs of these expenditures. It is this distribution of the costs of services that lies at the heart of most tax problems.

If everyone were served equally and at equal cost by the government, and particularly if everyone had equal ability to pay, the problems of taxation would be relatively simple. In such case the total expenditures could be divided by the population and all would pay poll taxes of equal amounts. Even then some might prefer installment payments rather than one lump sum each year; others might prefer to have their shares added to the prices of their tobacco, sugar, or gasoline. They might even be willing to pay three times as great a total in order to have the taxes come in the form of small sugar-coated pills.

In actual life, however, the distribution of taxes is not simple, largely because services received, costs of services, and abilities to pay are very unequal and also very difficult to measure. Furthermore, even if we could determine equitable quotas with accuracy, we would encounter many questions of practicability in the administration. Practicability and equity are two criteria that should never be lost sight of. With respect to equity it is generally held that taxes to pay costs of services should be allotted according to benefit received, or, if this is impractical, according to ability to pay. The promotion of the public welfare is the final test in all cases, though it is easier to state this principle than to apply it.

No service should be performed unless it is worth what it costs. This implies that it is worth these costs to somebody. What is more equitable than that the beneficiaries should pay for what they get? A general system of getting or giving something for nothing is contrary to all principles of economy and to most principles of human progress and advancement. It makes for extravagant rather than economical utilization of resources. It discourages rather than rewards intelligence and effort directed toward the increase of human satisfactions, for every time somebody gets something for nothing somebody else gives up something for nothing. Few things are more fundamental to economic progress than that beneficiaries should pay providers for the costs of benefits sought and received.

There are, however, situations in which it is more practicable, or more in accord with public welfare, to distribute costs on the basis of ability to pay rather than on the basis of special benefits received. For example, a democratic society cannot afford to have its children grow up in ignorance and crime merely because their parents are unable to pay for the benefits of proper training. A state or a nation cannot stand idly by and let forests be consumed by fire or rivers flood the land periodically merely because those at the sources of these catastrophes cannot pay adequately for the special benefits of preventive services. When the benefits are general rather than special and when they are impossible of practicable allocation, it may well be in the interest of the public to distribute the costs generally.

In such cases it may be best to adopt some criterion of ability to pay. Even here, however, benefit is assumed; the solidarity of interests of the people of the state or nation are taken for granted. The expenditure is justifiable only in case it does not exceed the value of benefits. Practically every taxpayer is supposed to get, directly or indirectly, benefits equivalent to what he pays, though many who pay nothing or little may get benefits for which they do not pay, or for which they pay less than the value of the benefits received.

Few, indeed, can truly claim that they pay more in taxes than the value of government services to them. Those who are most able to pay taxes are generally also most able to benefit from good government. Let them consider what would be the profits of their business, the value of their property, or the safety of their lives if there were no government, or let them consider how much it would cost them to obtain for themselves individually the services provided by government. Thus, even if taxes are distributed on some other basis than benefits, they cannot normally be said to exceed the value of benefits. In a good tax system both the criteria of benefit and of ability to pay are duly considered in the attempt to promote the public welfare. All government services cost somebody something. Those who fail to pay their share of costs according to some criterion are public parasites and should be so recognized.

We have seen that government is an organization to perform certain services. Taxes for its support and also the means for all private services and undertakings must come from the same general source, namely, out of the people's income. It is often asked, "What proportion of the total should be taken for government purposes?" All, and no more than, the people's cooperative agency, called the government, will use for them better than they will use it for themselves in other ways. In other words, taxes are too high only when they turn over to public servants funds that could be used to better advantage for other services or through other agencies. "Better" as used above must be defined in terms of long-time public welfare, rather than in terms of immediate advantage to any particular individual.

Some of the most serious practical problems of public as well as of private finance arise from the fact that incomes are not stable but fluctuate greatly from year to year and from period to period. Everybody knows this and yet every period of depression finds governments as well as individuals hard pressed, with funds inadequate for badly needed services. In fact, the funds that are available are not put to the best use because planning and management are not as wise and economical as they might be. Good finance, therefore, requires foresight, control of expenditures, reserves, sound debt policy — in a word, far-sighted and courageous budgeting policy and practice. Furthermore, good finance is almost impossible in a world whose economic and social systems are subject to frequent unpredictable upheavals by war and violently fluctuating monetary and credit systems.

Requisites of a Good Tax System

But assuming that civilization is not to commit suicide and that we may have sufficient stability to make possible a reasonable measure of planning, the outstanding requisites of a good tax system are adequacy, equity, economy, and practicability.

A few other characteristics of a good tax system may be added by way of amplification. The tax system should be a real system; that is, the different taxes should form a harmonious whole and not a mere collection of unarticulated taxes. For example, an income tax of unstable yield may be corrected by a property tax; a regressive property tax may be compensated for by a progressive income tax; each may reach abilities that the other fails to reach, and one may take account of benefits that the other slights or overlooks. The combination is better than either tax alone.

In a good system the taxes of a state will harmonize not only with those of its own subdivisions, but also with those of sister states and the national government. Proper cognizance will be taken of respective needs and resources, and there will be a happy medium between home rule and central coordination. The "Model System of State and Local Taxation" as proposed by the Committee of the National Tax Association is one of the most notable and suggestive attempts to meet the requirements outlined above. It was prepared after mature consideration by some of the best authorities and practical tax administrators in the country; it has been discussed at length before the conferences of the National Tax Association; and it has received general approval for a dozen years. The "model system" deals with large matters of principle and policy rather than with details. Perhaps no sounder advice can be given to any state than to consider to what extent it is feasible to bring its tax system into line with this "model system." In fact, this might well be considered every time that important tax modifications are contemplated. It is not meant that any two states should have exactly the same tax system, but there are fundamental guiding principles that should be observed at all times.

To remain satisfactory a tax system should be gradually but continuously adapted to changing conditions. Too frequent radical changes are upsetting and should be avoided. The usual presumption is in favor of old taxes to which competition has forced the adjustment of business and investment. On the other hand, no change means no progress. A happy mean should be the rule here also. Unfortunately, laws and customs generally, including tax laws and practices, often lag in the mud-road stage long after science and industry have advanced to the age of automobiles and airplanes. Our most progressive modern industries would not be where they are today if they still followed the lax and inexact methods of a century ago, if they made as little use of scientific research and expert administration as do some government administrators.

A good tax system will not only be conservatively progressive and as equitable as possible to every taxpayer, but it will also have regard for the prosperity of every farmer, every laborer, every manufacturer, every merchant, every professional man, and every other producer in the state. The government is a partner of every one of these; its aim is to promote their welfare. By providing the conditions under which they can prosper, it assures itself of funds for its own support. Those planning the finances of the state should consider the effect of each tax and each expenditure upon the future prosperity of the state. This does not mean, however, that business men and industries should be exempt from taxation. If they were, funds would be so inadequate that the government could not provide the services necessary for their own greatest prosperity, to say nothing of the welfare of the people as a whole. A poor government is one of the most expensive of luxuries. However little it may cost directly, its indirect cost will be very great.

Broad Social and Economic Requirements

A proper tax system will promote social and political cooperation, rather than excessive friction; it will enable the state to perform its proper functions efficiently; it will work for the prosperity of agriculture, industry, and commerce; it will aid in the best utilization of human capacities and natural resources; it will promote the public welfare generally.

It has been said that there is an Old World economy and a New World economy; that if pressed for means the citizen of the Old World tightens his belt, whereas the citizen of the New World bestirs himself to produce more so that he can continue to maintain and even expand his standard of living. This characterization may be unfair to the citizen of the Old World, but in any case it illustrates a point. If Minnesota's citizens are sufficiently alert, clever, and persevering, they may meet their tax problems in large part through better utilization of resources — that is, through increasing their wealth and income rather than through the elimination of valuable services. Of course it is desirable to eliminate waste and extravagance, but no one welcomes the idea of lower standards with respect to schools, highways, care of the unfortunate, police, etc.

This is the age of steel. Chemistry and electricity are the wizards of the present generation. The vast iron deposits and other resources of Minnesota appear to offer a fertile field for the researches of the University and other schools of the state as well as for the researches and investments of leading private industries. No one can tell what romances they may bring forth. One has but to review the scientific and industrial advance of the world during the past few years to sense the possibilities.

But the greatest resource of the state consists of its people; the development of other resources depends upon their capacities, their energies, and their training. Four hundred years ago the potential resources of North America were as great as they are today, but the Indians were roaming the plains and forests quite unaware of these riches. Nor were Europeans of that day aware of or prepared to take advantage of them. A German economist remarked to the writer that if the people of the United States and Russia had exchanged countries a century or two ago, this would now be Russia and what is now Russia would be the United States. During the worst financial throes of France following the late war, a French economist said that what France needed most was not foreign loans that would have to be repaid, but scientific, inventive, alert, and shrewd citizens who would discover oil, or make inventions, or otherwise increase the internal wealth of France.

It is not possible for Minnesota or any other state to solve tax problems and other financial problems by magic or overnight. There may be many times when it will be necessary to resort to the painful process of restriction, at least for short intervals when income will not go around. But it is obvious that its long-run plans should be directed as much toward the development of resources as toward tightening its belt.

Of course, a perfect tax system never did and probably never will exist. Nevertheless, it is well to have standards or criteria in mind as guides to action. In any particular situation where attempts at improvements are being made, one must always be guided by what is practicable.

We shall next turn our attention to the tax system of Minnesota as it now exists. Later we shall consider how it may be improved to the end that the state and its people may make the most of their possibilities.

CHAPTER 3

FARM REAL ESTATE ASSESSMENT IN MINNESOTA[1]

Plan and Scope of Study

The general property tax is the main source of public revenue in most states and their local subdivisions. In order that it may operate equitably as between the owners of various types of property and between the different owners of any one class of property the assessments upon which it is based must be made with at least a moderate degree of uniformity.

In assessing real property the assessor is not confronted with the problem of discovering the existence of property, as in the case of intangibles, but his chief problem is to determine the taxable value. In normal times the turnover of real estate is not rapid, and consequently the assessor can rely on sales data only to a limited extent. Furthermore, property that is sold is frequently not very comparable with adjoining property. The factors that determine value are numerous; they include fertility, proximity to markets, market value of the normal produce, type and repair of buildings and other equipment, and others. Even though the assessor has all these factors in mind, to apply them in proper proportion in a given case is not a simple task.

Although rural real estate must, according to law, be assessed at 33⅓ per cent of its value, in order to determine the proper assessed value the assessor must list its "true and full value." The latter phrase is interpreted to mean "the usual selling price at the place where the property to which the term is applied shall be at the time of the assessment, being the price which could be obtained therefor at private sale, and not at forced or auction sale." [2]

If all property were equally under- or over-assessed, little inequality would ensue. The rates of levy would merely have to be

[1] Mr. C. Z. Smith of the College of Agriculture, University of Minnesota, is primarily responsible for the preparation of this chapter. Much assistance in collecting and analyzing the data has been given by Professor George A. Pond, Professor W. L. Cavert, and a number of graduate students of the College of Agriculture. Professor E. P. Schmidt of the School of Business Administration has assisted in the presentation of the material. A more extended treatment of this subject is found in "An Analysis of Farm Real Estate Assessments in Minnesota," a thesis prepared by Mr. Smith, now on file at the University of Minnesota.

[2] Minnesota Tax Commission, *Assessors' Manual, Including Assessment Laws* (St. Paul, 1930), p. 39.

adjusted to offset the incorrect valuations. But when assessments are not uniform with respect to true value, tax burdens are not equal, and this lack of equality is increased by the numerous tax jurisdictions — state, county, township, city, and school district, all of which overlap more or less and each of which subjects its taxpayers to a different and independent rate of levy.

The purpose of this chapter is to determine the extent of, and to indicate some reasons for, deviations of assessment values from market or sales values. The data used have been gathered from four sources as Table 1 shows.

TABLE 1. — SOURCES OF DATA ON ASSESSMENTS FOR EACH OF THE DISTRICTS

District	Survey Schedules		Owner-Operator Farm Accounting Records	Sales Data	Total
	Owner-Operator	Farm-Landlord			
I	...	228	180	775	1,183
II	128	483	...	734	1,345
III	110	410	...	384	904
IV	153	87	26	791	1,057
V	144	145	23	248	560
VI	...	...	...	401	401
Total	535	1,353	229	3,333	5,450

A survey was made in the summer of 1931 of 535 farms operated by the owners. A group of experienced farm men, under the direction of Professor George A. Pond of the Division of Agricultural Economics of the University of Minnesota, inspected each farm and placed an appraised value thereon with the aid of soil maps, interviews with the owners and local bankers, and real estate agents who were familiar with the situation in each case.[3] While there is nothing final about the appraisals of these investigators and local men, it is believed that they are the result of unbiased, considered analyses. Information for 1,353 rented farms was obtained in the same way from landowners or agents who had supervised the property long enough to know it well. A third source of data were the records kept by 229 farmers under the supervision of the Department of Agriculture of the University of Minnesota for periods of from one to three years. These records are especially valuable, inas-

[3] See page 67.

FIGURE 1.—DISTRIBUTION OF MINNESOTA TAX SURVEY DATA ON REAL ESTATE BY COUNTIES AND DISTRICTS

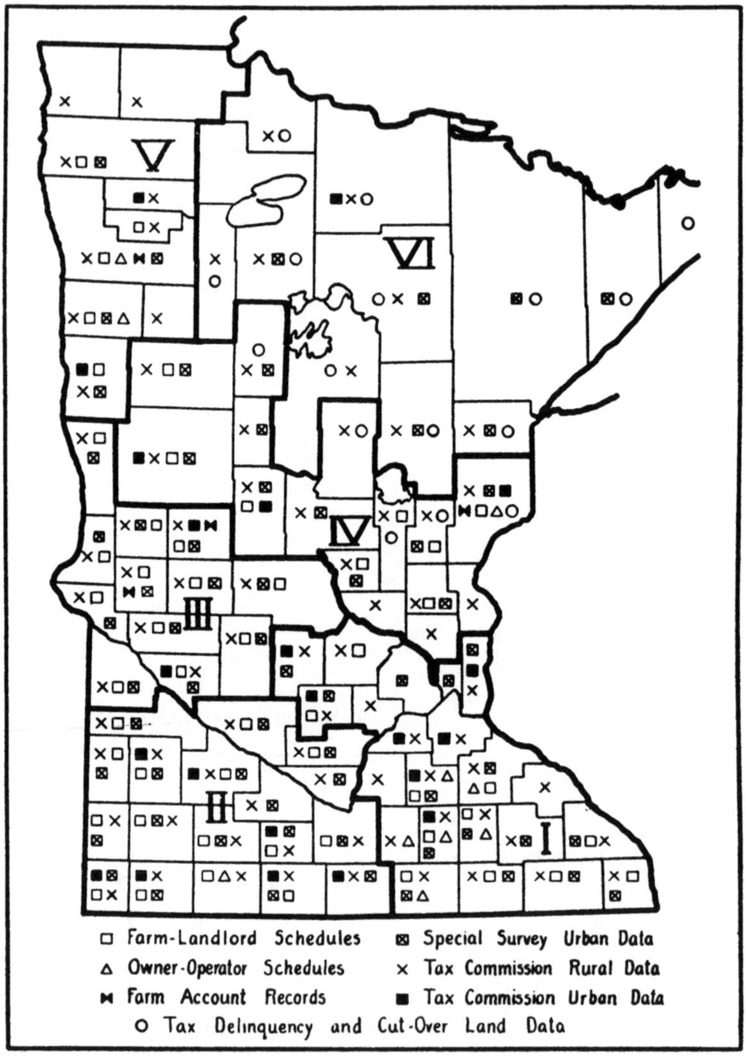

much as they comprise detailed accounts kept over a period of years. The three sources together furnished data in regard to the value of 2,117 farms in various parts of the state.

In addition to these schedules, sales information was furnished by the Minnesota Tax Commission, which has kept a record of bona fide sales in nearly all counties since its establishment in 1907. Sales figures for the years 1928 and 1929 were procured and were compared with the 1928 assessments. From this source the value of 3,333 farms was obtained.

For convenience the state was divided into the same districts used by G. B. Clarke and O. B. Jesness in their study of taxation and assessments during the period from 1924 to 1927.[4] The location of these districts is shown in Figure 1. It should be emphasized throughout that conclusions are most dependable where the size of the sample is adequate; in others, the sample may be merely indicative.

District I, in the southeast, is the oldest and most intensive dairy region of the state. District II, in the southwest, is the corn, hog, and beef area. District III, in the central and western part of the state, is a general farming region. Dairy products, potatoes, and small grain are produced in District IV, in the east and north-central part, where much of the soil is light. In District V (chiefly the Red River Valley) potatoes and small grain are the important crops. District VI, the northeastern section of the state, includes the cut-over region and the iron mines; what farming is carried on is devoted chiefly to small grain, potatoes, and dairying.

Comparison of Assessments with Appraised Values

The farms included in the samples are believed to be representative except that those in District I are of higher quality and are more improved than the average for the district. It should be noted, too, that appraisals in this district were made from January, 1928, to January, 1930, when prices were dropping, whereas most of the appraisals in other districts were made in 1931. Over-assessment would normally be more common in the case of the properties appraised most recently, because market values have declined faster than assessors' valuations.[5]

[4] G. B. Clarke and O. B. Jesness, *A Study of Taxation in Minnesota with Particular Reference to Assessments of Farm Lands* (University of Minnesota Agricultural Experiment Station Bulletin No. 277, St. Paul, 1931), p. 8.

[5] See B. R. Stauber, *The Farm Real Estate Situation, 1930–31* (United States Department of Agriculture Circular 209, 1931).

In making the comparison of assessed with appraised values, the farms were classified according to what percentage of appraised value was represented by assessed value and grouped in classes with a range of 10 per cent each, as indicated in Table 3 on page 42. The data pertain to 2,117 farms, of which 408 were in District I, 611 in District II, 520 in District III, 266 in District IV, and 312 in District V. In District III one farm was assessed between 20 and 30 per cent of the appraised value, another between 30 and 40 per cent, and 85 farms were assessed between 110 and 120 per cent of the appraised value. These few explanations should make the rest of the table clear. The data in Table 3 are summarized in Table 2.

TABLE 2.—COMPARISON OF ASSESSED WITH APPRAISED VALUES OF 2,117 MINNESOTA FARMS, 1928–1930 [a]

District	Farms Under-Assessed		Farms Assessed within 10 Per Cent of Appraised Value		Farms Over-Assessed					
					Total		50–100 Per Cent		100 Per Cent or More	
	No.	Per Cent	No.	Per Cent	No.	Per Cent	No.	Per Cent	No.	Per Cent
I	217	53.18	108	26.47	191	46.82	45	11.03	7	1.71
II	113	18.49	161	26.35	498	81.51	141	23.07	28	4.58
III	132	25.38	113	21.73	388	74.62	96	18.46	31	5.95
IV	117	43.98	65	24.43	149	56.02	28	10.53	0	.00
V	57	18.26	65	20.83	255	81.74	78	25.00	16	5.13
Total area	636	30.04	512	24.18	1,481	69.96	388	18.32	82	3.87

[a] The dividing line between under-assessment and over-assessment is 100 per cent of the appraised value. This is a summary of Table 3.

These tables reveal a great spread between assessed and appraised values. Only 512 farms, or 24 per cent of the total, were assessed within 10 per cent of the appraised value. Seventeen farms were assessed at 50 per cent or less of their appraised value, whereas 82 were over-assessed by 100 per cent or more; 18 of these latter were over-assessed by more than 160 per cent. As Table 2 indicates, the deviation of assessment from appraised value varied considerably in the different districts. In District II, 161 farms, or 26 per cent of the total, were assessed within 10 per cent of the appraised value. In District V only 21 per cent were assessed within 10 per cent of the appraised value.

FIGURE 2. — RELATION OF ASSESSED TO APPRAISED VALUES OF 2,117 MINNESOTA FARMS, 1931 [a]

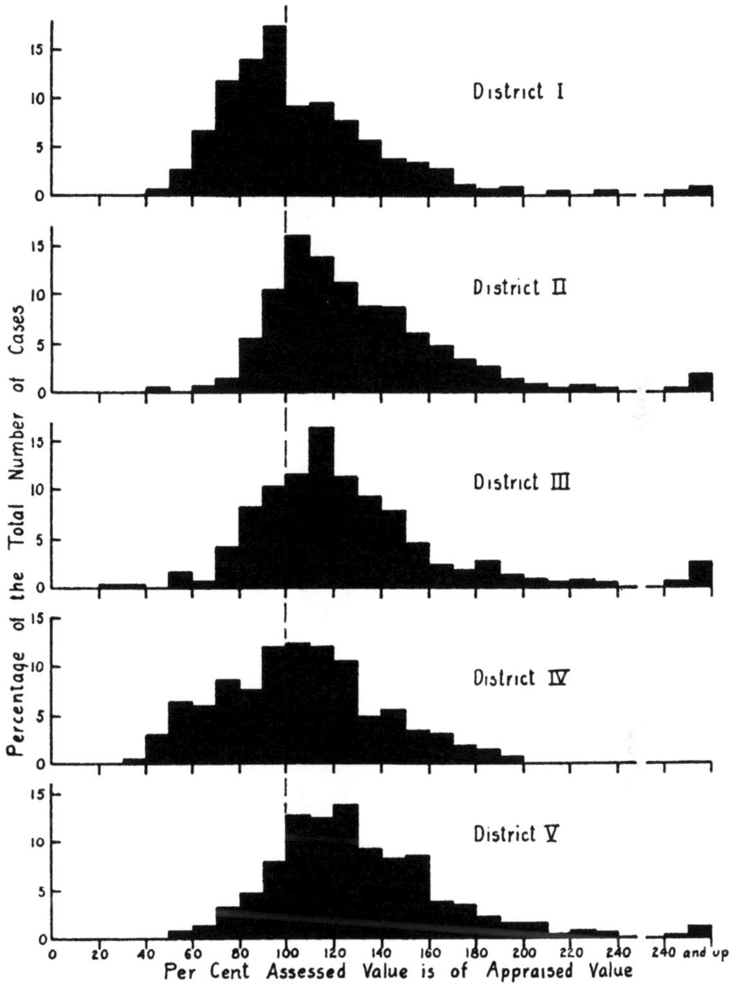

[a] Based on Table 3, page 42. For the explanation of this figure see the explanation of Figure 2 in Chapter 1, page 13.

TABLE 3.—DISTRIBUTION OF 2,117 MINNESOTA FARMS ACCORDING TO RATIOS OF ASSESSED TO APPRAISED VALUES, 1928–1930

PERCENTAGE OF APPRAISED VALUE	DISTRICT I	DISTRICT II	DISTRICT III	DISTRICT IV	DISTRICT V
20–30	..	..	1	..	..
30–40	..	..	1	1	..
40–50	3	3	..	8	..
50–60	11	..	8	17	3
60–70	27	4	3	16	4
70–80	48	8	23	23	10
80–90	57	35	43	20	15
90–100	71	63	53	32	25
100–110	37	98	60	33	40
110–120	39	84	85	32	39
120–130	31	68	58	28	43
130–140	23	54	48	13	29
140–150	16	53	41	15	26
150–160	14	38	24	9	27
160–170	12	30	12	8	12
170–180	5	21	9	5	11
180–190	3	16	14	4	7
190–200	4	8	6	2	5
200–210	..	6	5	..	5
210–220	2	3	3	..	1
220–230	..	5	4	..	3
230–240	2	3	3	..	2
240–250	2	2	3	..	1
250–260[a]	1	9	13	..	4
Total number of farms	408	611	520	266	312
Average percentage of appraised value	106.27	129.25	125.93	105.71	130.88

[a] Including 18 cases over 260 per cent.

In Districts II and V, 18 per cent of the farms were under-assessed,[6] whereas in District I, 53 per cent of the farms were under-assessed. Of the group of farms as a whole 30 per cent were under-assessed. If it is assumed that there is a reasonable degree of accuracy in the independent appraisals, Tables 2 and 3 clearly indicate a great range of deviations between assessments and actual values. It is not claimed that the appraised value is the correct value in each case, since this must always be a matter of opinion and varies greatly with costs, prices, freight rates, and so forth, but the appraisals are assumed to be reasonably reliable.

[6] The term "under-assessment" is used in this chapter to mean assessments under 100 per cent of sales or appraised value.

Ratios of Assessed to Sales Values

A comparison of assessed values with actual sales figures, where the latter are available, indicates similar disparities. (See Tables 4 and 5.) Of a total of 3,333 farms for which assessment and sales figures were available only 814, or 24 per cent, were assessed within 10 per cent of the sales figures. Of these, 471 were under-assessed and 343 were over-assessed. Apparently the most accurate assessment was made in District II, where 36 per cent of the farms were assessed within 10 per cent of the sales figures. The greatest disparities occurred in Districts V and VI, where only 14.5 and 16.2 per cent, respectively, of the farms were assessed within 10 per cent of the sales prices. Of the farms in all the districts 213 were assessed at 50 per cent or less of the sales figures. On the other hand, 65 farms were assessed at 100 per cent or more in excess of the sales figures. In three of these cases the excess was 160 per cent or more.

Table 5 reveals further disparities. The extent of under-assessment varied considerably in the different districts. In District V just over 50 per cent of all the farms were under-assessed, whereas in District I nearly 70 per cent were under-assessed, probably because the sales values are of an earlier date.[7] In District II, 265 farms were assessed within 10 per cent of the sales value, yet 66.89 per cent of the total number were under-assessed. Very exaggerated under-assessment occurred in District VI, where 21.94 per cent of all farms were assessed at 50 per cent or less of the sales value; in District II only 1.37 per cent of the farms were assessed at this low ratio.

Appraisals of farms in District VI are not available, but sales for the period from 1924 to 1927 show that the same situation existed during these years, when the average assessment for the district was 84.1 per cent of sales values.[8] No doubt the extreme under-assessment in District VI is due in part to the unsettled conditions in the northern part of the state, where farms differ radically in type and improvement. As a whole District V is over-assessed;[9] all the others are under-assessed, the greatest under-assessment occurring in District VI, where the average assessment

[7] See page 39.
[8] Clarke and Jesness, p. 14. See also the tables on pages 134, 157, and 158.
[9] But note that the number of farms in the sample is small.

TABLE 4.—DISTRIBUTION OF 3,333 MINNESOTA FARMS ACCORDING TO RATIOS OF ASSESSED TO SALES VALUES, 1928 AND 1929

PERCENTAGE OF SALES VALUE	DISTRICT I	DISTRICT II	DISTRICT III	DISTRICT IV	DISTRICT V	DISTRICT VI
20–30[a]	..	1	..	10	3	13
30–40	7	1	5	14	2	22
40–50	22	8	7	33	12	53
50–60	53	24	19	80	16	44
60–70	86	52	37	103	18	35
70–80	129	117	62	96	23	38
80–90	125	137	65	98	30	27
90–100	115	151	65	80	25	35
100–110	74	114	46	68	11	30
110–120	57	46	29	41	21	23
120–130	48	35	16	40	18	16
130–140	20	16	10	37	15	10
140–150	13	11	12	22	9	13
150–160	7	5	6	19	7	5
160–170	5	1	1	5	13	8
170–180	4	4	3	10	6	6
180–190	..	3	1	7	3	1
190–200	1	3	..	8	4	3
200–210	2	1	..	7	2	5
210–220	4	2	..	5	1	6
220–230	2	2	..	3	2	5
230–240	1	..	..	2	3	3
240–250	..	..	..	1	3	..
250–260[b]	..	..	..	2	1	..
Total number of farms	775	734	384	791	248	401
Average percentage of sales value	91.14	92.37	92.05	93.88	108.34	89.08

[a] Including 9 cases under 20 per cent. [b] Including 3 cases over 260 per cent.

TABLE 5.—COMPARISON OF ASSESSED VALUES WITH SALES PRICES OF 3,333 FARMS, 1928 AND 1929[a]

DISTRICT	FARMS UNDER-ASSESSED		FARMS ASSESSED WITHIN 10 PER CENT OF SALES PRICES		FARMS ASSESSED AT 50 PER CENT OR LESS OF SALES PRICES		AVERAGE ASSESSED VALUE IN TERMS OF PERCENTAGE OF SALES PRICES
	No.	Per Cent	No.	Per Cent	No.	Per Cent	
I	537	69.29	189	24.38	29	3.74	91.14
II	491	66.89	265	36.10	10	1.37	92.37
III	260	67.71	111	28.90	12	3.13	92.05
IV	514	64.98	148	18.71	57	7.20	93.88
V	129	52.02	36	14.51	17	6.85	108.34
VI	267	66.58	65	16.20	88	21.94	89.08
Total area	2,198	65.94	814	24.42	213	6.39	

[a] This is a summary of Table 4 above.

was 89.08 per cent of sales values; the greatest proportion of farms under-assessed was in District I.

The higher ratio between assessments and appraisals in 1931 than between assessments and sales in 1928 and 1929, as shown in Tables 3 and 4, is just what one would expect, since assessors' valuations are inclined to lag behind actual price movements, particularly when changes are as rapid as they have been during the past few years.

RATIOS OF ASSESSED TO SALES VALUES IN VARIOUS COUNTIES

In the light of the considerable variations existing between assessed and market values in the various districts, one might assume that similar variations must exist among the counties. Table 6 shows the number of counties in which the average assessed values of the farms for which data are available bear certain specified

TABLE 6.—NUMBER OF COUNTIES HAVING SPECIFIED AVERAGE RATIOS OF ASSESSED TO SALES VALUES, 1928 AND 1929

DISTRICT	ASSESSED VALUES IN TERMS OF PERCENTAGES OF SALES VALUES							TOTAL
	50–60	60–70	70–80	80–90	90–100	100–110	110–120	
	No. of Counties							
I	..	..	4	6	7	2	1	20
II	..	..	1	9	8	..	..	18
III	..	..	..	7	4	1	..	12
IV	..	1	3	8	3	..	..	15
V	..	..	..	1	3	3	1	8
VI	2	1	3	1	1	..	..	8
Total	2	2	11	32	26	6	2	81

ratios to sales values. The figures would be more valuable if more data were available. Some data are available for 81 of the 87 counties of the state. In 2 counties the average assessed value was only from 50 to 60 per cent of the sales value, which is of course gross under-assessment. In 32 counties, or 39 per cent of the total, the average assessment was within 10 per cent of the sales values.

The reader may suspect that this great discrepancy exists only between widely separated counties, but Table 7 indicates that marked variations between assessment and sales values occur in contiguous counties. The lowest average ratio between assessment and sales value occurred in Itasca County, where the farms were assessed at only 56.79 per cent of the sales value; in the neighboring

TABLE 7.—COMPARISON OF ASSESSED VALUES WITH SALES PRICES IN ADJOINING COUNTIES, 1928 AND 1929

DISTRICT	COUNTY	NO. OF SALES [a]	AVERAGE PERCENTAGE OF SALES PRICES	DISTRICT	COUNTY	NO OF SALES [a]	AVERAGE PERCENTAGE OF SALES PRICES
I	Dodge	26	114.34	IV	Anoka	9	98.12
	Steele	35	91.92		Isanti	43	89.09
II	Brown	34	87.49	V	Polk	47	94.27
	Redwood ..	56	95.10		Red Lake..	12	100.08
					Norman ...	42	91.19
III	Pope	20	80.81				
	Stearns ...	106	84.24	VI	Aitkin	70	76.88
	Stevens ...	34	92.92		Itasca	70	56.79

[a] Total sales reported in these counties, 1928 and 1929. They are insufficient in number to form a reliable guide, though they are indicative.

TABLE 8.—COMPARISON OF ASSESSED VALUES WITH SALES PRICES IN NINE COUNTIES, 1928 AND 1929 [a]

COUNTY	FARMS ASSESSED WITHIN 10 PER CENT OF SALES PRICES		FARMS ASSESSED AT 70 PER CENT OR LESS OF SALES PRICES		AVERAGE PERCENTAGE OF SALES PRICES
	No.	Per Cent	No.	Per Cent	
Marshall	4	14.28	7	25.00	97.68
Itasca	8	11.42	42	60.00	56.79
Becker	13	25.00	9	17.30	93.13
Aitkin	9	12.85	26	37.14	76.88
Steele	14	40.00	3	8.57	91.92
Redwood	29	51.78	4	7.14	95.10
Goodhue	13	35.13	3	8.10	98.25
Carver	13	40.62	2	6.25	91.95
Nobles	22	40.74	1	1.85	88.63
Total area	125	28.80	97	22.35	

[a] This table is based on data given in Table 16 on page 58.

county, Aitkin, the average ratio of assessment to sales value was nearly 50 per cent higher, namely 76.88 per cent. Even this figure indicates serious under-assessment. Dodge County had a high average, though situated in District I, where the average ratio of assessment to sales value was lower than in most districts. In general, the counties in this table having the poorest land show the highest assessment ratios. Table 8 gives the ratios of assessments to sales values in nine counties.

In Itasca County only 11.42 per cent of the farms were assessed within 10 per cent of the sales values, while in four counties—

FIGURE 3. — RELATION OF ASSESSED TO SALES VALUES IN FOUR COUNTIES [a]

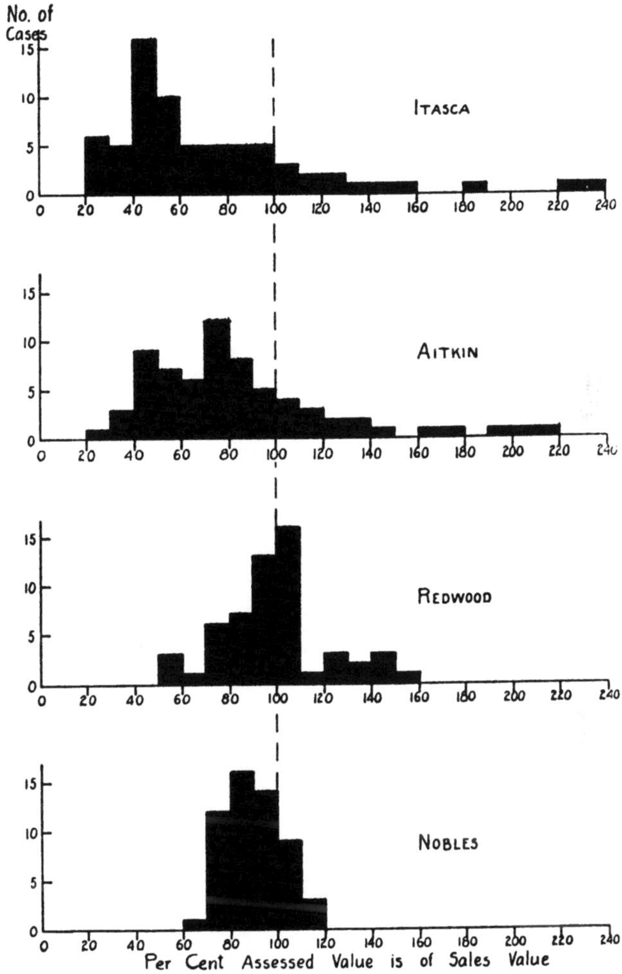

[a] Based on Table 16 on page 58. For the explanation of this figure see the explanation of Figure 2 in Chapter 1, page 13.

Steele, Redwood, Carver, and Nobles—over 40 per cent of the farms were so assessed. Itasca also has a very extensive range from extreme under-assessment to extreme over-assessment; 60 per cent of the farms in that county covered in this survey were assessed at 70 per cent or less of the sales values. In Aitkin County, where the next greatest amount of under-assessment occurred, only about half as great a proportion of farms were so under-assessed, namely 37.14 per cent. In Nobles County only 1.85 per cent of the farms were under-assessed by as much as 30 per cent or more. Itasca County had the lowest average ratio of assessments to sales values, namely, 56.79 per cent, as previously noted, whereas Goodhue and Marshall counties had the best averages, namely, 98.25 per cent and 97.68 per cent, respectively. These high averages may be occasioned by the small number of cases available. The range or scatter of assessments in Marshall County indicates very great lack of uniformity. (See Table 16, page 58.) It should be emphasized again that however accurate the *average* may be, there still may be wide under-assessment of some farms and equally wide over-assessment of others. A good county average is no consolation to the farmer whose farm is extremely over-assessed.

Figure 3 shows graphically the range of assessment of farms in four counties included in this survey. The greatest range and the least concentration at the point of accurate assessment occurs in Itasca; the highest average assessment is in Redwood; Nobles County has the most uniform valuations.[10] (See page 47.)

Influence of Value of Property upon Accuracy of Assessment

A further study of the data when arranged according to the value of the farms seems to indicate a strong tendency for the assessor to over-assess the least valuable farms a great deal more than the more valuable ones. This is indicated in Table 9.

In District I only 22.22 per cent of the farms worth less than $5,000 were under-assessed, whereas 81.48 per cent of the farms worth between $25,000 and $30,000 were under-assessed. Likewise in District II the tendency to under-assess the more valuable farms is very marked; only 2.44 per cent of the farms worth less than $5,000 were under-assessed, but 30.23 per cent of the farms valued

[10] For a comparison of farm real estate assessments in other states the reader is referred to Whitney Coombs, *Taxation of Farm Property* (United States Department of Agriculture Technical Bulletin No. 172, 1930). Inequalities in assessment are not confined to Minnesota.

TABLE 9.—RELATION OF FARM VALUE TO ACCURACY OF ASSESSMENT, 1931[a]

Appraised Value in Dollars	Percentage of Farms Under-Assessed		Percentage of Farms Assessed within 10 per cent of Appraised Value	
	District I	District II	District I	District II
Under 5,000	22.22	2.44	11.11	2.44
5,000–10,000	35.55	10.81	18.88	19.81
10,000–15,000	42.27	16.66	24.74	29.88
15,000–20,000	61.46	23.23	38.54	32.39
20,000–25,000	70.91	26.78	25.45	33.92
25,000–30,000	81.48	30.23	25.92	32.55
30,000–35,000	75.00	25.00	33.33	25.00
35,000–40,000	80.00	....	60.00	....
40,000–45,000	50.00	....	....	....
45,000–50,000	100.00	....	....	....
50,000–55,000	100.00	50.00	....	....
Over 55,000	100.00	100.00	....	....
District as a whole	53.18	18.49	26.47	26.35

[a] Table 9 is based on data summarized in Table 17 on page 59.

between $25,000 and $30,000 were under-assessed. In spite of this strong tendency to over-assess the less valuable farms it appears that the greater proportion of the more valuable farms were assessed within 10 per cent of the appraised value. An analysis of the data from the other districts yields similar results.

INFLUENCE OF VALUE PER ACRE ON ACCURACY OF ASSESSMENT

In order to determine the influence of the value per acre on the accuracy of assessment the farms were grouped according to the value per acre of land and improvements. Table 10 shows that there is a distinct tendency for the ratio of assessment to appraised value to decrease as the value per acre increases. In every district except IV and V the farms with a low value per acre show a variation of over 100 per cent in favor of those with a high value. Only one general conclusion can be drawn from this table, namely, that the farmer owning acreage with a low value is more likely to be over-assessed than the farmer with acreage of high value. The second column in the table, showing the percentage of farms under-assessed in District I, indicates likewise that the farmer owning land with a low value per acre had a much smaller chance of being under-assessed than the one owning land valued at $100 or more per acre.

Table 10.—Relation of Value per Acre to Accuracy of Assessment, 1931[a]

Value per Acre in Dollars	Percentage of Farms Under-Assessed in District I	Average Assessed Value in Terms of Percentage of Appraised Value: District I	District II	District III	District IV	District V
15–25	....	225.0	....	219.3	142.9	156.8
25–35	16.66	183.3	250.0	159.5	115.0	130.8
35–45	30.77	156.5	193.3	135.8	104.1	119.4
45–55	20.00	138.3	155.8	117.8	92.8	102.6
55–65	7.69	133.4	138.4	104.3	76.5	
65–75	4.00	135.8	122.8	100.0		
75–85	18.64	116.8	114.2			
85–95	61.76	101.4	108.1			
95–105	65.00	96.5	98.9			
105–115	76.00	88.2				84.0
115–125	90.69	83.8		88.2	68.0	
125–135	89.65	79.6				
135–145	100.00	73.3	99.2			
145–155	92.86					
155–165	100.00	72.0				
Over 165	100.00					

[a] This table is based on data summarized in Table 18 on page 60.

Table 11.—Relation of Size of Farm to Accuracy of Assessment, 1931[a]

Size in Acres	Average Assessed Value in Terms of Percentage of Appraised Value: District I	District II	District III	District IV	District V
20–60	....	128.0	127.0	112.3	....
60–100	101.7	133.1	123.1	103.6	123.5
100–140	111.8	118.2	126.3	110.8	135.0
140–180	108.6	123.2	131.8	103.1	134.5
180–220	102.3	129.3	125.4	96.1	130.5
220–260	107.9	125.9	120.8	102.2	128.6
260–300	114.1	127.3	119.5		122.9
300–340	93.5	130.6	120.8		123.5
340–380		129.4	138.6		138.3
380–420		131.9	111.3		132.2
420–460		121.3			134.0
460–500		155.6		129.7	151.3
500–540	106.3				
540–580			136.3		
580–620		160.0			126.9
620–660					
Over 660					

[a] This table is based on data summarized in Table 19 on page 61.

Influence of Size of Farm on Accuracy of Assessment

In order to determine what influence the size of a farm might have on the mind of the assessor all the farms in each district were arranged in groups according to size. Table 11 indicates that over-assessment is the rule, but it does not show that mere size causes the assessor to have any outstanding bias. The average assessments show no trend either toward increase or decrease in going from small to large farms. Table 12 shows the percentages of farms under-assessed in Districts I and II and indicates that there was about as great a proportion of small farms under-assessed as of large ones.

Table 12.—Percentages of Farms of Various Sizes Under-Assessed in Districts I and II, 1931[a]

Size in Acres	District I	District II
20–60	....	20.00
60–100	58.90	16.66
100–140	48.21	25.00
140–180	49.62	19.59
180–220	59.61	25.49
220–260	53.19	17.33
260–300	33.33	11.76
300–340	65.00	19.74
Over 340	57.14	22.22

[a] This table is based on data summarized in Table 19 on page 61.

Accuracy of Assessment of Bare Land

So far the land and the buildings have been included in the value per acre. In order to determine what influence the presence of buildings might have, the next analysis concerns itself exclusively with the accuracy of bare land assessments. Table 13 presents the results of this calculation.

This table, like the preceding tables, reveals a tendency for assessors to favor the more valuable land. About 5 per cent of the farms in District I valued between $15 and $25 an acre were under-assessed, but 54.84 per cent of the farms valued from $75 to $85 an acre were under-assessed. Apparently if the bare land had a value in excess of $100 an acre it was almost certain to be under-assessed. The same situation is evident in the other districts. The less valuable land seems always to be subject to a tendency toward over-assessment. The bias in assessment is more extreme when

Table 13. — Relation of Appraised Value per Acre to Assessment of Land Exclusive of Improvements, 1931

Value per Acre in Dollars [a]	Percentage of Farms Under-Assessed in District I	Average Assessed Value in Terms of Percentage of Appraised Value				
		District I	District II	District III	District IV	District V
5–15	....	....	....	313.7	251.2[b]	280.0
15–25	5.26	259.7	323.0	211.9	214.1	218.1
25–35	4.16	199.1	217.4	162.2	161.1	179.2
35–45	7.14	167.8	183.1	128.4	141.5	155.1
45–55	0.00	159.2	153.1	115.9	137.0	143.8
55–65	16.66	125.4	138.8		105.9	118.3
65–75	29.33	110.1	118.1			
75–85	54.84	100.4				
85–95	75.00	92.8				
95–105	100.00					
105–115	80.00			111.1	86.5	104.4
115–125	100.00		100.0			
125–135	100.00	78.3				
135–145	100.00					
Over 145	50.00					

[a] Does not include improvements. This table is based on data given in Table 20 on page 62. See also Table 6 in Chapter 5, page 134.
[b] Because of the low value per acre in Districts IV and V, the gradations ought properly to be by $5 rather than by $10 units.

comparison is made with bare land alone. The averages in District I showed a difference of 153 per cent between the most valuable and the least valuable groups when analysis was made of land and improvement combined. When the comparison is based on bare land only, the difference between the low and high value groups is 181.4 per cent. This condition prevails also in the other districts. Therefore improvements tend to compensate for some of the variation between the assessments of farms of low value per acre and those of high value. The average ratio of assessment to appraised value of bare land is higher in all districts than that of assessments to appraised value of land and improvements combined. District I has the lowest average, 117.5 per cent. The other district averages are considerably higher. If bare land has a higher assessment ratio than land and improvements, then improvements must have a low assessment ratio.

Assessment of Farm Improvements

Table 14 gives the ratios of the assessed values of farm improvements to the appraised values. The most obvious fact to be deduced from this table is that improvements do not tend to be assessed at nearly 100 per cent of their appraised value. Under-assessment seems to be the predominant tendency, although there are numerous cases in which the independent appraisers found considerable over-assessment by the local assessor. Where over-assessment was found, it was nearly always in connection with farms having a small amount of improvement, usually less than $1,000 worth. The assessment ratio here too has a bias in favor of the

TABLE 14.—RELATION OF ASSESSED TO APPRAISED VALUES OF FARM IMPROVEMENTS, 1931[a]

Appraised Value of Improvements	Average Assessed Value of Improvements in Percentage of Appraised Value				
	District I	District II	District III	District IV	District V
$0–$1,000	....	103.8	115.0	89.6	100.6
1,000– 2,000	93.4	71.8	89.5	63.1	87.2
2,000– 3,000	70.6	71.6	67.1	55.4	74.6
3,000– 4,000	61.6	63.5	56.7	52.2	70.1
4,000– 5,000	61.7	58.5	53.9	40.0	62.2
5,000– 6,000	57.8	53.4	46.7		61.5
6,000– 7,000	57.0	46.4			
7,000– 8,000	53.1	41.6		36.0	
8,000– 9,000	53.5				46.5
9,000–10,000			40.8		
10,000–11,000					
11,000–12,000		40.8			
12,000–13,000	50.6				
13,000–14,000					
14,000–15,000					
Over 15,000					
Average	56.5	51.7	51.9	49.6	65.1

[a] This table is based on data summarized in Table 21 on page 63.

more valuable improvements, but the bias is not so extreme as in the case of bare land.

All districts show the same general pattern. District IV has the least scatter, but it shows about the same bias as do the other districts. The average ratios of assessed to appraised values of buildings are fairly consistent between the different districts. District V has the highest average, 65.1 per cent, and District IV the lowest average, 49.6 per cent. On page 42 it was shown that District V had the highest assessment average, 130.88 per cent, and District IV the lowest, 105.71 per cent. Improvements have helped to create these differences between districts. This is illustrated in Table 23 on page 65.

Before turning from this part of the discussion it is well to find out what relation improvements bear to value per acre. In considering this question scatter diagrams were prepared in which the vertical scale showed the total value per acre and the horizontal scale the value of improvements per acre. Table 22 on page 64 shows this relationship for Districts II and V. The other districts showed the same general tendency, differing only in degree, according to the number of buildings the different types of farming required. District II indicates an average value of $29.21 an acre for improvements and District V only $10.37 an acre, a normal difference between an area devoted to dairying and one devoted to grain.

The scatter diagrams (Tables 17–22, pages 59–64) show that the higher land values are made up in part of the value of buildings per acre. Assessment bias in favor of the more valuable property may be due, therefore, to two reasons: first, to the high value of improvements per acre and, second, to the high value of land per acre. In the case of property having a high value per acre as well as valuable improvements there would be two causes of under-assessment.

Data presented in this section show that land is over-assessed and buildings are under-assessed. There is also a bias in assessment in favor of property of high value. Assessments do not favor the more valuable property because of its size but because of the high value per acre. On a basis of value per acre the bare land is favored to a greater extent than the land and improvements. Improvements are under-assessed as compared with land, and the percentage of under-assessment increases as the value of improvements increases. These variations indicate that the assessing of property requires considerable skill and should be done by highly trained men.

Variations in the Assessment of Farms of Different Classes of Operators

To determine variations in the assessment of farms of different classes of operators, comparisons were made between farms operated by resident owners, by nonresident owners, and by tenants. The average value per acre of each of these three groups was computed in order to make a more careful comparison, inasmuch as the

TABLE 15.—RELATION OF ASSESSED TO APPRAISED VALUE PER ACRE OF OWNER-OPERATED, NONRESIDENT OWNED, AND RENTED FARMS, 1931

Type of Farm	Average Value per Acre			Average Assessed Value in Terms of Percentage of Appraised Value			No. of Farms
	Land	Improvements	Land and Improvements	Land	Improvements	Land and Improvements	
District I							
Owner-operated	$76.92	$34.82	$111.74	98.47	56.07	85.25	180
Rented	51.02	24.32	75.34	142.68	57.10	115.10	228
Nonresident owned[a].	46.80	16.50	63.30	.....	....	136.70	17
District II							
Owner-operated	58.78	29.34	86.13	145.15	60.83	117.07	128
Rented	49.32	15.79	65.11	153.46	48.58	128.00	483
Nonresident owned..	46.25	10.16	56.41	.....	....	148.50	196
District III							
Owner-operated	30.95	17.61	48.56	147.82	64.36	117.56	110
Rented	27.73	13.12	40.85	149.67	48.15	117.06	410
Nonresident owned..	28.02	14.26	42.28	.....	....	150.70	95
District IV							
Owner-operated	16.22	18.73	34.95	153.91	53.20	99.90	179
Rented	27.59	16.66	44.25	118.93	44.00	90.70	87
Nonresident owned..	23.21	13.04	36.25	.....	....	121.10	33
District V							
Owner-operated	22.55	11.10	33.65	149.60	74.20	124.80	167
Rented	20.96	9.45	30.41	151.90	51.30	120.70	145
Nonresident owned..	18.25	7.01	25.26	.....	....	129.50	53

[a] Owned by a resident of another county.

higher acre values are favored in assessment. Table 15 above and Figure 4 on the next page show these comparisons by districts.

Owner-operated farms were worth more per acre in all districts except District IV. In this district the owner-operated schedules were obtained in Pine County, in the eastern part of the district, and most of the renter schedules were secured in Becker and Otter Tail counties, in the western part, where agricultural conditions are similar to those of District III. Comparisons can hardly be made because of these differences.

In Districts I and II the ratio of assessed to appraised values is lower for owner-operated farms than for rented farms. In the other districts the assessment ratio is slightly in favor of rented farms, but this may be accounted for by variations of sampling. As noted

FIGURE 4.—RELATION OF ASSESSED TO APPRAISED VALUE PER ACRE OF OWNER-OPERATED, NON-RESIDENT OWNED, AND RENTED FARMS, 1931

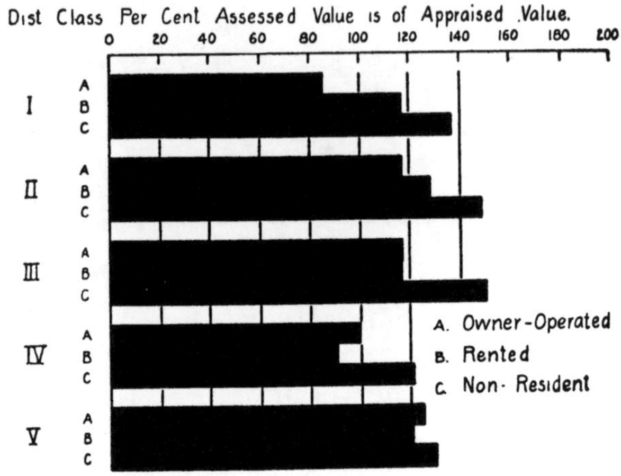

above, the owner-operated farms in all districts except District IV have a higher value than the rented farms. These differences are sufficient to lead one to expect a lower assessment ratio for owner-operated farms, on the ground that there is an assessment bias in favor of high values per acre. Considering all districts, the conclusion seems warranted that there is no discrimination in assessment of property because it is rented property. The differences are more likely due to differences in values per acre.

INFLUENCE OF NONRESIDENT OWNERSHIP ON ASSESSMENT

A second analysis was made of the rented farms to determine what differences might be due to the location of the property owner. Many landlords live in the same assessment unit or in the same county in which their rented property is located. This places them on much the same basis as the owner-operator farmers, inasmuch as they are acquainted with the assessor and frequently are present when the assessment is made. The nonresident owner is seldom able to be present at the time of assessment and must leave representation to an agent or not be represented at all.

The assessments of the rented farms owned by nonresidents were compared with the average for all rented farms. By nonresident owners are meant those residing outside the county in which their property is located. Table 15 on page 55 and Figure 4 give the results of this comparison. Except in District III farms owned by nonresidents are worth less per acre, both in land and improvements, and in District III there is only a slight difference between the value of nonresident owners' property and the average of all rented farms. In every case the assessment ratio is higher for nonresident owners' farms. This difference is as great in District III, where the values are similar to those of the other districts. The inequalities are great enough and consistent enough in all districts to warrant the conclusion that part of the bias in assessments arises from the fact that some owners are resident and others nonresident. The differences are not usually removed by the town and county boards of equalization.

Conclusions

1. There is great lack of uniformity in the assessment of farms in Minnesota. Many are under-assessed and many over-assessed.

2. Comparisons with other studies reveal that these inequalities are similar to those in other states.

3. Farms of high value tend to be under-assessed and those of low value over-assessed.

4. Further analysis shows that under-assessment usually accompanies high value per acre but that size of farm has little effect upon assessment.

5. When the assessments of bare land are studied separately from the assessments of improvements, improvements are seen to be under-assessed as compared with bare land, but in both cases the more valuable properties are most likely to be under-assessed.

6. There seem to be no general differences in the quality of the assessments of rented land and owner-operated land, at least in Districts III, IV, and V.

7. Land owned by nonresidents is usually over-assessed as compared with that owned by residents of the county in which it is situated.[11]

A more detailed presentation of the data upon which the foregoing analysis is based is found on pages 58 to 66. See also page 36, note 1. Suggestions for the improvement of assessments are made on pages 222 to 227.

[11] The main conclusions in this chapter, particularly those with respect to variations in assessments and the tendency to discriminate against property with a low value per acre, are in line with those of an earlier study covering more cases and a different period. See note 4.

TABLE 16. — NUMBER OF FARMS IN EACH OF NINE COUNTIES ASSESSED AT SPECIFIED PERCENTAGES OF SALES VALUES [a]

County	Total No. of Farms	0–30	30–40	40–50	50–60	60–70	70–80	80–90	90–100	100–110	110–120	120–130	130–140	140–150	150–160	160–170	170–180	180–190	190–200	200–210	210–220	Over 220 [b]	Average	Total Range
		Assessed Value in Percentage of Sales Value																						
		No. of Farms								No. of Farms														
Marshall	28	2	1	1	2	1	..	3	3	1	2	5	1	1	..	2	..	..	..	1	..	3	97.68	228
Itasca	70	6	5	16	10	5	5	5	5	3	2	2	1	1	1	..	..	1	..	..	..	2	56.79	215
Becker	52	..	3	2	3	1	5	5	8	5	4	4	4	2	4	..	..	..	2	..	..	..	93.13	158
Aitkin	70	1	3	9	7	6	12	8	5	4	3	2	2	1	..	2	2	..	1	1	1	..	76.88	211
Steele	35	..	..	..	2	1	7	5	11	3	..	2	..	3	..	1	..	..	..	..	..	..	91.92	106
Redwood	56	..	..	..	3	1	6	7	13	16	1	3	2	3	1	..	..	..	..	..	..	..	95.10	101
Goodhue	37	..	..	1	..	2	3	5	8	5	5	6	2	..	..	..	..	..	..	..	..	..	98.25	95
Carver	32	..	..	..	..	2	5	6	10	3	2	4	3	1	..	..	..	..	..	..	..	..	91.95	65
Nobles	54	..	..	..	..	1	12	16	13	9	3	..	..	..	..	..	..	..	..	..	..	..	88.63	50

[a] These data would probably be more representative if there were more cases for each county.
[b] Including 4 cases over 230 per cent.

TABLE 17.—COMPARISON OF ASSESSED WITH APPRAISED VALUES OF LAND AND IMPROVEMENTS ON 2,117 FARMS GROUPED ACCORDING TO VALUE, 1931 [a]

APPRAISED VALUE	ASSESSED VALUE IN PERCENTAGE OF APPRAISED VALUE																								TOTAL NO. OF FARMS
	30–40	40–50	50–60	60–70	70–80	80–90	90–100	100–110	110–120	120–130	130–140	140–150	150–160	160–170	170–180	180–190	190–200	200–210	210–220	220–230	230–240	240–250	Over 250	
	No. of Farms							No. of Farms																
$0–$5,000	..	2	4	9	11	14	28	38	40	41	25	30	26	18	16	12	9	5	6	6	7	3	23	373
5,000–10,000	..	5	14	14	26	35	59	73	86	72	49	58	49	27	18	16	12	5	3	..	3	4	2	630
10,000–15,000	2	2	7	6	29	34	59	67	76	62	52	32	19	11	6	5	2	2	..	7	..	..	1	481
15,000–20,000	..	3	5	11	17	48	57	58	45	34	23	14	9	9	3	3	1	3	..	..	..	..	3	346
20,000–25,000	..	1	3	8	9	20	20	16	15	13	6	11	2	3	1	1	..	..	..	..	..	1	..	130
25,000–30,000	..	..	2	3	11	10	13	10	6	3	8	1	2	3	4	1	2	1	..	..	..	..	..	80
30,000–35,000	..	..	1	1	2	6	6	5	6	1	2	1	3	2	3	1	..	..	..	..	..	..	..	40
35,000–40,000	..	..	..	2	1	1	2	1	4	1	..	2	2	1	..	1	..	..	..	..	..	..	..	18
40,000–45,000	..	..	..	..	2	1	..	..	1	1	2	..	..	..	..	..	..	..	..	..	..	..	..	7
45,000–50,000	1	1	1	..	1	..	..	..	..	..	..	1	..	..	..	..	..	..	..	..	..	..	..	5
50,000–55,000	..	..	..	..	1	1	..	..	..	..	..	1	..	..	..	..	..	..	..	..	..	..	..	3
55,000–60,000	..	..	1	..	2	..	..	..	..	..	..	..	..	..	..	..	..	..	..	..	..	..	..	3
Over 60,000	..	..	1	..	..	..	..	..	..	..	..	..	..	..	..	..	..	..	..	..	..	..	..	1
Total	3	14	39	54	112	170	244	268	279	228	167	151	112	74	51	40	26	16	9	13	10	8	29	2,117

[a] Tables 17–22 are summaries of tables originally prepared for each of the six districts. To save space these summary tables are presented rather than all the original district tables, which are contained in the thesis referred to in note 1, page 36. One district table is presented on page 66 as a sample.

TABLE 18. — COMPARISON OF ASSESSED WITH APPRAISED VALUES OF LAND AND IMPROVEMENTS ON 2,117 FARMS GROUPED ACCORDING TO VALUE PER ACRE, 1931 [a]

APPRAISED VALUE PER ACRE	ASSESSED VALUE IN PERCENTAGE OF APPRAISED VALUE																							TOTAL NO. OF FARMS
	30–40	40–50	50–60	60–70	70–80	80–90	90–100	100–110	110–120	120–130	130–140	140–150	150–160	160–170	170–180	180–190	190–200	200–210	210–220	220–230	230–240	240–250	Over 250	
	No. of Farms							No. of Farms																
$5–$15	..	..	..	..	..	..	1	1	..	..	1	..	1	1	..	2	1	1	1	..	..	..	3	13
15– 25	..	..	2	2	..	1	3	6	8	15	8	12	14	8	9	6	4	6	2	6	4	4	12	132
25– 35	..	1	3	3	5	7	18	30	32	33	23	23	25	15	9	6	6	2	4	2	4	2	8	261
35– 45	..	1	3	4	6	14	29	35	42	44	35	25	18	16	12	17	10	7	2	3	2	2	5	332
45– 55	..	1	4	5	11	21	23	33	37	26	29	31	18	18	16	7	5	..	..	1	..	..	..	286
55– 65	..	..	5	6	14	24	22	31	37	21	24	30	21	12	4	2	..	..	..	..	..	..	..	253
65– 75	1	2	3	2	9	7	22	21	32	29	21	19	9	2	..	..	..	..	..	1	..	..	1	181
75– 85	..	1	3	..	12	13	22	48	40	35	19	7	3	2	..	..	..	..	..	..	..	..	..	205
85– 95	..	1	1	3	4	16	26	20	23	16	3	2	..	..	1	..	..	..	..	..	..	..	..	116
95–105	..	5	5	9	10	34	44	27	16	8	3	2	1	..	..	..	..	..	..	..	..	..	..	164
105–115	..	..	..	3	7	7	8	10	6	..	1	..	..	..	..	..	..	..	..	..	..	..	..	42
115–125	..	..	1	6	14	10	14	3	3	1	..	..	..	..	..	..	..	..	..	..	..	..	..	52
125–135	1	..	..	3	10	10	8	3	2	..	..	..	2	..	..	..	..	..	..	..	..	..	..	39
135–145	..	..	5	3	5	4	2	..	..	..	..	..	..	..	..	..	..	..	..	..	..	..	..	19
145–155	..	1	1	4	3	2	2	..	1	..	..	..	..	..	..	..	..	..	..	..	..	..	..	14
155–165	1	..	..	..	1	..	..	..	..	..	..	..	..	..	..	..	..	..	..	..	..	..	..	2
Over 165	..	1	3	1	1	..	..	..	..	..	..	..	..	..	..	..	..	..	..	..	..	..	..	6
Total	3	14	39	54	112	170	244	268	279	228	167	151	112	74	51	40	26	16	9	13	10	8	29	2,117

[a] See footnote to Table 17.

Table 19. — Comparison of Assessed with Appraised Values of Land and Improvements on 2,117 Farms Grouped According to Size, 1931[a]

Size of Farm in Acres	Assessed Value in Percentage of Appraised Value																						Total No. of Farms
	30–40	40–50	50–60	60–70	70–80	80–90	90–100	100–110	110–120	120–130	130–140	140–150	150–160	160–170	170–180	180–190	190–200	200–210	210–220	220–230	230–240	240–250	Over 250	
	No. of Farms							No. of Farms																
20– 60	..	2	1	1	3	3	2	3	4	5	1	3	1	..	2	1	..	..	..	1	..	..	1	34
60–100	1	2	8	13	24	30	37	39	30	31	13	18	10	11	6	7	1	..	..	..	..	..	6	287
100–140	..	3	4	6	14	17	28	21	30	18	15	10	10	4	2	1	5	..	1	..	..	..	5	194
140–180	1	3	11	16	27	40	80	97	99	66	50	40	35	21	16	11	7	4	6	2	6	3	10	651
180–220	1	2	4	8	14	20	21	16	23	24	15	19	10	5	6	1	6	2	..	..	1	..	2	200
220–260	..	1	4	6	12	12	31	35	26	23	19	13	12	8	5	5	1	1	1	2	2	2	..	221
260–300	..	..	1	2	2	11	4	11	9	14	11	10	4	2	1	..	1	..	..	1	..	1	..	85
300–340	..	1	1	1	10	27	28	32	31	28	20	19	13	10	2	6	..	3	1	4	1	..	2	240
340–380	..	..	1	..	..	2	6	2	2	3	4	..	4	2	..	1	1	..	..	..	..	..	..	28
380–420	..	..	2	..	1	3	3	5	9	4	8	6	2	..	1	1	..	2	..	..	..	..	..	47
420–460	..	..	..	..	1	2	1	1	3	2	2	..	2	..	..	1	1	..	..	..	..	..	..	16
460–500	..	..	..	..	1	..	1	2	5	4	1	4	3	4	..	2	1	2	..	3	..	..	1	34
500–540	..	..	1	1	..	..	..	..	2	..	..	1	..	1	1	..	..	..	..	..	..	..	1	8
540–580	..	..	..	..	1	..	..	1	1	1	1	2	1	..	4	..	..	..	..	..	..	2	..	14
580–620	..	..	1	..	..	1	..	..	1	2	1	1	..	..	..	..	..	..	..	..	..	..	..	7
620–660	..	..	..	..	1	2	..	1	2	1	3	3	4	6	5	3	2	2	..	..	..	..	1	36
Over 660	..	..	..	..	1	..	2	2	2	2	3	2	1	..	..	..	..	..	..	..	..	..	..	15
Total	3	14	39	54	112	170	244	268	279	228	167	151	112	74	51	40	26	16	9	13	10	8	29	2,117

[a] See footnote to Table 17.

TABLE 20. — COMPARISON OF ASSESSED WITH APPRAISED VALUES OF LAND ONLY OF 2,117 FARMS GROUPED ACCORDING TO VALUE PER ACRE OF BARE LAND, 1931 [a]

Appraised Value per Acre	Assessed Value in Percentage of Appraised Value																									Total No. of Farms
	30–40	40–50	50–60	60–70	70–80	80–90	90–100	100–110	110–120	120–130	130–140	140–150	150–160	160–170	170–180	180–190	190–200	200–210	210–220	220–230	230–240	240–250	250–260	260–270	Over 270	
	No. of Farms							No. of Farms																		
$5–$15	..	..	..	..	..	1	1	1	..	1	3	4	6	3	10	6	12	9	5	8	7	3	10	7	38	135
15– 25	..	..	1	3	3	3	7	11	15	23	28	32	40	37	21	27	24	26	19	13	14	17	6	7	26	403
25– 35	..	..	2	2	4	4	18	13	27	30	35	39	40	40	39	16	11	14	15	11	9	2	9	3	8	391
35– 45	..	..	5	4	9	7	16	15	28	29	28	12	30	34	27	31	28	19	10	8	4	3	1	1	2	351
45– 55	..	..	4	3	..	9	10	13	18	27	36	42	41	43	34	15	11	3	3	..	..	..	..	..	1	313
55– 65	..	..	1	1	2	6	10	12	28	41	33	41	45	9	3	..	..	..	..	..	..	..	..	..	..	232
65– 75	..	..	2	1	5	8	22	34	25	20	16	7	1	..	1	2	1	..	..	..	..	..	..	..	..	145
75– 85	..	..	1	2	5	13	22	14	16	3	3	..	..	1	..	..	..	..	..	..	..	..	..	..	..	80
85– 95	..	..	..	1	4	9	10	6	2	2	..	..	..	..	..	..	..	..	..	..	..	..	..	..	..	34
95–105	..	..	1	3	9	6	2	..	..	..	..	..	..	..	..	..	..	..	..	..	..	..	..	..	..	21
105–115	..	..	..	1	2	1	..	1	..	..	..	..	..	..	..	..	..	..	..	..	..	..	..	..	..	5
115–125	..	..	1	..	2	..	..	..	..	..	..	..	..	..	..	..	..	..	..	..	..	..	..	..	..	3
125–135	..	..	1	..	..	..	..	..	..	..	..	..	..	..	..	..	..	..	..	..	..	..	..	..	..	1
135–145	..	..	..	..	..	..	1	..	..	..	..	..	..	..	..	..	..	..	..	..	..	..	..	..	..	1
Over 145	..	..	..	..	..	1	..	..	1	..	..	..	..	..	..	..	..	..	..	..	..	..	..	..	..	2
Total	..	..	19	21	45	68	119	120	160	176	182	177	203	167	135	97	87	71	52	40	34	25	26	18	75	2,117

[a] See footnote to Table 17.

Table 21. — Comparison of Assessed with Appraised Values of Improvements on 1,821 Farms Grouped According to Total Value of Improvements, 1931 [a]

Appraised Value of Improvements	Assessed Value in Percentage of Appraised Value																							Total No. of Farms
	0–10	10–20	20–30	30–40	40–50	50–60	60–70	70–80	80–90	90–100	100–110	110–120	120–130	130–140	140–150	150–160	160–170	170–180	180–190	190–200	200–210	210–220	Over 220	
	No. of Farms										No. of Farms													
$0–$1,000	..	3	3	2	9	5	4	4	3	3	2	1	3	1	3	3	2	1	1	2	..	1	8	64
1,000– 2,000	..	7	12	15	24	28	21	20	22	14	10	14	9	4	5	1	1	2	..	3	2	..	1	215
2,000– 3,000	..	6	16	27	42	35	39	41	27	16	22	6	3	4	2	1	1	..	..	..	..	..	1	289
3,000– 4,000	1	3	14	40	72	64	50	26	31	15	12	6	5	2	1	1	..	..	..	..	..	..	..	343
4,000– 5,000	1	5	29	50	76	46	54	28	23	15	4	..	3	7	1	1	1	..	..	..	..	..	..	344
5,000– 6,000	1	1	17	46	52	28	31	21	10	5	1	..	..	2	1	..	..	..	..	..	..	..	..	216
6,000– 7,000	..	3	13	35	36	22	12	8	..	4	2	..	..	1	..	..	..	..	..	..	..	..	..	136
7,000– 8,000	1	5	8	16	13	15	5	3	5	..	1	..	..	..	..	..	..	..	..	..	..	..	..	72
8,000– 9,000	..	..	10	17	16	11	2	2	..	1	..	..	..	..	..	..	..	..	1	..	..	..	..	60
9,000–10,000	..	3	4	8	9	3	2	1	1	..	..	..	1	..	..	..	..	..	..	..	..	..	..	32
10,000–11,000	..	..	..	6	3	4	3	2	..	..	..	..	..	..	..	..	..	..	..	..	..	..	..	18
11,000–12,000	..	..	4	7	..	..	..	1	..	..	..	..	..	..	..	..	..	..	..	..	..	..	..	12
12,000–13,000	..	..	1	2	..	..	1	..	..	..	1	..	..	..	..	..	..	..	..	..	..	..	..	5
13,000–14,000	..	..	4	1	..	..	..	..	1	..	..	..	..	..	..	..	..	1	..	..	..	..	..	7
14,000–15,000	..	..	1	..	1	..	1	..	1	..	..	..	..	..	..	..	..	..	..	..	..	..	..	4
Over 15,000	..	..	2	..	1	1	..	..	..	..	..	..	..	..	..	..	..	..	..	..	..	..	..	4
Total	4	36	138	272	354	262	225	157	124	73	55	27	24	21	13	7	5	4	2	5	2	1	10	1,821

[a] See footnote to Table 17.

Table 22.—Relation of Improvements per Acre to Total Value per Acre[a]

Value of Land and Improvements per Acre	Value of Buildings per Acre: $0–$5	5–10	10–15	15–20	20–25	25–30	30–35	35–40	40–45	45–50	50–55	55–60	60–65	65–70	70–75	75–80	80–85	Over 85	Average Value per Acre: District II	District V	Total No. of Farms
	No. of Farms																				
$5–$15	4	2	1	..	..	..	..	..	..	..	..	..	..	..	..	..	..	..	....	$1.78	7
15– 25	17	12	26	5	1	..	..	..	..	..	..	..	..	..	..	..	..	..	....	5.00	61
25– 35	12	10	42	46	6	..	..	..	..	..	..	..	..	..	..	..	..	..	$1.00	9.39	116
35– 45	25	21	16	44	32	11	1	..	..	..	..	..	..	..	..	..	..	..	2.34	14.28	150
45– 55	20	26	10	17	15	10	5	1	..	..	..	..	..	..	..	..	..	..	6.42	20.10	104
55– 65	13	13	8	20	14	17	4	2	..	..	..	..	..	..	..	..	..	..	12.06		91
65– 75	2	3	5	15	24	26	16	9	3	..	..	..	..	..	..	..	..	..	20.15		103
75– 85	..	1	1	8	18	28	25	15	12	4	..	..	..	..	..	..	..	..	25.00	24.50	114
85– 95	..	..	..	2	11	7	18	9	14	10	4	..	..	..	..	..	..	..	31.31		73
95–105	..	..	1	..	4	5	11	12	13	12	7	3	..	1	..	..	..	..	35.44		69
105–115	..	..	..	..	..	1	3	2	4	1	..	1	3	2	..	..	..	..	41.91		17
115–125	..	..	..	..	..	..	2	..	..	1	..	..	..	1	3	2	..	..			9
125–135	..	..	..	..	..	..	..	..	1	..	..	1	4	..	2	..	..	..			8
135–145	..	..	..	..	..	..	..	..	..	..	..	..	..	..	..	..	..	..	58.30		0
145–155	..	..	..	..	..	..	..	..	..	..	..	..	..	..	..	..	..	..			0
155–165	..	..	..	..	..	..	..	..	..	..	..	..	..	..	..	..	..	..			0
Over 165	..	..	..	..	..	..	..	..	..	..	..	..	..	..	..	..	..	1			1
Total	93	88	110	157	125	105	85	50	47	28	11	5	7	4	5	2	..	1	$29.21	$10.37	923

[a] See footnote to Table 17.

Table 23. — Summary Comparison of Assessed with Appraised Values of Land and Improvements on Farms, Grouped According to Total Value, 1931

Appraised Value	Average Assessed Value in Percentage of Appraised Value				
	District I	District II	District III	District IV	District V
$0–$2,500	152.2	172.1	169.8	126.3	151.7
2,500– 5,000	....	....	....	113.1	....
5,000– 7,500	122.1	137.7	123.8	94.6	131.2
7,500–10,000	....	....	....	93.4	....
10,000–12,500	110.2	124.5	117.8	71.4	117.7
12,500–15,000	....	....	....	....	....
15,000–17,500	97.5	121.6	104.3		115.8
17,500–20,000	....	....	....	73.3	
20,000–22,500	94.4	118.7	111.1		
22,500–25,000	....	....	....		
25,000–30,000	86.1	126.6			106.6
30,000–35,000	90.0	126.1			
35,000–40,000			96.8		
40,000–45,000					
45,000–50,000		128.1			
50,000–55,000	75.0				
55,000–60,000					
Over 60,000					
Average	106.27	129.25	125.93	105.71	130.88

Table 24. — Summary Comparison of Assessed with Appraised Values of Bare Land of Farms, Grouped According to Value per Acre, 1931

Value per Acre	Average Assessed Value in Percentage of Appraised Value				
	District I	District II	District III	District IV	District V
$5–$10	....	....	313.7	251.2	280.0
10– 15	....	....	....	214.1	218.1
15– 20	259.7	323.0	211.9	161.1	179.2
20– 25	....	....	....	141.5	155.1
25– 30	199.1	217.4	162.2	137.0	143.8
30– 35	....	....	....	105.9	118.3
35– 40	167.8	183.1	128.4		
40– 45	....	....	....		
45– 50	159.2	153.1	115.9		104.4
50– 55	....	....		86.5	
55– 60	125.4	138.8			
60– 65	....	....	111.1		
65– 75	110.1	118.1			
75– 85	100.4	100.0			
85– 95	92.8				
95–105					
105–115					
115–125	78.3				
125–135					
135–145					
Over 145					
Average	117.5	151.9	149.3	134.7	150.5

TABLE 25. — COMPARISON OF ASSESSED WITH APPRAISED VALUE OF LAND AND IMPROVEMENTS OF 408 FARMS IN DISTRICT I GROUPED ACCORDING TO VALUE PER ACRE, 1931

Appraised Value per Acre	Assessed Value in Percentage of Appraised Value																			Total No. of Farms	Average Percentage of Appraised Value
	40–50[a]	50–60	60–70	70–80	80–90	90–100	100–110	110–120	120–130	130–140	140–150	150–160	160–170	170–180	180–190	190–200	200–210	210–220	Over 220		
	No. of Farms						No. of Farms														Per Cent
$15–$25	..	..	..	..	..	..	..	..	..	..	..	..	..	..	..	..	..	1	1	2	225.0
25– 35	..	1	..	..	..	..	..	..	..	..	..	..	1	..	1	..	..	1	2	6	183.3
35– 45	1	..	..	..	1	2	..	..	..	1	..	..	2	1	1	2	..	..	2	13	156.5
45– 55	..	..	1	1	1	..	..	2	..	2	1	2	2	1	..	2	..	..	..	15	138.3
55– 65	..	..	1	..	1	1	4	4	5	8	5	4	3	2	1	..	..	..	..	39	133.4
65– 75	..	..	..	..	..	1	1	3	6	2	5	5	2	..	..	..	..	..	..	25	135.8
75– 85	..	..	..	1	6	4	10	13	11	7	4	1	2	..	..	..	..	..	..	59	116.8
85– 95	..	..	2	2	4	13	3	4	3	2	..	..	..	1	..	..	..	..	..	34	101.4
95–105	1	1	4	5	16	25	11	9	5	1	1	1	..	..	..	..	..	..	..	80	96.5
105–115	..	..	2	6	7	4	4	2	..	..	..	..	..	..	..	..	..	..	..	25	88.2
115–125	..	1	6	13	7	12	2	1	1	..	..	..	..	..	..	..	..	..	..	43	83.8
125–135	..	..	3	10	8	5	2	..	..	..	..	..	..	..	..	..	..	..	..	29	79.6
135–145	..	4	3	5	4	2	..	..	..	..	..	..	..	..	..	..	..	..	..	18	73.3
145–155	1	1	4	3	2	2	..	1	..	..	..	..	..	..	..	..	..	..	..	14	
155–165	..	..	..	1	..	..	..	..	..	..	..	..	..	..	..	..	..	..	..	1	72.0
Over 165	..	3	1	1	..	..	..	..	..	..	..	..	..	..	..	..	..	..	..	5	
Total	3	11	27	48	57	71	37	39	31	23	16	14	12	5	3	4	0	2	5	408	106.27

[a] No cases under 40 per cent.

CHAPTER 4

THE TAX BURDEN OF AGRICULTURE[1]

Two measures of the tax burden of agriculture commonly used are the proportion of the farmer's net income that he is required to pay as taxes on the property he uses in production and the proportion of the net income of farm real estate that is required to pay the real estate tax. Whether or not these are valid measures of the farmer's tax burden, at least it is important to farmers that the net income they have left after paying taxes and other expenses shall not decline rapidly or for a long period. The general property tax forms the bulk of farmers' taxes in Minnesota and throughout the United States. This is true in income tax states as in others, because few farmers have incomes in excess of personal exemptions permitted under income tax laws.[2]

Except for a limited number of financial accounts kept by small groups of farmers in cooperation with and under the supervision of the Division of Agricultural Economics of the Minnesota Agricultural Experiment Station, there are no data available as to the net incomes of farmers or of farm land in Minnesota. It was, therefore, necessary to undertake a field study to secure information bearing on the tax burden of agriculture.

SOURCES OF DATA

Number and Kind of Records Secured

The number and kinds of records used in this study are indicated in Table 1. Accounting records were available relating to 251 farms in twelve different counties. These records were kept in cooperation with the Division of Agricultural Economics of the Minnesota Agricultural Experiment Station. They were kept under the supervision of field men who visited these farms at intervals during the year to assist the farmer and to check them for completeness, uniformity, and accuracy. They include records of all items of in-

[1] Professor George A. Pond of the Division of Agricultural Economics, University of Minnesota Agricultural Experiment Station, wrote this chapter and directed the collection of data on which it is based. He was assisted by a staff, as indicated in the text, notably by Mr. Don S. Anderson, who prepared most of the tables.

[2] See Appendix A, page 547.

come and expense, both cash and non-cash, as well as complete farm inventories made at the beginning and end of each year. These records were scattered over the period from 1925 to 1931. Consecutive yearly records for at least three years are available for each group of farms.

TABLE 1.—NUMBER OF FARM RECORDS SECURED FOR OWNER-OPERATED AND FOR RENTED FARMS IN EACH DISTRICT

DISTRICT	OWNER-OPERATED FARMS		RENTED FARMS	TOTAL
	Farm Accounting Records	Survey Schedules [a]	Survey Schedules [a]	
I	180[b]	...	228	408
II	22[c]	128	483	633
III	..	110	411	521
IV	26[d]	179	87	292
V	23[e]	167	145	335
Total	251	584	1,354	2,189

[a] Records for the year ending June 30, 1931.
[b] Records for the calendar years of 1928, 1929, 1930, and 1931.
[c] Records for the years ending February 28, 1930, February 28, 1931, and February 29, 1932.
[d] Records for the calendar years of 1925, 1926, and 1927.
[e] Records for the years ending February 28, 1927, February 29, 1928, and February 28, 1929.

In order to secure a larger and more representative sample of farm incomes, a farm survey was undertaken in the summer of 1931; 584 owner-operators in six different counties were visited, and a record of their farm business for the year ending June 30, 1931, was taken by the survey method.[3] Each man was visited by a carefully trained enumerator, who secured a record of all items of income and expense, both cash and non-cash, for the year studied, as well as data regarding the size and quality of the farm, amount of livestock, value of machinery and equipment, value of real estate and real estate improvements, indebtedness, interest payments, ditch liens, and similar information bearing on the farmer's earning and taxpaying ability. Items of income and expense

[3] For further details as to the survey method see W. J. Spillman, *The Validity of the Survey Method* (United States Department of Agriculture Bulletin No. 529, 1917) and G. F. Warren, "Some Methods Used in Agricultural Economics Research," Proceedings of the First International Conference of Agricultural Economists, 1929.

were given by the farmer from memory with the assistance of such records as he had kept. All valuations were carefully checked and revised on the basis of current market prices in the area studied. The experience of the enumerators and the thorough system of checking and revision by experienced supervisors made it possible to secure a high degree of accuracy in the individual reports. These records served as a basis for studying the net income of farmers.[4]

Farm landlords and their agents were also interviewed to secure information regarding the net income of farm land. The federal census reports that 45 per cent of all agricultural land in Minnesota was operated by tenants in 1930. Reports covering 1,354 rented farms for the year ending June 30, 1931, were secured. Data covering the gross income of the landlords of these farms and the expenses incurred by them were obtained by the survey method. In a considerable proportion of cases this information was obtained from accounting records kept by the landlord or his agent. Descriptions of the farms and estimated values of the land and improvements were secured. The valuations were checked by the same methods as those used for the owner-operated farms. In addition to the reports obtained for the year 1930, records relating to a group of 178 farms totaling 46,087 acres were secured for each of the years from 1923 to 1930 inclusive from accounts kept by agents in charge of the farms.

Location of Farms Studied

The location of the farms from which records were obtained is shown in Figure 1 on page 38. The state was divided roughly into six districts on the basis of type of farming, soil, and other natural and economic conditions. No records were obtained from District VI because of its minor importance in Minnesota agriculture.[5] Representative counties in each of the five other districts were selected for the owner-operated farm study, and the farms to be visited were picked at random. No owner-operated farm records were taken in District I because of the accounting records available from that section. In Pine County, in District IV, 26 farms for which accounting records were available for the years from 1925 to 1927 were surveyed in order to determine the trend in income. For the same reason survey records were obtained from 23 farms in

[4] See page 73.

[5] This district is covered partly in Chapter 5, the study of tax delinquency in the cut-over region, and partly in Chapter 6, on the taxation of forests.

Polk County in District V for which accounting records for the years from 1926 to 1928 were available.

Records of rented farms were obtained in each of the first five districts. The number obtained was roughly proportional to the number of rented farms in each district. The rented farms were selected at random within the district.

TABLE 2.—AVERAGE ACREAGE AND INVESTMENT PER FARM AND TOTAL VALUE PER ACRE OF 764 OWNER-OPERATED FARMS, 1931

DISTRICT	NO. OF FARMS	AVERAGE NO. OF ACRES PER FARM			AVERAGE INVESTMENT PER FARM					VALUE PER ACRE OF LAND AND IMPROVEMENTS
		Total	Tillable	In Crops	Land	Buildings and Improvements	Equipment	Livestock	Total	
I..........	180	183	139	128	$14,074	$6,373	$1,998	$3,636	$26,081	$112
II..........	128	170	142	127	10,019	5,002	945	2,015	17,981	88
III..........	110	210	165	160	6,491	3,691	980	1,888	13,050	48
IV..........	179	115	40	43	1,860	2,148	406	1,070	5,484	35
V..........	167	304	262	236	6,855	3,368	1,240	1,711	13,174	34
Total area	764	195	147	135	$7,863	$4,110	$1,136	$2,091	$15,200	$61

DESCRIPTION OF FARMS STUDIED

Owner-operated farms.—The number of farms surveyed in each district and the average acreage and investment per farm are shown in Table 2. The tillable acreage is the total acreage that could be cropped without additional drainage or clearing. The crop acreage is the amount of land actually in crops in 1930. Except in District I the size of farm and the proportion of the total acreage in crops is about the same as the average for all farms in the counties in which they are located. As already noted, the group of farms in District I is a selected one, the operators of which are cooperating with the Minnesota Agricultural Experiment Station in an accounting study of their farm business. This factor of selection tended to secure not only farmers of more than average ability but also farms of more than average size.

The value of land as shown in Table 2 covers only the bare land. All improvements such as buildings, fences, drains, and water systems are included under the heading "Buildings and Improve-

TABLE 3.—AVERAGE ACREAGE AND INVESTMENT PER FARM AND TOTAL VALUE PER ACRE OF OWNER-OPERATED FARMS IN FOUR COUNTIES, 1925–1931

COUNTY AND YEAR	NO. OF FARMS	AVERAGE NO. OF ACRES PER FARM	AVERAGE INVESTMENT PER FARM: Land	Buildings and Improvements	Machinery and Equipment	Livestock	Total	VALUE PER ACRE OF LAND, BUILDINGS, AND IMPROVEMENTS
Pine County								
1925	27	104	$5,874	$4,578	$ 936	$1,385	$12,773	$101
1926	24	111	6,448	4,627	1,001	1,474	13,550	100
1927	25	115	6,485	4,419	1,019	1,425	13,348	95
1930	26	107	3,524	3,359	920	1,283	9,086	64
Polk County								
1926	15	380	21,398	6,883	2,343	2,585	33,209	74
1927	18	342	19,448	7,434	2,385	2,814	32,081	79
1928	20	349	21,381	7,407	2,893	2,532	34,213	82
1930	23	396	11,175	5,126	1,987	2,035	20,323	41
Rock and Nobles counties								
1929	22	323	32,183	5,763	1,967	7,176	47,089	117
1930	22	360	30,915	5,570	2,029	6,262	44,776	101
1931	22	344	20,640	6,007	1,984	4,338	32,969	77
Eight counties in southeastern Minnesota[a]								
1928	124	162	13,079	6,130	1,751	3,428	24,388	119
1929	171	177	13,979	6,310	2,017	3,829	26,135	115
1930	180	183	14,075	6,372	1,998	3,636	26,081	112
1931	147	198	11,005	7,132	2,146	3,470	23,753	92

[a] Dodge, Freeborn, Goodhue, Le Sueur, Mower, Rice, Steele, and Waseca counties.

ments." The value per acre of land, buildings, and improvements is somewhat higher in District I than the average reported by the 1930 federal census for the counties in which the farms studied are located. This is due to the method of selection mentioned in the previous paragraph, which tended to include a larger proportion of farms with land of better than average quality and improvements. In the four other districts the value per acre of land and improvements on the farms studied is slightly below the average of the federal census for the counties in which they are located.

TABLE 4.—AVERAGE ACREAGE AND INVESTMENT PER FARM AND TOTAL VALUE PER ACRE OF 1,354 RENTED FARMS, 1931

District	No. of Farms	Average No. of Acres per Farm: Total	Average No. of Acres per Farm: Tillable	Average Investment per Farm: Land	Average Investment per Farm: Buildings and Improvements	Average Investment per Farm: Total	Value per Acre of Land and Improvements
I	228	165	127	$8,453	$4,032	$12,485	$75
II	483	244	194	12,048	3,859	15,907	65
III	411	250	180	6,947	3,287	10,234	41
IV	87	168	106	4,650	2,809	7,459	44
V	145	271	236	5,672	2,556	8,228	30
Total area	1,354	231	177	$8,737	$3,507	$12,244	$53

Since these valuations were made in 1931 and the census valuations in 1930, the difference can be accounted for by the decline in land prices during the year.

Equipment includes not only all machinery and tools but also tractors, gasoline engines, motors, trucks, and such share of the automobile as represents its proportionate use in the farm business. The values are based on current resale prices. Livestock is valued at the current market prices of June 30, 1931.

Some data descriptive of four groups of owner-operated farms for which income figures are available for more than one year are shown in Table 3. All these data are from accounting records, except the 1930 figures for Pine County, which are included in the averages for District IV given in Table 2, and the 1930 figures for Polk County, which are included in the averages for District V.

Rented farms.—The number, size, and average investment per farm of the 1,354 rented farms studied are shown by districts in Table 4. These farms average somewhat larger than the owner-operated farms described in Table 2. This is to be expected because there is a larger proportion of rented farms in those counties and districts in which the average size of farm is larger than the average for the whole state, and also because within the same district or county, as shown by the federal census, the average size of rented farms is larger than the average size of owner-operated farms. The value per acre of the bare land of the owner-operated farms is only

TABLE 5.—AVERAGE ACREAGE AND INVESTMENT PER FARM AND TOTAL VALUE PER ACRE OF 178 RENTED FARMS IN SOUTHWESTERN MINNESOTA, 1923–1930

YEAR	AVERAGE NO. OF ACRES PER FARM	AVERAGE INVESTMENT PER FARM			VALUE PER ACRE OF LAND, BUILDINGS, AND IMPROVEMENTS
		Land	Buildings and Improvements	Total	
1923	259	$17,732	$1,310	$19,042	$74
1924	259	16,485	1,369	17,854	69
1925	259	16,124	1,436	17,561	68
1926	259	15,041	1,347	16,388	63
1927	259	14,560	1,357	15,917	61
1928	259	14,319	1,701	16,020	62
1929	259	13,838	1,705	15,543	60
1930	259	12,033	1,869	13,902	54

slightly higher than that of the rented farms, but the value per acre of the farm with buildings and improvements is materially higher on the owner-operated farms because of the larger investment in buildings and other improvements.

Records of income for the years from 1923 to 1930 inclusive were obtained for 178 rented farms in District II. These were obtained in the survey study from accounting records kept by agents of the owners. These farms are included in the District II group for which average figures are shown for the year 1931 in Table 4. The average size and investment of these farms for each of the eight years is shown in Table 5.

FARMER'S NET INCOME AND THE NET INCOME OF REAL ESTATE

FARMER'S NET INCOME

The average gross income, expense, and net income per farm of 764 owner-operated farms are shown in Table 6. The gross income

TABLE 6.—GROSS INCOME, EXPENSES, AND FARMER'S NET INCOME PER FARM OF 764 OWNER-OPERATED FARMS FOR YEAR ENDING DECEMBER 31, 1930, OR JUNE 30, 1931

DISTRICT	GROSS INCOME PER FARM					EXPENSES PER FARM			FARMER'S NET INCOME	
	Livestock	Crops	Miscellaneous	Family Living	Total	Cash	Non-cash	Total	Per Farm	Per Acre
I	$3,800	$436	$262	$559	$5,057	$1,613	$483	$2,096	$2,961	$16.18
II[a]	2,129	404	80	479	3,092	978	354	1,332	1,760	7.96
III	1,651	516	68	451	2,686	784	320	1,104	1,582	7.53
IV	822	154	67	352	1,395	446	173	619	776	6.77
V	1,110	1,316	85	509	3,020	1,033	375	1,408	1,612	5.30
Total area	$1,925	$568	$119	$471	$3,083	$987	$342	$1,329	$1,754	$8.99

[a] Includes twenty farms for which the data cover the year ending February 28, 1931.

is classified as to source. The item "miscellaneous" includes largely receipts for work done by the farmer for hire and for the rent of power and equipment used by others. The first three items represent cash receipts. The fourth item is a non-cash item. It includes the value of milk, cream, butter, eggs, meat, vegetables, and other farm-raised produce used by the farm family. This produce is valued at the current farm price. This item also includes an estimated rental value of the farmhouse used by the farmer and his family. This rental is computed at 10 per cent of the estimated value of the house.

The cash expense includes current operating expense. It includes no property taxes, no interest, principal, or rent payments, no items of capital investment, and no expense for labor other than hired labor. It does not include the cash cost of family living nor the personal expenses of the farmer and his family. Non-cash expense includes depreciation of buildings, improvements, and machinery. This depreciation is computed on the basis of the present value and the estimated length of life.

The net income as computed is the return the farmer gets for his services as a laborer and manager, for the labor of members of his family who receive no regular wage, and for the use of his capital in the form of machinery and livestock as well as for his land. If his farm and personal property are free from indebtedness, it represents what he has for personal and family expenditures, for the payment of taxes, and for savings and investment. Obviously not all of this net income is available for tax payments or other expenditures, since it includes family living consumed currently. On the other hand, the non-cash item of depreciation does not necessarily represent a deduction each year. In actual practice the farmer will spend considerable sums for building construction or machinery one year and may not make further expenditures for several years. In the long run, however, this depreciation must be provided for if the farmer is to continue in business.

Incomes both on a per farm and a per acre basis are much higher in District I than in the other districts. This is due in part to the more intensive methods of farming practiced and to the fact that the prices of the products raised in this section were relatively higher than those in the other districts. Prices received for products sold were also higher because of the difference in the time period covered. Records for District I were for the calendar year

1930 and for the other districts for the year ending June 30, 1931. Severe price declines occurred during the period from January 1 to June 30, 1931, which were reflected in the lower average gross incomes of Districts II to V. This difference in incomes was also due in a measure to the fact that these men were a carefully selected group who were studying their business with the help of accounting records and, undoubtedly, were receiving larger incomes than the average for all farmers in this section.

In all studies of farmers' incomes a wide variation is found between individuals even in the same community where soil, weather, and market conditions are fairly uniform. The variations in average net income per farm in each district are shown in Table 7. In order to eliminate the effect of size of farm from this comparison, the net income per acre for each district is shown in Table 8. These figures indicate a wide variation among farmers in their earning and consequently in their taxpaying ability.

The receipts, expenses, and net incomes of the same groups of farmers for several years are shown in Table 9. There is some change in the farms included in each group in succeeding years, but in all cases farms of approximately the same size and type were selected, so that these figures represent fairly accurately changes in the farmer's net income in each county or group of counties. With the exception of Polk County, incomes in 1930 were materially lower than in any of the previous years and in 1931 they were markedly lower. The 1926 income figure for Polk County is abnormal because of abnormally low yields of most of the crops that year in the area where this study was made. Low crop yields in 1931, due to drouth and hot weather, accounted in part for the lower earnings in 1931. These income data are computed on the same basis as those shown in Table 6.

Since 1929 the prices of all farm products have been falling rapidly. The prices of goods and services that the farmers use in production have fallen much less rapidly. As a result the gross income of these farmers was decreased relatively more in 1930 and 1931 as compared with previous years than were the expenses. This corresponds with the trend in the net cash income of agriculture in Minnesota as shown on pages 104 and 547. In fact, the effect of the decline in prices on the farmer's financial position is more serious than shown in these income figures. Not only has his net income been reduced but his investment in live-

TABLE 7.—DISTRIBUTION OF 764 OWNER-OPERATED FARMS ACCORDING TO FARMER'S NET INCOME PER FARM, 1930–31

Farmer's Net Income per Farm	District I	District II	District III	District IV	District V	Total Area
Loss	1	..	..	1	4	6
$0–$500	2	9	10	48	12	81
500–1,000	2	20	22	89	36	169
1,000–1,500	7	35	30	29	40	141
1,500–2,000	28	20	21	9	24	102
2,000–2,500	35	18	10	2	20	85
2,500–3,000	28	10	8	1	13	60
3,000–3,500	20	8	5	..	9	42
3,500–4,000	18	3	2	..	6	29
4,000–4,500	12	1	..	..	1	14
4,500–5,000	9	3	1	..	1	14
5,000–5,500	5	..	..	..	1	6
5,500–6,000	6	..	..	..	..	6
6,000–6,500	3	1	..	..	..	4
6,500–7,000	2	..	1	..	..	3
Over 7,000	2[a]	..	..	..	..	2
Total	180	128	110	179	167	764

[a] $8,645; 7,690.

TABLE 8.—DISTRIBUTION OF 764 OWNER-OPERATED FARMS ACCORDING TO FARMER'S NET INCOME PER ACRE, 1930–31

Farmer's Net Income per Acre	District I	District II	District III	District IV	District V	Total Area
Loss	1	..	..	1	4	6
$0–$2	2	7	4	9	13	35
2– 4	..	3	12	28	33	76
4– 6	1	16	26	45	42	130
6– 8	5	12	22	27	40	106
8–10	10	20	15	28	21	94
10–12	18	17	13	14	7	69
12–14	18	17	4	10	5	54
14–16	23	15	9	7	1	55
16–18	16	8	3	3	..	30
18–20	19	2	..	..	1	23
20–22	11	5	2	2	..	20
22–24	17	2	..	2	..	21
24–26	12	1	..	..	..	13
26–28	8	2	..	..	..	10
28–30	7	..	..	..	..	7
30–32	4	..	..	..	..	4
32–34	4	..	..	..	..	4
34–36	2	1	..	2	..	5
Over 36	2[a]	..	..	..	..	2
Total	180	128	110	179	167	764

[a] $39; 58.

TABLE 9.—RECEIPTS, EXPENSES, AND FARMER'S NET INCOME PER OWNER-OPERATED FARM IN SPECIFIED COUNTIES OF MINNESOTA, 1925–1931

County and Year	Receipts			Expenses	Farmer's Net Income	
	Cash	Non-cash	Total		Per Farm	Per Acre
Pine County						
1925	$2,724	$425	$3,149	$1,375	$1,774	$17.13
1926	3,137	441	3,578	1,610	1,968	17.74
1927	2,780	416	3,196	1,799	1,397	12.17
1930	1,819	476	2,295	1,176	1,119	10.46
Polk County						
1926	4,456	615	5,071	2,945	2,126	5.60
1927	5,062	680	5,742	2,932	2,810	8.22
1928	5,668	748	6,416	3,580	2,836	8.11
1930	3,718	793	4,511	2,310	2,201	5.55
Rock and Nobles counties						
1929	9,289	646	9,935	4,951	4,984	15.44
1930	8,090	599	8,689	4,509	4,180	11.61
1931	5,328	524	5,852	3,638	2,214	6.43
Eight counties in southeastern Minnesota[a]						
1928	4,353	554	4,907	2,181	2,726	16.84
1929	5,040	507	5,547	2,258	3,289	18.62
1930	4,498	559	5,057	2,096	2,961	16.18
1931	3,804	482	4,286	1,824	2,462	12.43

[a] Dodge, Freeborn, Goodhue, Le Sueur, Mower, Rice, Steele, and Waseca counties.

stock and machinery as well as in land and improvements has depreciated very materially. The depreciation in the value of land and land improvements is shown in Table 3 on page 71. In 1930 the value of livestock, machinery, and feeds on hand on the farms studied in Rock and Nobles counties declined $1,858 per farm and in 1931, $2,623. Part of this decline was due to reduced quantities of feed on hand resulting from lower yields. Similar losses occurred in the other counties. None of these inventory losses due to declining prices are reflected in any of the income figures presented in this study. They should be kept in mind, however, in studying the farmer's financial status and in interpreting relations to be discussed later in this chapter.

THE NET INCOME OF REAL ESTATE

Owner-operated farms.—The real estate tax comprises the major portion of the general property tax on farm property. It is primarily a tax on the income of real estate, though for temporary periods it does not vary as does current income. The farmers' net incomes presented in the preceding pages include the income to be credited not only to real estate but also to the labor of the farmer and his family and to working capital invested in livestock and machinery. In order to determine the net income due to the land only, it is necessary to make some division of the farmer's net income. This has been done by deducting from this income figure an estimated charge for the labor of the farmer and his family and a charge for the use of the capital invested in livestock

TABLE 10.—RECEIPTS, EXPENSES, AND NET INCOME OF REAL ESTATE OF 764 OWNER-OPERATED FARMS, 1930–31

District	Gross Income per Farm [a]	Expenses per Farm: Farm Operating Expense	Expenses per Farm: Personal Property Tax	Expenses per Farm: Charge for Family Labor	Expenses per Farm: Charge for Use of Working Capital	Expenses per Farm: Total	Net Income of Real Estate: Per Farm	Net Income of Real Estate: Per Acre
I	$5,057	$2,096	$31	$1,101	$282	$3,510	$1,547	$8.45
II	3,092	1,332	24	1,035	148	2,539	553	3.25
III	2,686	1,104	23	1,035	143	2,305	381	1.81
IV	1,395	619	13	990	74	1,696	—301 [b]	—2.62 [b]
V	3,020	1,408	19	1,080	119	2,626	394	1.30
Total area	$3,083	$1,329	$22	$1,050	$155	$2,556	$527	$2.70

[a] Same as in Table 6. [b] Minus (—) indicates loss.

and machinery. The labor was valued at the current wages paid hired help in the counties from which records were obtained. A charge of 5 per cent on the inventory value was made for use of the capital invested in machinery and livestock. The personal property tax was also added to the expenses since this is levied against the working capital used in the farm business. Table 10 shows the net income of real estate computed on this basis for the 764 owner-operated farms for which farmers' net incomes are shown in Table 6. Because of the relatively large labor charge in District IV resulting from intensive methods of production, the income was insufficient to cover the other expenses and leave any return for land.

In Table 11 is presented the net income from the real estate of the owner-operated farms for which the farmer's net income is

TABLE 11. — RECEIPTS, EXPENSES, AND NET INCOME OF REAL ESTATE PER OWNER-OPERATED FARM IN SPECIFIED COUNTIES OF MINNESOTA, 1925–1931

County and Year	Gross Income per Farm [a]	Expenses per Farm					Net Income of Real Estate	
		Farm Operating Expense [a]	Personal Property Tax	Charge for Family Labor	Charge for Use of Working Capital	Total	Per Farm	Per Acre
Pine County								
1925	$3,149	$1,375	$17	$985	$116	$2,493	$656	$6.31
1926	3,578	1,610	21	937	124	2,692	886	7.98
1927	3,196	1,799	23	953	122	2,897	299	2.60
1930	2,295	1,176	25	870	110	2,181	114	1.07
Polk County								
1926	5,071	2,945	22	1,151	246	4,364	707	1.86
1927	5,742	2,932	22	1,194	260	4,408	1,334	3.90
1928	6,416	3,580	28	1,148	271	5,027	1,389	3.98
1930	4,511	2,310	32	1,196	201	3,739	772	1.95
Rock and Nobles counties								
1929	9,935	4,951	37	1,308	457	6,753	3,182	9.85
1930	8,689	4,509	50	1,152	415	6,126	2,563	7.12
1931	5,852	3,638	37	826	316	4,817	1,035	3.01
Eight counties in southeastern Minnesota [b]								
1928	4,907	2,181	27	1,074	260	3,542	1,365	8.43
1929	5,547	2,258	27	1,081	292	3,658	1,889	10.67
1930	5,057	2,096	31	1,101	282	3,510	1,547	8.45
1931	4,286	1,824	37	867	281	3,009	1,277	6.45

[a] Same as in Table 9.   [b] Dodge, Freeborn, Goodhue, Le Sueur, Mower, Rice, Steele, and Waseca counties.

shown in Table 9. This is computed by the same method as that used for the 764 owner-operated farms presented in Table 10.

Rented farms.—Records of landlords' receipts and expenses on rented farms form another source of data covering the net income of farm real estate. In many ways these furnish a more satisfactory method of measuring the net income of land than owner-operator records, since it is unnecessary to estimate large items of expense such as unpaid family labor and the charge for the use of working capital. The net income of the real estate on 1,354 rented farms for the year ending June 30, 1931, is shown by districts in Table 12.

TABLE 12.—RECEIPTS, EXPENSES, AND NET INCOME OF REAL ESTATE OF 1,354 RENTED FARMS, 1930–31

District	Gross Income per Farm			Expenses per Farm			Net Income of Real Estate	
	Cash	Share	Total	Cash	Non-cash	Total	Per Farm	Per Acre
I	$606	$74	$680	$111	$161	$272	$408	$2.47
II	476	492	968	175	148	323	645	2.64
III	239	351	590	138	119	257	333	1.33
IV	194	157	351	98	99	197	154	.91
V	110	488	598	217	93	310	288	1.02
Total area	$369	$357	$726	$153	$132	$285	$441	$1.91

Some of these farms were rented for cash, some for a share of the crop, and the rest for a combination of the two. The gross income includes the cash rent received and the cash value of the share received, whether sold or used otherwise. The cash expenses include repairs of buildings and fences, other land improvements, and the cash cost of supervision whether rendered by the owner or his agent. The non-cash expense includes only depreciation of buildings, fences, and other land improvements. The net income is the excess of gross receipts over expense. This may be considered the net earnings or net income of the real estate.

The net income per acre of real estate of rented farms is somewhat lower in each of the districts than that of the owner-operated farms reported in Table 10. This may be explained at least in part by the fact that the value of the land and improvements of the owner-operated farms as shown in Table 2 was somewhat higher than that of the rented farms shown in Table 4. Apparently the higher values reported for the first group reflected greater produc-

TABLE 13.—DISTRIBUTION OF 1,354 RENTED FARMS ACCORDING TO NET INCOME OF REAL ESTATE PER FARM, 1930–31

NET INCOME OF REAL ESTATE PER FARM	DISTRICT I	DISTRICT II	DISTRICT III	DISTRICT IV	DISTRICT V	TOTAL AREA
Loss	5	12	20	14	17	68
\$0–\$125	21	31	60	30	45	187
125– 250	45	53	98	23	32	251
250– 375	60	67	88	11	17	243
375– 500	26	74	49	6	12	167
500– 625	34	48	46	2	4	134
625– 750	9	58	19	..	5	91
750– 875	14	36	13	1	5	69
875–1,000	4	29	8	..	1	42
1,000–1,125	3	18	6	..	2	29
1,125–1,250	4	11	1	..	1	17
1,250–1,375	1	6	1	..	1	9
1,375–1,500	2	8	..	..	..	10
1,500–1,625	..	5	2	..	..	7
1,625–1,750	..	6	..	..	1	7
1,750–1,875	..	7	..	..	..	7
1,875–2,000	..	3	..	..	..	3
2,000–2,125	..	2	..	..	..	2
2,125–2,250	..	2	..	..	..	2
2,250–2,375	..	4	..	..	..	4
Over 2,375	..	3[a]	..	..	2[b]	5
Total	228	483	411	87	145	1,354

[a] \$2,500; 2,610; 2,901. [b] \$3,196; 3,938.

TABLE 14.—DISTRIBUTION OF 1,354 RENTED FARMS ACCORDING TO NET INCOME OF REAL ESTATE PER ACRE, 1930–31

NET INCOME OF REAL ESTATE PER ACRE	DISTRICT I	DISTRICT II	DISTRICT III	DISTRICT IV	DISTRICT V	TOTAL AREA
Loss	5	12	20	14	17	68
\$.00–\$.50	4	7	33	18	39	101
.50–1.00	13	16	69	16	30	144
1.00–1.50	25	45	81	13	23	187
1.50–2.00	32	63	63	14	11	183
2.00–2.50	37	70	66	6	9	188
2.50–3.00	26	73	36	2	7	144
3.00–3.50	31	68	17	3	2	121
3.50–4.00	17	49	13	1	3	83
4.00–4.50	17	39	5	..	2	63
4.50–5.00	10	22	..	..	1	33
5.00–5.50	6	13	4	..	1	24
5.50–6.00	2	3	..	..	..	5
6.00–6.50	..	..	1	..	..	1
6.50–7.00	1	1	..	..	..	2
7.00–7.50	..	..	2	..	..	2
Over 7.50	2[a]	2[b]	1[c]	..	..	5
Total	228	483	411	87	145	1,354

[a] \$8.00; 14.50. [b] \$7.63; 8.10. [c] \$8.12.

tivity. Some of this difference in net income of real estate between the owner-operated and the rented farms may also be interpreted to indicate that the estimates of the value of labor and the use of working capital made in case of the owner-operated farms were rather conservative.

There was a wide range between different rented farms in the net income to real estate just as there was in the case of the farmer's net income on the owner-operated farms reported in Tables 7 and 8. This range is shown on a per farm basis in Table 13 and on a per acre basis in Table 14.

RELATION OF TAXES TO INCOME AND TO VALUE OF REAL ESTATE

Owner-Operated Farms

The tax burden of agriculture, as already mentioned, may be measured by the relation of the general property tax to the farmer's net income or by the relation of the real estate tax to the net income of real estate. It may also be measured by the ratio of real estate taxes to the value of real estate. The ratio of property taxes to the farmer's net income for 764 owner-operated farms is shown in Table 15. Personal property and real estate taxes are shown separately. In general the higher the net income per farm, the smaller is the percentage of that income that is required to pay the

Table 15.—Relation of Property Taxes to Farmer's Net Income on 764 Owner-Operated Farms, 1930–31

District	No. of Farms	Farmer's Net Income per Farm [a]	Real Estate Taxes			Personal Property Taxes per Farm	Total Taxes	
			Per Farm	Per Acre	Percentage of Net Income		Per Farm	Percentage of Net Income
I	180	$2,961	$236	$1.29	8.00	$31	$267	9.02
II	128	1,760	197	1.15	11.20	24	220	12.50
III	110	1,582	182	.87	11.50	23	205	12.90
IV	179	776	103	.90	13.30	13	116	15.00
V	167	1,612	196	.65	12.20	19	215	13.40
Total area	764	$1,754	$182	$ .93	10.40	$22	$204	11.40

[a] Farmer's net income includes the income from the labor of himself and family as well as income from investment in farm and equipment. This is, of course, different from income from real estate only. See further explanations in the text and in the other tables, especially pages 73 to 81.

Table 16. — Distribution of 764 Owner-Operated Farms According to Amount of Real Estate Tax per Farm, 1930–31

Tax per Farm	District I	District II	District III	District IV	District V	Total Area
$0–$25	..	..	..	3	..	3
25– 50	..	2	4	27	1	34
50– 75	..	2	7	37	9	55
75–100	9	7	10	34	20	80
100–125	13	14	11	21	20	79
125–150	11	11	17	26	21	86
150–175	26	22	9	9	15	81
175–200	26	20	9	9	20	84
200–225	21	11	15	6	11	64
225–250	13	11	8	3	9	44
250–275	7	11	3	2	13	36
275–300	15	5	4	..	4	26
300–325	8	1	5	1	5	20
325–350	5	2	3	1	5	16
350–375	8	2	1	..	1	12
375–400	4	1	..	..	5	10
400–425	6	3	1	..	1	11
425–450	1	1	1	..	1	4
450–475	3	1	1	..	1	6
475–500	1	1	1	..	..	3
Over 500	5[a]	..	..	..	5[b]	10
Total	180	128	110	179	167	764

[a] $500; 527; 537; 634; 906. [b] $517; 521; 581; 671: 1,043.

Table 17. — Distribution of 764 Owner-Operated Farms According to Amount of Real Estate Tax per Acre, 1930–31

Tax per Acre	District I	District II	District III	District IV	District V	Total Area
$.00–$.25	..	..	..	..	1	1
.25– .50	..	..	2	23	32	57
.50– .75	6	3	35	61	90	195
.75–1.00	27	22	41	28	28	146
1.00–1.25	61	66	20	19	10	176
1.25–1.50	36	20	10	12	3	81
1.50–1.75	22	12	2	17	3	56
1.75–2.00	14	3	..	12	..	29
2.00–2.25	5	1	..	5	..	11
2.25–2.50	4	1	..	1	..	6
2.50–2.75	2	..	..	..	..	2
2.75–3.00	..	..	..	1	..	1
3.00–3.25	2	..	..	..	..	2
3.25–3.50	..	..	..	..	..	..
3.50–3.75	1	..	..	..	..	1
Total	180	128	110	179	167	764

tax. On the average, 10.4 per cent of the farmer's net income on the 764 farms was needed to pay the real estate tax and 11.4 per cent to pay the total property tax.

The amount of total property taxes varies widely among different farms. The range is shown by districts in Table 16. Since a considerable proportion of this variation is due to differences in size of farm and in the amount of personal property taxes, as well as to differences in rates, the range in real estate taxes is shown on an acre basis in Table 17. The real estate tax per acre varies more widely within the district than do the averages of the different districts. In every case the amount of both the personal property tax and the real estate tax was taken from the county records, so that none of this variation is due to errors of estimate. Payments of interest and principal on ditch liens were not included in the real estate tax. They were recorded separately and will be discussed later.

The range in the percentage of the farmer's net income required to pay the total property tax is shown in Table 18. The range is comparatively narrow in Districts I and II, but it increases materially in Districts IV and V, where agricultural conditions are more variable and incomes average somewhat lower. In five cases there was no net income and in nine others the net income was less than the amount of the property tax. On less than one-third of the farms did the tax exceed 16 per cent of the farmer's net income, and on only 5 per cent did it exceed 41 per cent.

The relation of the real estate tax to the value and to the net income of real estate for the 764 owner-operated farms is shown in Table 19. Since the net income of real estate varies more between districts than does the farmer's net income, the proportion of the net income of real estate needed to pay the real estate tax also varies more widely. In District IV there was no net income to real estate. For the entire group of farms the real estate tax amounted to 34.5 per cent of the net income of real estate.

Rented Farms

The amount of property taxes per farm and per acre and their relation to the value of the real estate and to the net income is shown in Table 20 for 1,354 rented farms. Only the real estate tax is given, since only the income of real estate is being considered. In each district the tax per acre is lower than it is in the case of the

Table 18. — Distribution of 764 Owner-Operated Farms According to Proportion of Farmer's Net Income Required to Pay Total Property Tax, 1930–31

Percentage of Net Income Required to Pay Total Property Tax	District I	District II	District III	District IV	District V	Total Area
0– 6	36	4	6	14	8	68
6–11	91	49	33	45	58	276
11–16	39	37	35	47	43	201
16–21	8	15	19	19	23	84
21–26	1	7	6	15	10	39
26–31	..	6	4	6	7	23
31–36	1	2	2	12	2	19
36–41	..	..	..	9	4	13
41–46	..	1	..	6	..	7
46–51	..	..	1	..	1	2
51–56	..	..	..	4	3	7
56–61	..	..	1	..	2	3
61–66	..	1	1	..	1	3
66–71	..	..	..	1	..	1
71–76	..	1	..	..	1	2
76–81	..	..	..	..	..	..
81–86	1	..	..	..	..	1
86–91	..	..	..	1	..	1
91–96	..	..	..	..	..	..
96–101	..	..	..	..	..	..
Over 101	2[a]	5[b]	2[c]	..	..	9
Net loss farms	1	..	..	1	4	5
Total	180	128	110	179	167	764

[a] 115; 145. [b] 144; 153; 197; 295; 434. [c] 102; 120.

Table 19. — Relation of Real Estate Taxes to Value of Farm and to Net Income of Real Estate of 764 Owner-Operated Farms, 1930–31

District	No. of Farms	Value per Farm	Net Income of Real Estate per Farm[a]	Real Estate Taxes		
				Per Farm	Percentage of Value	Percentage of Net Income[a]
I	180	$20,441	$1,547	$236	1.15	15.30
II	128	15,021	553	197	1.30	35.60
III	110	10,182	381	182	1.80	47.80
IV	179	4,008	— 301[b]	103	2.60	....[c]
V	167	10,223	394	196	1.90	49.70
Total area	764	$11,973	$527	$182	1.52	34.50

[a] Note that income in this table is income to real estate; it does not include the labor and other income included in farmer's net income. See the distinctions made between "farmer's net income" and "net income of real estate" in Tables 10 and 15 and in the text above.
[b] Minus (—) indicates loss. [c] No net income.

TABLE 20.—RELATION OF REAL ESTATE TAXES TO VALUE OF FARM AND TO NET INCOME OF REAL ESTATE OF 1,354 RENTED FARMS, 1930–31

DISTRICT	NO. OF FARMS	VALUE PER FARM	NET INCOME OF REAL ESTATE PER FARM	Real Estate Taxes: Per Farm	Per Acre	Percentage of Value	Percentage of Net Income
I..........	228	$12,485	$408	$187	$1.13	1.50	45.80
II..........	483	15,907	645	258	1.06	1.60	40.00
III..........	411	10,234	333	173	.69	1.70	52.00
IV..........	87	7,459	154	115	.68	1.55	74.70
V..........	145	8,226	288	171	.63	2.10	59.40
Total area	1,354	$12,244	$441	$202	$ .87	1.65	45.80

TABLE 21.—DISTRIBUTION OF 1,354 RENTED FARMS ACCORDING TO AMOUNT OF REAL ESTATE TAX PER FARM, 1930–31

TAX PER FARM	DISTRICT I	DISTRICT II	DISTRICT III	DISTRICT IV	DISTRICT V	TOTAL AREA
$0–$25...........	1	1	3	1	1	7
25– 50...........	3	6	15	9	4	37
50– 75...........	8	20	20	15	22	85
75–100...........	31	19	53	16	18	137
100–125...........	24	24	56	11	24	139
125–150...........	34	59	60	14	19	186
150–175...........	25	53	45	10	8	141
175–200...........	20	39	32	4	14	109
200–225...........	15	33	29	5	6	88
225–250...........	13	42	26	..	5	86
250–275...........	16	30	21	..	3	70
275–300...........	8	25	5	..	4	42
300–325...........	6	23	13	..	2	44
325–350...........	6	18	8	..	2	34
350–375...........	8	18	7	1	3	37
375–400...........	4	12	1	..	2	19
400–425...........	3	7	4	..	..	14
425–450...........	1	5	4	..	..	10
450–475...........	..	3	3	1	2	9
475–500...........	..	5	2	..	1	8
Over 500	2[a]	41[b]	4[c]	..	5[d]	52
Total...........	228	483	411	87	145	1,354

[a] $645; 801.

[b] $500; 508; 511; 512; 513; 519; 522; 525; 538; 539; 543; 552; 551; 555; 565; 570; 577; 587; 626; 672; 685; 693; 720; 730; 742; 748; 750; 798; 802; 806; 809; 815; 836; 848; 872; 983; 1,012; 1,154; 1,284; 1,532.

[c] $528; 540; 584; 677.

[d] $543; 552; 597; 767; 1,077.

owner-operated farms, as reported in Table 15. This bears out the previous observation that the rented farms were lower in productivity and hence in value than the owner-operated farms studied. The latter have a higher value per acre and a higher net income per acre, and it is only reasonable to tax them somewhat more heavily. However, the percentage of the net income required to pay the taxes is greater than in the case of the owner-operated farms. All these comparisons make it apparent that the tax burden is falling most heavily on farms in Districts III, IV, and V, where land values are low. It is obvious from these data that real estate taxes are not closely adjusted to the earning power or net income of land. (See Chapter 3, especially pages 48 to 50.)

TABLE 22.—DISTRIBUTION OF 1,354 RENTED FARMS ACCORDING TO AMOUNT OF REAL ESTATE TAX PER ACRE, 1930–31

Tax per Acre	District I	District II	District III	District IV	District V	Total Area
$.00–$.25	..	..	..	1	3	4
.25– .50	5	4	33	23	51	116
.50– .75	16	63	166	32	53	330
.75–1.00	63	197	127	15	26	428
1.00–1.25	64	108	37	7	9	225
1.25–1.50	42	36	26	7	..	111
1.50–1.75	16	32	12	1	2	63
1.75–2.00	11	14	5	1	1	32
2.00–2.25	4	14	4	..	..	22
2.25–2.50	4	8	1	..	..	13
2.50–2.75	1	3	..	..	..	4
2.75–3.00	1	3	..	..	..	4
3.00–3.25	..	..	..	..	..	..
3.25–3.50	1	..	..	..	..	1
3.50–3.75	..	..	..	..	..	..
3.75–4.00	..	1	..	..	..	1
Total	228	483	411	87	145	1,354

Real estate taxes vary widely from farm to farm in each district, as shown in Table 21. This variation is similar to that for owner-operated farms, as shown in Table 16. The range in real estate taxes per acre is shown in Table 22. The range in the percentage of the net income of real estate needed to pay the real estate tax is shown by districts in Table 23. There was no net income to real estate on 5 per cent of the farms and insufficient income to pay the tax on an additional 16 per cent.

FIXED OBLIGATIONS AFFECTING THE FARMER'S TAXPAYING ABILITY

An important factor affecting the farmer's taxpaying ability is the amount of fixed obligations other than taxes that must be paid from his net income. In this survey a record was taken of all in-

TABLE 23.—DISTRIBUTION OF 1,354 RENTED FARMS ACCORDING TO THE PROPORTION OF NET INCOME OF REAL ESTATE REQUIRED TO PAY REAL ESTATE TAX, 1930–31

PERCENTAGE OF NET INCOME REQUIRED TO PAY REAL ESTATE TAX	DISTRICT I	DISTRICT II	DISTRICT III	DISTRICT IV	DISTRICT V	TOTAL AREA
0– 6	..	..	..	..	..	..
6–11	..	2	2	..	2	6
11–16	4	4	7	2	4	21
16–21	7	26	15	2	6	56
21–26	22	64	27	4	8	125
26–31	24	56	39	4	4	127
31–36	18	57	30	..	5	110
36–41	24	51	34	3	12	124
41–46	20	47	28	5	11	111
46–51	21	33	23	1	5	81
51–56	13	19	16	2	4	54
56–61	5	13	16	2	5	41
61–66	9	8	18	3	2	40
66–71	6	10	14	5	4	39
71–76	9	12	11	2	5	39
76–81	2	9	9	2	1	23
81–86	4	6	8	2	3	23
86–91	4	4	9	4	2	23
91–96	2	1	2	2	1	8
96–101	2	3	8	2	1	16
Over 101	27[a]	47[b]	75[c]	26[d]	43[e]	218
Net loss farms	5	11	20	14	17	67
Total	228	483	411	87	145	1,354

[a] 103%; 108; 110; 107; 111; 112; 119; 122; 123; 123; 126; 135; 139; 146; 155; 157; 162; 169; 168; 199; 205; 230; 239; 266; 351; 11,567.

[b] 100%; 102; 102; 103; 104; 107; 107; 110; 111; 112; 112; 113; 115; 115; 116; 120; 120; 121; 121; 128; 131; 141; 141; 144; 145; 146; 147; 155; 155; 158; 162; 163; 165; 170; 172; 194; 202; 208; 215; 209; 273; 307; 495; 569; 592; 1,077; 3,533.

[c] 101%; 101; 101; 102; 104; 104; 104; 106; 108; 108; 109; 110; 111; 112; 112; 113; 113; 114; 117; 117; 118; 119; 123; 124; 129; 130; 138; 139; 139; 140; 144; 146; 150; 150; 152; 156; 158; 159; 160; 165; 166; 168; 169; 170; 176; 178; 188; 189; 197; 202; 205; 207; 215; 240; 270; 286; 286; 358; 359; 373; 396; 405; 418; 425; 457; 467; 546; 644; 691; 870; 902; 1,514; 1,533; 1,800; 2,166.

[d] 103%; 104; 112; 112; 130; 131; 131; 138; 145; 147; 162; 166; 170; 171; 202; 206; 219; 225; 265; 267; 279; 297; 314; 587; 870; 1,062.

[e] 104%; 105; 105; 110; 113; 113; 113; 115; 117; 127; 133; 137; 139; 139; 143; 146; 154; 165; 168; 172; 182; 190; 194; 204; 209; 230; 240; 280; 288; 294; 297; 298; 313; 332; 404; 419; 473; 483; 696; 725; 985; 1,257; 4,766.

debtedness of both owner-operated and rented farms, including real estate mortgages, ditch liens, chattel mortgages, notes, and other obligations necessitating regular payments of interest or principal or both. No indebtedness not directly associated with the farm business was listed. The ditch liens were taken from the county records and the other indebtedness was given by the farmer. The data included the principal of the debt and the amount of both principal and interest due during the year ending June 30, 1931. Principal payments were listed only in case of amortized mortgage loans.

TABLE 24.—RELATION OF REAL ESTATE MORTGAGE INDEBTEDNESS TO VALUE OF FARM FOR 764 OWNER-OPERATED FARMS, 1931

District	No. of Farms	No. of Farms Mortgaged	Percentage of Farms Mortgaged	Value of Real Estate per Mortgaged Farm	Real Estate Mortgage Debt	
					Per Mortgaged Farm	Percentage of Value
I	180	85	47	$21,337	$8,827	41
II	128	95	74	15,112	8,372	55
III	110	60	55	10,445	6,141	59
IV	179	117	65	4,287	2,673	62
V	167	101	60	10,442	5,948	57
Total area	764	458	60	$11,861	$6,174	52

REAL ESTATE MORTGAGES

Data regarding the real estate mortgage indebtedness of 764 owner-operated farms is shown in Table 24. Sixty per cent of the farms studied were mortgaged, and the average mortgage indebtedness was 52 per cent of their estimated value. Variations in the amount of debt per farm are shown in Table 25. The range in ratio of real estate mortgage indebtedness to total value of real estate is shown by districts in Table 26. Seven per cent of the total number of farms and 12 per cent of the mortgaged farms were mortgaged in excess of their present value. In these cases the farmer's equity has been wiped out by declines in land values since the loan was made.

The real estate mortgage indebtedness of the 1,354 rented farms is shown in Table 27. A smaller proportion of these were mortgaged than of the owner-operated farms, but the relative equity of the owners of mortgaged land was less. The variations in the

Table 25. — Distribution of 764 Owner-Operated Farms According to Amount of Real Estate and Mortgage Indebtedness, 1931

Amount of Debt	District I	District II	District III	District IV	District V	Total Area
None	92	22	46	60	42	262
$0–$1,000	1	13	5	14	26	59
1,000– 2,000	5	4	4	32	7	52
2,000– 3,000	7	5	7	36	6	61
3,000– 4,000	2	5	9	18	11	45
4,000– 5,000	7	9	8	8	16	48
5,000– 6,000	12	10	5	4	15	46
6,000– 7,000	3	9	6	1	13	32
7,000– 8,000	8	5	7	2	7	29
8,000– 9,000	5	7	3	2	4	21
9,000–10,000	2	6	1	..	6	15
10,000–11,000	9	8	2	1	5	25
11,000–12,000	7	5	4	..	3	19
12,000–13,000	3	2	2	1	3	11
13,000–14,000	3	3	..	..	2	8
14,000–15,000	2	3	..	..	..	5
15,000–16,000	2	5	..	..	..	7
16,000–17,000	2	2	..	..	..	4
17,000–18,000	1	..	..	..	..	1
Over 18,000	7[a]	5[b]	1[c]	..	1[d]	14
Total	180	128	110	179	167	764

[a] $22,658; 19,000; 21,676; 18,400; 19,000; 19,340; 25,000.
[b] $32,000; 29,689; 27,317; 18,450; 20,186. [c] $40,786. [d] $19,500.

Table 26. — Distribution of 764 Owner-Operated Farms According to Ratio of Total Real Estate Indebtedness to Appraised Value, 1931

Percentage of Indebtedness	District I	District II	District III	District IV	District V	Total Area
None	92	22	45	60	42	261
0– 10	5	13	7	4	25	54
10– 20	11	6	2	6	6	31
20– 30	14	8	3	6	4	35
30– 40	10	10	8	13	11	52
40– 50	14	11	12	12	13	62
50– 60	14	15	6	20	16	71
60– 70	12	15	5	16	13	61
70– 80	2	8	7	6	10	33
80– 90	1	8	5	10	4	28
90–100	2	3	2	5	8	20
100–110	1	4	4	6	5	20
110–120	1	2	2	4	2	11
120–130	1	..	2	5	..	8
130–140	..	2	..	1	2	5
140–150	..	1	..	2	2	5
Over 150	..	..	..	3[a]	4[b]	7
Total	180	128	110	179	167	764

[a] 165; 170; 206. [b] 154; 155; 167; 187.

amount of mortgage debt on farms in the different districts are shown in Table 28. The range in ratio of indebtedness to value of real estate is shown in Table 29. The mortgage exceeds the value of the farm in the case of 4 per cent of the total number of rented farms and in the case of 11 per cent of those mortgaged.

TABLE 27.—RELATION OF REAL ESTATE MORTGAGE INDEBTEDNESS TO VALUE OF FARM IN THE CASE OF 1,354 RENTED FARMS, 1931

District	No. of Farms	No. of Farms Mortgaged	Percentage of Farms Mortgaged	Value of Real Estate per Mortgaged Farm	Real Estate Mortgage Debt	
					Per Mortgaged Farm	Percentage of Value
I	228	72	32	$13,899	$7,826	56
II	483	182	38	15,968	10,069	63
III	411	198	48	10,654	6,855	64
IV	87	36	41	8,509	4,855	57
V	145	41	28	9,557	6,707	70
Total area	1,354	529	39	$12,693	$7,946	63

DITCH LIENS

The ditch lien indebtedness of the 764 owner-operated farms is shown in Table 30 and of the 1,354 rented farms in Table 31. Twenty per cent of all farms in each group bear ditch liens, but the principal of these liens is relatively small. Most of the liens are in the western part of the state where large areas of low, wet land have been drained.

INDEBTEDNESS OTHER THAN REAL ESTATE INDEBTEDNESS

The amount of indebtedness other than real estate indebtedness for the 764 owner-operated farms is shown in Table 32. These debts include chattel mortgages, notes, store bills, and other accounts. The chattel mortgages and notes involved interest payments but usually no interest was paid on the store bills and accounts.

SUMMARY OF INDEBTEDNESS AND ITS RELATION TO FARM VALUES

The indebtedness of the 764 owner-operated farms and its relation to the value of the farm are summarized in Table 33. The real

TABLE 28. — DISTRIBUTION OF 1,354 RENTED FARMS ACCORDING TO AMOUNT OF REAL ESTATE MORTGAGE INDEBTEDNESS, 1931

AMOUNT OF DEBT	DISTRICT I	DISTRICT II	DISTRICT III	DISTRICT IV	DISTRICT V	TOTAL AREA
None	150	227	182	48	55	662
$0–$1,000	2	40	17	4	48	111
1,000– 2,000	7	24	11	4	1	47
2,000– 3,000	8	8	19	4	6	45
3,000– 4,000	4	12	22	7	6	51
4,000– 5,000	13	11	22	7	3	56
5,000– 6,000	5	10	26	1	2	44
6,000– 7,000	5	15	26	2	5	53
7,000– 8,000	2	23	20	5	8	58
8,000– 9,000	5	12	8	3	2	30
9,000–10,000	2	13	10	..	1	26
10,000–11,000	7	22	17	..	2	48
11,000–12,000	2	11	6	..	..	19
12,000–13,000	3	6	9	..	2	20
13,000–14,000	1	11	4	1	2	19
14,000–15,000	4	3	1	..	..	8
15,000–16,000	4	5	3	..	..	12
16,000–17,000	1	2	5	..	1	9
17,000–18,000	..	4	..	1	..	5
Over 18,000	3[a]	24[b]	3[c]	..	1[d]	31
Total	228	483	411	87	145	1,354

[a] $19,000; 20,000; 34,000.
[b] $18,000; 18,303; 18,294; 18,688; 18,500; 19,164; 19,301; 19,920; 20,000; 20,000; 20,000; 21,000; 20,456; 21,254; 22,192; 22,900; 22,031; 23,000; 24,000; 24,856; 26,410; 30,000; 30,000; 30,578.
[c] $18,000; 18,300; 20,000.
[d] $20,452.

TABLE 29. — DISTRIBUTION OF 1,354 RENTED FARMS ACCORDING TO RATIO OF TOTAL REAL ESTATE INDEBTEDNESS TO VALUE OF FARM, 1931

PERCENTAGE OF INDEBTEDNESS	DISTRICT I	DISTRICT II	DISTRICT III	DISTRICT IV	DISTRICT V	TOTAL AREA
None	150	227	182	48	55	662
0– 10	4	53	15	3	41	116
10– 20	4	12	7	2	6	31
20– 30	12	11	12	3	2	40
30– 40	8	10	16	4	..	38
40– 50	10	23	28	4	5	70
50– 60	10	33	24	6	6	79
60– 70	8	34	36	9	10	97
70– 80	8	30	25	3	6	72
80– 90	3	24	24	2	3	56
90–100	4	13	17	..	1	35
100–110	3	2	10	2	5	22
110–120	1	4	5	..	..	10
120–130	1	2	1	..	3	7
130–140	2	3	2	1	..	8
140–150	..	..	2	..	..	2
Over 150	..	2[a]	5[b]	..	2[c]	9
Total	228	483	411	87	145	1,354

[a] 154; 184. [b] 153; 153; 156; 156; 187. [c] 166; 185.

TABLE 30. — DITCH LIEN INDEBTEDNESS OF 764 OWNER-OPERATED FARMS, 1931

DISTRICT	NO. OF FARMS	Farms with Ditch Liens: No.	Per Cent	Average Amount of Lien per Farm	Average Percentage of Value of Farm
I	180	11	6	$1,676	8
II	128	49	38	479	3
III	110	13	12	361	4
IV	179	4	2	144	4
V	167	77	46	191	2
Total area	764	154	20	$402	3

TABLE 31. — DITCH LIEN INDEBTEDNESS OF 1,354 RENTED FARMS, 1931

DISTRICT	NO. OF FARMS	Farms with Ditch Liens: No.	Per Cent	Average Amount of Lien per Farm	Average Percentage of Value per Farm
I	228	7	3	$1,426	11
II	483	128	27	1,404	9
III	411	74	18	991	10
IV	87	3	3	137	2
V	145	60	41	315	4
Total area	1,354	272	20	$670	5

TABLE 32. — INDEBTEDNESS OTHER THAN REAL ESTATE INDEBTEDNESS OF 764 OWNER-OPERATED FARMS, 1931

DISTRICT	NO. OF FARMS	Farms with Indebtedness: No.	Per Cent	Average Amount per Farm
I	180	150	83	$2,047
II	128	65	51	929
III	110	64	58	758
IV	179	96	54	633
V	167	96	57	1,138
Total area	764	471	62	$1,234

estate mortgages and ditch liens are related to the value of the real estate, but the total indebtedness is related to the total farm investment, including livestock and machinery.

The indebtedness of the 1,354 rented farms is summarized in Table 34. The rented farms carry slightly less encumbrance of debt than the owned farms. The average debt per farm of those farms reporting debts is greater than it is in the case of the owner-operated farms, but a smaller proportion of them are encumbered with debt.

Interest and Principal Payments

The annual interest payments due on real estate mortgages, the property taxes, and the relation of these two items to income and to each other are shown in Tables 35 and 36 for all mortgaged farms included in this study. The farmer's net income is used as the measure of income for the owner-operated farms, and the total property tax includes both personal and real estate taxes. Net income of real estate and real estate taxes are used in the case of the rented farms. These two classes of farms are therefore not directly comparable with respect to the relation of taxes and interest to income and to each other. It is apparent, however, that interest payments are a more serious burden to the owner of a mortgaged farm than are taxes. In the case of the rented farm practically the entire income is needed to pay the interest bill, and the landowner must have an additional source of income if he is to pay both interest and taxes.

In addition to interest on the real estate mortgage the landowner has other fixed payments to meet, such as payment on the principal of amortized real estate loans and interest and principal on ditch liens. The owner-operator may also have interest to pay on chattel mortgages and notes. The extent to which such items were encountered on the farms studied and the amount of these items are shown by districts for both owner-operated and rented farms in Tables 37 and 38. Forty-two per cent of all real estate mortgages reported by owner-operators, but only 9 per cent of those reported by landlords, were of the amortized type. Most of the amortized type were made by the Federal Land Bank and the State Rural Credits Department and such loans are available to owner-operators only. Principal payments were made on part of the ditch liens. On some of them only interest was paid.

TABLE 33.—SUMMARY OF INDEBTEDNESS AND OF RATIO OF INDEBTEDNESS TO VALUE OF 764 OWNER-OPERATED FARMS, 1931

DISTRICT	NO. OF FARMS	AVERAGE REAL ESTATE INVESTMENT PER FARM	AVERAGE TOTAL INVESTMENT PER FARM	REAL ESTATE MORTGAGE PER FARM		DITCH LIEN PER FARM		TOTAL REAL ESTATE INDEBTEDNESS PER FARM		OTHER INDEBTEDNESS PER FARM	TOTAL INDEBTEDNESS PER FARM	
				Average Amount	Average Percentage of Value	Average Amount	Average Percentage of Value	Average Amount	Average Percentage of Value		Average Amount	Average Percentage of Total Investment
I........	180	$20,447	$26,081	$4,168	20.4	$102	.5	$4,270	20.9	$1,706	$5,976	22.9
II........	128	15,021	17,981	6,214	41.4	183	1.2	6,397	42.6	472	6,869	38.2
III........	110	10,182	13,050	3,349	32.9	43	.4	3,392	33.3	399	3,791	29.0
IV........	179	4,008	5,484	1,747	43.6	3	.1	1,750	43.7	340	2,090	38.1
V........	167	10,223	13,174	3,597	35.2	88	.8	3,685	36.0	654	4,339	32.9
Total area	764	$11,793	$15,200	$3,700	30.9	$81	.7	$3,781	31.6	$760	$4,541	30.0

TABLE 34.—SUMMARY OF INDEBTEDNESS AND OF RATIO OF INDEBTEDNESS TO VALUE OF 1,354 RENTED FARMS, 1931

DISTRICT	NO. OF FARMS	AVERAGE REAL ESTATE INVESTMENT PER FARM	REAL ESTATE MORTGAGE PER FARM		DITCH LIEN PER FARM		TOTAL INDEBTEDNESS PER FARM	
			Average Amount	Average Percentage of Value	Average Amount	Average Percentage of Value	Average Amount	Average Percentage of Total Investment
I..........	228	$12,485	$2,471	19.8	$43	.3	$2,515	20.1
II..........	483	15,907	3,794	23.9	372	2.3	4,166	26.2
III..........	411	10,234	3,302	32.3	178	1.7	3,480	34.0
IV..........	87	7,459	2,008	26.9	4	.1	2,012	27.0
V..........	145	8,226	1,896	23.0	130	1.6	2,026	24.6
Total area	1,354	$12,244	$3,104	25.4	$208	1.6	$3,312	27.0

Table 35.—Total Property Tax and Annual Interest Payments on Mortgage, per Farm, and the Ratios of These to Farmer's Net Income from 458 Mortgaged Owner-Operated Farms, 1931

District	No. of Farms	Farmer's Net Income per Farm[a]	Total Property Tax per Farm			Mortgage Interest Payment per Farm	
			Average Amount	Average Percentage of Net Income[a]	Average Percentage of Interest	Average Amount	Average Percentage of Net Income[a]
I	85	$3,083	$269	8.7	54.7	$492	16.0
II	95	1,738	220	12.7	49.3	446	25.7
III	60	1,825	215	11.8	69.6	309	16.9
IV	117	855	124	14.5	82.7	150	17.5
V	101	1,692	211	12.5	64.9	325	19.2
Total area	458	$1,763	$202	11.4	60.3	$335	19.0

[a] Farmer's net income includes income from labor and equipment besides income from real estate. See Tables 10 and 15, pages 79 and 83.

Table 36.—Real Estate Tax and Annual Interest Payments on Mortgage, per Farm, and Ratios of These to Net Income from Real Estate of 529 Mortgaged Rented Farms, 1931

District	No. of Farms	Net Income of Real Estate per Farm[a]	Real Estate Tax per Farm			Mortgage Interest Payment per Farm	
			Average Amount	Average Percentage of Net Income[a]	Average Percentage of Interest	Average Amount	Average Percentage of Net Income[a]
I	72	$442	$194	43.9	43.6	$445	100.7
II	182	616	260	42.2	47.7	547	88.8
III	198	342	173	50.4	45.8	378	110.5
IV	36	193	115	59.6	41.7	276	143.0
V	41	403	182	45.2	43.9	415	103.0
Total area	529	$444	$202	45.5	45.8	$441	99.3

[a] Note that the net income of real estate only is shown in this table. See Tables 12 and 20, pages 81 and 87.

A summary of principal, interest, and tax payments and their relation to net income is shown in Table 39 for the 764 owner-operated farms. Nearly 80 per cent of the average net income of real estate in the whole group is required to pay these three items; 76.6 per cent is required to pay interest and taxes only. In Districts II, IV, and V the net income was insufficient to cover the three items; in Districts IV and V, insufficient to cover interest and taxes. Nothing was left to make payments on the principal of non-amortized mortgages. As has already been noted, the relatively better showing of the farms in District I is due to the fact that not only were better than average farms selected in this district but the time covered by the records was slightly different from that for the other districts. (See pages 68 to 70.)

TABLE 37.—SUMMARY OF ANNUAL PRINCIPAL AND INTEREST PAYMENTS OTHER THAN INTEREST ON MORTGAGES ON OWNER-OPERATED FARMS, 1931

DISTRICT	REAL ESTATE MORTGAGE		DITCH LIENS			INTEREST ON OTHER DEBTS [a]	
	No. of Farms	Average Payment	No. of Farms	Principal Payment	Interest Payment	No. of Farms	Average Payment
I	19	$90	11	$106	$94	150	$122
II	26	171	49	100	35	65	69
III	17	60	13	74	21	64	43
IV	75	30	4	36	10	96	42
V	55	92	77	39	11	96	76
Total area	192	$75	154	$66	$26	471	$78

[a] Includes chattel mortgages and notes.

TABLE 38.—SUMMARY OF ANNUAL PRINCIPAL AND INTEREST PAYMENTS OTHER THAN INTEREST ON MORTGAGES ON RENTED FARMS, 1931

DISTRICT	REAL ESTATE MORTGAGES		DITCH LIENS		
	No. of Farms	Average Payment	No. of Farms	Principal Payment	Interest Payment
I	..	....	7	$187	$77
II	33	$144	128	172	78
III	9	95	74	104	49
IV	5	64	3	91	29
V	1	72	60	63	19
Total area	48	$125	272	$129	$56

TABLE 39. — SUMMARY OF PRINCIPAL AND INTEREST PAYMENTS AND TAXES PER FARM AND THE RATIOS OF THESE TO NET INCOME OF 764 OWNER-OPERATED FARMS, 1931

	DISTRICT I	DISTRICT II	DISTRICT III	DISTRICT IV	DISTRICT V	TOTAL AREA
Number of farms	180	128	110	179	167	764
Farmer's net income	$2,961	$1,760	$1,582	$776	$1,216	$1,754
Net income of real estate	1,547	553	381	—301[a]	394	527
Real estate taxes	236	197	182	103	196	182
Ratio to net income of real estate	15.3%	35.6%	47.8%	.....[b]	49.7%	34.5%
Total property taxes	$267	$220	$205	$116	$216	$204
Ratio to farmer's net income	8.0%	11.2%	11.5%	13.3%	12.2%	10.4%
Interest and principal payments on real estate indebtedness						
Real estate mortgage						
Principal	$ 10	$ 35	$ 9	$12	$ 30	$ 19
Interest	232	331	168	98	197	201
Ditch lien						
Principal	7	38	9	1	18	13
Interest	4	14	3	...[c]	5	5
Total	$253	$418	$189	$111	$250	$238
Ratio to net income of real estate	16.4%	75.6%	49.6%	.....[b]	63.5%	45.2%
Interest on other indebtedness	$102	$35	$25	$22	$44	$48
Total interest and principal payments due annually	$355	$453	$214	$133	$294	$286
Ratio to farmer's net income	12.0%	25.7%	13.5%	17.1%	24.2%	16.3%

[a] Minus (—) indicates loss. [b] No net income. [c] Less than one dollar.

A similar summary for the 1,354 rented farms is shown in Table 40. Only in Districts I and II were the incomes sufficient to cover interest and tax payments, to say nothing of principal. Only 10 per cent of the average net income per farm for the whole group was available for principal payments or as a return for the owner's equity in the farm. In the case of owner-operated farms interest on mortgages and ditch liens amounted to 113.2 per cent of the real estate taxes and in the case of rented farms to 90.6 per cent of such taxes. In the case of both owner-operated and rented farms the fixed obligations of principal payments and interest took a heavier toll from the net income than did taxes. They are an important factor in making it difficult for the farmers to meet their tax payments out of the earnings of the land.

TABLE 40.—SUMMARY OF PRINCIPAL AND INTEREST PAYMENTS AND TAXES PER FARM AND THE RATIOS OF THESE TO NET INCOME OF 1,354 RENTED FARMS, 1931

	DISTRICT I	DISTRICT II	DISTRICT III	DISTRICT IV	DISTRICT V	TOTAL AREA
Number of farms	228	483	411	87	145	1,354
Net income of real estate	$408	$645	$333	$154	$288	$441
Real estate taxes	187	258	173	115	171	202
Ratio to net income of real estate	45.8%	40.0%	52.0%	74.7%	59.4%	45.8%
Interest and principal payments on real estate indebtedness						
Real estate mortgages						
Principal	....	$ 9	$ 2	$ 3	$ 1	$ 4
Interest	$140	206	182	114	117	172
Ditch liens						
Principal	5	46	18	3	26	26
Interest	2	20	8	1	8	11
Total	$147	$281	$310	$121	$152	$213
Ratio to net income of real estate	36.0%	43.6%	90.4%	78.6%	52.8%	48.3%

TRENDS IN TAXES AND INCOMES

The data showing the relation of farm taxes to income that have been presented thus far have been for the crop year of 1930. Since it is impossible in a survey to cover more than the previous year's business, the only data that would show the trend in taxes and earnings are those to be found in such accounting records as are available. One set of data covers groups of owner-operated farms in four different sections of the state, another covers a group of rented farms in southwestern Minnesota. Some descriptions of these two groups of farms have been presented in Tables 3 and 5.

The trend in net income, taxes, and the ratio of taxes to net income is shown for the owner-operated farms in Table 41. These data are presented on a "per acre" basis in order to eliminate the effect of size, since there is some variation in size from year to year in each of the groups. In general the net incomes of farmers in Minnesota varied comparatively little from 1925 to 1929 but dropped sharply in 1930 and even more in 1931. (See the two tables on pages 104 and 547.) With few exceptions the incomes of these farms followed this trend. Local drouths reduced the incomes sharply in Pine County in 1927 and in Polk County in 1926. Incomes in southeastern Minnesota were relatively higher than the state average in 1930 because of the large proportion of receipts

TABLE 41.—RELATION OF TAXES TO NET INCOME OF OWNER-OPERATED FARMS IN SPECIFIED COUNTIES OF MINNESOTA, 1925–1931

County and Year	Farmer's Net Income per Acre	Taxes per Acre: Real Estate	Taxes per Acre: Personal Property	Taxes per Acre: Total	Ratio of Total Taxes to Farmer's Net Income	Net Income of Real Estate per Acre	Ratio of Real Estate Taxes to Net Income of Real Estate
Pine County					Per Cent		Per Cent
1925	$17.13	$1.45	$ .23	$1.68	9.8	$6.31	23.0
1926	17.74	1.53	.21	1.74	9.8	7.98	19.2
1927	12.17	1.57	.22	1.79	14.7	2.60	60.4
1930	10.46	1.57	.23	1.80	17.3	1.07	146.8
Polk County							
1926	5.60	.87	.06	.93	16.6	1.86	46.8
1927	8.22	.85	.07	.92	11.1	3.90	21.8
1928	8.11	.86	.06	.92	11.3	3.98	21.6
1930	5.55	.69	.07	.76	13.7	1.95	35.4
Rock and Nobles counties							
1929	15.44	1.07	.13	1.20	7.8	9.85	10.9
1930	11.61	1.02	.13	1.15	9.9	7.12	14.3
1931	6.43	1.14	.10	1.24	19.3	3.01	37.9
Eight counties in southeastern Minnesota[a]							
1928	16.84	1.25	.17	1.42	8.4	8.43	14.9
1929	18.62	1.33	.15	1.48	7.9	10.67	12.4
1930	16.18	1.29	.17	1.46	9.0	8.45	15.3
1931	12.43	1.39	.19	1.58	12.7	6.44	21.6

[a] Dodge. Freeborn, Goodhue, Le Sueur, Mower, Rice. Steele, and Waseca counties.

from livestock and the fact that the prices of livestock and livestock products dropped less than the prices of crops. Crop yields in this section were also less affected by the heat and drouth than were yields in most of the rest of the state. Low crop yields due to heat and drouth coupled with a severe decline in the prices of all farm products accounted for the very low net incomes of 1931. Except in Polk County the real estate tax and the total property tax for the last year covered by these records were as high as or higher than for any of the earlier years reported. Whether measured by the ratio of the total property tax to the farmer's net income or by the ratio of the real estate tax to the net income of real estate, the tax burden increased in 1930 and even more sharply in 1931 in those localities for which 1931 data are available.

TABLE 42.—RELATION OF REAL ESTATE TAXES TO NET INCOME PER ACRE OF 178 RENTED FARMS, 1923–1930

YEAR	NET INCOME PER ACRE OF REAL ESTATE	REAL ESTATE TAX PER ACRE	RATIO OF TAXES TO NET INCOME
			Per Cent
1923	$3.07	$1.02	34.0
1924	3.02	.93	31.0
1925	3.21	.95	29.5
1926	2.97	.87	29.4
1927	2.73	.96	35.2
1928	3.27	.89	27.3
1929	2.83	.93	33.0
1930	2.31	.91	39.2

The trend in the net income of real estate and in real estate taxes and their relation to each other in a group of 178 rented farms for the years 1923 to 1930 are shown in Table 42. These farms are all in District II. While there was a slight downward trend of taxes during the period the net change was small after 1924. Incomes, on the other hand, showed no definite trend up to 1928. Since then the trend has been downward and the percentage of the net income required to pay taxes has increased. The net income of real estate on rented farms is not so sensitive to changes in the prices of farm products as is that of owner-operated farms. From one-third to one-half of the gross income of these farms was derived from cash rent. Since cash rental rates are adjusted to price changes slowly and with considerable lag, the income tends to be more stable than if share rent were used exclusively.

The same tendency for the rate of taxation, as measured by ratio of tax to income, to increase with falling incomes that was noted in the case of owner-operated farms is apparent in the case of these rented farms. This illustrates a fundamental characteristic of the general property tax. As the income from property falls, the rate at which such income is taxed tends to be increased because the tax burden on property is not adjusted quickly to its income. The point has been frequently made that taxes levied directly on income yield revenue that fluctuates in amount as income changes. It usually is regarded as impracticable to raise rates as incomes fall in order that revenue may be sustained. As far as the farmer is concerned the general property tax operates in just this way because with a falling income he pays a larger proportion of his income for taxes on property. In any period characterized by a decline in all prices, the prices of farm products, like the prices of other raw materials, tend to fall first and farthest. In such a period, the general property tax proves especially burdensome to the farmer.

SUMMARY

Following are some of the outstanding facts shown by the preceding analyses of farm data secured for this investigation.

In the case of the owner-operated farms, real estate taxes took an average of 10.4 per cent of the farmer's net income. Real estate and personal property taxes together took 11.6 per cent of this income. In order to compare owner-operated farms with rented farms, it is necessary to estimate the income of real estate alone by subtracting from the farmer's net income the value of the labor of the farmer and his family and a proper amount for equipment used on the farm. In the case of owner-operated farms real estate taxes took an average of 34.5 per cent, and in the case of rented farms 45.8 per cent, of the income attributable to real estate alone.

The taxes on real estate averaged 1.52 per cent of the appraised value of owner-operated farms and 1.65 per cent in the case of rented farms.

Only 39 per cent of the rented farms were mortgaged as compared with 60 per cent of the owner-operated farms, but the mortgages on the latter averaged 52 per cent of their appraised value as compared with 63 per cent of the value of rented farms. Ditch lien indebtedness averaged only 3 per cent of the appraised value of owner-operated farms and 5 per cent of that of rented farms. Of

TABLE 43. — COMPARISON OF MINNESOTA FARM PRICES AND INCOMES [a]

Year	Value of Farm Land per Acre, U. S. Census		Index of Farm Land Value per Acre, U. S. Dept. of Agriculture [b]		Index of Prices of Minnesota Agricultural Products, U. of Minn. [c]	Net Cash Income per Farm, U. of Minn. Estimate	Purchasing Power of Average Net Farm Income [d]
	Land Only	Land and Buildings	United States	Minnesota			
1900	$21.31	$25.51	...	...	....	....	....
1910	36.82	45.62	...	...	75.7	$601	$613
1911	....	....	...	...	69.5	440	440
1912	....	....	97	95	70.9	509	504
1913	....	....	100	100	70.1	582	582
1914	....	....	103	105	73.5	561	550
1915	....	....	103	107	74.0	606	566
1916	....	....	108	122	89.9	698	558
1917	....	....	117	138	133.8	1,015	686
1918	....	....	129	155	146.9	1,644	913
1919	....	....	140	167	155.9	1,411	659
1920	91.00	109.23	170	213	144.9	892	393
1921	....	....	157	212	82.3	241	146
1922	....	....	139	187	81.6	465	291
1923	....	....	135	177	83.6	539	335
1924	....	....	130	170	88.7	837	517
1925	59.76	79.63	127	159	104.3	1,072	650
1926	....	....	124	155	107.6	1,113	679
1927	....	....	119	145	103.0	927	576
1928	....	....	117	140	101.7	944	583
1929	....	....	116	138	105.9	1,000	625
1930	47.03	68.74	115	133	88.8	873	578
1931	....	....	106	116	60.3	409	317
1932	....	....	89	98	....	...	...

[a] Compiled from data furnished by Professor Warren C. Waite. [b] Average value, 1912–1914=100. [c] 1924, 1925, and 1926=100.
[d] Purchasing power of net cash income, computed by Division of Agricultural Economics of the Minnesota Agricultural Experiment Station on the basis of the United States Department of Agriculture index of prices of things purchased by farmers.

the owner-operated farms 62 per cent had other indebtedness than that on real estate. This averaged $1,234 per farm.

In the case of the owner-operated farms that were mortgaged, it took 11.4 per cent of the farmer's net income to pay the taxes and 19 per cent to pay interest on mortgage debt, or 30.4 per cent to pay both. In the case of rented farms that were mortgaged it took on the average 45.5 per cent of the net income of real estate alone to pay taxes and 99.3 per cent to pay interest on mortgage debt, or 144.8 per cent to pay both. In other words, mortgaged rented farms made just about enough to pay interest only, or to pay taxes and half the interest on the mortgage debt. It is to be remembered that the income from rented farms did not include labor and equipment incomes as did the income of owner-operator farmers.

The preceding paragraphs deal with averages for all of the state covered in this part of the investigation. The situations in many individual cases and in various counties and districts are, of course, very different from the averages, some being much better and some much worse.

Income for the year covered (1930 or 1930–31) was lower than for the years immediately preceding but higher than for 1932 and about the same as for pre-war years. It makes a great deal of difference, however, whether income is calculated in dollars or in terms of purchasing power. (See pages 104 and 547.)

The data presented in earlier parts of this chapter, particularly those showing trends of farm taxes, may be supplemented by brief summary data from the reports of the Minnesota Tax Commission and the United States Department of Agriculture. Tables 45 and 46 present a comparison of farm land taxes per acre in Minnesota and other north-central states from 1913 to 1930. The Minnesota data in Table 45 may be compared with similar data based on Minnesota Tax Commission statistics. (See Table 44.)

It will be observed that according to both sources there was a big jump in the tax per acre from 1919 to 1920, also from 1922 to 1923, but a sudden drop in 1924. There appears to have been considerable fluctuation from year to year, the heaviest levies occurring most frequently in odd-numbered years. The data of the Tax Commission and those of the United States Department of Agriculture for the years from 1919 to 1925 show reasonable similarity,

TABLE 44. — TAXES PER ACRE ON MINNESOTA FARM LANDS, 1919–1925

YEAR	MINNESOTA TAX COMMISSION DATA	U. S. DEPT. OF AGRICULTURE DATA	YEAR	MINNESOTA TAX COMMISSION DATA	U. S. DEPT. OF AGRICULTURE DATA
1919	$.595	$.61	1926	$.700	$.76
1920	.701	.73	1927	.750	.77
1921	.750	.75	1928	.714	.80
1922	.715	.73	1929	.747	.86
1923	.782	.80	1930	.732	.83
1924	.702	.71	1931	.701	...
1925	.750	.75			

but for later years they show a substantial divergence, the former showing a downward trend since 1927 and the latter a distinct upward trend. The trend shown in the data of the Tax Commission is similar to that for the years from 1923 to 1930 shown in Table 42 above, but somewhat different from that shown in Table 41. According to the Tax Commission data, farm taxes per acre were the same in 1920 and 1931; according to United States Department of Agriculture data, they have been appreciably higher in recent years than they were a decade ago. Studies of farm operations made by the University of Minnesota Agricultural Experiment Station show that after the war farm taxes increased much more in the southwestern than in the southeastern counties. By 1924 they had reached approximate parity in the two sections and, for the farms studied, the taxes per acre continued to increase after that date.

A somewhat different picture is presented by Table 47, which shows state totals rather than taxes per acre. According to these data, taxes on township real estate (mostly farm real estate)[6] were about 13 per cent less in 1931 than in 1921, but about 57 per cent more than in 1918. On the other hand, taxes on city and village

[6] The Minnesota Tax Commission divides real estate into (1) that in townships and (2) that in cities and villages. Another classification is into (1) "unplatted" (mostly farm land in townships); (2) "platted" (mostly urban, nonagricultural land, though some farm land within some municipalities is platted); and (3) "unmined iron ore." Each classification is presumed to cover all real estate. "Township real estate" consists mostly of farms but includes part of the "unmined iron ore"; "city and village real estate" also includes some "unmined iron ore." If some allowance is made for the *proportion* that "unmined iron ore" forms of the total, one can get an approximate idea of the trend of total farm land assessed values and taxes by studying the township and unplatted real estate data; similarly the trends for urban land can be approximated by analyzing the city and village (mostly "platted") real estate data. (See Table 47.)

TABLE 45. — TAXES PER ACRE ON FARM LAND IN MINNESOTA AND NEIGHBORING STATES, 1913–1930 [a]

YEAR	MINN.	WIS.	MICH.	IOWA	ILL.	IND.	N. D.	S. D.
1913......	$ .29	$ .47	$ .54	$ .56	$ .49	$ .59	$ .15	$ .15
1914......	.33	.45	.55	.56	.46	.59	.17	.15
1915......	.33	.49	.63	.60	.52	.66	.20	.17
1916......	.37	.53	.65	.64	.61	.73	.21	.18
1917......	.46	.58	.74	.74	.68	.76	.21	.22
1918......	.45	.62	.80	.76	.65	.79	.25	.26
1919......	.61	.89	1.07	.94	.81	.90	.43	.35
1920......	.73	1.04	1.23	1.10	.99	1.26	.44	.45
1921......	.75	1.08	1.32	1.20	1.05	1.41	.45	.41
1922......	.73	1.05	1.31	1.26	1.06	1.41	.43	.41
1923......	.80	1.07	1.29	1.25	1.02	1.45	.38	.43
1924......	.71	1.03	1.24	1.23	1.08	1.45	.38	.43
1925......	.75	.96	1.26	1.15	1.15	1.40	.37	.44
1926......	.76	.98	1.27	1.14	1.13	1.38	.37	.44
1927......	.77	1.07	1.35	1.14	1.12	1.36	.39	.44
1928......	.80	1.09	1.35	1.15	1.11	1.38	.39	.45
1929......	.86	1.13	1.38	1.22	1.15	1.39	.38	.46
1930......	.83	1.07	1.34	1.24	1.16	1.41	.38	.44

[a] Eric Englund, United States Department of Agriculture mimeographed bulletin, August, 1932, pp. 3–4.

TABLE 46. — INDEX OF TAXES PER ACRE ON FARM LAND IN MINNESOTA AND NEIGHBORING STATES, 1913–1930 [a]
(1913=100)

YEAR	MINN.	WIS.	MICH.	IOWA	ILL.	IND.	N. D.	S. D.
1913......	100	100	100	100	100	100	100	100
1914......	114	95	101	100	94	99	110	99
1915......	117	104	116	108	106	111	128	110
1916......	129	113	120	115	124	123	134	117
1917......	161	122	137	132	138	128	138	145
1918......	158	132	149	136	132	133	162	172
1919......	212	188	198	169	165	151	277	226
1920......	254	220	227	197	202	212	284	289
1921......	264	228	244	215	214	238	292	265
1922......	255	223	242	225	215	237	281	268
1923......	281	226	238	224	208	245	249	278
1924......	250	218	228	220	220	244	245	276
1925......	261	202	233	206	233	236	243	287
1926......	268	208	234	204	230	232	242	284
1927......	270	226	249	203	227	228	253	283
1928......	282	230	248	206	226	233	252	290
1929......	302	238	256	218	233	234	246	298
1930......	291	226	247	222	235	237	248	288
Ratio of Taxes to Value of Land and Buildings, 1929								
	1.25%	1.44%	2.06%	.99%	1.07%	1.95%	1.54%	1.26%

[a] Eric Englund, United States Department of Agriculture mimeographed bulletin, August, 1932, pp. 3–6.

TABLE 47. — COMPARISON OF STATE AND LOCAL PROPERTY TAXES IN MINNESOTA, 1914–1931 [a]

	1914	1918	1921	1924	1931
Total general property taxes	$48,229,918	$68,507,529	$108,087,336	$113,033,552	$120,382,993
Assessed valuation [b]					
Real estate	1,274,159,395	1,481,544,677	1,757,560,396	1,708,434,922	1,680,184,868
Personal property	228,893,671	268,636,274	269,233,314	242,871,326	204,058,784
Total	$1,503,053,066	$1,750,180,951	$2,026,793,710	$1,951,306,248	$1,884,243,652
Assessed valuation of real estate					
Platted	$400,354,035	$477,402,770	$562,838,059 [c]	$641,895,625	$728,239,422 [c]
Unplatted	603,718,885	710,350,747	904,113,804 [c]	786,345,688	717,933,881 [c]
Unmined iron ore	270,086,475	293,602,140	282,595,821 [c]	280,301,853	229,044,834 [c]
Total	$1,274,159,395	$1,481,355,657	$1,749,547,684 [c]	$1,708,543,166	$1,675,218,137 [c]
Amount of taxes on					
Township real estate		$21,782,708	$39,409,598	$34,378,686	$34,175,296
Urban real estate [d]		34,664,799	58,126,880	62,007,425	70,645,639
All real estate		$56,447,507	$97,536,478	$96,386,111	$104,820,935
Percentage of total valuation on					
Townships		49.99%	51.34%	45.84%	42.92%
Urban centers		50.01	48.66	54.16	57.08
Total		100.00%	100.00%	100.00%	100.00%
All real estate	84.77%	84.65%	86.72%	87.55%	89.17%
All personal property	15.23	15.35	13.28	12.45	10.83
Total	100.00%	100.00%	100.00%	100.00%	100.00%

[a] Compiled from reports of the Minnesota Tax Commission. "General property taxes" shown in the first line include taxes on money and credits and on grain, and certain distributions of electric power company taxes, which items appear to be omitted from other figures shown in the table. These items do not affect totals greatly, e.g., about 2 per cent in 1931.

[b] Assessed valuations in this table refer to legal fractional valuations upon which tax rates are calculated, and not to "full and true" assessed values, which are referred to in most cases in this report, particularly in Chapters 3, 7, and 8. See page 576.

[c] Based on assessment of the previous year.

[d] "Urban" is used to describe the property the Tax Commission lists for cities and villages. See note 6.

	1914	1918	1921	1924	1931
Percentage of state and local levies on					
Townships		36.52%	37.42%	33.08%	30.79%
Urban centers		63.48	62.58	66.92	69.21
All real estate		100.00%	100.00%	100.00%	100.00%
Percentage of state and local taxes borne by					
Township real estate		32.28%	34.43%	30.77%	28.77%
Urban real estate		51.37	50.78	55.49	59.48
All real estate		83.65%	85.21%	86.26%	88.25%
Percentage Increase in 1931, as Compared with Years Indicated [e]					
Total general property taxes	149.60	75.72	11.38	6.50	
Assessed valuation					
Real estate	31.87	13.41	− 4.40	− 1.65	
Personal property	−10.85	−24.04	−24.21	−15.98	
Total	25.36	7.66	− 7.03	− 3.44	
Assessed valuation of real estate					
Platted	81.90	52.54	29.39	13.45	
Unplatted	18.92	1.07	−20.59	− 8.70	
Unmined iron ore	−15.19	−21.99	−18.95	−18.29	
Total	31.48	13.09	− 4.25	− 1.95	
Amount of taxes on					
Township real estate		56.89	−13.28	− 0.59	
Urban real estate		103.80	21.54	13.93	
All real estate		85.70	7.47	8.75	

[e] Minus (—) indicates a decrease.

TABLE 48. — COMPARATIVE ASSESSED VALUE OF FARM (UNPLATTED) REAL PROPERTY AND URBAN (PLATTED) REAL PROPERTY, 1920–1932 [a]

(000 omitted)

YEAR	FARM REAL PROPERTY		URBAN REAL PROPERTY		FARM AND URBAN REALTY COMBINED
	Amount	Per Cent of Total Real Property	Amount	Per Cent of Total Real Property	
1920..........	$904,114	61.63	$562,838	38.37	$1,466,952
1922..........	833,180	58.44	592,510	41.56	1,425,690
1924..........	786,346	55.06	641,896	44.94	1,428,241
1926..........	768,221	52.93	682,949	47.07	1,451,170
1928..........	751,537	51.28	714,149	48.72	1,465,686
1930..........	717,934	49.64	728,239	50.36	1,446,173
1932..........	552,547	44.68	684,272	55.32	1,236,819

[a] Compiled by the Minnesota Tax Commission. Unmined iron ore is not included in this tabulation.

"It is interesting to note that in the 12 year period between 1920 and 1932 the assessment shows a decrease in farm and urban real property of $230,133,296, or 15.69 per cent. The decrease in farm real property in this period was $351,567,116, or 38.88 per cent. This decrease was somewhat off-set by an increase in urban real property of $121,433,820 in the same period."—Extract from comment of the Minnesota Tax Commission.

real estate were about 22 per cent higher in 1931 than in 1921 and 104 per cent higher than in 1918. Table 47 shows that the great increases in property taxes came in the decade prior to 1921; the increases during the past decade have been relatively moderate; in fact, there has been an appreciable decline in total taxes on township real estate. The data in Table 47 are confirmed by those in Table 48 above. It is entirely possible, however, for total taxes to decline while taxes per acre of operated land are rising, especially in areas and in periods of increasing tax delinquency. Falling prices and tax delinquency act something like rolling snowballs in piling up tax burdens on those who continue to pay taxes.

In other words, prices, incomes, and taxes increased greatly during and immediately following the war, price increases preceding tax increases. War-time inflation and high prices of farm products led to great increases in speculation, prices of land, and mortgage debt and interest. The precipitate price declines of 1920–21 and 1929–1932 removed the foundations upon which land prices and mortgage debts were built up and left the farmer with higher standards of living and with increased fixed debt and tax charges but with little income to pay his obligations. That is, during the last decade in which Minnesota farmers' total taxes on real estate have decreased somewhat in dollars, the tax *burdens* of those who have continued to pay have greatly increased, chiefly because of the revolutions in prices of farm products.

The elimination of all property tax increases, in fact, entire exemption from taxation, would not solve the farmers' difficulties. The same may be said of many others besides farmers. This is not an argument against proper tax reduction, rather it is an indication that something more important than tax reduction is required. Neither agriculture, nor industry, nor commerce will pay taxes, or even continue to exist, where net losses are incurred indefinitely. Unless net income can be increased, taxes must necessarily be decreased.

The chief considerations concerning taxes on farmers' land are that they shall be predictable and planned properly with respect to average income over a long period of years. But ordinarily net incomes depend much more upon prices than upon taxes.[7] Land prices represent the capitalization of expected net incomes. So long as taxes on land are less than the net rent of land, the owner's chief concern is that they shall be stable or predictable. Unpredictable tax increases confiscate land values; predictable taxes can be discounted.

Prices of farm products during the past few years have dropped so much, or rather the prospects of future income from land are so poor, that land values have declined greatly, thus seriously aggravating farmers' difficulties. Heavy taxes have been a factor in the decline of these values, but they have caused the decline only to the extent that they have reduced the net income of land more than was expected. The elimination of unnecessary public expenditures and the development of other taxes to take the place of a substantial part of the taxes on realty can furnish appreciable relief to owners of land, but both the decline in land values and the increase in the burdensomeness of landowners' taxes have been due far more to the decline in prices of products than to the amount of taxes. No satisfactory solution of landowners' tax problems can be found without some solution or betterment of the general price situation.

[7] Population trends, production in this and other parts of the world, in fact, everything that affects supply and demand, affects prices and consequently the farmer's income and his ability to pay taxes. A reading of Chapter 2 will aid in an understanding of some matters discussed here.

CHAPTER 5

TAX DELINQUENCY AND THE CUT-OVER LAND PROBLEM IN NORTHERN MINNESOTA[1]

THE RISE OF A NEW PUBLIC DOMAIN

The United States is witnessing today the creation of a new public domain. The process by which the federal public domain was disposed of is now being reversed; land that a few decades ago was given away by the federal government as homesteads or as grants to the states, and later was passed on by the states to lumber companies and railroads, is now coming back to public ownership by the hundreds of thousands of acres. It is coming back stripped of its timber and drained of its natural wealth. This general reversion is taking place in consequence of tax delinquency and abandonment by the owners.

Tax delinquency and land abandonment are not confined to any geographical region, but the reversion is probably more advanced in the cut-over regions of the Lake States than in any other locality. It has been estimated that there are at least eighteen million acres, or nearly 34 per cent of the forested area of Michigan, Wisconsin, and Minnesota, that are tax delinquent and for the most part largely abandoned by their owners.

Tax delinquency has already caused the northern counties much difficulty in balancing their budgets. In some localities there is real financial embarrassment, which has resulted in a steady increase in tax rates and in valuations on remaining property. The large acreage of idle and unproductive land has a depressing influence on agriculture in the cut-over region. It is like an army of unemployed which depresses the wages of those who are employed. The reversion of this land creates new responsibilities for the states and counties. It overwhelms the state with a large acreage of land that can be brought back into productivity only by a considerable

[1] Contribution of the Lake States Forest Experiment Station, University Farm, St. Paul, of which Raphael Zon is director, R. N. Cunningham, forest economist, and Bernard Frank, assistant forest economist. The Station wishes to acknowledge the valuable assistance given in this study by the county commissioners and other county officials in the counties visited, as well as by county agents, state and federal forest rangers, and a number of interested citizens. Mr. George Empey of Hinckley gave particularly valuable advice and help.

outlay of hard cash, an investment that will be without tangible returns for many years to come.

What are the reasons for this delinquency? What is the outlook with respect to further abandonment? What is the effect on local communities and on county governments? What is the effect upon the tax base, the rate of taxation, and the valuation of the remaining property? What adjustments can be made and what remedies can be offered?

To obtain at least partial answers to these questions the Forest Service of the United States Department of Agriculture was given a special appropriation in 1931 to undertake studies of land reversion in various regions, including the Lake States region. The work was begun in sixteen northeastern cut-over counties[2] of Minnesota, and the present report embodies a summary of the findings of the first year's work.

Although each county presents different conditions and different local problems, there are several primary causes that seem to underlie the situation in all counties and call for general remedial treatment. The present study deals more with these general regional problems than with special local conditions which can be treated only after intensive study of each individual case.

The work of the Station was not concerned with the short-time delinquencies and tardy tax payments that are common at any time and may assume serious proportions in a time of general depression, such as has existed for the past two years. There is no need to call particular attention to the effects of the present depression upon tax revenues in the northern counties. In fact, there is reason to believe that the depression has had relatively less effect upon tax payments in these counties than in the richer and more densely settled regions, and certainly less than in some of the large cities of the country. The study deals rather with the long-time delinquencies and complete abandonment of land, phenomena characteristic of the cut-over forest lands of the northern Lake States. Short-time delinquency is a fiscal problem. Long-time delinquency and wholesale abandonment is a fiscal problem, a land problem, and a social problem.

[2] The counties included in this survey are Cook, Lake, St. Louis, Itasca, Koochiching, Beltrami, Lake of the Woods, Hubbard, Clearwater, Cass, Crow Wing, Kanabec, Pine, Mille Lacs, Carlton, and Aitkin. See Figures 1 and 13, pages 114 and 144.

FIGURE 1. — TAX DELINQUENCY IN SIXTEEN NORTHEASTERN COUNTIES

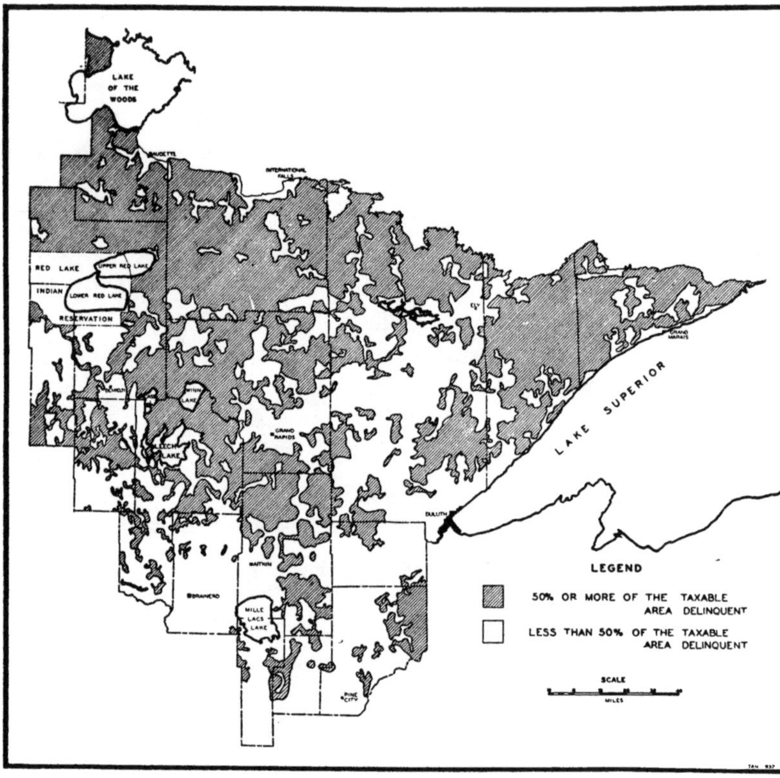

THE TAX SITUATION

One of the main purposes of the study was to determine the extent to which the lands within each county contribute to its support. The lands fall into three classes as regards the contribution of tax revenue: (1) land exempt by law from paying taxes — remnants of the federal public domain not allotted for any purpose, federal public domain allotted for special purposes such as national forests, Indian reservations, and state public domain, including state forests, state parks, and other land used by the state; (2) tax-delinquent land, that is, land privately owned the taxes on which have been in arrears for one or more years, including lands that have been delinquent for four years or longer and after 1933 will pass into the control of the state, the new public domain; and (3) individually or corporately owned land that is paying taxes.

Tax-Exempt Land

Of the total 19,021,000 acres of unplatted property in the sixteen counties, 3,815,240 acres are exempt from taxation. The acreage by counties and by ownership is shown in Table 1. There are 1,121,920 acres of federal land in the Superior and Chippewa National Forests, including unperfected claims. There are still 203,320 acres of unreserved federal public domain. There are 529,560 acres belonging to the Indians. The state retains 1,960,440 acres from the swamp land grant and other grants from the federal government. (See Figure 13, page 144.)

Tax-exempt lands in the sixteen counties comprise one-fifth of the total land area. Although no taxes are paid on these lands, they are not a burden to the local communities or the counties, since highway construction, fire protection, policing, and so on, are financed by the federal or state government. If they were privately owned, these lands would probably be on the tax-delinquent list.

National forests.—The national forests contribute 25 per cent

Table 1.—Acreage of Tax-Exempt Lands in Sixteen Northeastern Counties, 1931

County	State Land [a]	Federal Public Domain [b]	National Forest [c]	Indian Lands [d]	Total
Aitkin	70,760	680	.....	.....	71,440
Beltrami	30,080	22,560	5,800	297,000	355,440
Carlton	10,440	280	.....	440	11,160
Cass	79,760	1,360	104,120	39,240	224,480
Clearwater	26,720	160	.....	120,000	146,880
Cook	133,880	.....	305,480	11,560	450,920
Crow Wing	11,880	.....	.....	.....	11,880
Hubbard	9,520	.....	.....	.....	9,520
Itasca	223,960	2,000	81,760	14,760	322,480
Kanabec	200	40	.....	.....	240
Koochiching	740,200	75,800	.....	33,920	849,920
Lake	167,160	920	402,800	.....	570,880
Lake of the Woods	.....	84,040	.....	.....	84,040
Mille Lacs	560	.....	.....	.....	560
Pine	3,960	240	.....	.....	4,200
St. Louis	451,360	15,240	221,960	12,640	701,200
Total	1,960,440	203,320	1,121,920	529,560	3,815,240

[a] From records of the state auditor. Does not include lands that have been sold on contract and later abandoned, except where the state has definitely reclaimed the area.

[b] From records of the General Land Office, Cass Lake, Minnesota.

[c] From status records of forest supervisors at Cass Lake and Duluth.

[d] From plat books of the Indian Service at Cass Lake and Red Lake.

of their gross income from timber sales and all other sources to the state, and these funds are distributed to the counties in which the forests lie for the maintenance of schools and roads. Other large expenditures are made directly by the federal government for construction and maintenance of roads, fire protection, forest planting, and general administration of the lands. Not including expenditures for purchase of lands nor the $103,205 paid directly to the state for the protection of state and private lands from fire, a sum of $388,683 was spent in the state in 1931 for administration, protection, and development of the national forests. This is equal to about thirty-five cents for every acre of land under the jurisdiction of the Forest Service, a much larger contribution for the upkeep of local functions than is made by the owner of comparable private land.

State lands.—Approximately two million acres of the original acreage coming to the state from various land grants now remain in state ownership. The income from these state lands is accumulated in trust funds, the interest from which is used for the upkeep of the common schools and certain other state institutions. The income from the common school fund is now very large and the amounts distributed to the counties help materially in the maintenance of rural schools. Thus, the state lands contribute to the cost of local government. The poorer counties are favored in many kinds of state aid and, with the exception of St. Louis County, all of the sixteen northern cut-over counties receive more state aid than they pay in taxes. In fact, in a few cases the state aid amounts to seventeen or eighteen times the amount of the state tax levy.

The state spends from three hundred thousand to five hundred thousand dollars a year for forest-fire protection in the northern counties. This amounts to from fifteen to twenty-five cents per acre of state-owned land. Its expenditures for forest planting, forest management, and administration of the lands have been extremely small up to the present time, but with the development of the conservation program authorized by the 1931 legislature, these activities may be expected to expand.

Other public lands.—The federal public domain in northern Minnesota now amounts to only 203,320 acres, and it can be generally stated that all land of any prospective value for farming or other private enterprise has been taken up. The remaining land is

Figure 2. — Percentage of Taxable Area Tax Delinquent in Sixteen Northeastern Counties

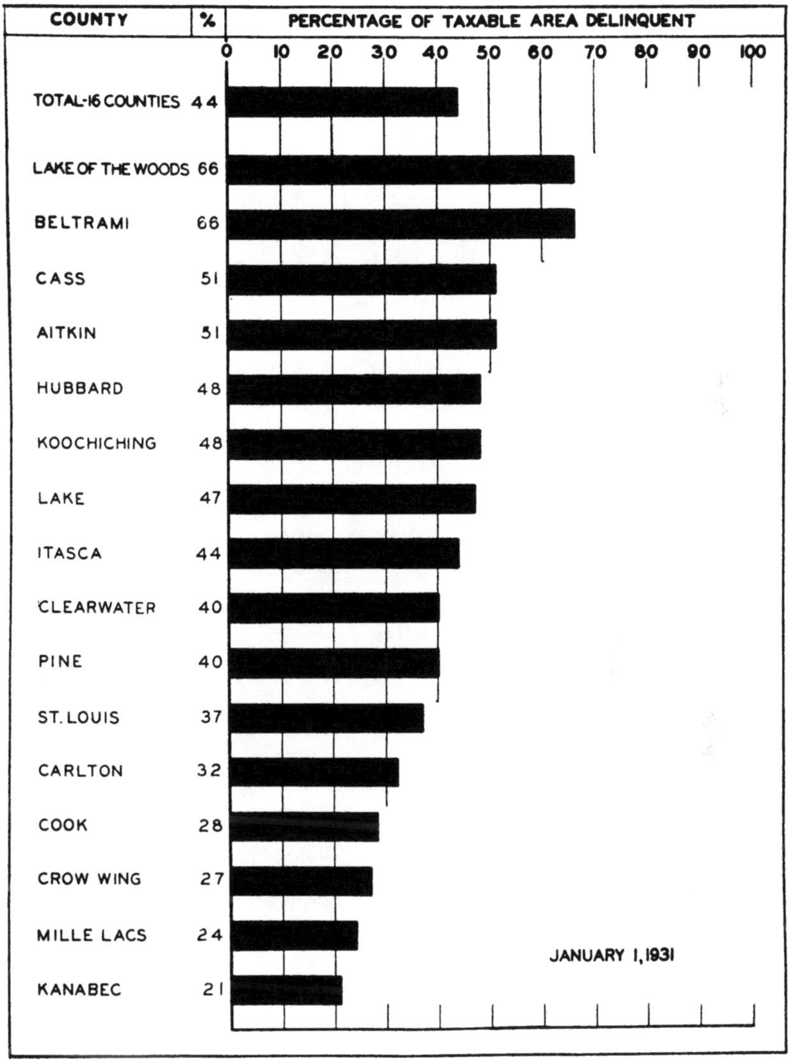

primarily poor swamp land of practically no value for private utilization but possibly of some value for water control and game production.

The Indian land remaining in these counties now amounts to only 529,560 acres, most of the good land having found its way into private ownership.

Tax-Delinquent Land

About 44 per cent of the total taxable area in the sixteen counties was tax delinquent on January 1, 1931. In two counties two-thirds of the taxable area was delinquent. In six counties about one-half, in six counties more than one-quarter, and in two counties about one-fifth was delinquent on this date. These figures include all the tax-delinquent land, irrespective of how long it has been delinquent. The exact percentage of taxable land delinquent on January 1, 1931, in each county is shown in Figure 2 on page 117. Figure 3 shows the acreage tax delinquent.

Table 2 gives the total acreage of tax-delinquent land in each county, classified according to the period for which it has been delinquent. In the entire group of counties, it will be seen, four million acres have been delinquent for over four years. Some of

Table 2.—Acreage of Tax-Delinquent Lands in Sixteen Northeastern Counties by Years

County	Acreage Delinquent for Taxes Levied in				Total Acreage Delinquent on January 1, 1931
	1926 and before	1927	1928	1929	
Aitkin	317,520	79,400	70,000	94,320	561,240
Beltrami	592,480	78,040	66,240	73,920	810,680
Carlton	96,920	22,160	17,240	35,360	171,680
Cass	373,400	74,560	49,080	79,640	576,680
Clearwater	107,120	20,600	28,680	47,280	203,680
Cook	88,360	18,160	20,800	15,840	143,160
Crow Wing	87,160	20,320	22,880	52,040	182,400
Hubbard	211,080	34,640	15,440	31,840	293,000
Itasca	390,000	75,200	73,840	93,000	632,040
Kanabec	20,800	18,680	9,960	22,600	72,040
Koochiching	369,200	57,360	52,680	81,960	561,200
Lake	252,600	33,560	37,200	40,080	363,440
Lake of the Woods	382,200	45,520	36,000	49,120	512,840
Mille Lacs	43,440	13,040	16,240	17,440	90,160
Pine	237,240	40,600	31,640	51,840	361,320
St. Louis	469,760	101,640	396,640	327,240	1,295,280
Total	4,039,280	733,480	944,560	1,113,520	6,830,840

Figure 3.—Percentage of Total Area Tax Delinquent, Non-Taxable, and Taxpaying in Sixteen Northeastern Counties

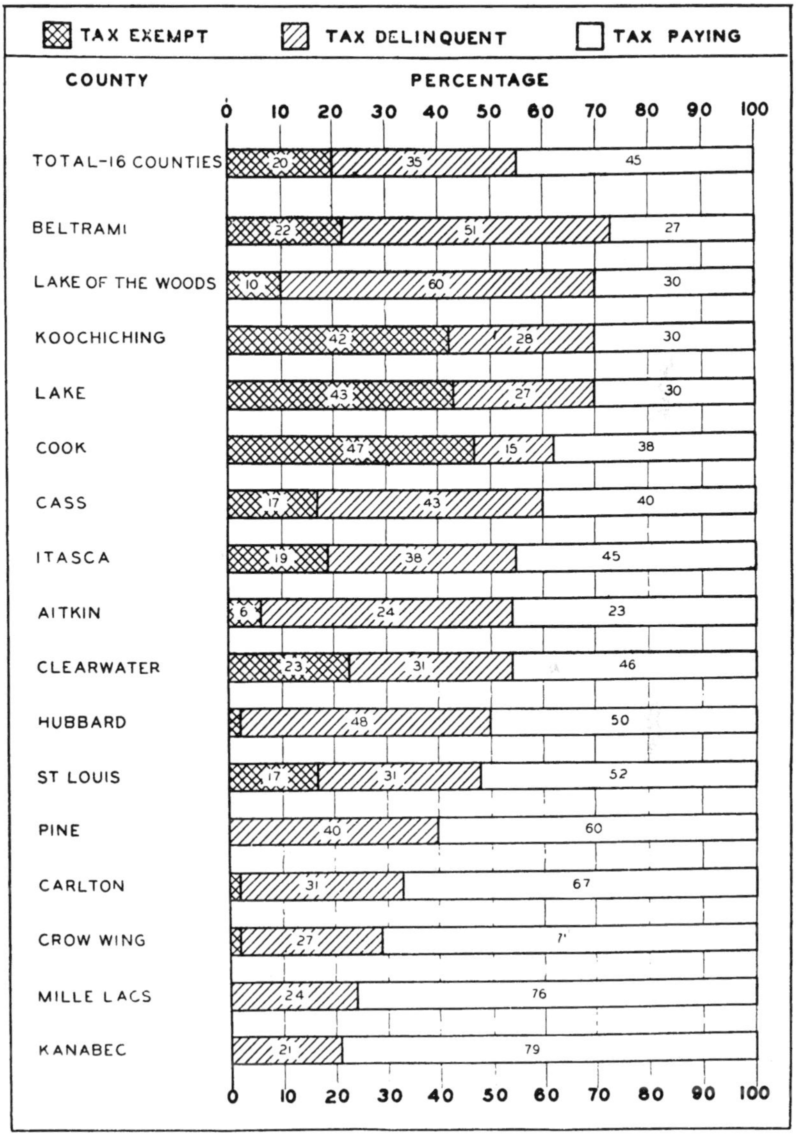

this delinquency extends back from twelve to fifteen years. In 1927 another 733,480 acres were added, making a total of 4,772,760 acres that have been delinquent for three years or more. The acreage added in 1928 was somewhat larger (944,560) and in 1929 still larger (1,113,520), making a grand total of 6,830,840 acres delinquent on January 1, 1931. Taxes payable in 1929 had been legally delinquent for approximately one year as of January 1, 1931, since the first date of legal delinquency for such taxes was the first Monday in January, 1930. There is, of course, more likelihood of redemption of the lands that have been delinquent for only one year, but even so there seems to be an accelerating tendency that has considerable significance.

Tax delinquency as related to tax levies.—The accumulated total of unpaid taxes and special assessments in the sixteen counties amounted to $21,874,033 in January, 1932. This almost equals the total delinquency in all the remaining seventy-one counties of the state.

The total amount of uncollected taxes in each of the sixteen counties and that for 1930 alone is shown in Table 3. The per-

TABLE 3.—EXTENT OF TAX DELINQUENCY IN SIXTEEN NORTHEASTERN COUNTIES AS OF JANUARY, 1932[a]

County	1930 Taxes Uncollected		Total Uncollected Taxes, 1930 and Before
	Amount	Per Cent	
Aitkin	$517,601	55.61	$2,626,499
Beltrami	414,130	53.05	3,849,944
Carlton	114,215	12.18	636,242
Cass	330,331	48.56	1,630,331
Clearwater	107,330	36.53	377,617
Cook	79,735	38.62	581,400
Crow Wing	152,732	12.93	707,662
Hubbard	138,738	39.34	543,447
Itasca	256,707	10.00	1,457,478
Kanabec	56,583	19.74	201,999
Koochiching	452,718	45.00	1,976,302
Lake	89,274	22.89	652,976
Lake of the Woods	230,830	68.46	1,442,030
Mille Lacs	83,709	18.27	312,355
Pine	228,418	30.76	970,611
Total 15 counties	$3,253,051	29.18	$17,966,893
St. Louis County	1,060,684	4.54	3,907,140
Rest of state	8,273,864	8.47	22,829,111
Grand total	$12,587,599	9.52	$44,703,144

[a] Data obtained from the Minnesota Tax Commission.

FIGURE 4. — ACREAGE TAX DELINQUENT IN SIXTEEN NORTHEASTERN COUNTIES, JANUARY 1, 1931

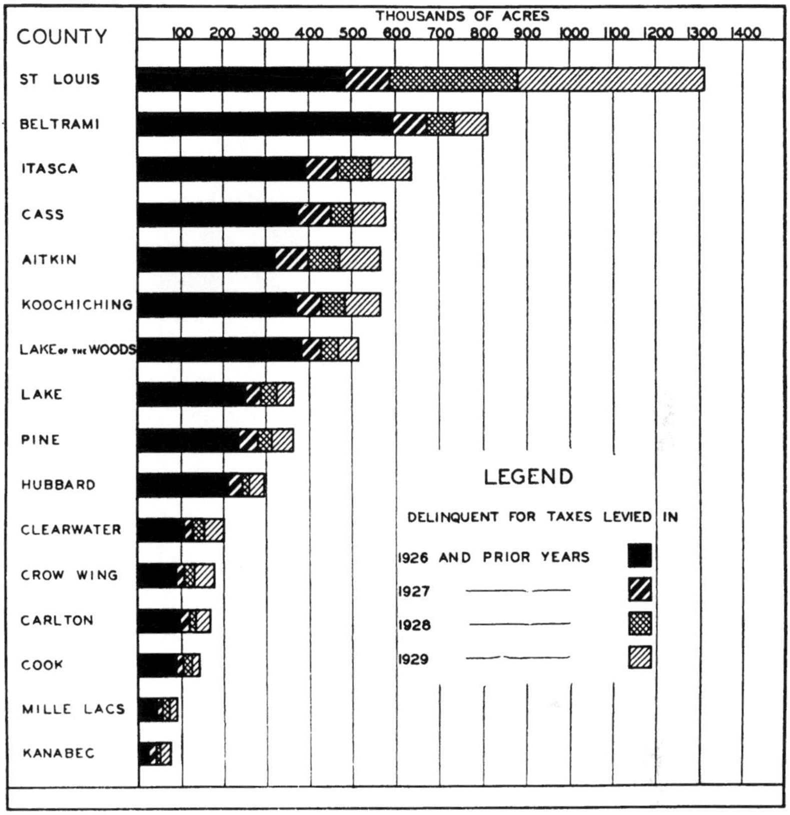

centage of the total levy that is delinquent varies greatly in the different areas — from 4.54 per cent in St. Louis County to 68.46 per cent in Lake of the Woods County. If St. Louis County is omitted from the group, the amount of the 1930 levy remaining unpaid in January, 1932, was 29.18 per cent of the total levy.

LAND THAT PAYS TAXES

By deducting from the total land area the public land that is exempt from taxation and the tax-delinquent land, the approximate acreage of taxable land is obtained. (See Figure 4.)

If we exclude state aid and the contribution of the national forests toward the upkeep of local governments, then only 45 per cent of the total unplatted land area in the sixteen counties as a whole was actually paying taxes as of January 1, 1931. The percentage varies greatly in individual counties. For instance, in Beltrami County owners of only 27 per cent of the land pay taxes. In Lake of the Woods, Koochiching, and Lake counties only 30 per cent of the land is taxpaying. In only six of the more southerly counties is more than 50 per cent of the land contributing to the county upkeep.

Figures 5 to 11, pages 123 to 129, show the location of the tax-delinquent, tax-exempt, and taxpaying lands in six of the counties most seriously affected by delinquencies. Similar records are available for the other counties. In some counties, such as Pine, the delinquency is more or less localized and can be associated with certain characteristics of the land, while in some other counties the delinquency has advanced so far as to lie like a blanket on the entire area.

REASONS FOR TAX DELINQUENCY

The widespread tax delinquency in northern Minnesota is largely a result of wasteful use of natural resources and a wrong appraisal of future trends in agriculture. The factors that have contributed to the present tax situation are deforestation, which has resulted in the closing of industries dependent on wood and a consequent enormous shrinkage in taxable values, colonization of land unsuited to agriculture, and large public expenditures resulting from the belief that most of the cut-over lands would soon be taken up as farms.

Destruction of Forests

It is unnecessary to go into the details of forest devastation in northern Minnesota. The great forests of pine and spruce are practically gone. In their place are extensive areas of cut-over and badly burned land. The belief that the plow would follow the axe disarmed public criticism and permitted the rapid and practically complete destruction of one of the greatest natural resources of the state. What timber was not cut by lumbermen was destroyed in slash fires or was burned off by settlers attempting to clear land.

Without provision for future forest regrowth, taxable values have almost disappeared. For example, in Townships 54 and 55 North, Range 14 West, in St. Louis County, real property was

Figure 5. — Tax-Delinquent, Non-Taxable, and Taxpaying Lands in Lake of the Woods County

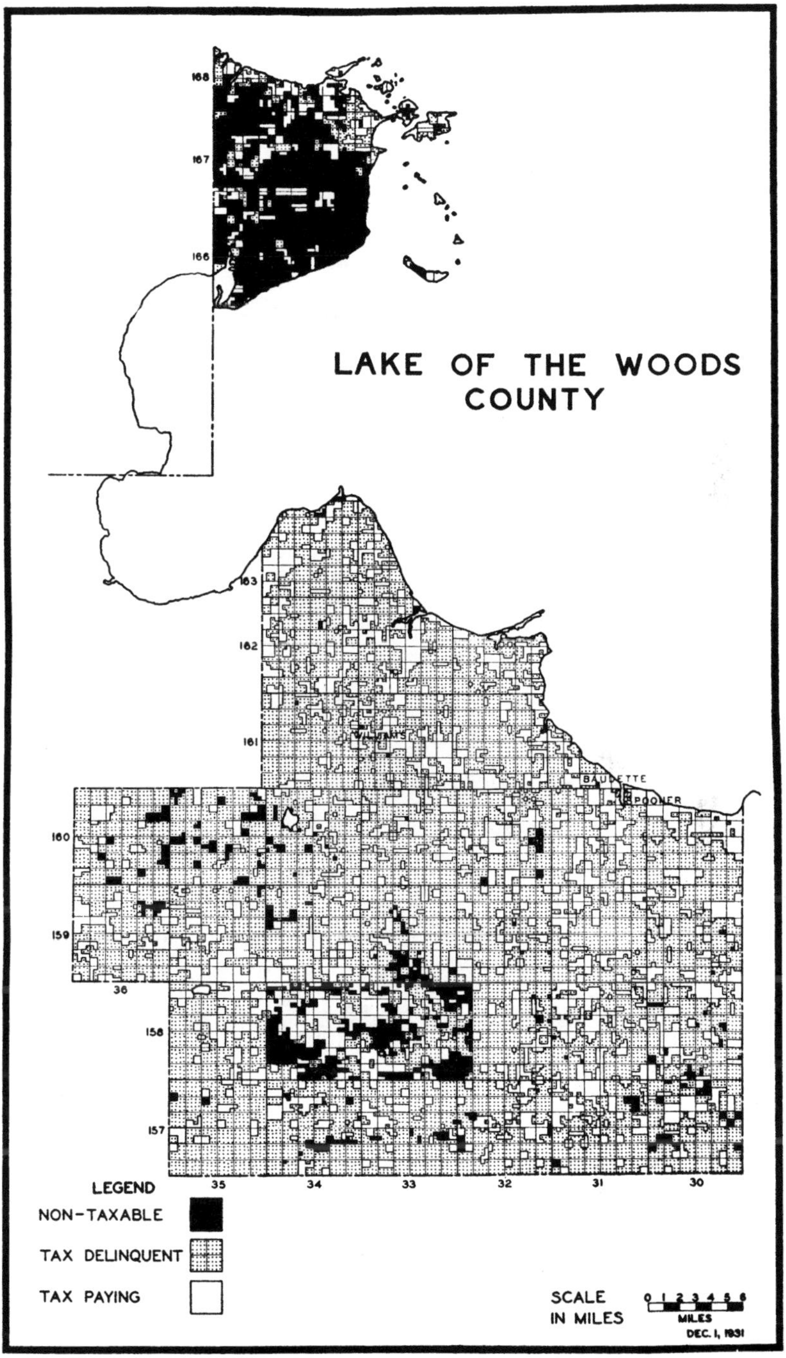

Figure 6. — Tax-Delinquent, Non-Taxable, and Taxpaying Lands in Beltrami County

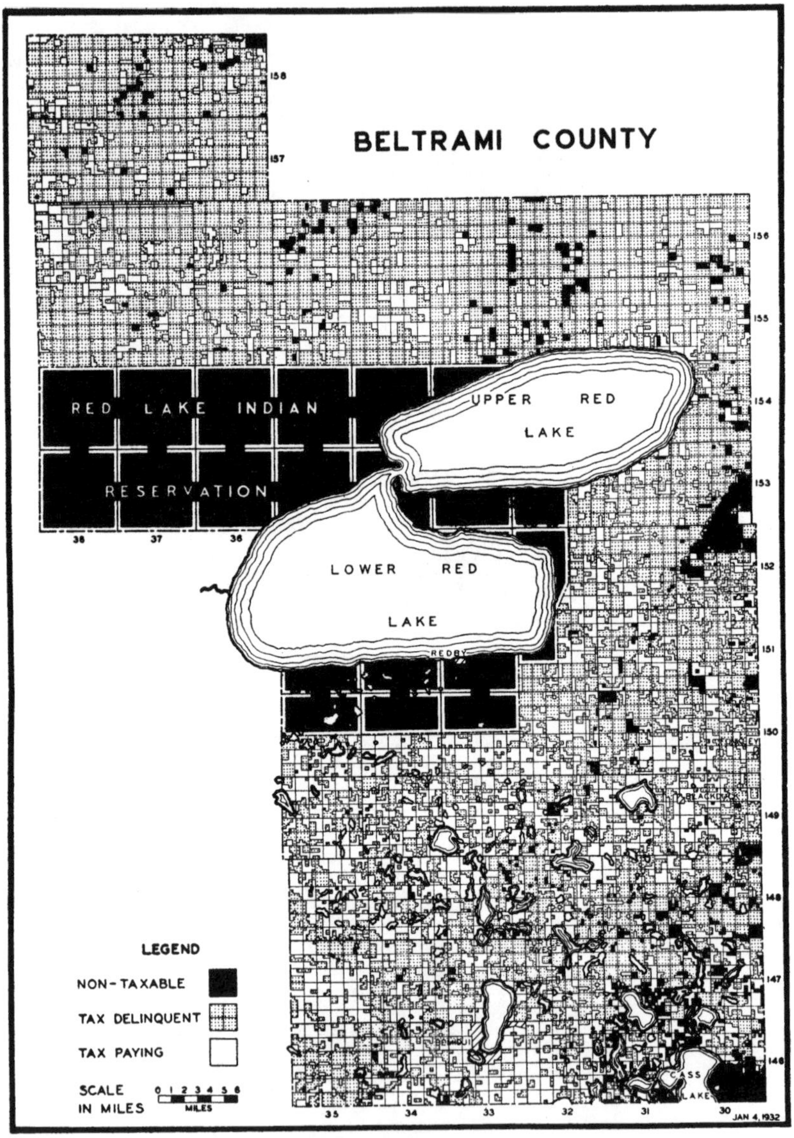

Figure 7. — Tax-Delinquent, Non-Taxable, and Taxpaying Lands in Cass County

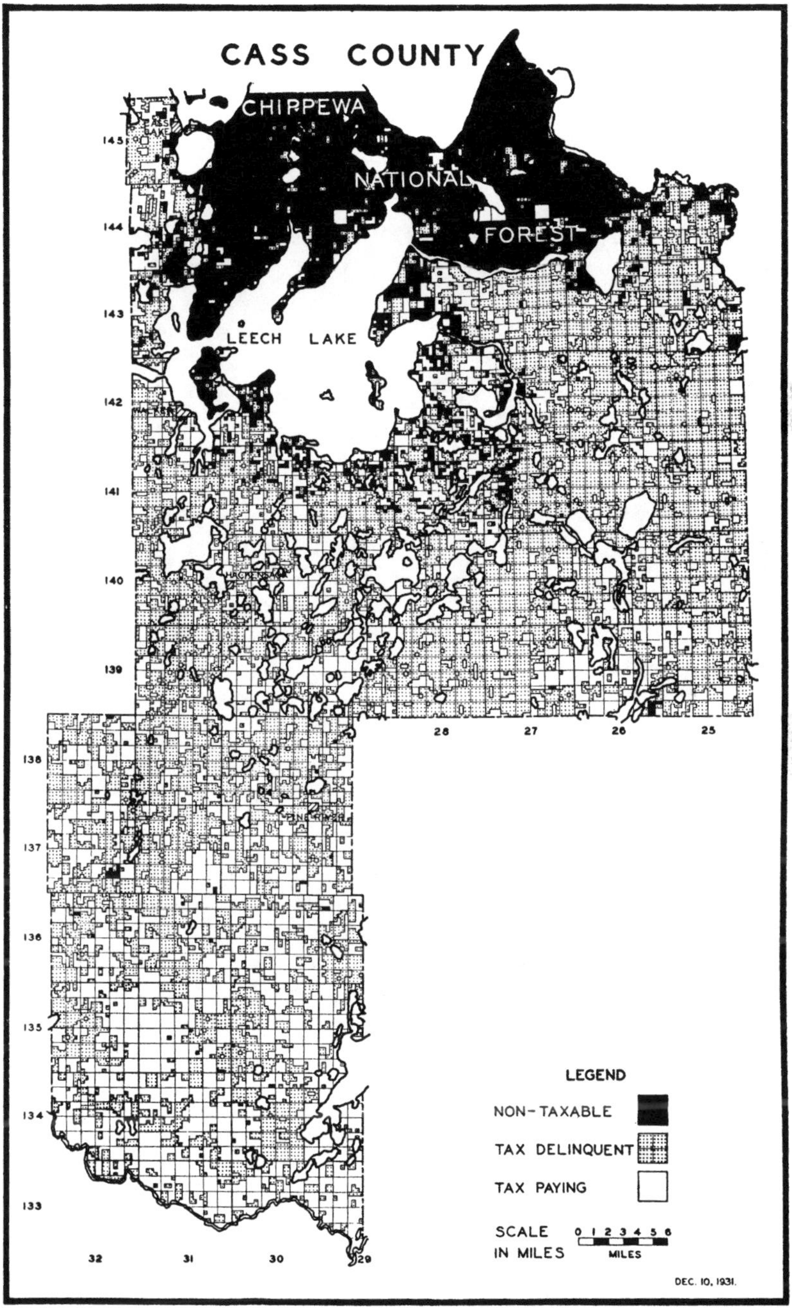

Figure 8. — Tax-Delinquent, Non-Taxable, and Taxpaying Lands in Aitkin County

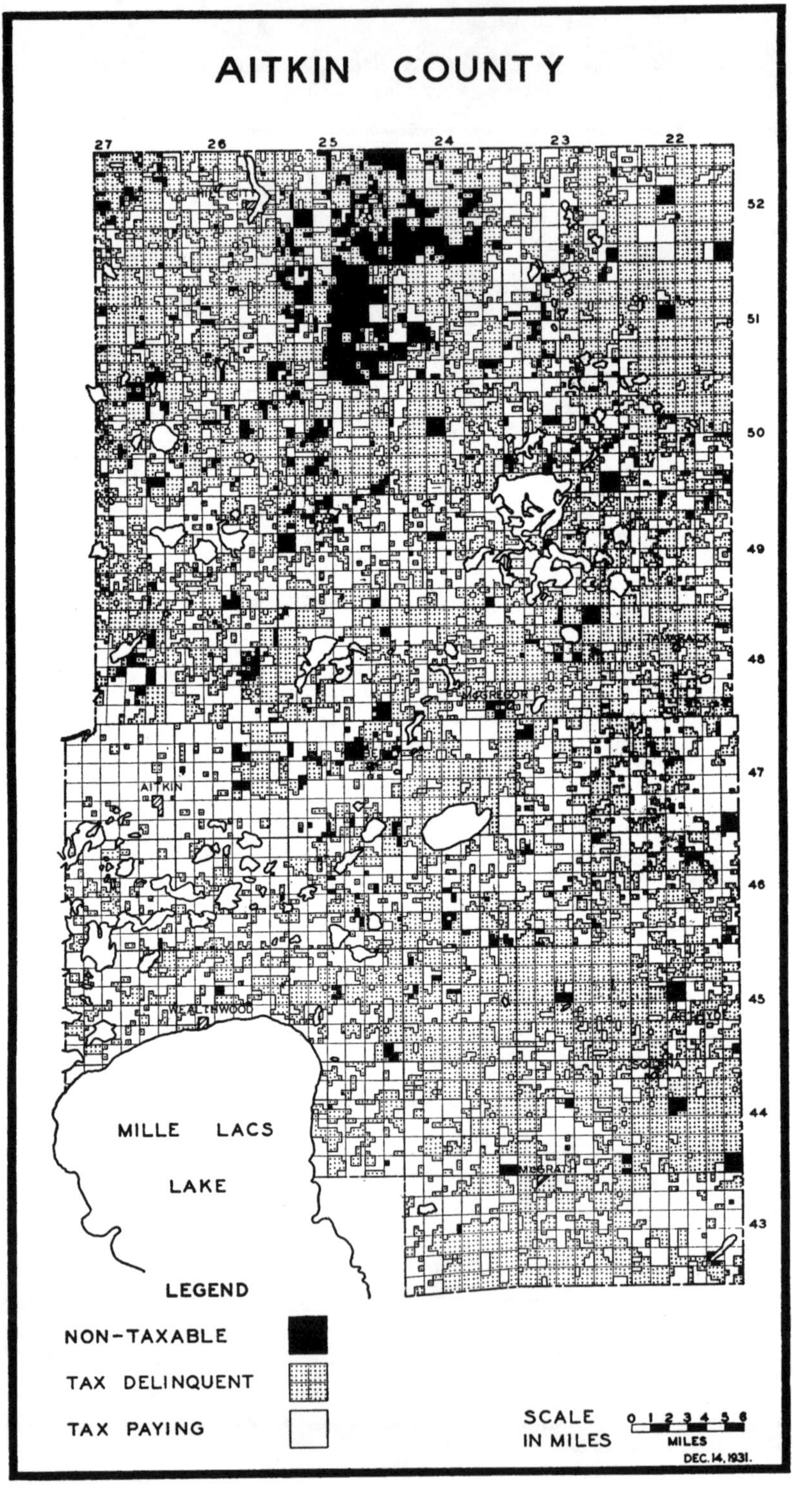

FIGURE 9. — TAX-DELINQUENT, NON-TAXABLE, AND TAXPAYING LANDS IN PINE COUNTY

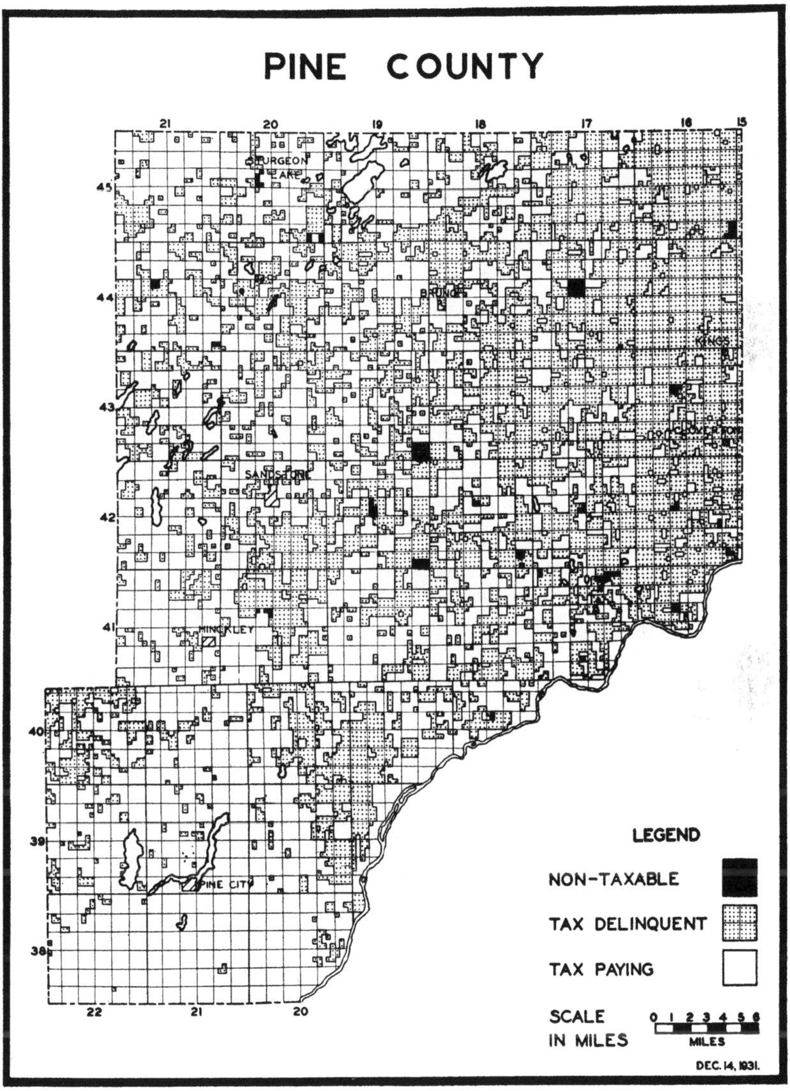

Figure 10. — Tax-Delinquent, Non-Taxable, and Taxpaying Lands in Northern St. Louis County

Figure 11. — Tax-Delinquent, Non-Taxable, and Taxpaying Lands in Southern St. Louis County

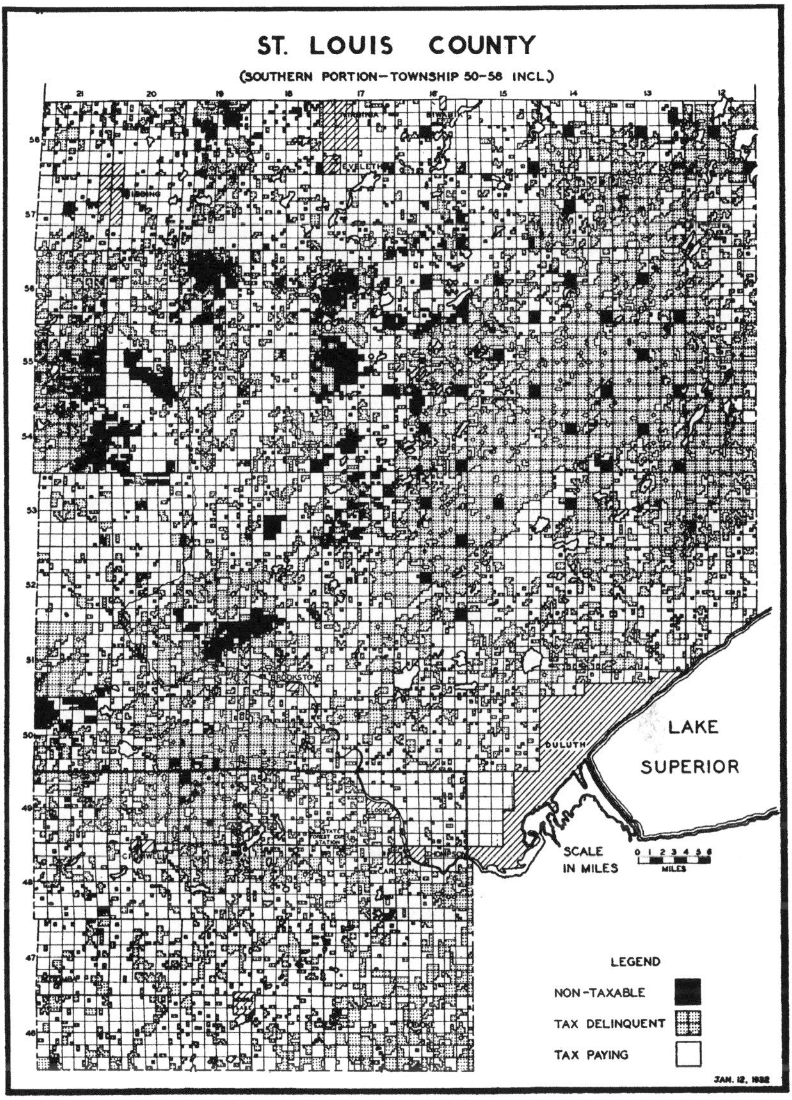

appraised at $1,129,558 in 1916.[3] As the timber was cut the valuations dropped to $297,296 in 1920 and to $261,290 in 1926. Taxes on other property had to be increased and tax delinquency resulted. In 1931, 85 per cent of the taxable area was delinquent in these townships. Taxable valuations in Townships 67 and 68 North, Range 20 West, decreased from $737,073 in 1914 to $72,301 in 1926. Seventy-seven per cent of the taxable area of the county was delinquent in 1931.

The town of Wilma in Pine County furnishes another example of the effects of destructive lumbering on tax delinquency. Once containing fine stands of pine and hardwoods, the township has been thoroughly stripped and a rich source of taxable income has almost completely disappeared. Now only 121 acres of merchantable timber remain. The entire acreage of cut-over lands, amounting to 21,700 acres, although taxed from 44 to 45 cents per acre, yields less than $4,000 in taxes because of extensive delinquency. Tax receipts in this township have dropped off steadily during the past six years, the deficiency in collection rising from 37 to 62 per cent during that period.

Not only has the rapid cutting of the timber reduced the taxable resources of the northern counties but the closing down of sawmills and logging camps has removed an important local market for farm crops and logs from the uncleared part of the farm. Farm produce must now be shipped long distances to an already glutted market. Moreover, there is now no opportunity for the farmer to do outside work in the woods during the winter months. The passing of the lumber industry has made it much more difficult for a new settler to maintain a home while he is clearing up and developing a farm and has had a depressing effect upon agriculture throughout the region.

One of the areas selected by the Forest Taxation Inquiry for special study in 1926[4] and revisited in the summer of 1931 was Township 59 North, Range 8 West, a part of Beaver Bay in Lake County. It lies near the center of the county, about fifty miles from the county seat. A small Finnish farming community settled here just after the first logging operations were begun. Of a total

[3] R. C. Hall and P. A. Herbert, "Property Taxation in Selected Towns in the Forest Land Regions of Minnesota," a mimeographed progress report of the Forest Taxation Inquiry issued by the United States Forest Service, Washington, D. C., July, 1930.

[4] *Ibid.*

of thirty families reported as living here twenty years ago only thirteen remain. The census for 1930 shows 2,043 acres in farms in the township, but interviews with settlers revealed that only 832 acres were owned by operating farmers and only 138 acres were cleared. Only one of the remaining settlers obtained a major part of his income from farming; of the others, one derives his income from storekeeping, one from carpentry, and the rest chiefly from outside jobs, such as road work, fire-fighting, trapping, guiding, and so forth. In the opinion of an original settler this community will largely disappear with the death of the old people.

Over-Expansion in Agriculture

The agricultural boom, which did not really come to an end until after the war, had several undesirable effects. In the first place, it resulted in the settlement of a great deal of sandy, swampy, and otherwise poor land in a region where only first-class land can be farmed at a profit. Often the prices paid were so out of proportion to the earning capacity of the land that the returns were insufficient to cover interest on capital outlays, not to mention wages for labor expended. It stimulated the building of schools, the construction of roads, and other rural development to take care of an expected growth of population. It created fictitious speculative values for all types of land, values that are still reflected in some of the tax assessments. It prompted some unwise ventures into swamp drainage. It retarded the adoption of any sound and comprehensive plans for utilizing land for timber growing by the state.

Swamp drainage.—Special mention needs to be made of the difficulties arising from the extensive drainage projects in the Red Lake and Swan River swamps. Beginning about 1908, laws were enacted by the legislature authorizing the construction of ditches upon the petition of a few landowners and ordering the county commissioners to issue bonds for the cost of construction. The expenses were to be assessed against the benefited lands. Some 1,487 miles of such ditches were constructed in Lake of the Woods and Beltrami counties alone, at an average cost of about eleven dollars an acre.

As a rule the benefits expected from drainage have not materialized. Much of the land against which assessments are levied has never been settled. Other large areas have been abandoned when it has been found that the land would not produce enough to carry the heavy drainage charges. The percentage of tax delinquency is enormous, and in Lake of the Woods County the total outstanding ditch indebtedness is now over half the assessed value of all the property paying taxes.

The township of Pioneer (Township 157 North, Range 33 West), twenty-five miles south of Baudette, illustrates the effects of injudicious drainage on tax delinquency and land abandonment. Despite the fact that some twenty-seven miles of ditches were dug, there is not a single settler living on swamp land. Two vacant buildings,

TABLE 4. — EXTENT OF TAX DELINQUENCY IN PIONEER TOWNSHIP, LAKE OF THE WOODS COUNTY, JANUARY 5, 1931[a]

	Year of Levy					
	1925	1926	1927	1928	1929	1930
Ordinary taxes	$5,385	$4,490	$4,124	$2,931	$2,868	$2,645
Ditch assessments	5,770	5,565	5,706	5,488	5,258	5,021
Total	$11,155	$10,055	$9,830	$8,419	$8,126	$7,666
Receipts from levies	3,756	2,935	2,779	2,155	1,820	
Percentage of deficiency in collection	66	71	72	74	78	

[a] From county abstract of tax lists.

one a school, are the only structures that remain. In 1910 the township listed forty-six inhabitants; now it can claim only fourteen. There are six farms aggregating 840 acres, of which 77 acres are crop land, but these farms are confined to ridges of sandy loam along the streams. As shown in Table 4, tax delinquency in this township is very great. In addition to ditch assessments totaling over $5,000 a year, there are some twenty-one miles of roads to keep up, schools to provide for, and so on. In spite of all possible economies these costs are bound to fall heavily upon a small and shrinking tax base.

In this township one-fourth of the land in farms was on the delinquent list in 1930. Merchantable spruce pulpwood, which was taxed about 48 cents an acre on the average, was likewise only 23 per cent delinquent. Delinquencies on cut-over land, which was taxed from 9 to 16 cents an acre, totaled 80 per cent, however.

HIGH TAXES AND INEQUALITIES IN TAXATION

A by-product of the agricultural boom has been a certain amount of public extravagance and an extension of public services beyond what the actual resources of the region can comfortably support. Increasing public expenditures in recent years are not peculiar to northern Minnesota, but the effects of such increases are more striking in a sparsely settled region. While tax rates have been more than doubled in the state as a whole in the past twenty years, in the northern counties they have been quadrupled. (See Table 5.) Many projects have been financed by bond issues, the retirement provisions and the interest charges for which still make up a large share of the current cost of local government.

TABLE 5. — COMPARISON OF AVERAGE TAX RATES IN NORTHEASTERN MINNESOTA AND REST OF STATE [a]

YEAR	16 NORTHEASTERN COUNTIES	REST OF STATE	WHOLE STATE
	Mills	Mills	Mills
1910	25.94	28.74	27.92
1915	34.84	34.91	34.89
1920	70.78	46.69	52.43
1925	73.04	55.40	59.72
1930	104.24	54.56	64.20

[a] Data for 1910–1925 from Progress Report No. 5 of the Forest Taxation Inquiry; for 1930, from the Minnesota Tax Commission.

Some of these public expenditures have been fully justified by the economic benefits that have accrued to the community. Expenditures for much-needed roads, better schools, and protection of health were the price paid for a higher rural civilization, and in spite of their cost were undoubtedly a benefit to the local communities. Some projects, however, such as the drainage of swamps in anticipation of the future expansion of agriculture, the erection of public buildings far beyond public needs, some over-ambitious road construction not justified by economic demands, and similar public investments based upon anticipated needs of the future rather than upon current requirements have put a heavy burden upon the finances of northern communities and are now a source of financial embarrassment because many of the obligations are fixed charges that cannot be scaled down.

The lowest average rate in any of the northern counties in 1930 was 62 mills in Hubbard and St. Louis counties. The highest was 177 mills in Koochiching County. This latter rate is nearly three times the state average. The lower average rate in St. Louis County is made possible by the presence of large taxable values in iron mines and mining property. This advantage, however, extends only to the townships in which such property lies, and the rate in some of the other townships runs from 130 to 140 mills per dollar of assessed value.

Not only are tax rates high in these northern counties, but valuations placed by assessors upon lands of low value are extremely high in most localities. In eleven townships in which valuations were checked by the United States Forest Service in 1926, it was found that the valuations placed by the assessors upon cut-over

TABLE 6.—COMPARISON OF ASSESSED VALUES WITH APPRAISED VALUES IN 4 NORTHERN COUNTIES, 1926[a]

County and Township	Average Assessed Value in Percentage of Appraised Values				
	Farm Property			Timber	Cut-Over Forest
	Land	Improvements	Total		
Beltrami County					
Eckles	88	13	73	...	140
Frohn	78	8	60	...	177
Hagali (part)	121	14	74	...	279
Hubbard County					
Clay	192	54	157	...	296
Crow Wing	104	50	95	...	289
Lake Emma	115	52	94	...	194
Schoolcraft	183	34	120	245	306
Lake County					
Beaver Bay (part)	38	22	34	106	92
Cramer (part)	..	..	..	...	252
Silver Creek (part)	68	30	51	...	128
St. Louis County					
Embarrass	26	27	26	...	65
Toivola	51	36	46	...	153
T. 54–55 N., R. 14 W.	..	..	..	110	216

[a] Hall and Herbert, "Property Taxation in Selected Towns in the Forest Land Regions of Minnesota" (mimeograph). Appraised values based on sales prices.

land ran from two to three times the actual sales value, while farm property valuations were often placed below their sales value. (See Table 6.) Farm improvements were invariably given a low valuation. Not infrequently cut-over wild land was given the same valuation per acre as developed farm land.

In many parts of the region, particularly in the mining districts, there are great differences in tax rates and valuations in adjoining townships. Undoubtedly, inequalities of this kind have contributed to the tax delinquency in the poorer districts.

At first, tax delinquency was confined largely to poor farm land and smaller tracts of cut-over swamp. Large landowners, as a rule, held on and owners of the better farms were able to pay taxes. But each case of delinquency has added a still heavier burden to the remaining taxpayers. The process works in a vicious circle, delinquency causing higher taxes and higher taxes causing more delinquency. Good land and bad alike are gripped by these unfortunate circumstances. In the past year some comparatively good farms have been given up in despair. Large landowners likewise have begun to lose hope of any remedial treatment and have begun to slough their holdings by the hundreds of thousands of acres. With the movement thus gaining momentum, there is little reason to hope that it will stop far short of complete reversion to public ownership unless remedial action is taken within a very short time.

The township of Frohn, which was mentioned by the Taxation Inquiry in 1926 as an area representing the better type of farming country in Beltrami County,[5] is an example of how comparatively good farming sections are being affected. It was described as "located close to Bemidji, with which it is connected by state highway, . . . also as having railroad facilities which permit it to send its farm products to the south and east and its woodlot products to the west, . . . a farming community which is apparently fairly prosperous and where a small expansion in agricultural development can be expected."

In 1926 only 879 acres were on the "unredeemed" list in the township of Frohn. In spite of the favorable circumstances described above, 2,800 acres were "unredeemed" in 1931, and the total delinquency amounts to 6,040 acres, or nearly a third of the township.

Deflation of Speculative Values

Speculation in agricultural lands has led to over-development and in the end to tax delinquency and land abandonment. Speculation in other lines has to some extent acted as a retardant on tax delinquency. Taxes on property valued for mining, water power, and recreation have been maintained to a greater extent than on common wild land, but in the past few years there has been a noticeable increase in tax delinquency even on this type of land.

[5] Hall and Herbert, "Property Taxation in Selected Towns in the Forest Land Regions of Minnesota" (mimeograph).

As a sample of an area containing values of a speculative character, a study was made of Township 62 North, Range 14 West, the township of Breitung in St. Louis County. This is another of the townships previously investigated by the Forest Taxation Inquiry in 1926. It is a cut-over area on one of the iron ranges in which there are several small lakes and several resort developments, but no farms. There are no operating mines in the township, but there is a general belief that the area is underlaid with iron and nearly 85 per cent of the area is assessed as mineral land. In 1930 the tax per acre for mineral land averaged 71 cents, for resort land 53 cents, and for cut-over land 10 cents. That faith in future mining values was beginning to weaken under the influence of high taxes was evidenced by the fact that 61 per cent of the area assessed as mineral was delinquent for the taxes of 1929. Forty-five per cent of the resort land was also delinquent. None of this delinquent area was favorably located for commercial development.

The township of Woodrow in Cass County, near Hackensack, is another newly developed recreational region. There are about ten thousand "lake shore" lots in this township, but on about 65 per cent of them, according to the town clerk, no taxes have been paid during the past year. Between 1928 and 1931 the taxable valuation of the township fell from $141,097 to $87,357. A possible clue to some of the large delinquency in recreational property is the fact that many of the "lake shore" lots sold in recent years are from several hundred yards to a half mile back from the lake. Recreation has been oversold.

Recreational development has been looked to as one of the most promising fields for the future employment of land in the northern counties. Commercial resorts, private summer homes, public camp grounds, all bring money into the country and help to support local communities and local industries. There has been a mushroom growth of the tourist and resort business in the past few years and the possibilities have only been touched. But if the experience with timber and with land colonization means anything, a measure of caution is in order. Recreational development should proceed soundly, with due consideration to the maintenance of the resources upon which it is founded and with some regard to the rights of the general public. If unrestricted development results in all the choice and accessible lake shore properties being monopolized by undesirable hotels and cabin camps, bent only on swindling

FIGURE 12. — PRIVATELY OWNED, STATE, AND FEDERAL LANDS IN NORTHEASTERN COUNTIES

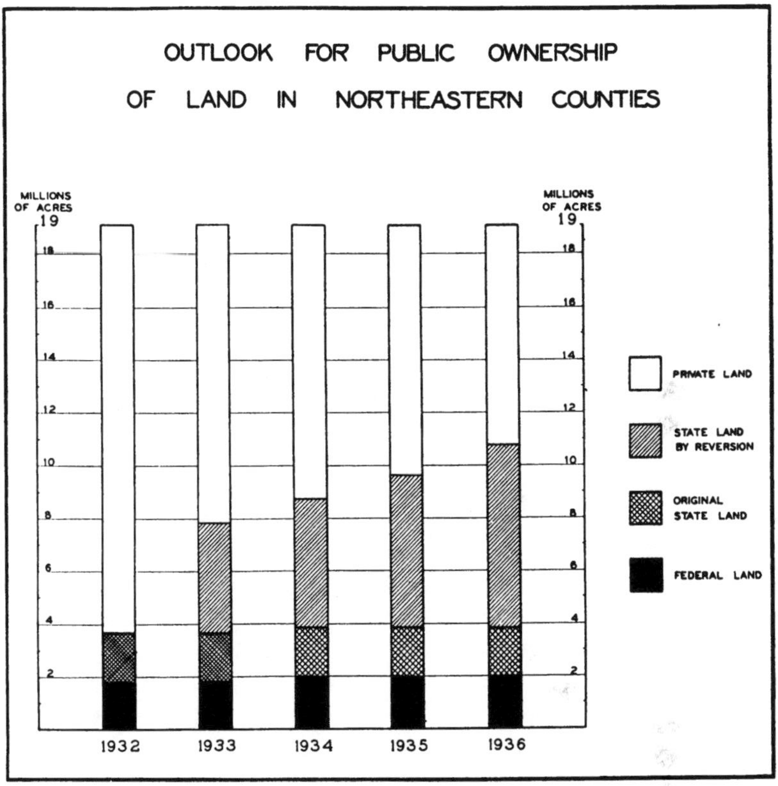

the traveling public, the industry will very soon destroy itself. Fortunately there is still time to institute some regional planning in this important field and to start recreational development along sound, constructive lines.

TRENDS IN TAX DELINQUENCY

The United States Forest Service made its first study of tax delinquency in northern Minnesota, Wisconsin, and Michigan in 1926–27.[6] In 1927, 4,127,831 acres were delinquent in northern Minnesota, but only 1,781,820 acres had been delinquent for more than three years and could thus be classified as "unredeemed."

By 1931 the total delinquency had grown to 6,830,840 acres, or

[6] H. H. Chapman and Daniel Pingree, "Tax Delinquency in the Forest Counties of the Lake States" (mimeographed Progress Report No. 10 of the Forest Taxation Inquiry, United States Forest Service, Washington, D. C.).

nearly three-quarters of a million acres a year, and the area that had been delinquent for more than three years amounted to 4,039,280 acres in January, 1931. On the basis of Table 2 on page 118 it is possible to forecast approximately, without allowing for some small redemption, the acreage that will become state property in the next four years.

The significance of this rapid accumulation of delinquencies can be appreciated only when considered in connection with the law of 1927,[7] which provides that land that is bid in for the state at sales of tax-delinquent property shall at the expiration of five years become the absolute property of the state.

Judging by the acreages that are now delinquent and for which there seems little prospect of redemption or sale, the state will come into possession of about 4,000,000 acres in 1933 and 1,000,000 acres more in each succeeding year. (See Figure 12, page 137.) By 1936 about 8,500,000 acres will be owned by the state. The public land will then total nearly 11,000,000 acres, or 55 per cent of the entire unplatted area of the region. What the trend will be after that will depend upon the amount of delinquency in 1932 and succeeding years. If the future trend should be the same as in the few years preceding 1933, the state may, in less than a decade, come into possession of a public domain of 12,000,000 acres in the sixteen northern counties. The economic and social significance of such a large public domain in the economic life of the state would be far-reaching.

Attempts to halt the abandonment of land.—Past efforts to arrest the reversion of tax-delinquent land to public ownership have taken the form of laws allowing redemption of the land under lenient terms or permitting sale of the forfeited lands for less than the amount of accrued taxes. Every possible effort has been made during the past decade to keep the lands on the tax rolls. As late as 1931 an act[8] was passed, to be effective for one year, providing

[7] Session Laws of Minnesota, 1927, Ch. 129, as amended by Session Laws, 1929, Ch. 415, provides in part that "parcels of land hereafter duly sold at the annual delinquent tax sale, whether so sold to an actual purchaser or bid in for the State as provided by law, shall, at the expiration of five years from the date of such sale, become and be the absolute property of the purchaser or of the State or of his or its assigns, without the doing of any act or thing whatsoever, without any right of redemption . . .

"The title to each and every parcel of land thereby acquired by the State shall be held by it in trust for each and all the taxing districts interested in the taxes and assessments, penalties, interest, and costs accrued therein at the time of such forfeiture in the proportion of their respective interests."

[8] Session Laws of Minnesota, 1931, Ch. 129.

that taxes delinquent for 1928 and 1929 might be paid without interest and penalty and that taxes delinquent for 1926 and 1927 might be cleared up by paying three-fifths of the original tax.

These laws were frequently abused. A man could deliberately let his taxes go for a number of years and then redeem the land by paying up a fraction of the accumulated taxes. Anyone might buy these bargain-counter lands on the installment plan, hold them only long enough to strip off the timber, and again let them become delinquent.

Altogether, legislation of this kind has done great harm by discriminating against taxpayers who pay promptly and by holding out as an inducement not to pay promptly the hope that existing penalties may be reduced or repealed by the legislature or simply not enforced by the administrative officers. This has been found to be a potent cause of delinquency all over the United States.

THE WAY OUT

There is no simple remedy in sight for the situation in northern Minnesota. The present difficulties have their roots in mistakes and wasteful exploitation extending back over forty or fifty years, and it is too much to expect that these conditions can be righted overnight. However, with the facts of the situation definitely known, there are steps that can be taken to reverse the undesirable tendencies and lay the basis for a more sustained though gradual development of the region.

Recent studies in the Lake States and elsewhere where the problem of tax delinquency is acute indicate the types of remedy that may be attempted. Some reorganization of local governments and many governmental economies are needed. Unquestionably state aid will be required to help some of the counties through this trying period. Better assessment methods will have to be worked out. Taxes in different parts of the region should be equalized. The burden of taxation on real property must be shifted to some extent by finding new sources of tax revenue. These are the kinds of reform that are being considered in almost every state in the Union. They are proposals that are likely to find favor in the northern communities where present taxes on real property are confiscatory. It is not within the field of this study to recommend definite changes but merely to point to the obvious fact that if private ownership of property is to be made possible in these cut-over regions, some radical adjustments must be made.

Economies in Government

The modernization of local government along the lines of greater simplicity and efficiency will doubtless effect economies in the local budgets and will be reflected in lower taxes. There is considerable logic in many of the plans put forward for county consolidation, curtailment of township activities, consolidation of school districts, and so on. But even these changes will not be sufficient to extricate some of the local districts from their present financial predicament. Many of the districts, especially in the swamp regions, have a heavy bonded indebtedness and have certain fixed charges that cannot be dodged by any reorganization of tax units. Modernization of local government is desirable, but it is not a cure-all.

The measures that may be taken to improve local government and reduce the cost thereof can only be mentioned in a general way. They include such possibilities as the following:

1. *Consolidation of school districts.*—Lake County has gone so far as to consolidate all districts into a county system, and it claims an improvement in standards as well as reduction in costs. Koochiching County likewise has effected large savings by closing some schools and transporting pupils. Consolidations on a smaller scale are being made throughout the state.[9]

2. *Reorganization of townships.*—There have been many proposals, ranging from complete abolition of townships to leaving them as they are. Even staunch friends of the township form of government recognize the desirability of certain changes—for example, altering the boundaries of townships to make them coincide better with natural trade areas, enlarging these units in sparsely settled regions, and possibly transferring certain of their functions to the counties.

3. *Consolidation of counties.*—This will be more difficult, even where the desirability is not open to argument. Although consolidations of counties have been under discussion for over a decade, only a few isolated consolidations have been put into effect anywhere in the United States. There are, however, many opportunities for adjoining counties to cooperate and consolidate some of their functions, and certain other functions might be absorbed by the state.

4. *Centralization of administrative responsibility.*—The city manager plan has been adopted by a number of Minnesota munici-

[9] See page 458.

palities, but it is new in county administration. Centralization of responsibility is possible under a commission form of government, but it will require legislation fixing such responsibility and making such positions as those of clerk, sheriff, and attorney appointive rather than elective.

5. *Change in methods of assessing and collecting taxes.*—Some municipalities are following with considerable success methods similar to the sales practice of manufacturers. Provision is made for monthly installments on taxes and a regular follow-up system of collection, including personal calls as necessary. The payment of taxes should be made as easy as possible.

6. *Zoning the state.*—The Institute of Public Administration of New York City has made the proposal that the state of New York be zoned into four classes of territory as follows: (a) unorganized territory, where governmental activities should be carried on directly by the state; (b) large cities, where county government should be abolished; (c) smaller cities, villages, and suburban territory, which require municipal government; and (d) sparsely settled rural territory, which does not warrant the maintenance of any local government except that of the county itself. Essentially the same types of area are to be found in Minnesota.

State Aid

State aid has already been extended to a few counties that have been unable to meet the principal and interest charges on drainage bonds. The Red Lake Game Preserve Act of 1929 provides that the state shall take over the delinquent land within certain drainage districts and assume the responsibility for the drainage charges against the lands. An area of 1,500,000 acres is involved. Similar aid was extended to other counties needing relief from ditch obligations by the act of April 25, 1931,[10] permitting the establishment of state reforestation or flood control projects. Six areas, aggregating 435,000 acres, have already been proposed in Aitkin County, and at least two other counties are expected to apply for aid under this act.

State aid to counties for this purpose is undoubtedly justifiable, both as a means of protecting the credit of the state and in recognition of the state's moral responsibility in helping out drainage projects developed as a part of a definite state policy. Such aid

[10] Session Laws of Minnesota, 1931, Ch. 407.

should be given frankly as a subsidy, however, and should not be disguised as a conservation measure. The danger is that the public approval that will be needed later to institute real forestry and conservation work for the rebuilding of the natural resources in the cut-over sections will have become weakened by the millions of dollars of so-called "conservation" appropriations poured into bankrupt drainage enterprises.

Equalization of Taxes

Property should pay taxes in proportion to its true worth. But it does not work out this way in northern Minnesota. Cut-over wild land fares particularly badly in this respect. At present cut-over land has little if any sales value, and yet its "full and true" assessment for taxation purposes is commonly from $3 to $10 an acre. In some townships wild land is taxed as much as developed farm land. Taxes on the same kind of land vary greatly in adjacent townships. These striking inequalities, which seem to be inherent in the present system of assessment, have led some to recommend the abolition of the township as a tax-levying unit. Some means of dividing the tax load more equitably would undoubtedly help to check tax delinquency.

New Tax Sources

Modernization of local government, better distribution of taxes, and state aid will help, but still the burden of taxes upon real property may be too great for property owners to bear. There is a growing belief that new sources of tax revenue, such as an income tax or sales taxes, must be found to ease the burden on real property. The taxes from these new sources could be used by the state to displace local taxes for state purposes such as highway construction, education, health protection, and so forth, and to facilitate state subsidies to counties if these be necessary.

Land Classification

The conditions offering the greatest opportunities for remedial treatment in the northern Lake States are those arising from the indiscriminate use of the land resources in the past. Today there are farms scattered widely over areas that under present economic conditions are unsuited to agricultural use. Miles of road have been built and maintained to serve only one or two settlers on remote stump ranches. Some rural schools serve only one or two families.

There are organized townships with only a dozen families or so. Of course these conditions cannot be overcome immediately, but some changes can be made and in the future a more planwise development can be substituted for the haphazard colonization of the past.

In Wisconsin rural planning has been authorized by law, and the local governments are beginning to exercise their power of segregating land suitable for agriculture from forest, recreational, and wild land. In Minnesota there is not as yet a law authorizing such planning, but the counties can accomplish much indirectly by discouraging settlement on wild, undeveloped land unsuited to agricultural use and by offering the advantages of better highways and better schools in other portions of the county. There is also the possibility of the voluntary relocation of settlers by using tax-forfeited land as a means of exchange.

If agricultural settlement can be concentrated on the areas of better soil and more favorable location with respect to roads and markets, many of the present difficulties will disappear. Not only will the farmers themselves be more prosperous but the large present expense for rural schools and roads will be materially reduced and taxes can be correspondingly cut. If, in addition, the remaining land not devoted to agriculture can be allotted to its most productive use and developed as forest, recreational area, game refuge, or whatever else is desirable, the ultimate prosperity of the region will be more assured.

What is needed as a first step in such planning is a classification of the land in the whole area in accordance with the purpose for which it is best suited. Such classification for preliminary planning need not be in extreme detail. It should include an inventory of the natural resources, a reconnaissance of soil conditions, an appraisal of the economic conditions bearing upon land use, and an analysis of local budgets. Such a survey, costing possibly a cent an acre, could doubtless be completed for all the counties in four or five years. It would lay the foundation for a systematic development of the county resources in the future.

Public Forests

The national and state governments must play an increasing part in rehabilitating the nonagricultural land in northern Minnesota. Figure 13 (page 144) shows the areas already designated as

FIGURE 13.—PUBLIC FORESTS IN MINNESOTA

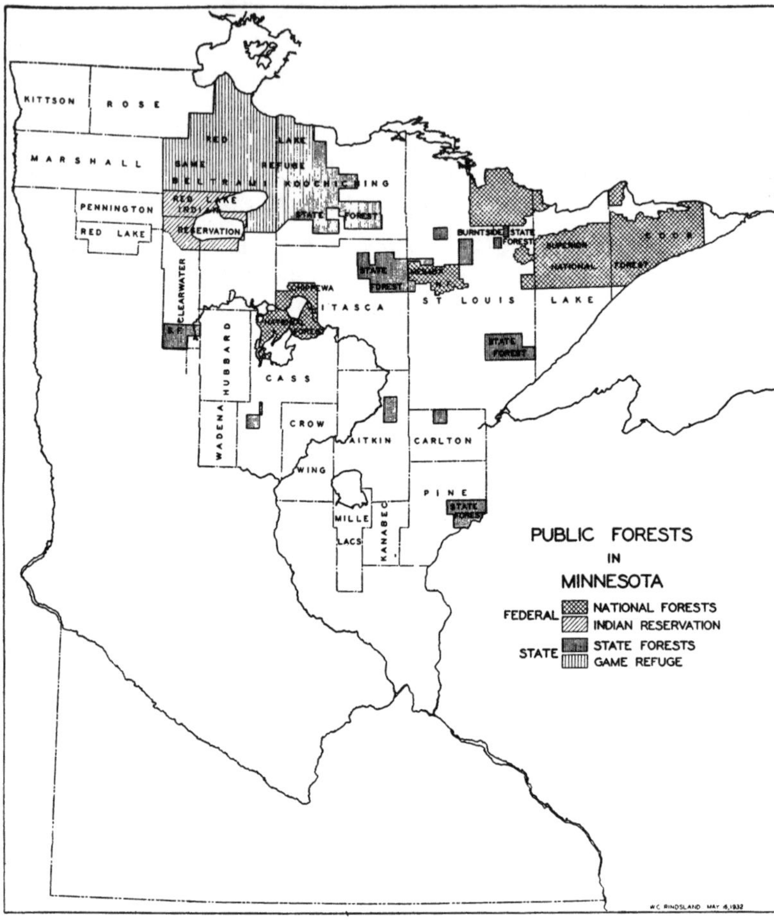

public forests. In 1933, when the new law regulating the transfer of title of tax-delinquent land to the state becomes operative, the state will come into the possession of some four million acres, largely swamp and cut-over forest land. In less than a decade, unless conditions change radically, it will have become the owner of twelve million acres, or well over half the entire area embraced within the northern sixteen counties. What to do with this land will become a pressing problem. The state itself will be the largest single landowner in Minnesota and will therefore be in a position to make or break any land policies that may be proposed.

There undoubtedly will be pressure brought by local authorities to return this land to private ownership and restore it to the tax rolls either by remitting earlier taxes or by other inducements. Should the present industrial depression continue for some time, there may be a concerted movement to place the unemployed on land. Such a movement, unless carefully planned and controlled, may lead again to unwise settlement with all its consequent hardship and misery. In short, from almost every standpoint, the indiscriminate return of this reverted land to private ownership would appear to be a mistaken public policy. All things considered, it would seem desirable that the lands reverting to the state for nonpayment of taxes should be held in public ownership until there is definite evidence of their need for private development.

One proposal frequently advanced is that the reverted lands should be designated as state forests and developed for timber growing. In this connection it must be remembered that, at least until recently, the state has lacked funds for the proper management of the few existing state forests, which were less than 10 per cent as extensive as the area now in process of reversion. The designation of large areas of cut-over land as state forests without provision for their rehabilitation and development will not change the areas into economically productive forest land. The Conservation Commission, therefore, will be limited in the creation of productive state forests by the funds available for their rehabilitation.

A logical public policy can be based only on a scientific classification of the land and a realistic appraisal of the public funds that can be used for their development. The possibilities of the entire area of nonagricultural land should be studied and the most promising use of each tract determined. Some areas will be of value for growing commercial forests, some for watershed protection, some for game propagation, and so on. With the desirable uses of the land determined, a decision can be reached as to what agency can best care for them and where public funds should be invested.

With such a vast acreage to choose from, it is natural that in creating new forest units the public agencies should concentrate their efforts first on land on which present management promises early benefits, that is, on land strategically located with reference to existing or prospective wood-using centers and on recreational areas accessible to the public.

There is much wild land in northern Minnesota, much swamp,

rock ledge, and barren plain for the immediate utilization of which there is no magic formula. Nothing is gained by ignoring the existence of such submarginal areas. These remaining lands should be retained in public ownership to prevent unwise speculative development and to conserve such values as they have. They should be handled at a minimum of public expense under a very extensive form of forest management so that the more promising areas can be more intensively developed. They should be protected from fire and trespass, but otherwise left to nature to heal the wounds as best she can. Gradually, as economic conditions change, other lands now submarginal may be brought under more intensive management.

If the state had ample funds for the rehabilitation of all the lands in the near future, it would be a short-sighted policy to allow any land to remain only partially productive when it could be made fully productive. With only limited funds available for the development of these lands, however, it is simply a matter of necessity and common sense to concentrate development first on the most promising land and to extend more intensive management to other lands as funds become available and economic conditions justify it.

Situation Not Hopeless

It would be erroneous to conclude from the large acreage of tax-delinquent land in northern Minnesota that the region is poor. Northern Minnesota still has enormous natural wealth. It has the richest iron mines on the American continent. It has sixteen million acres of naturally productive forest land. With its "ten thousand lakes" it has almost unlimited recreational possibilities. Agriculture, properly correlated with other uses of land, has a very promising future. The problem at the present time is to utilize fully the potential natural wealth of the region. The remaining natural resources must be conservatively used, those replaceable resources that have been run down must be rebuilt, and the lands of the region must be put to their best possible use. If met with courage and foresight, the great tide of land reversion may prove a blessing in disguise.

CHAPTER 6

TAXATION OF FOREST PROPERTY[1]

FUNDAMENTAL CHARACTERISTICS OF LUMBER PRODUCTION

One of the fundamental characteristics of lumber production is the long period of time required for the production of the forest crop, a period varying in Minnesota from a minimum of fifty years for jack pine or white spruce pulpwood to a maximum of perhaps a hundred years or more for good quality Norway pine saw logs. Another characteristic is that timber is a replaceable natural resource. In the past we in the United States have depended for the satisfaction of our needs upon the supply of timber stored up for us by nature before our arrival. In the comparatively near future we must depend upon a timber supply grown under more or less intensive human control.

After the merchantable timber is cut, a long period of time usually must elapse before the next succeeding stand becomes merchantable and can be converted into cash. During this period the direct costs of the enterprise, namely, the cost of establishing the crop, taxes, protection, and so forth, continue to accumulate until the time when the mature crop is converted into cash income. If there is to be any profit to the owner, this cash income must exceed the sum of the costs. Furthermore, forestry is not advantageous to the owner if it will not yield interest on expenses invested during the many years prior to the harvest of the crop. This interest factor is particularly important but usually underestimated.[2]

THE FOREST TAXATION PROBLEM IN MINNESOTA

The forest and unimproved cut-over lands of Minnesota cover an area of approximately 21,900,000 acres,[3] or 42.3 per cent of the total land area of the state. By far the greater part of this area is cut-over forest land and is now covered with brush or young

[1] This chapter was prepared by Professor John H. Allison of the Division of Forestry, University of Minnesota.

[2] R. C. Staebner, "The Problem of Interest in Forestry," *Journal of Forestry*, 29: 763–767 (1931).

[3] United States Forest Service, Lake States Forest Experiment Station, "Forest Statistics for the Lake States," p. 9. This is a mimeograph issued in 1931.

timber of inferior quality. Approximately four-fifths of the area is concentrated in the northeastern two-fifths of the state, within the boundaries of the sixteen cut-over counties.[4]

Outside the boundaries of the sixteen cut-over counties the forested area of the seventy-one counties comprising the rest of the state totals approximately 4,630,000 acres, or only about 15 per cent of the land area of these seventy-one counties. Most of it is owned in connection with operated farms; over half, 2,488,000 acres, is pastured, and ultimately much of it will be converted into improved land. The taxation of this forest land is a minor part of the general problem of rural taxation and can be solved by better assessment, that is, by a more careful determination of the real capital value of such land.

Within the boundaries of the sixteen cut-over counties, forest lands cover an area of approximately 17,270,000 acres, or 90.8 per cent, of the total unplatted (rural) land area. Approximately 13,455,000 acres[5] is privately owned, most of it in units of less than 400 acres.[6]

These forest lands have always been subject to the ad valorem property tax, which must be paid semi-annually. Insufficient consideration is given to the fact that the forest owner must pay the taxes accruing against his forest land long before the timber can be cut and converted into cash. Land used for agriculture generally produces an annual income out of which taxes may be paid. This difference between forest and agricultural land makes the taxation of forest land a different problem from that involved in the taxation of agricultural land.

Forest lands located within the cut-over counties are assessed very generally at acre valuations nearly equal to the acre valuations placed upon the intermixed agricultural lands.[7] The tax rates applying to these valuations are also very high. In 1926 they

[4] Aitkin, Beltrami, Carlton, Cass, Clearwater, Cook, Crow Wing, Hubbard, Itasca, Kanabec, Koochiching, Lake, Lake of the Woods, Mille Lacs, Pine, and St. Louis counties. See Figures 1 and 13, pages 114 and 144.

[5] Computed from the figures given in "County Table I," *Fifteenth Census of the United States,* 1930: *Agriculture,* 1: 810, and in Table 1 on page 115 above.

[6] Fred R. Fairchild, "Forest Taxation in a Cut-Over Region," Proceedings of the National Tax Association, 1927, pp. 367–394.

[7] R. C. Hall and P. A. Herbert, "Property Taxation in Selected Towns in the Forest Lands Regions of Minnesota" (Forest Taxation Inquiry, United States Department of Agriculture, Forest Service, mimeographed Progress Report No. 9, July 1, 1930). This statement is also verified with reference to portions of Hubbard County by D. C. Dvoracek in his preliminary (1931) report on "The Economic Survey of Hubbard County" (MS), pp. 70–109.

varied from a minimum of 58.33 mills in Hubbard County to a maximum of 157.31 mills in Koochiching County.[8] That this combination of high assessments and high tax rates is placing an unbearably heavy tax burden upon the privately owned forest lands of this section of the state is clearly indicated by the large amount of tax delinquency in this class of ownership. On January 1, 1931, approximately 6,830,000 acres had been tax delinquent for a year or more, and by January, 1932, accumulated unpaid taxes amounted to nearly $22,000,000.[9] Privately owned forest lands are an important source of public revenue in each of the cut-over counties except St. Louis and Itasca. In twelve[10] counties rural land, which is approximately 90 per cent forest land, made up over 50 per cent of the total assessed value of each county in 1926.

The very large area still remaining in forest land, the important position that these lands hold in the total taxable valuation of twelve of the sixteen cut-over counties, the large area of forest land that on January 1, 1931, had been tax delinquent for a period of a year or more, and the very considerable sum to which the delinquent taxes on these lands then totaled, indicate clearly that the taxation of forest property in the cut-over counties has become a problem of major importance not only to these counties themselves but also to the whole state.

Objectives in Taxation of Forest Property

Northeastern Minnesota was formerly covered with a magnificent forest, the greater part of which was transferred from public to private ownership between 1840 and 1900. Following this transfer in ownership, the commercial timber was rapidly cut to supply both the local and the general market. Both the cut-over lands and the uncut forest were subjected to repeated fires, which effectively prevented nature from replacing the former forest with a new one. Until about 1920 comparatively few people cared whether or not the forest replaced itself, because it was generally believed that most of the cut-over or burned forest land would soon be cleared for agriculture. This belief has not proved to be well

[8] Fred R. Fairchild, director of the Forest Taxation Inquiry, United States Department of Agriculture, Forest Service, mimeographed Progress Report of September 5, 1928, Tables 3 and 22.

[9] See Tables 2 and 3, pages 118 and 120 above.

[10] Aitkin, Beltrami, Cass, Clearwater, Cook, Hubbard, Kanabec, Koochiching, Lake, Lake of the Woods, Mille Lacs, and Pine counties.

founded. Only a small portion of this area has as yet been cleared and put into crops. As will be shown below (pages 154–158), much of it will not be used for farming for a long time to come, if ever.

But another use of this section of the state is developing. In fact, it is now being used extensively for recreational purposes. The forest is important as a cover for game and fish. Hence the renewal of the forest will be a real aid in perpetuating and increasing the recreational value of this section.

Minnesota consumes large quantities of wood in various commercial uses. For eighty years (1838–1917) the cut-over counties produced as much lumber as was consumed within the state, and for a long period (1870–1914) much more than that. Now these counties are producing only about 40 per cent of the lumber requirements of the state, and the percentage is falling from year to year. With protection from fire, which is now being given fairly well by the Conservation Department, and with efficient management, the forest lands within the cut-over counties could again be made to produce a volume of timber products sufficient to supply the needs of the state. Freight charges are high enough to afford considerable protection to producers and still permit the lower prices to consumers that would follow the increased supply. For example, upon the lumber consumed within the state in 1924 the freight charge averaged $4.91 per thousand feet board measure on that part originating within the state as against $14.05 per thousand feet on that part originating outside the state.[11] Substantially this spread in rates is still in effect.

Because of the importance of the forest cover in attracting the tourist and because of the possibility of supplying the greater part of the timber requirements of the state from this section, it is assumed that the re-establishment of the forest cover upon much of the area within the sixteen cut-over counties will ultimately become the most important objective of the state's forest policy. The achievement of this objective, and its cost to the public, may be markedly affected by the methods followed in the taxation of forest property.

If it is to be accomplished under public control, the aim should be to transfer the forest lands to public ownership as effectively, as quickly, and as cheaply as possible. This can be accomplished

[11] United States Forest Service, *American Forest and Forest Products* (United States Department of Agriculture Statistical Bulletin No. 21, Washington, D. C., 1927), Table 63.

to a considerable extent by simply doing nothing to relieve the forest owner from his present tax burden, which seems to him so confiscatory that he is letting his forest property become tax delinquent. This of course means bringing about public ownership of this class of property through the extinguishment of private property rights by the imposition of unbearable taxes. One must not forget that this course of procedure will, in the comparatively near future, very greatly reduce both local and county public revenues within most of the cut-over counties and will probably make it necessary for the people in other parts of the state not only to pay directly the entire cost of re-establishing the forest upon the reverted forest lands, but also to assume a very considerable portion of the expense of maintaining local government and education.

If, on the other hand, the state wishes the private owner to share the cost of re-establishing the forest cover and to contribute to the maintenance of local government in this region, the tax burden placed upon forest property should be so limited as to enable a considerable number of owners to retain their ownership of such lands. This would not relieve the state from the probable necessity of helping several of the forest counties and many of the local communities to meet the cost of local government for many years to come, but it should enable the state to get the private owner of forest land to share in both the cost of local government and the cost of re-establishing a satisfactory forest cover. Both these costs will be large and may assume such proportions that even the state will find them burdensome.

Furthermore, it would seem advantageous to the state to have a considerable area of forest land in private ownership in order to measure the efficiency of the public management of forest property. This is the policy followed in those countries of Europe where forestry is most intensively and successfully practiced. (See Table 1.) In this discussion it will be assumed that the public desires to have a considerable portion of the forest lands retained in private ownership and that this desire will determine the tax policy followed with respect to this class of property.

In order to see the problem in its proper perspective it is necessary to consider briefly the forest products industries of Minnesota, the utilization of land in the cut-over counties, the tax burden now resting on forest lands in these counties, the tax burden resting on forest property in places where forestry is being practiced, and the attempts made there to adjust the tax burden carried by

TABLE 1.—PUBLIC AND PRIVATE OWNERSHIP OF FOREST LAND IN REPRESENTATIVE COUNTRIES OF EUROPE[a]

Country	Total Acreage of Forest Area	Percentage in Private Ownership	Percentage in Public Ownership
Hungary	3,148,000	88.0	12.0
Norway	14,059,734[b]	78.0	22.0
Sweden	55,550,000[b]	76.4	23.6
Poland	24,131,900	69.6	30.4
Holland	622,235	69.4	30.6
Finland	37,523,098[b]	64.9	35.1
Austria	7,599,449	64.4	35.6
Czechoslovakia	12,354,000	63.9	36.1
France	25,508,420	63.5	36.5
Belgium	1,321,243	61.9	38.1
Italy	14,249,000	50.3	49.7
Germany	30,905,839	47.3	52.7
Denmark	872,000	47.0	53.0
Switzerland	2,342,239	27.5	72.5

[a] W. N. Sparhawk and R. Zon, *Forest Resources of the World* (New York, 1923), 1: 72–349.
[b] These figures apply only to what is classed as "productive forest."

TABLE 2.—THE DEVELOPMENT OF THE LUMBER INDUSTRY IN MINNESOTA, 1849–1929[a]

Year	Lumber Cut M Ft. B.M.	Value of Products	No. of Persons Engaged	Salaries and Wages Paid	Capital Invested
1849	....	$57,800	.....	....	....
1859	....	1,245,303	1,155[b]	$365,712[b]	$1,342,620
1869	242,390	4,538,804	3,010[b]	905,550[b]	3,454,540
1879	563,974	7,366,038	2,854[b]	924,473[b]	6,771,145
1889[d]	1,084,377	25,075,132	**25,715**	6,166,266	28,321,062
1899[d]	**2,342,338**	47,080,000	23,241	11,182,000	35,662,000
1904	1,942,248	42,033,000	21,878	11,558,000	34,884,000
1909	1,561,508	42,353,000	22,304	12,378,000	**49,128,000**
1914[d]	1,312,230	44,674,948	22,316	13,696,451	38,587,782
1919[d]	699,639[c]	**52,579,620**	16,860		38,601,513
1925	578,703	26,132,487	9,168	8,622,388	....
1929	357,180	14,744,351	4,589	5,191,901	....

[a] From federal census reports. Peaks are indicated by figures in boldface.
[b] Including wage earners and wages paid at mills only.
[c] Of this amount 540,146 thousand feet were cut by the seventeen mills that cut over 10,000 thousand feet a year.
[d] Taxes paid, state and federal: $165,098 (1889); $339,448 (1899); $624,098 (1914); $2,164,442 (1919). See Table 3.

forest property to the owners' conception of its ability to pay. Then, on the basis of this analysis, an attempt will be made to develop the points that should be included in a remedial forest tax measure.

The Forest Products Industries of Minnesota

Commercial lumbering in Minnesota began in the St. Croix Valley during the winter of 1837–38. The settlement and development of the central Mississippi and lower Missouri valleys provided a large and accessible market for the lumber cut from the Minnesota forests. A great volume of high-grade commercial pine timber was available, and the lumber industry grew rapidly. Table 2 shows that the peak of production occurred in 1899, and that the cut in 1929 was only about 15 per cent as large as in 1899.

The forest products industries represent more accurately the industrial value to the state of the forest as a source of raw material than does the lumber industry alone. These industries are summarized statistically in Table 3.

Table 3.— Development of the Forest Products Industries in Minnesota, 1859–1929[a]

Year	Value of Products	No. of Persons Engaged	Salaries and Wages Paid	Capital Invested	Federal, State, and Local Taxes Paid
1859	$1,458,879	1,393[b]	$456,156	$1,480,370	....
1869	5,776,786	3,910[b]	1,257,057	4,258,658	....
1879	10,360,375	4,794[b]	1,792,198	8,209,075	....
1889	26,975,947	26,845	6,854,472	42,498,106	....
1899[c]	67,755,305	30,079	14,311,964	64,418,220	$399,325
1904[c]	53,610,000	29,340	15,726,000	45,588,000	....
1909[c]	59,846,000	31,688	18,397,500	67,725,000	....
1914[c]	66,504,776	**34,135**	20,881,497	84,351,475	896,556
1919[d]	**89,650,615**	24,022	**25,187,575**	**87,992,401**	**3,451,839**
1925[d]	78,508,194	17,930[b]	18,877,868	....	....
1929[d]	79,044,626	15,334	20,826,842	....	....

[a] Compiled from the federal census reports. Industries and products included are lumber and timber products, planing mill products, cooperage, furniture, railroad car construction and repair, boat and shipbuilding, wood boxes, wood pulp and paper, wagons, and wood goods not included elsewhere in this list. ("Wood goods" does not appear in the 1919 and later census reports.) Peaks are indicated by figures in boldface.

[b] Figures for wage earners and wages are exclusive of those for men working in the woods.

[c] Including one-half of the railroad car construction and repair industry.

[d] Not including the railroad car construction and repair industry because of the extensive substitution of steel, the very high wages and salaries paid, and the high value assigned to the products produced.

Among these industries the wood pulp and paper industry should be given special consideration. Its development is shown in Table 4. This industry is particularly important to the forest owner because it may utilize small trees, either those removed as thinnings to enable the remaining trees to reach a larger size in a shorter period or those produced in short rotations. Perhaps other cellulose-using industries will be developed later, thus increasing the market for small material and thereby making forestry more attractive to the private owner of forest land.

TABLE 4.—DEVELOPMENT OF THE WOOD PULP AND PAPER INDUSTRIES IN MINNESOTA, 1904–1929[a]

YEAR	VALUE OF PRODUCTS	NO. OF PERSONS ENGAGED	SALARIES AND WAGES PAID	CAPITAL INVESTED	AMOUNT OF TAXES PAID (STATE AND FEDERAL)
1904	$1,146,000	418	$265,000	$1,491,000	....
1909	2,385,000	640	425,000	3,235,000	....
1914	5,572,537	1,417	1,161,666	16,540,268	**$86,260**
1919	20,138,482	2,771	3,618,666	**24,634,705**	748,238
1925	20,320,392	2.767	4,126,535	....	....
1929	**28,316,883**	**2,811**	**4,145,738**	....	....

[a] Compiled from the United States census reports. Peaks are indicated by figures in boldface.

UTILIZATION OF LAND IN THE SIXTEEN CUT-OVER COUNTIES

The data presented in the preceding pages indicate that it would be of great advantage to the state to have forest on most of the cut-over area in the northeastern counties unless the land is needed for agriculture. We must now determine to what extent these lands will be so needed.

A summary of the ownership and utilization of the unplatted lands in the cut-over counties is given in Table 5. If we convert certain of these figures into acreages we find that, of the 15,206,000 acres of unplatted lands in private ownership in this section, 14,030,000 acres (including approximately 1,700,000 acres of forest land in farms) are wild. These lands have been converted into improved farm lands at the rather slow average net rate of 26,254 acres a year during the decade from 1900 to 1910; 42,171 acres a year from 1910 to 1920; and 25,548 acres a year from 1920 to 1930. The annual net increase in the area added to the improved farm lands of this section reached its peak in the agriculturally prosperous decade from 1910 to 1920; since then it has fallen off markedly. The total area in farms increased rapidly from 1900 to 1920, slowly from 1920 to 1925, and has since fallen off slightly. The total number of farms increased from 9,321 in 1900 to 16,573 in 1910, to 25,846 in 1920, and to 32,785 in 1925, then decreased to 29,554 in 1930. These figures show a marked slackening in the rate of agricultural expansion in this section during the last ten years as compared with the period from 1900 to 1920.

How much of the 14,030,000 acres of the privately owned forest land still available in these counties will agriculture need in the next fifty years? It is impossible to answer this question with certainty. But certain physical characteristics of the land within these counties, combined with certain general trends in land utilization, should enable us to guess at the answer with sufficient accuracy to decide whether or not the agricultural need for these lands will be great enough to shelve the need for reform in the taxation of forest lands if any considerable portion of them are to be kept in private ownership.

Let us consider the physical situation first. The Bureau of Agricultural Economics of the United States Department of Agriculture

TABLE 5. — OWNERSHIP AND UTILIZATION OF UNPLATTED LANDS IN THE SIXTEEN FOREST COUNTIES [a]

CLASS OF UNPLATTED LANDS	PERCENTAGE OF TOTAL UNPLATTED LAND IN 1900	1910	1920	1925	1930
As to ownership					
In farms	6.3	11.2	16.6	18.6	18.0
Non-farm privately owned	34.1 [b]	49.5 [b]	59.2 [b]	59.9	61.9
Publicly owned	59.6 [c]	39.3 [c]	24.2 [c]	21.5	20.1 [d]
Total	100.0	100.0	100.0	100.0	100.0
As to utilization					
Improved land	1.2	2.6	4.8	5.5	6.2
Unimproved land	98.8	97.4	95.2	94.5	93.8
Total	100.0	100.0	100.0	100.0	100.0

[a] From the federal census. The land area of these counties totals 19,301,120 acres. Platted land and highway and railroad rights of way account for about 280,000 acres; thus the total unplatted area covers approximately 19,021,000 acres.

[b] Based upon the figures for the unplatted taxable area within the sixteen counties here under consideration as given under "Assessment and Taxation" in the biennial reports of the state auditor covering the years 1899, 1910, and 1919. The areas given in this table are arrived at by subtracting from the "number of acres of land exclusive of town lots," given by the auditor, the number of acres in farm ownership given in the United States census report for the nearest census year. The areas thus determined are probably somewhat smaller than the actual nonfarm acreage in private ownership.

[c] Approximations only. Based upon the state auditor's figures.

[d] Based on Table 1, page 115.

estimated about 1923 that there were in these counties 4,153,000 acres of land that were too rough and too poor ever to be used by agriculture under conditions at present conceivable; that 4,398,000 acres of land were in need of drainage before they could be used by agriculture; and that there were 9,018,000 acres that could be used without drainage.[12] At that time it was estimated that there were 3,098,000 acres of unimproved lands in other parts of the state that could be used by agriculture without drainage. It was also estimated that by 1950 the state would require for agriculture only about 2,200,000 additional acres of land over that in use in 1920.[13]

But during the last ten years great changes have occurred in the United States both in the trend of population and in the demand for agricultural products. Apparently our population is not going to increase to the numbers anticipated, and other parts of the world will not take our agricultural products as freely as they did before 1920.[14] These changes are now being reflected in the cut-over counties. The total population of these counties has remained almost stationary during the last ten years.[15] As a result it now appears probable that only a relatively small number of new farms will be carved out of the wild lands of the cut-over counties during the next two decades. Possibly this condition will hold true for a much longer period of time.

The area in improved land in these counties may, however, increase appreciably even without an increase in the number of farms, because the average area per farm now in improved land is less than is needed to carry on farming to the best advantage. This is indicated by the fact that there is an average of only 39.8 acres of improved land out of a total of 116.1 acres per farm in the cut-over counties as compared with an average of approximately 65.0

[12] Fred R. Fairchild, director of the Forest Taxation Inquiry, United States Department of Agriculture, Forest Service, mimeographed Progress Report of September 5, 1928, Table 10.

[13] *Ibid.*, pp. 5–7. See also L. C. Gray and others, "The Utilization of Our Lands for Crops, Pasture, and Forests," Yearbook of the Department of Agriculture, 1923, pp. 415–506.

[14] O. E. Baker, "The Trend of Land Utilization in the United States and the Present Situation," Proceedings and Papers of the First Congress of Soil Science, 1927 (Washington, D. C.), 1: 90–98, and O. E. Baker, "Changes in Production and Consumption of Our Farm Products and the Trend in Population. Do We Need More Land?" Annals of the American Academy of Political and Social Science, 152: 97–146 (1929).

[15] Based upon results obtained in the study of population trends made in 1932 by Richard E. Scammon and Marie Ness of the Medical School of the University of Minnesota.

acres of improved land out of a total of 123 acres per farm in the region of relatively well-developed farms in the formerly wooded country directly to the southwest of the cut-over counties. For some years to come most of the improved land to be added to that already in existence in the cut-over counties will come from the wild land area already in farm ownership. Hence we may assume that the privately owned non-farm lands, totaling approximately 11,775,000 acres, will remain in forest or brush indefinitely.

How much of this land will remain in private, taxpaying ownership depends very largely upon the tax burden placed upon it. Does the present tax burden leave for the owner any part of the prospective future income? To answer this question we must consider the tax burden currently placed upon these lands and the

TABLE 6.—COMPARISON OF ASSESSOR'S "FULL AND TRUE" VALUES WITH APPRAISED VALUES OF SPECIFIED CLASSES OF PROPERTY IN THIRTEEN TOWNSHIPS IN MINNESOTA, 1926[a]

Township	Assessor's "Full and True" Value in Percentage of Appraised Value					
	Farms		Cut-over Holdings		Resort Property	Total
	Operated	Abandoned	Small	Large		
Beltrami County						
Eckles	64	111	140	...[b]	...[b]	92
Frohn	60	...[b]	175	215	72	86
Hagali	72	...[b]	278	...[b]	106	116
Hubbard County						
Clay	158	...	292	301	147	247
Crow Wing Lake	90	181	294	...[b]	106	131
Lake Emma	92	...[b]	187	206	84	116
Schoolcraft	107	...[b]	300	336	360	272
Lake County						
T. 59 N., R. 8 W.	34	...[b]	90	95	...[b]	92
T. 58 N., R. 6 W.	...[b]	...[b]	250	272	...[b]	236
T. 54 N., R. 10 W.	51	...[b]	127	133	...[b]	100
St. Louis County						
Embarrass	26	...[b]	60	75	...[b]	36
Toivola	46	...[b]	106	180	...[b]	100
Unorganized T. 54 and 55 N., R. 14 W.	...[b]	...[b]	215	216	...[b]	197

[a] Jens P. Jensen, *Property Taxation in the United States* (University of Chicago Press, 1931), Table 54, p. 230, quoted by special permission of the publisher. The data upon which this table is based was obtained from several tables in R. C. Hall and P. A. Herbert, "Property Taxation in Selected Towns in the Forest Lands Regions of Minnesota" (Forest Taxation Inquiry, United States Department of Agriculture, Forest Service, mimeographed Progress Report No. 9, July 1, 1930). See also Chapter 3 above, especially page 43.

[b] Data not available.

TABLE 7.—COMPARISON OF ANNUAL TAX BURDEN PER ACRE OF SPECIFIED CLASSES OF PROPERTY IN THIRTEEN TOWNSHIPS IN MINNESOTA, 1926[a]

Township	Farms		Cut-over Holdings		Resort Property	Weighted Average
	Operated	Abandoned	Small	Large		
Beltrami County						
Eckles	$ .36	$ .35	$ .35	....[b]	$ .47	$ .36
Frohn	.56	.49	.52	$ .47	.48	.54
Hagali	.62	.54	.57	.68	.66	.61
Hubbard County						
Clay	.28	.29	.26	.26	.28	.26
Crow Wing Lake	.46	.22	.23	.20	.29	.32
Lake Emma	.36	.26	.26	.25	.41	.31
Schoolcraft	.33	.26	.31	.30	.37	.31
Lake County						
T. 59 N., R. 8 W.	.22	....[b]	.19	.22	.18	.20
T. 58 N., R. 6 W.	.25	....[b]	.30	.30	....[b]	.30
T. 54 N., R. 10 W.	.44	....[b]	.31	.32	....[b]	.33
St. Louis County						
Embarrass	.27	....[b]	.19	.17	....[b]	.22
Toivola	.46	....[b]	.35	.33	....[b]	.36
Unorganized						
T. 54 and 55 N., R. 14 W.	.22	....[b]	.17	.17	.30	.17

[a] Adapted from the report of R. C. Hall and P. A. Herbert cited in connection with the preceding table.
[b] Data not available.

prospective income the owner may hope to get out of them if they are devoted to the production of timber.

TAX BURDEN CARRIED BY FOREST LANDS IN MINNESOTA

Most of the 11,775,000 acres of non-farm privately owned forest land is cut-over land devoid of merchantable or near merchantable timber. The burden of taxation now resting upon these lands, relative to that resting upon farm and resort lands, is indicated by a comparison of the assessed "full and true" value of these different classes of property with their appraised value in the thirteen selected townships covered in Table 6. These townships were selected at random but are believed to be representative of conditions throughout the cut-over counties. Within this group of townships the actual tax burden per acre on the cut-over land varied from a minimum of 17 cents for cut-over holdings in St. Louis County[16] to a maximum of 68 cents for large cut-over holdings in Hagali, Beltrami County. Taxes of from 20 to 40 cents an acre

[16] Townships 54 and 55 North, Range 14 West, St. Louis County (unorganized).

predominated. The burden per acre in the thirteen townships examined by the Forest Taxation Inquiry is shown in Table 7. The large area (6,830,000 acres) already tax delinquent in the sixteen forest counties indicates clearly that the tax burden resting upon these lands is confiscatory.

According to the Forest Taxation Inquiry the tax burden resting upon the "wild lands" of the sixteen cut-over counties amounted on the average to 28 cents an acre in 1926.[17] This tax burden has not changed greatly since. Let us assume that fifty years is the minimum period within which merchantable pulpwood or box bolts can be grown, that the timber grower is entitled to interest upon the taxes that he must advance from year to year during this period, and that 6 per cent is a reasonable rate upon such payments. Let us assume also that the assessor does not increase the assessment, so that the tax does not increase as the timber approaches fifty years of age. Then, with interest compounded at 6 per cent, the cost of taxes, at 28 cents an acre annually, at the end of fifty years equals $\frac{\$0.28\ (1.06^{50}-1)}{.06}$ or \$81.29.[18] Similarly:

With interest at 5 per cent the cost of taxes at the end of 50 years = \$58.63.
With interest at 4 per cent the cost of taxes at the end of 50 years = \$42.75.
With interest at 3 per cent the cost of taxes at the end of 50 years = \$31.58.

Let us assume also that a reasonably full stand of white spruce, on land suitable to white spruce, or jack pine on land suitable to jack pine, is immediately established, and that, at the end of the fifty-year period, the white spruce produces twenty-five cords and the jack pine thirty cords of pulpwood per acre.[19] Then the cost of taxes to the forest owner on the pulpwood produced would be:

With interest at 6 per cent: spruce, \$3.25, jack pine, \$2.71 per cord
With interest at 5 per cent: spruce, \$2.35, jack pine, \$1.95 per cord
With interest at 4 per cent: spruce, \$1.71, jack pine, \$1.42 per cord
With interest at 3 per cent: spruce, \$1.26, jack pine, \$1.05 per cord

But there are many townships in the cut-over counties where the taxes amount to 60 cents or more per acre annually and where the cost of taxes is correspondingly larger.

[17] Herman H. Chapman, "Tax Base Continued, Tax Rates, and Tax Burden on Wild Lands" (Forest Taxation Inquiry, United States Department of Agriculture, Forest Service, Progress Report No. 5, November 1, 1929), Table 9.

[18] In fifty years the total cash tax payments made by the landowner at \$0.28 an acre annually amount to \$14.00; in eighty years to \$22.40. Similarly at \$0.60 an acre, the cash cost of taxes will total \$30.00 in fifty years and \$48.00 in eighty years.

[19] Joseph Kittredge, Jr., *Forest Planting in the Lake States* (United States Department of Agriculture Bulletin No. 1497, 1929), Tables 15, 16, and 17

In order to produce saw timber of satisfactory size a cropping period of not less than eighty years is probably necessary. For medium white pine and Norway pine soils, assumed to produce a yield of 25,000 feet board measure per acre at eighty years of age,[20] the cost to the forest owner of taxes at 28 cents per acre at 6 per cent, as calculated above, would amount to $19.56 per thousand feet board measure. Reducing the interest rate to 4 per cent would reduce this cost to $4.12 per thousand feet board measure. Increasing the tax burden to 60 cents per acre would increase the cost per thousand feet board measure to $41.92 with interest at 6 per cent, and to $13.23 with interest at 4 per cent. It should be noted that none of these figures includes any of the expenses of production other than taxes and interest on taxes. For the period from 1925 to 1930 inclusive the weighted average stumpage prices received by the state of Minnesota were $7.72 per thousand feet, board measure, for white pine and $2.12 per cord for spruce pulpwood.[21] Judged on the basis of the probable income to be derived from the use of these lands for the production of timber, the tax burden now resting upon most of these "wild lands" is unquestionably excessive.

The average tax in 1926 of 28 cents per acre upon the "wild lands" located in this section was assessed upon a land valuation based upon a combination of prospective agricultural, recreational, and other than forest values, and upon public expenditures, which were relatively large in relation to the population and the total sum of taxable values. The greater part of these public expenditures were for schools, roads, and the drainage of wet lands. Quite possibly the tax burden that would rest upon these "wild lands," if they were assessed at their true timber-producing value alone, would not seem excessive to their owners. But how convince the local assessor that, for the greater part of the "wild land" area, there is little or no agricultural, recreational, or other value than that based upon the ability of the land to produce timber? How determine the true value of these lands for timber production? And how convince the assessor that the latter values, even if they could be calculated with a reasonable degree of certainty, are reasonable?

Furthermore, no matter what the tax burden per acre may be when the forest is established, there is a strong probability, under

[20] *Ibid.*

[21] Data furnished by the Timber Department, Office of the State Auditor.

the normal operation of the ad valorem tax, that the tax will be increased from time to time by the addition of the anticipated stumpage value of the growing timber to the value of the land itself. Since the growing of a stand of merchantable timber requires from fifty to one hundred years, there is no possibility that the private owner can estimate accurately the total tax burden that will rest upon his forest property, nor is there much possibility of his being able to convert his growing timber advantageously into cash and quit production during this long period, no matter how confiscatory the forest tax burden may become.

Examples of Tax Burdens Being Successfully Carried by Forest Property

In Maine there is a total area of about six million acres of privately owned forest land upon which more or less intensive forestry is now being practiced.[22] These lands are covered with a second growth that has been selectively logged for a hundred years or more. Although this forest has been cut again and again, it continues to provide raw material for a permanent wood pulp and paper industry. Most of this area is located within the boundaries of the unorganized townships, where it is subject only to state, county, and forestry district taxes. The average assessed value per acre and the state, county, and forestry district taxes within the unorganized townships are shown by counties in Table 8. There are no other taxes applying to these lands except local road taxes, which apply to 46 of the 366 unorganized townships. Under

Table 8.—Average Annual Tax Burden per Acre on Lands, Mostly Forest Bearing, in Five Counties in Maine, 1931[a]

County	Assessed Value per Acre	Tax Burden per Acre for Indicated Purposes			
		State	County	Forestry District	Total[b]
Aroostook	$8.08	$.05656	$.017776	$.0181800	$.0925160
Franklin	8.95	.06265	.031325	.0201375	.1141125
Penobscot	6.35	.04445	.011303	.0142875	.0700405
Piscataquis	8.00	.05600	.012600	.0180000	.0866000
Somerset	9.37	.06559	.018740	.0210825	.1054125

[a] Data obtained from the Bureau of Taxation, Maine.
[b] Exclusive of local road taxes, which apply to 46 of a total of 366 unorganized townships.

[22] From an unpublished report upon industrial forestry prepared by Shirley W. Allen, chairman of the Industrial Forestry Committee, Society of American Foresters, in 1930.

conditions as they exist in Maine, forest property is carrying successfully a total tax burden the county average of which, exclusive of local road taxes, varies from a minimum of 7 to a maximum of 11.5 cents per acre annually.

Sweden is one of the most important competitors of the United States in the lumber-importing markets of the world. Several hundred thousand tons of Swedish wood pulp are usually marketed in the United States itself every year. Over four-fifths of the total Swedish timber cut comes from privately owned, second-growth forests upon which fairly intensive forestry is practiced. The area of these privately owned forest lands totals 42,450,000 acres.[23]

In Sweden agricultural and forest real estate is now assessed under the law of 1921. Forest property is assessed at its ordinary local sales value when such a value is clearly established by sales. But for most forest property there is no clear sales value. In such cases the theoretical value of the property for assessment purposes is determined by capitalizing at 6 per cent the annual net income which it is estimated the property can produce if properly managed. Eighteen per cent of the value thus determined is then assigned to the land as its taxable value. The estimated annual net income to be thus capitalized is determined by multiplying the merchantable annual growth by its average stumpage value. The assessors are provided with much material covering both these factors together with detailed instructions as to how to use it. In order to complete the assessment of a forest property, the estimated value of the timber growing on the land included in the property is added to the assessed value of the land itself. If the land carries a definite building or industrial site value, that value is added also.[24]

The total taxable value thus arrived at is subject to: (1) the county council tax; (2) the assize house tax; and (3) the road tax, all of which are levied at the same rate upon both land and timber; and to (4) the commercial real estate tax, in which the rate levied upon the assessed value of the timber is two-thirds of that levied upon the assessed value of the land. In addition, the net income which it is estimated the forest ought to produce is subject to (5) the forest excise tax, in which the rate levied on the income assigned to the growing timber is two-thirds of that on the income

[23] See Table 1 on page 152.

[24] Tor Jonson, "New Bascs for the Assessment of Forest Property," *Journal of Forestry*, 23:795–811 (1925), as translated from *Skogen*, 1921, pp. 169–183, by Mary E. Lagenby, Research Translation Service, Washington, D. C.

assigned to the land. The income from this tax is assigned to the tax-spending units within which the forest property is located. The stumpage value of the timber cut annually from the forest is subject to (6) the forest conservation tax. This tax is used for the maintenance of the work of the forest conservation agencies. All these taxes are levied directly on the forest property and are a lien against it rather than against its owner. Hence these taxes as a group can be considered as a substitute for our ad valorem tax.

Under the Swedish method of assessment a privately owned forest property of 988 acres located near Stockholm was assessed in 1928 at $37.39 an acre, the land being assessed at $6.56 and the growing forest at $30.83. The taxes levied in that year directly against this property, namely, taxes 1 to 6 as listed above, totaled $.3046 an acre. This property was covered with a spruce-pine forest in which all age classes, from seedlings to eighty-year-old timber, were represented. The growth amounted to about 500 cords of merchantable products annually with an average stumpage value of $6.35 a cord.[25]

How Shall Forest Property Be Taxed?

In Sweden the capital value of forest property is carefully determined, the expected net income to be produced by the forest being used as a base. The value thus determined is subject to the same tax rates as adjoining agricultural property values or to certain definite proportions of those rates. The application of this method places a total property tax burden of about 30 cents an acre annually upon well-developed, productive forest property located near Stockholm. This burden is almost identical with that now carried by the "wild lands" of the sixteen forest counties of Minnesota. In Sweden speculative values based upon the possible future use of forest land by agriculture are not allowed to creep into the assessment. Under the Swedish method of taxation forest property is kept productive. At the same time it is providing much public revenue.

In Maine the lack of speculative agricultural or other value in the unorganized townships has kept the assessments at or near the value of the property for timber-growing purposes. The lack of speculative value has limited the demand for public expenditures in this section. The resulting tax burden of from 7 to 12 cents per

[25] James W. Toumey and Erik Lindeberg, "An Example of Forest Taxation in New Hampshire as Compared with an Example in Sweden," *Journal of Forestry*, 28: 199–211 (1930).

acre per year is not heavy enough to prevent the owners from keeping their forest property in a productive condition.

In Minnesota the forest taxation problem is primarily one of getting the tax burden now resting upon "wild lands" reduced to a point where some of the expected income to be produced by this land will be left in the possession of the landowner after he has paid his taxes.

This problem could be solved administratively without any change in our present laws by eliminating the unjustifiable speculative agricultural values that have been and are still being included in the assessed value of the forest lands, and reducing local public expenditures correspondingly. Such a solution would require the setting of the "full and true" assessed value of these lands at the capitalized value of the net income which they could reasonably be expected to produce when used for the growing of timber alone. Such an assessed value would probably be nominal. Limitation of the area within which schools and roads would be provided for settlers in this section of the state is another necessity if the local public expenditures are to be held within limits bearable by owners of the forest land.

But there are serious obstacles to this solution. It does not now seem possible to get the assessed value of the forest lands reduced to true value. It could be done by entrusting it to the Tax Commission if the commission were given sufficient funds to employ expert appraisers. But Minnesota clings to its local assessors. They and their neighbors still feel that there is an agricultural value inherent in these lands and they will give up this idea with great reluctance, if at all.

In this connection attention should be called to the fact that in the past very real relief has frequently been offered to the owners of tax-delinquent lands in the form of laws authorizing the settlement of the delinquent tax liability for varying portions of the amount of the delinquency. Such laws seem very unfair to those who pay their taxes as they come due.

The Minnesota Auxiliary Forest Tax Law

For the reasons mentioned above it seems necessary under present conditions to give the forest owner who is interested in utilizing his wild lands for timber growing the encouragement and protection of a special forest taxation law, a law that will fix rather definitely the amount of the taxes he is to pay on his forest property during the period of time required for the growing of merchantable timber and will definitely postpone the payment of a considerable portion of the taxes on his forest property until the timber is convertible into cash.

The Minnesota Auxiliary Forest Tax Law is intended to be of this type. It was originally passed in 1927, following the passage in 1926 of a constitutional amendment authorizing a separate classification for forest property and the subjection of the property so classed to a low annual tax, plus a yield tax to be paid at the time the timber was cut. The law of 1927 [26] differed from the present law in setting the annual tax on accepted auxiliary forest land at eight cents on each dollar or fraction thereof of assessed value (excluding value of mineral rights).

No forest owners attempted to utilize this law, so in 1929 it was revised.[27] In the revised form it authorizes a specific annual property tax of five cents an acre, plus an annual fire-protection fund tax of three cents an acre (which does not apply to farm wood lots), plus a 10 per cent yield tax, payable at the time of cutting, on the full and true stumpage value of the timber cut, except that which was merchantable at the time of classification or that cut for the owner's use. The receipts from the yield tax are to be divided among the tax districts in which the auxiliary forest is situated in proportion to their several interests in the ad valorem property taxes.

To have his lands classified as auxiliary forests the forest owner must apply first to the county commissioners and, if they approve, then to the state commissioner of forestry. To be eligible for such classification, commercial forest tracts must have an area of not less than 160 acres with a full and true surface value of from $3.00 to $10.00 an acre. Farm wood lots may contain from 20 to 40 acres and be of unlimited value. The lands approved must contain, or immediately be planted with, sufficient young growth of merchantable species so that a commercial forest will develop upon them. The forest thus established must be managed under a definite plan covered by a fifty-year contract between the state and the owner. This contract must embody the plan of management and be drawn up by the commissioner of forestry and the chief of the Division of Forestry of the University of Minnesota. Cutting is permitted only with the permission of and under regulations laid

[26] Session Laws of 1927, Ch. 247.
[27] Session Laws of 1929, Ch. 245.

down by the commissioner of forestry. Declassification of approved auxiliary forest land is provided for.

No land has yet been classified under the provisions of this law. The lumber companies located at Cloquet applied to the county commissioners of St. Louis County to have a tract of approximately 172,000 acres of cut-over lands, located for the most part in unorganized townships, classified as an auxiliary forest under the provisions of this law. Interests hostile to the lumber companies, or to this form of land utilization, stirred the settlers adjacent to and for some distance around this tract to active and vigorous opposition to its classification. The settlers and their leaders attended the several hearings which the county commissioners held on the application, with the result that action by the county commissioners was postponed from time to time until the lumber companies withdrew their application.

Points to Be Considered in the Next Revision of the Minnesota Auxiliary Forest Law

From many points of view the present Minnesota Auxiliary Forest Tax Law is a good one. But the responsibility for classifying the eligible land should be shifted from the county commissioners to a state officer or commission. The other provisions of the law ought to be reviewed at the time this change is made. The following points merit particular consideration.[28]

1. *Lands classifiable.*—(a) Should all wild lands, unless more valuable for some other purpose than timber production, be classifiable, no matter what their present condition, or (b) should classification be limited to lands that carry a sufficient stand of suitable forest trees so distributed that one may expect a stand of merchantable timber to develop within a reasonable period of time? Most states, including Minnesota, that have passed forest yield tax laws specify (b), but Oregon and Washington specify (a). If the forest tax law is considered as a special concession, that is, as a form of subsidy, to the forest owner, then (b) should be specified; but if the law is considered to be primarily a method of equalizing the tax burden carried by forest land with that carried

[28] Anyone interested in the revisions here proposed should consult "Digest of Forest Tax Laws in the United States in Effect January 1, 1932" (mimeographed Progress Report No. 16 of the Forest Taxation Inquiry, 1932). This 72-page report, prepared by Louis F. Murphy, P. A. Herbert, and Wade E. DeVries, contains a complete summary of all the forest tax laws in force in the United States.

by other lands, then (a) should be specified. There is much to be said in favor of (a).

2. *Procedure followed in making classification.*—Most of the states having special forest tax laws, including Minnesota, require that the owner of forest land request classification in order to utilize the law. This optional feature is objectionable because it puts the forest owner in the position of asking a special favor, which, if granted, may subject him to the hostility of his neighbors and to all the inconvenience that goes with such hostility. In Oregon and Washington the forest owner has nothing to do with the classification of his land; classification is made by the state forestry board and checked by the state tax commission, the forestry board being required to cover all eligible lands as rapidly as possible. The advantages and disadvantages of automatic as against optional classification should be given careful consideration.

3. *Modification of the tax system.*—(a) The property tax. More than twenty states have laws on their statute books that modify the property tax as it applies to forest property. These states either exempt growing timber entirely from taxation under the property tax or exempt it from such taxation for a period of years. Most of these states also limit the amount of the tax on the land either by specifying the valuation, usually one dollar an acre, at which the land shall be taxed, or by specifying the actual amount of the annual tax (or "fee") per acre. At present Minnesota is following the latter plan, specifying an annual tax of five cents an acre. Oregon also specifies five cents, whereas Michigan and Wisconsin specify ten cents an acre. The other states having forest tax laws follow the former plan. It is a moot question as to which of these methods is the better.

(b) The yield tax. Yield taxes are provided for in the forest tax laws of sixteen states because of the fear that the forest owner may pay too little under the modified property tax system (a). The Minnesota law provides for a yield tax at the rate of 10 per cent on the full stumpage value of the timber at the time it is cut. This is the rate most frequently authorized by other states, although such rates vary from a minimum of less than 1 per cent, where the growing timber put under the law is already approaching maturity, up to a maximum of 12.5 per cent (in Idaho, Oregon, and Washington). Several states specify rates of 5 or 6 per cent. Rates of 10 per cent or more are probably excessive.

4. *Division of the revenue.*—Ordinarily the division of the receipts obtained under both the property and the yield tax should be apportioned among the various eligible tax-spending units in the same proportion as the ad valorem taxes. However, the state may be justified in taking the whole or a major part of the yield tax if it advances special aid to the local tax-spending units within which forest tax law lands are found.

5. *Control by the state of the management of forests entered under forest tax laws.*—Many of the forest tax laws, including Minnesota's, require some control by the state of the management of the forest grown on the land entered under the forest tax law. Such control can be justified now only on the ground that the forest owner who utilizes the forest tax law is receiving a special favor. Even though that be the case, provisions relating to management greatly complicate the administration of a forest tax law and may prevent many owners from utilizing it. Hence it may be better policy not to include such provisions. They have been omitted in the Oregon, Washington, Maine, and Connecticut laws. They appear in only very limited form in the Massachusetts and New York laws.

6. *Contracts between the state and the forest owner.*—Most of the states having yield tax laws, including Minnesota, require or permit the state to enter into contractual relations with the forest owner if his land is entered under the forest tax law. These contracts usually run for a period of fifty years, and in some states they may be renewed for a second fifty years. Such contracts should not be required unless they are necessary in order to make legal the entry of land under the forest law. However, they are of some advantage to the forest owner.

7. *Should the state directly subsidize the local tax-spending units?*—The Michigan and Wisconsin laws subsidize the local tax-spending units by providing for the annual payment of ten cents an acre by the state to such units. The inclusion of such a provision in a forest tax law seems unwise. After the principle of making such payments was established, it would probably not be very difficult to increase the rate from time to time. Ultimately the payments called for might become very burdensome to the state, with the result that the legislature either might refuse to make the required appropriations or might repeal the forest tax law altogether.

Furthermore, it is quite probable that a provision of this kind in the forest tax law would encourage local communities to urge the inclusion in state forests of lands such as muskegs which are too poor to produce even a forest. Moreover, an automatic subsidy might provide the greatest state assistance to areas with least need of such assistance. It is often argued that the state owes the local tax-spending units this kind of subsidy in areas where it retains or acquires ownership of land, since by such ownership of land it reduces the total taxes that such communities can collect. But do the local communities have any real tax equity in such lands? Such a tax equity cannot exist unless such lands are now producing or in the near future can be made to produce a net income at least sufficient to pay the taxes levied against them.

While it is true that many of the local tax-spending units in the cut-over counties are badly in need of aid, such aid as they must have may be granted them by the state from biennium to biennium as long as the urgent need exists and may then be discontinued. Ultimately a plan may be developed under which the counties in which state forests are located will participate in the returns from such forests.

8. *Tax for protection of the forest property against fire.*—The present Minnesota law includes a tax of three cents an acre annually for fire protection. Such a tax does not appear in any other forest tax law. Some consider it unreasonable to subject the auxiliary forest owner to this charge.

In conclusion, it seems to the writer that the administrative solution of this problem is the most logical one under our tax system. But that solution, assessment at true value, does not seem attainable under current assessment conditions in the cut-over counties. It now seems possible only after the present owners have been almost entirely eliminated in consequence of tax delinquency. Then, if any considerable portion of these lands again pass into private ownership, it will be much easier to hold their assessed values down to approximately their real capital values than it would be now to get the present assessed values down to such levels. If it is impracticable to authorize the Tax Commission to assess these lands and to give the commission sufficient funds for appraisers, it seems advisable to have a yield tax law that will enable private forest owners to retain their forest property, if they so desire, and to share with owners of other classes of property and with the state in providing the revenue required by the local tax-spending units.

CHAPTER 7

URBAN REALTY ASSESSMENTS AND TAX BURDENS[1]

The assessments and tax burdens of farm real estate have been treated in Chapters 3 and 4 above. Chapters 5 and 6 discuss the related problems of forest taxation and of cut-over lands and tax delinquency, and Chapter 9 treats the taxation of iron ore. This chapter presents data relative to the other most important class of real estate, namely, that located in cities and villages.

The importance of urban real estate is indicated by the fact that in 1931 it represented about 86 per cent of the total property tax base in urban areas and that it paid approximately 59 per cent of the total taxes paid on state and local property in Minnesota. The same year rural real estate paid about 29 per cent of the total state and local property taxes. Ten years previously, urban realty paid 51 per cent and rural realty 34 per cent of such taxes.[2]

This chapter will consider primarily: (1) the inequalities of assessments within each of 143 municipalities of the state; (2) the inequalities of assessments among the several cities and villages; and (3) the relation of taxes to the income of real estate in different municipalities.

Character and Distribution of Data

This study of the taxation of urban realty is based on 6,508 properties in 143 municipalities of the state. Of these sample cases, 849 were collected in Minneapolis for a university thesis in 1929–30; 4,839 were collected especially for this study in 133 other cities and villages of the state in 1931–32; and 820, representing 25 cities, were taken from the records of the Minnesota Tax Commission. (Data for 1928–29 were collected in 1930.)

The Tax Commission data compare assessments with sales prices; the other data compare assessments with appraised values of properties, though these appraised values are based chiefly upon the

[1] Most of the data in this chapter for the larger municipalities were collected and analyzed in part by Mr. J. R. McFadyen, former graduate student in taxation. Most of the special survey data for the smaller municipalities were collected by the field staff that collected the agricultural data under the direction of Professor George A. Pond. Miss Violet Johnson performed much of the statistical work in connection with both sets of data but particularly with the latter.

[2] See Table 47 on page 108 for additional comparisons.

sales of the property in question or of similar property in the same community. The tax survey staff secured data in 16 of the 25 cities for which Tax Commission data are shown. The distribution of these data and other pertinent facts regarding them are summarized in Tables 2, 3, and 4, pages 194–197. (See also page 38.)

Everyone familiar with real estate knows that it is difficult to get accurate appraisals and that most records of sales do not disclose true considerations. Furthermore, conditions have been very abnormal during the past few years; free sales (as opposed to forced sales) have been relatively few, values have been dropping rapidly, and uncertainty as to values has prevailed generally.

The limitations just mentioned undoubtedly affect the information gathered for this study, but special effort has been made to get accurate and reliable appraisals, sales values, and other data. Owners, renters, real estate men, bankers, loan agents, auditors, assessors, and others have cooperated in checking them. Several times as many cases were discarded as were selected for use because it was decided after preliminary investigation that certain facts or the lack of certain facts made it doubtful whether they were representative. Within the limits of time and means available it has been possible to get much better and more adequate samples in some cities than in others. In a number of cities and villages the samples are too few in number to permit any certainty that they are truly representative of these particular municipalities, but when they are grouped by districts, or when all are put together, we believe that the figures here presented give a true picture of the situation in the state.

In comparing the different cities, note should be taken of the fact that assessors' valuations usually tend to lag behind changes in actual values. This is particularly important in a period of rapid changes, such as that under consideration, though the figures here presented seem to call for this caution less than do the agricultural data in Chapter 3. The Tax Commission data included for checking purposes are for a period two or three years earlier than that of most of the data obtained especially for this study; hence one would expect them to show assessors' valuations relatively low as compared with sales or appraisals.

Different Assessment Valuations

The law requires that assessors list property at what it would bring in case of a free sale, that is, a sale between a willing buyer

TABLE 1.—CLASSIFICATION AND DISTRIBUTION OF PROPERTIES INVESTIGATED IN MINNEAPOLIS[a]

Class	Kind of Real Estate	Assessed Value	Land Only	Improvements	Land and Improvements[b]	
			No.	No.	No.	Assessed Value
1	Residential	$0–$5,000	98	79	137	$ 399,810
2	Residential	5,000–10,000	226	226	275	1,391,543
3	Residential	10,000–20,000	71	68	133	1,409,390
4	Residential	Over 20,000	15	18	30	730,235
Total (1–4)			410	391	575	$ 3,930,978
5	Hotels, apartments, and fraternal properties	$0–$50,000	51	49	66	1,409,750
6	Hotels, apartments, and fraternal properties	50,000–200,000	36	35	44	2,897,350
7	Hotels, apartments, and fraternal properties	Over 200,000	10	10	9	2,817,890
8	Commercial: stores, office buildings, etc.	$0–$100,000	28	11	16	425,785
9	Commercial: stores, office buildings, etc.	Over 100,000	15	14	11	9,900,430
10	Commercial: garages, warehouses, etc.	$0–$50,000	26	13	12	372,575
11	Commercial: garages, warehouses, etc.	Over 50,000	20	10	9	865,345
Total (5–11)			186	142	167	$18,689,125
Grand total (1–11)			596	533	742	$22,620,103

[a] The same classification was used in Duluth and elsewhere, but samples of data according to classes are shown in this chapter for Minneapolis and Duluth only. In the case of other cities all classes are summarized rather than shown separately.

[b] These last two columns do not represent the sum of preceding columns, but only those properties for which usable appraisals were obtainable for both land and improvements. For example, a property for which a usable appraisal of the land only was obtained is not included here, though it is included in the column under "Land Only" and is used elsewhere herein in arriving at the ratio between assessed values and appraised values of "land only." This explanation applies to following tables and figures also.

and a willing seller, neither of whom is forced to make the transaction. This is what is called the assessor's "full and true" value and is not to be confused with the 40 per cent of this value upon which the tax rate for platted land is calculated.[3] Unless otherwise noted, it is this "full and true value," not the 40 per cent, that is referred to wherever assessed value is discussed in this chapter.

Equitable property taxation according to the legal concept is not attainable unless all property is assessed alike, that is, at the same percentage of true value. All property in one city or community may be assessed uniformly at 50 per cent of its true value; but if property in another city in the same county is assessed uniformly at 100 per cent of its true value, the two cities are not uniformly assessed as compared with each other. The citizens of the latter will have to pay twice as much in state and county taxes per dollar of property owned as the citizens of the former. If all the property of all the citizens of the state were assessed at the same percentage of true value, assessments would be uniform even though all were assessed much below full value. If, however, all were assessed uniformly at 25 per cent, the rate of tax levied upon the assessed values would have to be four times as high, if the same amount of revenue were to be raised, as if the assessed values were at 100 per cent, as required by law. The important thing is not so much the height of assessments as their uniformity, both among individuals within a community and among different townships, villages, cities, and counties.

A comparison of assessments in the cities and villages of Minnesota shows great lack of uniformity both between the different municipalities and between the different properties within the same municipality. These disparities are shown most fully in this chapter in Tables 2 to 8, but they can be shown more clearly and strikingly by means of figures or diagrams. There is not space enough to give graphs for all cities, but a sufficient number of samples are shown to give a good idea of the situation throughout the state. The data in the figures will be supplemented later by further comment on the fuller data in the tables.

Assessments in Minneapolis

More time was spent in collecting information in Minneapolis than in any other city, and the appraisals made for comparing assessments in this city were among the best. It was possible also to

[3] See Appendix, page 576.

get more auxiliary data here than elsewhere. The properties investigated in Minneapolis and other larger cities were divided into eleven classes according to character and valuations. These classes and their distribution in Minneapolis are shown in Table 1, page 172.

EXPLANATION OF ILLUSTRATIVE FIGURES

Charts for Minneapolis and other cities are given below. They will perhaps be made clearer by means of the two charts representing hypothetical cases. Figure 1 represents a fairly good assess-

FIGURE 1.—AN ILLUSTRATION OF A FAIRLY GOOD ASSESSMENT ACCORDING TO EXISTING STANDARDS

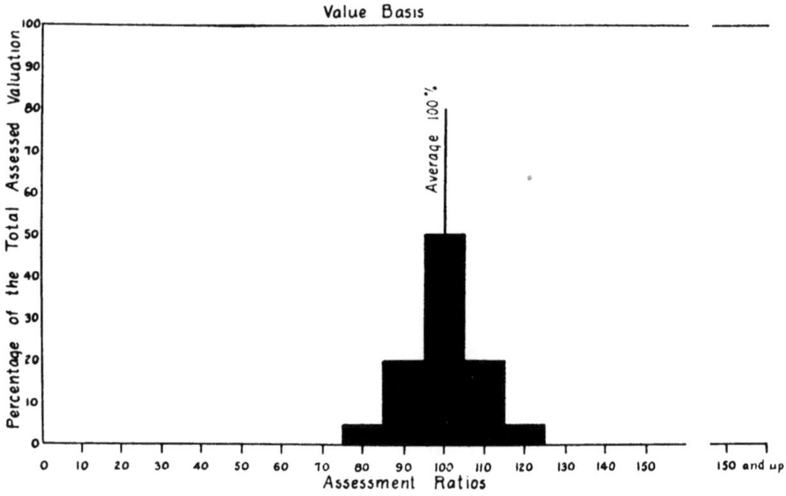

ment according to existing standards of assessment, which are not very high. The percentages of true value at which properties are assessed are represented at the bottom by the positions of the bars on the horizontal base; the percentages of the total amount of property assessed at the several ratios of assessment to appraised value are represented by the length of the lines or bars as measured on the vertical scale at the left. Figure 1 represents a district in which 50 per cent of the property (see the vertical scale at the left) is assessed at between 95 per cent and 105 per cent of its true value (shown on the horizontal scale at the bottom); 20 per cent of the total is assessed at between 85 per cent and 95 per cent of its true value; another 20 per cent at between 105 and 115 per cent;

5 per cent at between 75 per cent and 85 per cent; and the remaining 5 per cent at between 115 per cent and 125 per cent.

In Figure 2 the vertical line in the middle of the bar represents a perfect assessment. By its length and position this line shows that 100 per cent of the property (see the vertical scale at the left) is assessed at 100 per cent of its true value (see the horizontal scale at the bottom). If instead of the line (Figure 2) we take the bar enclosing it, we have a nearly perfect assessment, because all property, as represented by this bar, is assessed at valuations between 95 per cent and 105 per cent of its true value.

FIGURE 2. — AN ILLUSTRATION OF A PERFECT ASSESSMENT

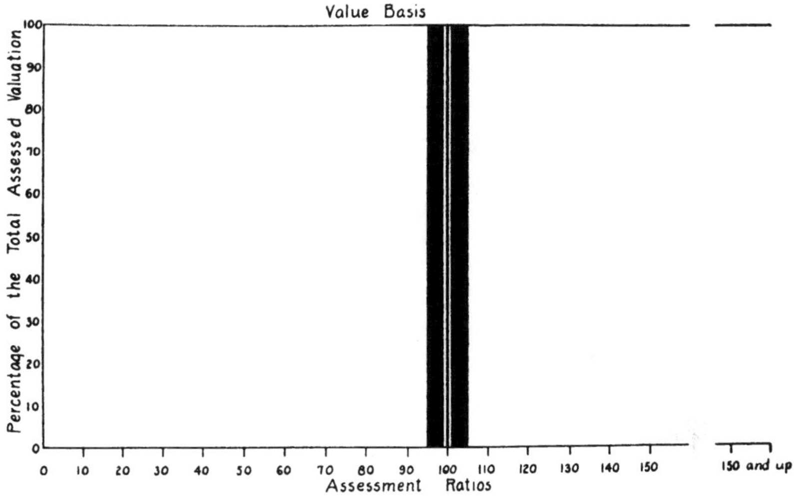

The sum of the five bars in Figure 1 is equal to the bar in Figure 2. The average assessment in the two cases is the same, namely, 100 per cent of true value, but the assessment represented in Figure 1 is far inferior because of its lack of uniformity. An average is very misleading; it conceals the inequalities that make taxes on property so unfairly distributed. For example, two similar properties of equal value might be assessed at 40 per cent and 160 per cent of their respective values. The average would be a perfect 100 per cent; but the owner of the second would be required to pay four times as heavy taxes as the owner of the first. The 5 per cent of property in Figure 1 that centers over 120 per cent (on the horizontal scale) pays one and one-half times as much in taxes as the

5 per cent centering over 80 per cent, though the average assessment of these two 5 per cent groups is a perfect 100 per cent.

FIGURES SHOWING ASSESSMENTS IN MINNEAPOLIS

Figure 3 represents the assessments of properties in Minneapolis designated as Class 1 in this study, namely, 137 residential properties assessed at less than $5,000 each. It will be noted that the average assessment of this class is 74.60 per cent of the appraised value and that nearly 30 per cent (see the scale at the left) of the total property in this class is assessed at a figure near this average. Almost as large a proportion (27 per cent) is assessed at between 60 and 70 per cent, and 9 per cent of the total is assessed at between 50 and 60 per cent of appraised value. The distribution of the rest of this class is clear. The distribution of properties shown in Figure 3 is not so good as that in the hypothetical assessment shown in Figure 1 for at least two reasons: first, the average is 74.6 per cent, 25.4 per cent below the 100 per cent legally required; and second, the assessments do not "peak up," or form a high, pointed, even-sided triangle, thus: △, but tend to flatten out, thus: ⏜.

As indicated by the captions, Figures 3 to 6 represent assessments of Minneapolis residences in various value groups, while Figures 7 and 8 represent the several value classes of hotels, apartments, and fraternal properties. No charts are presented for the other five classes of Minneapolis properties listed in Table 1, partly because the number of properties obtained in these classes is relatively small and partly because of lack of space. The five classes of which the assessments are not charted include hotels, apartments, and fraternal properties assessed at over $200,000 each, stores, office buildings, garages, warehouses, and other commercial properties, as classified in Table 1 on page 172.

Let us compare the quality of assessments represented in Figures 3 to 8. Figure 8 shows the highest average (nearest the legal requirement) and in that one respect is best. But it shows great lack of uniformity in the valuations of different properties in this class. The largest percentage of the total property in this class of residential property that was assessed in any one 10 per cent range was assessed at between 70 and 80 per cent of appraised value. But only a little over a quarter (27 per cent) of the total class was assessed in this 10 per cent range. The proportions assessed between 100 and 110 per cent and above 150 per cent are smaller but far too large. Figure 4, which represents residences assessed at

FIGURE 3. — COMPARISON OF ASSESSED WITH APPRAISED VALUES OF CLASS 1 REAL ESTATE IN MINNEAPOLIS (RESIDENCES ASSESSED UNDER $5,000), 1928–1930

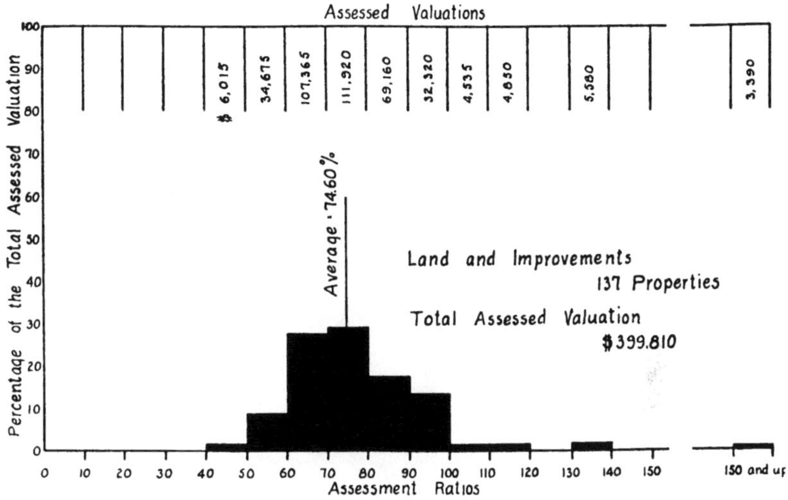

FIGURE 4. — COMPARISON OF ASSESSED WITH APPRAISED VALUES OF CLASS 2 REAL ESTATE IN MINNEAPOLIS (RESIDENCES ASSESSED AT $5,000–$10,000), 1928–1930

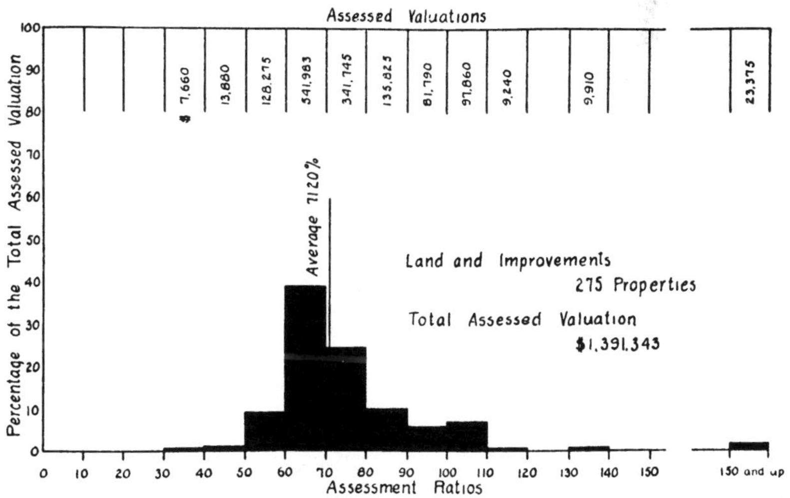

FIGURE 5. — COMPARISON OF ASSESSED WITH APPRAISED VALUES OF CLASS 3 REAL ESTATE IN MINNEAPOLIS (RESIDENCES ASSESSED AT $10,000–$20,000), 1928–1930

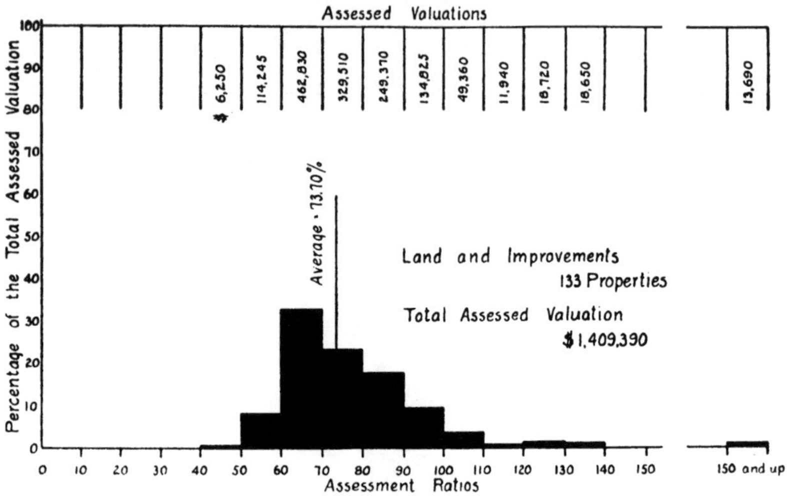

FIGURE 6. — COMPARISON OF ASSESSED WITH APPRAISED VALUES OF CLASS 4 REAL ESTATE IN MINNEAPOLIS (RESIDENCES ASSESSED AT OVER $20,000), 1928–1930

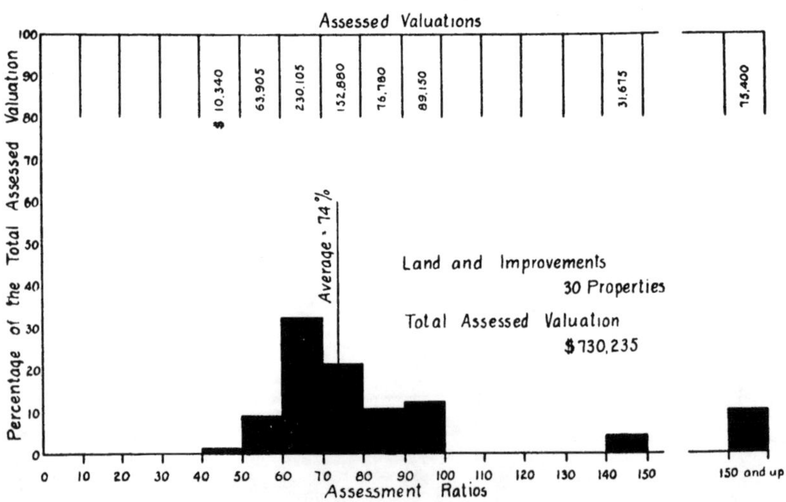

FIGURE 7. — COMPARISON OF ASSESSED WITH APPRAISED VALUES OF CLASS 5 REAL ESTATE IN MINNEAPOLIS (HOTELS, APARTMENTS, AND FRATERNAL PROPERTIES ASSESSED UNDER $50,000), 1928–1930

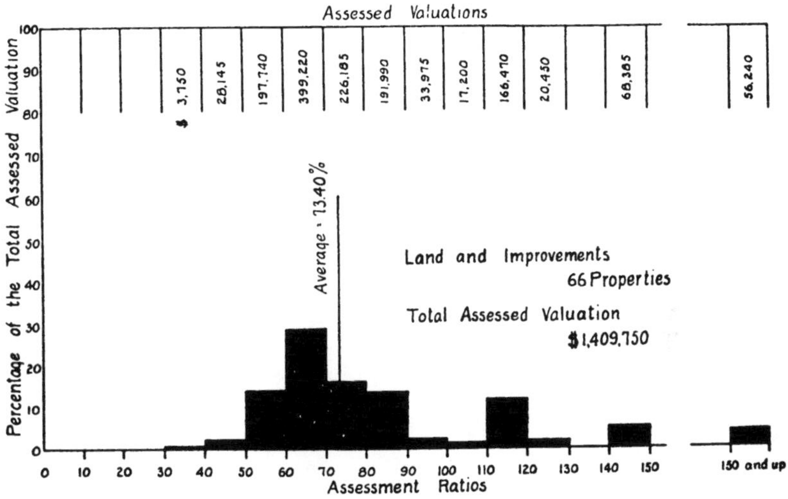

FIGURE 8. — COMPARISON OF ASSESSED WITH APPRAISED VALUES OF CLASS 6 REAL ESTATE IN MINNEAPOLIS (HOTELS, APARTMENTS, AND FRATERNAL PROPERTIES ASSESSED AT $50,000–$200,000), 1928–1930

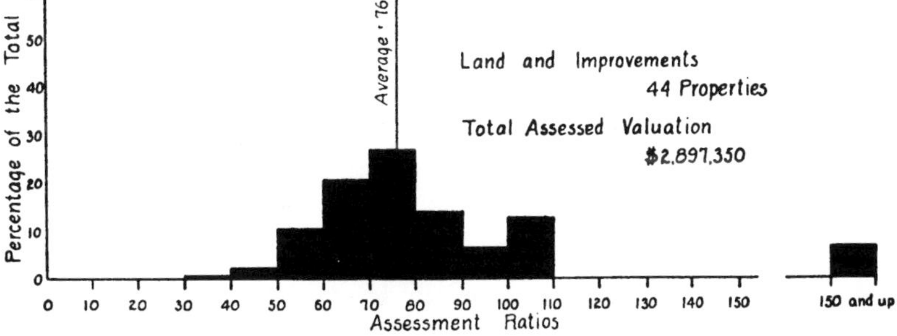

FIGURE 9. — COMPARISON OF ASSESSED WITH APPRAISED VALUES OF LAND, OF IMPROVEMENTS, AND OF LAND AND IMPROVEMENTS COMBINED, MINNEAPOLIS RESIDENTIAL REAL ESTATE (CLASSES 1–4), 1928–1930

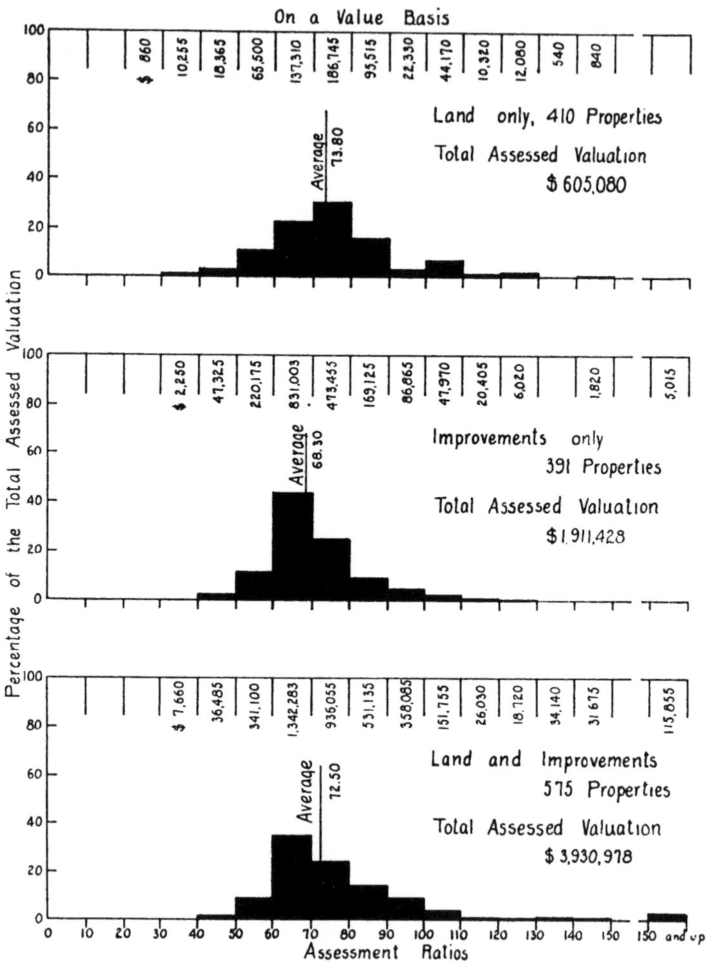

between $5,000 and $10,000 each, "peaks up" much better than Figure 8, which represents hotels, apartments, and fraternal properties assessed at between $50,000 and $200,000 each. That is, Figure 4 resembles Figures 1 and 2 more closely than does Figure 8 or any other of the six charts now under consideration. This means that the assessments are more uniform for Minneapolis residential

FIGURE 10.—COMPARISON OF ASSESSED WITH APPRAISED VALUES OF LAND, OF IMPROVEMENTS, AND OF LAND AND IMPROVEMENTS COMBINED, MINNEAPOLIS RESIDENTIAL AND COMMERCIAL REAL ESTATE (CLASSES 1–11), 1928–1930

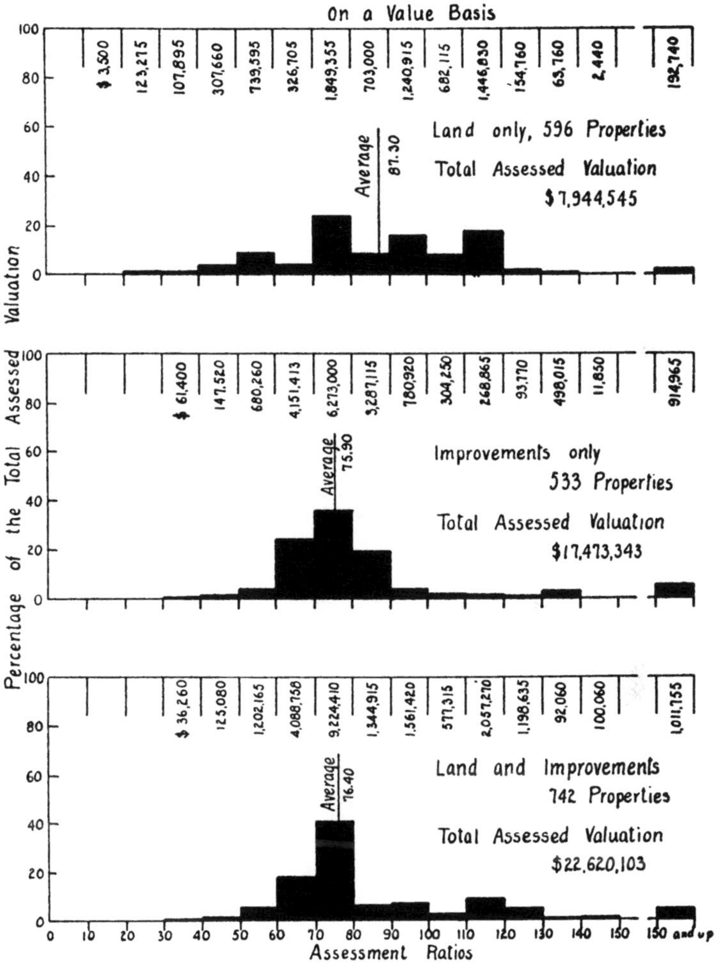

properties assessed between $5,000 and $10,000 than for the other classes, but even here too small a proportion of the total is assessed near the average and too large a proportion is assessed far from the average. (Note particularly how the proportion assessed at between 100 and 110 per cent violates the trend.) The average for this class is only 71.2 per cent of appraised values, that is, lower than the average for any other class of property shown in Figures 3 to 8.

Figure 9 summarizes assessments of Minneapolis properties in classes 1 to 4 combined; Figure 10 does the same for all classes, 1 to 11.[4] It will be observed with respect to Minneapolis residential properties (classes 1 to 4, Figure 9) that improvements are assessed at a lower average than "land only" (68.3 per cent as compared with 73.8 per cent) but that they are assessed much more uniformly as compared with appraised values. This greater uniformity is shown by the fact that bars for "improvements" form a higher and narrower peak than the bars for "land only."

The unpublished diagrams summarizing property classes 5 to 11 — hotels, apartments, and commercial properties — show that the average assessment of "land only" in these classes is much higher than of "land only" in the case of residential property (90.2 per cent as compared with 73.8 per cent) and also much higher than for improvements. Improvements among these commercial properties are assessed appreciably higher also than improvements in residential classes (76.6 per cent as compared with 68.3 per cent). These commercial properties are so much more valuable than residential properties that they dominate the diagrams in Figure 10, in which all classes are combined. In other words, summary diagrams of assessments of commercial property look very little different from those in Figure 10.

Duluth and Other Cities

Four summary charts are shown for Duluth (Figures 11 to 14) and one for each of sixteen other cities (Figures 15 to 30). The single charts for the sixteen cities correspond to the lowest diagram in Figure 10 for Minneapolis and with Figure 14 for Duluth. In making comparisons, attention should be paid to the number of cases, the years considered, and other factors noted at the beginning of this chapter. For example, the relative uniformity of assessments in Minneapolis as shown by the charts is probably due in part to the number of cases and in part to the superior appraisal data obtained for this city. Most of the Minneapolis data are for one or two years earlier than data for other cities. Hence the usual

[4] The footnotes to Table 1 should be read in connection with these figures. It should be noted especially that "Land and Improvements" is not the sum of the two items "Improvements" and "Land Only."

lag in assessments tends to make the assessment ratio in Minneapolis lower than it would be for later years. The preceding explanations of the charts for Minneapolis and the guide figures (1 and 2, pages 174 and 175)) make unnecessary any detailed comment upon the charts for Duluth and other cities which follow. Attention may be called, however, to a few outstanding points.

Altogether, the charts indicate great lack of uniformity in assessments within nearly every city and between different cities. Of the

FIGURE 11. — COMPARISON OF ASSESSED WITH APPRAISED VALUES OF RESIDENTIAL REAL ESTATE IN DULUTH (CLASSES 1–4), 1928–1931

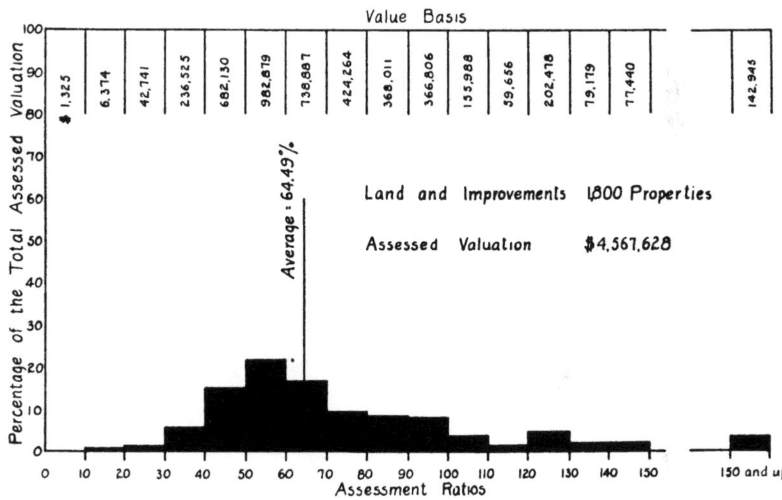

cities represented in the charts, if we omit the three largest cities, Brainerd, Hibbing, Two Harbors, Mankato, and Pine City have the most erratic assessments. There is more uniformity in Moorhead than in other cities, but assessments there are uniformly low, averaging only 47 per cent. Unimproved land in Duluth makes a bad showing on the score of uniformity, though the average is 90.98 per cent. Mankato's average is rather high despite the erratic character of the valuations. Fairmont presents a peculiar distribution. Wadena, Park Rapids, Bemidji, and Albert Lea show better than average assessments, though they are not very uniform.

Obviously there is not sufficient space to present charts for all the cities and villages in the state where data were obtained, but

FIGURE 12. — COMPARISON OF ASSESSED WITH APPRAISED VALUES OF UNIMPROVED LAND AND LAND AND IMPROVEMENTS IN DULUTH (CLASSES 5–11), 1928–1931

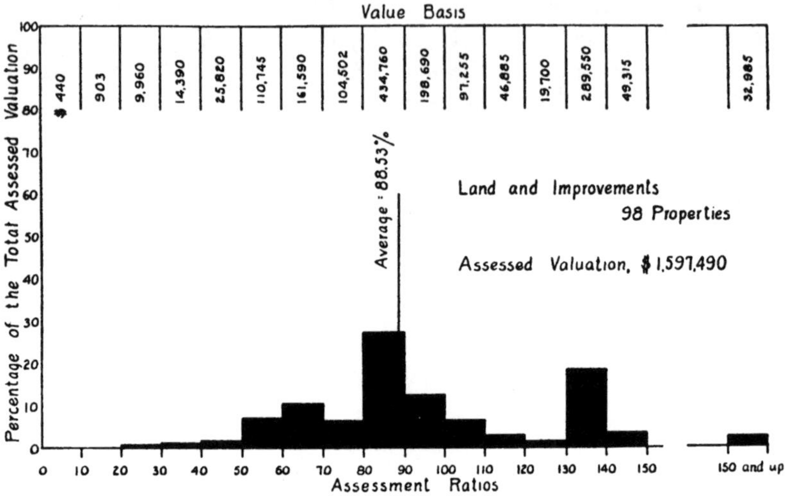

FIGURE 13. — COMPARISON OF ASSESSED WITH APPRAISED VALUES OF UNIMPROVED LAND IN DULUTH (CLASSES 1–11), 1928–1931

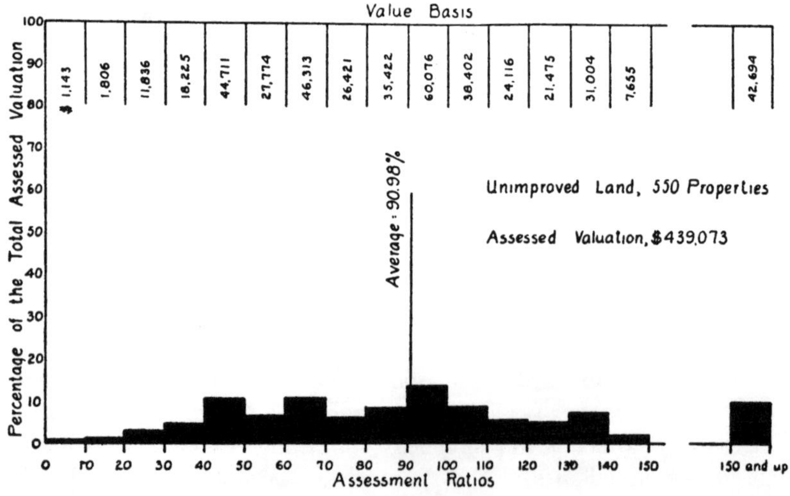

Figure 14. — Comparison of Assessed with Appraised Values of Land and Improvements Exclusive of Unimproved Land in Duluth (Classes 1–11), 1928–1931

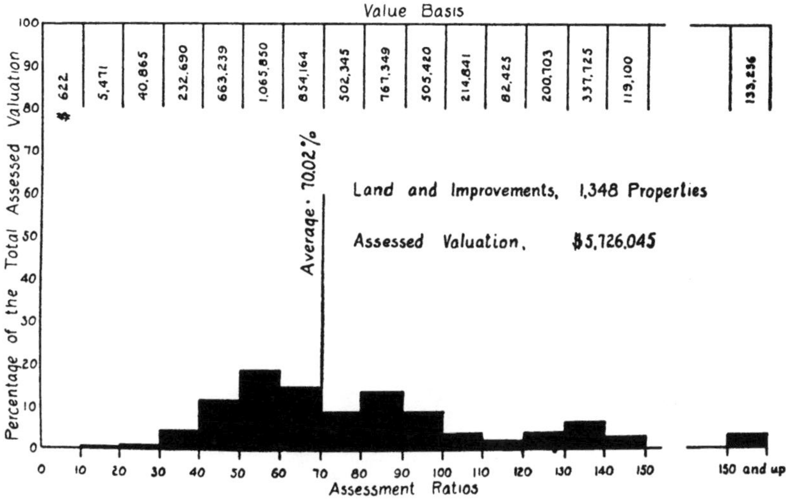

Figure 15. — Comparison of Assessed with Appraised Values of All Classes of Real Estate in St. Paul, 1928–1931

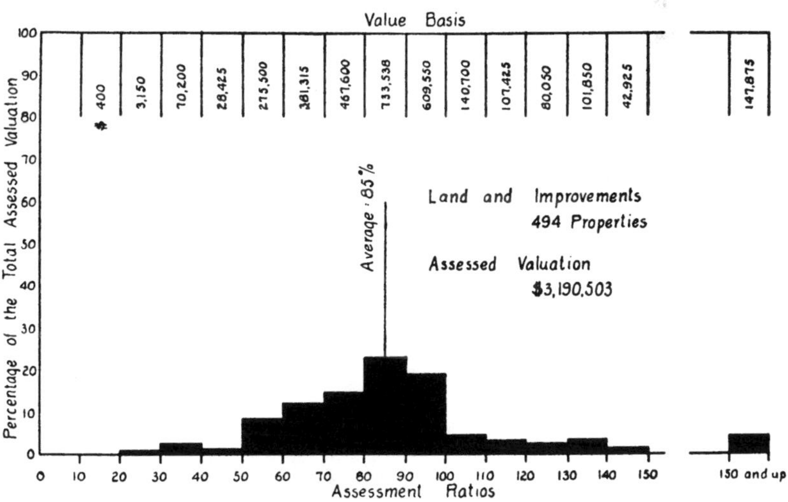

FIGURE 16. — COMPARISON OF ASSESSED WITH APPRAISED VALUES OF ALL CLASSES OF LAND AND IMPROVEMENTS IN ROCHESTER, 1928–1931

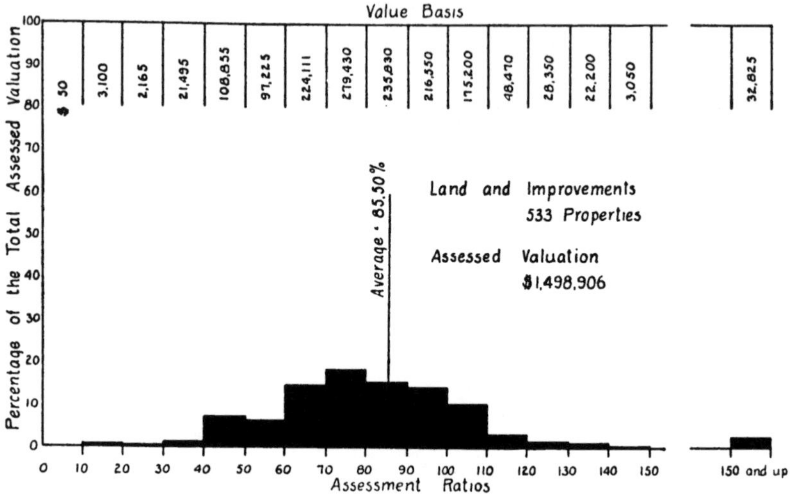

FIGURE 17. — COMPARISON OF ASSESSED WITH APPRAISED VALUES OF LAND AND IMPROVEMENTS IN RED WING, 1928–1931

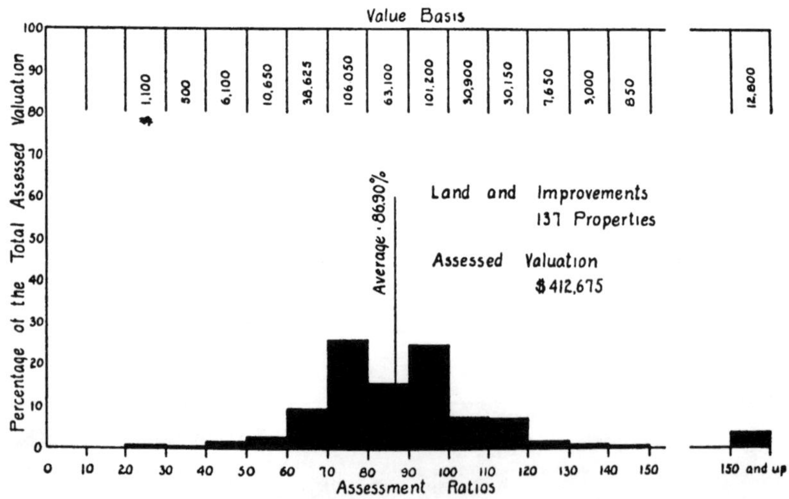

FIGURE 18. — COMPARISON OF ASSESSED WITH APPRAISED VALUES OF LAND AND IMPROVEMENTS IN WINONA, 1928–1931

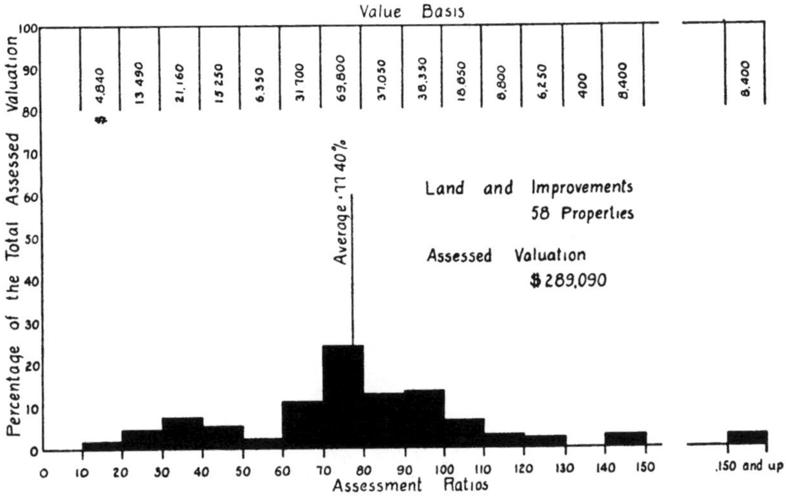

FIGURE 19. — COMPARISON OF ASSESSED WITH APPRAISED VALUES OF LAND AND IMPROVEMENTS IN ALBERT LEA, 1928–1931

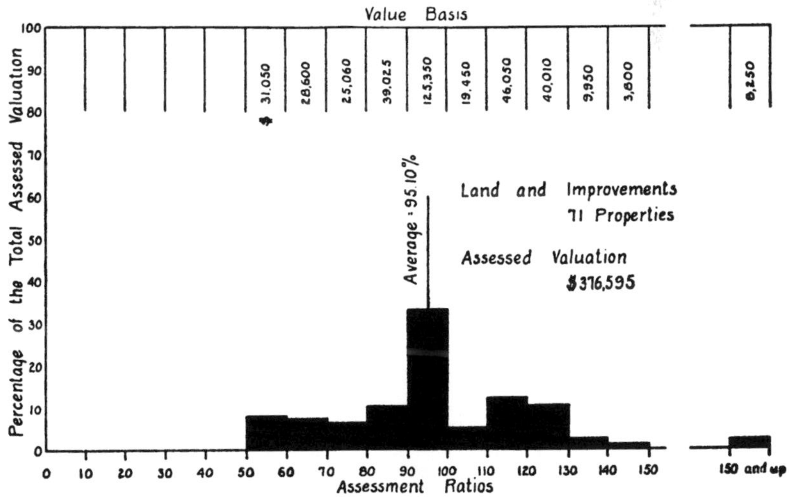

FIGURE 20. — COMPARISON OF ASSESSED WITH APPRAISED VALUES OF LAND AND IMPROVEMENTS IN MANKATO, 1928–1931

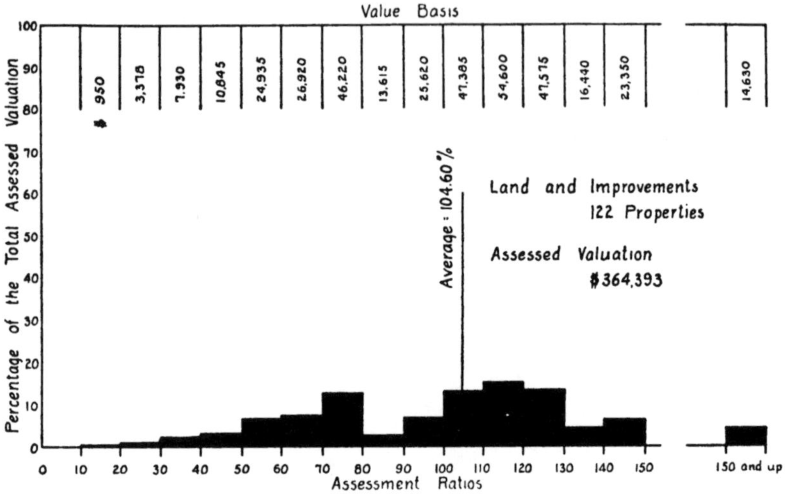

FIGURE 21. — COMPARISON OF ASSESSED WITH APPRAISED VALUES OF LAND AND IMPROVEMENTS IN ST. CLOUD, 1928–1931

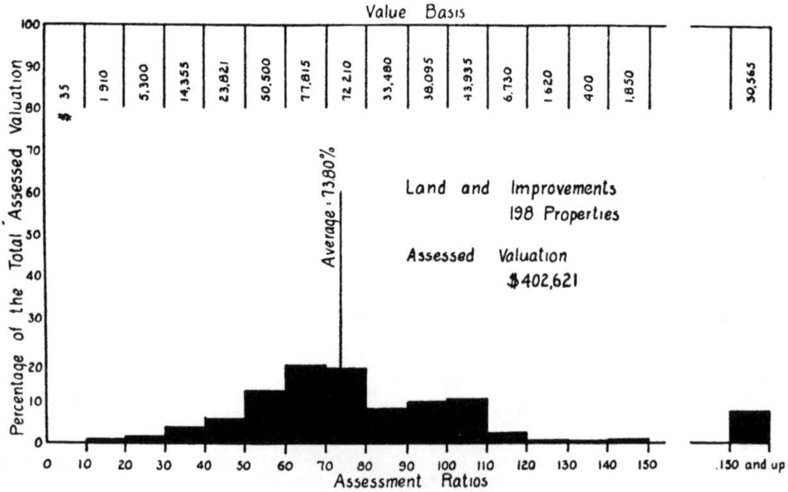

FIGURE 22.—COMPARISON OF ASSESSED WITH APPRAISED VALUES OF LAND AND IMPROVEMENTS IN BRAINERD, 1928–1931

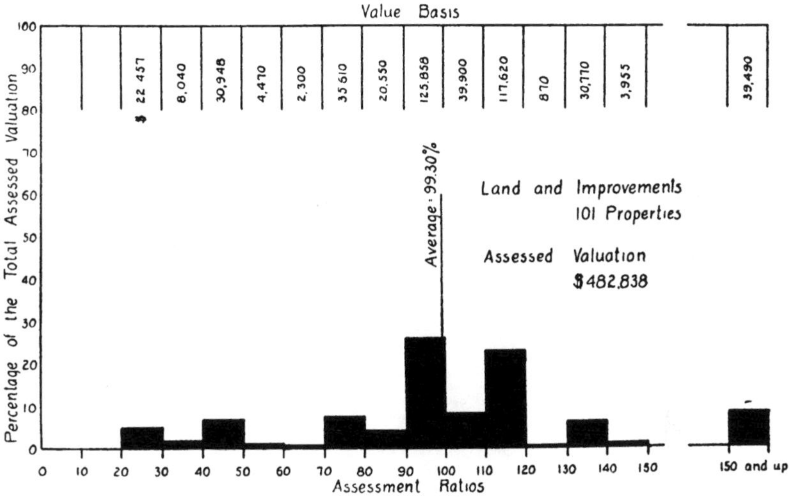

FIGURE 23.—COMPARISON OF ASSESSED WITH APPRAISED VALUES OF LAND AND IMPROVEMENTS IN WADENA, 1928–1931

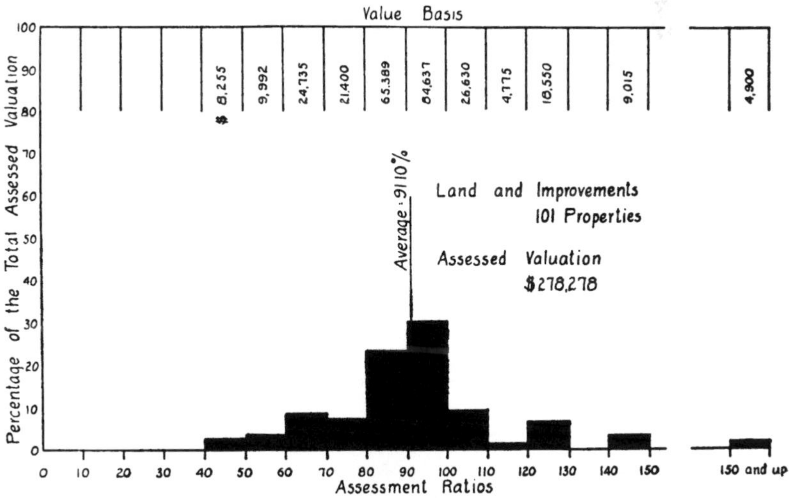

Figure 24. — Comparison of Assessed with Appraised Values of Land and Improvements in Park Rapids, 1928–1931

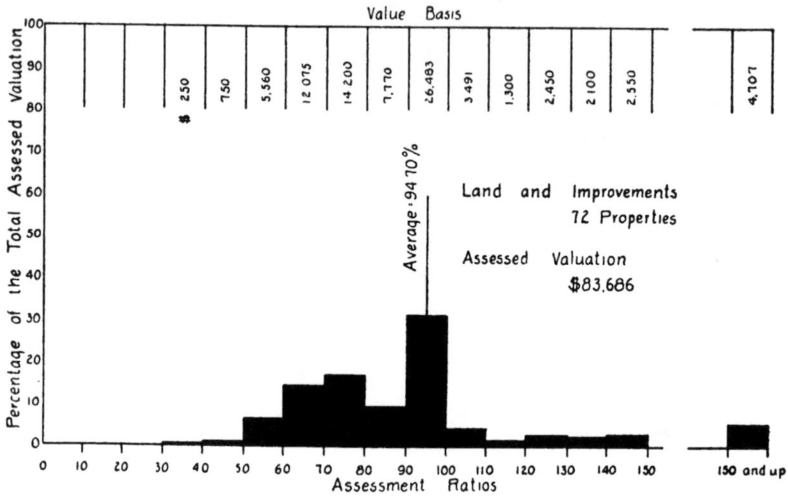

Figure 25. — Comparison of Assessed with Appraised Values of Land and Improvements in Bemidji, 1928–1931

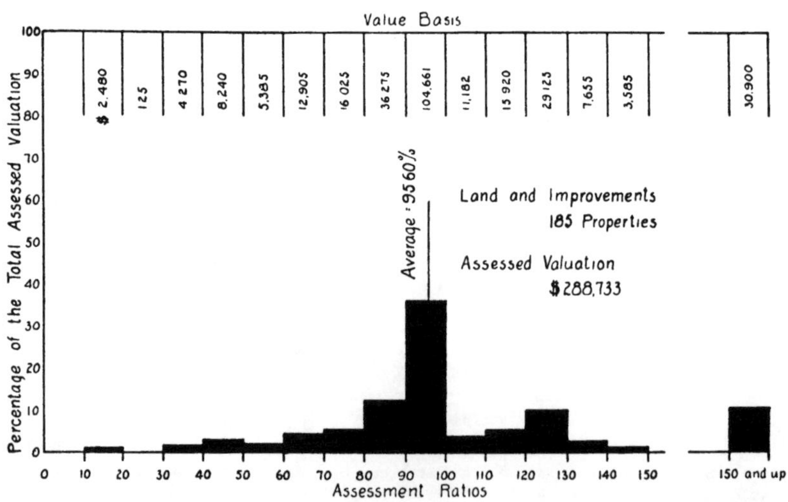

FIGURE 26. — COMPARISON OF ASSESSED WITH APPRAISED VALUES OF LAND AND IMPROVEMENTS IN HIBBING, 1928–1931

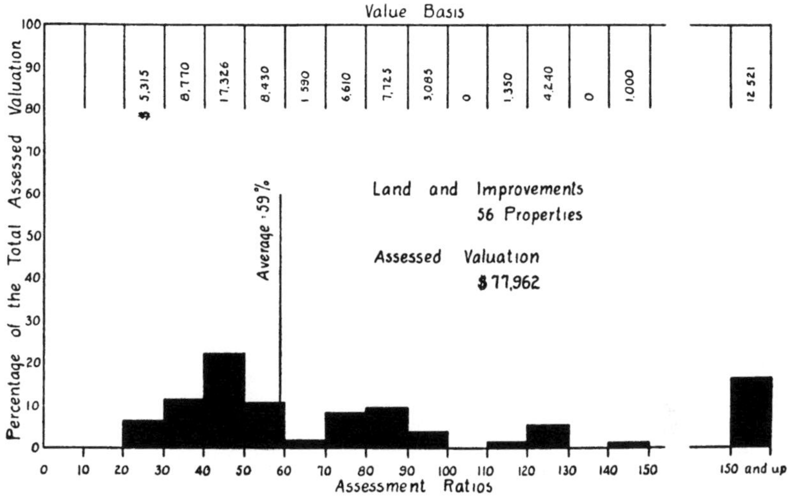

FIGURE 27. — COMPARISON OF ASSESSED WITH APPRAISED VALUES OF LAND AND IMPROVEMENTS IN TWO HARBORS, 1928–1931

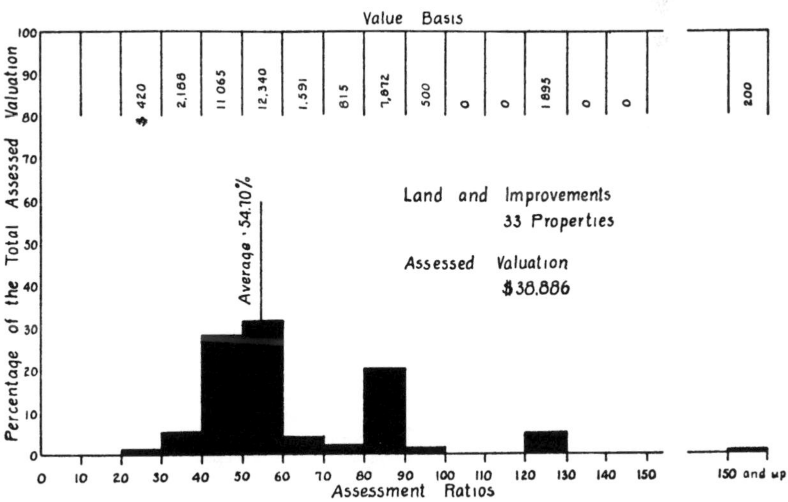

FIGURE 28. — COMPARISON OF ASSESSED WITH APPRAISED VALUES OF LAND AND IMPROVEMENTS IN FAIRMONT, 1928–1931

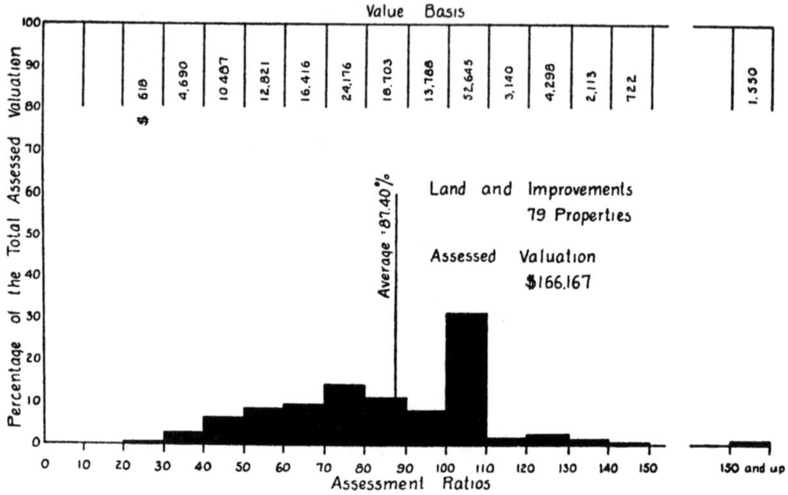

FIGURE 29. — COMPARISON OF ASSESSED VALUES WITH SALES PRICES IN MOORHEAD, 1928–1929

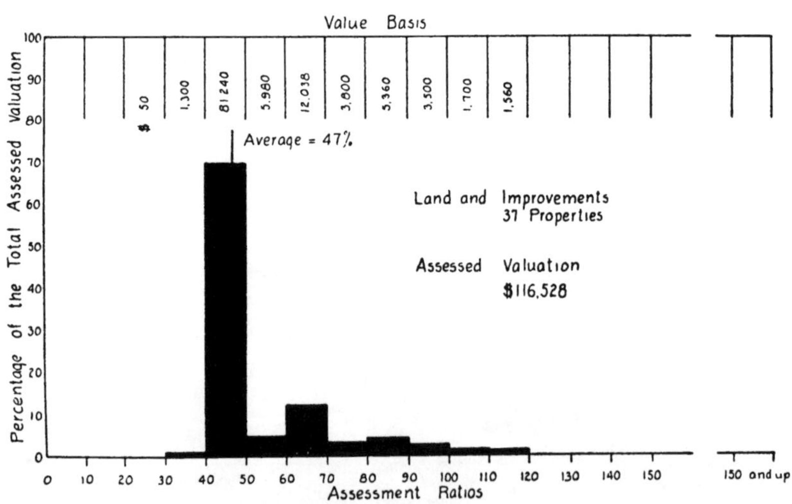

FIGURE 30. — COMPARISON OF ASSESSED VALUES WITH SALES PRICES IN PINE CITY, 1928–1929

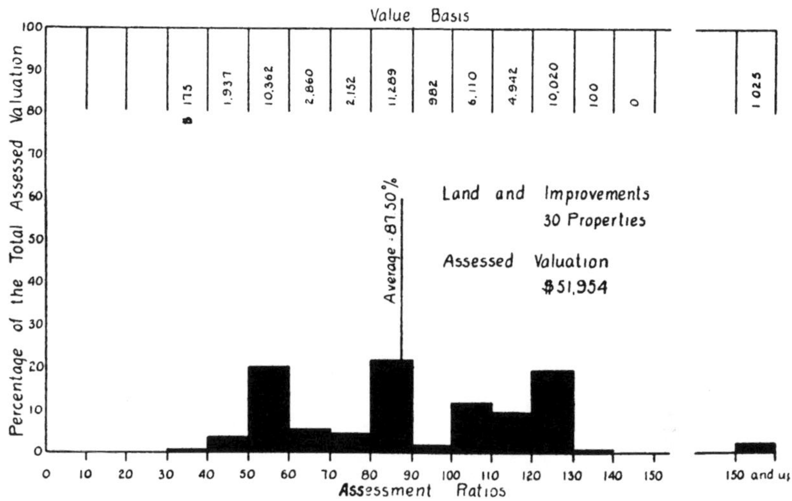

summaries of data for all are shown in Tables 2, 3, and 4. Table 2 presents data for 23 cities, for the most part the larger ones, and Table 4 covers data for 111 other cities and villages, most of which are small. Fewer samples were obtained in the latter cities; hence it appears to be statistically sounder to present them in groups, by population and by district, rather than separately. (See the map on page 38.) The data in Table 3, which cover 25 municipalities, refer for the most part to an earlier biennium, and they compare sales prices rather than appraised values with assessments. Later data for 16 of these 25 municipalities are included in Table 4. All the cities shown in Figures 3 to 30 are represented in Tables 2 and 3. (See pages 194 and 195.)

In judging whether the different cities pay their fair shares of state property taxes, comparison should be made of their averages; but in judging whether the citizens of a particular city bear equal burdens of local property taxes it is the scatter or range of assessments that is most important to observe. The range of assessments is shown in two different sets of columns. Columns 5 to 10 show the percentages of total property in the samples for each city that were assessed at the percentages of appraised (or sales) values indicated above the columns. For example, 64.7 per cent of the $22,620,103 of assessed value of the 742 Minneapolis properties in

TABLE 2. — COMPARISON OF ASSESSED VALUES WITH APPRAISALS AND SALES IN 23 MUNICIPALITIES[a]

City	Assessed Valuation of Sample	No. of Cases	Average Assessment Ratio[b] (Per Cent)	Percentage of Total Assessed Value of Sample Assessed at Following Percentages of Sales or Appraised Values[c]						Interquartile Range[d]	
				0–30	30–60	60–90	90–120	120–150	Over 150		
(1)	(2)	(3)	(4)	(5)	(6)	(7)	(8)	(9)	(10)	(11)	(12)
Minneapolis	$22,620,103	742	76.4	..	6.0	64.7	18.5	6.1	4.5	96.0—70.2 =	25.8
St. Paul	3,190,503	494	85.0	.1	11.7	49.7	26.9	7.0	4.6	97.1—70.8 =	26.3
Duluth	5,726,045	1,348	70.0	.8	34.3	37.1	14.0	11.5	2.4	103.0—64.6 =	38.4
Albert Lea	376,595	71	95.1	..	8.2	24.7	50.5	14.3	2.2	113.0—82.4 =	30.6
Austin	96,705	39	89.9	..	7.9	42.4	40.4	8.6	.7	106.2—80.8 =	25.4
Bemidji	288,733	185	95.6	.9	6.3	22.6	45.6	14.0	10.7	119.5—86.2 =	33.3
Brainerd	482,838	101	99.3	4.7	9.0	12.2	57.8	7.4	8.2	116.0—87.9 =	28.1
Cloquet	60,935	40	69.9	..	39.4	49.3	4.4	4.2	2.6	77.3—51.4 =	25.9
Grand Rapids	77,728	36	55.1	.5	69.7	15.8	7.6	5.2	1.1	71.9—39.5 =	32.4
Hibbing	77,962	56	59.0	6.8	44.3	20.4	5.7	6.7	16.1	98.7—43.1 =	55.6
Little Falls	103,530	77	89.0	.4	8.8	42.2	17.1	19.7	11.8	132.0—73.8 =	58.2
Mankato	364,393	122	104.6	1.2	12.0	23.8	34.9	24.0	4.0	122.3—73.5 =	48.8
New Ulm	321,283	111	98.8	.2	4.6	30.6	43.9	13.3	7.4	116.9—83.5 =	33.4
North Mankato	72,436	52	70.9	.4	22.5	46.3	18.2	12.0	.6	95.6—60.8 =	34.8
Park Rapids	83,686	72	94.7	..	7.8	40.7	37.4	8.4	5.6	98.4—71.6 =	26.8
Red Wing	412,675	137	86.9	.3	4.2	50.4	39.3	2.7	3.1	98.2—74.3 =	23.9
Rochester	1,498,906	533	85.5	.3	15.2	49.3	29.4	3.6	2.2	97.0—66.3 =	30.7
St. Cloud	402,621	198	73.8	1.8	22.0	45.5	22.0	1.0	7.6	96.0—60.6 =	35.4
St. Peter	103,312	49	97.1	..	15.7	26.5	27.0	5.3	25.5	150.0—67.8 =	82.2
Two Harbors	38,886	33	54.7	1.1	65.8	26.4	1.3	4.9	.5	80.9—46.4 =	34.5
Virginia	90,908	26	87.8	.3	19.8	31.0	24.1	24.8	...	119.9—64.0 =	55.9
Wadena	278,278	101	91.1	..	6.6	40.1	41.7	10.0	1.8	99.4—80.8 =	18.6
Winona	289,090	58	77.4	6.4	14.8	48.0	22.8	5.1	2.9	94.4—63.5 =	30.9

[a] Data for Minneapolis refer to the years 1928 to 1930; for other cities, assessments are for the years 1928 to 1931 and appraisals for 1931 and 1932, or of dates of sales where the latter are different.

[b] The assessment ratio is the assessed value divided by the sales or appraisal value.

[c] The figures in these six columns give the proportion of the assessed value of the sample in each city that was assessed at less than 30 per cent of its appraisal or sales value, the proportion assessed at from 30 to 60 per cent, etc. Thus 64.7 per cent of the assessed value of the Minneapolis sample was assessed at from 60 to 90 per cent of its appraised value.

[d] The variation in assessment of the central half of the sample. Thus if the central half of the property in a city were assessed at from 40 to 55 per cent of its appraised or sales value, the interquartile range would be 15 per cent (55—40=15).

TABLE 3. — COMPARISON OF ASSESSED VALUES WITH SALES PRICES IN 25 MUNICIPALITIES [a]

CITY	ASSESSED VALUATION OF SAMPLE	NO. OF CASES	AVERAGE ASSESSMENT RATIO [b] (Per Cent)	PERCENTAGE OF TOTAL ASSESSED VALUE OF SAMPLE ASSESSED AT FOLLOWING PERCENTAGES OF SALES PRICE [c]						INTERQUARTILE RANGE [d]	
				0–30	30–60	60–90	90–120	120–150	Over 150		
(1)	(2)	(3)	(4)	(5)	(6)	(7)	(8)	(9)	(10)	(11)	(12)
Alexandria	$40,670	30	71.7	..	13.0	70.3	12.0	...	4.6	83.1—63.5 =	19.6
Belle Plaine	25,750	25	88.4	..	16.3	35.2	37.2	.8	10.5	106.9—70.2 =	36.7
Blue Earth	62,400	34	82.2	..	11.1	57.7	21.3	8.2	1.6	101.3—70.7 =	30.6
Fairmont	166,167	79	87.4	.4	16.8	35.7	41.9	4.3	.9	104.4—67.9 =	36.5
Faribault	50,750	23	84.0	.7	6.9	63.9	15.1	13.4	...	93.0—75.1 =	17.9
Fergus Falls	60,770	41	69.4	..	26.8	56.2	8.7	3.4	4.8	79.6—58.7 =	20.9
Glencoe	62,460	27	81.6	..	12.2	55.5	18.6	12.9	.9	94.4—69.0 =	25.4
Hutchinson	73,742	28	86.7	..	1.9	54.6	30.9	7.5	5.1	104.2—75.4 =	28.8
International Falls	40,215	37	58.3	1.0	55.6	36.2	3.2	1.1	2.9	65.9—54.3 =	11.6
Litchfield	73,797	34	63.6	..	41.4	36.0	16.8	3.4	2.3	86.3—55.5 =	30.8
Long Prairie	26,970	22	92.4	..	12.0	27.8	45.0	3.0	12.2	98.2—76.0 =	22.2
Luverne	65,681	22	82.7	..	5.0	63.3	2.0	28.4	1.3	126.3—67.6 =	58.7
Marshall	95,850	33	85.5	1.6	22.2	30.0	10.2	33.9	2.1	132.7—60.7 =	72.0
Montevideo	45,690	29	83.9	.2	7.4	49.2	15.0	28.1	...	121.6—73.1 =	48.5
Moorhead	116,528	37	47.0	..	76.0	18.2	5.8	...	...	58.0—43.4 =	14.6
Owatonna	82,740	23	87.3	..	9.9	51.3	9.1	29.6	...	121.6—81.4 =	40.2
Pine City	51,954	30	87.5	..	24.0	31.3	23.2	19.5	2.0	116.3—61.8 =	54.5
Redwood Falls	92,200	35	85.5	..	8.8	53.0	31.9	...	6.3	96.9—74.8 =	22.1
St. James	32,930	23	72.5	..	22.6	55.9	10.8	6.5	4.2	84.3—61.2 =	23.1
South St. Paul	64,265	49	71.9	2.8	23.9	59.3	12.2	.9	1.0	78.3—59.0 =	19.3
Staples	53,305	40	68.7	..	40.6	27.3	11.6	6.5	14.0	102.6—53.6 =	49.0
Stillwater	38,210	20	83.2	..	6.5	59.6	25.8	2.3	5.5	93.7—74.9 =	18.8
Thief River Falls	50,280	26	89.4	.2	1.2	50.0	12.8	24.0	11.7	128.0—77.9 =	50.1
Tracy	54,600	26	107.2	2.6	4.2	13.9	54.8	17.0	7.5	119.7—100.0=	19.7
Worthington	156,712	47	106.4	..	3.0	28.1	35.2	16.3	17.5	128.9—86.1 =	42.8

[a] Data secured from the Minnesota Tax Commission's records of sales for 1928 and 1929.

[b] The assessment ratio is the assessed value divided by sales price.

[c] The figures in these six columns give the proportion of the assessed value of the sample in each city that was assessed at less than 30 per cent of its sales price, the proportion assessed at from 30 to 60 per cent, etc. Thus 70.3 per cent of the assessed value of the Alexandria sample was assessed at from 60 to 90 per cent of its sales prices.

[d] The variation in assessment of the central half of the sample. Thus if half the property in a city were assessed at from 40 to 55 per cent of its sales value, the interquartile range would be 15 per cent (55—40=15). See footnote 5, page 197.

TABLE 4.— COMPARISON OF ASSESSED WITH APPRAISED VALUES IN 111 MUNICIPALITIES, 1930 [a]

Group of Munici-palities	No. of Cases	Assessed Valuation of Sample	Average Assess-ment Ratio [b] (Per Cent)	Percentage of Total Assessed Value of Sample Assessed at Following Percentages of Appraised Value [c]						Interquartile Range [d]
				0–30	30–60	60–90	90–120	120–150	Over 150	
MUNICIPALITIES CLASSIFIED ACCORDING TO DISTRICTS [e]										
I	158	$954,141	82.07	.17	8.72	44.88	32.93	8.12	5.18	106.43— 69.99 = 36.44
II	254	1,269,930	86.83	..	8.79	40.22	34.33	7.00	9.65	111.86— 73.65 = 38.21
III	260	1,356,113	82.96	..	10.09	44.60	28.76	11.63	4.92	107.47— 72.51 = 34.96
IV	145	819,937	76.69	.19	21.02	43.70	21.10	8.08	5.92	105.08— 64.78 = 40.30
V	72	536,095	82.43	..	9.87	45.63	31.16	2.74	10.59	105.45— 71.72 = 33.73
VI [f]	11	35,165	75.14	..	27.39	59.11	2.70	...	10.81	87.36— 59.12 = 28.24
MUNICIPALITIES CLASSIFIED ACCORDING TO POPULATION										
Under 500	67	$182,608	94.11	..	12.76	20.98	24.24	14.06	27.96	158.59— 72.93 = 85.66
500– 1,000	176	659,888	88.83	.24	5.53	43.26	25.67	12.74	12.57	120.35— 74.68 = 45.67
1,000– 2,500	366	2,015,401	84.45	.06	10.34	39.93	33.78	7.33	8.55	110.93— 70.75 = 40.18
2,500– 5,000	159	1,153,680	77.16	.04	16.05	47.05	25.79	8.56	2.50	98.39— 71.05 = 27.34
5,000–10,000	119	875,104	77.69	..	12.73	56.02	24.85	4.93	1.46	101.65— 69.10 = 32.55
Over 10,000 [f]	13	84,700	104.57	..	....	9.62	83.77	6.61	....	108.80—101.70 = 7.10
All cities	900	$4,971,381	82.51	.06	11.36	43.65	29.78	8.17	7.00	107.72— 71.29 = 36.43

[a] Data secured by field survey.

[b] The assessment ratio is the assessed value divided by appraised value.

[c] The figures in these six columns give for each district the proportion of the assessed value of the sample in each district that was assessed at less than 30 per cent of its appraised value, the proportion assessed at from 30 to 60 per cent, etc. Thus in places of under 500 population, 12.76 per cent of the properties were assessed at between 30 and 60 per cent of appraised value; 20.98 per cent of the cases were assessed at between 60 and 90 per cent of appraised values; 24.24 per cent were assessed at between 90 and 120 per cent; and so forth.

[d] The variation in assessment of the central half of the sample. Thus if half the property in a city were assessed at from 40 to 55 per cent of its sales value, the interquartile range would be 15 per cent (55—40=15). See footnote 5, page 197.

[e] See the map on page 38.

[f] This group contains too few cases to be considered except as a part of the total.

the samples were assessed at between 60 and 90 per cent of their appraised values, and 18.5 per cent of these properties were assessed at between 90 and 120 per cent of their appraised values. The other figures show the percentages at which the rest of these Minneapolis properties were assessed, and the distributions for the other cities are shown similarly. The last two columns show the distributions by interquartile ranges.[5] The wider or larger these ranges, the less uniform the assessments.

Averages Conceal Inequalities

Examination of the tables reveals that a city may have a very high average and still have a very poor or erratic assessment because the high average is the result of a very low assessment of some property combined with a large over-assessment of other property, neither of which assessments is good. For example, in St. Peter (Table 2) the middle half of the samples were assessed at from 67.8 to 150 per cent; that is, the interquartile range was 150 per cent minus 67.8 per cent, or 82.2 per cent. This represents a very great scatter or lack of uniformity. It means also that one-fourth of the properties (on the basis of assessed value) were assessed at below 67.8 per cent and that one-fourth were assessed above 150 per cent of appraised value. Numerous interquartile ranges of 40 per cent or more show great lack of uniformity in individual cities. On the other hand, Wadena, International Falls, Moorhead, and some other cities show interquartile ranges of less than 20 per cent. This means more uniform assessments, though it will be noted that the averages in International Falls and Moorhead are very low. It should be remembered, however, that in cities where the number of samples is small it is not certain that they are fairly representative of all assessments. In such cases they are merely indicative.

Table 4, which with a few exceptions presents data for smaller cities and villages and includes a smaller number of cases from

[5] These interquartile ranges are the ranges of assessments of the second and third quarters (the middle half) of the properties. These are the two quarters divided by the average. For example, consider the interquartile range of Minneapolis properties in the table. The second and third quarters, or middle half, of Minneapolis properties in our samples, totaling $22,620,103 (assessed values), were assessed at between 70.2 per cent and 96 per cent of the appraised values. The average for this half as well as for the total was 76.4 per cent; but the range or scatter for this half was 96 per cent minus 70.2 per cent or 25.8 per cent. If all this half had been assessed at between 85 per cent and 95 per cent the assessment would have been much more uniform, since the range would have been only 10 (95 minus 85) instead of 25.8 per cent.

TABLE 5.—RELATION OF TAXES TO RECEIPTS AND EARNINGS OF CERTAIN URBAN PROPERTIES, 1930 AND 1931[a]

Properties and Year	No. of Cases	Gross Receipts	Gross Profits[b]	Net Receipts[c]	Tax	Assessed Valuation	Percentage Ratio of: Tax to Gross Receipts	Tax to Gross Profits[b]	Tax to Net Receipts[c]	Net Receipts to Assessed Valuation	Gross Receipts to Assessed Valuation
DULUTH PROPERTIES											
Total	159	$2,014,639	$1,094,559	$818,778	$423,578	$13,380,454	21.0	38.7	51.7	6.12	15.1
1930	127	1,608,312	755,571	533,709	306,363	9,569,829	19.0	40.5	57.4	5.58	16.8
1931	32	406,327	338,988	285,069	117,215	3,810,625	28.8	34.6	41.1	7.48	10.7
Properties reporting net receipts after paying taxes											
Total	113	1,506,665	981,450	806,313	334,351	10,533,009	22.2	34.1	41.5	7.66	14.3
1930	92	1,117,674	648,767	523,004	227,458	7,057,964	20.4	35.1	43.5	7.41	15.8
1931	21	388,991	332,683	283,309	106,893	3,475,045	27.5	32.1	37.7	8.15	11.2
Properties reporting deficits after paying taxes											
Total	46	507,974	113,109	12,465	89,227	2,847,445	17.6	78.9	715.8	.44	17.8
1930	35	490,638	106,804	10,705	78,905	2,511,865	16.1	73.9	737.1	.43	19.5
1931	11	17,336	6,305	1,760	10,322	335,580	59.5	163.7	586.5	.52	5.2

TABLE 5.—*Continued*

Properties and Year	No. of Cases	Gross Receipts	Gross Profits [b]	Net Receipts [c]	Tax	Assessed Valuation	Percentage Ratio of: Tax to Gross Receipts	Tax to Gross Profits [b]	Tax to Net Receipts [c]	Net Receipts to Assessed Valuation	Gross Receipts to Assessed Valuation
PROPERTIES IN CERTAIN MINNESOTA MUNICIPALITIES OF LESS THAN 30,000 POPULATION											
Total	108	132,970	98,208	73,818	33,613	915,774	25.3	34.2	45.5	8.06	14.5
1930	99	127,590	94,798	71,622	31,814	863,939	24.9	33.6	44.4	8.29	14.8
1931	9	5,380	3,410	2,197	1,799	51,835	33.4	52.8	81.9	4.24	10.4
Properties reporting net receipts after paying taxes											
Total	87	122,338	92,448	71,351	27,215	745,849	22.2	29.4	38.1	9.57	16.4
1930	82	118,928	90,283	69,662	26,301	719,549	22.1	29.1	37.8	9.68	16.5
1931	5	3,410	2,165	1,689	913	26,300	26.8	42.2	54.1	6.42	13.0
Properties reporting deficits after paying taxes											
Total	21	10,632	5,759	2,467	6,398	169,925	60.2	111.1	259.3	1.45	6.3
1930	17	8,662	4,515	1,959	5,512	144,390	63.6	122.1	281.3	1.36	6.0
1931	4	1,970	1,244	508	886	25,535	45.0	71.2	174.4	1.99	7.7

[a] In this table different properties are represented for 1930 and 1931.
[b] Gross profits = gross receipts minus all expenses except taxes and depreciation.
[c] Net receipts = gross receipts minus depreciation and all expenses except taxes.

each, shows that nearly all districts and nearly all population groups have rather wide ranges, that is, very unequal assessments within each group, though none of the averages run as low as for some of the individual cities shown in Tables 2 and 3.

As must be obvious to anyone who studies these tables, which represent 6,508 properties in 143 municipalities in the state, lack of uniformity between cities and inequalities within nearly every city give evidence of an extraordinary need for better qualified assessors.

Relation between Urban Realty Taxes and Income

Income data were obtained for about twelve hundred urban real estate properties, mostly for the one year 1930, though some are for 1931 and some are for both of these years. It is unfortunate that it was not feasible to secure more adequate and better distributed samples, though small samples were secured in 120 municipalities. More cases were obtained in Duluth than in any other city because of the unusual assistance given by Mr. J. A. Scott, city assessor; hence data for that city are shown separately in Tables 5 and 6.

It will be seen from Table 5 that between a third and a fourth of the Duluth properties did not earn enough to pay taxes. The properties for which income data were secured for both 1930 and 1931 paid an average of 57.9 per cent of net receipts for taxes in 1930 and 66.9 per cent in 1931. (See Table 6.)

The lower half of Table 5 shows a small number of samples from a few other cities. These would be combined with the data for

Table 6. — Comparison of Taxes and Incomes, 125 Duluth Properties, 1930 and 1931[a]

	1930	1931
Assessed valuation	$9,589,390.00	$9,398,725.00
Gross receipts	1,599,400.83	1,329,027.29
Ratio of gross receipts to assessed valuation	16.7%	14.1%
Net receipts[b]	$ 525,072.22	$ 429,260.07
Ratio of net receipts to assessed valuation	5.5%	4.6%
Ratio of net receipts to gross receipts	32.8	32.3
Taxes paid	$ 304,111.42	$ 287,276.89
Ratio of taxes to net receipts	57.9%	66.9%
Ratio of taxes to gross receipts	19.0	21.6
Net income capitalized at 6 per cent	$8,751,203.00	$7,154,334.00
Ratio of assessed valuation to capitalized net income	109.6%	131.4%

[a] In this table the same properties are used for 1930 and 1931.
[b] After deductions for depreciation but not for taxes.

TABLE 7.—APPRAISED VALUE, ASSESSED VALUE, NET INCOME, AND TAXES—PROPERTIES IN 111 CITIES AND VILLAGES CLASSIFIED ACCORDING TO DISTRICTS AND TO POPULATION, 1930–31

Group of Munici-palities	No. of Cases	Appraised Value			Assessed Value ("Full and True")			Net Income	Taxes
		Land	Improve-ments	Land and Improve-ments	Land	Improve-ments	Land and Improve-ments		
MUNICIPALITIES CLASSIFIED ACCORDING TO DISTRICTS									
I	158	$224,600	$938,032	$1,162,632	$218,518	$735,623	$954,141	$71,721	$32,067
II	254	288,600	1,173,925	1,462,525	271,041	998,889	1,269,930	94,312	41,997
III	260	325,780	1,308,850	1,634,630	319,534	1,036,579	1,356,113	106,612	48,044
IV[a]	145	208,715	800,410	1,069,125	188,171	588,516	819,937	80,075	32,682
V	72	151,950	498,450	650,400	133,540	402,555	536,095	42,723	20,003
VI[b]	11	13,700	33,100	46,800	11,425	23,740	35,165	3,721	1,732
Total	900	$1,213,345	$4,752,767	$6,026,112	$1,142,229	$3,785,902	$4,971,381	$399,164	$176,525
MUNICIPALITIES CLASSIFIED ACCORDING TO POPULATION									
Under 500	67	$18,390	$175,650	$194,040	$17,164	$165,444	$182,608	$10,386	$6,194
500– 1,000	176	108,350	634,550	742,900	106,064	553,824	659,888	44,838	20,990
1,000– 2,500[a]	366	416,425	1,970,107	2,386,532	408,696	1,606,705	2,015,401	165,773	72,383
2,500– 5,000	159	349,530	1,085,660	1,495,190	306,992	803,438	1,153,680	102,774	42,458
5,000–10,000	119	297,650	828,800	1,126,450	267,363	607,741	875,104	70,201	31,451
Over 10,000[b]	13	23,000	58,000	81,000	35,950	48,750	84,700	5,192	3,049
Total	900	$1,213,345	$4,752,767	$6,026,112	$1,142,229	$3,785,902	$4,971,381	$399,164	$176,525

[a] Because of differences in methods of classification, the total of "Land" and "Improvements" is not exactly equal to "Land and Improvements." For a map of districts see page 38.

[b] The cases are too few to use except in the totals.

TABLE 8.—RELATION BETWEEN APPRAISED VALUE, ASSESSED VALUE, NET INCOME, AND TAXES—PROPERTIES IN 111 CITIES AND VILLAGES CLASSIFIED ACCORDING TO DISTRICTS AND TO POPULATION, 1930–31

GROUP OF MUNICIPALITIES	PERCENTAGE RATIO OF ASSESSED TO APPRAISED VALUE			PERCENTAGE RATIO OF				
	Land Only	Improvements	Land and Improvements	TAX TO GROSS EARNINGS	TAX TO NET EARNINGS	NET TO GROSS EARNINGS	NET EARNINGS TO APPRAISED VALUE	NET EARNINGS TO ASSESSED VALUE
MUNICIPALITIES CLASSIFIED ACCORDING TO DISTRICTS								
I	97.29	78.42	82.07	23.66	44.71	52.92	6.17	7.52
II	93.92	85.09	86.83	22.96	44.53	51.57	6.45	7.43
III	98.08	79.20	82.96	21.69	45.06	48.13	6.52	7.86
IV	90.16	73.53	76.69	20.10	40.81	49.25	7.49	9.77
V	87.88	80.76	82.43	23.03	46.82	49.19	6.57	7.97
VI[a]	83.39	71.72	75.14	29.17	46.55	62.66	7.95	10.58
Average	94.14	79.66	82.50	22.20	44.22	50.19	6.62	8.03
MUNICIPALITIES CLASSIFIED ACCORDING TO POPULATION								
Under 500	93.33	94.19	94.11	26.22	59.64	43.97	5.35	5.69
500– 1,000	97.89	87.28	88.83	23.14	46.81	49.43	6.04	6.79
1,000– 2,500	98.14	81.55	84.45	22.22	43.66	50.89	6.95	8.23
2,500– 5,000	87.83	74.00	77.16	21.09	41.31	51.05	6.87	8.91
5,000–10,000	89.82	73.33	77.69	21.72	44.80	48.49	6.23	8.02
Over 10,000[a]	156.30	84.05	104.57	33.57	58.72	57.16	6.41	6.13
Average	94.14	79.66	82.50	22.20	44.22	50.19	6.62	8.03

[a] The cases are too few for consideration except in the totals.

other cities shown in Table 7 except that data in the two groups of cities were collected by different field men in somewhat different ways, with the result that while they are similar they are not exactly comparable. (See pages 201 and 202.)

Tables 7 and 8 classify samples of data from 111 cities and villages according to districts and population groups. It will be noted that the minimum percentage of net earnings taken for taxes in any group is 40.81 per cent and that in places of less than 500 population the figure is 59.64 per cent. The average for these properties is 44.22 per cent. The average percentage of taxes to appraised values for these properties is 2.89.

The assessment data obtained for urban real estate are fuller than those for agricultural real estate shown in Chapter 3. Both sets of data show erratic and extreme inequality. The income data for agricultural real estate are fuller and better distributed than those for urban real estate (see Chapter 4), a fact that should be considered in making comparisons. In all the cases presented, average real estate taxes in 1930 and 1931 took about a third of the net income of owner-operated farm real estate and about half the net income of rented farm and urban real estate. Most of the differences are among individual properties rather than between agricultural and urban real estate. The two outstanding facts are the high proportion of income taken by taxes and the unequal assessments, which make the tax burden all the heavier on those that are over-assessed.

CHAPTER 8

TAX ADMINISTRATION, WITH SPECIAL REFERENCE TO PERSONAL PROPERTY[1]

The general property tax is by far the most important source of revenue in Minnesota. It provided a sixth of the state revenues in 1931 and more than three-fourths of the much larger aggregate of local revenues.[2] Because of the important rôle that this tax plays and will continue to play in the economy of the state, it is especially important that it be well administered. The foundation of the property tax is laid by the local assessors. If their valuations are very unequal, tax burdens are unequal and the entire tax system is inequitable if not unsound. Chapters 3, 5, 6, and 7, as well as Chapters 8 to 11, indicate that assessments are far from equal in Minnesota; hence our tax system is seriously in need of improvement.

Efforts to meet the inequities and inadequacies of the property tax in Minnesota and other states have followed two main lines: first, the improvement of administration, and second, the substitution of other taxes for the property tax. Some of the substitute taxes have proved to be supplementary taxes, inasmuch as they have not generally reduced the former property tax very much, but have only relieved it of the necessity of full support of new as well as of old revenue requirements. Some of these substitute and supplementary taxes are discussed in other parts of this survey; this chapter will be concerned chiefly with attempts to improve the administration of the tax.

The main attempts to improve property tax administration in the United States may be classed under three heads: (1) separation of sources of state and local revenues; (2) classification and

[1] Most of the data in this chapter on Minnesota intangible and other personal property assessments were secured and analyzed by Mr. G. R. Treanor and assistants. Much of the subject matter of this chapter is treated more fully in Roy G. Blakey's *Report on Taxation in West Virginia* (1931), with which Professor L. A. Rufener assisted. Numerous points have been taken from the works of Professors E. R. A. Seligman and Mabel Newcomer, leading expositors of separation; Professors C. J. Bullock and S. E. Leland, advocates of classification; and others. For an outline of the Minnesota tax system, see the Appendix, page 576.

[2] An estimate only, since exact data for local revenues are not available. See page 580 in the Appendix.

differential taxation of property; and (3) centralized administration or supervision of administration. Minnesota has used all three methods; it has gone further than most states, particularly in the use of classification.

SEPARATION OF STATE AND LOCAL SOURCES OF REVENUE

The issue of separation has recently been raised again in Minnesota, this time by certain advocates of a state income tax and also by advocates of greater reductions in local expenditures.[3] By separation of the sources of state and local revenue is meant the assignment of certain sources of revenue to the state government and of other sources to the local governments. Separation may be complete or partial. It is complete when one class of sources is drawn upon exclusively by the state and another exclusively by the local tax units. It is partial when the state has one or more sources of revenue reserved exclusively for its use and shares other sources with the local units.

The ordinary method of separation has been to reserve for the state the taxes on public utility corporations, the inheritance tax, in some cases the income tax, and possibly some other taxes. The local units are left in possession of the general property tax, which is levied primarily upon real estate and localized tangible personal property. The principal arguments advanced in favor of separation during the early years of the present century were as follows:

1. The removal of the state tax on general property would eliminate the incentive to undervaluation by local assessors. Undervaluation is a device that has been used by assessors to reduce the burden of the state tax on their respective tax districts. And even if separation did not bring undervaluation to an end, it would at least do away with inequalities between counties in payment of the state tax.

2. Separation would be of advantage to the localities by giving them home rule, or local option, in taxation. Within their jurisdictions and for their own purposes the local governments could choose those taxes and methods of taxation best fitted to their peculiar conditions. Freed from the shackles of uniformity imposed from above, the localities might devise new and better methods of taxation.

3. Each tax could be assigned to that government agency best

[3] See page 519 with regard to Governor Olson's and other plans for distributing the proceeds of the proposed income tax.

fitted to administer it; for example, inheritance or income taxes to the state and taxes on real estate to the cities and counties.

4. The more efficient administration of the taxes assigned to the state, and the increase in revenue from these sources, would tend to relieve the burden of taxation on real estate.

5. Separation would permit the yield of taxes to be assigned to that unit of government the patronage of whose people occasions the value taxed. This argument applies, for example, to the taxation of valuable corporation property located in a tax district the needs of which are not in proportion to the value of the taxable property, as when a relatively undeveloped county includes within its borders long stretches of railroad tracks. Such property should be taxable for the benefit of the people of the state as a whole.

Having presented the main arguments in favor of separation, we may examine them critically and point out their weaknesses, noting incidentally a few positive arguments against separation:

1. The removal of the state tax on general property does not remove the incentive to undervaluation of real estate and personal property by local assessors; at most it tends in some small measure to diminish it. Undervaluation is the result primarily of causes other than the desire to reduce each tax district's share of the state tax. Each individual desires his assessment to be low as compared with his neighbor's, and each tax district within a county desires a low valuation of property in that district as compared with the valuation in other districts of the county. Since local taxes are greater than state taxes, most of the incentive to undervaluation still remains even if no state tax is levied on general property. The experience of various states has amply demonstrated, moreover, that in actual practice separation does not put an end to undervaluation. As will be pointed out later, state supervision of local assessment is much more effective in curing undervaluation than is separation.

Removal of the state tax on general property, regardless of its effect on local assessment, does abolish that particular type of inequality which arises from variations in the ratio of assessed value to full value among the several counties in the state. But the very separation of sources whereby this particular inequality is removed gives rise to the possibility of inequality of another kind — inequality between the rate levied on property taxed for state purposes and the rate levied on property taxed for local purposes only. This type of inequality has been a troublesome problem under separation in Minnesota, California, and elsewhere.[4]

2. Separation makes home rule possible, but there may still be state regulation of local taxation even if separation is adopted. Opponents of separation as a method of reform argue, moreover, that home rule is undesirable, since chaotic conditions often result when the various localities of the state experiment with diverse systems of taxation. Diverse systems of taxation in the several states already give rise to perplexing problems of double taxation, tax evasion, and the like, and diverse systems in the various tax districts of the same state would only make the confusion worse confounded. There is also the danger of majorities putting oppressive burdens upon unfortunately placed minorities. Experience teaches that more centralization rather than less is desirable in matters of taxation. The possibility of home rule cannot therefore be advanced as an entirely valid argument in favor of separation, although persons who desire home rule may wish to establish separation as a means of gaining their ends.

3. The argument that separation permits each tax to be assigned to the government agency best fitted to administer it has considerable force but can easily be overemphasized. If the state government is to retain for itself all revenue derived from those taxes that it can best administer, and the local units are likewise to retain for themselves all revenue derived from the taxes that they can best administer, we have complete separation of the sources of taxation, both in respect to collection and to use; but the revenue resources of the state and of the local governments will not be in proportion to their needs. Rather they will be determined by their relative efficiency in tax administration. Complete separation of the sources of taxation on this basis would produce inflexibility in the tax system.

This difficulty is overcome in part in Minnesota, Massachusetts, New York, and some other states by the distribution among the localities of part of the taxes collected by the state. When, however, part of the state-collected funds are distributed among the localities, separation of sources of taxation is no longer complete so far as disposal of the proceeds of the taxes is concerned, although complete separation may exist in respect to collection. In the case of certain taxes it may be most convenient for the government

[4] See Chapters 11 and 12 for discussions of proper rates of taxation on railroad and telephone companies.

that collects the taxes to retain them exclusively for its own use, but this is not advisable in all cases. Either the state or the local units might, under these conditions, obtain relatively too much or too little revenue. In short, it would seem that separation of sources of taxation as to collection only should be on the basis of administrative efficiency, and presumably it should be complete. After collection, however, that governmental agency, whether state or local, which has an excess of revenue in proportion to its needs should turn the excess over to the one which has a deficiency. It is difficult to fix the rates of all taxes equitably and to achieve such a nice balance that neither the state nor the local governments will have an excess or a deficiency. The experiences of Minnesota, New York, North Carolina, California, and other states illustrate this difficulty.

4. It is true that separation of sources of state and local taxation may reduce the tax burden on real estate, because along with separation new and additional taxes, such as the income tax or the corporation franchise tax, are usually developed and assigned to the state. The locally taxed real estate may thus be relieved of the burden of the state rate on real estate. But under separation it may happen, as in Minnesota, California, and other states, that some real estate is removed from the jurisdiction of the local tax districts to be taxed by the state, and thus the relief accorded by the removal of the state rate may be offset by the narrowing of the local tax base.

There is also the possibility mentioned by opponents of separation that when the local tax districts are relieved of the state rate, they will tend to increase the local rate up to the point where it will equal or exceed the former local rate plus the state rate, as the temporary relief of the tax burden may encourage extravagance It has also been argued that under separation the people through the legislature will increase state expenditures with the comfortable reflection that the rich, or the corporations, since they pay the special state taxes, will bear the burden.

Whatever the worth of these arguments, it may be noted that they are really arguments in favor of state administration of certain taxes other than real estate taxes. If the proceeds of such taxes should be distributed in part among the localities in respect to use — and this is the opposite of separation — the tax burden on real estate might be reduced even more than by complete separation.

5. The argument that separation would permit the yield of taxes to be assigned to that governmental unit the patronage of whose people occasions the value taxed, has some degree of validity when very valuable utility property happens to be located in a tax district with a small population that has no important direct relation to the property and no great need of revenue; for example, a hydroelectric plant or a railroad in a sparsely populated district. There are, however, logical difficulties in applying this rule to public utility property in a large city.

The full and proper discussion of separation would involve a treatment of all the fiscal and some of the other relations between state and local units of government. States usually require the local units to perform certain services, to levy certain taxes, and to stay within certain tax and debt limits; and in turn the states usually grant state aid for school, highway, and other purposes. The areas, main functions, and governmental administrations of most local units were laid out years ago. Since then changes in population, communication, and industry and commerce have been revolutionary in character and extent. Changes are likely to continue. Hence the whole question of state and local relations is a dynamic one and already encounters too much rigidity in state constitutions and in ordinary habits of thought. The discussion of these aspects of separation would require more space than is available.[5]

Several of the states that have adopted extreme forms of separation have since abandoned them or are now trying to abandon them for the reasons suggested above. Some other states with very moderate and partial separation are moving in the direction of more complete and rigid segregation of sources. But on the whole separation is not now regarded as the panacea it was once thought to be.

Minnesota has not adopted as rigid a system of separation as have California, North Carolina, and some other states; nevertheless, it has a very large degree of separation. Nearly all property taxes go to the local units, whereas the state gets its funds primarily from gross earnings and supplementary taxes. The local units share the state-administered taxes. In fact, the state aid to the local units amounts to much more than the property taxes that go to the state government.

[5] Fortunately, many of these matters are discussed in Professor William Anderson's forthcoming monograph on "Local Government and Finance in Minnesota," which makes unnecessary their treatment here, even if space were available

The two most prominent current arguments for further separation in this state are that (1) the replacement of the property tax levy by an income tax would relieve property and would prevent the income tax from becoming an addition to existing taxes and that (2) the elimination of the state property tax would make it clearer to citizens that the present tax burden of which so many complain is due primarily to local expenditures rather than to state expenditures.[6] If they paid no property taxes to the state it would be more obvious to them that the way to reduce taxes is to reduce local expenditures. These two arguments are not essentially different from those discussed above.

Conclusion as to Separation

A rather careful examination of arguments for separation and a survey of experience with it indicate that separation effects an improvement in the tax system primarily because it develops new taxes to supplement the unsatisfactory general property tax and places the administration of the new taxes in the hands of that governmental agency best fitted for the task, that is, the state. The real reform consists in the centralization of the taxing power. The separation is incidental, and may actually be harmful, if it is complete, by dividing the revenue raised between the state and the local units on the basis of administrative efficiency instead of fiscal requirements. In so far as separation is regarded as a reform in itself and causes the state to relax its supervision and control over local assessment of the property tax, local tax administration may tend to get worse rather than better. With or without separation, state supervision over local tax administration is necessary in the interest of fairness and efficiency.

CLASSIFICATION OF PROPERTY FOR TAXATION

Various economists and tax administrators, including those who are critical of separation, have advocated classification and differential taxation of property as an important means of improving the general property tax. They insist that different kinds of property should be taxed differently for reasons of expediency in administration if not as a matter of principle. Land will bear heavy levies, it cannot be moved to a more favorable tax jurisdiction; but personal property can be moved out, or may never be brought in, and intangibles can be hidden from the assessor. It is argued, therefore,

[6] See page 580.

that if taxes are made especially light on movables, particularly upon intangibles, owners will list them, capital and enterprise will be attracted, more revenue will be obtained than under higher rates which are evaded, and tax burdens will be distributed more equally. As a matter of principle, moreover, aside from the question of administration, most intangibles represent physical property already taxed, hence to tax them in addition means discriminatory double taxation.

At present in states that tax all property alike, few persons are taxed on their securities except widows and orphans whose property has recently gone through probate courts, some superconscientious individuals, and corporations that are compelled to make public reports of their holdings. To make matters more inequitable, the few securities that are assessed are listed at full value, whereas most other property is listed at fractions of its true value. The result is that in reality owners of securities are forced to conceal them or pay more taxes on them than do owners of equivalent values in land, livestock, merchandise, household goods, and other tangibles. Classification is held to be the best remedy for this situation.

Minnesota may be said to have adopted classification years ago with the substitution of gross earnings for ad valorem taxes on railroad property. This change simplified administration tremendously by obviating the necessity of valuing such property. This administrative consideration is still the strongest reason for maintaining the gross earnings measure. But classification in Minnesota is generally dated from the adoption of the "wide open" constitutional amendment of 1906. This made possible the mortgage registry tax (1907), the low rate tax on moneys and credits (1911), and general classification (1913).[7] Only four or five states besides Minnesota have general or comprehensive classification.[8] Most states, however, provide for the classification and low rate taxation of intangibles.

Effects of Low Rate Taxes upon Listing and Tax Yields

INTANGIBLES

The adoption of these low rate taxes on moneys and credits in this state was followed almost immediately by great increases in

[7] For a brief outline of classification in Minnesota, see page 576 below, or the Report of the Minnesota Tax Commission, 1926, p. 138.

[8] Montana, Kentucky, Virginia, and Ohio. J. P. Jensen adds Iowa to this list. See his *Property Taxation in the United States* (1931), p. 175.

the listings and by gradual increases in the revenues. The changes with respect to moneys and credits assessments and tax collections are shown in Table 1. Few other states have shown such favorable fiscal results from the lowering of rates on intangibles. In fact, Minnesota's experience has frequently been cited as the outstanding example and proof of the fiscal and administrative merits of this type of classification.[9]

TABLE 1.—MONEY AND CREDITS ASSESSMENTS AND TAX COLLECTIONS IN MINNESOTA, 1910–1931[a]

YEAR	NO. ASSESSED	AMOUNT OF ASSESSMENTS	TAXES COLLECTED
1910	6,200	$ 13,919,806	$ 379,754.00
1911	41,439	115,481,807	346,445.00
1912	50,564	135,369,314	406,107.00
1913	57,068	156,969,892	470,909.00
1914	73,266	195,549,307	589,644.00
1915	73,062	212,134,901	636,404.00
1916	74,219	234,186,268	702,588.00
1917	87,688	284,968,875	854,907.00
1918	98,502	330,300,219	990,900.00
1919	109,215	359,798,976	1,079,399.00
1920	127,471	437,628,871	1,312,886.00
1921	118,846	424,816,226	1,274,449.00
1922	109,081	400,688,948	1,202,066.00
1923	115,496	417,030,342	1,251,091.00
1924	109,969	405,480,155	1,216,440.00
1925	119,763	414,159,249	1,242,477.00
1926	115,190	414,072,314	1,242,217.00
1927	109,797	411,982,418	1,235,947.00
1928	102,720	416,914,484	1,250,743.00
1929	104,691	436,795,354	1,310,386.00
1930	98,961	441,920,557	1,325,762.00
1931	94,345	418,953,346	1,258,865.00[b]

[a] Reports of the Minnesota Tax Commission. [b] Preliminary figures.

It has often been asked, Do low rate taxes result in general listing or is there still much evasion? In order to get an objective answer to this question, a study has been made of inventories of the estates of deceased persons in the more populous cities and counties of Minnesota for the three-year period ending April 30, 1931.

All usable estates among those examined were compared, but many inventories had to be discarded because needed information concerning them was not available. After these eliminations there

[9] S. E. Leland, *Classified Property Tax in the United States*, pp. 144, 403; Jens P. Jensen, *Property Taxation in the United States*, pp. 177, 274.

remained 302 acceptable inventories for Hennepin County, 249 for Ramsey, 162 for St. Louis, and 92 for fifteen other counties of the state,[10] a total of 805 estate inventories from eighteen counties. (See Tables 2 to 7.)

It is unfortunate that so many inventories had to be excluded from the study. For example, one estate in St. Louis County was found to have money and credits assessments for 1927, 1928, 1929, and 1930 of $350,000, $450,000, $3,177,914, and $3,626,252, respectively. The owner died in September, 1929. Inasmuch as the assessments for 1929 and 1930 were made by the assessor in the name of the executor and were not independent valuations, this estate was excluded. One extremely unusual case from Ramsey County which could not be included contained taxable money and credits of $254,645, whereas the amount returned to the assessor on the preceding May 1 was over $2,000,000. In addition the same estate contained over $3,850,000 of nontaxable moneys and credits.[11]

TABLE 2. — MONEY AND CREDITS IN ESTATES OF DECEASED PERSONS COMPARED WITH RETURNS TO ASSESSOR IN EIGHTEEN COUNTIES, 1928–1931

COUNTIES	INVENTORIES OF MONEYS AND CREDITS			RETURNS TO ASSESSOR		
	No. of Estates	Total Amount	Amount Taxable	No. of Estates	Amount Listed	Percentage of Taxable Amount Listed
Hennepin	302	$25,590,320	$ 7,649,298	20	$ 879,030	11.49
Ramsey	249	25,204,964	11,171,661	64	1,436,802	12.86
St. Louis......	162	15,808,223	3,865,450	59	1,428,211	36.95
Total	713	66,603,507	22,686,409	143	3,744,043	16.50
Fifteen counties	92	3,490,174	1,693,070	36	481,864	28.46
Total for eighteen counties ..	805	70,093,681	24,379,479	179	4,225,907	17.33

Even in the inventories that were usable, there were many items about which there was doubt. These items were excluded from the list of taxables and designated as "Probably Taxable," "Probably

[10] Only the larger estates were examined in these fifteen counties, though they averaged smaller than those of the three most populous counties.

[11] Of course the amount of moneys and credits in an estate at the time of the owner's death is not necessarily the same as his holdings on the preceding May 1. It is assumed, however, that if 805 cases are taken, the average or total for the different dates probably will not vary greatly.

Nontaxable," or "Unclassified," as shown in the tables. In fact, every effort was made to exclude from the list of taxables all doubtful cases.[12]

The total money and credits in the usable inventories, the proportions taxable and nontaxable, and the number and amount of assessments are shown in Tables 2 to 7. It will be seen from Table 3 that only 34.78 per cent of the total money and credits in these estates was taxable, though 2.63 per cent additional was probably

TABLE 3.—PERCENTAGES OF TAXABLE AND NONTAXABLE MONEY AND CREDITS IN ESTATES OF DECEASED PERSONS IN EIGHTEEN COUNTIES, 1928–1931

COUNTIES	TAXABLE	PROBABLY TAXABLE	NON-TAXABLE	PROBABLY NON-TAXABLE	UNCLASSIFIED
Hennepin	29.89	1.04	57.95	6.84	4.28
Ramsey	44.32	2.52	41.37	8.49	3.29
St. Louis........	24.45	5.19	68.02	.97	1.36
Average	34.06	2.59	54.07	6.07	3.21
Fifteen counties..	48.22	3.37	39.25	5.91	3.25
Average for eighteen counties	34.78	2.63	53.30	6.07	3.22

taxable. The percentages taxable were much lower in St. Louis and Hennepin than in the other counties. Of the amount taxable, only 11.49 per cent had been listed for taxation in Hennepin and 12.86 per cent in Ramsey, as compared with 37 and 28 per cent in St. Louis and the other counties,[13] with the average of 17.33 per cent in eighteen counties. In other words, after eliminating doubtful cases from the group of taxables, so that the amount is probably understated, we still find only a little over one-sixth (17.33 per cent) of this amount listed with the assessors. Of the total holdings of money and credits, taxable and nontaxable, less than one-sixteenth (6.03 per cent) had paid the money and credits tax.

[12] As a matter of fact, the law should be clarified. Even the Tax Commission is unable to classify some items where there is no question as to the facts other than legal requirements.

[13] The percentage for Ramsey County and even that for the eighteen counties would have been affected considerably if the unique case cited on page 213 had been included, provided it alone and no other excluded cases to offset it had been included.

TABLE 4. — MONEY AND CREDITS IN ESTATES OF DECEASED PERSONS IN HENNEPIN, RAMSEY, AND ST. LOUIS COUNTIES COMPARED WITH RETURNS TO ASSESSORS ON MAY 1 PRIOR TO DEATH

(May 1, 1928, to April 30, 1931)

Classes by Amount Taxable	Inventories of Money and Credits			Returns to Assessor		
	No. of Estates	Total Amount	Amount Taxable	No. of Estates	Amount Listed	Percentage of Taxable Amount
Three largest counties combined						
All classes.......	713	$66,603,507	$22,686,409	143	$3,744,043	16.50
Under $1........	29	761,526	....	1	1,000	.....
$1– $1,000	95	1,116,611	48,104	7	9,233	19.19
$1,000– $10,000	331	9,144,962	1,332,966	48	217,938	16.35
$10,000– $50,000	191	12,753,603	3,988,459	49	626,033	15.70
$50,000–$250,000	52	15,335,502	5,247,816		889,485	16.95
$250,000–$500,000	10	11,068,126	3,902,873	38	1,402,244	35.93
Over $500,000...	5	16,423,177	8,166,191		598,110	7.32
Hennepin County						
All classes.......	302	25,590,320	7,649,298	20	879,030	11.49
Under $1........	10	432,987	....	0	....	.....
$1– $1,000	38	363,698	21,764	0	....	.....
$1,000– $10,000	143	6,124,847	609,568	6	7,880	1.29
$10,000– $50,000	90	6,316,946	1,923,582	6	40,900	2.13
Over $50,000....	21	12,351,843	5,094,384	8	830,250	16.30
Ramsey County						
All classes.......	249	25,204,964	11,171,661	64	1,436,802	12.86
Under $1........	13	180,569	....	0	....	.....
$1– $1,000	32	600,744	15,463	1	1,900	12.29
$1,000– $10,000	110	2,007,099	428,650	22	164,750	38.43
$10,000– $50,000	60	3,940,095	1,236,047	21	148,512	12.02
Over $50,000....	34	18,476,458	9,491,502	20	1,121,640	11.82
St. Louis County						
All classes.......	162	15,808,223	3,865,450	59	1,428,211	36.95
Under $1........	6	147,971	....	1	1,000	.....
$1– $1,000	25	152,170	10,877	6	7,333	67.42
$1,000– $10,000	78	1,013,017	294,748	20	45,308	15.37
$10,000– $50,000	41	2,496,562	828,830	22	436,621	52.68
Over $50,000....	12	11,998,504	2,730,994	10	937,949	34.34

If the inventories of money and credits are classified according to number of dollars taxable in each estate, we find a curious variation between the counties but a remarkable uniformity in the averages for the eighteen counties combined. (See Tables 4, 5, 6, and 7.) For example, in Hennepin County the largest percentage of taxable money and credits listed for assessment is found in the class of "Over $50,000" (16.30 per cent), whereas in Ramsey it is in the $1,000–$10,000 class (38.43 per cent), and in St. Louis in the class below $1,000 (67.42 per cent), though the $10,000–$50,000 class shows a relatively high percentage (52.68 per cent).[14] If the returns for these three counties are combined, we find the highest ratio of the amount assessed to the amount taxable in the $250,000–$500,000 class (35.93 per cent), with an average of 16.50 per cent for all classes. But when the returns from the eighteen counties are combined, all classes except the lowest are close to 17 or 18 per

TABLE 5.—MONEY AND CREDITS IN ESTATES OF DECEASED PERSONS IN FIFTEEN COUNTIES OTHER THAN HENNEPIN, RAMSEY, AND ST. LOUIS, COMPARED WITH RETURNS TO ASSESSOR ON MAY 1 PRIOR TO DEATH[a]

(May 1, 1928, to April 30, 1931)

Classes by Amount Taxable	Inventories of Money and Credits			Returns to Assessor		
	No. of Estates	Total Amount in Estate	Amount Taxable	No. of Estates	Amount Listed	Percentage of Taxable Amount
All classes	92	$3,490,174	$1,693,070	36	$481,864	28.46
Under $1	3	41,666	....	..	....	.....
$1– $1,000	9	95,749	2,806	..	....	.....
$1,000–$10,000	41	606,636	191,092	12	41,963	21.96
$10,000–$50,000	32	1,311,402	663,216	19	219,084	33.03
Over $50,000	7	1,434,721	835,957	5	220,817	26.41

[a] Data include one case in which death occurred on May 14, 1931.

cent. The minimum is 17.05 per cent; the maximum, 18.17 per cent. (See Table 6.)

These data indicate very definitely that although classification and low rate taxation of intangibles may have improved the administration of this tax greatly, brought in additional revenues, and set up Minnesota as the outstanding example of the success of classification, nevertheless this success in the one field in which classification is most generally advocated and insisted upon is not a record to boast of.

It is difficult to get complete data on this kind of property, but there is much fragmentary evidence to confirm that presented in the preceding pages. To do so one has only to talk with men familiar with this kind of property, compare listings of intangibles

[14] Note that classification here is by amount of taxable money and credits in each estate, not by total amount of money and credits nor by total amount of all property in estate.

with bank and other corporation statements, or examine what little published data there are on this subject.[15] If only 6.03 per cent of money and credits are taxed, or if only 17.33 per cent of those taxable are listed, in a good state, one may raise the question whether such property should not be taxed by some more successful method or removed entirely from the tax rolls. Inasmuch as the physical property underlying most of these intangibles is already taxed, perhaps they should not be taxed at all; or possibly

TABLE 6. — MONEY AND CREDITS IN ESTATES OF DECEASED PERSONS IN EIGHTEEN COUNTIES COMPARED WITH RETURNS TO ASSESSOR ON MAY 1 PRIOR TO DEATH

(May 1, 1928, to April 30, 1931)

CLASSES BY AMOUNT TAXABLE	INVENTORIES OF MONEY AND CREDITS			RETURNS TO ASSESSOR		
	No. of Estates	Total Amount	Amount Taxable	No. of Estates	Amount Listed	Percentage of Taxable Amount
All classes.........	805	$70,093,680	$24,379,479	179	$4,225,907	17.33
Under $1..........	32	803,192	....	1	1,000	.....
$1– $1,000....	104	1,212,360	50,910	7	9,233	18.14
$1,000–$10,000....	372	9,751,598	1,524,058	60	259,901	17.05
$10,000–$50,000....	223	14,065,005	4,651,675	68	845,117	18.17
Over $50,000......	74	44,261,525	18,152,836	43	3,110,656	17.14

the taxpaying capacity represented by them can be reached more equitably and practically through an income or other tax.

As mentioned above (page 211), Minnesota went beyond the classification of intangibles and adopted classification of general property in 1913. In so doing this state went much further than most states. This adoption of general classification in Minnesota (in addition to previously adopted low rate taxation of intangibles) was a curious perversion of a recommendation of the Tax Commission. Assessors in Minnesota, like those in other states, were competing with each other in the under-valuation of property, although the statute called for full valuation. As a result, great inequalities existed and ordinary methods of equalization were ineffective. Soon after the Tax Commission was created it asked the legislature to make it practicable for the commission to enforce statutory full valuation or, if that seemed too heroic, to provide for

[15] See the statement of Secretary Fiterman of the Minneapolis Mayor's Tax Commission referred to in the *Minneapolis Tribune* of July 31, 1932 (news section, p. 2).

uniform fractional valuation. It suggested 50 per cent for all property; uniformity was the end sought. The legislature struggled over the details for three biennial sessions, and finally agreed upon classification substantially as outlined on pages 576 to 579. This was essentially a crystallization into law of something approximating the normal practice before that time, though there was no such uniformity in practice as the statement might imply.

The Tax Commission has never justified the details of this classification. The commission claims, however, that it has resulted in

TABLE 7.—PERCENTAGES OF TAXABLE AND NONTAXABLE MONEY AND CREDITS IN ESTATES OF DECEASED PERSONS IN COUNTIES OTHER THAN HENNEPIN, RAMSEY, AND ST. LOUIS

(May 1, 1928, to April 30, 1931)

CLASSES BY AMOUNT TAXABLE	TOTAL AMOUNT OF MONEYS AND CREDITS IN ESTATES	TAXABLE	PROBABLY TAXABLE	NON-TAXABLE	PROBABLY NON-TAXABLE	UNCLASSIFIED
All classes	$3,490,174	48.22%	3.37%	39.25%	5.91%	3.25%
Under $1	41,666	....	...	100.00	...	...
$1- $1,000	95,749	2.90	.08	86.10	...	10.92
$1,000-$10,000	606,636	31.08	2.77	56.71	8.75	.68
$10,000-$50,000	1,311,402	50.25	2.32	41.47	1.58	4.39
Over $50,000	1,434,721	58.27	4.96	24.54	9.37	2.87

an improvement over the old situation: it can now enforce uniformity within each class, and while this is not all that was desired, it is better than the chaos that existed before. In other words, Minnesota already had special treatment of intangibles before this general classification. The main benefit obtained from the general classification was not from the increase of differential taxation at all, but from exactly the opposite, that is, from the measure of *uniformity* that this classification made possible.

HOUSEHOLD GOODS

In the general classification of property in Minnesota household goods were put in the lowest or most favored class.[16] This is an unstandardized class of property, and it is difficult to make a fair and comprehensive test of assessments to discover whether or not

[16] This excepts intangibles, which were classified before general property, and it excepts a later amendment which put farm implements and certain other personal property of farmers on a still more favorable basis. See page 576 in the Appendix.

classification brings about improvement in the uniformity and completeness of the assessment. Certain tests are possible, however.

Independent comparisons have been made in Minneapolis, St. Paul, and Duluth of assessments, insurance carried, and appraisals made by fire insurance appraisers and fire department officials. Besides data obtained from state and city officials, additional information has been secured from private sources. Admittedly, insurance on and appraisals of household goods or other property do not bear fixed and definite relations to full and true value at the date of the latest assessment. There will be great variations from case to case. But the data in Tables 8 to 14, including the averages, are indicative of the character of tax administration.

Our samples of household goods contain 913 cases in which appraisals were obtained from official sources in three larger cities and 893 cases from independent sources not allocated by location, a total of 1,806. Investigators were instructed to omit cases in which household goods were appraised at $500 or less, though they did include a few at $500.[17] The other cases range as high as $60,000, though the number above $8,000 or $10,000 is relatively small. (See Tables 8 to 14, pages 220–233.)[18]

The average ratios of insurance to appraised value, of assessed value to insurance, and of assessed value to appraised value, indicate that the samples are reasonably representative. There are differences between the cities and between the different classes of properties but only such differences as might be expected from other data shown in this survey and elsewhere.[19]

The most striking thing shown in these tables is the great number of the properties in each city that were missed by the assessor, even though most of the small properties were not included in the sample. (See Table 9.)[20] In St. Paul 72 per cent were missed. St. Paul shows the largest ratios of assessed value to insurance and of assessed value to appraised value, however, in the few cases that were assessed. Its showing is quite the reverse, however, in the larger percentage of cases not assessed; here the ratio of insurance to appraised value is lower than in the other cities.

[17] In Minneapolis, 19; in St. Paul, 15; and in Duluth, 3, a total of 37 out of 1,213; also 47 of these small properties among the 893 of the independent group.

[18] See pages 228 to 231 for details.

[19] See especially Chapters 3 and 7, parts of Chapters 11 and 12, and earlier parts of this chapter.

[20] The showing is a little better in the independent samples not allocated by cities. (See Table 13 on page 232.)

TABLE 8.—ASSESSMENTS OF HOUSEHOLD GOODS COMPARED WITH APPRAISALS AND INSURANCE CARRIED[a]

SAMPLE	PROPERTIES ASSESSED					PROPERTIES MISSED BY ASSESSORS		
	No. of Cases	Total Appraised Value	Total Insurance Carried	Total Assessed Value[b]	Percentage[b] Ratio of Assessed to Appraised Value	No. of Cases	Total Appraised Value	Total Insurance Carried
					Per Cent			
Minneapolis	206	$729,200	$442,850	$169,460	23.24	239	$463,750	$286,410
St. Paul	56	124,500	100,800	42,900	34.46	144	213,700	99,925
Duluth	125	357,567	261,506	87,836	24.56	143	374,063	260,000
Total for three cities	387	$1,211,267	$805,156	$300,198	24.78	526	$1,051,513	$646,335
Independent samples[c]..	521	....	862,750	338,440[d]	....	372	....	455,400
Grand total	908	....	$1,667,906	$638,638	....	898	....	$1,101,735

[a] See Tables 9 to 14 on pages 221 and 228–233 for fuller data and dates.
[b] "Full and true" value reported by assessors for May 1 preceding the fire.
[c] No fires reported in these cases. [d] As of May 1 of the year insured.

It will be observed that in Minneapolis and Duluth, where less than half of the properties were assessed, the "full and true" assessed value of those that were listed averaged less than 25 per cent of the appraised value; whereas in St. Paul the fourth (28 per cent) that were listed had a "full and true" assessed value of 34.46 per cent of appraised values, with some indication that appraised values were low. (See Table 9.)

Ampler and better data for all classes of property throughout the state would be desirable but enough has been said in this and other chapters, particularly in Chapters 3 to 7, to show that assessments in this state are far from what they should be. The available evidence in this and other states indicates that classification of intangibles brings about some improvement, but that if the administration is lax,[21] most owners do not list such property even if the rate is low. If we continue to tax such property as property we should take adequate steps to see that listing is general, instead of simply putting a law on the statute books and expecting it to enforce itself.

TABLE 9.—ASSESSMENTS OF HOUSEHOLD GOODS COMPARED WITH APPRAISALS AND INSURANCE CARRIED: SUMMARY IN PERCENTAGES [a]

	MINNEAPOLIS [b]	ST. PAUL [b]	DULUTH [b]
	Per Cent	Per Cent	Per Cent
Properties assessed	46.29	28.00	46.64
Average ratio of insurance to appraised value	60.73	80.96	73.13
Average ratio of assessed value to insurance.	38.27	42.56	33.59
Average ratio of assessed to appraised value	23.24	34.46	24.56
Properties not assessed	53.71	72.00	53.36
Average ratio of insurance to appraised value	61.76	46.76	69.51

[a] Based on Tables 10 to 12. Data in Tables 13 and 14 are not allocated by cities and hence are not included in this table. See the text for explanations. Assessed value is "full and true" value, not 25 per cent thereof.

[b] Minneapolis and St. Paul, 1930; Duluth, 1930–1932.

Leland has suggested the following devices for uncovering intangibles: checking estate, divorce, bankruptcy, guardianship, and trustee records; compelling corporations to pay taxes for shareholders in the state or to give information about them; requiring banks to file lists of collateral given as security for loans; compel-

[21] See Leland, *Classified Property Tax in the United States* (1928), and Jensen, *Property Taxation in the United States* (1931).

ling brokers to furnish accounts of transactions; and requiring the opening of safety vaults to assessors.[22]

As was mentioned earlier, the Minnesota Tax Commission has expressed the opinion that classification of general property has led to improved assessments, though the exact form of classification in Minnesota can be defended only as the best compromise politically possible at the time it was adopted. Though this classification ought to be changed, the danger is that change might result in as great evils as those that exist now. To begin comprehensive or radical changes would be to set all the conflicting interests in the state pulling and hauling against each other. Property values and business generally tend to adjust themselves to existing and predictable conditions. A stable and predictable tax system if not too bad makes for economic and social stability. On the other hand, no change means no progress. The happy medium is conservative but progressive adaptation to changing conditions. Fortunate is the state that can achieve this happy mean.

CENTRALIZED SUPERVISION OF ADMINISTRATION

Boards of Review

One of the most appropriate methods of striking this happy mean at the present time would be the improvement of administrative personnel and organization. Such improvements will now be considered.

Some of the evils of the general property tax, as we have seen, are alleviated or removed by the device of separation of sources of state and local taxation accompanied by the introduction of new and additional taxes as sources of state revenue. Some of its evils are likewise diminished or abolished by the device of classification, with low rate taxes on intangibles. But neither of these devices singly nor both combined will provide any state with a reasonably satisfactory tax system if not accompanied by effective centralized control and supervision over local assessment.

Fortunately, during the last forty years there has developed a strong movement in the United States toward such central control and supervision. The first step taken was the establishment of local boards of review and equalization by towns, cities, and counties, whose primary purpose was to smooth out some of the inequalities of assessment among individuals of the same tax district and, in

[22] *Op. cit.*, p. 146

the case of the county boards, inequalities among the tax districts of the same county. The creation of these local boards with their limited powers to wipe out the inequalities arising from inefficient original assessment was followed by the establishment of state boards of equalization for the primary purpose of securing a more equitable distribution of the state tax. The state boards of equalization were ordinarily composed of ex officio members holding other important state offices and burdened with too many other duties to give sufficient attention to the serious business of equalization. Moreover, these boards were given powers and jurisdiction wholly inadequate for the proper performance of their duties; hence they made little headway in developing a reasonably satisfactory system of taxation. A further hampering circumstance was the fact that frequently they were chosen for office for reasons or qualifications other than proficiency in matters relating to tax administration. Political considerations rather than sound and effective tax administration were too often guiding motives.

A further step in administrative reform was represented by the growth of state control of the assessment of corporate property, particularly of the property of railroads and certain other public utilities, including telegraph, telephone, and car companies. It was in the assessment of the property of these corporations that the farcical nature of local assessment without state supervision first became glaringly obvious.[23]

With the development of new and additional taxes to meet the increasing demand for both state and local revenue, it became apparent that more effective administrative machinery was required than the ramshackle system represented by unsupervised local tax officials plus ex officio politically minded state boards of equalization. This led to the introduction of the professional state tax commission, of which the first was that of Indiana, created in 1891. Minnesota reached this stage with the appointment of its tax commission in 1907.

The Local Assessor and His Work

Under the general property tax the most important single administrative feature is, of course, the original assessment by local tax officials. When assessment is done badly the evil results cannot be undone by equalizing and reviewing. It is universally agreed

[23] See pages 308–317.

that so-called good equalization can never be a satisfactory remedy for poor assessments generally. This is true because many equalization boards do not take their work very seriously. They commonly make few corrections except in the case of complaints, which are comparatively rare. Even these few corrections are not always made carefully. When blanket increases are made, they may be made to increase revenues rather than to accord with real values.

One very useful method adopted by the Minnesota Tax Commission in checking assessors' valuations is the regular checking of sales against assessments. This would be much easier and cheaper, and data would be much more complete if all deeds of sale were required to name the true consideration. If there is too much objection to this, each seller could be required to file a confidential affidavit that would be open only to the inspection of tax officials and the courts. This is a very little thing that offers large possibilities if properly used. A federal tax law repealed in 1926 provided for a tax on transfers in proportion to the amount of the consideration in each case. This afforded an opportunity to check sales with assessments up to that time. The federal revenue act of 1932 contains a similar provision and will be useful in this way while it is in force, though this law is presumed to be effective for one year only.

Local assessment is exceedingly important because it is the local property tax assessed by local officials that represents the heaviest burden on the average taxpayer in the United States, not excepting the average taxpayer in Minnesota. Removing the state levy on general property does not lighten this burden a great deal because ordinarily the state levy is only a small fraction of the local levies.

In view of the significant place that local assessment occupies in the tax systems of the various states, it is unfortunate that it is almost universally poorly done. The task of a conscientious assessor who regularly and carefully examines and accurately appraises all the properties in his district without fear or favor is usually a very difficult and thankless one; in fact, such assessment is impossible for one not qualified both by temperament and by training. The bad results actually obtained in practice are, however, often more the fault of the system than of the tax officials themselves. The faults of the system can be readily pointed out and practicable remedies for some of them can be suggested. Although political conditions preclude the application of an ideal system, experience shows that local assessment can be considerably improved, that it need not be so badly done as it usually is.

QUALIFICATIONS OF ASSESSORS

The greatest single cause of defective local assessment is the method of choosing local assessors by election for relatively short terms. The natural result of this method of choice is that a large proportion of the assessors are without special training or experience that fits them for their task, and they are subject to political pressure and biased by desires to favor their political supporters and their localities. The low compensation offered and the short tenure of office do not encourage men of great ability and proper training to run for office, nor do the voters always act with discrimination and select the best of the various candidates that enter the race. The evils of this method of selecting assessors are naturally greater in states like Minnesota, which make the township the tax unit, than in states which elect county assessors.[24]

Since the first requirement in obtaining a good assessment is an assessor qualified by training and experience to do his work, and since elected county, township, or city assessors are unlikely to be so qualified, there is a strong tendency for tax experts to recommend that the local assessor, a purely administrative official having nothing to do with governmental policies, should be appointed by the state tax commission. Since, however, such appointment of assessors is not likely to be favored by the people, it becomes necessary to compromise between political expediency and efficiency, and to get the best possible results from elective assessors.

It has been suggested that better assessors might be secured if the candidates for office were required to pass a qualifying examination demonstrating their ability to do reasonably good work in assessment, such examinations to be set by the state tax commission at convenient times and places. If such examinations were properly conducted, and if all assessing were under efficient state supervision, great improvement could be brought about. Salaries large enough to attract properly trained men would be a real economy under such conditions. But such proposals may be too advanced to receive immediate public approval.

A change to the county assessor system has been advocated persistently by the Minnesota Tax Commission ever since it was

[24] See page 607 relative to the qualifications of Minnesota assessors.

created. This improvement has the support of the best tax authorities elsewhere, but old habits and prejudices have so far prevented its adoption in Minnesota. Of course there is little merit in the county assessor system per se. Unless he is properly qualified, has qualified assistants, and works under proper conditions, a county assessor will not get good results. In any case, guidance and supervision by a tactful but firm state tax department is absolutely essential to uniform and equitable administration. Obviously, under present limitations it is impossible for the Minnesota Tax Commission to exercise proper guidance and supervision over 2,800 assessors who devote only a few weeks each year to their work. But if there were only eighty-seven county assessors and they were well qualified, and if the Tax Commission had a few good district supervisors, great improvements in administration could be effected.

The attempt to secure county assessors should not be abandoned, but if this change is to be postponed longer, it will be well meanwhile to take a leaf out of Wisconsin's experience and provide a number of full-time supervisors appointed by and under the direction of the Tax Commission.[25] The commission could in this way exercise tactful and helpful guidance without undue show of authority and thus gradually improve the entire system of local assessing.

PRESENT SYSTEM ANTIQUATED

We have reached a stage in our economic and social development where haphazard methods are no longer tolerable. The most successful business concerns carefully select their staffs and continue to train them afterwards. The more efficient state and municipal governments are following the same practices in more and more of their departments. Every sane person recognizes the importance of training for physicians, lawyers, engineers, teachers, and other professional groups. But in many places we are lagging woefully behind in the matter of public administration. In no field is this more important, in none does it touch us vitally in more places than in the field of taxation. We have tried palliatives long enough. Our tax system has now reached a situation where real reforms in administration are imperative.

Whatever good may result from devices such as separation and classification or from the adoption of substitute and supplemen-

[25] See page 492 relative to experience in Wisconsin. Some additional suggestions with regard to general administrative needs are made on page 24.

tary taxes, the most effective method of improving taxation in Minnesota is to revamp the administrative organization and particularly to provide for more adequate and systematic supervision over local tax administration. The burden of locally assessed taxes is relatively so heavy that when the local administration is poor the whole tax system is poor; and good local administration seems to be impossible without state supervision — supervision that aids the local tax officials and at the same time brings pressure upon them to do their work well.

The Minnesota Tax Commission has given valiant service. It ranks high among the commissions in the United States. It needs more support, however, in the form of funds and, most of all, a public opinion that appreciates and demands a qualified personnel and an adequately supervised organization from the bottom up. The people of the state may be assured that they will get on the average about the kind of tax system and tax administration that they insist upon and deserve.

Table 10.—"Full and True" Assessed Values of Household Goods in Minneapolis, Appraised Values, and Insurance Carried, 1930 [a]

Appraised Value of Each Property	No. of Cases	Total Appraised Value	Total Insurance Carried	Total Assessed Value	Average Assessed Value	Percentage Ratio of Assessed to Appraised Value
ASSESSED PROPERTIES						
$1,000........	14	$14,000	$9,800	$11,090	$792.14	79.21
1,200........	1	1,200	800	560	560.00	46.67
1,500........	23	34,500	25,600	16,460	715.65	47.71
2,000........	76	152,000	88,300	42,180	555.00	27.75
2,500........	12	30,000	19,500	6,780	565.00	22.60
3,000........	34	102,000	58,650	22,550	663.24	22.11
3,500........	3	10,500	7,700	1,820	606.67	17.33
4,000........	12	48,000	34,000	15,400	1,283.33	32.08
5,000........	10	50,000	33,000	9,680	968.00	19.36
6,000........	4	24,000	18,000	5,060	1,265.00	21.08
7,000........	2	14,000	5,500	1,520	506.67	10.86
8,000........	4	32,000	15,500	4,140	1,035.00	12.94
10,000........	7	70,000	31,500	16,040	2,291.43	22.91
12,000........	1	12,000	10,000	840	840.00	7.00
15,000........	1	15,000	5,000	1,360	1,360.00	9.07
60,000........	2	120,000	80,000	13,980	6,990.00	11.65
$3,539.81 (average)	206	$729,200	$442,850	$169,460	$822.62 (average)	23.24 (average)

Average ratio of insurance to appraised value: 60.73 per cent.
Average ratio of assessed value to insurance: 38.27 per cent.

Appraised Value of Each Property	No. of Cases	Total Appraised Value	Total Insurance Carried
PROPERTIES MISSED BY ASSESSORS			
$500........	5	$2,500	$4,700
800........	14	11,200	8,450
1,000........	61	61,000	39,300
1,200........	4	4,800	3,800
1,250........	1	1,250	1,250
1,500........	63	94,500	58,110
2,000........	47	94,000	53,300
2,500........	9	22,500	17,500
3,000........	18	54,000	31,000
4,000........	4	16,000	10,500
5,000........	6	30,000	18,500
7,000........	2	14,000	7,500
8,000........	1	8,000	6,500
10,000........	2	20,000	15,000
15,000........	2	30,000	11,000
$1,940.38 (average)	239	$463,750	$286,410

Average ratio of insurance to appraised value: 61.76 per cent.

[a] Appraised value as determined by fire insurance appraisers for fires occurring in 1930. "Assessed" value is the "full and true" value reported by assessors on May 1 preceding the fire.

TABLE 11.—"FULL AND TRUE" ASSESSED VALUES OF HOUSEHOLD GOODS IN ST. PAUL, APPRAISED VALUES, AND INSURANCE CARRIED, 1930[a]

Appraised Value of Each Property	No. of Cases	Total Appraised Value	Total Insurance Carried	Total Assessed Value	Average Assessed Value	Percentage Ratio of Assessed to Appraised Value
ASSESSED PROPERTIES						
$500........	1	$500	$1,500	$500	$500.00	100.00
1,000........	12	12,000	3,700	6,400	533.33	53.33
1,500........	11	16,500	26,300	9,120	829.09	55.27
2,000........	19	38,000	28,800	15,900	836.84	41.84
2,500........	4	10,000	6,500	2,120	530.00	21.20
3,000........	2	6,000	4,500	1,520	760.00	25.33
3,500........	1	3,500	4,000	1,100	1,100.00	31.43
4,000........	2	8,000	3,000	1,280	640.00	16.00
6,000........	2	12,000	7,500	1,240	1,875.00	10.33
8,000........	1	8,000	5,000	1,600	5,000.00	20.00
10,000........	1	10,000	10,000	2,120	2,120.00	21.20
$2,263.16 (average)	56	$124,500	$100,800	$42,900	$766.08 (average)	34.46 (average)

Average ratio of insurance to appraised value: 80.96 per cent.
Average ratio of assessed value to insurance: 42.56 per cent.

Appraised Value of Each Property	No. of Cases	Total Appraised Value	Total Insurance Carried
PROPERTIES MISSED BY ASSESSORS			
$500........	14	$7,000	$4,000
600........	5	3,000	1,400
800........	3	2,400	800
1,000........	55	55,000	20,425
1,200........	3	3,600	1,000
1,500........	26	39,000	22,600
1,800........	2	3,600	2,500
2,000........	19	38,000	25,300
2,500........	7	17,500	11,900
2,800........	2	5,600	2,000
3,000........	3	9,000	6,500
4,000........	3	12,000	1,500
8,000........	1	8,000	....
10,000........	1	10,000	....
$1,484.03 (average)	144	$213,700	$99,925

Average ratio of insurance to appraised value: 46.76 per cent.

[a] Appraised value as determined by fire insurance appraisers for fires occurring in 1930. "Assessed" value is the full and true value reported by assessors on May 1 prior to the fire.

TABLE 12.—"FULL AND TRUE" ASSESSED VALUES OF HOUSEHOLD GOODS IN DULUTH, APPRAISED VALUES, AND INSURANCE CARRIED, 1930–1932 [a]

Appraised Value of Each Property	No. of Cases	Total Appraised Value	Total Insurance Carried	Total Assessed Value	Average Assessed Value	Percentage Ratio of Assessed to Appraised Value
ASSESSED PROPERTIES						
$500........	1	$500	$500	$468	$468.00	93.60
800........	3	2,400	2,300	1,380	460.00	57.50
1,000........	7	7,000	6,100	3,216	459.43	45.94
1,200........	3	3,600	3,000	1,524	508.00	42.33
1,400........	1	1,400	1,000	456	456.00	32.57
1,500........	24	36,000	25,100	12,412	517.17	34.48
1,700........	1	1,700	1,700	948	948.00	55.76
1,800........	2	3,600	3,000	928	464.00	25.78
2,000........	19	38,000	25,626	10,952	576.42	28.82
2,217........	1	2,217	1,300	464	464.00	20.93
2,450........	1	2,450	2,000	450	450.00	18.37
2,500........	19	47,500	33,000	10,616	558.74	22.35
3,000........	15	45,000	31,700	11,552	770.13	25.67
3,500........	10	35,000	25,500	6,826	682.60	19.50
4,000........	1	4,000	2,500	1,732	1,732.00	43.30
5,000........	6	30,000	25,500	5,076	846.00	16.92
5,500........	1	5,500	4,300	712	712.00	12.95
5,700........	1	5,700	4,500	1,200	1,200.00	21.05
6,000........	1	6,000	4,000	460	460.00	7.67
7,000........	1	7,000	1,980	460	460.00	6.57
7,500........	2	15,000	13,500	6,556	3,278.00	43.71
10,000........	2	20,000	20,000	2,300	1,150.00	11.50
11,000........	1	11,000	5,000	1,624	1,624.00	14.76
12,000........	1	12,000	9,400	3,600	3,600.00	30.00
15,000........	1	15,000	9,000	1,924	1,924.00	12.83
$2,860.54 (average)	125	$357,567	$261,506	$87,836	$702.69 (average)	24.56 (average)

Average ratio of insurance to appraised value: 73.13 per cent.
Average ratio of assessed value to insurance: 33.59 per cent.

[a] Appraised value as determined by fire insurance appraisers for fires occurring in 1930–1932. "Assessed" value is the full and true value reported by assessors on May 1 prior to the fire.

TABLE 12.—*Continued*

Appraised Value of Each Property	No. of Cases	Total Appraised Value	Total Insurance Carried
PROPERTIES MISSED BY ASSESSORS			
$500	2	$1,000	$1.000
600	1	600	650
700	3	2,100	1,500
800	1	800	1,000
1,000	33	33,000	26,500
1,200	3	3,600	2,300
1,500	27	40,500	28,600
1,800	2	3,600	2,700
2,000	20	40,000	26,200
2,100	1	2,100	1,050
2,200	1	2,200	1,500
2,300	1	2,300	2,600
2,500	12	30,000	16,900
2,940	1	2,940	1,000
2,976	1	2,976	3,500
3,000	10	30,000	20,200
3,500	2	7,000	4,500
3,536	1	3,536	4,000
4,000	3	12,000	10,000
4,500	2	9,000	6,500
5,000	3	15,000	12,500
5,057	1	5,057	3,500
5,500	1	5,500	1,500
6,000	3	18,000	13,800
7,000	1	7,000	5,000
7,300	1	7,300	4,500
8,000	3	24,000	12,000
17,954	1	17,954	17,000
20,000	1	20,000	3,000
25,000	1	25,000	25,000
$2,615.83 (average)	143	$374,063	$260,000

Average ratio of insurance to appraised value: 69.51 per cent.

TABLE 13.—"FULL AND TRUE" ASSESSED VALUES OF HOUSEHOLD GOODS, COMPARED WITH INSURANCE CARRIED, 1929–1931

(Independent and supplementary data)

Amount of Insurance	Total No. of Cases	Total Insurance Carried	Properties Assessed			Properties Missed by Assessors		Ratio of Assessed Value to Insurance	
			No. of Cases	Insurance Carried	Assessed Value [a]	No. of Cases	Insurance Carried	All Cases	Assessed Cases
								Per Cent	Per Cent
$500	47	$29,200	16	$10,300	$8,440	31	$18,900	28.90	81.94
1,000	488	500,150	246	252,750	138,780	242	247,400	27.75	54.91
1,500	166	252,000	111	168,400	66,300	55	83,600	26.31	39.37
2,000	114	228,200	83	166,200	53,100	31	62,000	23.27	31.95
2,500	22	55,100	15	37,600	12,100	7	17,500	21.96	32.18
3,000	28	84,000	25	75,000	20,460	3	9,000	24.36	27.28
3,500	3	10,500	3	10,500	2,040	..	.....	19.43	19.43
4,000	8	32,000	7	28,000	4,960	1	4,000	15.50	17.71
4,500	2	9,000	2	9,000	1,660	..	.....	18.44	18.44
5,000	3	15,000	2	10,000	5,000	1	5,000	33.33	50.00
5,500	..	.....	..	.....	.....	..	.....	.....	.....
6,000	2	12,000	2	12,000	4,440	..	.....	37.00	37.00
6,500	1	6,500	1	6,500	2,600	..	.....	40.00	40.00
7,000	2	14,000	2	14,000	2,300	..	.....	16.43	16.43
7,500	1	7,500	1	7,500	1,040	..	.....	13.87	13.87
8,000	2	16,000	1	8,000	5,000	1	8,000	31.25	62.50
9,000	..	......	..	......	.....	..	.....	.....	.....
10,000	2	20,000	2	20,000	4,320	..	.....	21.60	21.60
12,000	1	12,000	1	12,000	3,140	..	.....	26.17	26.17
15,000	1	15,000	1	15,000	2,760	..	.....	18.40	18.40
Total	893	$1,318,150	521	$862,750	$338,440	372	$455,400		
Average								25.68	39.23

[a] Assessments of May 1 of year insured.

TABLE 14.—"FULL AND TRUE" ASSESSED VALUES OF MISCELLANEOUS PERSONAL PROPERTY IN MINNEAPOLIS, ST. PAUL, AND DULUTH, APPRAISED VALUES, AND INSURANCE CARRIED, MAY 2, 1930, TO JULY 28, 1931

KIND OF ESTABLISHMENT	APPRAISED VALUE OF CONTENTS [a]	ASSESSED VALUE OF CONTENTS [b]	RATIO OF ASSESSED VALUE TO APPRAISAL	INSURANCE ON CONTENTS [b]	RATIO OF ASSESSED VALUE TO INSURANCE
Foundry	$300,000	$17,720	5.91%	$200,000	8.86%
Foundry	25,000	4,240	16.96	15,000	28.27
Laundry	7,000	None	....	4,000	....
Hotel	3,000	400	13.33	2,000	20.00
Factory	500	None	....	500	....
Print shop	60,000	3,000	5.00	46,000	6.52
Confectionery	8,000	1,680	21.00	3,000	56.00
Clothing store	600,000	150,630	25.10	600,000	25.10
Store	4,000	None	....	2,500	....
Beauty shop	3,000	None	....	2,000	....
Overall factory	100,000	124,435	124.43	60,000	207.39
Recreation parlors	10,000	2,500	25.00	8,000	31.25
Beauty shop	10,000	1,200	12.00	7,000	17.14
Food manufacturer	7,000	1,920	27.43	5,000	38.40
Shoe factory	120,000	42,840	35.70	70,000	61.20
Restaurant	10,000	1,000	10.00	4,000	25.00
Restaurant	15,000	2,000	13.33	8,000	25.00
Clothing store	60,000	18,015	30.02	50,000	36.03
Auto polish manufacturer	3,000	1,040	34.67	2,000	52.00
Bedding manufacturer	10,000	11,145	111.45	1,100	1,013.18
Old rags warehouse	25,000	1,980	7.92	18,000	11.00
Paint shop	4,000	510	12.75	3,500	14.57
Barber shop	600	None	....	1,000	....
Auto paint shop	10,000	330	3.30	7,000	4.71
Filling station	800	300	37.50	600	50.00
Paper box and envelope manufacturer	70,000	6,150	8.79	60,000	10.25
Store	2,250	1,842	81.87	2,250	81.87
Auto supply store	22,469	None	....	16,500	.....
Fur store	4,500	None	....	1,500	.....
Store	1,000	600	60.00	600	100.00
Store	1,500	300	20.00	700	42.86
Manufacturer	23,461	15,957	68.02	22,200	71.88
Store	6,000	3,600	60.00	6,000	60.00
Manufacturer	1,000	None	....	1,050	....
Restaurant	4.250	801	18.85	4,000	20.02
Hotel	150,000	3,000	2.00	130,000	2.31
All establishments	$1.682,330 [b]	$419,135	24.91	$1,365,000 [b]	30.71

[a] Assessments made three months or less before date of fire. [b] Average ratio of insurance to appraised value=81.14 per cent.

CHAPTER 9

IRON ORE AND MINING TAXES[1]

The state of Minnesota is fortunate in possessing one of the principal deposits of high-grade iron ore known to geologists. Not only have the three ranges lying about the head of Lake Superior contributed the major portion of the iron ore used by the American iron and steel industry during the past generation, but in 1928, 22 per cent of all the iron ore mined in the world was taken from the relatively small area about Duluth. Since the first iron range, the Vermilion, was opened in 1884, nearly a billion tons of ore have been shipped from Minnesota to the blast furnaces. Although the richer mines are now being rapidly exhausted, it has been estimated that in 1926 about 1.8 billion tons remained in reserve.[2]

The importance of mine taxation in Minnesota arises in part from the size of the deposits of iron ore lying within its borders. But it arises also from the peculiar difficulties involved in applying the general property tax to such properties. It has been usual to assess mining properties at their capital values and to apply to them the rates of the general property tax. But although this was the original basis of mine taxation in the United States, there has been in the past fifty years a persistent tendency to differentiate ore bodies from other property. This differentiation arises partly from the economic peculiarities of mines, which, unlike agricultural and urban land, are productive only for limited periods, and partly from the administrative difficulties encountered in applying ad valorem taxation to these properties. These difficulties are inherent in part in the nature of mine deposits, which cannot in most cases be accurately measured, and in part in the tenure under which mines are held. A mine is always a speculation because no one can predict accurately how much mineral may lie beneath a given superficial area. This uncertainty increases the difficulty of assessment and it gives rise to the so-called royalty contracts

[1] This study was made by Mr. Glen R. Treanor of the School of Business Administration of the University of Minnesota. For critical and constructive suggestions and special assistance in presentation, the obligations to Professor F. B. Garver are especially great.

[2] O. R. Kuhn, "World's Iron Ore Resources Now Exceed 57,000,000,000 Tons," *Engineering and Mining Journal*, 122:84–93 (July 17, 1926).

whereby the owner of ore property, instead of parting with the fee simple to the mining company, engages to permit the extraction of the ore for a compensation of so much per ton.

The discussion of the problem of mine taxation, which has been carried on in various quarters for many years, raises the following questions: (1) Should mines be taxed by a method different from that applied to other property? (2) Should they be taxed at a higher rate than other property if they are taxed in the same manner? (3) If mines and minerals are not to be taxed in the same manner as other property, what method of taxation should be used? The purpose of this study is to seek an answer to these questions as they apply to the mine taxation policy of the state of Minnesota.

PRESENT STATUS OF MINE TAXATION IN MINNESOTA

The mining industry in Minnesota is now subject to three different kinds of taxes. Ad valorem taxes for state and local purposes are levied on the value of the real and personal property used in mining. Real estate in the form of unmined iron ore is taxable on 50 per cent of full value. Personal property in the form of mined iron ore is also taxable on 50 per cent of full value, but other personal property is taxed on 33⅓ per cent. In addition to the ad valorem taxes, the operator must pay an occupation tax of 6 per cent on the value[3] of the iron mined during the year and the owners of the mineral land are liable to a tax of 6 per cent on royalties received during the year.

PROBLEMS INVOLVED IN THE AD VALOREM SYSTEM

VALUATION OF IRON ORE IN THE GROUND

Under the ad valorem tax, the assessors are required to value mines at "such a price as such property, including the mine or quarry, would sell at a fair, voluntary sale, for cash." But a direct sale of an iron mine is seldom made; the ore is usually sold on a royalty basis.

At the present time, the valuation of mines is based on a consideration of future profits, the following factors being involved:[4]

[3] Certain specified deductions for most expenditures of production, commonly comprising from 80 to 90 per cent of such expenditures, are allowed in determining this value, which might more properly be termed "net profit." See pages 236, 247, and 250–254 below.

[4] For a description of the method of valuation see the Report of the Minnesota Tax Commission for 1930, page 46.

the tonnages and analyses of ores; the cost of delivering the ore to Lower Lake Ports, including the cost of development, mining, and beneficiation and the cost of rail and lake transportation; the market value or selling price at the Lower Lake Ports; the profit per ton; the present value per ton, obtained by discounting the profit per ton over the exhaustion period of the mine.

The three Minnesota iron ranges are considered as separate units because of the differences in type and structure of the ore and in cost of mining. The profit per ton is obtained by subtracting the cost of production and transportation from the market price of the ore. For costs of production "averages over a past period of years for each range are used," and variations from the average are determined in individual cases. The market value is taken as the price at the Lower Lake Ports, which is "assumed to truly represent all elements entering into the value of the ore, influenced as it is not only by the sources of supply, both domestic and foreign, but also by the demand for steel and its products." When, in the opinion of the Tax Commission, the market price at the Lower Lake Ports does not reflect the market value of an ore, a price is set that will represent such value. Average profits for each range are used as bases for valuation. The profits over the life of the mine, or exhaustion period, are discounted at a "proper rate of interest." The life of the mine is taken as the average exhaustion period of the whole range. This is obtained by dividing the total remaining tonnage of the range by the "estimated annual future shipments," which are based upon shipments of previous years. Occasional exceptions are made in the case of properties nearing exhaustion.

In the case of iron ore reserves, the same factors are taken into account as in the case of operating mines, but the commission also takes into account the fact that it would not be commercially profitable to develop and mine all deposits of ore in any one year. The rates of valuation per ton applied to reserve properties are therefore different from those applied to operating properties, even though the ores in the two classes of properties may be of the same character.

The official reports of the Tax Commission do not tell us what "past period of years" is used in obtaining estimates of the cost of production, nor what kind of an average is used— that is, whether the average is a simple average or a weighted average. The same is true of the price at the Lower Lake Ports.

ESTIMATING TONNAGE IN THE GROUND

The brief summary given above does not give a complete picture of the problem involved in the valuation of iron ore properties for purposes of taxation. Estimating the tonnage of various ore bodies is not a simple matter. The method of making an estimate may be briefly described. Prospecting for ore is usually done by sinking drill holes. Ore samples are taken at five-foot intervals, and these samples are analyzed. In this manner the depth and grade of each layer of ore and the thickness of intervening layers of other materials is ascertained. The outline of the ore body is established from the drill holes.

Difficulties arise in connection with the estimation of the tonnage of underground mines, especially where the drill-hole data are inadequate or entirely lacking. The problem is to estimate the depth to which an ore body extends below the bottom of a mine shaft. In the absence of reliable information to the contrary, it is customary to assume that the ore body extends one hundred feet below the bottom of the shaft. This rule is especially applicable to mines on the Vermilion Range. But there still remains the matter of the number of cubic feet per ton. This necessarily involves some kind of assumption. In recent years the Tax Commission has attempted to place a value on unexplored properties where adjacent properties are known to contain ore. In such cases it is necessary to make certain assumptions based upon the drill-hole records of the adjacent properties.

Because of peculiarities arising from geologic formations the accurate estimation of the tonnage of an ore body may be very difficult, even for experts. This is especially true of tonnage estimates on the Cuyuna and Vermilion ranges. Estimates may result in either over-assessment or under-assessment. The "remaining tonnage" decreased from 1,468,574,970 tons in 1914 to 1,228,003,755 tons in 1930, or 240,571,215 tons, but over 600,000,000 tons of ore were shipped from this state during that period. In Table 1 the tonnage assessed is compared with the actual tonnage, as determined by subsequent shipments from the mine, for a selected group of mines during the period from 1917 to 1931, inclusive. The figures seem to indicate that some mine owners, or the lessees, have paid taxes for rather long periods on iron ore that never existed. We cannot be sure of this, however, until the mines in question have been exhausted. It seems also that some mine owners or lessees

Table 1. — Comparison of Tonnage Assessed with Actual Tonnage for Certain Selected Iron Ore Properties in Minnesota, 1917–1931 [a]

(000 omitted)

Properties	1917	1918	1919	1920	1921	1922	1923	1924	1925	1926	1927	1928	1929	1930	1931
Arcturus Mine: SE–SW and S½–SE, S. 13 and N½–NE and NE–NW, S. 24, T. 56, R. 24															
Tonnage shipped in season	314	295	543	584	6	173	718	32	....	1,275	487	501	499	446	....
Tonnage assessed, May 1	7,424	7,405	7,111	6,832	6,307	6,301	6,175	5,798	5,773	5,773	5,773	5,815	5,495	5,105	4,737
Actual tonnage, May 1	10,616	10,301	10,006	9,462	8,878	8,872	8,699	7,980	7,948	7,948	6,672	6,184	5,682	5,183	4,737
Bennett Mine: NE¼, N½–NW, S. 24, T. 57, R. 22															
Tonnage shipped in season	784	871	552	576	350	605	778	603	633	656	612	499	738	512	....
Tonnage assessed, May 1	20,809	20,027	19,117	18,553	18,104	17,754	17,103	15,864	15,252	14,567	11,505	10,861	10,392	9,628	9,201
Actual tonnage, May 1	17,978	17,193	16,322	15,769	15,192	14,841	14,236	13,458	12,854	12,220	11,564	10,952	10,452	9,713	9,201
Chisholm Mine: W½–NE, S. 28, T. 58, R. 20															
Tonnage shipped in season	382	322	295	294	278	376	320	251	217	128	201	177	....	....	....
Tonnage assessed, May 1	3,058	2,586	2,266	1,973	1,743	1,583	1,082	842	596	519	386	198	154	154	154
Actual tonnage, May 1	3,399	3,017	2,694	2,399	2,105	1,827	1,450	1,130	879	661	532	271	154	154	154
Bruce Mine: E½–NW, S. 27, T. 58, R. 20															
Tonnage shipped in season	....	....	....	....	....	....	....	....	....	6	213	225	249	132	....
Tonnage assessed, May 1	9,446	7,443	8,238	6,525	5,647	5,647	5,647	5,647	5,647	5,647	5,283	5,013	4,747	6,368	6,193
Actual tonnage, May 1	7,020	7,020	7,020	7,020	7,020	7,020	7,020	7,020	7,020	7,020	7,014	6,801	6,575	6,326	6,193
La Rue Mine: S½–SE, S. 29; and NW–NE, NE–NW, S. 32, T. 57, R. 22															
Tonnage shipped in season	330	295	234	247	135	....	183	132	287	301	418	433	387	358	....
Tonnage assessed, May 1	4,723	3,495	4,457	4,096	3,974	3,814	1,740	1,557	1,220	932	952	542	954	558	278
Actual tonnage, May 1	4,026	3,696	3,400	3,165	2,918	2,782	2,782	2,599	2,466	2,179	1,877	1,458	1,025	637	278

[a] Taken from compilations of Mr. H. M. McCraw, a member of the staff of the Minnesota Tax Commission, and from the Mining Directory of Minnesota, a bulletin of the University of Minnesota Mines Experiment Station. Iron ore "in stockpile" was not included in "Tonnage assessed, May 1." This table is given to indicate the difficulties of assessing iron ore, which arise from the nature of the deposits, changing technique, and other unknown factors. It is not suggested that ores be assessed before they are discovered or before there is some practicable basis of valuation, or that when discovered they shall be assessed for "back taxes." See page 240.

Orwell Mine: S½–SW, S. 21; N½–NW, S. 28; NE–NE, S. 29, T. 56, R. 24															
Tonnage shipped in season......	....	....	....	....	....	....	....	....	....	....	....	....	201	151	....
Tonnage assessed, May 1.......	4,786	4,786	4,786	6,268	6,268	6,268	6,268	6,268	6,268	6,268	6,268	4,879	4,879	4,677	4,635
Actual tonnage, May 1.........	4,988	4,988	4,988	4,988	4,988	4,988	4,988	4,988	4,988	4,988	4,988	4,988	4,988	4,786	4,635
Scranton Mine: SW–NE and N½–NE, S. 12, T. 57, R. 21															
Tonnage shipped in season......	....	....	....	....	....	....	402	318	387	404	404	404	607	465	....
Tonnage assessed, May 1.......	18,046	18,046	18,046	18,046	18,046	18,046	18,046	17,643	17,325	16,937	16,152	15,701	15,169	14,577	14,111
Actual tonnage, May 1.........	17,506	17,506	17,506	17,506	17,506	17,506	17,506	17,103	16,785	16,397	15,993	15,589	15,184	14,577	14,111
Pioneer Mine:[b] SW¼, S. 27, T. 63, R. 12															
Tonnage shipped in season......	352	260	376	441	509	634	511	473	683	718	564	671	897	1,006	....
Tonnage assessed, May 1.......	5,194	4,839	4,507	4,356	6,817	7,206	6,799	6,409	6,194	5,550	4,948	6,943	7,780	7,109	7,449
Actual tonnage, May 1.........	15,551	15,198	14,937	14,561	14,119	13,610	12,976	12,464	11,990	11,307	10,588	10,024	9,352	8,455	7,449
St. James Mine: NE–SW, S½–SW, S. 3, T. 58, R. 15															
Tonnage shipped in season......	184	242	77	379	....	636	603	519	....	....	....	....	....	....	....
Tonnage assessed, May 1.......	5,794	5,670	5,429	5,306	4,941	4,942	4,293	3,716	3,229	3,535	3,535	3,535	3,535	3,535	3,535
Actual tonnage, May 1.........	6,179	5,994	5,752	5,674	5,294	5,294	4,658	4,054	3,535	3,535	3,535	3,535	3,535	3,535	3,535
Soudan Mine:[b] N½–SW; NW–SE, S. 27; SE–NE, NE–SE, S. 28; T. 62, R. 15															
Tonnage shipped in season......	150	124	110	142	78	131	136	59	98	129	158	164	161	140	....
Tonnage assessed, May 1.......	353	413	487	372	591	498	414	393	383	331	712	612	653	650	582
Actual tonnage, May 1.........	2,371	2,220	2,095	1,984	1,842	1,764	1,632	1,496	1,436	1,338	1,208	1,049	884	723	582
Union Mine: NE–NW, S. 9, T. 58, R. 17															
Tonnage shipped in season......	229	222	191	184	....	....	....	....	....	....	135	8	201	144	....
Tonnage assessed, May 1.......	1,116	878	656	552	368	368	546	546	546	546	546	440	408	314	169
Actual tonnage, May 1.........	1,488	1,258	1,036	844	660	660	660	660	660	660	660	525	516	314	169
Wabigon Mine: SE–SE, S. 17, T. 58, R. 19															
Tonnage shipped in season......	....	....	....	....	....	....	....	....	357	406	477	599	398	96	....
Tonnage assessed, May 1.......	7,910	7,910	7,910	7,904	7,904	7,904	7,904	6,107	5,998	5,641	5,208	4,757	4,721	4,017	3,921
Actual tonnage, May 1.........	6,257	6,257	6,257	6,257	6,257	6,257	6,257	6,257	6,257	5,900	5,493	5,016	4,416	4,017	3,921
Wade Mine: N½–NW, S. 13, T. 58, R. 19															
Tonnage shipped in season......	....	67	211	200	....	....	35	11	5	24	141	298	160	99	....
Tonnage assessed, May 1.......	2,140	2,153	2,925	2,729	2,534	2,622	2,622	2,611	2,611	2,561	2,342	2,201	1,902	1,639	1,460
Actual tonnage, May 1.........	2,918	2,850	2,638	2,437	2,237	2,237	2,237	2,201	2,190	2,185	2,160	2,018	1,720	1,559	1,460

[b] The Pioneer and Soudan mines are deep underground mines located on the Vermilion Range.

have escaped paying taxes on large tonnages as a result of an underestimate of tonnage. Eleven of the mines represented in Table 1 are located on the Mesabi Range, where it is comparatively easy to make reasonably accurate estimates of tonnage. The Pioneer and Soudan mines are located on the Vermilion Range, where the ore deposits are usually deep. In the case of the Soudan Mine, the mining shaft extends down 2,300 feet and the ore "in sight" seldom exceeds 400,000 tons. In the case of mines on the Vermilion Range, the ore is known only as it is developed by the progress of the underground workings, and it is impossible at any time to determine the tonnage that may ultimately be produced.

It is not suggested, however, that any ores or values should be assessed before they are discovered. In fact, the ores are non-existent from the standpoint of practical taxation until they are discovered and until economical methods of utilization give promise of rendering them economically profitable. Estimates of tonnage must be revised and new tonnages added or subtracted as more information is gathered. In some instances mines have been idle for considerable periods, yet the estimated tonnage has been changed because of additional information. This is illustrated by the tonnage estimates of the Bruce and Orwell mines given in Table 1. Frequently tonnage is added as a result of a change in market conditions or in the methods of mining or treating the ore. For example, large tonnages were added in 1910, and have been added since then, because it was discovered that large amounts of ore on the Mesabi Range could be utilized if it were washed.[5] In some instances certain low-grade ores were not included in the estimate because they had no market value by themselves. Later it was found that these ores could be used by mixing them with the higher grade ores in the mine. When this was done, shipments tended to exceed tonnage estimates. Finally, a certain margin of safety in estimating tonnage is perfectly justifiable. Estimates of "hairbreadth" accuracy would probably result in a great deal of injustice; that is to say, there would be more over-assessments. In spite of the difficulties noted above, the estimates of tonnage in the ground are probably reasonably accurate. The purpose of Table 1 is to illustrate the difficulties of valuation due to the nature of ore deposits, changing technique, and other unknown factors. The table is, however, somewhat misleading in that it

[5] Report of the Minnesota Tax Commission, 1922, pp. 30–40.

tends to show that overestimates and underestimates are equally common, whereas there are probably more underestimates than overestimates.

RELATION OF LAKE ERIE PRICE TO MARKET VALUE

No difficult problems are involved in ascertaining the cost of mining ore. These costs are made available to the Tax Commission by the reports required under the Occupation Tax Law, and they can be verified by the commission with comparatively little difficulty. But a real difficulty is encountered in determining the value of the ore. The commission uses the so-called "Lake Erie price," which is a series of quotations for ores of various grades at the Lower Lake Ports.[6] A controversy has developed as to whether these quotations actually represent the true or market value of the ore. Some mine operators defend the use of this price. They point out that long-term contracts for the sale of ore and commercial valuations for mergers are based on it; that sliding-scale royalty contracts use it; and that sales are actually made at this price and determine it. On the other hand, it has been asserted that the Lake Erie price does not represent the true market value of Minnesota iron ore, because only a very small portion of all the ore shipped from the Lake Superior district is sold in the open market. It has been contended that the price of iron ore is manipulated by the larger operators in order to reduce the taxes levied upon them. On the other hand, mine operators insist that the Lake Erie price does represent the market value of Minnesota ores.

Effect of consolidations upon price.—It has been said that the business of mining "no longer exists as a separate and distinct unit." "Mines, ships, docks, railroads, blast furnaces, steel plants, and mills have become so linked by purchases and mergers that for all practical purposes they are one single, integrated industry"[7] and "more than 95 per cent of the ore now is mined by the same interests who convert all, or nearly all of it, in their own blast furnaces."[8] In 1924 four of the leading companies in the ore business accounted for 73 per cent of all the ore mined in the Lake Superior district. In 1915 the same companies shipped 64 per cent. The

[6] Report of the Minnesota Tax Commission, 1930, pages 46 and 57.

[7] "Survey of Low-Grade Ore Deposits Important" (editorial), *Steel,* June 4, 1931, p. 34.

[8] "How Consolidations Affect Ore Prices" (editorial), *Iron Trade Review,* January 22, 1925, p. 269. This is also the authority for most of the statements in this paragraph.

increase in the percentage shipped by the group from 1915 to 1924 was due to consolidations. The question arises as to the effect of these consolidations, and the resulting concentration of control over ore shipments, upon the Lake Erie price. From the same source we find that "the price reaction has been opposite from that which might naturally be expected under the circumstances." Since the principal shippers are also large consumers, "low prices charged by them against this raw material have been applied to the open market, and thus have been of advantage to furnace interests less fortunately situated, although a disadvantage to small ore producers who have to meet sharp price reductions in quiet years."

Another characteristic of the Lake Erie price is its remarkable stability.[9] From 1925 to 1928, inclusive, it did not change; there was an increase of 25 cents a ton in 1929 over the 1928 price; and since 1929 there has been no change, in spite of the adverse business conditions faced by mine operators in 1930 and 1931. The tendency was for the prices of ore to follow the trend of iron and steel prices from 1919 to 1925, "when ownership of mines became more centralized in the hands of the leading iron and steel producers."

The volume of open market sales ten years ago was "about 5,000,000 tons, and in recent years, less than 1,000,000 tons."[10] The largest purchaser of iron ore in the open market is the Ford Motor Company. In 1928 the Ford Company asked for bids on about 400,000 tons of ore of various grades.[11] The company contracted for 441,000 tons in 1930 and for between 190,000 and 200,000 tons in 1931.[12] The total shipments of ore from the Lake Superior district in 1928 and 1930 were, in round numbers, 55,000,000 and 47,000,000 gross tons, respectively. Shipments in 1931 were 17,309,211 gross tons. Evidently a very small part of the total tonnage shipped from the Lake Superior district is effective in determining the Lake Erie price.

Definite statements as to the representative character of the Lake Erie price would be justified only after a more exhaustive study of the subject than is possible at this time. Certain weaknesses in the arguments advanced by the defenders of the Lake Erie price should, however, be noted. First, the mere fact that many contracts for ore are based on the Lake Erie price is not

[9] "Ore Prices Re-Established; Long Trend toward Stability" (editorial), *Steel*, April 23, 1931, p. 29.

[10] *Ibid*, p. 29.

[11] *Iron Trade Review*, March 1, 1928, p. 589.

[12] *Ibid.*, April 3, 1930, p. 117; *Steel*, April 23, 1931, p. 29.

important. If there are many contracts between subsidiary companies and their parent or controlling companies, such contracts must certainly affect the representative character of the Lake Erie price, for they are not made in a competitive market. It makes little difference what price is used in effecting mergers and consolidations so long as all merging mines are valued on the same basis. The fact that the Lake Erie price is used as a bookkeeping price by some large operators indicates only that they have confidence in the usefulness of that price, although it is difficult to see the relationship between bookkeeping and price determination. Finally, anyone who is familiar with price movements knows that a price with the remarkable stability of the Lake Erie price in recent years is open to suspicion.

RELATION OF ASSESSED VALUE TO LAKE ERIE PRICE

The relationship between the assessed rates (assessed valuation) per ton of the various classes of iron ore properties and the Lake Erie price is of some significance. The Tax Commission still adheres to the policy adopted at its inception with respect to the classification of ore properties. Class rates and groups are changed from time to time, but the classification in use during a certain period "represents the general average value of ores for that period," and the classification furnishes a "guide to be followed in establishing rates for taxable purposes, regardless of the fact that there may be as many individual rates as there are individual ore deposits."[13]

The assessed values per ton have not been changed since they were increased in 1920. The classifications were modified in 1924 and two new classes added to provide for properties in which the ore is of mixed grade and requires beneficiation and for properties requiring special treatment. Yet the Lake Erie price of iron ore has declined considerably since 1920.

In 1928 the mine operators requested the commission to "make a substantial general reduction in the value of all iron ore properties in the state,"[14] but the commission replied that time was lacking to make the necessary surveys and provide a new assessment for that year. But they added:

> The Tax Commission realizes, however, that the mining industry of the state is bearing a heavier burden, based on value, than other forms of taxable prop-

[13] Report of the Minnesota Tax Commission, 1930, p. 44.

[14] *Ibid.*, 1928, p. 135. They are requesting a 20 per cent reduction now also (October, 1932).

erty. . . . Finally, in the opinion of this commission, any reduction in the taxable value of iron ores that could be made under existing laws would afford but little relief to the mining industry. It is not so much a matter of valuation as it is of excessive taxation.[15]

The theory of the ad valorem tax is that the mines shall be taxed on their fair sales values. Since the value of a mine depends on the value of the ore that may be taken from it, its value would be expected to change with changes in the trends of ore prices, particularly if these trends give promise of long continuance. The Lake Erie price of Mesabi non-bessemer ore decreased $2.05 per ton between 1920 and 1931. Similar decreases took place in the prices of other ores. Moreover, the net taxable value of a ton of ore as computed for the levy of the occupation tax declined from $2.16 per ton in 1921 to $1.38 in 1929.[16] The reports of the Tax Commission show that the average assessed value per ton of ore (determined for the ad valorem tax) fell from $.2195 in 1920 to $.1914 in 1930. During the same period the reserve tonnage declined 106,457,028 tons. One cannot be certain that the decrease in the valuation per ton was due entirely to the decrease in reserves. Yet the rates of assessment per ton remained the same.

HOOVER SYSTEM OF VALUATION

Valuations based upon the Hoover system, used by Finlay in Michigan and in its modified form in Minnesota, have been rather severely criticized. One critic contends that "estimates of further extensions" of ore and of "the average content of valuable minerals" are usually nothing but guesswork; that the factor of average price to be obtained for the product in the future is a "presumption and nothing else"; and that the other factors are estimates subject to many errors.[17] He concludes that not even the most ardent "advocates of mine taxation on a valuation basis" can "contend that an equitable distribution of tax burdens can be accomplished by this method."[18] Another objection is that assessments based on the methods in use in Minnesota and Michigan "put a tax on the development of reserve ore, inactive mines, in advance of present

[15] Report of the Minnesota Tax Commission, 1928, p. 139.

[16] *Ibid.*, 1930, p. 97.

[17] Heath Steele, "Mine Taxation," *Engineering and Mining Journal*, 98:381 (1914).

[18] Steele, *op. cit.* For further argument against this system of valuation see O. D. Skelton, "The Taxation of Mineral Resources in Canada," Proceedings of the National Tax Association, 2:392 (1908); and E. D. Boyle, "Mine Taxation," Proceedings of the National Tax Association, 9:86 (1915).

workings, and consequently operate to the detriment of an efficient and progressive company."[19]

The arguments of the proponents of the ad valorem method of taxing mining properties, with valuations based upon the Hoover method, have been forcefully presented in the reports of two committees on mineral taxation to the National Tax Association in 1913 and in 1920.[20] The committee reporting in 1920 expressed its opinion as follows: "If, then, mines should pay to state and local governments a tax commensurate with that paid by other real estate, how should the tax on mines be imposed and collected? Our answer is, in precisely the same manner that taxes are imposed and collected on other real estate."

Arguments in favor of the ad valorem system presented by the committee are as follows:

1. The equalization of the taxes "on mines with those on other real estate requires that no exception be made in the case of mines."

2. If the ad valorem tax on mines "is abandoned in favor of a tax on income or product, the local community will lose control of its main source of revenue, and in lieu of the ad valorem tax it will receive such portion of the tax on income or product as may be prorated to it by the state; and this portion will be an annually fluctuating sum, large in periods of flush production, small in periods when the mines are operating at part capacity, and nothing at all when the mines are closed." The interests of the "local taxing jurisdictions are paramount in any system of taxation devised for the American state."

3. The committee was not impressed with the claim that "ad valorem taxation for revenue only, at the same rate as other real estate, restrains to a too serious extent the development of the ore reserves in advance of current requirements and discourages exploration for and development of new mines," for "after all the tax is merely an element of cost and will be reckoned with precisely as other costs are." Hence there is no "pyramiding of the taxes on unmined mineral as an actual fact of accounting and finance."

The method of ascertaining the taxable value of mines in

[19] W. L. Uglow, *A Study of Methods of Mine Valuation and Assessment with Special Reference to the Zinc Mines of Southwestern Wisconsin* (Wisconsin Geological and Natural History Survey Bulletin No. 41, Economic Series No. 18, Madison, Wisconsin, 1914), p. 42.

[20] "Report of Committee on Taxation of Mines and Mineral Lands," Proceedings of the National Tax Association, 7:387 (1913); "Report of Special Committee on Mine Taxation," *ibid.*, 13:406 (1920).

Michigan, Minnesota, and Wisconsin has had the general approval of mine operators in the Lake Superior district. In 1920 the leading operators of the district submitted to the United States Bureau of Internal Revenue recommendations for the valuation of ore properties.[21] These recommendations were based on the Hoover method of valuation.

Administration of the Occupation Tax

The Occupation Tax Law had hardly come into operation in 1922 when it was attacked in the federal courts. But a year later its validity was sustained by the United States Supreme Court.[22] The commission then determined the amount of the tax due for the years 1921 and 1922. The policy pursued by the commission in administering the Occupation Tax Law is set forth in the following quotation from its biennial report in 1924:

> In construing the law, however, the commission resolved every reasonable doubt in favor of the state. As a result, there was a wide difference of opinion between the commission and the mining companies as to the amount of tax due under the law, but the commission persisted in its own construction of the law and certified taxes on that basis. . . .
>
> The total difference for the two years in the figures of net taxable values of mining companies and the tax commission amounted to $49,271,996, with a difference in taxes of $2,956,319.[23]

The following excerpt from the same report illustrates the administrative problems involved in the enforcement of the Occupation Tax Law:

> Shortly after the taxes were certified to the state auditor and state treasurer, the mining companies filed petitions with the commission requesting deductions in taxable values of more than $10,000,000 and aggregating more than $600,000 in taxes. They also asked for the abatement of penalties attempted to be imposed under the law. The principal allegations of the petitioners were that the published Lake Erie base values, which had been used by the commission, were higher than the actual prices for which the ore sold; that large quantities of ore were sold on long-time contracts at much less than the published market price, and payments made, therefore, in monthly instalments extending over twelve months' period; that no allowance had been made for excess silica, which reduces the value of the ore; that proper allowance had not been made for depreciation of plant and equipment; that a loss in one mine had not been offset against the profit of another mine operated by the same company; that no allowance had been made for actual commissions paid for selling the ore, for cargo analysis, or for personal property taxes paid on stockpiles and movable mine equipment assessed as personal property; that penalties could not be imposed under the law and decisions of the courts until the amount of the tax had been ascertained and an opportunity to pay the same given the taxpayer.[24]

[21] "Outline Iron Mine Tax Methods" (editorial), *Iron Trade Review,* March 11, 1920, p. 788.

[22] 262 U. S. 172 (1923).

[23] Report of the Minnesota Tax Commission, 1924, pp. 98, 99.

[24] *Ibid.,* p. 99.

Some of these questions have been settled by amendments to the law, others by decisions of the Supreme Court of this state.

The Tax on Royalties

The tax on royalties received "for permission to explore, mine, take out, and remove ore from land in this state" presents no complex administrative problems.[25] In fact, most of the problems arising in connection with royalties have been those relating to the occupation tax. In theory the royalty tax is a direct tax upon the lessors or other persons owning interests in ore lands from which royalty is received for the privileges of mining. In actual practice we find that most of the royalty taxes are paid by the mine operators. Such items as "minimum royalties" and "royalty bonuses," which were paid before the enactment of the Royalty Tax Law, cannot be taxed under that law, although they have been held to be deductible as royalty under the Occupation Tax Law. At the present time attempts are being made to impose the tax on "royalty commissions." These commissions are paid for services rendered to fee owners or others in negotiating mineral leases. They are usually assumed by the operating lessee. From the point of view of the lessee-operator, the payments are "royalty" and should therefore be deducted in determining the occupation tax. There is considerable doubt as to whether they can be taxed as "royalty." In some instances royalty payments are made either before or after mining, but if the tax is not levied in one year it is levied in another, and the state ultimately receives the same revenue. From what has been said thus far, it is clear that the annual royalty tax cannot be levied upon the same amount of royalty as is deducted in the same year in determining the occupation tax.

Reasons for Special Mine Taxation

The special taxes levied on the mining industry were the outgrowth of a general opinion in certain parts of the state that the mining companies were not required to pay as much as they should under the general property tax then in force. The natural heritage and diminishing value theories, and especially the belief that foreign corporations made large profits from Minnesota ores, probably had much to do with creating a public opinion in favor of special mine taxation. This opinion first found expression in the

[25] The following discussion of the royalty tax is based on the Tax Commission's report for 1930, pages 101–102.

Classified Assessment Law, which provided that iron ore, both mined and unmined, should be valued and assessed at a higher percentage of full and true value than any other form of property. But the extra burden put upon the mining industry by this provision was not sufficient to satisfy the demand. It was therefore urged that a special tax, in addition to all other taxes, be levied on the industry. The product of this agitation was the Occupation Tax Law of 1921 and its complement, the Royalty Tax Law of 1923.

The arguments for and against a special or additional tax on the mining industry in Minnesota have been elaborately presented by the Tax Commission in its biennial report for 1920 and need not be repeated here.[26]

At different times different arguments have been advanced to justify unusually heavy taxes on mines. The so-called "natural heritage" argument asserts that because the mines are a gift of nature they should be subject to heavier taxes than property that has been created by human effort and saving. But the same argument would apply also to agricultural land and to manufacturing sites on navigable waters, as well as to forests. It might even be logically extended to cover the earnings of human beings who possess unusual talents that are the result of inherited characteristics. A more practical view of the problem must, moreover, take account of the fact that the development of a mining center adds to the opportunities for labor, merchandising, transportation, and all other economic enterprises. It must be remembered too that mining is usually a speculative venture, more hazardous to capital than are most economic activities. Too often men are inclined to look only at the enormous profits made in successful ventures and to ignore the losses of the unsuccessful. Our conclusion is that the natural heritage argument is not a strong one and that it does not of itself justify heavier taxation of mines.

Somewhat more substantial is the contention that because mining exhausts the wealth that is both the support of all private enterprise and the revenue of the state, a severance tax should be imposed. As far as the state is concerned, this tax should not be regarded as revenue for current expenditures but as a trust fund to be invested for the benefit of future generations.[27] But it must be

[26] Page 27. See also Paul Armitage, "Tax Problems in Relation to Reserves and Depletion of Natural Resources," *Mining Congress Journal*, 10:251.

[27] Cf. Roy G. Blakey, *Report on Taxation in West Virginia*, p. 155.

TABLE 2.—COMPARISON OF TOTAL VALUE OF IRON ORE SHIPMENTS, TOTAL TAXES LEVIED, AND RATIO OF TAXES TO VALUE IN MICHIGAN AND MINNESOTA, 1920–1929

YEAR	VALUE OF ORE SHIPPED [a] (000 OMITTED)		TOTAL STATE AND LOCAL TAXES LEVIED [b] (000 OMITTED)		PERCENTAGE RATIO OF TAXES TO VALUE	
	Michigan	Minnesota	Michigan	Minnesota	Michigan	Minnesota
1920......	$85,749	$163,538	$3,799	$20,840	4.43	12.74
1921......	18,481	62,781	4,044	20,423	21.88	32.53
1922......	43,450	98,903	3,931	21,852	9.05	22.09
1923......	54,110	158,403	3,999	26,810	7.39	16.93
1924......	36,606	93,311	4,125	22,492	11.27	24.10
1925......	40,926	96,083	3,688	21,732	9.01	22.62
1926......	43,933	103,716	3,975	20,904	9.05	20.16
1927......	37,135	87,935	3,879	20,443	10.45	23.25
1928......	37,040	94,259	3,569	20,190	9.64	21.42
1929......	47,598	121,776	3,708	22,083	7.79	18.13
Average for 10 years	$44,503	$108,071	$3,872	$21,777	8.70	20.15

[a] Data are from the United States Department of Commerce, Bureau of Mines, *Mineral Resources of the United States.* "Value of ore shipped" is value "at the mine."

[b] Data for Michigan were supplied by Mr. F. G. Pardee, mine appraiser, Michigan Department of Conservation, Geological Division. Data for Minnesota are from the reports of the Minnesota Tax Commission.

admitted that it is difficult to discover any method by which the state could preserve intact the wealth originally existent within its borders. Moreover, the history of public trust funds does not warrant placing too much reliance upon them.

Finally, one further authority may properly be quoted. The National Tax Association Committee on Mines Taxation of 1920 stated its opinion of super-taxes as follows:

> We believe that mines should be taxed for revenue only and condemn the super-taxation of mines on the one hand, and on the other hand, exemption or under-taxation. A classification of real estate for taxation opens the door to exploitation of the numerically weaker elements in the population by the dominant elements. . . . *The developments in Minnesota* should be carefully pondered by those who would give into the hands of state legislatures the power of classification of real estate for taxation through constitutional amendment.[28]

EFFECT OF THE TAX SYSTEM UPON LOCAL EXPENDITURES

We have seen that under the Classified Assessment Law the iron ore lands of this state are taxed on 50 per cent of full and true

[28] "Report of Special Committee on Mines Taxation," Proceedings of the National Tax Association, 1920, p. 407. (Italics the author's.)

TABLE 3.—ESTIMATES OF COSTS OF PRODUCTION, NET VALUE, AND OPERATOR'S PROFIT PER TON, BASED ON STATUTORY DEDUCTIONS UNDER THE OCCUPATION TAX LAW, AND PERCENTAGE OF TAX TO OPERATOR'S PROFIT PER TON, 1921–1929

Year	Average Statutory Cost per Ton [a]	Estimated Total Costs per Ton, Based on Deductions of			Value per Ton at Mouth of Mine [a]	Estimated Net Value per Ton at Mouth of Mine, Based on Deductions of			Average Cost per Ton of All Taxes [a]	Estimated Operator's Profit per Ton, i.e., Net Value plus Average Tax per Ton, Based on Deductions of			Tax per Ton in Percentage of Estimated Operator's Profit, Based on Deductions of		
		80 Per Cent	85 Per Cent	90 Per Cent		80 Per Cent	85 Per Cent	90 Per Cent		80 Per Cent	85 Per Cent	90 Per Cent	80 Per Cent	85 Per Cent	90 Per Cent
1921.....	$1.592	$1.990	$1.873	$1.769	$3.754	$1.764	$1.881	$1.985	$1.167	$2.931	$3.048	$3.152	39.82	38.29	37.02
1922.....	1.434	1.793	1.687	1.593	3.439	1.646	1.752	1.846	.760	2.406	2.512	2.606	31.59	30.25	29.16
1923.....	1.395	1.744	1.641	1.550	3.682	1.938	2.041	2.132	.598	2.536	2.639	2.730	23.58	22.66	21.90
1924.....	1.406	1.758	1.654	1.562	2.958	1.200	1.304	1.396	.694	1.894	1.998	2.090	36.64	34.73	33.21
1925.....	1.309	1.636	1.540	1.454	2.458	.822	.918	1.004	.578	1.400	1.496	1.582	41.29	38.63	36.54
1926.....	1.251	1.564	1.472	1.390	2.427	.863	.955	1.037	.502	1.365	1.457	1.539	36.78	34.45	32.62
1927.....	1.295	1.619	1.524	1.439	2.397	.778	.873	.958	.567	1.345	1.440	1.525	42.16	39.38	37.18
1928.....	1.211	1.514	1.425	1.346	2.359	.845	.934	1.013	.524	1.369	1.458	1.537	38.28	35.94	34.09
1929.....	1.190	1.488	1.400	1.322	2.566	1.078	1.166	1.244	.471	1.549	1.637	1.715	30.41	28.77	27.46

[a] Taken from the reports of the Minnesota Tax Commission. See also Table 4 of this chapter and explanations in the text.

value, while urban and rural real estate are assessed and taxed on 40 and 33⅓ per cent of full and true value, respectively. Apparently the legislature of 1913 failed to foresee that classification would give the local governmental units on the iron ranges a greater assessed valuation upon which to levy taxes. Taxes levied even at very moderate rates have yielded more revenue in some instances than was needed for ordinary purposes. Another result of the law has been to increase the tax liability of owners of iron ore properties and to decrease that of owners of other forms of property in communities where the mines are located. But because the taxes are levied by the owners of other forms of property, the taxpayers and the tax-spenders became different groups. The result has been that the average per capita expenditures of range towns and cities have been far greater than those of other municipalities in Minnesota; in 1930 they were from about two and one-fourth to four times the average per capita expenditures of communities of comparable size in the rest of the state. (See page 600.)

Tax Burden of the Mining Industry

The average annual tax bill of the mining industry in Minnesota during the period from 1920 to 1929, as shown in Table 2, amounted to about 20 per cent of the value of the average annual shipments of iron ore. The average costs per ton of ore distributed to various items during the period from 1921 to 1929 are shown in the report of the Tax Commission for 1930.[29] During the five-year period from 1925 to 1929 we find that taxes amounted to $.524 per ton, while the labor cost per ton was $.322. Taxes exceeded labor costs by about 63 per cent. The average cost of development, labor, supplies, and other items during the same five-year period was $.686 per ton. The taxes imposed amounted to a little over 70 per cent of all production costs.

Another and better method of measuring the tax burden on the mining industry would be to determine what percentage of the surplus above expenses of production was absorbed by taxation. Complete data on expenses of production are not available in the form required for such a computation. Data published by the Tax Commission, however, show the deductions permitted in computing the annual occupation tax levies. In 1924, according to the Tax Commission, the deductions allowed under the Occupation Tax Law represented approximately 83 per cent of the total expenses of

[29] Page 98.

production, exclusive of interest on investment and charges for depletion of capital. This percentage has been somewhat higher in recent years on account of amendments to the law and court decisions that have increased the number of deductible items. Since 1924 deductions have averaged between 85 and 90 per cent of the total expenses of production, exclusive of interest on investment and depletion. In addition to the deductions permitted under the Occupation Tax Law, data for the value of the ore at the "mouth of the mine" are also given in the reports of the Tax Commission.

On the basis of the data described above, three different estimates have been made of the total cost of production per ton and of net profit * per ton in each year from 1921 to 1929. The three sets of estimates were based upon different assumed percentages of deductions under the Occupation Tax Law to total expenses of production as reported to the Tax Commission by the mine operators. The percentages assumed were 80, 85, and 90 per cent, respectively. These estimates are tabulated in Table 3. The estimates of total costs per ton were obtained by dividing the average statutory cost per ton, that is, the average deduction per ton under the Occupation Tax Law, by the assumed percentages and multiplying the result by 100. Estimates of net profit per ton were obtained by subtracting the estimated total cost of production per ton from the value per ton at the "mouth of the mine."[30] The percentages of average tax per ton of ore produced to net profit per ton for each of the three sets of estimates are also given in Table 3. We find on the basis of the three assumptions as to percentage of total expenses deducted under the Occupation Tax Law that the percentage of taxes to net profit varied from 23.58, 22.66, and 21.90 per cent, respectively, in 1923 to 42.16, 39.38, and 37.18 per cent, respectively, in 1927. A conservative estimate of the average percentage of taxes to net profit per ton during the entire period would be not less than 30 per cent. (See Table 3 opposite.)

We must remember, however, that the estimates of total cost of production include royalties paid by the mine operators. The estimates of net profit represent net profit to the mine operator only. In reality the payment of royalties represents a division of profit between the mine operator and the fee owner, and to obtain an

* "Value" in the law, but see note 3 on page 235 above.

[30] A great deal of iron ore is sold at a small margin below the Lake Erie price. It must be kept in mind that the value at the "mouth of the mine" does not include any allowance for this factor.

estimate of the total surplus above expenses of production, royalties should be added to the net profit to the mine operator. The "true" net profit, which is obtained by adding the average royalty paid per ton of ore mined, is shown in Table 4 for the period from 1923 to 1929. The average royalty per ton mined was obtained by dividing the total royalty payments as reported to the Tax Commission by the number of tons mined. The ratios of taxes per ton to "true" net profit according to the three sets of estimates described in the preceding paragraph are also shown in

TABLE 4.—AVERAGE ROYALTY PER TON, ESTIMATED "TRUE" NET PROFIT, AND THE PERCENTAGE OF TAXES TO "TRUE" NET PROFIT, 1923–1929

Year	Average Royalty Paid per Ton [a]	"True" Net Profit, i. e., Estimated Net Profit Plus Average Royalties Based on Deductions of			Tax in Percentage of "True" Net Profit Based on Deductions of		
		80 Per Cent	85 Per Cent	90 Per Cent	80 Per Cent	85 Per Cent	90 Per Cent
1923	$.382	$2.918	$3.021	$3.112	20.49	19.79	19.22
1924	.461	2.355	2.459	2.551	29.45	28.22	27.21
1925	.375	1.775	1.871	1.957	32.56	30.89	29.54
1926	.364	1.729	1.821	1.903	29.03	27.57	26.38
1927	.419	1.764	1.859	1.944	32.14	30.50	29.17
1928	.380	1.749	1.838	1.917	29.96	28.51	27.33
1929	.371	1.920	2.008	2.086	24.53	23.46	22.58

[a] Total royalties paid, as reported to the Tax Commission, divided by total tonnage produced. See also Table 3 above and explanations in the text.

Table 4 except for the years 1921 and 1922. These percentages show that the average annual tax payments during the seven-year period from 1923 to 1929 absorbed from 20 to 30 per cent of the total surplus above the expenses of production. But the real burden of taxation is on the mine operators, for, as we have seen, most of them have agreed to pay all taxes levied upon royalties.

The foregoing calculations are subject to two qualifications. First, no allowance has been made for interest on invested capital, except capital invested in mine equipment and in beneficiation plants, nor for depletion of capital. The inclusion of these items would increase the percentages of taxes to net profit and "true" net profit as noted above. The second qualification is that the calculations of net profit and "true" net profit are based on the Lake Erie price, the validity of which is dependent on whether this price represents the true market value of Minnesota iron ores. But even with this qualification in mind, we are safe in concluding that the tax burden on the mining industry is a heavy one.

RELATION OF TAXES TO GROSS VALUE

The basis for the statement that the "iron ore companies operating in Minnesota pay the heaviest taxes of any industry in the world" is the fact that "the average rate of all state and local taxes for all industry and trade in the United States is in the neighborhood of 1.5 per cent of the gross value of the product at the point of production and the rate on all mining and quarrying operations is less than 2.5 per cent," whereas "the Minnesota state and local taxes on the iron mining industry are more than 22 per cent."[31] Although the facts may be as stated, it does not necessarily follow that the iron ore industry in Minnesota pays the heaviest taxes of any industry in the world. The percentage of taxes to gross value is not the proper basis for comparing relative tax burdens as between the iron ore industry and other industries or as between iron mines in the same state or in different states. Costs of production absorb different proportions of gross value in different industries and in different concerns within the same industry. Hence the percentage of taxes to gross value may be high in one industry and low in another while the actual burden of taxation may be heavier on the industry having the lower percentage of taxes to gross value, because taxes may absorb a higher percentage of the net value or net income of that industry. This is true also with respect to iron mines in different states and to different mines in the same state. With this point in mind, let us examine the facts.

DEVELOPMENTS IN MINNESOTA AND MICHIGAN COMPARED

The fallacy involved in the use of the percentage of taxes to gross value as a measure of the burden of taxation[32] can be shown by comparing the tax burden on the iron mines of Michigan with that on the iron mines of Minnesota. The average percentages of

[31] "Lake Superior Iron Ore Reserves" (editorial), *Trade Winds*, Vol. 10, no. 10, p. 10, October, 1931.

[32] The terms "burden of taxation" and "tax burden," as used in this paper, refer to the amount of taxes levied on the industry in proportion to ability to pay. In other words, they refer to the relationship between taxes and the income from which taxes must be paid. A tax may be large in absolute amount and yet the "burden" of the tax may be light because only a relatively small portion of the net income is required to pay the tax.

taxes to gross value during the period from 1920 to 1929, tabulated in Table 2, were 8.70 per cent in Michigan and 20.15 per cent in Minnesota. One might conclude from this that the tax burden on iron mines of Minnesota is twice that on the mines of Michigan. But this conclusion would overlook important considerations.

A comparison between the tax per ton of iron ore mined in Michigan and that for ore mined in Minnesota might lead us to the same erroneous conclusion. Table 5 shows that the average tax per ton of ore mined in Minnesota was a little over twice as

TABLE 5. — COMPARISON OF AVERAGE TAX PER TON OF ORE MINED IN MICHIGAN AND IN MINNESOTA, 1921–1929 [a]

YEAR	TOTAL TONNAGE PRODUCED		TOTAL STATE AND LOCAL TAXES		AVERAGE TAX PER TON	
	Michigan	Minnesota	Michigan	Minnesota	Michigan	Minnesota
1921....	7,283,492	17,495,578	$4,044,380	$20,423,484	$.555	$1.167
1922....	10,453,578	28,770,120	3,930,512	21,852,097	.376	.760
1923....	14,174,468	44,843,457	3,999,132	26,809,558	.282	.598
1924....	12,350,755	32,401,584	4,125,371	22,491,916	.334	.694
1925....	14,490,529	37,580,850	3,687,674	21,732,333	.254	.578
1926....	15,248,254	41,662,490	3,975,012	20,903,627	.261	.502
1927....	15,075,079	36,474,549	3,878,600	20,442,515	.257	.560
1928....	13,676,984	38,532,003	3,568,767	20,190,126	.261	.524
1929....	15,456,397	46,922,911	3,707,698	22,082,748	.240	.471

[a] Data for Minnesota are from the reports of the Minnesota Tax Commission. Figures for tonnage produced in Michigan are from the United States Department of Commerce, Bureau of Mines, *Mineral Resources of the United States*. Figures for the total state and local taxes paid by iron mines of Michigan were supplied by Mr. F. G. Pardee, mine appraiser in the Michigan Department of Conservation.

great as the average tax per ton of ore mined in Michigan during that period. But this does not mean that the tax burden on the mining industry in Minnesota is twice as great as in Michigan. The iron ore reserves in Minnesota are much larger than the reserves in Michigan. The ratio of ore produced by mines in Minnesota to ore produced by mines in Michigan is much smaller than the ratio of reserves in Minnesota to reserves in Michigan. Thus an ad valorem tax levied on the mines of the two states at the same rate would result in a larger tax per ton of ore produced in Minnesota than in Michigan.

In Table 6 the taxes levied on the iron ore industry in Minnesota and in Michigan are compared on the basis of the tax per dollar of full and true value. This table shows that the average tax per dollar of full and true value during the period from 1920 to

1930 was about 7.5 per cent greater in Minnesota than in Michigan. But this does not necessarily mean that the burden of taxation on iron mines is less in Michigan than in Minnesota. A great deal depends upon the relative accuracy of the mine valuations in the two states. Although the methods of valuation are substantially the same in that they are based upon a consideration of

TABLE 6.—COMPARISON OF TAXES LEVIED PER DOLLAR OF "FULL AND TRUE" VALUE ON IRON MINES IN MICHIGAN AND IN MINNESOTA, 1920–1930[a]

Year	True and Full Value (000 omitted)		Total Taxes Levied (000 omitted)		Tax per Dollar of Value		Percentage Ratio of Michigan Tax per Dollar to Minnesota Tax
	Michigan	Minnesota	Michigan	Minnesota	Michigan	Minnesota	
1920	$113,977	$597,594	$3,799	$20,840	$.0333	$.0349	95.42
1921	117,199	570,989	4,044	20,423	.0345	.0358	96.37
1922	113,948	562,415	3,931	21,852	.0345	.0389	88.69
1923	113,676	576,961	3,999	26,810	.0352	.0464	75.70
1924	113,373	584,286	4,125	22,492	.0364	.0385	94.55
1925	109,325	560,527	3,688	21,732	.0337	.0388	86.86
1926	100,273	542,146	3,975	20,904	.0396	.0386	102.59
1927	99,031	514,452	3,879	20,443	.0392	.0397	98.70
1928	93,597	506,568	3,569	20,190	.0381	.0399	95.49
1929	89,758	495,439	3,708	22,083	.0412	.0446	92.60
1930	89,908	479,295	3,923	20,789	.0436	.0432	100.46
Average					.0368	.0398	92.71

[a] Figures for Minnesota are from reports of Minnesota Tax Commission; figures for Michigan were supplied by Mr. F. G. Pardee, mine appraiser, Department of Conservation, Geological Division of the state of Michigan.

the same factors, these factors are not considered in the same way, nor are the same persons making the valuations in the two states.[33] Hence there may be a margin of error between the results obtained.

RELATION OF TAXES TO NET PROFIT

Taxes took about 25 per cent of "true" net profit, that is, of the surplus above the expenses of production, of iron mines in Minnesota during the period from 1923 to 1929. Table 7 shows that

[33] In Michigan the iron mines are treated as separate units. Estimated future cost of mining and marketing, the exhaustion period, and the estimated future profits of a mine are based upon the performance of that mine during the previous five years. The value is obtained by reducing estimated future profits to present worth by using a 6 per cent interest rate and allowing 6 per cent for return of capital (depletion). The corresponding percentages for Minnesota are "about 7.5 per cent" in the case of each of these items.

during the same period state and local taxes on iron mines in Michigan also absorbed about 25 per cent of the "true" net profit. In other words, state and local taxes absorbed about the same percentage of the surplus above expenses of production in Michigan as they did in Minnesota. No allowance was made for the siliceous open-pit mines in Michigan in making the calculations of "true"

TABLE 7.—ORE COSTS, LAKE ERIE VALUE, "TRUE" NET PROFIT, STATE AND LOCAL TAXES PER TON OF ORE MINED, AND PERCENTAGE OF TAXES TO "TRUE" PROFIT PER TON FOR UNDERGROUND IRON MINES OF MICHIGAN, 1921–1929[a]

YEAR	COSTS OF PRODUCTION, TRANSPORTATION, MARKETING[b]	AVERAGE LAKE ERIE VALUE PER TON	"TRUE" NET PROFIT PER TON[c]	STATE AND LOCAL TAXES PER TON	PERCENTAGE RATIO OF TAXES TO "TRUE" NET PROFIT
1921	$4.7779	$5.5561	$.7782	$.5044	64.82
1922	3.8815	5.1429	1.2614	.3675	29.13
1923	3.9121	5.6100	1.6979	.2702	15.91
1924	3.9233	4.9334	1.0101	.3098	30.67
1925	3.6794	4.3615	.6821	.2472	36.24
1926[d]	3.3714	4.1796	.8082	.2511	31.07
1927	3.4784	4.3200	.8416	.2486	29.54
1928	3.4774	4.3959	.9185	.2618	28.50
1929	3.3568	4.5838	1.2270	.2366	19.28

[a] Data for 1921 to 1924, inclusive, are from L. P. Barrett, "Taxes Overburden Iron Mines," *Iron Trade Review,* 77:621. Data for 1925 to 1929 were supplied by Mr. F. G. Pardee, mine appraiser, and Mr. W. Osgood, geologist, in the Michigan Department of Conservation, Geological Division.

[b] Includes cost of mining, deferred mining cost, general overhead, and transportation and marketing costs. No allowance is made for interest on borrowed funds.

[c] Includes royalties and taxes.

[d] All mines are included in the data for 1926.

net profit for iron mines in that state. During the five-year period from 1926 to 1930, however, the average cost per ton for producing siliceous ores was $2.1460; the Lake Erie value per ton was $2.2998.[34] Hence the "true" net profit during this period was $.1538. The average state and local tax per ton was $.0514 per ton; that is, taxes absorbed over 33 per cent of the "true" net profit in the case of siliceous open-pit mines in Michigan during the five-year period from 1926 to 1930. It appears, therefore, that there is little if any difference between the tax burdens borne by the mining

[34] F. G. Pardee and W. Osgood, *General Statistics Covering Costs and Production of Michigan Iron Mines* (Michigan Department of Conservation, 1930), Table VII.

industry in the two states.[35] It is evident that Minnesota is not the only state that levies heavy taxes on the iron ore industry.

EFFECTS OF HEAVY TAXES AND OTHER FACTORS

Effects of Taxation on Production

The heavy burden of taxes levied upon the mining industry in this state is said to have produced the following results:

1. Operators of rich mines with low costs of production and large reserves are forced to produce large tonnages to pay the taxes levied on their reserves.[36] This situation has resulted in lower prices and has forced mines having high costs out of business. It is said that the taxes levied on the mines of the Mesabi Range have forced many of the iron mines on the Cuyuna Range to cease producing.

2. It is said that the cumulative nature of the ad valorem taxes hastens the utilization of the best ores — that only the best and most favorably located deposits can be mined to best advantage and that lower grade and underground ores of higher cost, which ought to be mined with and mixed with the ores of lower cost and better grade, are often left untouched. As a result the aggregate cost of recovering the ore will be higher in the future and the total efficiency will be lower.

3. It is held also that the heavy ad valorem taxes levied on the iron mines have discouraged the exploration and development of new bodies of ore.

4. The heavy taxes levied on the iron ore industry are said to place the iron mines in Minnesota at a disadvantage in competing with the mines of other states and of foreign countries.

Data bearing on the first two alleged results of heavy taxation are shown in Table 8. These data show a decrease in the number of mines shipping ore from this state and an increase in the shipments per mine. It appears that mines with high costs have been forced to cease shipping, whereas the mines with lower costs and the richer mines have increased their shipments.

The data in Table 8 show also that the number of mines shipping ore from the Cuyuna Range increased from 1 in 1911 to 29 in 1918, then decreased to 8 in 1921. Since then the number has

[35] It may be well to note that the difference in the probable life of the mines in the two states does not invalidate this comparison.

[36] Note the text explanations as to how taxes are affected by the differences between the reserve situations in Minnesota and in Michigan (page 255).

TABLE 8.—IRON ORE TONNAGE SHIPPED FROM MINNESOTA MINES, 1910–1931 [a]

YEAR	MESABI RANGE		VERMILION RANGE		CUYUNA RANGE		TOTAL		TONNAGE SHIPPED PER MINE
	Tonnage Shipped	No. of Mines	Tonnage Shipped	No. of Mines	Tonnage Shipped	No. of Mines	Tonnage Shipped	No. of Mines	
1910....	29,194,534	104	1,203,177	6	....	..	30,397,711	110	276,343
1911....	22,093,532	93	1,088,930	7	147,431	1	23,329,893	101	230,989
1912....	32,047,409	95	1,844,981	8	305,111	4	34,197,501	107	319,603
1913....	34,038,643	112	1,566,600	7	733,021	8	36,338,264	127	286,128
1914....	21,465,967	94	1,016,993	6	859,404	7	23,342,364	107	218,153
1915....	29,756,689	95	1,733,595	7	1,136,113	10	32,626,397	112	291,307
1916....	42,525,612	108	1,947,200	8	1,716,218	19	46,189,030	125	369,512
1917....	41,445,211	123	1,530,692	8	2,422,884	22	45,398,787	153	296,724
1918....	40,396,711	97	1,192,908	8	2,478,800	29	44,068,419	134	328,869
1919....	31,997,699	117	929,049	7	1,861,165	27	34,787,913	141	246,723
1920....	37,149,277	112	1,007,435	7	2,191,528	24	40,348,240	143	282,156
1921....	16,350,696	71	869,313	4	488,562	8	17,708,571	83	213,356
1922....	28,055,394	92	1,211,467	6	1,497,615	15	30,764,476	113	272,252
1923....	41,814,463	100	1,278,598	8	2,220,745	15	45,313,806	123	368,405
1924....	29,141,665	89	978,097	5	1,468,940	13	31,588,702	107	295,222
1925....	35,889,988	88	1,437,577	5	1,509,217	13	38,836,782	106	366,385
1926....	38,249,793	79	1,586,054	5	2,079,276	15	41,915,123	99	423,385
1927....	32,974,157	86	1,547,732	5	1,982,302	14	36,504,191	105	347,659
1928....	35,398,648	72	1,671,327	5	2,093,479	15	39,163,454	92	425,690
1929....	43,007,015	80	1,873,548	5	2,603,753	14	43,737,220	99	441,790
1930....	31,067,050	72	1,884,412	5	1,928,027	17	34,879,489	94	383,291
1931 [b] ..	15,270,411	54	1,140,710	4	898,090	19	17,309,211	77	224,795

[a] From the *Iron Trade Review*.
[b] Data for 1931 are from *Skillings' Mining Review*, February 22, 1932, p. 5.

varied from 13 to 19, the average for the period from 1922 to 1930 being about 15. The number of mines shipping from the Vermilion Range has varied from 4 in 1921 and 1931 to 8 in 1912, 1916, 1917, 1918, and 1923. From 1924 to 1929 only 5 mines were making annual shipments. The number of mines shipping iron ore from the Mesabi Range fluctuated considerably during the twenty-year period from 1911 to 1930, increasing from 93 in 1911 to 123 in 1917. During the ten-year period 1921 to 1930 the average number of mines shipping from the Mesabi Range was about 93. The actual number decreased from 100 in 1923 to 54 in 1931.

From the foregoing discussion it is clear that in recent years iron ore shipments from Minnesota have been from the richer and more advantageously located mines; that the number of mines shipping from the Cuyuna Range in recent years is one-half the number in the peak year, 1918; and that during the period from 1922 to 1930 there was practically no change in the number of mines shipping from the Cuyuna and Vermilion ranges. Persons familiar with mining conditions on the three ranges in Minnesota state that little or no exploration and development of new bodies of ore has been carried on in recent years.

Factors Other than Taxation Affecting Production

With the facts as stated, does it follow that the conditions described above can be attributed solely to the heavy tax burden on the mining industry? The answer to this question requires a consideration of other factors, the effects of which cannot be measured separately from the effects of taxation. If we turn again to Table 8, we note that the total number of mines shipping ore from this state increased from 101 in 1911 to 153 in 1917 and then decreased to 83 in 1921. These changes were chiefly the effect of the war boom and the post-war depression. After the war, mines having lower costs of production and an excessive productive capacity tended to force the mines with higher costs out of business. The overdevelopment of the iron mines has tended also to decrease the necessity for further exploration and development of new ore bodies. Another result of overdevelopment has been the increase of taxes levied on the mining industry. Ore bodies that have been proved and developed are relatively easy to assess.

Another factor to be taken into account is the changing demand for iron ore.[37] The increased use of scrap in recent years has resulted in a decrease in the amount of iron ore required in the production of iron and steel. In 1912, 1.47 tons of iron ore were required for each ton of merchant iron and steel produced in the United States, whereas only 1.14 tons of ore were required in 1929. In 1920, 1.14 tons of Lake Superior iron ore were produced to every ton of merchant iron and steel. This ratio had decreased to .99 by 1929. Had it been the same in 1929 as in 1920, the Lake Superior mines would have supplied 73,254,760 tons of ore instead of the 63,662,346 tons actually consumed. The data show that the ratio of Lake Superior ore consumed to total pig iron produced has been declining at almost the same rate as the ratio of the total ore consumed to the total iron and steel produced. Had the ratio of Lake Superior ore consumed to total pig iron produced been the same in 1929 as in 1920, the mines would have furnished 66,051,700 tons

[37] For an interesting discussion of this factor see A. J. Hain, "Scrap Conserving the Nation's Ore Resources; Large Tonnage Added Yearly to Record of Lake Reserves," *Steel,* January 1, 1931.

of ore for the production of pig iron instead of the 63,662,346 tons actually used. The result of this change in demand has been to check the normal rate of increase in shipments from mines and to reduce the market for Minnesota iron ores. Obviously the mines with the lower costs of production and the better grades of ores have advantages over other mines in supplying ore for this narrower market.

Still another factor that must be taken into account to explain the increase in the rate of extraction of ores from the richer mines is the nature of the mining leases. It is customary for mining leases to provide for the payment of minimum royalties by the operators. The purpose of this provision is to insure the lessor-owner an annual income under the lease. These leases are made for periods of different lengths, ranging from twenty or twenty-five years to ninety-nine years. The royalties are usually based on an agreed rate of royalty, certain minimum requirements as to tonnage and the amount of the royalty being stipulated. These minimum royalties frequently accrue in substantial amounts long before ore is actually shipped from the property. In such cases, if no provision is made to the contrary, it is customary for the lessee-operator to apply royalties from ore mined and in excess of the annual minimum royalty to the credit of these accrued minimum royalties.

Leases usually contain a provision requiring the lessee-operator to mine the ore in a "workmanlike" manner. Some leases contain specific directions as to the handling of low-grade ores. For example, a lease may specify that low-grade ores must be put in a stockpile or that a certain number of tons of low-grade ore must be removed for each ton of high-grade ore mined. In some leases provision is made for beneficiating the ore, and the royalty is paid only upon tonnage actually shipped and not on that mined. Most fee owners have an engineer of their own at their mines whose duty it is to inspect the work of the operating company and to decide which material is to be discarded as waste and which is to be placed in stockpiles for possible future use. Hence we may conclude that there is little wasteful mining at the present time. It is probably true, however, that less low-grade ore is mined than would be mined under a more economic system of taxation.

Another factor that affects the rate at which some mines are being exhausted is the fact that many long-term leases are about to expire and will not be renewed except at a higher royalty. This causes the operator to extract as much ore as he can before his lease runs out. Mr. Charles M. Schwab is authority for the statement that in the "old days" he could get leases for royalties of from 10 to 25 cents a ton that would have cost from $1.25 to $1.50 in 1926.[38]

In the foregoing discussion the intention is not to minimize the effects of heavy taxes on the utilization of iron ore in this state but rather to point out that there are other factors in the situation that tend to affect the utilization of the ore; and that the effects of these factors cannot always be distinguished from the effects of taxation.

Effects of Taxation on the Competitive Position of Minnesota Iron Mines

It is said that heavy taxation has put the iron ore industry in Minnesota at a disadvantage in competing with the mines of other states and of foreign countries. But if we examine the statistics of production of iron ore in the United States, we find little evidence to substantiate this claim. The data show that there was little or no change in the percentage of ore coming from the Lake Superior district from 1921 to 1930 and that Minnesota mines did not decline in relative importance as producers of iron ore during that period. In 1919 Minnesota shipments constituted 61.49 per cent of the total shipments in the United States, and in 1930, 61.89 per cent. The average percentage for the entire period was a little over 61.6. In spite of the heavy taxes imposed upon them Minnesota mines have been able to retain their relative position as producers of iron ore in the United States.

There is little evidence to show that taxation is at present an important factor in the competition between Minnesota mines and foreign mines. In 1913 Mr. J. R. Finlay stated that "Cuban ores will meet Lake Superior ores at about one hundred miles east of Pittsburgh on even terms and east of that will have an advantage" and that "Brazil cannot compete even on tide-waters."[39] Ore imports into the United States have tended to increase since the World War. The average number of tons imported annually during the five-year period from 1910 to 1914 was 2,090,539; the average

[38] "An 'Iron Age' Interview with Mr. Schwab" (editorial), *Iron Age,* January 7, 1926, p. 11. We have heard a great deal about the increase in taxes and very little, if anything, about the increase in royalties. One effect of the present depression has been a decline in the value of royalties.

[39] J. R. Finlay, "The Valuation of Iron Mines," Transactions of the American Institute of Mining Engineers, 45:289 (1913).

for the period from 1926 to 1930 was 2,708,653. During the war, imports of iron ore fell off considerably, as might be expected. Cuba was the principal source of foreign ore before and during the war, supplying during the period from 1910 to 1920 over half the iron ore imported into the United States. Since 1920 less than half the imports have come from Cuba, and there has been a great increase in imports from Chile. In 1921 imports of Chilean ore into the United States amounted to 8,000 tons; in 1930, to 1,689,071 tons. At the present time about 60 per cent of the total tonnage of iron ore imports into the United States comes from Chile. Imports from Spain and Sweden varied greatly during the twenty-one year period from 1910 to 1930, inclusive, but the average annual tonnage imported into the United States since 1923 is slightly under the pre-war level of imports from these countries. There has been a great increase in imports of iron ore from Australia in recent years, from 5,000 tons in 1927 to 219,926 tons in 1930.

Of late years, especially since 1923, the average annual shipments of iron ore into the United States from countries that were important sources of iron ore imports before the war have been less than before the war. This decrease has been offset by the imports from Chile since 1921. The largest decrease in absolute amount has been in the imports of iron ore from Cuba. The ownership or control of iron ore deposits in Cuba and Chile may help explain this situation. About 90 per cent of the total reserve of Cuba, which is estimated at three billion tons, is owned by three American steel companies. The Bethlehem Steel Corporation through its subsidiaries controls over 80 per cent.[40] It also owns the only opened iron ore deposits in Chile, the Tofo Mines, all the ore from which is shipped to the United States. These mines contain about sixty million tons of ore assaying 67.50 per cent natural iron.[41] On the other hand, while some Cuban ores run as high as 63 per cent iron, the larger portion of them assay less than 50 per cent natural iron. The decrease in imports from Cuba and the increase from Chile is due largely to the fact that Chilean ores are of higher quality. Persons who point to the increase in imports from Chile as evidence of the competitive superiority of foreign ores over Lake Superior ore frequently overlook the decrease from other sources.

[40] Olin R. Kuhn, "Iron Ore Deposits of Cuba," *Engineering and Mining Journal,* 121:607 (1926).

[41] F. S. Warner, *Future Movement of Iron Ore and Coal in Relation to the St. Lawrence Waterway* (Philadelphia, 1930), p. 82.

There has been no great change in the pre-war ratio of imports to the production of Minnesota mines. The average ratio of total imports to shipments from Minnesota during the period from 1910 to 1914 was 7.08 per cent, while the average ratio for the period from 1926 to 1930 was 6.90 per cent. Minnesota iron mines have been able to hold their position with respect to foreign competitors in spite of the heavy taxes levied upon them in recent years. It is significant that they have done so in view of the fact that the tariff of fifteen cents a ton on imported ore of which the iron mines in the United States had the benefit before the war was repealed in 1913, and since then iron ore has been on the free list.

Conclusions as to the Effect of Taxation

We may summarize our conclusions with reference to taxes on mines in Minnesota as follows: (1) The mining industry is without doubt the most heavily taxed major industry in the state. (2) It is undoubtedly true that heavy taxation has tended to force some mines with high costs to cease producing. (3) Heavy taxation has caused uneconomic utilization of iron ore. (4) When we consider the effects of taxation on the mining industry, certain other factors, such as the overdeveloped condition of the industry, the changing demand for iron ore, and the nature of the mining leases, must also be taken into account. We cannot measure the effects of these factors separately from those of taxation. (5) There is little evidence to show that heavy taxes have had an appreciable effect on the competitive position of iron mines in this state. On the contrary, Minnesota mines have retained their position in spite of heavy taxes.

FUTURE OF THE IRON MINING INDUSTRY IN MINNESOTA

We have already seen that the heavy ad valorem taxes levied on the iron mines in this state have tended to result in uneconomic utilization of the iron ore. Such taxes will continue to have this result as long as they are levied and they may result in materially shortening the life of the mining industry. The possibility of exhausting the "actual" ore reserves of the state in the relatively near future is a matter of serious concern to all the people of the state as well as to the mining communities. The term "actual" refers to ore that has been proved to exist or is indicated by explorations to be probably existent and capable of being mined. About 3.2 per cent of the "actual" iron ore reserves of the world are in Minnesota. If we consider the "possible" reserves of the state, that is, "low-grade ores that are not available at present but will be used in the future — ore that is not proved but the existence of which is indicated by the formation, and ore that cannot be mined or used under present conditions or methods,"[42] we find that Minnesota has about 24 per cent of the world's "possible" reserves within its borders. The future tax policy of the state will have an important bearing upon the utilization of both the "actual" and the "possible" reserves of the state.

The future of the iron and steel industry depends very largely on a supply of good, relatively inexpensive, iron ore. The part that Minnesota is to play in the supply of ore is difficult to forecast. The opinions of different authorities are at variance. Dr. C. K. Leith sets twenty years hence as the date when the output of the mines in this state will begin to diminish.[43] Another geologist, Mr. M. C. Lake, after considering probable future demands, concludes that the present reserves of high-grade ore will be exhausted by 1945 or 1950.[44] On the other hand, another geologist, Mr. Carl Zapffe, is more hopeful. He believes that new deposits will continue to be discovered and that merchantable ore in the Minnesota ranges will last for an indefinite period.[45] He emphasizes the possibility of using low-grade ores and the more economical combination of low- and high-grade materials. Mr. E. W. Davis, of the University of Minnesota Mines Experiment Station, who is an expert on beneficiation, summarizes the situation as follows:

> The industry is in no immediate need of merchantable ore. Reserves are available to maintain the present grade of shipping product for a long time. These reserves are not inexhaustible, however, and the time when the high-grade ores will be depleted can be anticipated. Tremendous tonnages of high-silica ores are available, however, but no method has been perfected by which any considerable

[42] Olin R. Kuhn, "World's Iron Ore Reserves Now Exceed 57,000,000,000 Tons," *Engineering and Mining Journal,* 122:84 (July 17, 1926). The total reserves of the United States are estimated at 10,450,000,000 tons of actual ore averaging about 50 per cent iron and 83,970,000,000 tons of possible ore carrying from 25 to 30 per cent of iron. It is extremely difficult, if not impossible, to get accurate information as to iron content in many cases.

[43] *World Minerals and World Politics* (New York, 1931), p. 24.

[44] "Economic Aspects of Lake Superior Iron Ore Beneficiation," *Mining and Metallurgy,* Vol. 7, no. 236, p. 325 (August, 1925). See also W. O. Hotchkiss, "Lake Superior Iron Ore Reserves," *Mining and Metallurgy,* Vol. 7, no. 236, p. 339 (August, 1926) and O. R. Kuhn, "World's Iron Ore Resources Now Exceed 57,000,000,000 Tons," *Engineering and Mining Journal,* 122:84 (July 17, 1926).

[45] See his discussion of Mr. Lake's paper on "The Future of the Lake Superior District," Proceedings of the Lake Superior Mining Institute, 24:63 (August, 1925).

proportion of this material can be utilized. Moreover, it will probably take at least ten years to perfect and establish commercial plants that can produce any considerable tonnage of low-silica ore from the low-grade reserves. In ten years or possibly less time, many of the operators will be running short of merchantable ore.[46]

We have already indicated that there is a possibility that the iron and steel industry will have to relocate its plants in places convenient for the importation of foreign ores. There is some evidence that this process of relocation has already begun. Mr. Charles M. Schwab, when questioned as to the reason why the Bethlehem Steel Corporation was enlarging its plants at Sparrows Point, Maryland, replied as follows:

> My hope is that eventually we shall have at Sparrows Point the greatest steel plant in the world. . . . Eastern steel plant development is in response to the growing demand for steel from the great consuming districts of the country. . . .
>
> Looking toward Lake Superior, I saw costs steadily advancing and the quality of the ore steadily declining. . . . In the old days I could get ore properties there at royalties ranging from 10 to 25 cents; today these royalties have gone to $1.25 and $1.50. Taxes on Lake ores have increased several fold, and there have been successive advances in labor cost. On the other hand are the low mining costs in Chile, which have been stable over a long period, and substantially that is the case in Cuba. Our Chilean ore runs 67 per cent in iron, whereas Lake ores that once averaged about 60 per cent in iron are now down between 50 and 55 per cent. Chilean ore hauled 4,400 miles can be laid down at Sparrows Point at $6 for the ore required to make a ton of pig iron, or about 6 cents per unit. While Pittsburgh has its advantage on fuel, the ore advantage of the Eastern seaboard plant is such that pig iron can be made more cheaply at Sparrows Point than at any point in the Middle West.
>
> The marked advance in rail transportation cost is another factor in the greater future of the Eastern steel industry. When I started making steel at Pittsburgh we had a $2 freight on finished steel to the Atlantic seaboard. Today the rate is $7 per ton.[47]

On the other hand, since 1902 the production of pig iron has shifted toward the West.[48] In 1902 the district including eastern Pennsylvania, Maryland, Maine, Massachusetts, and Connecticut produced 11.71 per cent of the total pig iron output of the United States; by 1930 the percentage had decreased to 9.12. In 1910 New York and New Jersey produced 8.07 per cent of the total, but in 1930 only 6.46 per cent. Western Pennsylvania, Kentucky, West Virginia, and Ohio produced 57.65 per cent of the total in 1902 and 51.09 per cent in 1930. We note similar decreases in Virginia and

[46] E. W. Davis, "Progress in the Beneficiation of Minnesota Iron Ores," *Mining and Metallurgy*, Vol. 7, no. 235, p. 280 (July, 1926).

[47] "An 'Iron Age' Interview with Mr. Schwab" (editorial), *Iron Age*, January 7, 1926, p. 11.

[48] *Steel*, June 11, 1931, p. 15.

the southern states — from 3.01 and 10.66 per cent, respectively, in 1902 to .30 and 7.57 per cent, respectively, in 1930. The only district that increased in importance as a producer was that composed of Illinois, Indiana, and Michigan; this district produced 10.58 per cent of the total pig iron output in 1902 and 22.92 per cent in 1930. In other words, the district that depends almost entirely upon the Lake Superior mines for its supply of iron ore has increased in relative importance, whereas all other districts, except the western states, have decreased. This would seem to indicate that producers of iron ore have faith in the ability of the Lake Superior district to supply them with iron ore for a long time in the future.

Mr. Warner states that certain conditions will tend to hold the steel industry in the Lake Erie district.

> While there are potential tendencies for the industry to move to the Atlantic coast, there are several which tend to hold it, as well as to increase its importance, in the Lake Erie district. First, a tremendous sum of fixed capital is invested, and this capital is relatively immobile. Second, it is located between two great markets, the eastern and middle western, while the industry itself and the district it is in also furnish a large market. Third, it is located at the present center of transportation costs of fuel, ore, and fluxes. It is also at a convenient center for shipping the finished and semi-finished products. Fourth, it is located close to a supply of high-grade coke for smelting purposes. Fifth, if our foreign trade continues to develop in the steel industry, it will be at an advantageous shipping point by water for eight months of the year with the prospect of loading steel at ocean rates.[49]

In the foregoing discussion concerning the future of the Lake Superior iron mines we have presented the opinions of the leading authorities on the subject. While it is probably true that "few individuals have a clear conception of the total amount of merchantable reserves now available, and none can possess a knowledge of how far into the future the vast deposits of 'lean' iron ore will take us,"[50] it seems highly improbable that the present reserves of high-grade ore in Minnesota will last longer than thirty-five or forty years. But in the last analysis the life of the mining industry in the state will depend largely upon whether or not the low-grade ores can be utilized profitably. It will depend also, in part at least, upon the state's policy of mine taxation. The total cost of mining and ore beneficiation, royalties, taxes, transportation, and overhead, per unit of iron at Lake Erie, must not exceed the cost per unit of ore from other sources.

[49] F. S. Warner, *Future Movement of Iron Ore and Coal in Relation to the St. Lawrence Waterway* (Philadelphia, 1930), p. 74.

[50] A. J. Hain, "Scrap Conserving the Nation's Ore Resources; Large Tonnages Added Yearly to Record of Lake Resources," *Steel*, January 1, 1931, p. 325.

SUGGESTIONS FOR A FUTURE TAX POLICY

Fundamental Questions

If we turn now to a consideration of the three fundamental questions stated on page 235 our answer to the question "Should mines and minerals be taxed by a method different from that applied to other property?" is emphatically in the affirmative. The ad valorem tax as it now stands on the statute books of Minnesota is not consistent with the economic conditions peculiar to the mining industry. The principal arguments advanced by proponents of the ad valorem system of taxing mines are based on the desire for equality in taxation and for local control of local finances. As far as equality in the treatment of mining and other properties is concerned, it is a desire that is impossible of realization. Anyone familiar with the political situation in Minnesota knows how utterly hopeless it is for mine owners to expect mining property to be taxed on the same basis as other property. Equality in taxation can never be attained, moreover, even if the legislature repeals the present discriminatory taxes against the mining industry and places the property of the industry on a basis of equality with other property for purposes of taxation. The valuations computed by the Tax Commission are at best only approximations. We do not mean by this that the Tax Commission is inefficient. There are many uncertainties connected with the valuation of iron mines, the principal one perhaps being the future price of the ore. As the amount of ore sold on the open market diminishes, the Lake Erie price will become more unsatisfactory as a measure of the true market value of Minnesota iron ore, and the error in valuations based on it will increase. This factor alone is sufficient to produce gross inequality in taxation as between mining property and other property.

The argument for local control over local finances encounters certain difficulties. The situation in Minnesota clearly illustrates what usually happens when the taxpayer and the tax-spender are different persons. When local taxing jurisdictions spend large sums in excess of their legitimate needs and the funds are raised by means of heavy taxes that tend to result in the uneconomic utilization of a natural resource of such far-reaching importance as iron ore, the interests of those local taxing jurisdictions are no longer paramount. The argument for local control of local finances overlooks the fact that local governmental units in mining districts may not know what is best for them in the long run. There is ample evidence to show that some mining communities in this state do not.

As for the second fundamental question, "Should mines and minerals be taxed at a higher rate than other property if they are taxed in the same manner?" it must be answered in the negative. To tax mining property at a higher rate than other property is to increase the evils resulting from the ad valorem tax.

The third question, "If mines and minerals are not to be taxed in the same manner as other property, what method of taxation should be used?" is not easy to answer. The answer should, however, be based upon a consideration of the following points:

1. The present system is well established and the industry has developed business policies to accord with the system. Hence any change in the system of taxation may result either in penalizing certain mine operators or in giving them a bonus.

2. The present reserves of high-grade ores will probably be exhausted within thirty-five or forty years. A continuation of the mining industry in this state on a large scale will depend, therefore, upon whether the vast deposits of low-grade ores can be mined economically. By its policy of taxation the state may either encourage or discourage the development of these deposits of low-grade ore. In the long run the state would undoubtedly gain by encouraging development.

3. The assessed valuation of mining property as fixed by the Tax Commission constitutes a relatively large proportion of the total assessed value of all property in the state. This assessed value is certain to diminish as the deposits of high-grade ore become depleted. If the state continues the present system of taxation, it will lose a fairly large portion of its tax base and in consequence will be forced to look elsewhere for revenue. Consequently the exhaustion of the high-grade ore deposits will shift part of the burden of state taxes to other forms of property.

4. Under the present system of mine taxation almost all receivers of royalties escape taxation for state and local purposes because their leases require the lessees to pay such taxes. Some lessees now find themselves saddled with a royalty charge that they cannot escape except by surrendering the lease. In fact, some operators have requested the Tax Commission to reduce their assessed valuations because they could not operate at a profit while paying

royalties to the fee owner. This is equivalent to asking to escape the penalty of past business errors by means of a lower tax levy. What a fine world this would be if all business men could recoup the losses resulting from their own mistakes simply by obtaining reduced tax levies!

5. Every year less ore is sold on the open market, and soon the amount will be negligible. The Lake Erie price will therefore become progressively less dependable as a basis for determining the value of iron ore properties.

6. Although it is a matter of minor importance, some consideration ought to be given to the matter of mineral reservations on the cut-over timber lands of this state. In disposing of this land many of the former owners reserved the rights to any minerals that might be discovered therein. Since the present owner of the surface does not have a clear title to the land, the reservations tend to detract from the value of the surface. The net result is to decrease the size of the property tax base, because these mineral reservations commonly have no determinable taxable value.

A Suggested Method of Taxation

On the basis of these points the following plan of iron ore taxation is proposed as one worthy of consideration. If others have better plans to meet the serious defects of the present system, or if the discussion of this plan brings forth a better one, well and good. But some important positive action should be taken soon, lest the indefinite continuance of the present system of taxation hinder the future economical development and utilization of the vast potential resources of the state. The future as well as the present must be taken into account. The plan outlined here applies to the taxation of iron ore and iron mines generally, but in so far as it concerns vested interests, reasonable expectations, and certain other factors, some of which are mentioned below, it may be considered primarily with reference to the taxation of low-grade ores.

It is suggested that the state obtain its revenues from the iron ore properties in the same way that the fee owners get their royalties. Fee owners usually lease their properties to mine operators on the condition that a certain minimum royalty be paid annually, whether any ore is mined or not. These minimum royalties are usually based upon a prearranged rate of royalty and on the tonnage in the mine. They frequently accrue in substantial amounts long before a property actually begins to ship ore. In such cases, if the lease so provides, it is customary for the lessee-operator to apply royalties from ore mined in excess of the annual minimum royalty to the credit of the accrued minimum royalties.

The state may obtain its revenue from the mines in a similar manner. It may abolish all the present taxes for state and local purposes and levy in their place a graduated tonnage tax on all ore produced. At the present time the active mines and the inactive or reserve ore properties are classified according to costs of mining and the grade of the ore. Under the plan suggested this classification would be retained, and a tonnage tax would be levied on all iron ore produced, different rates being levied on the several classes. Inactive or reserve ore properties in the several classes would pay a minimum annual tax corresponding to the minimum royalties paid to the fee owners by the operators. This minimum annual tax would be based upon the tonnage tax rate for active mines of the given class and the tonnage in the particular mine. For example, suppose the active mines in a given class were required to pay a tax of $.25 on each ton of ore produced and that a given inactive or reserve ore property in the same class contained, say, 1,000,000 tons of ore. This inactive or reserve ore property would pay a minimum annual tax of perhaps 2½ cents, or some other fractional part of $.25, for each ton of ore in the property—that is, a total minimum annual tax of $25,000.

Obviously, if this inactive or reserve ore property lies idle for any period of time and pays taxes, the minimum annual taxes will accrue. In acordance with the practice followed in the case of accrued minimum royalties, after the mines become active the tax payable on ore produced during a given year and in excess of the minimum annual tax would be applied to the credit of the accrued minimum taxes. To illustrate, let us suppose that the total tax payable on ore produced during a given year is $15,000 and that the minimum annual tax is $10,000. The tax payable on ore produced exceeds the minimum annual tax by $5,000. If the mine operator has paid the minimum annual tax for, say, two years, the accumulated minimum taxes will amount to $20,000. In that case the mine operator would pay only the minimum annual tax of $10,000 and apply the $5,000 to the credit of the $20,000 in accrued minimum taxes. This process would continue until all accrued minimum taxes had been credited, or offset, by the excess of taxes payable on ore produced over the minimum annual tax.

Since there are eight classes of active and reserve ore properties, not including special classes, there would be eight tonnage tax rates on ore produced by mines in the various classes and also eight minimum annual tax rates per ton for reserve ore properties. The minimum annual tax rate per ton for reserve ore properties would be fixed at the same proportion, one-tenth or some other fraction, of the tonnage tax per ton of ore mined in all classes.

The actual determination of the tonnage tax rates and of the minimum annual taxes is a matter to be decided by experts after a careful study of the available data of past production and past costs. The rates should be adjusted, however, so as not to result in any large increase or decrease in the average annual tax bill of the iron mining industry.

The plan is based upon the assumption that a large part of the revenue from this graduated tonnage tax would be placed in a permanent trust fund, as in the case of the occupation tax, and that the earnings from this fund would be used for current governmental expenditures. As this fund grew and the annual earnings from it increased, ad valorem taxes on iron ore for local purposes would be reduced and finally abolished. The local governments would obtain their revenue from taxes on other property and from the allocation of the earnings of the permanent trust fund.

ADVANTAGES OF THE PROPOSED PLAN

The proposed system of mine taxation has several advantages:

1. Many of the difficulties involved in the valuation of iron ore properties would be avoided. The principal data required would be the estimates of the tonnage and grade of the ore in the ground, the analysis of the ore, and the data on costs of production. The system would be easy and economical to administer after it was properly established.

2. The graduated tonnage tax would have little if any effect on the development of a body of reserve ore in advance of requirements, and it could not be avoided by increasing the rate of removing the ore. Thus the tendency would be to conserve the supply of iron ore.

3. The graduated tonnage tax would be equitable as between mine operators. Thoroughly explored bodies of ore would not pay a greater proportion of their earnings in taxes than bodies less thoroughly explored. In addition, the present discrimination would not exist between underground and open-pit mines with respect to the stockpile tax. The tax, being graduated, would take into ac-

count differences in ability to pay. Efficient operators would not be required to pay more taxes per ton than inefficient operators in the same class.

4. The graduated tonnage tax, as described above, would reach all classes of mineral property.

5. The system provides a method for checking the extravagant expenditures of the local mining communities. Incidentally, the loss in revenue to the state from depletion of the mines would be offset by revenue from the permanent funds.

6. There is no reason to believe that the yield of the tax would be more unstable than the yield of the present system. The annual minimum tax yield would vary but little from year to year, and the earnings from the permanent fund would be relatively stable. The average annual yield might well be greater than under the present system.

7. As the mines become depleted, costs of mining increase. This increase in costs of mining would be offset in part by a decrease in the tonnage tax rate, for the mines would be shifted from a class having relatively low costs to a class having higher costs.

DISADVANTAGES OF THE PLAN

There are certain difficulties involved in the plan, but they do not seem to be insuperable. First, there are always difficulties involved in the allocation of revenues. Perhaps the biggest difficulty is to determine the basis for apportioning the revenue from the permanent trust fund. This apportionment might be made in any one of several ways. It might be based upon (1) the assessed valuation of property other than iron ore property in the mining communities; upon (2) the percentage of total tonnage taxes paid by iron mines in the various communities; or upon (3) the per capita expenditures in the mining communities.

The second disadvantage of the plan is that it contemplates the accumulation of a permanent trust fund. It would be necessary, if it were deemed wise to create such a fund, to amend the state constitution in order definitely to assure the permanency of the fund.

A third disadvantage is the fact that if the plan were to be put into operation at once, or within the next decade, the effect would be to shift a portion of the tax burden from the mining companies having large reserves to those having small reserves. This follows from the fact that output is not proportional to reserves. This disadvantage would be offset in part by the minimum annual tax and in part by the fact that the plan would enable small mining companies to increase their reserves without making the large expenditures for taxes that are necessary under the present system.

It may not be feasible to apply the plan outlined above to all ores immediately. As suggested earlier, owners, mining companies, state and local industries and governments, and others have all made plans and investments based on the existing system. It may not be wise or practical to upset all calculations by sudden and radical changes. But it is important to plan now for the future welfare of the state instead of merely drifting along forever with a tax system not in harmony with the best utilization of the state's resources.

It is therefore suggested that if the tonnage tax plan outlined above involves too radical a change to apply to all ores in the state at the present time, the present tax system with certain modifications be allowed to continue as far as the high-grade ores are concerned, but that the proposed plan be applied to the low-grade ones that do not now have any substantial value and thus do not form an appreciable part of the present tax base.[51] The dividing line between high and low grades might be 35 or 40 per cent. The system may be applied to all grades of ore as soon as conditions will permit.

Obviously this compromise involves certain disadvantages, but it appears to harmonize various interests and factors in the situation in a reasonable and practical manner. As a matter of fact, it involves no radical changes for the present. It does, however, involve changes in the future, but changes that will be better for both public and private interests. And, what is very important, it involves making these changes now, before this enormous reserve of low-grade ore has taken on value and before vested interests, public and private, have become so great that the inauguration of a proper tax system will become very disturbing and difficult.

STEPS REQUIRED TO PUT PLAN INTO OPERATION

It cannot be stressed too emphatically that policies for the future should not be delayed but should be made now. Perhaps the first step is to obtain the necessary constitutional amendment. This would probably require a more or less extended campaign of education to show the people of the state the need for such a system of mine taxation. Another step is to provide proper per capita or

[51] See Report of the Minnesota Tax Commission, 1920, p. 51.

other limitations upon local expenditures and debts, as well as upon tax rates, and also to tax iron ore on the same percentage of full value as other real property. If it should prove that local governments are unable to derive sufficient revenue for reasonable local needs from an ad valorem tax on surface valuations, the state could allocate a part of the tonnage tax revenue back to the localities on one of the bases suggested above. The mining communities would then have a relatively fixed income from this allocated portion of the tonnage tax. The elasticity desired for local revenues would be provided for by the local general property tax on surface valuations.[52]

SUMMARY

In this study only a few of the more important aspects of the problem of mine taxation in Minnesota have been touched upon. A thorough investigation of the problem would require the expenditure of more time and funds than are available.

Emphasis has been placed upon the fact that the present system of mine taxation is out of date and unsuitable to the economic conditions peculiar to the mining industry. Although the present situation cannot be said to be serious, it promises to develop into something serious in the not very distant future. In ten years or possibly less time, many operators will be running short of merchantable ore. These operators will have two alternatives; they may (1) increase their reserves by acquiring large tonnages of low-grade ore in this state, or (2) they may acquire large tonnages of high-grade ore in foreign countries. The operators are reluctant to acquire large tonnages of low-grade ore in Minnesota for two reasons. Under the present system of taxation they are required to expend large sums in taxes while carrying these reserves, long before they can be utilized. Moreover, the operators have no assurance that the state and the mining communities are not going to increase the super-taxes on iron ore. As far as foreign ores are concerned, Dr. Leith contends that the mining companies have reached the "jumping off" stage.[53] He says that English and American capitalists are planning to spend from sixty to eighty million dollars in putting Brazilian mines into a productive state. Brazilian ore can be quarried at low cost. The mine operators must have reserves. In most cases large investments in steel plants

[52] We must not lose sight of the fact, however, that the present system has an advantage in that the mining companies are vitally interested in local taxes.

[53] Interview, December 14, 1931.

are dependent upon the ability of mine operators to increase their reserves. If these reserves cannot be obtained in Minnesota, the operators must go elsewhere. An equitable policy of taxation on the part of the state will encourage them to invest large sums in the development of low-grade ores. Moreover, the state is facing the possibility of losing a considerable portion of its tax base through the rapid depletion of the high-grade mines unless it becomes possible to utilize the low-grade ores.

It is very doubtful if equality in taxation as between iron ore and other property can be attained with public opinion in its present state, no matter how desirable it may be in the long run from the economic point of view. This is, however, a relatively unimportant matter. The truly important need for the future is the proper utilization of the vast reserves of low-grade ore. If the state is to encourage the proper utilization of this ore and to avoid the dangers pointed out in this study, it is essential that changes be made that will enable the mining companies to develop these deposits at a profit.

CHAPTER 10

BANK TAXATION[1]

LEGAL POWERS OF THE STATES

The problem of bank taxation is greatly complicated by the multiplicity of franchising authorities, each jealous of its sovereignty and insistent upon its legal rights and the correctness of its viewpoint. As a result, the primarily economic nature of the problem has been obscured to a serious extent.

The forty-eight states possess the power to tax banks and other financial institutions operating under state charter.[2] But since the famous case of McCulloch v. Maryland[3] in 1819, the courts have recognized that a national bank is a legal means of carrying out powers delegated to Congress, in consequence of which the states' power to tax national banks is greatly restricted. At present such limitations are embodied chiefly in Section 5219, United States Revised Statutes, as interpreted by the courts.[4] Further restrictions exempt federal reserve banks,[5] federal land banks,[6] federal intermediate credit banks,[7] and national farm loan associations[8] from taxation by states except upon real property.

In brief, the law permits the states to tax national banks only to the extent and in the manner permitted by Congress. There are now four methods from which to choose. The states "may (1) tax said shares [of national banking associations located within state limits], or (2) include dividends derived therefrom in the taxable income of an owner or holder thereof, or (3) tax such associations

[1] This chapter was prepared by Professor Walter R. Myers of the School of Business Administration of the University of Minnesota.

[2] The Kansas case, Voran v. Wright (1930), 284 Pac. 807, indicates a legal restriction upon a state's right to tax its own banks at a higher rate than national banks. Cited by Jens P. Jensen, *A Survey of Bank Taxation in the United States* (American Bankers Association, Committee on Taxation, 4th ed., September, 1931), p. 7. Cf. note 27 below.

[3] 4 Wheat. 316 (1819).

[4] For a chronological index of United States Supreme Court decisions on the taxation of national bank shares and additional federal and state court decisions involving Sec. 5219 U. S. R. S., see United States House of Representatives, 71 Congress, 2 Session, Hearings on H. R. 7752 (H. R. 12490), a bill to amend Sec. 5219 U. S. R. S., p. 162.

[5] Federal Reserve Act, Sec. 7 (1913).

[6] Federal Farm Loan Act, Sec. 26 (1916).

[7] *Ibid.*, Sec. 210 (1916).

[8] *Ibid.*, Sec. 26 (1916).

on their net income, or (4) according to or measured by their net income," provided certain conditions are met. Each method is exclusive of the others, but all permit local taxation of real property in addition.[9] Since the states have not wished to handicap their own creatures in competition with national banks, taxes upon the latter permitted by Congress have generally determined the taxation of state banks also.

Taxation of Bank Shares

Until 1923 only the first of the four methods was available for taxation of national banks, "subject only to the two restrictions, that the taxation shall not be at a greater rate than is assessed upon other moneyed capital in the hands of individual citizens of such state, and that the shares of any national banking association owned by non-residents of any state shall be taxed in the city or town where the bank is located and not elsewhere."[10] The first of these two conditions has caused extensive readjustments in state tax laws, as well as the amendment of Section 5219. In 1921 in the case of Merchants National Bank v. City of Richmond[11] it was represented that state and national bank shares were taxed at a much higher rate than some six million dollars' worth of bonds and notes owned by individual citizens, and the Supreme Court upheld the contention that "moneyed capital in the hands of individual citizens" includes not only investments in the shares of state banks and trust companies competing with national banks but also funds invested in private banks and investments of individuals in securities that represent money at interest and other evidences of indebtedness such as normally enter into the business of banking.

TAXATION OF INTANGIBLES

The enormous development of industry in the last quarter of the nineteenth century and the accompanying increase in corporate and government financing created a large volume of securities in the hands of corporations and of private individuals. The general ad valorem property tax, which carried a relatively high rate when applied to this class of personal property, resulted in wholesale tax evasion, so that proceeds were insignificant. As a practical measure to protect their revenue many states legalized the classification of

[9] Sec. 5219 U. S. R. S.; but see page 286 below.
[10] Sec. 5219 U. S. R. S. as amended in 1868.
[11] 256 U. S. 619.

property, making the rates on "intangibles" sufficiently low to induce owners to declare them. In 1907 Minnesota established a low registry tax[12] in lieu of all other taxes on mortgages and in 1911 a money and credits tax of 3 mills on the dollar. Both measures have been followed by greatly increased proceeds to the state and have probably served to encourage domestic mortgage loan activities and the deposit of private funds in banks.[13] On the other hand, evasion is probable in the case of the money and credits tax; hence this may be said to be in effect upon a voluntary basis and therefore not comparable to a property tax on real estate.[14] This situation is in a sense parallel to the current "taxation" of banks in Minnesota, whereby the banks voluntarily pay, by compromise with the state, 75 per cent of the assessed tax.

The Supreme Court decision in the Richmond case essentially invalidated the bank tax law of Minnesota and most other share-tax states, as well as that of Virginia. Minnesota took the lead in an attempt made by several of the states concerned to secure such amendment of Section 5219 as would permit continued taxation of intangibles at low rates while bank shares were taxed at general property rates. The plan to substitute for the "other moneyed capital" restriction a clause permitting taxation of national bank shares at a rate no higher than that imposed upon state bank shares or upon other moneyed capital *employed in the business of banking* was successfully opposed by the American Bankers' Association, which urged that such provision would single out banking capital for special tax treatment, without limitations. As adopted, the amendment of 1923 reads:

> In the case of a tax on said shares, the tax imposed shall not be at a greater rate than is assessed upon other moneyed capital in the hands of individual citizens of such state coming into competition with the business of national banks: Provided, That bonds, notes, or other evidences of indebtedness in the hands of individual citizens not employed or engaged in the banking or investment business and representing merely personal investments not made in competition with such business, shall not be deemed moneyed capital within the meaning of this section.

But in 1927 the Supreme Court in its decision of First National Bank of Hartford v. City of Hartford[15] affirmed that this amend-

[12] At present 15 cents per $100 if the term is less than five years, otherwise 25 cents per $100.

[13] State tax yields from mortgages increased from less than $100,000 in 1906 to $316,761 in 1929; proceeds from money and credits increased from $380,000 in 1910 to $1,323,857 in 1929. Report of the Minnesota Tax Commission, 1928, pp. 143–145; 1930, p. 385. See Table 1 on page 212.

[14] See pages 212–218 and 284.

[15] 273 U.S. 548 (1927).

ment merely stated explicitly what repeated decisions of the Court had implied, and thus the law was unchanged. The Court held that "Section 5219 is violated whenever capital, substantial in amount compared with the capitalization of national banks, is employed either in a business or by private investors in the same sort of transaction as those in which national banks may engage and in the same locality in which they do business." It was not necessary to show that the banks and the "competing" capital were soliciting the same customers. Further, in the case of Minnesota v. First National Bank of St. Paul,[16] decided along the same lines, the Court found that in the field of bonds, mortgages, cattle loans, and other promissory notes investments in substantial amounts, listed for taxation at low rates as "moneys and credits," were in competition with bank capital, which was taxed at the high general property rate.[17]

The effect of these decisions was to void the bank tax laws of Minnesota and other states having both a general property tax on bank shares and materially lower rates on certain intangibles. As a result at least forty states found their statutes to be in conflict with the federal law as interpreted, mainly in one or more of the following respects: (1) Mortgages were exempt or (2) subject to a low registry tax; or (3) money and credits were exempt or (4) taxed at a low rate or at a fraction of their value or (5) were subject to deduction of debts before taxation; while capital invested in banks was taxed without deductions and/or at higher rates.[18] Minnesota is at fault in respect to the second and fourth items in this list.

DISADVANTAGES OF TAX ON BANK SHARES

Aside from the immediate difficulty presented by the "other moneyed capital" clause, the general property tax on bank shares involves numerous disadvantages. In theory it confuses economic goods with the documentary evidence of temporary transfer of such goods; that is, it confuses securities and other credits with the physical property "represented" by these credits. Inasmuch as the physical properties are taxed as property at least once, it means discriminatory double taxation to tax also the "representative"

[16] 273 U.S. 561 (1927).
[17] 273 U.S. 561 (1927).
[18] J. G. Armson, "Condensed Summary of States in Which the Tax on Bank Shares Is Apparently Higher Than the Tax on Certain Competitive Capital," *Brief on Amending Subdivision B, Paragraph 1, Section 5219, R. S. 1927*, pp. 62–66.

property.[19] The holdings of banks, aside from real estate, are chiefly of this "representative" character.[20] A further practical error lies in the fact that a property tax based upon capital and surplus amounts to an extra levy, or fine, upon conservatively managed banks. From the standpoint of safety to depositors the results would be disadvantageous. Considerable evidence of the practical significance of this fact seems to be available.[21]

Another objection to the share tax is that it is high, either as a percentage of the profits or of the property of banks.[22] Woosley shows that in thirty states in 1926 the percentage of reported state taxes to net profits of national banks ranged from a low of 13 to a high of 281 (see Table 1). This percentage in Minnesota was 37.[23] Corporation income tax returns in 1926 show uniformly much higher percentages of total state and local taxes to total net income for all banks than for all other corporations; in Minnesota the percentages were 27.90 for banks and 13.34 for other corporations.[24] Table 2 shows that in Minnesota in the year 1930 the percentage of taxes to net income in the case of banks having a net income was lower than the average for all other corporations. Woosley's comparison of the percentage of state taxes to book value of banks under the share tax and the excise tax in Massachusetts and New York shows clearly the far greater tax burden borne by bank

[19] Jensen, *A Survey of Bank Taxation*, p. 7. See pages 288–289 below.

[20] An important cause of inequality in bank taxation is the misconception prevalent in some states concerning the economic nature of bank resources. Part of the proprietors' share in the assets of a bank (capital, surplus, and undivided profits) is invested in bank premises and other real estate. The remainder is not kept in cash but is invested in evidences of indebtedness, such as acceptances, promissory notes, and bonds. Lawmakers have often failed to distinguish between the two kinds of property as bases of taxation. Real estate is a physical factor in economic production and is capable of paying a tax because of, and in proportion to, its economic productivity. A bond or a promissory note is merely the legal evidence of a temporary transfer of economic goods and the conditions of the transfer. In itself it is economically unproductive, except as it may result in more efficient use of the goods involved. During its life the bond or note represents to the owner an annual income, but only a *contingent* claim to the actual economic goods (the capital transferred or the goods purchased therewith). Only when the note matures are the economic goods or their value transferred back to the lender, who then must resume the tax burden.

[21] Cf. Thornton Cooke, "Taxes and Bank Failures," appended to *Survey of Bank Taxation in United States*, pp. 49–51. See note 19 above.

[22] Cf. Hearings on H. R. 7752 (H. R. 12490), p. 29.

[23] John Brooks Woosley, "State Taxation of National Banks" (manuscript dissertation, University of Chicago, 1931), Table XXIV, p. 346. Compiled from the Report of the United States Comptroller, 1926, and reported taxes for federal income tax returns as shown in Hearings on H. R. 7752 (H. R. 12490), pp. 30–65. See Table 1, including footnote, on the next page.

[24] As quoted in Hearings on H. R. 7752, pp. 30–65.

TABLE 1.—RATIO OF TOTAL STATE AND LOCAL TAXES TO NET PROFITS OF BANKS IN THIRTY STATES USING THE PROPERTY TAX ON SHARES, 1926[a]

STATE	REPORTED STATE TAXES	NET PROFITS	RATIO OF TAXES TO NET PROFITS
			Per Cent
Alabama	$535,000	$2,610,000	20
Arizona	110,000	199,000	55
Arkansas	736,000	791,000	93
Colorado	879,000	1,131,000	77
Florida	847,000	6,141,000	13
Georgia	755,000	1,812,000	42
Idaho	180,000	64,000	281
Illinois	5,693,000	16,484,000	34
Indiana	1,484,000	4,168,000	35
Iowa	884,000	458,000	193
Kansas	1,113,000	1,219,000	91
Louisiana	765,000	1,407,000	54
Michigan	1,749,000	5,042,000	34
Minnesota	1,764,000	4,688,000	37
Mississippi	418,000	909,000	45
Missouri	1,674,000	5,271,000	31
Montana	210,000	411,000	51
New Mexico	112,000	52,000	215
North Carolina	385,000	1,995,000	19
North Dakota	279,000	110,000	253
Ohio	2,991,000	9,074,000	32
Oklahoma	1,158,000	1,856,000	62
South Carolina	496,000	388,000	127
South Dakota	157,000	62,000	254
Tennessee	808,000	2,465,000	32
Texas	3,379,000	11,098,000	30
Utah	165,000	496,000	33
Washington	966,000	2,821,000	34
West Virginia	564,000	1,908,000	29
Wyoming	126,000	252,000	50

[a] Woosley, "State Taxation of National Banks" (manuscript dissertation, University of Chicago, 1931), Table XXIV, p. 346. Compiled from the Report of the United States Comptroller, 1926, and from reported taxes for federal income tax returns as shown in Hearings on H. R. 7752 (H. R. 12490), pp. 30–65. Mr. Woosley notes (pages 345–346) that "in some states where the ratio of taxes to income is the highest, banks have been suffering from a severe agricultural depression and in many cases have had to take over substantial amounts of real property on default of interest and principal. Allowing for such situations, and for possible inaccuracies in the data, it may still be maintained that banks are subject to an unduly heavy tax burden when both their shares and real property are assessed at full property rates."

property under the share tax system. (See Tables 3, 4, and 5.) If the excise tax is just, the share tax is excessive. Excessive taxation may have contributed to recent bank failures, though probably not more than to failures in other classes of business.[25]

[25] Cf. Cooke, *op. cit.*, pp. 49–51.

TABLE 2.—STATE AND LOCAL TAXES AND NET INCOMES OF BANKS COMPARED WITH THOSE OF OTHER CORPORATIONS IN MINNESOTA, 1930 [a]

ALL CORPORATIONS, THOSE REPORTING PROFITS AND THOSE SHOWING LOSSES

CLASSES OF CORPORATIONS	No.	NET INCOME OF ALL CORPORATIONS	TAXES	RATIO OF TAXES TO NET INCOME
				Per Cent
National banks	233	$7,098,142.86	$1,487,119.23	20.95
State banks	661	3,052,264.04	688,205.41	22.54
Other financial	264	4,528,951.81	1,374,419.77	30.34
Mercantile corporations	1,375	12,197,298.24	3,935,966.07	32.26
Manufacturing corporations	641	13,026,690.76	4,175,121.80	32.05
Public utilities	31	18,343,531.92	4,063,254.67	22.15
Mining corporations	66	38,328,899.54	16,593,133.86	43.29
Other corporations	899	9,238,515.88	3,012,404.06	32.60
Total	4,170	$105,814,295.05	$35,329,624.87	33.38
Total of banks	894	10,150,406.90	2,175,324.64	21.43
Total of other corporations	3,276	$95,663,888.15	$33,154,300.23	34.65

CORPORATIONS SHOWING PROFITS

CLASSES OF CORPORATIONS	NO. OF CORPORATIONS SHOWING PROFIT	NET INCOME	TAXES	RATIO OF TAXES TO NET INCOME
				Per Cent
National banks	193	$7,114,720.67	$1,440,306.14	20.24
State banks	563	3,094,252.16	633,169.96	20.46
Other financial	147	4,839,387.77	922,159.49	19.06
Mercantile corporations	878	16,760,110.06	2,599,558.13	15.51
Manufacturing corporations	319	19,803,659.44	2,131,989.41	10.76
Public utilities	18	18,485,656.61	4,031,234.99	21.80
Mining corporations	47	38,343,286.08	16,543,334.88	43.14
Other corporations	579	10,541,960.04	1,838,945.15	17.44
Total	2,744	$118,983,032.83	$30,140,698.15	25.33
Total of banks	756	10,208,972.83	2,073,476.10	20.31
Total of other corporations	1,988	$108,774,060.00	$28,067,222.05	25.80

[a] Statement of net income and taxes in 1930 of corporations having their principal place of business in Minnesota, showing separately (1) all corporations included in the tabulation and (2) only corporations reporting profits for the year. Compiled by the Minnesota Tax Commission pursuant to the provision of Chapter 278, Laws of Minnesota, 1931. For additional data see also pages 298–299 below.

TABLE 3.—EXCISE AND SHARE TAXES ON NATIONAL BANKS IN MASSACHUSETTS [a]

Year	Amount of Tax	Net Income [b]	Book Value of Banks	Ratio of Taxes to Net Income [b]	Ratio of Taxes to Book Value
Excise tax				Per Cent	Per Cent
1926......	$561,000	$14,725,000	$167,281,000	3.81	.33
1927......	515,000	11,046,000	176,738,000	4.66	.29
1928......	514,000	15,288,000	290,425,000	3.36	.18
Share tax					
1920......	$2,843,000	$11,061,000	$140,171,000	25.70	2.01
1921......	2,716,000	15,817,000	152,983,000	17.11	1.77
1922......	2,784,000	11,466,000	149,772,000	24.28	1.85

[a] Adapted from Woosley, Table VI, p. 247. Compiled from reports of the comptroller of currency and of the commissioner of corporations and taxation.
[b] Before taxes are deducted.

TABLE 4.—FRANCHISE AND SHARE TAXES ON NATIONAL BANKS IN NEW YORK [a]

Year	Amount of Tax	Net Income [b]	Book Value of Banks	Ratio of Taxes to Net Income [b]	Ratio of Taxes to Book Value
Franchise tax				Per Cent	Per Cent
1927......	$2,528,000	$87,867,000	$744,250,000	2.88	.34
1928......	2,694,000	83,778,000	877,959,000	3.21	.30
Share tax					
1925......	$6,639,000	$94,294,000	$667,222,000	7.04	.99
1926......	7,002,000	76,236,000	711,850,000	9.20	.98

[a] Adapted from Woosley, Table VII, p. 247. Compiled from reports of the comptroller of currency and of the state tax commission.
[b] Before taxes are deducted.

Further, since bank shares are of record, and therefore, unlike other intangibles, easily and surely assessable, and since local assessors are likely to be influenced by the popular notion that because banks hold large sums of money they can well afford to carry a heavy share of the tax load, local administration of the property tax upon shares is likely to increase the discrimination against banks.[26]

ADVANTAGES OF TAX ON BANK SHARES

On the other hand, the outstanding advantages of the property tax on shares are: (1) productivity, (2) simplicity, (3) economy,

[26] Jensen, *Survey of Bank Taxation*, p. 7.

and (4) ease in administration.[27] It has yielded from three to five or six times as much as the income or excise taxes. It is easy to obtain the book value, evasion is nearly impossible, assessment and collection at the source insure economy of administration, and there is no requirement for comparison with other taxation on the basis of complicated statistical data. It has been said further that local taxation of banks on a property tax basis is in harmony with

TABLE 5.—TAX BURDEN ON THE AVERAGE NATIONAL BANK IN THE UNITED STATES UNDER THE SEVERAL OPTIONS [a]

Kind of Tax	Percentage Rate	Estimated Taxes Payable: Business Tax [b]	Estimated Taxes Payable: Real Estate Tax [c]	Ratio of Business Tax to Net Profits [d]	Ratio of Total Tax to Net Profits
				Per Cent	Per Cent
Income	6.0	$1,405	$2,064	4.0	9.8
Excise	5.0	1,756	2,064	5.0	10.8
General property....	2.5	9,542	2,064	27.0	33.0

[a] Adapted from Woosley, *op. cit.*, Table XL, p. 450; computed from Report of Comptroller of Currency, 1928. The average national bank in 1928 had a capital of $464,307, net profits of $35,126, an investment in real estate of $110,116, and total assets of $3,706,701.

[b] Business tax refers to taxes other than on real estate.

[c] The assessment of real estate is based upon 75 per cent of the book value of this item, and the tax rate is assumed to be 2.5 per cent in each instance.

[d] It is assumed that one-third of the net profits of the average national bank came from tax exempts and are, therefore, not taxable (Woosley).

the unit or local type of bank in the United States; that is, the assets of the banks are local and therefore should be taxed locally. This rather doubtful claim will be examined later.[28] These advantages are of a nature to commend the property tax on bank shares to a taxing body faced with the practical problem of securing a certain revenue. Doubtless they account in large part for the tenacity with which the states have clung to this method of taxing banks.

INCOME TAX METHOD OF TAXING BANKS

Two other methods of taxing national banking associations were offered the states in the amendment of 1923. The dividends from such shares might be included in the taxable income of the owner or holder, or the state might levy a tax on the net income of the

[27] Woosley, *op. cit.*, chapter on Taxation of Bank Shares.

[28] See below, page 304.

banks, but at a rate no greater than that "assessed upon other financial corporations nor higher than the highest of the rates assessed by the taxing state upon the net income of mercantile, manufacturing, and business corporations doing business within its limits."[29] In 1926 Section 5219 was further amended to permit taxation of national banks *according to* or *measured by* their net income "received from all sources," the so-called excise plan. Precisely the same limits were set to the rate of this tax as in the case of the tax upon income, and the same permission was given in the two cases to tax individuals' dividend income from national banks if and as such dividends from other financial, mercantile, manufacturing, and business corporations are taxed.[30] This last provision is equivalent to combining the second with the third or the fourth tax methods of Section 5219. Income "received from all sources" appeared to include the income from federal bonds exempt by law from a direct income tax. Otherwise the fact that banks hold large amounts of such securities, while most corporations subject to an income tax hold a relatively small proportion of tax exempts, would result in essential reduction of taxes on banks even though taxation were at the same rate.

Since the third and fourth choices of Section 5219 permit conditional combination with the second, the states have turned logically to those choices. Wisconsin adopted a general income tax in 1911 but did not apply it to banks until 1927, under "compulsion" of the Hartford decision (273 U. S. 548), which declared the Wisconsin bank share tax invalid. The tax base is a three-year average of income with a graduated rate running from 2 per cent on the first $1,000 to 6 per cent on all above $7,000 net income.[31] In his intensive study of state bank taxation Woosley shows that the new tax produces approximately one-fifth the revenue to the state that the old share tax would yield.[32] Since the prime object of the tax is to produce revenue, the results are unsatisfactory. A further fault of the tax has been the inequality of incidence resulting from the exclusion of income from tax-exempt securities held in quantity by some banks.

[29] Sec. 5219 as amended in 1923 (U. S. C. A., Title 12, §548).

[30] Sec. 5219 U. S. R. S., Subsection 1c.

[31] See page 514 concerning Wisconsin's tax and averaging system, including recent modifications, which eliminate "averaging" after 1932.

[32] Woosley, *op. cit.*, chapter on Income Tax on Banks; Wisconsin Statutes, 1931 (11th ed.), Sec. 71.06, Subsection 2.

The Excise Method of Taxing Banks

The states that have attempted the excise plan have experienced varying degrees of difficulty. The Massachusetts law, which was designed to take advantage of the excise clause of the federal law, was made invalid with respect to the income from tax exempts by the Supreme Court decision in the case of Macallen Company v. Massachusetts.[33] The Court held that states may not levy a tax upon income from United States bonds or other tax-exempt securities, whether or not such tax is called an excise tax measured by or according to net income, if it is the *clear intent* of the tax to reach such tax-exempt securities. The Massachusetts law was, therefore, amended in 1930 to exclude from net income the income from tax exempts.

The New York law was drawn in 1926 immediately after the passage of the federal amendment and prescribed a 4.5 per cent tax on net income. This law likewise was considered invalidated by the Macallen decision with respect to the income from exempt securities. In the case of Educational Films Corporation v. Ward, however,[34] in which taxable income included income from copyrights, which are governmental instrumentalities, the Supreme Court held that a corporate franchise tax measured by total net income was valid. A similar case now before the Supreme Court is Fox Film Corporation v. Tax Commissioners of Georgia, in which royalties from copyrights included in the basis of the Georgia gross receipts tax are the cause of action. Hence the status of income from tax-exempt securities as a base for measuring the excise tax on banks may be said to be uncertain at present.

California amended its constitution in 1928 and in 1929 levied an excise tax of 4 per cent on the net income of the previous year. The definition of income includes tax-exempt securities. The attorney-general of California ruled that the Macallen decision does not apply to the California law. His view was sustained by the California courts; later, by the United States Supreme Court.[35]

In 1929 the states of Washington and Oregon passed excise tax laws, in each case levying a tax of 5 per cent on net income including tax exempts. The Washington law was held invalid by the state courts.[36] Banks in Washington can be taxed only on their real

[33] 279 U.S. 620 (1929). [34] 282 U.S. 379 (1931).

[35] Pacific Company Ltd. v. Johnson (1931), 298 Pac. 489. See footnote 87 below.

[36] Aberdeen Savings and Loan Association v. Chase (1930), 157 Wash. 351.

estate and tangible personal property. National banks cannot be required to pay taxes on tangible personal property under Section 5219 but are said to be doing so.[37] Oregon raised the rate to 8 per cent in 1931.[38]

The establishment in 1931 of taxation of banks on an income basis in Idaho, Oklahoma, and Utah has not yet allowed time to determine the degree of its effectiveness in operation. Yet the fact that six states have in the last three years surrendered the property tax on shares in favor of an income basis may indicate a trend. Minnesota has authorized[39] a vote in the 1932 election upon a constitutional amendment authorizing the legislature to "enact any law required to make the taxation of national banking associations conform to the laws of the United States," and further generally authorizing taxes "upon incomes and on franchises and privileges measured by income . . . and such taxes may be in lieu, in whole or in part, of taxes on any class or classes of real estate or personal property as the legislature may determine."[40]

It appears that this amendment if approved will give the legislature very wide latitude. If necessary it could revamp the tax laws so that a really productive excise tax might be applied both to banks and to other corporations, though it is not implied that satisfactory revamping would be an easy task. As it stands now it seems doubtful whether Minnesota has the legal authority to levy adequate taxes upon banks without abandoning low rate taxation of competing capital or without a satisfactory revision of Section 5219. Neither alternative promises certain, practical, and satisfactory relief soon; hence the desirability of the proposed amendment.

ADVANTAGES OF THE EXCISE TAX METHOD

Aside from the advantage of legality, the excise tax method has the weight of sound theory in its favor. It is reasonable to tax the holder of "representative" property upon or in proportion to his income from such rights or claims, rather than to tax the rights as property, in which case double taxation of property results. The holder of the bonds receives an income and on that basis may be taxed. As the lender he has a mere contingent claim upon the

[37] Jensen, *Survey of Bank Taxation,* p. 4.
[38] *Ibid.,* p. 5. See also Table 32 on page 539.
[39] Session Laws of Minnesota, 1931, Ch. 420. For text of amendment see Chapter 15, footnote 466, below.
[40] Session Laws of Minnesota, 1931, Ch. 420.

tangible property. As long as the stipulated payments are made (income to the lender), the right to the use of the tangible property remains with the borrower, who is justly subject to taxation thereon.[41]

Two sound reasons, however, might justify a light property tax upon the holder of representative property: (1) his representative property right is protected by government quite as much as the tangible property right of the owner of real estate; (2) income tax laws regularly exempt small incomes while exemption from taxes on real estate is exceptional. Thus the taxpayer who owns no real property enjoys a preferred position.[42]

Finally, the right to operate a banking business is valuable because of the normal income earned and may therefore logically be taxed on an income basis. Woosley reminds us[43] that banks are privileged to do business with a relatively small percentage of proprietor's capital investment (13 per cent of total assets of national banks are furnished by shareholders compared with 66 per cent in the case of 493 selected industrial corporations); that the United States comptroller's reports show that average earnings of national banks were fairly stable from 1914 to 1929;[44] and that business depressions probably cause less decline in incomes of banks as a class than in incomes of other classes of corporations.[45] These facts testify to the desirability of the privilege of operating a banking business. To be sure, many banks have failed, but probably a higher percentage of other types of business have failed in all periods of the business cycle.

WEAKNESSES OF EXCISE TAX METHOD

In practice the excise method has given evidence of certain weaknesses.[46] The meaning of net income is not yet clear, as shown above. This method, moreover, has resulted in greatly reduced income to the state. Woosley finds[47] that in Massachusetts the reduction was about 80 per cent from the years immediately preceding introduction of the new tax plan. He shows that in New

[41] Jens P. Jensen, *Property Taxation in the United States* (1931), p. 205. See also Report of the Minnesota Tax Commission, 1928, p. 4.

[42] Harley L. Lutz, *Public Finance* (1929), p. 384.

[43] Woosley, *op. cit.*, chapter on Franchise Tax on Banks.

[44] Cf. also the Report of the United States Comptroller of the Currency, 1930, p. 77. The ratio of net additions to profits to capital and surplus ranged from 7.08 per cent to 12.78 per cent (averaging about 9 per cent) between 1914 and 1930.

[45] W. I. King, *The National Income and Its Purchasing Power* (1930), p. 278.

[46] Woosley, *op. cit.*, chapter on Franchise Tax on Banks.

[47] See Table 3, page 284 above.

York the reduction was about 62 per cent. "In both states a four-mill tax on total book value of shares would have raised much more revenue." In California he finds the loss of revenue still greater, upwards of 85 per cent, with the yield equal to a property tax of 1.2 mills on the book value of shares of national banks.[48] Further, under the excise plan the yield of this tax has been greatly affected by the offset of real estate taxes, as in California.[49] Utah, with a 3 per cent rate, permits various offsets up to one-third of the tax.[50] The tax rate upon banks cannot be raised in California in order to produce larger returns because Section 5219 stipulates that "the rate shall not be higher than the rate assessed upon other financial corporations nor higher than the highest of the rates assessed by the taxing state upon mercantile, manufacturing, and business corporations," and since these other corporations are usually subject to multiple taxation, a higher rate of excise tax would be unfair to them. Thus the excise method as applied in California favors the banks at present.[51]

Further difficulties may be encountered through litigation over definitions of such concepts as "other financial corporations." The attorney-general of Massachusetts has defined this term to include corporations employing moneyed capital in substantial competition with any phase of national banking activity[52] but not insurance companies, savings banks, cooperative banks, or credit unions. This definition does not appear to be in harmony with the Supreme Court's interpretation of the intent of the law with respect to moneyed capital in the Hartford case[53] and the St. Paul case.[54] Such ruling would require a tax rate upon national banks no higher than the rate upon state and private commercial banks, trust companies, investment banks, mortgage loan companies, all other loan or finance companies, stock building and loan associations, stock savings banks, investment trusts, holding companies, or insurance companies — in fact, all types of companies organized to conduct or actually conducting the business of loaning, discounting, or investing funds in substantial amounts.

Insurance companies, through the Association of Life Insurance

[48] Woosley, *op. cit.*, chapter on Franchise Tax on Banks.
[49] *Ibid.*
[50] Jensen, *Survey of Bank Taxation*, p. 45. See also page 484 below.
[51] But see pages 297–298, including note 81.
[52] Report of the Massachusetts Commissioner of Corporations and Taxation, 1927, p. 98.
[53] 273 U.S. 548 (1927). [54] 273 U.S. 561 (1927).

Presidents, have expressed a desire to be omitted from the comparison.[55] But in view of their enormous volume of investments and short-time loans, and especially of the fact that their activities in some cases approach those of investment trusts or even of holding companies for bank stock,[56] the presumption is strong that they could properly be included among financial corporations competing with national banks. Expert opinion, however, seems to be that the problem of determining net income of insurance companies for state tax purposes is too complicated to make an income base feasible for such tax.[57]

It is deserving of note, however, that the famous principle of equality of tax burden between national banks and competing moneyed capital *in the hands of individuals* so consistently required by the Supreme Court in its interpretation of the property tax on bank shares is completely lost sight of in the income and excise methods of taxation permitted by Section 5219 and upheld by the courts.[58] This fact may conceivably provide greater freedom for the states in taxing national banks under the excise tax upon an income base.

MINNESOTA'S ALTERNATIVES

Minnesota, having adhered to the principle of the general property tax as applied to bank shares, is now confronted with a seeming impasse. The tax on bank shares is uncollectible because of the low registry tax on mortgages and the 3-mill tax on money and credits. The latter taxes are defended by the tax authorities of the state. Their combined yield in 1929 was $1,640,618,[59] or about three-fourths the compromise tax of $2,175,324 paid by all banks of this state in 1930.[60] Exemption of mortgages and money and credits would be costly, and furthermore would supply no solution to the problem, since it would increase the inequality of taxation of competing moneyed capital. The three other methods of taxing national banks provided by Section 5219 may be illegal in Minnesota at present because of constitutional limitations.[61] Further-

[55] Hearings on H. R. 7752 (1930), pp. 154, 155.

[56] Gaines T. Cartinhour, *Branch, Group, and Chain Banking* (New York, 1931), p. 77.

[57] Jensen, *Survey of Colorado Tax System* (Denver Chamber of Commerce, 1930), p. 149.

[58] Cf. Harley L. Lutz, *Public Finance* (1929), p. 490.

[59] Report of the Minnesota Tax Commission, 1930, p. 385.

[60] See Table 2 above. See also Table 1 in Chapter 8, page 212.

[61] Leading legal opinion in Minnesota indicates the full legality of an excise tax upon national banks under the present state constitution.

more, the experience of other states, already referred to, does not entirely warrant the expectation of comparable returns from an excise or an income tax on banks.

Likelihood of Federal Action

Congress may at some future time modify the requirements of Section 5219. The history of attempts by the states to effect such changes has shown three facts: solid opposition by both national and state banks, which have urged the necessity for protection against excessive state taxation of banks as a class; the apparent conviction of Congress that such protection is needed; and Supreme Court interpretation of the law in support of the banks' contentions.

Various plans for modification have been presented in congressional hearings. The most sweeping proposal would repeal the detailed instructions of Section 5219, leaving to the states the right to tax national banks as they tax other moneyed capital engaged in the business of banking. This proposal seems to leave to the banks only the protection of the courts under the Fourteenth Amendment. The Minnesota plan embodied in H. R. 12490, passively approved by the bankers and presented at the hearing on May 9, 1930, proposed to permit the states which tax intangibles ad valorem at fixed rates less than the rate on tangible property to tax shares of national banks "at a rate no higher than the rate assessed upon the shares of other financial corporations, nor upon the net assets of individuals, partnerships, or associations employed or engaged in the banking, loan, or investment business, nor higher than the rate assessed by the taxing state upon mercantile, manufacturing, and business corporations having their actual principal place of business within such state." For purposes of such comparison totals or aggregates are to be used.[62] This proposed amendment to Section 5219, especially drawn to remove the conflict of authorities in Minnesota, would likewise give relief to several other states in which existing bank tax laws are unenforcible.[63]

The same bill, H. R. 12490, included a fifth optional method of taxing national banks, a *specific* tax on shares based upon annual increase in net worth plus dividends, the rate of tax being made comparable with the taxes on incomes paid by other corporations.

[62] Hearings on H.R. 7752 (H.R. 12490), p. 6, Sec. 1b. See also page 298 below.
[63] *Ibid.*, pp. 99, 101, 102.

This specific tax base would include income from tax exempts, and in the opinion of competent counsel would be legal because levied upon the shares of the stockholder rather than upon the income of the corporation.[64]

With respect to these two proposals it is only fair to state that members of the House committee conducting the hearings criticized them for verbal complexity and called attention to the probability of renewed litigation over the definition of such terms as "other financial corporations," which would cause further uncertainty and ineffectiveness in bank taxation. Are insurance companies, investment trusts, holding companies, bond and commercial-paper houses, auto finance companies, trust companies, savings banks, and building and loan companies all "financial corporations" or "engaged in the banking, loan, or investment business"? If so, the lowest rate of assessment upon any of them would determine the maximum rate of tax upon national banks.

At present Minnesota does not class these corporations with commercial banks for purposes of taxation but does tax mortgage loan companies in the category with banks. Insurance companies pay a 2 per cent tax on gross premium earnings in the state.[65] Trust companies that do not accept demand deposits are taxed 5 per cent on gross earnings.[66] Savings banks, stockbrokers, and commercial-paper houses, note brokers, and investment bankers are grouped in one class, as are finance companies and building and loan associations. The reports of the United States comptroller indicate a different classification, and the usages of the states seem to vary. Therein appears to lie endless opportunity for litigation.

At the current hearings before committees of Congress,[67] several new drafts of amendments to Section 5219 were proposed. No action has been taken to date. All that can be said at this time is that no clear-cut solution has been presented to Congress that will at once explicitly protect the national banks against unequal taxation and leave the states entire freedom in methods of taxation. Until such a solution is found it seems safe to predict that Congress will not materially alter its limitations. Discussion of certain possible changes in federal bank policy and the consequent changes in bank taxation is reserved until later in this survey.

[64] Hearings on H.R. 7752 (H.R. 12490), pp. 20–24.
[65] Tax Laws of the State of Minnesota, 1930, Sec. 423 and 372.
[66] *Ibid.*
[67] April, 1932.

Reduction of the Property Tax on Shares in Minnesota

Should no relief come from Congress during the current session, three practical forms of revision of bank taxation by the next legislature seem to remain to Minnesota: (1) to retain the present invalid share tax but at a sufficiently lower rate that the banks will not care to litigate, even though the low taxes on mortgages and money and credits are maintained; (2) to raise the tax on money and credits to 4 or even 5 mills, as recommended by the Tax Commission in its 1930 report, with the same rate of tax on book value (or true value) of bank shares without deductions; or (3) to substitute the excise tax for the ad valorem property tax on bank shares. Objection may be made to all three measures for various reasons and in different degrees, as examination will show.[68]

Eight or more states have at present a moderately low tax rate on bank shares, ranging from New Jersey with a rate of 7.5 mills to Maine with 15 mills.[69] The base is generally the book value or the true value of the shares minus the assessed or real value of bank-owned real estate, which is taxed at local real estate rates. These states either exempt mortgages and other intangibles or tax them at a low rate.[70] In these states in which a moderate rate is levied, the banks have paid the tax without litigation.[71] Presumably results would be similar in Minnesota.

ESTIMATED YIELD

What would such a tax with higher rates yield in Minnesota? Reckoning book value of national banks at $68,882,000 and of state commercial banks at $30,105,000, the total book value is $98,-987,000.[72] Deducting the estimated full value of bank-owned real estate of $30,000,000,[73] $68,987,000 remains as a base for calculating the property tax on shares. In Minnesota, with the general property rate determined locally, reduction to the level of the current compromise may be secured by transferring bank stock to the class of property taxable at 25 per cent of true value. On this basis, at

[68] The proposal to raise the tax rate in Minnesota on "competing moneyed capital" to the level of the tax on bank shares is probably impractical, for reasons suggested in the Report of the Minnesota Tax Commission, 1928, pp. 143–145.

[69] In five other states the tax rate on bank shares is extremely low; in Pennsylvania and Rhode Island, 4 mills; in Delaware, Florida and Ohio, 2 mills.

[70] Woosley, *op. cit.*, pp. 219–222, Table III.

[71] Hearings on H.R. 7752, pp. 75, 94; Jensen, *Survey of Bank Taxation*, p. 6.

[72] Report of the United States Comptroller, 1930, p. 664; Minnesota Bank Call No. 193, December 31, 1930.

[73] On the basis of figures for state commercial banks in the Report of the United States Comptroller, 1930, pp. 78, 745.

an average general property tax rate for the state of 65 mills, the total bank tax including tax on real estate would amount to $1,859,633.[74] Assuming an average tax rate of 70 mills, the total yield would reach $2,002,682, while an average rate of 75 mills would produce $2,145,731. The 1930 tax was compromised at over $2,175,000.

Because of the "other moneyed capital" clause the tax law would be no more legal than now. But as a temporary measure such a plan would probably operate without objection from banks, and thus for a time both litigation and further compromise legislation by the state authorities would be avoided.

A notable modification of the ad valorem tax on bank shares obtains in Ohio under the system adopted in 1931. Although too new to be judged upon the basis of its effectiveness in operation, the Ohio plan is of interest because it "employs three devices to differentiate the tax burden on property, namely, differential tax rates, differential assessment ratios, and income taxation."[75] The plan seems to present some real contribution toward the solution of the bank tax problem. In passing, it seems desirable to compute the probable proceeds if the Ohio tax system were applied to banks in Minnesota.

A tax of 2 mills on the full value of shares (using book value, $98,987,000) would produce the sum of $197,974. Bank deposits amounting to $844,000,000,[76] taxed at the same rate, would yield $1,688,000. The total bank tax, therefore, would be $1,885,974, in addition to taxes on real estate at general property rates. These taxes are paid by the bank for the shareholder and the depositor. "Shares of, and capital employed by, dealers in intangible property, which includes brokers, finance companies, mortgage companies, and investment companies, are taxable at the rate of 5 mills.

[74] The Report of the United States Comptroller, 1930, pp. 78, 745, records total real estate holdings of banks in Minnesota as follows:

Type of Bank	Banking Premises	Other Real Estate
National banks	$13,007,000	$2,761,000
State banks	7,741,000	6,429,000
Total	$20,748,000	$9,190,000

Roughly speaking, the first category consists of urban real estate taxed in Minnesota on 40 per cent of true value, and the second group consists of agricultural land taxed on one-third of its true value. Combining the values assessed at these percentages results in a total assessed value of approximately $11,363,000.

[75] Jensen, *Survey of Bank Taxation,* p. 8.

[76] Cf. note 72. Concerning tax rates and classes in Ohio see Section 5638 of Laws of Ohio, 114 (1931).

Money and credits not otherwise specified take a rate of 3 mills. Investments consisting of stocks and bonds are taxable at 5 per cent of the income yield, but if not income-producing, at 2 mills per dollar of value."[77] This plan probably would increase somewhat the tax burden on banks in Minnesota while still making a distinction between bank capital and other moneyed capital, and thus might lead to renewed litigation.

Adoption of a Uniform Rate on Bank Shares and Intangibles

Pennsylvania is the outstanding example of the operation of this type of tax measure. The book value of shares is taxed at 4 mills. No deductions are made from the base. Since the rate is the same for bonds, mortgages, and other intangibles, the Pennsylvania law seems to be in harmony with Section 5219. The Minnesota Tax Commission believes it is feasible to increase the rate on money and credits to 5 mills without disturbing the total of declarations.[78] If this rate were applied successfully to money and credits and bank shares in Minnesota, it would yield a total revenue of approximately $2,649,935. To this should be added the tax on bank-owned real estate, or $739,535, making a total of $3,389,470. In 1930 the bank tax amounted to $2,175,000, and the money and credits tax yield was $1,323,000, or a total of $3,498,000. The application of the uniform rate, therefore, would result in a moderate reduction of the total and a shifting of the major burden from banks to money and credits. If the 5-mill rate were applied to mortgages also, as in Pennsylvania, the total tax would be materially increased. But Minnesota would doubtless hesitate to levy an annual tax of even $5.00 per $1,000 upon mortgages. If the 5-mill tax were not made uniform upon mortgages also, a loophole would be left for litigious banks. However, the probability of refusal to pay such a low bank tax on the sole pretext that mortgages were not taxed at the same rate as bank shares, would be very small indeed.

Against the adoption of either of these alternatives as a practical tax measure in Minnesota the argument is potent that neither plan is as productive of revenue to the state as the present compromise basis. Furthermore, the first certainly and possibly the second could be successfully opposed in the courts by individual banks, even though the banks might offer no concerted opposition.

[77] Jensen, *Survey of Bank Taxation*, p. 8.

[78] Report of the Minnesota Tax Commission, 1930, pp. 2, 150.

Neither the banks nor any great number of well-informed individuals advocate abandoning the low rate taxation of intangibles if a better solution of the bank tax problem can be found.

Substitution of the Excise Tax Method

From the preceding comparison of the income and excise methods of taxing banks it appears that the latter has all the advantages of the former and in addition the possibility that future interpretation by the Supreme Court may permit inclusion of income from tax exempts in the base upon which the excise tax on banks is calculated. Since Minnesota has made no use of income as a tax basis except in the case of the gross earnings tax, the development of a system of taxation based upon income would be relatively free from complications. It appears, however, that the nature of the excise tax upon banks would be greatly influenced by the interpretation put by the legislature and the courts (1) upon the phrase "other financial corporations" (see above, pages 290 and 293), and (2) especially upon the word "rate" in the restrictions imposed by Congress if the excise method of taxing national banks is employed.

MEANING OF LIMITATIONS CONDITIONING USE OF EXCISE TAX

In the case of an income tax or an excise tax on national banks, the statute provides that the rate shall not be higher than the rate assessed upon other financial corporations nor higher than the highest of the rates assessed by the taxing state upon mercantile, manufacturing, and business corporations doing business within its limits. At least two divergent interpretations of "rate" have been advanced. The attorney-general of Massachusetts seems to define rate as the ratio of *a* tax paid to net income of the corporations considered. This reading might be so interpreted as to limit the excise tax rate on national banks to the excise tax rate on "other financial corporations" and the *highest similar rate* assessed upon mercantile, manufacturing, and business corporations.[79] This interpretation appears to be supported by the preponderance of legal opinion, though it results in taxation fully as unjustifiable as that which recently caused the United States Supreme Court to reverse its former position on another matter.[80] The dilemma of California illustrates the difficulties under this interpretation.[81]

[79] Hearings on H.R. 8727 (May 10, 1928), p. 20.

[80] See Farmers Loan and Trust Co. v. Minnesota (1930), 280 U. S. 204, and a series of subsequent decisions along this line.

[81] *U. S. Daily*, April 4, 1932, p. 2. In the hearings on S. 4291 the point was urged that the present excise tax on banks measured by net income in California

The other definition of "rate" was offered by Philip Nichols, counsel for the Massachusetts National Bankers' Association, in his testimony before the House Committee on Banking and Currency, and interprets "rate of tax" as "tax load," or percentage of total taxes paid (any number, any kind) to net income.[82] If the manufacturing and mercantile corporations of a state, for example, paid an aggregate tax per year (aside from real estate, which is separately taxed in the case both of banks and of business corporations) equivalent to 15 per cent of their income, whether or not such taxes were based upon income, then the national banks might be subjected to an excise tax of 15 per cent of their net income in addition to their tax on real estate. In Mr. Nichols' words, "the tax on the income of banks shall not be greater than the proportion of income which manufacturing and mercantile corporations pay in taxes to the state and its political subdivisions." The comparison sought is one of aggregate tax burdens. To the humble layman this interpretation appears to be reasonable and equitable and to present a possibility that should not be overlooked.

ESTIMATED YIELD

If this interpretation is valid, Minnesota already has the essential data for the establishment of an excise tax upon banks. Under Chapter 278 of the Session Laws of 1931, "each bank and each financial, mercantile, manufacturing, and business corporation having its actual and principal place of business within this state" is required to file with the Minnesota Tax Commission a statement of its net income and net profits as last reported in its income tax return to the United States Government, together with a statement of its total taxes on real property, and total taxes other than on real property, imposed by the state during the given period. The published summary for 1930 given above (Table 2, page 283) shows the percentage of taxes to net income to be approximately the same for national and state banks; the tax on national banks is slightly lower (20.95 and 22.54, respectively). The corresponding percentage for all "other financial corporations" is considerably

must be at a rate not higher than the excise rate on business, mercantile, and manufacturing institutions, which in addition pay real estate and property taxes. The 4 per cent rate (the only tax on banks) cannot be raised without the same increase being applied to 37,000 business corporations subject to multiple taxation. Whether or not this interpretation of Section 5219 is correct, California's present bank tax seems to be based upon it.

[82] Hearings on H.R. 8727 (May 10, 1928), p. 139. See also a further elaboration of the same idea in hearings on the Goodwin substitute bill, H.R. 12490 (May 9, 1930), p. 18.

higher than that for banks (30.34). The percentage for all corporations other than banks is still higher (34.65). The mining corporations have a higher percentage than any other single class of corporations (43.29).[83]

It appears that at least the present tax burden upon national banks would be maintained through the levying of an excise tax at a rate equal to the difference between the percentage of total taxes and the ratio in which real estate taxes stand to net income.[84] In addition, experience might show that some increase would prove equitable. The fact that the national banks in Minnesota have continued for several years by gentleman's agreement to pay on a compromise basis the taxes assessed under the general property tax law suggests that the banks see no serious inequality in the present tax burden. A 15 per cent excise tax in 1930 would have produced approximately $1,522,000. Adding to this the tax upon real estate, amounting to approximately $739,000, we get a total tax burden upon banks by this method of approximately $2,261,000, or essentially what was paid in 1930. Conceivably the excise tax return might be raised somewhat and still be legal.

Summary of Feasible Measures in Minnesota

Assuming that no change is made in federal statutes and that by 1933 an income base for taxation will be legal in Minnesota, the excise tax upon banks has most to recommend it of the four plans open to Minnesota. As described above it would be fully in harmony with Section 5219, as two of the plans would not be. It entirely escapes the troublesome comparison with competing moneyed capital in the hands of individuals. It seems more likely than other methods to yield returns comparable with present taxes, or even higher. There is an excellent chance also that if a Minnesota excise tax law is properly drawn it may be interpreted by the Supreme Court to include all bank income from whatever source in calculating net income as a base. The language of the Court in the Macallen decision indicates that Massachusetts overreached itself in its

[83] Against the inclusion of the percentage for mining corporations in the total for all corporations the point is made that tax rates upon industries that deplete natural resources are not strictly comparable with other rates. If we exclude this item we find a percentage for "all other corporations" of 29.88. (See Table 2, page 283.)

[84] To illustrate: In 1930 the average percentage of total taxes to net income of national and state banks in Minnesota was 21.745. Estimating real estate taxes on these banks at a rate of 65 mills on an assessed valuation of $11,363,000 results in a percentage of real estate taxes to net income of 7.27. The difference in percentages is thus 14.475. See Table 2 and footnote 74 in this chapter.

eagerness to include certain income from tax exempts; its statute was obviously directed at government securities. The decision of the Court may have been intended to parry this direct thrust at federal tax exempts, which aimed frankly to take advantage of a seeming conflict in the laws. Certainly in the case of Educational Films Corporation of America v. Ward the Court clearly says that in the Macallen case the law was *specifically* worded so as to include an income that previously had not been included in the measure.[85] "But a tax may very well be upheld as against any casual effect it may have upon the bonds of the United States when passed with a different intent and not aimed at them." Further, the Court says that the Macallen decision is not a "departure" from the principle laid down in Flint v. Stone Tracy, "that a non-discriminating tax upon corporate franchise is valid, notwithstanding the inclusion of tax exempt property or income in the base of it."[86]

An act that does not discriminate against tax-exempt securities by specific or veiled allusion to them, especially if drawn like the New York tax law, which requires payment of the franchise tax in advance for the current year though based on income for the past year, seems to meet the requirements of the Court; for it would be a tax "which can in no case have any incidence, unless the taxpayer enjoys a privilege which is a proper object of taxation, and which would not be open to question if its amount were arrived at by any other non-discriminating method." The Georgia case and the California case further clarify this question, especially since the latter case involves tax-exempt securities of a bank.[87]

If the Nichols interpretation of Section 5219 is not legally valid, as the preponderance of legal opinion seems to hold, it appears that

[85] 51 Sup. Ct. 173 (1931).

[86] 220 U. S. 154, 172 (1911).

[87] Pacific Co. Ltd. v. Johnson, decided by the United States Supreme Court on April 12, 1932, after the above was written. As quoted in the *U. S. Daily* of even date, the Court said that "the privilege of doing business in corporate form, which is a legitimate subject of taxation, does not cease to be such because it is exercised in the acquisition and enjoyment of non-taxables." The reasoning applied in the case of Educational Films Corporation of America v. Ward was sustained and emphasized. The Court said: "The owner may enjoy his exempt property free of tax, but if he asks and receives from the state the benefit of a taxable privilege as the implement of that enjoyment he must bear the burden of the tax which the state exacts as its price." See 52 Sup. Ct. 424. This decision appears to establish fully the legality of using the full net income of banks as a proper basis for the franchise tax. The Pacific Company is, of course, a state corporation. The question may be raised whether in the case of a corporation having a federal charter, such as a national bank, the decision of the Supreme Court would be similar.

Minnesota cannot tax national banks adequately or satisfactorily without a revision of Section 5219 or the adoption of the pending amendment or some similar amendment to the state constitution.

PROBLEMS OF ADMINISTRATION

In the case of the excise tax particularly, and probably in the other plans indicated also, the tax should be levied and collected by the state government. Real estate taxes might still be administered locally. But the calculation of rates of excise tax could be accomplished satisfactorily only through a central commission. A part or all of the collected tax could then be distributed to the local government divisions where the banks are situated, in proportion to debits to individual accounts or on some other satisfactory basis.

COMPLICATIONS DUE TO CHANGES IN CHARACTER OF FINANCIAL INSTITUTIONS

Minnesota has not yet been confronted to any great extent with certain situations which have developed in some other states and which will perhaps result in revising the classification of "other financial corporations" with reference to the banking business. Savings banks have been developing the use of checks, while commercial banks have for two years or more shifted deposits from demand to time classification as far as possible. Savings banks have in recent years enormously increased the proportion of their assets represented by short-time paper in order to secure greater liquidity. The McFadden Act greatly increased the powers of national banks to make loans on real estate and to invest in long-term securities other than federal bonds. Most building and loan associations do a large savings banking business. Life insurance companies have an enormous volume of short-time loans to policy-holders in competition with commercial banks. That a large volume of credits was withdrawn from New York banks and loaned on the call market in 1928 and 1929 by insurance companies and other "non-banking" corporations in direct competition with the banks is well known. As certain of these institutions take on more unmistakably the functions of commercial banking, the class of "other financial corporations" must necessarily become more inclusive.[88] The use of the income basis of taxation seems to solve most of the problems involved in such changes.

[88] Cf. Hearings on H. R. 12490 (May 9, 1930), p. 77. Mr. Blodgett, state tax commissioner of Connecticut, discusses possible interpretations of this phrase in another connection.

Complications Due to Group, Chain, and Branch Banking

The problem of administration is complicated somewhat by recent developments in bank organization. Branch banking is technically nonexistent in this state at present, although "banking offices" having most of the functions of branches are maintained. Branches of foreign banks do not exist in Minnesota. In the case of group and chain banks each bank legally retains its corporate identity, and the excise tax paid by each corporation could easily be returned to the proper local government unit. Real estate taxes would raise no question. A natural person owning shares of a chain of banks and a holding company holding shares of the members of the group might both be taxed upon their shares of the stock of state banks situated outside Minnesota, such stock being classified as money and credits.[89] Furthermore, if Minnesota should establish a general income tax upon the income of individuals from corporations whose stock they hold, there is nothing in Section 5219 to prevent such levy upon the income from shares of national bank stock, whether held by natural persons or by corporations such as holding companies. In the case of a Minnesota bank owned by an individual or a holding company situated elsewhere than in Minnesota, both excise tax and real estate tax would be levied upon and collected from the Minnesota corporation by the state of Minnesota.

EFFECT OF GROWTH OF BRANCH BANKING UPON THE BANK TAX PROBLEM

At present the legal question of situs for tax purposes is often complicated enough, though recently it has been simplified somewhat by Supreme Court decisions. The legal fiction is that a tax on the stock of a bank is really a tax upon the stockholder but that for convenience it is levied upon the corporation and paid by it.[90] But since legally the tax is upon the shareholders, shall the proceeds of the tax (when collected by the state) go to the city where the bank is situated or to the place of residence of the stockholder?

In the case of domestic corporations owned by their own citizens

[89] Minnesota Revised Statutes, 1927, Sec. 2337. For recent developments with respect to the power of the states to tax intangibles of nonresidents see R. J. Traynor, "Taxation Problems in Branch Banking," *Minnesota Law Review,* 15:770 (June, 1931); Henry Rottschaefer, "Power of the State to Tax Intangibles," *Minnesota Law Review,* 15:741 (June, 1931); and below, page 303.

[90] McCulloch v. Maryland (1819), 4 Wheat. 316; Van Allen v. The Assessors (1865), 3 Wall. 573.

the states differ in their practices. In the case of shares owned by citizens of other states, the tax goes to the state government that levied the tax and in whose territory the bank has its legal situs. States sometime tax securities of a foreign corporation held by their own citizens. This frequently involves double taxation. In states that permit state-wide branch banking the question of allocation of tax proceeds other than real estate taxes is more complicated. Two principles have been tried: distribution of the tax funds on the basis of capital employed by or assigned to the various branches and distribution on the basis of the total deposits or total resources at the various branches. The latter method appears to be more sound, inasmuch as it seems to use a better measure of the business done at a given branch. A still more accurate measure would be the proportion of local to total net income earned by the branch and the bank.

At present it appears as if in the near future we shall have at least a moderate development of interstate branches of national banks. Such a condition raises at once the question of authority to tax. The ownership lies unquestionably in the head office. A branch has no legal existence of itself. Could Iowa tax a Minnesota national bank upon its branch located in Iowa? Iowa might further wish to impose excise or income taxes upon the business of branches in Iowa. This might induce attempts to use such taxation to practically exclude such branches. Federal action could probably be relied upon to prevent that danger, but the controversies might involve considerable friction between states and between state and nation. Conceivably such questions could be settled amicably, but a spirit of good will and equity does not always exist in practice. Since, moreover, forty-nine different codes of banking and as many of taxation would have to be reckoned with, the possibility of serious and costly differences is greatly increased.[91]

ULTIMATE SOLUTION

Efforts to solve the vexing problem of state taxation of national banks have in the past sought to sweep away any vital assertion of congressional authority or to modify the federal restrictions so as to permit each state to pursue its own tax preference. Either attempt if successful necessarily results in a maze of tax regula-

[91] For further discussion of possible legal difficulties compare R. J. Traynor, "Taxation Problems in Branch Banking," *Minnesota Law Review*, 15:770 (June 1931).

tions, which vary from state to state. Ultimate solution of the problem must follow the lines of simplicity and uniformity. Sound principles of taxation do not vary according to latitude and longitude. A scientific tax devised, levied, and collected by a single authority would have enormous advantages over the present conflict of authorities and diversity of methods and efficiency. Equitable division and distribution of proceeds among state and local government units could be made on the basis of local bank deposits as a measure of business, or better still on the basis of debits to individual accounts within a period, as a more accurate measure of banking activity.

The view that banks should be taxed locally because their business is local is becoming less and less tenable. No community lives unto itself. Local banks mobilize and energize local credit, but they serve also to import and export credit — purchasing power — for village, state, and nation. Wisely managed local banks diversify their assets geographically as well as according to types of securities. Bonds, commercial paper, and acceptances owned by a local bank may represent loans of local funds to enterprises in other states or in the antipodes. Correspondent relations with other banks, domestic and foreign, are vital to the local customer who wishes to send or collect credits elsewhere, yet such relations require the local bank to deposit part of its funds with its correspondents. The conclusion is inevitable that the service which one bank can give locally depends in part upon the services of banks elsewhere, and that the more prosperous a community becomes, the greater the exchange of goods with other localities and hence the more vital the dependence upon banks of other cities and states. The actual medium of exchange in the United States has ceased to be primarily money and has become largely bank credit, which circulates throughout the country with remarkable ease and rapidity. In fact, it is generally recognized that without this recently developed circulating medium modern business would be seriously restricted. No doubt the service rendered to commerce could be materially improved if regulation and taxation of banking were uniform.

Uniformity of taxation of national banks might be obtained in two ways. (1) Congress might permit the states only one prescribed form of tax at a uniform rate low enough to favor the national banks, or it might withdraw from the states all power to tax the national banks and itself write a uniform law.[92] (2) The more recently developed possibility of uniform bank taxation rests upon the proposed complete substitution of national for state banking. The conflict of sovereignties has resulted in banks operating under a multiplicity of systems, and consequently varying standards and restrictions have obtained in different areas in the United States. Under the so-called "parity principle" Congress has attempted to adjust national banking laws to the forty-eight state systems. Repeatedly the requirements for national banks have been made "easier" so that national banks might compete on an equal basis with state-chartered institutions.[93] The parity principle has effected equalization of banking standards downward.[94] Elimination of state banking would leave one system of commercial banks under a single authority. The authority to create, to franchise, carries with it the power to tax and otherwise to regulate. A uniform national tax on national banks might be used as a source of federal income, replacing other tax income, or the proceeds might be distributed to state and local governments on the basis of local banking activity as suggested above.

The Federal Reserve Board is quoted in the *United States Daily*[95] as believing that unification of the banking system is "essential to sound banking in the United States." "A plan to bring all banks of the country into one system under Federal con trol is being drafted in the offices of the Federal Reserve Board." The board states further that "no serious constitutional impediment stands in the way of simplifying the country's banking system under national authority." A strong array of Supreme Court decisions may be cited in support of this view.[96] There are some indications that leading members of Congress favor such a measure.[97] If such a measure should be adopted, great care should be taken, of course, to safeguard the legitimate rights of the individual states, of their business interests and the interests of their

[92] Cf. an editorial in *Bankers' Magazine*, 58:15 (January, 1899).

[93] Cf. the McFadden Act (1927) with respect to loans on real estate and investment in securities.

[94] See Charles W. Collins, *Rural Banking Reform* (1931), pp. 139, 154.

[95] April 5, 1932, p. 1.

[96] The following decisions in particular: McCulloch v. Maryland (1819), 4 Wheat. 316; Osborn v. United States Bank (1824), 9 Wheat. 738; Veazie Bank v. Fenno (1869), 8 Wall. 533; Casey v. Galli (1876), 94 U. S. 673; First National Bank of Bay City v. Fellows (1917), 244 U. S. 416; First National Bank of St. Louis v. Missouri (1924), 263 U. S. 640.

[97] *United States Daily*, April 5, 1932, p. 1.

citizens; but in any case comprehensive action is hardly to be expected for several years.

If all banking should be put under federal authority, bank taxation could and doubtless would be greatly simplified. Duplication and conflict of authority would be eliminated and unequal taxes making for unfair competitive situations would not be permitted. The contingent problem of equitable taxation of intrastate and interstate group systems would no longer exist.

The simplification and uniformity that federal control would bring about should not, however, be used to deprive the states of revenue that they need more than does the federal government. There are several possible solutions of this problem. One has been suggested above, namely, distribution of proceeds to the state and local governments. Another would be the relinquishment of inheritance, income, or other taxes to the states or distribution of a part of the proceeds of these taxes. In fact, one of the greatest tax needs before the country today is the adjustment of federal and state tax systems as a whole. The harmonization of bank taxation is a part of this problem.

While federal control of all banking may prove to be the ultimate solution, the most practical path to early and substantial improvement of the present bank tax situation appears to be along the lines of the excise plan discussed above, provided the pending amendment to the state constitution is approved. If it is not approved, an amendment concerned with the bank taxation issue alone ought to be submitted as soon as is practicable.

CHAPTER 11

RAILROAD TAXATION[1]

To a total of about ten billion dollars in taxes collected by all governments and political units in the United States in 1929, the Class I railroads of the country contributed nearly four hundred million, or slightly over 4 per cent.[2] In the same year the railroads of Minnesota contributed to the state $8,142,000, or about 5 per cent of the entire revenue collected from taxpayers in the state.[3] Because of the importance of railroad taxes, a study of their growth, equity, and administration is especially appropriate.

That railroad taxes are excessive and that they have increased more rapidly than taxes on other property is an allegation frequently heard. From 1890 to 1928 the population of the United States increased 90 per cent, but railroad taxes increased 1,220 per cent and other taxes increased 952 per cent. Yet during this same period railroad property investment increased only 203 per cent, gross earnings increased 501 per cent, and net earnings, 382 per cent.[4] While these figures bear out the charge of increasing tax burdens thrust upon railroads, the analysis does not tell the whole story. In 1890 the taxation of railroads had not yet begun as a serious business. Thousands of miles of line were exempt from taxation and many states had adopted low rates in order to induce railroad construction. The country was unexploited. Distances were enormous and communication was difficult. Many states built canals and railroads. Subsidies running into millions of dollars and guaranties of tax exemptions and low tax rates in perpetuity or for given periods were part of the program. Some eight hundred miles of railroad in Georgia are still exempt, and Maryland and New Hampshire have exemptions for railroads. It is clear, therefore, that a mere increase in the tax rate or tax burden is no proof of excessive taxation.

[1] This chapter was prepared by Professor Emerson P. Schmidt of the School of Business Administration, University of Minnesota.

[2] National Industrial Conference Board, *Cost of Government in the United States, 1928–29* (New York, 1931), pp. 57, 70.

[3] Report of the Minnesota Tax Commission, 1930, p. 385.

[4] *Railway Taxation, 1930,* p. 6, published by the Bureau of Railway Economics, Washington, D. C.

The fact that some $5,800,000,000 additional funds were invested in the railroad industry from 1920 to 1930 indicates that capitalists did not regard the return from the investment as unduly low before the present extraordinary depression. The comparison in Table 1 of the cost of new capital to municipalities, railroads, other utilities, and other industries does not show that capital funds have veered away from the railroads. From 1920 to the middle of 1928

TABLE 1.—AVERAGE COST OF NEW CAPITAL, 1922–1929 [a]

	PER CENT
Municipal bonds	4.3
Railroad bonds	5.2
Other utility bonds	5.7
Industrial bonds	6.2

[a] Moody's *Public Utility Securities,* 1931, p. xix. Based on weighted averages of yields of newly issued bonds.

the cost of railway capital declined continuously. In 1920 every dollar raised by the roads cost them 7.29 per cent; by 1928 this cost had fallen to 4.78 per cent.[5]

THE AD VALOREM TAX SYSTEM

At present there are three main systems of railroad taxation in operation: ad valorem, stock and bond, and earnings. Few states have only one of these, but in most states one system predominates. Furthermore, with the exception of net income taxes levied by the federal government and a few states, the above-mentioned taxes are in nearly all states a revised form of general property tax. The criticisms usually leveled against the general property tax frequently apply with even greater force when that tax is applied to railroads.

GENERAL PROBLEMS

DIFFICULTY OF ASSESSING RAILROAD PROPERTY

A building or a farm may be a unified going concern and have a value as such. A railroad extends in narrow strips through many assessment districts and is commonly interstate. Its value depends on its ability to perform transportation services over an economic

[5] Roy L. Reierson, "Cost of Railway Capital," *Journal of Land and Public Utility Economics,* 6:98–101 (1930).

region and can be determined only when considered as a whole. Local assessment has usually resulted in very great inequalities; for example, in 1874 the assessment in New York ranged from $400 to $23,000 a mile. The qualifications of the majority of local assessors have never been very high. Their judgments are largely the judgments of the man in the street. And when it comes to appraising a piece of property that is a minute section of a large going concern, the value of which concern depends on many non-local factors, their judgments are likely to be more faulty than usual.

A railroad may have a taxable value in excess of or less than the bare cost of constructing the property. This fact gives rise to such concepts as franchise value, goodwill value, corporate excess, and obsolescence. These elements of value are likely to elude the local assessor entirely and can be determined only by an appraisal of the property as a whole. The Adams Express Company in 1895 reported $5,189,000 of real and personal property but the aggregate market value of its shares amounted to over $16,000,000. The difference, or the intangible value of the property, arose from the unity of use; a share, therefore, of this intangible value, proportionate to the mileage in the state, was held to be taxable by the state, according to the decision of the court.[6] Obviously a local assessor would have great difficulty in discovering this value and above all in determining its amount. In Texas the central board of assessors assesses only this intangible property. The balance is still assessed by the counties as required by the constitution and is not subjected to review or equalization.

The local assessors likewise run into great difficulty in assessing the rolling stock of a railroad. Their technique for arriving at the value of a locomotive or a box car is inadequate. They need also to figure the depreciation, always a difficult task. An assessor would have to decide too when a locomotive or box car should be subject to local assessment in his district. Assessors in neighboring districts may assess the same rolling stock. Clearly this part of the company's equipment must be centrally assessed if the ad valorem method is to be retained.

ARGUMENT FOR UNIT ASSESSMENT

Regional or system assessment of a railroad is as logical and as necessary as was the departure from local assessment. In one

[6]Adams Express Company v. Ohio (1896), 165 U. S. 194.

respect it is perhaps more necessary, since under the present method of state assessment each state is tempted to reach out and import a part of the value of the railroads in other states. Arizona boasts of such importation of value from other states for taxation purposes. The state tax commission capitalizes the net income of a railroad as a whole at 8 per cent; its proportionate value is then allotted to Arizona on a mileage basis. "In this way Arizona gets a portion of the earnings of the railroads in the more populous states as well as a portion of the earnings of their large terminals, such as Chicago, Kansas City, and Los Angeles."[7]

THE COURTS FAVOR CENTRAL ASSESSMENT

The courts have not opposed state central assessment. The rule appeared first in 1875 in Illinois and in Missouri in the valuation of intrastate railroad property and was approved by the federal Supreme Court as reasonable and within the powers of the state.[8] In later cases it was extended to include interstate property.[9] That is, the value of the intrastate property of an interstate railroad may be determined upon the basis of information concerning the total mileage of the road and the market value of the securities of the company. The rule is not intended to extend the jurisdiction of any state to tax property it could not otherwise tax, that is, to import property for taxation.[10]

From the standpoint of raising additional taxes, central assessment has been eminently satisfactory. In North Dakota under local assessment certain designated public utility property was assessed at $7,899,000 in 1928; after two years of activity by the state board of equalization the assessment was increased about 50 per cent, to $11,863,559.[11] Lutz gives abundant evidence of similar increases that occurred earlier in other states. In Illinois, for instance, railroad assessments jumped from $25,500,000 in 1872 to $133,500,000 in 1873. In Indiana the assessment jumped from $66,000,000 in 1890 to $161,000,000 in 1892. In both these cases there was, of course, some slight increase in railroad mileage in these years.[12]

[7] Report of the Tax Commission of Arizona, 1930, p. 9.

[8] Harshman v. Bates County (1876), 92 U. S. 575.

[9] Cincinnati, New Orleans, and Texas Pacific Railroad Company v. Kentucky (1885), 115 U. S. 321.

[10] Great Northern Railway v. Minnesota (1929), 278 U. S. 503.

[11] Report of the Tax Commission of North Dakota, 1930, p. 49.

[12] H. L. Lutz, *The State Tax Commissioner* (Harvard University Press, 1918), p. 73.

WHAT DOES VALUE MEAN?

Assuming that central assessment is desirable, the assessing authorities must have some theory of value. Actually, most of the authorities seem to have a multiplicity of theories and methods of determining value. Usually a statute or the constitution gives some general directions as to the determination of values when applied to railroad assessment.

Terminology varies considerably in the several states with reference to such phrases as real value, actual value, market value, cash value, sale value, true value, fair cash value, fair cash market value, and others.[13] The constitution of Oklahoma requires all property to be assessed at its fair cash value, the estimated price that it would bring at a fair voluntary sale. But, "as a matter of fact," writes the chairman of the Oklahoma Tax Commission, "property is not assessed in Oklahoma at its full value, and it is variously estimated that it is assessed from 40 to 100 per cent."[14]

All the diverse definitions of value probably mean approximately the same thing, namely, the value of the property at a free voluntary sale. But railroads are rarely sold. When they are sold it is often at a forced sale. Furthermore, railroad property differs so radically from other types of property that comparisons are difficult. Sale values, moreover, are not the same under all circumstances. For instance, in the sale of shares of stock the price will differ according to whether the transaction involves odd lots, lots of a hundred shares, or from 25 to 100 per cent of the outstanding shares. Numerous opinions are bound to arise as to what constitutes the sale value of a railroad company, especially when there is no semblance of perfect competition and no actual sale has taken place.

Another question that arises is whether the assessed value should be equal to the sale value or to the value to the owner. The New York Stock Exchange erected its own building, which was highly specialized for its own use. The Exchange argued that the assessment should be on a basis of sale value and not value to the owner. Since there is no other use for the building and no potential buyer, there is really no reasonable sale value. Thus the sale value would be materially below the economic value of the property to the Exchange. Why a building or any other structure that is especially

[13] G. G. Tunell, "Value for Taxation and Value for Rate Making Purposes," Proceedings of the National Tax Association, 1927, p. 263.

[14] Letter to the author from Chairman Melven Cornish, January 18, 1932.

adapted to the use of one particular owner should be taxed, not on the basis of its value for that particular use, but rather on its much lower value for some other hypothetical use, is beyond comprehension. In this case the court decided that the assessment should be made on the basis of value to the owner and not sale value.[15] Wisconsin requires an opposite interpretation.

Up to the present time no rational formula for determining the taxable value of a railroad has been discovered. North Dakota uses two criteria: stock and bond value and capitalized value. The weight to be given each of these is not stated, and the rate of capitalization is admitted to be arbitrary.[16]

The Administrative Burden of the Ad Valorem System to the Railroads

Another objection to the ad valorem system is the excessive burden it frequently places on the railroads in the way of making calculations, preparing reports, sending payments, attending hearings, and perhaps keeping a watchful eye on the ratio of assessment of other property to its full value. In some states, for instance, a railroad must certify to each county not only the length of its lines in that county but also the portion of the line in each local tax district. The line may run through several dozen overlapping tax districts in each county. A check for the amount due is sent to each county in question, and the proper county official then divides the proceeds among these numerous tax districts according to the mileage contained in each. The addition of a few extra feet to a line in a given district and the abandonment of a part of a line elsewhere must be taken into account the following year. Every change in the boundary of every political subdivision from year to year necessitates a new survey to determine the percentages of the line located in these changed subdivisions of the state.

Mr. E. A. McCrary, tax commissioner of the Northern Pacific Railway Company, says that all the states through which its lines operate require different reports.[17] Several states require reports running into hundreds of pages of detailed figures. Many costs are

[15] People ex rel. New York Stock Exchange Building Company v. Cantor et al. (1927), 223 New York Sup. Ct. 64. Somewhat similar issues have been raised with respect to the Minneapolis Federal Reserve Bank Building and other Minnesota properties.

[16] Report of the Tax Commissioner of North Dakota, 1930, p. 50.

[17] Interview.

required to be allocated in a way that would make any first-class cost accountant lose his temper.

Many of these administrative burdens imposed on the railroad companies are not inherent in the ad valorem system. In Michigan they are diminished somewhat by the fact that the proceeds from the ad valorem railroad tax are returned to the local areas in proportion to school population in each. In Wisconsin practically the entire sum collected from railroads remains in the state treasury.

The Wisconsin Ad Valorem System

THE CRITERIA OF VALUE USED

Wisconsin, after trying the gross earnings tax, reverted to the ad valorem system. There the state tax commission is required to assess all railroad property at its true cash value, that is to say, at what it ordinarily would sell for at private sale. The commission recognizes that railroads are seldom sold. It therefore asks itself, What investigation would a prospective purchaser make?

> Very naturally, he would scrutinize the earnings of the utility. He would also desire to know the amount of the investment and the cost of replacing the property at present-day prices and in its present condition. But the earnings would undoubtedly be considered by him and influence his valuation of the property as much as or more than any other element. Hence the commission uses as one of the bases of determining the value of a utility system the capitalization of its earning power.[18]

Because of fluctuating earnings the commission normally utilizes average earnings over a period of "from three to five years. . . . The rates of capitalization vary, depending upon the size, strength, earning power, and financial prospects of the company in question. The rate at which earnings should be capitalized in each case should be the rate which would invite capital for investment in the enterprise under consideration."

Another element considered by Wisconsin in the assessment of utility property is the market value of the securities of the company.[19] Under normal conditions this market value represents a composite estimate of the investing public as to the worth of the entire property. This method of assessment has received judicial sanction.[20] Because of price fluctuations the commission here, too, uses a three- to five-year average. Moreover, it uses "figures repre-

[18] Report of the Wisconsin Tax Commission, 1930, p. 86.

[19] See footnote 33 below.

[20] State Railroad Tax Cases (1876), 92 U. S. 575, 605.

senting both the cost of the property and the depreciated book value. . . . In addition, whenever it is possible to do so, the data relating to cost of reproduction new, less depreciation, is compiled. . . . In each case under consideration, no one basis is used to the exclusion of all others. All possible information is secured and carefully weighed before the final assessment is made." Much of the information on which the Wisconsin commission relies is obtained from elaborate reports supplied by the railways.

SOME CRITICISMS OF THE WISCONSIN SYSTEM

We are not told what weight is accorded each of the factors enumerated. In the case of a given railroad it is quite possible that the book value might be $1,000,000, the capitalized value $2,000,000, the cost of reproduction new, less depreciation, $1,500,000, and the value of securities on the exchanges $2,500,000. What, in such a case, would the commission decide to be the value for taxation purposes? When it was suggested to one of the commissioners that the procedure and the results of the evaluating procedure must be purely arbitrary if there is no definite formula for determining value, the commissioner replied that if a formula were used, *then* the results *would* be arbitrary. As now determined, he argued, the results are due to a proper weighing of the varying factors and a reasonable value emerges.[21] It has been suggested by one authority that the reluctance of the various tax commissions to adopt a definite formula for determining assessed value and to disclose the weight accorded each factor of value is due to their fear that such precision will only result in endless litigation.[22]

The Michigan system is even more vague than that of Wisconsin; there the commission never discloses the criteria on which the assessment is based.[23] In fact, the Michigan assessment body has admitted that to reveal its methods would expose it to attack by the railroad attorneys.[24] In both Michigan and Wisconsin the public is kept ignorant of the real process and of the factors that finally determine the assessment. Mr. J. T. Waddill of the Missouri Tax Commission states that the value determined by the commission "is an arbitrary value fixed by the road's physical

[21] Interview with Commissioner Charles D. Rosa.

[22] Jens P. Jensen, *Property Tax in the United States* (University of Chicago Press, 1931), p. 429.

[23] Hsien-Ju Huang, *State Taxation of Railways in the United States* (Columbia University Press, 1928), p. 119.

[24] Report of the Minnesota Tax Commission, 1912, p. 203.

value, its earning power and its financial condition, stock market, *etc.*"[25] If the method is not known to the people it is not subject to their scrutiny. Furthermore, so long as no exact rule prevails by law there is every inducement for the railroads to get into politics. This is well borne out by experience.

It is an enormous task to assess the railroads in a state such as Wisconsin, in which there are eight thousand miles of line owned by some thirty railroads, most of which are interstate. If the market value of the securities is one of the criteria, that value must be apportioned to the state in accordance with some rule. If net earnings are used as a basis of assessment, a portion of those earnings must be allocated to Wisconsin and, in addition, the commission is confronted with the difficult task of determining a rate of capitalization. Furthermore, the commission admits the use of varying rates of capitalization from year to year and for different companies. Should it use annual earnings or an average of three or five years? Again the commission admits that it has no uniform practice. Cost of property, cost of reproduction, and cost of reproduction minus depreciation are all utilized. As is well known, to find cost or reproduction cost is a process involving enormous expense and a great deal of guesswork. Valuation by the cost of reproduction method usually involves the imaginary blotting out of the property and the calculation of what it would cost to bring it back into existence. The land would have to be acquired. But at what price? At the present price of adjoining land? If that is the assumption, then the charge is made that these prices are dependent on the presence of the railroad and so the valuation involves circular reasoning.[26] The calculation of depreciation is also largely a matter of guesswork and experts almost never agree on the amount to be deducted, if any. Because of the technical changes that occur no railroad would be built exactly as it exists today. Should such factors be considered in calculating cost of reproduction?

One advantageous feature of the Wisconsin and Michigan systems, however, is that the property is viewed as a whole. In Illinois, New Jersey, and a few other states the state board has adopted a much more piecemeal system of assessment. Real property may be assessed separately, then personal property, and,

[25] From a report to the writer. Italics not in the original.

[26] Homer B. Vanderblue, *Railroad Valuation* (Houghton Mifflin Company, 1917).

finally, franchise value. This system involves much more work and violates the unit assessment idea. In some instances this simply means that a state assessor has been substituted for the local assessors. Thus, while it has some merit, the method does not go far enough.

Improving the Ad Valorem System

CAN THE AD VALOREM SYSTEM BE MADE WORKABLE?

To a great extent the difficulties of valuing railroad property discussed above arise from faulty theory and poor administrative methods. In determining the base for *rate-making* purposes the courts have largely neglected earning capacity and market value (and rightly so) and have concentrated on historical cost and cost of reproduction. It appears that the tax commissions have frequently been influenced too much by the theories and methods of the courts in *rate cases* and too little by earning capacity, the most important determinant of *taxable value.* They have insisted too strenuously on making an inventory of the physical units of property. Every new machine purchased, or bridge erected, or car put into service has been a cause for concern. Likewise, every locomotive retired or every station abandoned has meant a decreased assessment whether or not the earning power of the road was decreased or increased by such abandonment or purchase.

Many states now do take earnings into account as one of the criteria of value, but the bulk of the administrative cost of assessment goes into the making of inventories. It seems obvious that a railroad may have a reproduction cost of $100,000,000, but because of its strategic location, easy grades, and skilled management, it may have a capitalized value of twice that figure. On the other hand, the capitalized value may be a great deal less than the original or the reproduction cost. Taxable value is market value or the capitalization of all expected future net income. It is this aspect on which the tax commission should concentrate.[27] The difficult problems of settling upon a rate of capitalization and of allocating an appropriate part of the system value to the state would still have to be faced. But these problems are believed to be easier to solve than the problem of physical valuation by the piecemeal inventory method.

[27] It is not implied that past income, "physical value," and many other factors should not be *considered* by the tax commission. Everything that affects future net income, or that helps in estimating it, is pertinent.

Table 2. — Percentage of Tracks Operated, of Car and Locomotive Mileage, Etc., of the Great Northern Railway Company in the Several States, 1930[a]

Item	Percentage in Each State											
	Wisconsin	Minnesota	Iowa	North Dakota	South Dakota	Montana	Idaho	Washington	Oregon	Manitoba	British Columbia	Other
All tracks operated	1.97	26.44	.96	20.18	3.43	22.27	1.15	16.24	2.07	1.67	3.62	...
Car and locomotive mileage	2.36	32.78	1.01	19.58	.91	27.89	2.41	12.16	.36	.21	.33	...
Ton and passenger miles	3.81	38.24	.79	18.24	.62	24.46	2.33	10.91	.32	.08	.20	...
Gross operating revenues	4.15	35.31	.84	17.79	.85	22.95	2.01	14.64	.46	.31	.63	.06
Net railway operating revenue	4.15	59.18	.49	18.42	2.26[b]	14.64	3.22	4.38	.36[b]	.12[b]	1.28[b]	.40[b]
Average	3.29	38.39	.82	18.85	.71	22.44	2.22	11.67	.57	.43	.70	.07[b]

[a] Data from W. L. Schoettler, Great Northern Railway Company. [b] Deficit.

AN IMPROVED METHOD OF ALLOCATING THE TAXABLE VALUE OF A RAILROAD

After the market or taxable value of a railroad or other utility has been determined for the system as a whole, we still have the problem of allocation to the several states or other jurisdictions concerned. It is impossible to secure an allocation formula that is always both practical of administration and unassailable from the standpoint of economic theory. The proper thing to do is to choose the best possible practical criteria of allocation, criteria that will conform fairly well to net earnings, that will prevent an unreasonable importation of value or of multiple taxation, and that will not result in unduly erratic or absurd results. It is believed that no single measure of allocation is likely to be so satisfactory generally as a composite criterion, particularly if this is used by all the different taxing jurisdictions. Whether the so-called physical inventory of plant is used or not, it would probably be well to include in the composite unit of allocation some such factors as the following: miles of track operated, car mileage, locomotive mileage, revenue traffic units, gross operating revenues, and net revenues from railway operations. Many, if not all, railroads gather state figures on these matters for their own uses. In Table 2 such data are shown for the Great Northern Railway for 1930. To eliminate violent fluctuations, a three- or five-year average could be used. If adopted generally, this system would avoid "the importation of value" from other states and consequent duplicate and unequal taxation. While an apportionment of the company's property according to this composite method would allot a higher tax yield to Minnesota than is collected at present, these figures are not intended to show that Minnesota undertaxes this railroad. It is as justifiable to argue that the taxes in other states are too high. The purpose of these tabulations is merely to show the unsoundness of present physical appraisal methods of assessment and allocation.[28] (See page 317.)

Table 3 indicates the percentage of the Great Northern Railway Company's taxes actually collected by each of the states in which the company operates and the percentage that would have been collected under the scheme suggested in the following table.[29]

[28] The writer is making a further investigation into this problem of determining the value of a railroad and apportioning it to the states through which it operates, with the hope of developing a formula that will take account of ability to pay, equity, governmental needs, and ease of administration.

[29] The details of this plan would need to be carefully scrutinized and perhaps appropriate weights assigned to the various items suggested. Other items might be included.

TABLE 3.—PERCENTAGE OF 1930 TAXES OF GREAT NORTHERN RAILWAY COMPANY ACTUALLY COLLECTED IN EACH STATE AND THEIR DISTRIBUTION UNDER PROPOSED PLAN

STATE	PERCENTAGE ACTUALLY COLLECTED	PERCENTAGE UNDER PROPOSED PLAN
Wisconsin	3.19	3.29
Minnesota	21.28	38.39
Iowa	.54	.82
North Dakota	20.61	18.85
South Dakota	1.42	.71
Montana	24.95	22.44
Idaho	2.03	2.22
Washington	22.90	11.67
Oregon	.99	.57
Manitoba	.23	.43
British Columbia	1.80	.70
Total	100.00	100.00

THE AD VALOREM SYSTEM AND ABILITY TO PAY

RELATION OF TAX TO GROSS AND NET RAILWAY REVENUES

Mr. H. A. Thomson, tax commissioner of the Soo Line, informed the writer that in a number of states in which that company operates the tax paid bears no logical relation to the value of the property either in good or in bad years. In one year the ad valorem taxes paid by the company in Montana amounted to about 75 per cent of the gross receipts. Table 4 shows the relation between gross earnings and taxes paid in the various states in which the company operated.[30] The rate ranged from about 5 per cent in Minnesota to 62 per cent in Montana.[31]

An analysis of the ratio of state and local taxes to net operating

TABLE 4.—RATIO OF 1930 TAXES TO 1929 GROSS EARNINGS OF THE SOO LINE IN EACH STATE

STATE	PER CENT	STATE	PER CENT
Wisconsin	5.51	Illinois	5.45[a]
Minnesota	4.94	South Dakota	27.20
North Dakota	7.44	Montana	62.61
Michigan	10.43	System	5.98

[a] 1929.

[30] It should be noted that Minnesota is the only state where taxes are measured by gross earnings but calculations have been made for the other states.

[31] These figures are not quite accurate because in some instances gross earnings accrued from non-operating properties; otherwise the Minnesota rate would be exactly 5 per cent.

revenues in the several states through which the Great Northern and the Northern Pacific railways operate indicates that the taxes levied in those states bear no systematic relation to taxpaying ability. In many states these companies had no net railway operating income, that is, no income after all deductions except interest and dividends have been made. Yet in these states the companies had to pay millions of dollars in taxes. In the other states the ratio of taxes to net operating income varied from a low of 10.92 per cent for the Great Northern and 13.92 per cent for the Northern Pacific in Minnesota to a high of 66 per cent for the Great Northern and 73 per cent for the Northern Pacific in Washington, as indicated in Table 5.[32]

TABLE 5.—RATIO OF STATE AND LOCAL TAXES TO NET OPERATING REVENUES OF TWO RAILROADS IN VARIOUS STATES

STATE	NORTHERN PACIFIC RAILWAY, 1930	GREAT NORTHERN RAILWAY, 1929
	Per Cent	Per Cent
Wisconsin	Deficit	13.32
Minnesota	13.92	10.92
Iowa	.....	29.89
North Dakota	44.11	21.49
South Dakota	.....	Deficit
Montana	40.01	23.35
Idaho	2,209.35	15.19
Washington	73.02	52.62
Oregon	Deficit	207.35
Manitoba	Deficit	66.87
British Columbia	.....	337.00
System	42.54	21.36

ABILITY-TO-PAY THEORY NOT UNIVERSALLY ACCEPTED

While this constitutes a serious defect of both the ad valorem and the gross earnings taxes, the latter can be partially remedied by graduating the tax, by a supplementary net income tax, or by using a five-year average. It should be noted that the ability to pay is not universally or even usually accepted as the only criterion of obligation to support the government; a railroad that earns no net income in a given year enjoys, nevertheless, the protection and

[32] Mr. E. A. McCrary, tax commissioner of the Northern Pacific Railway, warned the writer that the allocation of earnings and expenses to the various states is on an arbitrary basis, although the same system applies in each state and therefore for a reasonably accurate general impression such allocation will suffice. Data for a longer period would be necessary of course for other than indicative purposes.

the advantages of government. It might be as logical to urge that in lean years a business should refrain from paying its rent or bond interest as to argue that because of no net income it has no obligation to pay taxes.

THE CAPITAL STOCK AND BOND SYSTEM OF TAXATION

Instead of making a direct valuation of railroad property a number of states levy a tax in accordance with the outstanding securities of the company. This is basically a property tax, the securities merely being a measure of the value. In some instances book value is used; in others, market value. Some states levy the tax on the stock only; in others, bonds, floating debt, and perhaps surplus are included. No state relies on this system exclusively, however, and the method is of declining importance.

New York, Pennsylvania, and Massachusetts are the three outstanding states using the capital stock tax for railroads. In New York the railroads have never been singled out for special taxation, but as the need for more revenue has occurred one tax after another has been placed on all corporations. At present the New York railroads pay three franchise taxes. The first of these is measured by the capital stock employed within the state; the second is actually a gross earnings tax; and the third is in reality a property tax. Finally, all tangible real and personal property is subject to state and local taxes assessed by the local authorities. A stranger mixture could scarcely be found.

In Massachusetts the railroad tax consists of a local tax on the real estate and machinery outside the right of way and another tax on the remainder of the property as indicated by the market value of the capital stock over and above the value of the property locally taxed. This represents an attempt to tax the property as a unit and to get at the value of the franchise or the value in excess of the mere physical property. The assumption seems to be that the market value of the stock gives a true indication of the value of the company.

One of the outstanding merits of the capital stock tax over the ad valorem is that it requires no complex process to determine the value of the property. Arbitrariness in the assessment is largely removed, however arbitrary the rate on the capital stock may need to be. A portion of the stock and bond value of an interstate railroad must be allotted to the state, and this also is likely to be done on an arbitrary basis. The taxing authorities are given a definite rule in regard to the method of determining the market, or par, or book value of the securities. But many problems remain to be solved. Shall par or market value be the criterion? If market value, should the value as of a certain day or week or the average for the year or a period of years be taken?[33] Should bonds, floating debt, and surplus be included?

On the average, nearly 60 per cent of the capitalization of the railroads is made up of bonds, but in a given state some companies have no more than 40 per cent in bonds and others have as much as 75 per cent. Clearly, a tax on capital stock exclusive of bonds will operate unequally. From an economic viewpoint, funds are devoted to the same use whether raised by sale of bonds or of stock. From the point of view of taxation, bonds are as important as stocks so far as the total value of the property is concerned.

It is simpler to determine the par value than the market value of securities. Par value, however, has no fixed relation to taxable value. Market value or value for taxation purposes depends, among other factors, on the freight and passenger rates and the amount of business available. Extensions made out of surplus earnings will be reflected in the market value of the securities but not in the par value unless stock dividends are paid.

The determination of taxable value by means of market value of securities has received judicial sanction in the state railroad tax cases in which Justice Miller said, "When you have ascertained the current cash value of the whole funded debt, and the current cash value of the entire number of shares, you have by the action of those who, above others, can best estimate it, ascertained the true value of the road, all its property, its capital stock, and its franchises."[34]

[33] Nebraska uses market value of stocks and bonds *on April 1* to determine the taxable value of railroads in the state, according to a letter from Mr. William H. Smith, Nebraska tax commissioner. How extreme absurdities may enter into the results is indicated by the Wisconsin method. There the tax commission found the average value of the Northern Pacific stock during 1931 to be $77,562,000. The method used was to multiply the number of shares actually sold each day by the average market price for that day and thus arrive at an average value throughout the year. The company itself took the average quoted price throughout the year, without regard to the number of shares that exchanged ownership, and by this method arrived at an average value of $94,550,000 for the same stock during the same year. Information supplied by Mr. E. A. McCrary, tax commissioner of the Northern Pacific Railway Company.

[34] 92 U. S. (1876), 575, 605.

While market value is likely to be the better test of tax value it too has its drawbacks. Speculation, rumors, and other special circumstances may cause the price of the stock to be depressed or elevated unduly. Some railroad stocks are very active on the exchanges; others are not — in fact some are not quoted at all. Here the determination of their taxable value becomes a special problem. In 1904 the Interstate Commerce Commission found that the securities of only 225 roads of a total of 2,000 could be valued according to market quotations.[35] Another difficulty of administering this tax is suggested by Professor Lutz in these words, "The complication of railroad security issues by reorganization, consolidation and operation of lines under long term leases makes stocks and bonds a doubtful, if not entirely worthless, index of values."[36] It has been pointed out that non-operating property, such as timber lands, mines, and hotels, are normally assessed locally in the various states, yet the value and earning power of these properties are frequently reflected in the security values of the railroads. Thus under this system of taxation proper deductions should be made to allow for local assessment and taxation of this type of property.

THE GROSS EARNINGS TAX

Early History of Gross Earnings Taxes

The first adoption of a gross earnings tax in the case of the railroad industry was that for the Illinois Central Railroad Company in 1851.[37] This company still pays on this basis, whereas other roads in Illinois are taxed on an ad valorem basis. In 1854 this principle was adopted in Wisconsin and in 1857 it was embodied in railroad charters in Minnesota. In 1871 it superseded the capitalization tax in Michigan for some of the roads.

At present six states, Minnesota, California, Connecticut, Maine, Maryland, and Ohio, rely wholly or to a considerable extent on this type of tax for railroads, and fourteen states or more use it in part, including Alabama, Georgia, Illinois (for one company), Louisiana, Mississippi, Missouri, New York, Oregon, Pennsylvania, Rhode Island, South Carolina, Tennessee, Virginia, and West Virginia.[38]

[35] Report of the Minnesota Tax Commission, 1912, p. 211. These 225 roads, however, probably comprised most of the mileage.

[36] H. L. Lutz, *Public Finance* (1924), p. 388.

[37] Guy E. Snider, "Taxation of Gross Receipts of Railways in Wisconsin," Publications of American Economic Association, 3d series, Vol. 7, no. 4, 1906, p. vii.

[38] Most states apply a gross earnings tax to car line and freight line companies.

Why Michigan and Wisconsin Rejected the Gross Earnings System

Michigan and Wisconsin reverted to the ad valorem system after having tried the gross earnings tax. Does this mean that there is some fundamental defect in the principle of the gross earnings tax? Peculiar and special political and administrative circumstances caused the overthrow of the tax in both states. Michigan utilized a capitalization tax until 1871, when the gross earnings system was adopted. Low rates of from 1.5 to 3 per cent were put into effect "with the deliberate intention of giving a concealed subsidy to the railroads; and powerful influences in the legislature were able to prevent any advance in the rate. . . ."[39] Under this system the railroad tax receipts fell off; in 1893 there was a drop of 25 per cent.

This decline occurred just at the time when there was a growing deficiency of revenue in the state treasury. Several court decisions hampered the operation of the tax. The tax law was re-enacted three times and frequently amended. The feeling prevailed that the the tax was, in fact, unconstitutional. In addition, there was no definition of gross earnings, of mileage, or of uniformity in railroad accounts and practically no machinery for supervision and administration of the tax. Some roads made questionable deductions before reporting their gross earnings. The tax was a graduated one, and since a slight reduction in the reported earnings per mile would often put a railroad in a lower tax bracket, there was this additional inducement to falsification. As a result, the tax virtually amounted to self-assessment, as charged by its opponents.

The opposition to the gross earnings tax in Michigan served to stimulate similar antagonism in Wisconsin, where the tax law became the subject of repeated law suits and legislative modification and thus was made a political football.[40] In both states there was a reform movement for "equality of taxation." The adoption of the general property tax uniformly applied was urged as the remedy for inequality. In 1898 the Wisconsin Tax Commission pointed out that the corporations taxed under this system were not taxed so heavily as other corporations and it mildly recommended a change.[41] In 1903 the Wisconsin gross earnings tax system was

[39] Report of the Minnesota Tax Commission, 1912, p. 201.
[40] Snider, *op. cit.*
[41] R. C. McCrea, "Taxation of Transportation Companies," Annals of the Academy of Political and Social Science, 15:43 (May, 1900).

replaced by an ad valorem system. In both Michigan and Wisconsin the people insisted on the abolition of the gross earnings taxes on grounds that would not bear critical analysis.[42]

The Minnesota Gross Earnings Tax

As previously indicated, Minnesota first used the gross earnings tax for railroads in 1857. While not all railroads have been subject to this tax since that time, there has never been any general departure from the system; more and more railroads were brought under it until in 1887 it was made compulsory for all of them.

The act incorporating the Minnesota and Pacific Railroad Company in 1857 imposed an annual gross earnings tax of 3 per cent on the company, the tax to be in lieu of all taxes and assessments, both state and local. This tax was levied in consideration of land grants, privileges, and franchises. The land granted to the company was to be exempt from taxation until sold. In the same year similar taxes and exemptions were applied to other roads, including the Transit Railroad Company, the Root River Valley and Southern Minnesota Railroad Company, and the Minneapolis and Cedar Valley Railroad Company.[43] Other railroads incorporated without land grants were required to pay the usual property tax.

In 1873 the St. Paul, Stillwater, and Taylor's Falls Railroad Company was exempted from other taxation and assessments forever in consideration of its agreement to pay a tax of 1 per cent on the annual gross earnings for three years, to be followed by 2 per cent for the next seven years and 3 per cent thereafter. Any other railroad could elect to come under this law and be exempted from all other taxes and assessments.[44]

In 1887 another law was passed requiring every railroad to be liable for the gross earnings tax in lieu of all other taxes and assessments unless it had accepted and become subject to the 1873 law mentioned above or to some special act or acts relating to taxation.

Until 1905 the gross earnings tax rate was 3 per cent after the tenth year of a railroad's operation. In 1903 the legislature voted to raise the rate to 4 per cent. But a constitutional amendment adopted in 1871 required that any proposed modification of the gross earnings tax for railroads be submitted to the people and

[42] Snider, *op. cit.*, p. 118. See also Bulletin of the National Tax Association, 7:282 (1922).

[43] Session Laws of the Territory of Minnesota, Extra Session, 1857, Ch. 1 and 2, Sec. 17 ff.

[44] Special Laws of Minnesota, 1873, Ch. 111.

approved by a majority of those voting at the election.[45] Consequently the 1903 measure did not become effective until 1905. Land grants were still exempted until sold.

In 1912 the Minnesota Tax Commission published in its annual report a very exhaustive study of the gross earnings tax on railroads by Professor E. V. Robinson. He not only endorsed the system as the best one available but also recommended an increase in the rate from 4 to 5 per cent, in order that railroad and other property should be taxed on more nearly equal bases.[46] This recommendation was adopted in 1913, but since that time there has been no increase in the rate. In 1919, however, the legislature took steps to remove the special assessment exemption enjoyed by practically all railroad property and in 1920 this proposal was ratified at a general election.

LEGALITY OF THE GROSS EARNINGS TAX

For many years the legality of the gross earnings tax as applied to the earnings of interstate railroads was in doubt. A number of statutes were found to interfere unduly with interstate commerce and were declared unconstitutional.

The Minnesota Supreme Court has repeatedly declared the gross earnings tax to be a property tax, the value of the property being measured by the gross earnings. In one case this Court said:

> If the gross earnings tax law is to be construed as a tax upon gross earnings, admittedly a tax upon earnings from interstate shipments is an interference with interstate commerce; but if such a law does not authorize a tax upon gross earnings, if it is a tax upon the property of the corporation within the state, its gross earnings within the state being merely a measure or method of arriving at the value of its property for taxation, it is equally clear that there is no interference with interstate commerce.[47]

Then the Court pointed out that it is not illegal for a state to tax property within its borders just because that property is used in interstate commerce and that courts have for many years recognized that the gross earnings taxes were not intended to create new taxes "but for the purpose of certainty were intended to change the method of computation."[48]

The federal Supreme Court has definitely disapproved a tax on gross earnings from interstate commerce in these words: "If it

[45] Constitution of Minnesota, Article IV, Sec. 32, adopted in 1871.

[46] Report of the Minnesota Tax Commission, 1912, p. 187.

[47] State v. U. S. Express Company (1911), 114 Minn. 346. (This interpretation is a typical legal fiction.)

[48] See also Minneapolis and St. Louis Railroad Company v. Koerner (1901), 85 Minnesota 148; Maine v. Grand Trunk Railway Company (1891), 142 U. S. 217.

[the gross earnings tax] is laid on earnings as such, they being derived largely from interstate commerce, it is an unconstitutional restraint or burden on such commerce and void."[49] The Court found an Oklahoma gross earnings tax unconstitutional. In this case, however, Oklahoma had levied a gross earnings tax in addition to the ad valorem tax on express companies and had expressly declared it to be an additional tax. The Court found it could not be sustained as a gross earnings tax and was not in lieu of a property tax, and it was therefore void.[50] On the same day that the preceding pronouncement was made the Court upheld the Minnesota gross earnings tax on express companies because the Minnesota statute definitely declared this tax to be in lieu of all other taxes, including those on property.[51]

THE ADMINISTRATION OF THE GROSS EARNINGS TAX

From the standpoint of administration the gross earnings tax is the simplest tax, both for the taxing authorities and the taxpayer. The Minnesota Tax Commission collects annually some seven or eight million dollars from the railroads at a nominal cost. The state public examiner makes a fairly thorough but inexpensive audit of railroad accounts. In the past two years the average cost of these audits for the whole state was only $4,022.[52]

The reporting of gross earnings to the taxing authorities entails little extra expense to the railroads. It is true that in Minnesota every company must keep an accurate record of every dollar collected from every shipment and every traveler. If the shipment or journey is wholly within the state the figures are merely added up. If such shipment or journey is interstate, the Minnesota portion of the freight or passenger charge must be calculated in terms of the proportion of Minnesota mileage to total mileage traveled. With the aid of Hollerith machines the tabulations are more or less automatically made, once the cards for the machines are punched. Mr. L. A. Behler, accountant in charge of this work for the Northern Pacific Railway Company, states that the task is simple and inexpensive. He states also that such calculations have to be made in any case for purposes of their own records and for the Interstate Commerce Commission, so that the Minnesota sys-

[49] Cudahy Packing Company v. Minnesota (1918), 246 U. S. 450. In this case, however, the gross earnings tax on car line companies was upheld.

[50] Meyer v. Wells Fargo and Company (1912), 223 U. S. 298.

[51] U. S. Express Company v. Minnesota (1912), 223 U. S. 335.

[52] Information supplied by E. J. Pearlove, Minnesota state comptroller.

tem constitutes in reality little extra burden to the company. It should be mentioned also that every other state through which the Northern Pacific Railway Company runs requires a similar report of gross earnings in addition to a voluminous amount of other data.

Mr. H. A. Thomson, tax commissioner for the Soo Line, also informs us that states having an ad valorem system still require from the company a report on gross earnings in order that the assessing authorities may better determine the tax value. Furthermore, for purposes of their own records the railroads tabulate this information in approximately the way usually required by law. Besides being precise and accurate, this type of tax has the advantage that it requires no valuation or assessment of the railroad property. A further advantage is that the state automatically shares in the increased earnings of the railroads without waiting for the action of a board of assessors. The gross earnings system also abolishes the complexities in connection with the taxation of franchises, which have given rise to a great deal of controversy.

Determination of a State's Portion of Gross Earnings

A state adopting the gross earnings tax must settle the question of how to determine the state's appropriate share of interstate gross receipts. In Minnesota a mileage system is used. If a railroad runs through a series of states of about equal development having similar economic conditions this system may operate equitably as between the states in question. If, however, such a state as New Jersey should adopt a gross earnings tax and determine its share of the gross receipts on a mileage basis, the amount of taxes collected would be considerably less than if an ad valorem tax determined in the usual way were in effect, because of the enormous terminal properties in that state. On the other hand, in South Dakota, in which very little traffic terminates or originates, a mileage apportionment of the gross receipts accruing from the shipments that travel in part in South Dakota may give the state an undue proportion of the gross receipts. At the same time the other states through which these shipments pass may, by virtue of denser population and denser traffic, receive an unduly small proportion.

Theory of the Gross Earnings Tax

Nearly a quarter of a century ago the Minnesota Tax Commission pointed out that a gross earnings tax altogether ignores the value of the property and the profit of the corporation and "discards all pretense of equity or of equality with other systems of taxation. It is not a tax upon property at all,[53] nor upon the profits arising from the use of property. It is essentially a business tax, a license to carry on the business for which the corporation is organized, and the amount of the tax is mathematically determined by the amount of business done. Like all other licenses the rate fixed is purely arbitrary. . . ."[54] This quotation points out at once the strength and weakness of the system.

There are three, or perhaps four, serious criticisms of the gross earnings tax. First, it discriminates against the weaker companies. Of two railroads operating in a state, one may barely earn a fair rate of return on its investment because of heavy grades, circuitous routes, and other operating difficulties, whereas the other, in consequence of good operating conditions, may have the same gross earnings and therefore the same tax, but will enjoy a wide margin of profit between gross income and expenses.

In Minnesota the railroads pay a tax of 5 per cent of their gross earnings. Yet in 1929 at least three important railroads showed no net operating revenue; on the contrary, they had a deficit. Furthermore, the 5 per cent tax on gross earnings for the other leading roads amounted to as little as 6.71 per cent of the net operating revenue for another road, as shown by Table 6. Wide variations occurred among the other companies. It should be mentioned, however, that the ad valorem system of taxation, as it operates in northwestern states, is possibly as defective in this connection as the gross earnings tax. The evidence for this was presented on pages 319 and 320.

A second criticism of the gross earnings tax is that it bears little relation to the taxpaying ability of the consumers of railroad services. This point is discussed below under railroad tax burdens.

A third objection to this tax is the instability of the yield. In this respect it stands between property and net income taxes. Taxpayers welcome a tax that relieves them from burdens when their earnings are low, though public officials do not usually welcome deficits or retrenchment. For public services that must be carried on in lean years it may be desirable to borrow funds to the extent necessary and repay in good years.

A fourth objection to the gross earnings tax is that the determination of the proper tax rate requires an appraisal of the prop-

[53] Yet it was held by the courts to be a property tax as previously indicated. See pages 326, note 47.

[54] Report of the Minnesota Tax Commission, 1910, p. 200.

erty if railroads are to be taxed on an equality with other property. If the tax value of other property is determined largely on the basis of earnings, then railroads may be appraised on the same basis. If physical valuation is the dominant method, then railroads will probably need to be assessed in the same way. No systematic appraisal has been made in Minnesota for over twenty years.

TABLE 6.—RATIO OF STATE TAXES TO NET RAILWAY OPERATING INCOME OF SPECIFIED RAILROADS IN MINNESOTA

COMPANY	1929[a]	1930[b]
	Per Cent	Per Cent
Chicago and North Western	Deficit	Deficit
Chicago, Burlington, and Quincy	Deficit	Deficit
Chicago Great Western	90.00	Deficit
Chicago, Milwaukee, St. Paul, and Pacific	14.20	21.58
Chicago, Rock Island, and Pacific	84.65	Deficit
Chicago, St. Paul, Minneapolis, and Omaha	18.36	61.45
Duluth, Mesabi, and Northern	6.71	13.99
Duluth, Winnipeg, and Pacific	32.59	406.10
Great Northern	13.95	13.04
Illinois Central	Deficit	Deficit
Minneapolis and St. Louis	35.82	329.47
Soo Line	15.30	21.66
Northern Pacific	15.31	14.65

[a] Calculated from reports submitted to the state auditor and to the Minnesota Railroad and Warehouse Commission. Taxes are deducted.

[b] Calculated from data secured from Mr. L. R. Bitney, statistician, Minnesota Railroad and Warehouse Commission. Taxes are deducted.

THE NET INCOME TAX FOR RAILROADS

The income tax is discussed in Chapter 15.[55] Its relation to the railroad industry may, however, be mentioned here. In order to avoid the defects of both the net income and the gross earnings tax, a special committee of the National Tax Association, which was rather favorable to the gross earnings tax, recommended that the net income tax be combined with the gross earnings tax:[56]

> A tax on net earnings could be imposed at a certain rate, with the proviso that the amount of the tax should never be less than a certain moderate percentage of the gross earnings. This is the same thing as providing two taxes, one on gross earnings, at a moderate rate, the other at a higher rate on net earnings, with the proviso that in each particular case the tax collected shall be the higher of the two. . . . Virtually, the same result could also be obtained by means of a gross

[55] Page 466. See also page 518.

[56] Proceedings of the National Tax Association, 1922, p. 173. A graduated gross earnings tax, the rate depending on the gross earnings per mile, has been suggested. This system would conform with ability to pay somewhat more closely in most instances than a straight gross earnings tax and would make unnecessary the determination of net income.

earnings tax at a progressive rate, starting with a moderate rate where net earnings bear a small ratio to gross or are non-existent and increasing with the increase in the ratio of net to gross.

It is well known that in the railroad industry freight rates in a given area must be the same for all competing railroads. This results in a large net income for some roads and a small net income for others. The net income tax or the gross-net tax could be readily utilized to make the system of rate regulation a little more precise, and the gains of the superior roads would be shared more readily with the public. The Interstate Commerce Commission has repeatedly recommended the repeal of the recapture clause of the federal transportation act.[57] Through this clause the surplus income of the more fortunate roads was to accrue to the benefit of the weaker roads and thence to the improvement of the transportation system of the country as a whole.[58] If this clause is abolished a state net income tax for railroads may be more appropriate than heretofore.[59]

RAILROAD TAX BURDENS

Who Bears Them?

In private industry taxes levied on specific persons or corporations frequently are shifted backward and forward to a long "waiting list" and finally settle in some proportion on stockholders, consumers, wage earners, wholesalers, and others. For instance, if the manufacturer of cigarettes is required to pay a tax of six cents on each package of twenty cigarettes, this tax tends to be shifted to the smoker in the form of a higher cigarette price, though manufacturer and dealers may absorb parts of the tax under certain conditions.

[57] The determination of gross earnings on a state basis is simple as compared with a similar determination of expenses. The allocation of costs, many of which are joint, to specific increments of business is impossible except on an arbitrary basis. The Minnesota Railroad and Warehouse Commission in its report for 1930, page 6, vehemently objects to the allocation of expenses by the railroads at present. For 1929 the Chicago, Burlington, and Quincy Railroad reported operating revenues for Minnesota as $860,000 and operating expenses as $1,536,000. The railroads in general tend to allocate to Minnesota the entire costs of maintenance and operation of the large railway terminal facilities located in St. Paul, Minneapolis, and Duluth. Obviously, these facilities are designed for the whole system, and if an income tax were to apply to railroads, a different allocation of costs should be made. If a net income tax is to be adopted by the several states their commissions should require the adoption of uniform methods of cost allocation.

[58] William J. Schultz states that there is no point in adopting any other tax, such as net income, in addition to gross earnings, since both are shifted in any case. (*American Taxation and Public Finance*, 1931, p. 517.) In the light of the problem of strong and weak roads this seems a dubious conclusion.

[59] Report of the Interstate Commerce Commission, 1930, p. 96. It is not intimated that the recapture clause has operated effectively to date.

Do shippers and travelers using railroad facilities ultimately bear the tax imposed on railroads? Under competitive conditions a uniform tax or a tax levied in accordance with output tends normally to result in higher prices to the consumer. The extent of the rise in prices depends primarily on the conditions of supply and demand, especially on the elasticity of demand. The high-cost or least efficient producer has his unit costs increased by approximately the amount of the tax, and if he is to remain in business he must raise his selling price. If the high-cost producer is forced out and the supply is thus decreased, the producers who remain can raise prices. Thus most of the tax probably passes on to the consumer.

The railroad industry is highly regulated, however. It was the intent of Congress that service rates be so fixed by commissions that railroads in a particular area can earn about 5.5 to 6 per cent on their rate base. If wages or other costs rise, it is the duty of the commissions to raise service rates so that the allotted rate of return can be earned. Similarly, if a state levies taxes on a railroad other than those on net income above a fair return, the total operating expenses will increase and the management will go to the commission for rate increases. To the extent that the traffic will bear these increases, they will be passed on to customers.[60] But normally there is a considerable lag before service rates are raised to compensate for tax increases and the adjustments can never be exact.

An examination of commission and court decisions supports this analysis. The Ohio Public Service Commission reckoned the operating costs of hauling a ton of coal from one town to another as follows:[61]

	Cents
Line hauling and assembling	51.29
Excise tax	3.20
Other taxes	1.50
Rentals	1.11
Switching charges	7.28
Total	64.38

Presumably, if the commission had found the excise tax to be 5.2 cents instead of 3.2 cents, it would have allowed the railroad to make a higher hauling charge. In a telephone case the Pennsyl-

[60] A similar view is expressed in the Report of the Tax Commission of North Carolina, 1928, p. 237.

[61] Herbert D. Simpson, "Taxation of Public Service Industries," *Journal of Land and Public Utility Economics*, 1925, p. 46.

vania Public Service Commission allowed the company to include in its operating expenses taxes on non-operating property, since the revenue from this property was included in the total revenue.[62] The Missouri commission allowed such a small item as an annual $50 occupational tax to be added to annual expenses.[63] However, the companies must show that an increase in taxes will cause an insufficiency in revenues.[64]

Comparative Railroad Tax Burdens in the Several States, with Special Reference to Minnesota

No study of railroad taxation would be complete without an inquiry into the relative burdens imposed by various states on their railroads. From a statistical standpoint this problem is made more difficult by virtue of the fact that the railroads are predominantly interstate in character and the economic conditions in the various states differ so widely that taxes paid per mile of line are not a satisfactory index of the different burdens. The net incomes of the railroads are not separated on a state basis and in many cases the data on the investment or reproduction value are not available by states. However, data in regard to railroad taxes in the various states are published annually.

TAXES PER MILE OF LINE IN THE SEVERAL STATES

As is indicated in Table 7, Column III, the average state and local tax in the United States per mile of line for all Class I railroads and their non-operating subsidiaries was $1,229 in 1929. The Minnesota rate ($988) was distinctly below the average. Sixteen states — Alabama, Arkansas, Colorado, Delaware, Georgia, Iowa, Maine, Missouri, Nebraska, New Hampshire, North Dakota, Oklahoma, South Dakota, Tennessee, Texas, and Vermont — had a lower rate per mile than did Minnesota. It will be noted that these states, with perhaps one or two exceptions, are more predominantly agricultural than is Minnesota. Thirty-one states and the District of Columbia had a higher rate than Minnesota.

[62] Erie v. Mutual Telephone Company, Public Utility Reports, Inc., 1931 A, p. 169.

[63] Public Utility Reports, Inc., 1930 E, p. 47.

[64] Public Utility Reports, Inc., 1929 E, p. 272. Many additional cases could be cited to support the position that taxes are normally shifted to consumers. The Interstate Commerce Commission selected 5.75 per cent as a fair rate of return after payment of the federal income tax, and 6 per cent as a fair rate prior to deduction of the tax. Reports of the Interstate Commerce Commission, 68:683. See also Galveston Electric Company v. Galveston (1922), 258 U. S. 388, the leading case on this point.

TABLE 7.—RAILROAD MILEAGE, TOTAL TAXES, TAXES PER MILE, AND THE RATIO OF TAXES TO VALUE OF RAILROAD PROPERTY IN THE UNITED STATES

State	I	II	III		IV	V	VI	VII	VIII	IX
	Miles of Line, 1930[a]	State and Local Taxes, 1930[b]	State and Local Taxes per Mile of Line[c]		Value of Railroads, 1922[d]	Ratio of Taxes to Value, 1922[e]	Value of Railroads, 1923[f]	Ratio of Taxes to Value, 1923[g]	Value of Railroads, 1931[h]	Ratio of 1930 Taxes to Value, 1931[i]
			1929	1930						
						Per Cent		Per Cent		Per Cent
Alabama	5,245	$3,681,000	$803	$797	$295,534,000	.82	$190,916,000	1.29	$196,157,000	1.87
Arizona	2,485	3,099,000	1,500	1,403	105,831,000	2.41	115,146,000	1.83	110,261,000	2.81
Arkansas	4,818	3,024,000	712	690	278,425,000	.98	177,281,000	1.49	169,716,000	1.78
California	8,206	13,210,000	1,846	1,842	710,573,000	1.70	....	....	687,509,000	1.92
Colorado	4,972	4,270,000	939	972	364,963,000	.98	159,646,000	2.20	172,658,000	2.47
Connecticut	968	1,672,000	2,086	1,737	179,075,000	1.07	....	....	403,677,000	.41
Delaware	325	166,000	565	567	21,919,000	.77	....	....	....	...
Florida	5,636	4,963,000	1,076	965	233,548,000	1.40	99,652,000	2.82	315,947,000	1.57
Georgia	6,664	3,966,000	711	719	319,619,000	.86	108,369,000	2.58	123,086,000	3.22
Idaho	2,965	3,244,000	1,239	1,219	159,946,000	1.86	168,732,000	1.71	170,000,000	1.90
Illinois	12,499	22,084,000	1,953	1,827	1,211,143,000	1.47	1,103,069,000	1.68	592,230,000	3.72
Indiana	7,106	13,852,000	2,026	2,011	790,298,000	1.35	563,553,000	2.04	501,552,000	2.76
Iowa	9,697	8,026,000	763	831	583,887,000	1.26	....	....	292,487,000	2.74
Kansas	9,338	8,870,000	997	968	666,315,000	1.01	377,036,000	1.91	412,866,000	2.14
Kentucky	4,042	5,372,000	1,561	1,411	314,731,000	.75	....	....	309,146,000	1.73
Louisiana	4,654	5,098,000	1,248	1,280	264,484,000	1.50	169,269,000	2.53	159,983,000	3.18
Maine	2,193	1,908,000	896	963	119,353,000	1.74	....	....	....	....
Maryland	1,441	2,075,000	1,813	1,829	183,100,000	1.09	....	....	179,104,000	1.15
Massachusetts	2,021	4,709,000	2,116	2,369	268,013,000	1.30	....	....	....	....
Michigan	8,071	10,815,000	1,313	1,469	571,827,000	1.23	308,627,000	2.23	318,570,000	3.40
Minnesota	8,778	6,778,000	988	823	554,570,000	1.37	485,489,000	1.75	542,590,000	1.25
Mississippi	4,191	5,046,000	1,389	1,322	213,021,000	1.84	132,757,000	2.99	100,000,000	5.04
Missouri	7,896	4,284,000	550	566	612,795,000	.50	275,487,000	1.15	254,067,000	1.68
Montana	5,228	5,177,000	1,003	1,016	318,993,000	1.57	231,234,000	2.02	233,743,000	2.21
Nebraska	6,173	4,622,000	747	749	380,413,000	1.28	314,739,000	1.55	252,841,000	1.82
Nevada	2,108	1,970,000	1,187	1,163	172,202,000	.92	75,440,000	2.24	....	....
New Hampshire	1,165	1,125,000	971	990	104,699,000	.92	42,107,000	2.36	39,729,000	2.83
New Jersey	2,298	20,441,000	9,342	9,951	572,263,000	2.58	520,582,000	2.94	507,392,000	4.02
New Mexico	2,972	2,785,000	1,016	993	207,660,000	1.07	122,178,000	1.59	98,109,000	2.84

New York	8,295	27,377,000	3,277	3,491	1,479,682,000	1.38	....	....	....	....
North Carolina	5,066	5,392,000	1,379	1,399	251,694,000	1.36	231,614,000	1.72	296,024,000	1.82
North Dakota	5,275	4,110,000	849	799	305,530,000	1.57	202,570,000	1.93	188,143,000	2.18
Ohio	8,804	19,927,000	2,288	2,334	1,009,197,000	1.80	812,005,000	2.35	847,520,000	2.35
Oklahoma	6,668	6,468,000	941	994	441,267,000	1.15	190,309,000	3.04	....	....
Oregon	3,456	3,063,000	1,267	1,119	365,252,000	.71	137,790,000	1.74	175,687,000	1.74
Pennsylvania	11,139	12,440,000	1,392	1,235	1,902,737,000	.55	....	....	....	....
Rhode Island	190	686,000	3,684	3,933	34,671,000	1.60	23,226,000	2.54	....	....
South Carolina	3,765	3,488,000	1,068	1,106	160,166,000	1.12	47,064,000	4.42	....	....
South Dakota	4,237	2,695,000	645	644	229,631,000	1.20	128,390,000	1.90	104,500,000	2.57
Tennessce	3,939	3,629,000	963	1,002	269,323,000	.94	161,079,000	1.80	....	....
Texas	16,982	7,614,000	484	494	640,968,000	.92	....	....	....	....
Utah	2,196	2,403,000	1,128	1,142	177,314,000	1.12	106,942,000	1.82	92,650,000	2.59
Vermont	1,056	406,000	517	540	53,953,000	.77	41,396,000	1.01	....	....
Virginia	4,515	7,317,000	1,686	1,759	501,972,000	.96	392,480,000	1.26	530,000,000	1.38
Washington	5,541	7,430,000	1,383	1,480	390,042,000	1.76	333,260,000	1.94	359,530,000	2.06
West Virginia	4,018	8,108,000	1,972	2,193	441,524,000	1.03	355,657,000	1.47	474,345,000	1.70
Wisconsin	7,288	7,201,000	1,002	1,034	396,746,000	1.80	348,105,000	2.09	341,566,000	2.10
Wyoming	2,035	1,970,000	1,064	1,071	128,700,000	1.08	86,488,000	1.84	90,057,000	2.18
District of Columbia	36	144,000	3,662	4,178	21,231,000	.50	14,982,000	.71	....	....
Total state and local		$308,220,000	$1,229	$1,341		1.24		2.01		2.31
Total United States government ...		40,985,000	395	178						
Total United States	248,676	$349,206,000	$1,731	$1,519						

[a] Interstate Commerce Commission, *Statistics of Railways in the U. S.*, 1930.

[b] Year ending December 31, 1930, Class I steam railway companies and their non-operating subsidiaries. *Statistics of Railways in the U. S.*, 1930.

[c] Class I steam railway companies and their non-operating subsidiaries. *Statistics of Railways in the U. S.*, 1929 and 1930. These figures do not agree exactly with those in the two preceding columns, which are from different sources.

[d] Estimate of the value of railroads and their equipment in 1922. Bureau of the Census, *Estimated National Wealth*, 1922.

[e] Estimated by the Bureau of the Census. Tax figures secured from *Statistics of Railways in the U. S.*, 1922.

[f] As reported to the Interstate Commerce Commission in response to the request of the United States Senate. 68 Congress, 2 Session, Senate Doc. 199, 1925.

[g] Tax figures secured from *Statistics of Railways in the U. S.*, 1923.

[h] True and full value of railroads as reported by state tax commissions in response to a questionnaire. In some instances only estimates were given; in others, tax commission figures; and in still others, public service commission figures. Owing to the variety of sources from which these figures were obtained too much reliance ought not to be placed on them.

[i] Ratio of Column II to Column VIII.

The instability of the returns from a gross receipts tax are indicated by the fact that in 1930 only ten states had a lower per mile tax than did Minnesota. The Minnesota rate dropped from $988 per mile in 1929 to $823 in 1930. This was a drop of 16.7 per cent in state and local taxes in one year, whereas the average for the United States actually increased 9.1 per cent, that is, from $1,229 per mile to $1,341. In 1929 the Minnesota rate was 19.6 per cent, and in 1930, 39 per cent, below the average rate for all states.

Ratio of Taxes to Value of Railroad Property

In 1922.—In 1922 the Bureau of the Census made an estimate of the national wealth in the various states which included separate figures for railroads.[65] From these census and tax figures (Table 7, Column V) we learn that the railroads paid state and local taxes to the amount of 1.24 per cent of their value as found by the census. The Minnesota rate was 1.37 per cent on the value of the roads. Thirty-one states and the District of Columbia collected a lower rate than did Minnesota, and sixteen states collected a higher rate. The lowest rate, .5 per cent, occurred in the District of Columbia and Missouri; the highest, 2.58 per cent, occurred in New Jersey. Figures for other states may be found in the same table.

In 1923.—In 1924 a Senate resolution requested data in regard to railroad valuation and taxation in the several states. The full values of the railroads in thirty-seven states and the District of Columbia were secured for 1923.[66] Data on taxes paid in 1923 were secured from the report of the Interstate Commerce Commission. An analysis of these figures indicates that the railroads in question paid 2.01 per cent on their full valuation, whereas the railroads in Minnesota paid only 1.75 per cent on their valuation. However, only twelve states paid a lower rate than did Minnesota, namely, Alabama, Arkansas, Idaho, Illinois, Missouri, Nebraska, New Mexico, North Carolina, Oregon, Vermont, Virginia, West Virginia, and the District of Columbia. Most of the states in which the lower rates prevailed are largely non-industrial. The highest rate, 4.42 per cent, occurred in South Carolina and the lowest, .71

[65] Bureau of the Census, *Estimated National Wealth,* 1922. The figures cover all steam railroads, whereas the tax data applied to these figures cover only Class I railways and their non-operating subsidiaries. This will account for some of the variations from other data.

[66] The figures for Maryland are omitted, being obviously in error.

per cent, in the District of Columbia; in Vermont the rate was 1.01 per cent.[67]

In 1931.—Letters addressed to all the tax commissions in the United States requesting information in regard to the full or true value of railroads within the states brought information from thirty-six states. In some cases the figures given (Table 7, Column VIII) are estimates; in others, they are the findings of the public service commission; and in still others, the equalized value as found by the tax commission. Because of these variations too much reliance must not be placed on them. They indicate, however, that the ratio of state and local taxes to the full value of the railroad property in the thirty-six states was 2.31 per cent for 1930. The Minnesota rate, figured on the basis of the 1925 valuation for the twelve leading roads and their taxes for 1930, was 1.25 per cent, that is, about 46 per cent below the average for the other states.[68]

Ratio of Taxes to Gross Earnings

In the five-year period ending December 31, 1930, the Class I railroads and their non-operating subsidiaries had total gross operating revenues of $30,191,692,741; they paid a total of $1,486,464,531 in the form of state and local taxes, as indicated in Table 8. Thus these taxes absorbed 4.93 per cent of the gross operating revenues. In 1929 these companies paid 4.88 per cent of their gross revenues to state and local governments; in 1930 these taxes amounted to 5.84 per cent because of the relative stability of taxes in the face of the decline in revenues. Since 1913 the Minnesota railroads have paid 5 per cent of their gross revenues to the state; thus for the five-year period ending in 1929 the state and local tax burden of the railroads as a whole in the United States was slightly lower than in Minnesota, but in 1930 the Minnesota burden was slightly lower than the national average.[69]

It should not be overlooked that in all these years the railroads paid considerable sums to the federal government. Including these

[67] 68 Congress, 2 Session, Senate Document 199, 1925. Apparently the Interstate Commerce Commission in fulfilling the Senate request accepted as the value of the railroads in the several states the figures reported by various tax or public service commissions. If so, the railroad property in the various states would obviously be valued through a great diversity of methods. This may account for the discrepancies between these figures and those found by the Bureau of the Census in 1922.

[68] It is not implied that the railroad tax rate in other states is a guide to the equity of the Minnesota rate, which declines greatly in depression years.

[69] The 1931 and 1932 depression figures will show Minnesota still lower relatively.

TABLE 8.—RATIO OF STATE AND LOCAL TAXES TO TOTAL OPERATING REVENUES, 1926–1930 [a]

YEAR	TOTAL OPERATING REVENUES	TOTAL STATE AND LOCAL TAXES	RATIO OF TAXES TO OPERATING REVENUE
			Per Cent
1926	$6,382,939,546	$279,941,982	4.38
1927	6,136,300,270	291,011,559	4.74
1928	6,111,735,511	300,720,300	4.92
1929	6,279,520,544	306,569,958	4.88
1930	5,281,196,870	308,220,732	5.84
Total	$30,191,692,741	$1,486,464,531	4.93

[a] Bureau of Railway Economics, *Statistics of Class I Railways in U. S., 1920–30* (Washington, 1931). These figures were taken from the official reports of the Interstate Commerce Commission.

sums the ratio of total taxes to operating revenues was 6.30 per cent for the period covered by Table 8, 6.60 per cent for 1930, and 7.25 per cent for 1931.

An examination of the accounts of individual railroad companies reveals that the ratio of taxes to gross earnings varies enormously in the various states through which such lines run, as indicated in Table 9. For instance, in 1930 the Northern Pacific Railway Company paid state and local taxes in Idaho amounting to 16.62 per cent of the gross earnings from the traffic in and through that state. The average for the whole system was 9.45 per cent. The rate in Minnesota is indicated as 4.90 per cent, whereas the legal rate is 5 per cent. This slight discrepancy is due to a certain accounting procedure that is of no concern here. With the exception of the rate paid by the Minneapolis and St. Louis Railroad in Illinois, the Minnesota rate was lower than any other.

As previously indicated, gross earnings are not necessarily a good criterion of taxpaying ability, nor are figures for a single year to be given too much weight. A comparison of the ratio of taxes to gross earnings of nineteen railroads in twelve states will give at least a general idea, however, of the severity of the tax burden imposed by these states. Table 10 presents such a comparison for 1926 and indicates that the taxes ranged from 2.11 per cent of the gross earnings in Missouri to 8.77 per cent in North Dakota. The Minnesota rate was 5.13 per cent.[70]

[70] Because of a slightly different method of calculating gross earnings in Minnesota than is usually used, the rate is not exactly 5 per cent. These data were compiled by the Minnesota Railroad and Warehouse Commission in a rate case and included the leading north-central and southwestern railroads.

TABLE 9. — RATIO OF STATE AND LOCAL TAXES TO GROSS REVENUES OF VARIOUS RAILROAD COMPANIES [a]

COMPANY	PERCENTAGE OF GROSS REVENUE PAID IN STATE AND LOCAL TAXES												
	System	Montana	Wisconsin	Minnesota	Manitoba	North Dakota	Idaho	Washington	Oregon	Michigan	Illinois	South Dakota	Iowa
Northern Pacific Railway Company [b]	9.45	7.70	14.31	4.90	18.73	10.47	16.62	13.50	8.11	....	....	....	....
Soo Line [c]	5.98	62.61	5.51	4.94	....	7.44	....	....	....	10.43	5.45	27.20	....
Minneapolis and St. Louis [d]	5.34	....	....	4.94	....	....	....	....	....	....	4.17	13.97	5.38
Great Northern [b]	8.30	8.85	6.28	4.91	6.11	9.43	8.24	12.74	17.74	....	....	13.61	5.27

[a] Data secured from the company in each case. [b] Figures are for the year 1930.
[c] The figures for Minnesota and Illinois are for the year 1929; all the others are for 1930.
[d] Figures are for the years 1926–1930.

THE RELATIVE TAX BURDENS OF MINNESOTA RAILROADS AND OTHER MINNESOTA PROPERTY

In a thorough study of the relative tax burdens on railroads and other property made by the Minnesota Tax Commission in 1912 it was shown that the rate of 4 per cent on the gross earnings would have to be raised to 5.74 per cent in order to place the railroads on an equality with other property. Since then the railroad rate has been increased 25 per cent whereas the average tax burden on other property, measured by millage levies, has grown from an average of 29.67 mills to 63.59 mills, an increase of 114 per cent.[71]

TABLE 10.—RATIO OF TAXES TO RAILWAY OPERATING REVENUE OF NINETEEN RAILROADS IN TWELVE STATES, 1926

STATE	PER CENT	STATE	PER CENT
Illinois	4.23	Missouri	2.11
Wisconsin	4.09	Nebraska	4.40
North Dakota	8.77	Kansas	5.46
Michigan	6.49	Colorado	5.67
South Dakota	7.51	Wyoming	2.96
Minnesota	5.13		——
Iowa	4.77	Average	5.13

The value of the Minnesota property of the twelve leading railroads,[72] as found by the Interstate Commerce Commission, was $542,590,882 in 1925.[73] In 1930 these roads paid a gross earnings tax of $7,759,556 to the state. This indicates a rate of 14.30 mills on railroad property as valued by the commission.

Table 11 indicates that taxes on all property in Minnesota subject to the ad valorem tax paid a rate of 23.33 mills on the full and true value in 1925. If special assessments are excluded, the rate amounted to 21.87 mills and to 21.77 mills for the period from 1922

[71] Report of the Minnesota Tax Commission, 1930, p. 158. See also Table 47 on page 108.

[72] Chicago and North Western; Chicago, St. Paul, Minneapolis, and Omaha; Chicago, Burlington, and Quincy; Chicago Great Western; Chicago, Milwaukee, St. Paul, and Pacific; Minneapolis and St. Louis; Duluth and Iron Range; Duluth, Mesabi, and Northern; Duluth, Winnipeg, and Pacific; Great Northern; Minneapolis, St. Paul, and Sault Sainte Marie; and Northern Pacific.

[73] This value is based on the Interstate Commerce Commission's tentative valuation of property used, plus additions and betterments, minus increase in depreciation reserve from date of valuation to December 31, 1925. It should be kept in mind, however, that actual or proper valuations for rate purposes do not necessarily coincide with actual or proper valuations for tax purposes. Hence the tax calculations based on rate valuations are approximate only.

to 1929. Had this latter rate of 21.77 mills been applied to the twelve leading railroads in Minnesota on the 1925 valuation, they would have paid $11,812,203 in 1930, instead of the $7,759,556 they paid under the 5 per cent gross earnings tax. In 1925 these roads had operating revenues of $156,034,399. To make the gross earnings tax equal to the general property levy on other property would have required a rate of 7.57 per cent.[74] Table 11 gives also the average rate of taxation on other property — 21.77 mills for the period from 1922 to 1929 and 23.35 mills in 1930.

TABLE 11. — AVERAGE TAX RATE BASED ON TRUE AND FULL VALUE OF PROPERTY IN MINNESOTA FOR SPECIFIED YEARS[a]

YEAR	VALUE OF PROPERTY	TOTAL TAXES	RATE IN MILLS	TOTAL TAXES EXCLUDING SPECIAL ASSESSMENTS	RATE IN MILLS
1925.......	$5,398,112,241	$125,951,488	23.33	$118,040,134	21.87
1922–1929[b]	5,395,725,852	125,413,609	23.24	117,475,522	21.77
1930.......	5,292,939,751	130,921,947	24.74	123,595,579	23.35

[a] Data secured from the reports of the Minnesota Tax Commission, 1922–1930, and biennial reports of the state auditor, 1923–1930. But see note 73 on page 340.
[b] Average.

Another method of comparing the relative burdens of gross earnings and property taxes is to capitalize the net earnings of the business paying gross earnings taxes. A formula for comparison on this basis was suggested by the Connecticut Tax Commission in 1913.[75] In this case the writer has taken 5.75 per cent as the rate for capitalizing the net railway operating income, which is the same as the net income before bond interest is paid. According to this formula the rate on the gross earnings of railroads in Minnesota would be 7.54 per cent.[76] It should be noted that if a higher or lower rate of capitalization had been employed the result

[74] $\frac{\$11{,}812{,}203}{\$156{,}034{,}399}$ of 100=7.57.

[75] $\frac{t\,r}{i} = x$ where x equals the rate on gross earnings that should be applied to equal the property tax rate, t equals the rate of property tax, r equals the ratio of net to gross earnings and i equals t plus the rate of interest at which the net income is computed. See C. J. Bullock, *Selected Readings in Public Finance* (1924), p. 638.

[76] $$\frac{21.87 \text{ mills} \times \frac{42{,}737{,}553}{156{,}034{,}399}}{21.87 \text{ mills} + 5.75} = 7.54 \text{ per cent.}$$

would have been different.[77] It is significant that both these methods indicate that if railroads are to be taxed on a parity with other property in the state, a rate of about 7.50 per cent would be required. See page 341.

At present (1932) the railroads and other industries are depressed. To increase their taxes now would probably not be the part of wisdom. It is barely possible that the railroads, unlike general industry, will face a permanent depression and may never again be able to earn 5 per cent on their present capitalization. Western civilization appears to be passing rapidly into an oil, rubber, and electricity stage to which railroads may not be wholly adaptable. This may require a wholesale capital charge-off and, if this fear is well grounded, the taxpaying ability of the railroads will be less rather than greater in the future.

SUMMARY OF CONCLUSIONS

The low cost of new capital for the railroad industry, at least up to the time of the present depression, does not indicate that the industry has been taxed excessively.

The ad valorem system of assessment, in so far as it relies on a physical appraisal, involves considerable arbitrariness and uncertainty. The weight to be given historical (investment) cost and cost of production, as well as depreciation, are matters of judgment causing serious difficulties in making valuations. If the ad valorem system is to be made reasonably satisfactory, able experts and additional appropriations for valuation purposes must be secured in most states. If net income is utilized to determine value, or at least chiefly used, the ad valorem system can be made workable.

Because of the numerous interpretations and statistical variations that may be applied to the stock and bond method of valuation, this plan has only very limited usefulness.

Gross earnings as a measure of taxation is the simplest measure

[77] The following table indicates the gross earnings tax rates that would apply under the varying rates of capitalization indicated:

Capitalization Rate	Equivalent Gross Earnings Tax Rate	Capitalization Rate	Equivalent Gross Earnings Tax Rate
Per Cent	Per Cent	Per Cent	Per Cent
5.00	8.33	6.50	6.89
5.25	8.05	6.75	6.70
5.50	7.79	7.00	6.52
5.75	7.54	7.25	6.35
6.00	7.32	7.50	6.18
6.25	7.10	....	....

to apply. It incurs little extra expense for railroads and tax commissions. It stands between the general property tax and the income tax with respect to stability of revenue.

If the state adopts an income tax, it might be applied to railroads as well as to other corporations.

Neither the ad valorem system as applied generally nor the gross earnings tax makes any serious pretense of conforming closely to ability to pay. However, every company receives certain benefits from government, and in any case its taxes ought to be sufficient to compensate governments for the cost of supplying these benefits.

Since the net income derived from Minnesota business by the companies is not calculated and since no appraisal of the property has been made recently, an accurate comparison of the tax burdens of railroads with those on other property is difficult to make. Such data as are available indicate that it would require an increase of about 50 per cent in the gross earnings rate on railroads to put them on a parity with other property. Owing to the business depression, and particularly to the uncertain future of the railroads, it would, however, be unwise to make such an increase in railroad taxes before the situation is somewhat clarified.

CHAPTER 12

THE TAXATION OF PUBLIC UTILITIES[1]

Increase in the Value of Public Utilities

In 1900 the railroads were regarded as the one great public utility. Today the term "public utility" is used frequently to apply exclusively to utilities other than railroads. The marked increase in the investments and earnings of public utilities has induced legislators to turn their attention more and more to this class of property for purposes of taxation. In 1902 the value of the plant and equipment of electric light and power establishments in the United States was about $504,000,000; by 1927 it had grown to $9,297,000,000, approximately one-half the investment in the railroad industry.[2] In 1902 these establishments paid $13,000,000 in taxes; in 1930, $203,000,000. Railroad taxes in 1902 were eight times those of power companies. In 1930 they were only one and three-quarter times as great, the railroads paying $353,000,000 and the electric companies $203,000,000. Remarkable developments of a similar though perhaps not quite so spectacular nature occurred in the telephone, telegraph, gas, and other utilities. Because of the growth and importance of the so-called "local" utilities, a study of the tax systems prevailing in the United States and especially in Minnesota is particularly appropriate.

Special Problems in the Taxation of Public Utilities

During the past sixty years nearly every state in the Union has recognized the impossibility of assessing and taxing locally the property of steam railroads. The discussion in Chapter 11, pages 307–343 of the taxation of railroads describes some of the special problems that confront the assessing authorities and the types of taxes operative in the United States. The present chapter deals with the taxation of local utilities, especially electric, gas, telephone, telegraph, and pipe line companies. Although very similar

[1] This chapter was prepared jointly by Mr. C. H. Nelson, engineer of the Minnesota Tax Commission, and Professor Emerson P. Schmidt of the School of Business Administration of the University of Minnesota. Some principles underlying discussions in this chapter are treated more fully in Chapter 11.

[2] United States Bureau of the Census, *Central Electric Light and Power Stations, 1927.*

basic principles of taxation might be applied to these utilities and to the steam railroads, technological and marketing differences are sufficient to warrant a separate chapter. The several local utilities not only differ in many respects from railroads; they differ from each other also. For instance, a plant that manufactures gas normally does not reach beyond a single assessment district, whereas an electric plant nearly always does. Furthermore, the continued local assessment and taxation of the majority of these utilities throughout the United States indicates that, at least until recently, legislatures and taxing authorities have regarded them as a separate class from steam railroads.

TABLE 1.—INTERSTATE TRANSMISSION OF ELECTRICITY IN THE UNITED STATES

Year	Kw. Hrs. Crossing State Lines	Percentage Ratio of Interstate Power to Power Generated	No. of Interstate Crossings
1926[a]	6,171,530,000	9.06	453
1928[b]	8,920,000,000	10.90	510
1930[c]	11,898,000,000	13.10	554
1931[c]	12,488,000,000	14.20	No data

[a] Bureau of Business Research, *Interstate Transmission of Power by Electric Light and Power Companies in 1926* (Harvard University, 1927).
[b] National Electric Light Association Statistical Bulletin No. 4, 1930.
[c] Letter from the National Electric Light Association. See also H. L. Elsbree, *Interstate Transmission of Electric Power* (Harvard University Press, 1931), p. 59.

"Local" Utilities Extend Their Marketing Area

Until about 1910 electric companies were local affairs. Since that time it has become the custom to dismantle local generating plants and erect high-tension transmission systems to supply numerous urban and rural communities from a single central station. That is, the property owned by a single company extends beyond the confines of any one assessment district. Indeed, much of this property is now interstate, as Table 1 shows. In 1926 one-third of the lines crossing state boundaries had been put into operation during the years from 1924 to 1926. During the next four years the amount of energy crossing state lines nearly doubled. Furthermore, the proportion of energy crossing state boundaries is on the increase.

Although the industry has expanded, the number of independent establishments has been decreasing. In 1902 there were 2,805 commercial electric light and power establishments; in 1927 there were only 2,137, although the gross revenues had increased from $78,000,000 to $1,841,000,000, or 2300 per cent. Obviously companies are becoming much larger. In Minnesota five or six large companies do possibly 95 per cent of the commercial business. The six largest companies own about 94 per cent of the personal property of electric companies (item 55 as defined by law) outside corporate communities.[3]

Similar technical and business interconnections have occurred to a considerable extent in the telephone, telegraph, and other utilities. In the last decade oil and natural gas pipe lines have been spread across many assessment districts as well as over state lines. Indications are clear that the natural gas industry is destined to develop increasingly along regional lines, a single system or company covering numerous states. Street railways, buses, and trucks frequently operate in a metropolitan area throughout which their property is widely scattered, and they derive their earnings from broad economic regions.

METHODS OF TAXING PUBLIC UTILITIES

Local Assessment

In short, "local" utilities have ceased to be local. The impracticability of local valuation of property located in more than one assessment district has been discussed elsewhere.[4] The local assessor does not have the knowledge, the data, or the facilities to make a proper appraisal of a mile of railroad track or transmission line. He lacks the ability to determine the value of an underground pipe line or of a substation standing at a country crossroad or on the edge of a village. In fact, these pieces of property, which may happen to have a situs in a particular assessment district, are worthless in most cases except for their interconnections with other property in neighboring districts. To find the market or taxable value of this class of property the entire aggregate of poles, wires, pipes, transformers, etc., belonging to each company must be viewed as a whole. Then only can all the factors bearing on value be seen in the proper perspective. To appraise the property of a farm, a store, or a building is a difficult task, but it is not beyond the ability of the local assessor, because he may view the property as a unit. But it is equally necessary that inter-assessment district property, such as modern public utilities, be

[3] Report of the Minnesota Tax Commission, 1930, p. 109. [4] See page 308.

appraised as a unit; the assessor must be able to secure data on the investment, receipts, expenses, and net income of the property as a whole if he is to make an appraisal that will stand the test of critical analysis. It is not implied that a public utility has a taxable value per se in excess of the value of the individual pieces of property. But if regulation of rates is lax or if the utility is serving a market that is becoming more and more restricted, as is the case with many street railways, the taxable value may be greater or less than a physical inventory would indicate.

Central Assessment of Public Utilities

In the light of these facts it is not surprising to find a strong trend away from local assessment of utilities in the several states. Only a few states, including Delaware, New Jersey, New York, and Texas, assess most of their utilities under the old system of local assessment. In Texas the intangible values of railroads and a few unimportant utilities are centrally assessed. In New Jersey only railroads and canal companies are so assessed. In Delaware all utilities are locally assessed. In Connecticut and Minnesota there is little central assessment; in these states, however, the extensive application of the gross earnings tax to numerous utilities makes central assessment somewhat less necessary.[5]

Central assessment of the property of electric companies obtains in thirty states. In a few, including Idaho and New Mexico, transmission lines alone are assessed by state authorities. In Mississippi and Utah the property of electric utilities is assessed locally except when the property extends beyond a single county. In some states, Massachusetts, for example, the corporate excess only is centrally assessed. In spite of these halfway measures and partial exceptions, the dominant tendency is away from local assessment. Moreover, the application of the gross earnings tax in almost all states to a few or many utilities actually circumvents the difficulties of local assessment. Wisconsin has perhaps departed from local assessment to a greater extent than any other state.

How Wisconsin Has Met the Problem of Local Assessment

Wisconsin has definitely recognized the grave difficulties involved in the local assessment of public utilities and the equity

[5] Other methods of meeting the difficulties of local administration have been suggested. For example, the land owned by utilities might be assessed and taxed at local rates and the state might levy an income tax for its own purposes.

and soundness of the unit system of assessment. The tax commission of the state is required to assess the property of the following companies: steam railroad, telegraph, street railway, electric, sleeping car, freight line and equipment, express, conservation and regulation. The non-operating property of the several utilities is locally assessed. Telephone companies pay a gross earnings tax and thus need not be assessed. The commission uses the following criteria to determine the taxable value of utility property: earnings, securities outstanding, investment, cost of reproduction, and cost of reproduction minus depreciation. The weight given each of these factors is not indicated in the commission's reports.[6]

All property of public utilities assessed by the commission is taxed at the average rate in the state, or approximately 2 per cent. The uniform rate, which was adopted largely as a matter of administrative expediency, is subject to a minor criticism. General property in one county may be taxed at an average rate of 1 per cent and in another county as high as 3 per cent, yet the property of public utilities in both counties will be taxed at about 2 per cent.

The commission seems to be reconciled to this method and is inclined toward the view that all tax receipts from centrally assessed public utilities should accrue to the state treasury. "If it is proper . . . to tax all utility property at the average state rate, then it would seem to be equally proper and fair and equitable to use all utility taxes for a state-wide purpose for the benefit of all citizens of the state and not attempt to administer a rather unwieldy method of apportionment of such taxes."[7] The difficulty of apportioning the receipts back to the several tax districts has been largely responsible for this conclusion.

No doubt in most cases central assessment is a first step in the process of depriving local communities of the tax receipts from property so assessed. But the state governments usually return a considerable proportion of these revenues directly or indirectly to the communities for highway, school, and numerous other local purposes. In fact, all money collected and expended by the state is presumably for state-wide purposes.

In Wisconsin the tax receipts from electric, street railway, gas, and water companies are distributed on the following basis: 15 per cent to the state treasury, 20 per cent to the counties, and 65 per

[6] Report of the Wisconsin Tax Commission, 1930. The difficulties of the ad valorem system of assessment are discussed on page 311.

[7] Report of the Wisconsin Tax Commission, 1930, p. 101.

cent to the municipalities in which the property is located. The same basis of distribution applies to the proceeds from portions of municipally owned utilities outside municipal boundaries. The proceeds from municipally owned utilities inside municipal boundaries remain within the municipality. The entire tax receipts from "inter-district" electric utilities are turned over to the state treasury. Recently this has meant a loss of nearly half a million dollars to the counties and municipalities and a corresponding gain to the state treasury. All taxes on railroads except those on terminal property are turned over to the state treasury. None of the tax receipts from telegraph, sleeping car, freight line and equipment, and express companies are available to the local communities. As mentioned elsewhere, municipally owned utilities are subject to the ad valorem tax in Wisconsin. The income tax applies to all utilities except those that are municipally owned and to steam railroad, express, and sleeping car companies.[8]

TABLE 2.—NUMBER OF STATES HAVING GROSS EARNINGS TAXES ON DESIGNATED UTILITIES, 1932[a]

UTILITY	NO. OF STATES	UTILITY	NO. OF STATES
Railroad	20	Telephone	17
Street railway	12	Electric	21
Express	30	Gas	19
Telegraph	20		

[a] Tax Research Foundation, *Federal and State Tax Systems* (Chicago, 1932), pp. 135–137.

THE GROSS EARNINGS TAX AS A METHOD OF ESCAPE FROM LOCAL ASSESSMENT

Perhaps the easiest escape from the problem of annual assessment, both local and state, is the adoption of a gross earnings tax. While every state in the Union taxes some of its utilities on the basis of the general property tax, only six states (Colorado, Iowa, Kentucky, Michigan, New Hampshire, and Utah) do not have a gross earnings tax on any utility. Idaho applies this tax to express companies only. Twenty states apply it to railroads in whole or in part and nineteen to gas companies, as Table 2 indicates. In the case of gas companies the rate varies from 7.5 per cent in California to less than 1 per cent in South Carolina and Mississippi. In at

[8] Letter from C. M. Chapman of the Wisconsin Tax Commission.

least six states the rates are progressive. In some cases the tax is placed on intrastate business only. Twenty-one states tax electric companies on a gross earnings basis with rates somewhat comparable to those on gas companies. Frequently this tax is levied in addition to the general property tax; in such cases it rarely amounts to as much as 1 per cent of the value of the property.[9]

The Net Income Tax

Twenty-one states apply a net income tax to some or all of the utilities operating within their boundaries. The rate usually varies from 1 to 6 per cent and is frequently graduated. In California and Connecticut the utilities that pay gross earnings taxes are exempt from the income tax. In many states, including Idaho and Montana, the general corporation net income tax has been extended to apply to utilities. In Wisconsin the income tax applies to most utilities. Pennsylvania and Virginia do not apply their corporate taxes to utilities. In some states, Tennessee and Oklahoma, for example, this tax applies to the income derived from intrastate business only. Apparently where the tax is applied to utilities it operates as an additional tax, although in a few states, Georgia, for example, a partial offset is allowed for other taxes paid.

Other Forms of Local Taxes

Other taxes than those discussed above are levied on utilities in many states and municipalities. The nomenclature is exceedingly varied and confused. Excises, special excises, franchise taxes, special franchise taxes, privilege taxes, privilege fees, and many others are employed. In some cases mileage taxes, based on miles of track, telephone, or electric lines are levied; in others, a pole tax; in some, a meter tax. Street cars are frequently taxed so much per car. In a number of cases fixed lump-sum taxes are levied on companies. One holding company found that eight of its subsidiaries paid "an average of eight different kinds of direct taxes and that in the aggregate there were some sixteen or seventeen different methods of inflicting the torture." The rates varied from a low of 3 per cent to a high of 13 per cent of the gross receipts.[10] In Virginia telegraph companies had five special taxes to pay in 1930.

Perhaps the most complex system of public utility taxation in the

[9] The principles of the gross earnings tax are discussed on pages 327–330.
[10] Proceedings of the National Tax Association, 1921, p. 361.

United States is found in New York. With one exception real estate is assessed locally; "special franchises" are classified as real estate and are assessed by the state tax commission. Such special franchises are taken to be the value of the company's right to occupy and use the highways and other public places. All transportation, telegraph, and telephone companies pay a general franchise tax on capital stock employed within the state, at a rate that varies with dividends, the relation of assets to liabilities, and the average market price of the stock; in addition they pay a franchise tax of from .5 to 1 per cent on gross earnings within the state. Water, gas, and electric companies pay from .5 to 1 per cent of gross earnings within the state, plus 3 per cent on dividends in excess of 4 per cent.[11] A more complex tax system or one involving more costly administration could scarcely be found. The net result of these laws "has been scandalous inequality and disgraceful discrimination."[12]

This brief review of the taxation of public utilities in the United States indicates clearly that no existing "system" of taxation is regarded as peculiarly appropriate to utilities. The general property and gross earnings taxes are the most popular—the former for historical reasons and the latter because of ease of administration.

TAXATION OF PUBLIC UTILITIES IN MINNESOTA

The Present System

Minnesota, like nearly all other states, has failed to adopt any consistent, coherent system of taxing public utilities. On the contrary, the laws and the administration of today are the result of expediency and of piecemeal development. Broadly speaking, two types of taxes obtain: the general property tax with local assessment and the gross earnings tax with no property assessment whatsoever. (See Table 3.) Railroad, sleeping car, express, freight line, and telephone companies do not have their property assessed but pay gross earnings taxes at varying rates.[13] With minor exceptions the proceeds from these companies all go to the state treasury. Telegraph companies are centrally assessed and the tax payments are

[11] Report of the New York State Commission for the Revision of Tax Laws, 1932 (Legislative Document No. 77, 1932).

[12] Report of Special Joint Commission on Taxation and Retrenchment (Albany, New York, 1922).

[13] By legal fiction the gross earnings tax is a property tax, as is pointed out in Chapter 11.

TABLE 3.—PUBLIC UTILITY TAX SYSTEM IN MINNESOTA, 1932 [a]

Utility	By Whom Assessed	Type of Tax	Rate	Distribution of Proceeds
Railroad	No assessment	Gross earnings	5%	State treasury
Sleeping car	No assessment	Gross earnings	5%	State treasury
Express	No assessment	Gross earnings [b]	8%	State treasury
Freight line	No assessment	Gross earnings	6%	State treasury
Telephone	No assessment	Gross earnings	4%	State treasury
Telegraph	Tax Commission	General property [c]	...	State treasury
Vessels [d]	No assessment [e]	Net tonnage	5c per ton	Local districts
Street railway	Local assessor or Tax Commission [f]	General property	Local	Local districts
Electric	Local assessor or Tax Commission [g]	General property	Local	Local districts
Manufactured gas	Local assessor	General property	Local	Local districts
Pipe lines:				
Gas	Local assessor	General property	Local	Local districts
Gasoline	Local assessor	General property	Local	Local districts

[a] Based on the report of the Minnesota Tax Commission for 1930 and on an interview with the commissioners.

[b] Minus the amount paid to railroads for transporting their freight in Minnesota.

[c] Rate not to exceed the average rate on all property throughout the state.

[d] Plying international waters.

[e] If the owner of the vessel fails to file a report, the property is assessed and taxed as other local property.

[f] Personal property is assessed by the Minnesota Tax Commission if the property is located in two or more assessment districts.

[g] Personal property, including transmission lines not located in a municipality, is assessed by the Tax Commission and taxed at the rate of the county in which it is located, the proceeds being turned over to the county and school funds in each case.

turned over to the state. A net tonnage tax on vessels navigating international waters is optional, the alternative being local property assessment. Street railway, electric, gas, and several other minor utilities are locally assessed except under certain conditions. For instance, the personal property of street railway companies is assessed by the Minnesota Tax Commission if the property is located in more than one assessment district.[14] The personal property of electric companies not located within a municipality is likewise assessed by the commission. All taxes paid by utilities under the general property tax, with the exception of those paid by telegraph companies, accrue to the local districts. With this one exception the state receives a share of these general property taxes through its own mill levy.[15]

[14] Personal property has been defined to include right of way, tracks, poles, wire, etc. See *Tax Laws of Minnesota*, 1930, Sec. 74.

[15] See page 354.

Before 1921 the personal property of electric utilities, regardless of situs, was assessed at the principal place of business. Because the Northern States Power Company had its headquarters in Minneapolis, for instance, property located in distant counties was assessed and taxed in Minneapolis. Some companies deliberately established their "principal" place of business in some small village where the tax rate was low, and thus the operation of the law was unfair to many localities. In 1921 the defect was remedied by a statute requiring this class of property to be assessed at its situs.

The property of all telegraph companies, of street railways operating in more than one assessment district, and, since 1925, the personal property of electric companies not having a fixed situs within a municipality, are assessed by the Minnesota Tax Commission. As previously noted, no property belonging to companies paying a gross earnings tax in lieu of all other taxes is subject to local or state assessment.

Suggested Improvements for Taxing Electric and Gas Property

CLASSIFYING PROPERTIES

The assessment laws and procedure in Minnesota do not operate entirely satisfactorily. The Minnesota Tax Commission must determine whether thousands of items of property are located within a municipality or outside it. Frequently neither the records of the company nor those of the municipality indicate the specific situs of a transformer, a converter, or some other property. If they are within a municipality they are assessed locally; if not, by the commission. Extensive field trips often are necessary to settle the question.

Many knotty problems arise in connection with legal distinctions between personal and real property. The legislature has classified the distribution systems of gas and electric companies and the right of way, tracks, poles, and wires of street railway companies as personal property. As such, it must be assessed at 40 per cent of its full and true value. Real property, which is defined for taxation purposes to include land and permanent improvements, is to be assessed at 40 or at 33⅓ per cent of its full and true value. In 1916 the Minneapolis Gas Light Company attempted to have its distribution system classified as manufacturers' machinery, assessable at 33⅓ per cent. The decision of the Tax

Commission requiring this property to be assessed at 40 per cent was sustained by the court.[16]

Power house structures and large substations are clearly to be classed as real estate, but much of the machinery and equipment in these buildings may be assessed as personal property by one assessor and as real property by another. Machinery, including boilers and engines permanently attached to a building, is to be regarded as a fixture and assessed as real estate at 33⅓ per cent.[17] In general all tools, implements, and machinery that may be removed without doing substantial damage to the building and without making it useless for the purpose for which it was constructed and is maintained are to be classed as personal property and assessed at 40 per cent.

Possibly these instructions are as explicit as can be given. Nevertheless, they leave a good deal to the discretion of the local assessor. Presumably a built-in lathe in a power plant would be real estate, whereas a portable lathe would be personal property. A carriage running on tracks held fast by cement structures would be real estate. A set of wheelbarrows used for the same purpose would be personal property. Substations range in size from elaborate steel structures to handle 110,000 V circuits, built on several acres of company-owned land, down to the familiar two-pole station on the roadside to serve some small community. Legally the first is real estate and the latter is personal property, although both serve the same purposes. Between these extremes are many stations difficult to classify.

The Minnesota Tax Commission has engaged an engineer to help solve these problems. After he has determined the situs of the various pieces of property and given a decision as to whether they are real or personal property, he must determine the full and true value and then assess each piece at either 40 per cent or 33⅓ per cent, as the case may be. The assessed value of personal property located outside incorporated communities is certified to the county auditor, and the property is taxed at the average tax rate levied for all purposes throughout the county. The law covering the assessment of electric property outside municipalities is so drawn as to prevent a portion of the tax on this property from

[16] Minneapolis Gas Light Company v. Minnesota Tax Commission (1916), 132 Minnesota 419. The same issue came up in St. Paul Street Railway Company v. Minnesota Tax Commission (1915), 128 Minnesota 384.

[17] Minnesota Tax Commission, *Assessors' Manual,* 1930, p. 25.

going to the state, which in this way sustains an annual loss of from $25,000 to $30,000.

Thus it is clear that the present procedure involves a good deal of uncertainty and possibly needless expense. Yet the solution seems simple enough. All land, buildings, substations, transformers, transmission lines, poles, pipe lines, etc., should be regarded alike, as parts of an economic unit contributing to a common end, namely, the production and distribution of utility services. It is impossible to find a satisfactory system of classifying the parts of such an integrated whole. The present arbitrary distinctions between rural and urban property and between real and personal property could be eliminated by a similar change in point of view.

CENTRAL ASSESSMENT

Central assessment of all the property of a particular company is the only method that will meet this problem effectively. As previously noted, Wisconsin and many other states have solved it; Minnesota has solved it only in part. Indeed, if the legislature does not meet this problem satisfactorily, economic and technological forces will bring about their own solution, without the desirable dispatch and uniformity, however. This statement is borne out by the numerous letters which the commission continually receives from local assessors seeking information as to the value of, say, 100 yards of gasoline pipe line or a mile of natural gas pipe line. The local assessors cannot make satisfactory appraisals of such property and they admit it.

The Minnesota Tax Commission is required to equalize the assessments made by local assessors, which include the property of public utilities. In making its review of the assessments the commission always finds a considerable number of omissions as well as of over- and under-assessments. In 1931 the commission found it necessary to make 320 changes in assessment; it ordered 8 assessments of omitted property and reviewed assessments in 658 municipalities.[18] (See Table 4.) Increasingly the local assessors are relying on the commission to make assessments of this class of property in the first place.

If the assessment of the property of public utilities in Minnesota were turned over to the Tax Commission, as it should be, a num-

[18] Report of the Minnesota Tax Commission, 1930, p. 108; and data in the files of the Minnesota Tax Commission.

ber of statutory changes would be necessary, and the commission would have to settle upon an effective method of making the appraisals. Ultimately all taxes are paid out of earnings, and these should be the chief guide to taxable valuations. The inventory or physical appraisal method gives little clue to earning power, yet it is used widely in Minnesota and elsewhere. Under this method a complete inventory must be made. Frequently the companies fail to list some property, and field trips are necessary for purposes of checking. Omitted property must be measured, often it must be weighed; in other instances name-plate data of machinery are obtained. Then the basic inventory must be compiled and rearranged for the application of unit prices, which must be carefully

TABLE 4.—EQUALIZATION OF ELECTRIC PROPERTIES WITHIN MUNICIPALITIES BY THE TAX COMMISSION, 1925–1931

YEARS	NO. OF VILLAGES AND CITIES	NO. OF CHANGES MADE BY COMMISSION	ASSESSMENTS OF OMITTED PROPERTY ORDERED
Average for 1925–1930	563	208	26
1930	623	207	21
1931	658	320	8

determined for each item. The determination of these prices must be based on the various factors influencing cost of materials, labor, overhead, etc. Obsolescence, depreciation, physical conditions, age, and maintenance must all be taken into consideration.[19]

Obviously such a procedure involves a great deal of guesswork and uncertainty. No two engineers appraising the same property are likely to come to the same conclusion. Wherever this method has been utilized, whether for tax or rate purposes, the subsequent litigation and dissatisfaction have been enormous.[20] Justice Brandeis of the United States Supreme Court in a dissenting opinion has the following to say of the method: "Gradually it came to be realized that the definiteness of the engineers' calculations was delusive, that they rested upon shifting theories, and their estimates varied so widely as to intensify, rather than to allay, doubts."[21] In a case involving a water company the several valua-

[19] Report of the Minnesota Tax Commission, 1930, p. 109.

[20] Report of New York State Commission for the Revision of Tax Laws, 1932, Part 2, p. 196.

[21] Southwestern Bell Telephone Company v. Public Service Commission (1923), 262 U. S. 276.

tions of five experts were $670,163, $723,001, $763,028, $919,204, and $1,031,436.[22] In another involving a gas and electric company, the several valuations of five experts ranged from a low of $547,488 to a high of $940,988.[23] In the Duluth Street Railway Company case the valuations of two experts, both employed by the state, were $600,000 and $1,100,000.[24] Many similar cases could be cited.[25] In the light of these facts the inventory or physical appraisal method is seen to be of doubtful validity. The ownership of physical property is not proof of earning power nor of taxpaying ability. Market or taxable value can best be determined by a study of earnings, past and prospective. This means that the taxing officials should be given complete authority to require uniform and complete reports from the public utilities; also that they should have some understanding of general economic conditions and of the prospects for the future of the properties to be assessed. Under such conditions a good commission could carry out the tax policy adopted by the state for the various public utilities.

Taxation of Water Power Rights

The appraisal of hydro-electric stations and flooded lands for tax purposes is a knotty problem confronting state tax commissions. In Minnesota the dams, power houses, and machinery have been appraised by the commission according to established principles. The value of the site and the flooded lands presents a greater difficulty, however. In states where electric rates are rigidly regulated and a rate base is determined along specific lines, the question of taxing the value of the property is readily settled. But in Minnesota there is no regulation of electric rates except by municipalities. Consequently the commission has been inclined to take the view that the value of the flooded lands and the valuable rights of using water power should be taxed.

There are several methods of arriving at the value of water power rights. One is to capitalize the earnings of the company where this is possible. This is more appropriate for determining the value of the system as a whole than for allocating values to parts of the system or to different tax areas in which the system is located or carries on business. This method assumes that complete data are available, as they are not in Minnesota, largely be-

[22] *Re* Marin Municipal Water District, Cal. P. U. R. 1915C, 433, 452.
[23] Ill. P. U. R., 1916C, 281, 307.
[24] Duluth Street Railway Co. v. Railroad Commission (1915), 161 Wis. 245.
[25] See Homer B. Vanderblue, *Railroad Valuation* (Houghton Mifflin Co., 1917).

cause of the absence of rate regulation. Though rate valuations and tax valuations are based on different considerations and should be arrived at by different methods, the data on the rate valuation are of assistance in determining value for tax purposes.

Another method sometimes employed is to use actual sales data for similar property sold in the vicinity and make comparisons on a horsepower basis. On account of the many divergencies of construction, depreciation, marketing, and other factors, the data necessary for this method seem unavailable.

A third method is to compare the cost of energy from water and steam plants under conditions regarded as comparable and then to capitalize the difference, if any, in favor of water power. This is the method that has been adopted by the Minnesota Tax Commission for the study of 16 hydro-stations.[26] Although this method may be the best of the three noted, it, too, is subject to much criticism. A rate of capitalization must be determined; detailed cost figures must be obtained; and the selection of plants for purposes of comparison must be defensible.

Taxation of Telegraph Companies

As previously noted,[27] the property of telegraph companies is assessed by the Minnesota Tax Commission, and the law requires that the tax rate on this class of property shall *not exceed* the average rate of taxes — general, municipal, and local — levied throughout the state. Such taxation is in lieu of all other taxes, and the proceeds are payable into the state treasury. Clearly this law suggests that the property of telegraph companies is to be appraised on the same basis as other property in the state. It then devolves upon the commission to determine the appropriate rate. Table 5 gives some data concerning the taxation of this class of property. Assuming that the appraisals of property are equally accurate, it appears that the property of telegraph companies in Minnesota is taxed approximately on a parity with other property.

Taxation of Telephone Companies

Telephone companies vary greatly in size. In Minnesota 1,884 companies filed reports with the Tax Commission in 1930. More than 18 per cent of these reported no gross earnings whatsoever.

[26] Report of the Minnesota Tax Commission, 1930, p. 116.
[27] See page 353.

Earnings from zero to $1,000 were reported by 83.5 per cent of the companies. No taxes at all were paid by 354 companies; 286 others paid an average tax of less than $1; and a very large number paid only a few dollars each. The bulk of the taxes came from three large companies. The Tax Commission points out that it would be in the interest of economy if a large portion of these small companies were not required to pay at all, and suggests that all companies be classified into two groups, commercial and non-commercial. The former are organized for profit and might well be taxed on a gross earnings basis. The latter are usually small,

TABLE 5.—COMPARISON OF GENERAL PROPERTY AND TELEGRAPH PROPERTY TAX RATES, 1922–1930 [a]

YEAR	TAXABLE ASSESSED VALUATION	TRUE AND FULL ASSESSED VALUATION	TAXES LEVIED	TAX RATE ON ASSESSED VALUE IN MILLS		TAX RATE ON FULL AND TRUE VALUE IN MILLS	
				General Property	Telegraph Property	General Property	Telegraph Property
Average for 1922–1929	$749,008	$1,872,115	$40,567	59.13	54.16	21.77	21.67
1930.......	743,952	1,859,883	40,917	64.20	55.00	23.35	22.00

[a] Reports of the Minnesota Tax Commission, 1922–1930.

rural, non-profit-making organizations; some of them are designed merely to connect subscribers with some central exchange and actually collect no money. The commission recommends that all companies be divided into two groups: those with gross earnings of $1,000 or less and those with gross earnings of over $1,000. This, it is believed, will with minor exceptions separate the commercial from the non-commercial companies. The former would pay a flat rate of 15 cents for each telephone station, the latter a gross earnings tax of 6 per cent.[28]

The gross earnings tax was first applied to telephone companies in Minnesota in 1887, the rate being 2 per cent. In 1891 the law was repealed because the tax burden was not considered commensurate with that on other property. In 1897 the gross earnings tax was again restored, but with a rate of 3 per cent. It remained at this figure until 1922, when it was raised to 4 per cent.[29]

[28] Report of the Minnesota Tax Commission, 1930, p. 156.
[29] *Ibid.*

TABLE 6.—COMPARATIVE TAX BURDEN OF TELEPHONE COMPANIES AND OF OTHER PROPERTY, 1922–1929[a]

Year	Fixed Capital	Telephone Taxes Actually Paid	Tax Rate[b]		Calculated Tax[c]	Loss in State "Potential" Revenues[c]	Calculated Equivalent Gross Earnings Tax Rate
			On Telephone Companies	On General Property			
1922[d]	$102,059,000	$1,153,015	11.29	19.93	$2,034,052	$881,037	7.08
1923	55,424,000	658,013	11.87	22.08	1,223,780	565,767	7.44
1924	56,873,000	677,457	11.91	20.99	1,193,772	516,315	7.05
1925	59,186,000	713,726	12.05	21.87	1,294,415	580,689	7.25
1926	61,634,000	744,791	12.08	21.30	1,312,825	568,034	7.05
1927	66,996,000	763,928	11.40	22.34	1,496,695	733,368	7.82
1928	67,266,000	787,643	11.70	22.47	1,511,487	723,844	7.67
1929	70,172,000	816,644	11.63	23.20	1,627,996	811,352	7.96
Average	$67,451,000	$789,402	11.70	21.77	$1,461,953	$672,551	7.44

[a] Compiled from the reports of the Minnesota Railroad and Warehouse Commission, 1922–1930, and those of the Minnesota Tax Commission for the same years.

[b] In mills on estimated true value.

[c] Amount payable if telephone property had been taxed at the same rate as other property. Based on fixed capital as shown in Burnett, *op. cit.*, p. 43. These figures have been rounded off in the first column.

[d] Data of 1922 include the entire Northwestern Bell system.

ARE TELEPHONE COMPANIES TAXED ON A PARITY WITH OTHER PROPERTY?

In 1918 the Minnesota Tax Commission published a study of the taxation of telephone companies in the state. In the case of the three largest companies then operating in the state it was shown on the basis of their own reports of invested capital minus depreciation that a rate of 6.45 per cent on gross earnings would be necessary if the tax burden were to equal the average tax burden of 37.66 mills imposed on other property in 1917. The average millage rate on other property increased from 37.66 in 1917 to 64.20 in 1930, an increase of over 70 per cent, whereas the rate on telephone property increased only 33⅓ per cent. According to this study it would require a rate of approximately 9 per cent on the gross earnings of telephone companies to equal the tax on general property.[30] The rate would vary somewhat from 9 per cent in some proportion to the size of the companies.

If we assume that the figures are reasonably accurate, Table 6 indicates clearly that the telephone industry has not paid taxes on a parity with other property in the state. The gross earnings taxes levied at 4 per cent have been equal to a rate of about 11.70 mills, whereas general property in the state paid a rate of about 21.77 mills on the full and true value during the period from 1922 to 1929. A simple calculation indicates that if telephone property had been on a par with other property during that period, a gross earnings rate of 7.44 per cent would have been necessary. According to this table the state lost "potential" revenues of $5,380,000 from 1922 to 1929, or an average of about $672,000 annually.[31]

Another method of measuring the relative tax burdens on general property and property paying a gross earnings tax is available, namely, capitalization of net income by means of a formula developed by the Connecticut Tax Commission.[32]

As previously indicated, the tax rate on the full and true value of general property averaged 21.77 mills for the period from 1922 to 1929. Other data used in applying the formula are given in

[30] Report of the Minnesota Tax Commission, 1930, p. 154.

[31] The writers are indebted for most of these data to Mr. Judson O. Burnett's unpublished report, "A Comparison of the Relative Tax Burden of Telephone Companies and General Property in Minnesota," which is on file at the University of Minnesota. Miss Violet Johnson and Mr. Elmer E. Hilpert also contributed much toward this study.

[32] C. J. Bullock, *Readings in Public Finance* (1924), p. 638. This formula is described and used in Chapter 11 on railroad taxation, page 341.

TABLE 7.—SUGGESTED GROSS EARNINGS TAX RATES CALCULATED ACCORDING TO CAPITALIZATION FORMULA[a]

Year	Gross Earnings	Net Operating Revenue	Per Cent of Net to Gross Earnings	Comparable Gross Earnings Tax Rate with Capitalization Rate of					
				4 Per Cent	5 Per Cent	6 Per Cent	7 Per Cent	7.5 Per Cent	8 Per Cent
1922[b]	$28,825,000	$8,041,000	27.90	9.28	7.95	6.96	6.18	5.86	5.56
1923	16,450,000	5,251,000	31.92	11.35	9.77	8.59	7.66	7.26	6.91
1924	16,936,000	5,545,000	32.74	11.25	9.69	8.49	7.56	7.16	6.81
1925	17,843,000	5,992,000	33.59	11.89	10.22	8.98	8.01	7.59	7.22
1926	18,619,000	6,372,000	34.22	11.90	10.22	8.97	7.98	7.57	7.19
1927	19,098,000	6,586,000	34.49	12.35	10.66	9.38	8.47	7.92	7.53
1928	19,691,000	6,910,000	35.10	12.67	10.92	9.59	8.55	8.12	7.72
1929	20,416,000	7,256,000	35.54	13.05	11.26	9.97	8.85	8.32	7.98
Average	$19,735,000	$6,494,000	32.90	11.58	9.98	8.75	7.80	7.40	7.04

[a] Burnett, *op. cit.* See footnotes on pages 341 and 361 above.
[b] Data for 1922 cover the entire Northwestern Bell system.

Table 7. Calculation indicates that if the net income of the telephone property is capitalized at 4 per cent, the gross earnings tax rate necessary to equalize the telephone tax burden with that on other property is 11.58 per cent. Undoubtedly this rate of capitalization is too low. For the convenience of the reader calculations have been made at varying rates of capitalization from 4 to 8 per cent. At the high rate of 8 per cent it would require a gross earnings tax rate of 7.04 per cent on telephone companies to equalize the tax burdens on this class of property with that on general property.

The telephone industry in Minnesota has been a profitable one. From 1922 to 1929 the net return on capital before taxes were deducted was 9.63 per cent. The return on capital stock during the same period was 19.54 per cent.[33] Taxes have amounted to 1.17 per cent, leaving an untaxed return on the investment of 8.46 per cent for the nine years. Had the property been taxed at the average rate obtaining in the state, the net return after payment of taxes would have amounted to 7.54 per cent. This is undoubtedly an unnecessarily high rate of return, but assuming that it is correct, a capitalization rate of 7.50 per cent should be used. This suggests that to place telephone property on a par with other property would require a gross earnings tax of 7.40 per cent.[34] (See Table 7 on the opposite page.)

TAXATION OF MUNICIPALLY OWNED UTILITIES

Considerable controversy surrounds the issue of taxing municipally owned utilities. Municipal officials and many students of local government are inclined toward the view that publicly owned utilities are in the same general category as streets, parks, schools, and libraries. It is claimed that municipally owned utilities are non-profit-making institutions conducted for the public good and that their services ought to be delivered at the lowest possible price and hence should not be taxed.

Although such reasoning has a certain plausibility, it rests on a weak foundation. Streets, parks, schools, and libraries render a type of public service that is given free to all citizens as a matter of public policy. With utility services the situation is different. The amount of gas or electricity a family uses is a personal matter,

[33] Burnett, *op. cit.*

[34] Because of great differences in the earnings of different companies, the suggested gross earnings rate would vary from 2.40 per cent in the smallest to 7.81 per cent in the largest groups. See Burnett, *op. cit.*, p. 39.

whereas the education and recreation of citizens have become matters of public concern. Should a public park or golf course be laid out for the special benefit of one section of the city, it would, however, be appropriate to have the taxpayers in that district bear the cost of acquiring and maintaining it. Similarly, if one municipality owns property in another municipality, the former should be required to pay a tax to the latter. Although it is true that publicly owned utilities are conducted for the public good, the same may be said in a measure of grocery stores, banks, manufacturing plants, and privately owned utilities. The consensus of opinion[35] is that under regulation a tax levied on a private utility tends normally to be shifted in large measure to the ultimate consumers, that is, the company makes its rate high enough to enable it to collect the tax from the customers; if publicly owned utilities are exempted from taxes simply because taxation would mean a rise in rates, privately owned utilities might equally well be exempted for the same reason.

Those who oppose the taxation of municipally owned utilities frequently recognize two exceptions. First, "so far as state taxes are concerned, there is justification for imposing upon municipally owned utilities the same burdens that are placed upon privately owned utilities. Unless there is such equalization, the communities which own their own gas and electric properties do not contribute their proportion to the state taxes."[36] Second, when a municipality owns and operates hydro-electric generating stations, transmission lines, street railways, or other utility property in another tax district, the latter district should be allowed to assess and tax such property within its boundaries. Clearly, if these two exceptions are not made, certain communities will not pay their full share of the cost of government.

Students of public finance feel that these two exceptions do not go far enough. Not all citizens within a municipality are direct users of gas, electricity, street railway services, or other specific utility services. There is an enormous difference, moreover, in the volume of these services used by different customers. Consequently, to exempt utilities from taxation would be to discriminate against the non-user or the small user of services. These utilities, whether privately or publicly owned, are responsible for certain necessary outlays for police and fire protection and for improvements of

[35] See page 331.
[36] Letter from John Bauer, May 6, 1932.

streets and alleys. The customers of the utilities who are the beneficiaries of these services should shoulder the entire expense that they entail; that is, neither privately nor publicly owned utilities should be tax exempt.

CONCLUSIONS

Throughout the United States the local assessment of public utility property is being abandoned. Minnesota has made progress in this direction, but additional legislation is needed. The assessing authority should place the chief emphasis on earning power rather than on physical appraisal. This involves the adoption of uniform methods of accounting and standardized reports for each class of utilities.

The gross earnings tax provides an easy method of escaping some of the difficulties of making appraisals. This tax, however, has certain important defects; it involves inequalities between companies and difficulties in determining rates that will place the several utilities on a par with other property. Because of the varying rates of capital turnover among the several utilities, a single gross earnings tax rate will not make for equality among them. California has found the following rates desirable: electric and gas, 7.5 per cent; railroads, 7 per cent; telephone and telegraph, 5.5 per cent; express, 1 per cent; and electric railway, 4.25 per cent. Another defect of this tax is that the burden is shifted to the ultimate consumers without regard to the taxpaying ability of such consumers. The adoption of the gross earnings tax does not mean that the proceeds must be turned over to the state treasury. The revenue may be apportioned back to the counties or other tax districts on the basis of the number of meters in use (this has been found to be a fairly accurate measure of property investment), or of gross receipts, or of miles of line in some cases. This apportionment must be settled for each utility individually.

In Minnesota the greatest need of further central assessment is in connection with electric and pipe line companies. Then a general property or gross earnings tax rate will need to be applied. In the United States as a whole electric companies paid an average of about 10 per cent on gross receipts from 1928 to 1930; in 1930 the rate was 10.2 per cent.[37] In arriving at a rate of taxation to be applied to the several utilities the incidence of the tax should not be ignored. For instance, in 1930 domestic consumers of electricity

[37] This information is supplied by National Electric Light Association. Federal income taxes are included in this figure.

constituted 83 per cent of all customers. They consumed only 14.8 per cent of the output, yet they contributed 33 per cent of the revenues.[38] In Minnesota the six largest private electric companies, which did about 95 per cent of the business, paid general property and other local taxes amounting to 8.59 per cent of their gross receipts from 1928 to 1931. (See Table 8.)

TABLE 8.—TAXATION OF SIX LARGEST ELECTRIC COMPANIES IN MINNESOTA, 1928–1931[a]

YEAR	WHOLE COMPANY			MINNESOTA PORTION		
	Gross Receipts	Taxes	Per Cent of Taxes to Gross Receipts	Gross Receipts	Taxes	Per Cent of Taxes to Gross Receipts
1928	$30,298,342	$2,326,220	7.68	$22,087,128	$1,846,368	8.36
1929	31,842,913	2,382,540	7.48	22,828,860	1,900,930	8.33
1930	32,403,636	2,455,397	7.58	23,312,161	2,080,119	8.93
1931	32,429,564	2,611,006	8.05	24,230,824	2,113,613	8.72
Average	$31,743,614	$2,443,791	7.70	$23,114,743	$1,985,254	8.59

[a] Data supplied by the Minnesota Tax Commission. These figures include all local property taxes and special franchise taxes, but they exclude federal and state income taxes. With two exceptions these companies are engaged in interstate business. The figures do not include the Minneapolis General Electric Company, the Wisconsin division of the Northern States Power Company, or numerous small companies throughout the state whose reports to the Minnesota Tax Commission are not sufficiently complete to be used in this analysis.

Assuming that these figures are accurate and that the property has been taxed by the local authorities on a par with other property, it would appear that a gross earnings tax rate of at least 8 per cent would be required to make such a tax equivalent to the property tax. Several municipalities, including Crookston and St. Paul, levied $401,931 in taxes in addition to the general property taxes on electric companies in 1931. Similar amounts were levied in the other years. If we deduct this figure, the regular taxes on the six largest companies in 1931 amounted to 7.06 per cent of the gross receipts instead of 8.72 per cent.

The available evidence indicates that the telephone industry in Minnesota has not been taxed on a par with other property. The statistical data presented suggest that it would be necessary to

[38] National Electric Light Association Statistical Bulletin No. 7, 1931.

raise the present rate of 4 per cent to about 7.4 per cent on the gross receipts in order to equalize tax burdens.[39]

Finally, it is the judgment of the writers that municipally owned utilities, with the exception of water perhaps, should be required to pay taxes on the same basis as private utilities, first, because this is necessary to equalize the contributions of the several communities to the state treasury, and second, because inequalities that would otherwise occur between large and small users and between users and non-users of utility services may thus be ironed out. Many publicly owned utilities, if successful, are destined to extend their property beyond the confines of the municipal boundaries; they will probably avoid considerable hostility if the users of their services pay the entire costs involved, including those of governmental protection.

[39] In 1930 the telephone companies in the United States paid about 5.74 per cent of their gross earnings in taxes, a tax equal to 15.63 mills on their fixed capital. Interstate Commerce Commission, *Telephone Companies, 1930.*

CHAPTER 13

HIGHWAY FINANCE [1]

The problem of highway expenditures has rapidly come to the fore as a major problem in governmental finance. During the early stages of highway improvement, before the demand for through highways, the county, the township, and the city were the important road-building agencies. State departments were organized as the demand for trunk highways developed. A national system of highways, to include 7 per cent of the total mileage, was authorized in 1915 by the federal government. Since that time, as motor vehicle traffic has developed, the highway costs imposed upon governments have increased enormously. From the standpoint of total expenditure involved, the problem of highway finance is now second only to that of education in state and local finance.

As organized at present, the rural highway system of the country as a whole may be divided roughly into two parts. The primary system, including the main routes and consisting of approximately 325,000 miles of state and federal highways, is administered through forty-eight state highway departments and the United States Bureau of Public Roads. The secondary system of local highways, consisting of approximately 2,700,000 miles, is administered principally through county, township, and district highway authorities. Then of course there are the city streets, most of which are not included in these two systems.

A bird's-eye view of the nation's sources of revenue for rural highways in 1930 and the nature of expenditures may be obtained from Tables 1 and 2. City streets, few of which are included in rural highway systems, are financed for the most part by property taxes and special assessments.

ORGANIZATION OF HIGHWAY ADMINISTRATION

PRESENT ORGANIZATION IN MINNESOTA

Minnesota has a State Department of Highways headed by a commissioner of highways appointed by the governor for a term of two years. The department includes a chief engineer, a construc-

[1] This study of highway finance was made by Professor Arthur Borak of the School of Business Administration of the University of Minnesota.

TABLE 1. — RECEIPTS FOR HIGHWAY PURPOSES IN THE UNITED STATES, 1930[a]

Source	For Use of State Highway Departments		For Use of Local Highway Authorities		Total	
	Amount	Per Cent	Amount	Per Cent	Amount	Per Cent
Tax funds[b]	$43,317,991	4	$494,633,325	60	$537,951,316	28
Motor vehicle registration tax[c] .	289,801,738	25	54,911,122	7	344,712,860	17
Gasoline tax ...	411,109,446	36	107,110,709	13	518,220,155	26
Bonds and notes	222,288,308	20	94,684,481	12	316,972,789	16
Federal aid	92,462,836	8	....	..	92,462,836	5
Fund transfers, local to state (or vice versa)	60,609,297	5	33,701,795	4	94,311,092	5
Miscellaneous ...	17,083,821	2	33,338,076	4	50,421,897	3
Total	$1,136,673,437	100	$818,379,508	100	$1,955,052,945	100

[a] From data compiled by the United States Bureau of Public Roads. Figures in this table represent funds actually received, some of which were derived from 1929 and some from 1930 funds.

[b] Highway levies and appropriations from general funds.

[c] This levy is sometimes designated as a license fee, but since the tax element has become predominant, it will be referred to as a tax.

TABLE 2. — CLASSIFICATION OF RURAL HIGHWAY DISBURSEMENTS IN THE UNITED STATES, 1930[a]

Purpose	By State Highway Departments		By Local Highway Authorities		Total	
	Amount	Per Cent	Amount	Per Cent	Amount	Per Cent
Construction	$713,117,045	64	$296,594,546	35	$1,009,711,591	51
Maintenance	191,683,477	18	284,228,960	33	475,912,437	24
Miscellaneous	24,529,184	2	37,066,817	4	61,596,001	4
Interest on bonds and notes	50,668,141	4	82,604,925	10	133,273,066	7
Total expenditures	$979,997,847		$700,495,248		$1,680,493,095	
Principal payment on bonds and notes	69,504,631	6	112,576,447	13	182,081,078	9
Transfers, local to state (or vice versa)	66,897,782	6	38,614,930	5	105,512,712	5
Total disbursements	$1,116,400,260[b]	100	$851,686,625	100	$1,968,086,885	100

[a] From data compiled by the United States Bureau of Public Roads.

[b] In addition, $23,276,341 was spent to defray other assumed obligations, including some obligations by law not directly related to state highway expenditures.

tion engineer, a maintenance engineer, and a bridge engineer. The highway commissioner has direct charge of the state trunk highway system, as provided in Article 16 of the state constitution, an amendment adopted in 1920. The constitution provides for a system of seventy routes to be constructed, improved, and maintained by the state. The main points on each route are named in the amendment, the location between the points being left to the highway commissioner. The routes named connect all the county seats and other principal communities. Only two communities of more than 1,000 population which are not suburbs of larger cities do not have a trunk highway. The streets in Minneapolis, St. Paul, and Duluth that connect trunk highway routes at the city limits are not included; such streets in other cities are included. New routes may be added by the legislature when a county seat is changed to a municipality not already on a trunk highway, when the county seat of a new county is not on a trunk highway, or when at least 75 per cent of the total number of miles embraced in the original system, including the above additions, "shall have been constructed and permanently improved . . . provided, however, that no such new routes shall be added until and unless the funds available for the construction, improvement, and maintenance of such additional routes shall be sufficient therefor in addition to the construction, improvement, and maintenance of the several routes hereinbefore specifically described." One route was added to the system in 1929 to connect the county seat of a new county with the seat of an adjoining county. After the passage of the trunk highway amendment in 1920, the trunk highway system was designated as the federal aid system. Of the 6,864 miles in this system, 3,978 miles had been improved with federal aid by January 1, 1931.

The county boards have general supervision of county roads. Every county must employ a highway engineer. He is appointed by the county board and *may* be selected from a list of eligible and competent highway engineers or road-builders submitted by the commissioner of highways upon request of the county board. The county highway engineer must prepare and submit to the county board and state highway commissioner a report of a construction job within thirty days after its completion and a report of all other work once a month. He must also prepare and submit to the county board and the state highway commissioner an annual report of all the highway work done in the county. The extent of the control exercised by the county board differs for the several classes of roads in the county. State-aid roads, which before the passage of the highway amendment in 1921 were the old state roads, are constructed, improved, and maintained by the county boards under the supervision of the state highway commissioner. The county board may request that certain roads be designated as state-aid roads, this request being subject to the approval of the state highway commissioner. The state highway commissioner establishes general regulations and standards and approves plans, and he must approve the work with respect to construction and maintenance before state aid can be paid to the counties. The state aid consists of allotments to the several counties from the proceeds of the state one-mill property levy, which partially finances this class of roads. The county board has general jurisdiction over the other county roads. These roads are established, constructed, and improved by the county boards, which may designate as county-aid roads any that are financed in part by allotments to the various counties from the proceeds of one-third of the gasoline tax. The state highway commissioner has no supervision over these or other county roads.

The town boards have general care and supervision of all town or township roads. The board appoints a town road overseer. The town may be divided by the board into road districts, not to exceed four in number, in which case a road overseer is appointed for each district. The state highway commissioner has no supervision over these roads. The county board may aid in their construction, repair, and maintenance. The town board may aid in the construction and improvement of county roads, including state-aid roads in the town. In counties having less than 150,000 population the town boards must, moreover, maintain all county roads except state-aid roads and county-aid roads. A town board may, however, with the consent of the county board, delegate to the county all or part of the construction, improvement, or maintenance for which the town is liable. Thus the provision and maintenance of highways other than those in the state trunk system is pretty much a cooperative affair between the county and the town.

The rural highway system consists, therefore, of state trunk highways, state-aid roads, county-aid roads, other county roads, and township roads.[2] The state finances and has absolute jurisdiction over the first, supervises and aids in financing the second, and aids in financing the third. Otherwise the counties and towns have

[2] A classification of Minnesota highways is presented in Table 5 on page 377.

jurisdiction and provide the funds. The tendency during the past two or three decades has been toward a greater extension of central authority over the whole system, a movement that ought certainly be carried further. Recent experience and practice in certain other states may suggest needed changes in Minnesota.

Recent Developments in Other States

The Bureau of Public Roads in cooperation with the Michigan State Highway Department carried on a comprehensive traffic survey in Michigan in 1930 and 1931.[3] Two regular counts were taken for each day of the week at approximately a thousand stations throughout the state, or fourteen counts at each station in the course of the year. Thus daily traffic fluctuations as well as seasonal variations were obtained. Practically all trunk-line routes and representative county and township roads in all sections of the state were covered. Information was obtained concerning the following classes of vehicles at each point: (1) out-of-state automobiles; (2) Michigan automobiles; (3) trucks of one and one-half tons and under; (4) trucks of over one and one-half tons; (5) trailers; and (6) buses. Information was collected on item 1 as to the time visitors to Michigan were to spend in the state, the amount of traveling they expected to do, and whether they were camping, stopping at hotels, staying with friends, or staying at their summer homes in the state. Classes 2 to 6, inclusive, were subdivided at each station into traffic originating in that individual township, in that county, and in other parts of the state. A one-month count was taken in seven representative cities to determine the percentage of traffic originating in those cities and the percentage of out-of-town traffic.

In 1930 a cooperative survey of the county-road mileage and financial operations of the counties of North Carolina was made by the Bureau of Public Roads, the state highway commission, and the state tax commission.[4] The results of the investigations are of

[3] The bureau has completed similar cooperative surveys in a number of states in recent years. The year of classification in Michigan ended July 15, 1931, but the results are not yet available. Comments on this survey appear in Grover C. Dillman, "Financing a Complete Highway System," Proceedings of the National Tax Association, 1930, pp. 119–121.

[4] "North Carolina County Road and Finance Survey," Report of the Tax Commission of North Carolina, 1930, pp. 41–103. Comments on the Survey appear in American Road Builders' Association, Report of the Committee on Administrative and Financial Relationship of State and County, January, 1932. See also O. Max

special interest in considering the situation in Minnesota at the present time. Among other things the investigators concluded that township administrative road units are not suited to modern needs when automobiles may cross a township in fifteen minutes and some counties in about half an hour. Rural highways are no longer the concern of townships only. They further concluded that township road officials who devote only part of their time to highway problems are not qualified to meet modern traffic needs, which require full use of modern equipment and technique. Even the county unit is too small for administrative purposes, in the opinion of these investigators. The county-road mileage is not sufficient to permit full utilization of the force and equipment required for economic and efficient highway construction and maintenance. Moreover, the unequal distribution of wealth among the various counties makes for a like inequality in ability to provide the most economic staff and equipment.[5] The investigators recommended the abolition of the township as a road-building unit, the vesting of control over roads in the county, and the extension of state supervision over county roads. But by action of the legislature the state highway commission of North Carolina assumed the financing and jurisdiction of the entire 45,000 miles of local or county highways. Thus North Carolina became the first state in the Union to eliminate the county as a road-building unit. Virginia has very recently taken somewhat similar action.

Several aspects of this problem of township highways in other states are worthy of mention. Twenty-eight states report no township highways, and with the exception of Pennsylvania and several New England states where township or town roads are closely affiliated with the state highway or are supervised by the state, there is little real township highway activity in the country. The million miles of township highways in the country are administered ineffectively. In Iowa counties have taken over the entire township mileage. Counties in Michigan will have done the same by 1936, and in New Jersey they will ultimately absorb the most important township highways. Similar movements are taking place in Illinois, Pennsylvania, Nebraska, and Oklahoma.

Gardner, "Extension of State Operation of Highways and Roads," Bulletin of the National Tax Association, 17:263–268 (June, 1932).

[5] It was found that 40 counties had 76.5 per cent of the total assessed valuation, leaving 60 counties with 23.5 per cent.

Needed Changes in Minnesota

The Minnesota State Department of Highways takes a classified traffic census during one week in August each year at points on the state trunk system, but this is inadequate. An occasional census like that of Michigan would be of great aid in determining needs more accurately and would be in the interests of economy. We ought to know not only what roads should be built, but which should be abandoned or maintained less intensively; and we ought to know more definitely how state aid should be distributed.

Minnesota should seriously consider a number of administrative changes. Some of these changes are not only warranted by the experience of other states but are logical and just in the light of facts and suggestions to be presented below concerning highway revenues in Minnesota.[6] In view of the improvement that has taken place in the state trunk highway system and of the difficulties of local governments in bearing their financial burdens, the inclusion of more mileage in the state trunk system seems wise. The additional mileage should usually consist of roads bearing the greatest burden of traffic, since these are the ones in which the state or general public has the greatest concern. The entire township mileage should be transferred to the counties. At most there are two logical road systems — state and county. The counties themselves, in many cases, might well be larger and consequently fewer in number. State supervision could very well be extended even beyond the field of state aid. No more local control over the selection of the county engineer is advisable than his selection by the county board from a list of eligible persons submitted by the state highway commissioner. The state highway commissioner should be appointed for a longer term than two years. The proper coordination of the highways and the economical expenditure of highway funds call for these changes.

COST OF HIGHWAYS IN MINNESOTA

At the close of the year 1931 there were 6,864 miles of road in the Minnesota state trunk highway system. At the close of 1930 there were 103,770 miles of local roads, including state-aid, county-aid, other county, and township roads. A classification of expenditures for these roads in the years indicated is given in Table 3.

These figures indicate that about 56 per cent of the total ex-

[6] See pages 390 and 414.

penditures for highways in the state at the present time is being concentrated on the trunk highway system, which contains 6 per cent of the total mileage of rural highways. Of this 6 per cent, 27 per cent is paved and over 99 per cent is surfaced either with pavement or with a lower type of finish. This situation is not exceptional with Minnesota. In the country as a whole, about 58 per cent of total expenditures for roads in 1930 was disbursed by state highway departments. According to Mr. W. C. Markham, secretary of the American Association of State Highway Officials,

TABLE 3.—CLASSIFICATION OF MINNESOTA HIGHWAY DISBURSEMENTS

PURPOSE	STATE HIGHWAYS, 1931[a]		LOCAL ROADS, 1930[b]	
	Amount	Per Cent	Amount	Per Cent
Construction	$23,923,999	70	$15,542,100	63
Maintenance	4,547,077	13	5,341,000	21
Administration and miscellaneous	217,479	1	2,458,000	9
Interest on bonds and notes	1,589,659	5	801,500	3
Total expenditures	$30,278,214		$24,142,600	
Principal payment on bonds and notes	3,946,893	11	1,148,500	4
Total disbursements	$34,225,107	100	$25,291,100[c]	100

[a] From data compiled by the Minnesota Department of Highways.
[b] From data compiled by the United States Bureau of Public Roads.
[c] In addition, there was $690,607 which the bureau represents as transfers to the state for work on state roads.

at the close of the year 1930 the average state had 6,569 miles of primary or state trunk highway out of an average total of 63,005 miles of rural highway—roughly, 10 per cent. Of this state trunk highway mileage 29 per cent was paved.

The sources of funds expended by the Minnesota State Department of Highways on the state trunk highway system in 1931 and by local authorities on the local rural highways in 1930 are shown in Table 4.

These figures indicate that the state trunk highway system is not financed by property levies or by appropriations from general funds. The state bonds issued to hasten construction will be retired out of motor vehicle and gasoline taxes. Receipts for the support of the State Department of Highways come from taxes on motor vehicles paid by users of the highways—to the extent of 83 per cent of the total receipts in 1931. On the other hand, the bulk of the receipts (87 per cent) for the maintenance of the local system comes from property taxes. Besides levies on county and township property, however, the local systems receive state aid from a state-wide one-mill property tax and a third of the receipts from the gasoline tax. The figures for bond sales indicate that the local authorities are not now incurring debt for any appreciable portion of their highway funds. As far as the past is concerned, however, the figures for outstanding local debt for highway

TABLE 4. — RECEIPTS FOR HIGHWAY PURPOSES IN MINNESOTA

SOURCE	FOR USE OF STATE HIGHWAY DEPARTMENT, 1931 [a]	PER CENT	FOR USE OF LOCAL HIGHWAY AUTHORITIES, 1930 [b]	PER CENT
Local road levy and appropriation from general fund	....	...	$17,845,613	69
Motor vehicle registration tax	$10,709,368	30	....	..
Gasoline tax	7,942,042	23	3,453,037	13
Bond sale receipts	10,060,200	28	1,045,000	4
Federal aid	5,443,400	17	....	..
Transfer funds from state for local roads	....	..	1,869,370	8
Miscellaneous receipts	509,876	2	1,590,000	6
Total	$34,664,886	100	$25,803,020	100

[a] From data compiled by the Minnesota Department of Highways.
[b] From data compiled by the United States Bureau of Public Roads.

purposes tell a different story. The bonds will probably be retired eventually out of property taxes. It is evident that operators of motor vehicles are directly financing the state trunk highways and that property is meeting the bill as far as local rural highways are concerned.

Minnesota has not neglected its local rural roads. At the close of 1930, according to figures compiled by the United States Bureau of Public Roads, 29 per cent of the local rural roads in Minnesota were surfaced as compared with an average of 17 per cent for all states. The state trunk highway program was stepped up to a faster pace in 1931 as compared with previous years to bring the system up to the status shown in Table 5, with more than one-fourth of the system paved and more than one-half either paved or bituminous graveled.[7] The trunk highway program for 1932

[7] *Minnesota Highway News*, December 12, 1931.

will bring the mileage of pavement to 2,400 and of bituminous-treated gravel to 2,700 — that is, to a total of 5,100 miles.[8] Recent state bond issues, increased federal aid, and favorable prices on materials have made this expansion possible.

Is Minnesota concentrating her highway expenditure too much on the state highway system? It is estimated that about 80 per cent of the local highway traffic moves on the state trunk system. Government studies have shown that the improvement of main roads tends to lessen the volume of traffic on local roads and thus reduces maintenance costs for local governments. It is interesting to note that even with the addition of 435 miles of pavement laid in 1931 Minnesota has only half as much pavement as Iowa or Wisconsin. Traffic on the paved routes of the Minnesota trunk system is more than three times as great as on the unpaved routes in the system, according to the traffic census of August, 1931. Vehicle counts taken at 95 points on paved routes showed an average traffic of 2,309 a day. Counts taken at 271 points on unpaved highways, including bituminous gravel routes, showed an

TABLE 5. — CLASSIFICATION OF RURAL HIGHWAYS IN MINNESOTA

Type	State Trunk Highways [a]	Local Highways: State-Aid Roads [a]	Local Highways: County Roads [b]	Local Highways: Township Roads [b]	Total [e]
Pavement	1,873	103	64	2	2,042
Bituminous gravel	1,872	215 }	5,555	6,183	30,199
Untreated gravel	2,971 [d]	13,403 }			
Sand-clay surfaced	91	289	1,380	4,243	6,003
Graded and unsurfaced	57	1,029	655	186	1,927
Partly graded and unsurfaced	....	.....	2,308	48,872	51,180
Unimproved	....	1,454	3,558	14,693	19,705
Total	6,864	16,493	13,520 [c]	74,179	111,056

[a] At the close of 1931. See *Minnesota Highway News,* December 12, 1931, in regard to trunk highways, and February 20, 1932, in regard to state-aid highways.
[b] At the close of 1930. *Ibid.,* August 8, 1931.
[c] Several county roads were designated as state-aid roads during 1931, but these were offset by a number of roads transferred from the state-aid to the county-aid class during the same year; thus the difference in dates is not serious.
[d] This figure includes 1,350 miles with gravel on standard grade and 1,621 miles with gravel on sub-standard grade.
[e] Exclusive of state-aid roads but including county-aid roads.

[8] Based on work completed by October 5, 1932.

average of 678 vehicles a day. According to this same census there were 40 points on the unpaved routes at which traffic averaged from 1,000 to 3,000 a day, indicating, according to the highway officials, that many unpaved routes ought to be paved.[9] These facts seem to show that concentration of expenditures on a small but well-chosen portion of the highways is warranted.

Certain other aspects of Minnesota highway costs are interesting. The State Department of Highways considers that an August

TABLE 6.—AVERAGE COSTS PER MILE OF STATE TRUNK HIGHWAYS IN MINNESOTA, 1931[a]

Item	Construction	Resurfacing	Maintenance of Surface or Slab	Total Maintenance[b]
Right of way, culverts, bridges, and miscellaneous structure....	$6,364	....	....	......
Grading	8,608	....	....	......
Graveling	757	....	....	......
Total for untreated gravel road	$15,729	$256[c]	....	$339.00[d]
Bituminous treatment on gravel..	1,307[e]	761[f]	$176.00	280.60
Concrete paving (20 feet wide, 9 inches at edges, and 7 inches in center)..................	22,920[g]	....	97.61	249.36

[a] See *Minnesota Highway News,* February 13 and March 5, 1932.
[b] Including roadside maintenance, removal of snow, and all other items.
[c] Regraveling on 1,601 miles.
[d] Includes all items except regraveling on 2,948 miles.
[e] Bituminous treatment only. [f] Bituminous retreatment only.
[g] Includes shouldering, curbs, drains, and all miscellaneous items.

traffic count of 400 or 500 vehicles a day indicates that bituminous treatment is warranted. Before it is decided to improve a road, however, the available source of the gravel for the particular highway is taken into account, as well as certain other factors, including present cost of maintenance. When it is a question of pavement, an August traffic count of 1,000 seems to be the critical point. Here again other factors, including present cost of maintenance, are considered.

Much of the work on the trunk highways is done in stages, but construction figures indicate that in 1931 the entire cost of a mile of paving was in the neighborhood of $38,000. On those unpaved portions of the highway where recent annual expenditures for

[9] *Minnesota Highway News,* October 3, 1931. See above, page 374.

maintenance exceed $1,000 per mile (there were 899 miles of such highways in 1930, of which 296 cost more than $1,500 and 92 more than $2,000), the savings in maintenance charges alone will justify to a considerable extent the higher construction cost of paving.

At the present time, figures as to costs of construction and maintenance are not compiled by uniform methods in the several states; hence comparisons are liable to much error. Table 7 should be read with this caution in mind.

TABLE 7.—COMPARISON OF AVERAGE UNIT COSTS ON CERTAIN ITEMS OF CONSTRUCTION IN MINNESOTA AND IN MICHIGAN, 1931

ITEM	MINNESOTA[a]	MICHIGAN[b]
Paving (except cement) per square yard[c]	$1.252	$.92
Cement for paving per square yard	.466	.43
Net per square yard, slab only	$1.718	$1.35
Gravel surfacing per cubic yard	.837	1.00
Grading excavation per cubic yard, including overhaul	.2486	.251

[a] *Minnesota Highway News,* February 13, 1932.
[b] From data compiled by the Michigan State Highway Department.
[c] Seven inches in center and nine inches at edges.

HIGHWAY REVENUES

PRINCIPLES AND PROBLEMS OF DISTRIBUTING COSTS

It is now generally agreed that the cost of constructing and maintaining highways should be covered by taxes imposed on those who benefit from these improvements, in proportion to the benefits received or to the costs occasioned, in so far as this is practicable. It may be assumed that benefits are of three kinds: (1) general social benefits; (2) special benefits to abutting property; and (3) benefits to the individual user of the road. The privately owned toll bridge and the turnpike highway have disappeared. Considerations of convenience and the American dislike for petty payments both favor free roads.

Provision of highway facilities has become a governmental function. Outside of federal aid, which may be justified on the basis of the first benefit mentioned above, the task of providing highway revenues has been and will continue to be left to the states or their political subdivisions. With the exception of a few miscellaneous sources of revenue that may be disregarded here, revenues have been obtained in the past two decades by means of general property taxes, special assessments, gasoline taxes, and motor registration taxes. One of the most important questions of theory and policy in highway finance is what part of the total highway bill is to be paid out of taxes on motorists and what part out of other revenues.[10] If this question is satisfactorily answered by showing that owners of automobiles are the direct and chief beneficiaries of highway improvements, another arises: What type of tax or taxes shall be imposed on the operator of a motor vehicle or user of the highways? Then follow questions as to the distribution of the tax or taxes among owners of vehicles of different types and uses, and questions as to the allocation of motor tax revenues or any revenues for highway purposes between the state and the local units. These questions will be taken up in the order mentioned. It is sufficient to say at this point, however, that as yet no clear-cut underlying principles have been worked out with respect to any of them. The maze of differences apparent in state laws, especially with respect to amounts of taxation of motor vehicles and the methods of allocating the proceeds among the different classes of roads, furnishes abundant evidence of the lack of generally accepted principles. So far as the country's expenditures for rural highways are concerned, the trend is in the direction of taxing motor vehicles for the larger portion of the total. According to figures compiled by the Bureau of Public Roads, the country as a whole derived from motor vehicle taxes 12.7 per cent of the total amount spent on state and local highways in 1921 and 50.5 per cent of the total in 1930.[11] Minnesota conforms fairly well to these averages. In 1930 the total receipts from the gasoline and motor registration taxes in Minnesota amounted to 44.2 per cent of the total expenditures for state and local rural highways and to 88.1 per cent of the highway expenditures of the state road department. Receipts from the gasoline tax amounted to 20.4 per cent, and receipts from the motor registration tax to 22.8 per cent, of the total state and local expenditures for rural highways, as compared with an average of 29.4 per cent and 21.1 per cent, respectively, for all states. Minnesota is far below the average with respect to the portion raised by the gasoline tax.

In its report of 1930 the National Tax Association's Committee

[10] A comprehensive list of printed references expressing various views on this point appears in the Report of the Committee on Taxation of Motor Vehicle Transportation, Proceedings of the National Tax Association, 1930, p. 135.

[11] See Table 14 on page 416 below.

on Taxation of Motor Vehicle Transportation approved the tendency to increase the proportion of highway revenue obtained from taxes on motor vehicles. It recommended that the increase in such revenues continue until special taxes on motor transportation pay all highway costs which would not have been incurred in the absence of motor vehicles and which are not more equitably and conveniently obtained by special assessments against property owners who derive indirect benefits.[12] The owners of motor vehicles are regarded as the direct beneficiaries. The committee believes, however, that in urban and suburban communities it is often more equitable and convenient to levy carefully applied special assessments than to tax owners of motor vehicles. The above suggestion calls for the classification of highways as local rural roads, rural motor highways, and urban and suburban streets. This suggestion is certainly a step forward in the formulation of principles of highway taxation, and the present movement in various states toward such classification is a progressive one.

According to figures compiled by the Bureau of Public Roads and the American Automobile Association in 1930, the total average tax per car in Minnesota was $29.22, as compared with an average of $37.72[13] in all states when personal property taxes on motor vehicles are included with gasoline and registration taxes. If we disregard the District of Columbia, only North Dakota, with $21.47, had a lower tax than Minnesota. The position of Minnesota is due largely to the fact that the state levies no property tax on motor vehicles other than that contained in the so-called registration tax.[14] If we consider only gasoline and registration taxes, the average tax per car in all states was $32.06.[15] On this basis only eleven states had a lower average tax than Minnesota. The registration tax in Minnesota averaged $15.09, as compared with a national average of $13.41; but the excess in this tax was more than counterbalanced by the gasoline tax, which averaged only $14.13 in Minnesota, as compared with a national average of $18.65, plus a personal property tax in 34 states averaging more than $5.00 per car. In 1931 a dozen states increased their gasoline

[12] Report of the Committee on Taxation of Motor Vehicle Transportation, Proceedings of the National Tax Association, 1930, p. 149.

[13] The average taxes in the several states are presented in Table 8, page 383.

[14] The states that do not levy a property tax on motor vehicles are designated in Table 8.

[15] In 1931 the average registration tax in all states was $13.34 and the average gasoline tax $20.83 per motor vehicle. *American Highways,* July, 1932, p. 8.

taxes and many states increased the registration tax on certain classes of vehicles. When the figures for 1931 are compiled it will be seen that Minnesota has fallen still further below the average. In view of these and other facts, Minnesota might well increase its taxes on motor vehicles, especially its gasoline tax.

Gasoline Taxes

RELATION TO HIGHWAY EXPENDITURES

State taxes on gasoline and motor registration taxes have come to stay. They are accepted as just and logical forms of taxation imposed upon owners of motor vehicles to meet at least part of the cost of highway improvements and extensions attributable to the demands of automobile traffic. With respect to these taxes the state may be said to act as an agent for the automobile owners, building the roads for them and collecting the costs from them. There is, however, no general agreement as to how levies should be apportioned between the gasoline tax and the registration tax. Nor is there agreement as to the proper rate of tax per gallon of gasoline, nor any generally accepted basis for determining the registration fees of the various classes of motor vehicles. Many state legislatures have, moreover, been unable to decide whether they are taxing according to the value of service or to the cost of service. Gasoline taxes are defended on both grounds.

Strictly speaking, to tax motor vehicles directly in proportion to benefit received is an impossibility. In a sense, however, taxation in proportion to damage to the highway is also in proportion to benefit received. Certainly it is not generally, and in the long run, in excess of benefit received or the operation of the vehicle would be discontinued. In any event, the best and most recent thought on the subject, whether embodied in statutes, court decisions, or journals, regards wear and tear on the roads and responsibility for highway expense as the proper basis for the distribution of the burden among the users of the road. According to studies made by the Bureau of Standards, the Bureau of Public Roads, and two committees of the National Tax Association, the major factors to be considered in taxing a vehicle are (1) the number of miles it travels; (2) the weight imposed on the road surface by the vehicle and its load; (3) the manner in which the load is distributed—that is, whether on four wheels with two axles or on six wheels with three axles; and (4) the type of tires with which the

TABLE 8.—STATE MOTOR VEHICLE TAXES IN 1930

(Average per car)

STATE	GAS TAX PER GALLON, 1932	GAS TAX RECEIPTS [a]	REGISTRATION TAX RECEIPTS [a]	REGISTRATION AND GAS TAX RECEIPTS [a]	PERSONAL PROPERTY TAX [b]	TOTAL TAX	RATIO OF TAX TO VALUATION [b]
							Per Cent
Alabama	$ .05	$24.90	$13.71	$38.61	$7.80	$46.41	22.5
Arizona	.05	24.16	6.65	30.81	8.80	39.61	19.2
Arkansas	.06	29.19	19.45	48.64	4.00	52.64	25.6
California	.03	17.08	4.83	21.91	15.00	36.91	17.9
Colorado	.04	19.92	6.16	26.08	9.36	35.44	17.2
Connecticut	.02	13.64	25.04	38.68	9.29	47.97	23.3
Delaware	.03	18.06	19.78	37.84	....	37.84	18.4
Florida	.07	41.66	14.68	56.34	10.00	66.34	32.2
Georgia	.06	39.33	13.12	52.45	6.90	59.35	28.8
Idaho	.05	22.93	16.78	39.71	....	39.71	19.3
Illinois	.03	16.77	11.26	28.03	9.37	37.40	18.2
Indiana	.04	19.59	7.25	26.84	5.24	32.08	15.6
Iowa	.03	13.60	16.31	29.91	....	29.91	14.5
Kansas	.03	15.34	10.23	25.57	5.16	30.73	14.9
Kentucky	.05	25.42	16.76	42.18	8.40	50.58	24.6
Louisiana	.05	27.41	16.74	44.15	6.64	50.79	24.7
Maine	.04	22.39	17.01	39.40	10.18	49.58	24.1
Maryland	.04	21.73	10.69	32.42	6.25	38.67	18.8
Massachusetts	.03	12.48	8.41	20.89	11.33	32.22	15.7
Michigan	.03	16.35	16.92	33.27	....	33.27	16.2
Minnesota	.03	14.13	15.09	29.22	....	29.22	14.2
Mississippi	.055	29.18	12.85	42.03	12.41	54.44	26.4
Missouri	.02	11.34	13.33	24.67	8.60	33.27	16.2
Montana	.05	21.76	11.71	33.47	3.00	36.47	17.7
Nebraska	.04	21.26	8.93	30.19	3.98	34.17	16.6
Nevada	.04	18.05	12.61	30.66	52.28	82.94	40.3
New Hampshire	.04	22.28	20.41	42.69	....	42.69	20.7
New Jersey	.03	13.34	18.03	31.37	....	31.37	15.2
New Mexico	.05	32.82	15.21	48.03	8.50	56.53	27.5
New York	.03	12.34	17.70	30.04	....	30.04	14.6
North Carolina	.06	27.65	15.08	42.73	3.38	46.11	22.4
North Dakota	.03	10.77	10.70	21.47	....	21.47	10.4
Ohio	.04	21.08	7.55	28.63	10.40	39.03	19.0
Oklahoma	.04	21.97	11.88	33.85	....	33.85	16.4
Oregon	.04	24.59	38.15	62.74	....	62.74	30.5
Pennsylvania	.03	19.17	18.88	38.05	....	38.05	18.5
Rhode Island	.02	12.72	16.72	29.44	20.00	49.44	24.0
South Carolina	.06	32.72	13.18	45.90	5.00	50.90	24.7
South Dakota	.04	17.08	14.43	31.51	....	31.51	15.3
Tennessee	.07	29.10	12.95	42.05	9.30	51.35	24.9
Texas	.04	21.62	10.22	31.84	3.28	35.12	17.1
Utah	.04	18.47	7.51	25.98	7.25	33.23	16.1
Vermont	.04	21.70	27.61	49.31	....	49.31	24.0
Virginia	.05	28.67	17.28	45.95	5.00	50.95	24.7
Washington	.05	16.26	17.07	33.33	10.87	44.20	21.5
West Virginia	.04	20.16	17.66	37.82	7.47	45.29	22.0
Wisconsin	.04	10.62	16.72	27.34	6.15 [c]	33.49	16.3
Wyoming	.04	23.53	11.24	34.77	9.10 [c]	43.87	21.3
District of Columbia	.02	10.21	4.06	14.27	3.75	18.02	8.8
Average	..	$18.65	$13.41	$32.06	$5.66	$37.72	18.3

[a] Compiled by the United States Bureau of Public Roads.

[b] Compiled by the American Automobile Association. In the last column an average retail value of $808 and an average value of $205.88 throughout an average life of seven years were assumed.

[c] Wisconsin and Wyoming have recently exempted motor vehicles from property taxation.

vehicle is equipped, pneumatic, solid rubber, or metal. A system that neglects any one of the four is inequitable; one that attempts to include more factors becomes unwieldy.

If only one motor vehicle tax were to be levied, and if cost of service were to be taken as the guide, the gasoline tax would be more suitable than the registration tax. Certainly the number of miles a car is driven bears a definite relation to the total damage it does to roads. The gasoline tax brings in more revenue per mile from the heavy truck than it does from the light passenger car, and it taxes the fully loaded vehicle more heavily than the empty one. The Bureau of Public Roads found in several experiments that the damage from impact or pounding of wheels on the road surface increases with the speed. Inasmuch as the amount of gasoline consumed increases with speed, the gasoline tax automatically "fines" the speeder. It is the only practicable method of taxing visitors and tourists who use the roads. The increase in the price of fuel, due to the tax, encourages greater economy in the design and operation of vehicles and penalizes the owner who operates a car that wastes the nation's fuel resources. In addition, the tax is conveniently paid, simple to collect, and inexpensive to administer. These factors have all contributed to the wide acceptance of the tax as eminently suited to meet the costs of establishing and maintaining the modern highways. No special interests have opposed its imposition. Earmarking of the funds collected for highway use has won the support of the motor industry and has disarmed the opposition even of the petroleum industry.

TABLE 9. — NET PROCEEDS OF THE GASOLINE TAX IN MINNESOTA, 1925–1932 [a]

YEAR	AMOUNT	YEAR	AMOUNT
1925	$3,068,209	1929	$8,892,125
1926	4,956,498	1930	10,359,111
1927	5,174,880	1931	11,070,422
1928	5,768,100	1932 (est.)	10,500,000

[a] Data for 1925 and 1926 are from the Minnesota State Department of Highways; for 1927 to 1930, from the Bureau of Public Roads; for 1931, from the Minnesota Division of Oil Inspection. Decrease to November 1, 1932, $445,207.

A gasoline tax has been in effect in Minnesota since May 1, 1925. The rate was 2 cents per gallon until May 1, 1929, when it was raised to 3 cents. The proceeds of this tax, after the deduction of refunds, are as shown in Table 9.

According to data compiled by the Bureau of Public Roads, the gasoline tax in 1932 was 2 cents in three states and the District of Columbia, 3 cents in twelve states, 4 cents in seventeen states, 5 cents in nine states, 5.5 cents in one state, 6 cents in four states, and 7 cents in two states. Only three states, Connecticut, Missouri, and Rhode Island, and the District of Columbia, all of which levy 2 cents, have a lower tax than Minnesota. (See page 383.)

EXEMPTIONS AND REFUNDS

The perplexing question of exemptions and refunds brings out the need for a clear understanding of the fundamental basis of the tax as well as the need for efficient administration. The state constitution states that the proceeds of the gasoline tax shall be used to defray highway costs. Statutes provide for the allocation of these revenues and for the refund of the tax paid on gasoline used for other than transportation purposes. These facts might indicate that it was considered a benefit tax. In so far as it can be considered something more than a special benefit tax, there is no necessity for a refund. Table 10 shows the percentages of refunds in recent years.

TABLE 10. — GASOLINE TAX REFUNDS IN MINNESOTA, 1929–1931[a]

Year	Gross Tax	Total Refunds		Agricultural Refunds		
		Amount	Per Cent	No. of Claims	Amount	Per Cent
1929	$ 9,631,151	$ 739,026	7.7	68,226	$ 497,715	5.2
1930	11,432,686	1,073,575	9.4	91,399	733,915	6.4
1931	12,543,077	1,472,655	11.7	133,800	1,031,795	8.2

[a] Data furnished by the Minnesota Division of Oil Inspection.

In 1931 the taxes on nearly 50,000,000 gallons of gasoline were refunded. Farmers received 71 per cent of the refunds and road contractors 15 per cent. Table 10 shows that refunds reduce revenues appreciably; it also shows that the percentage of refunds is increasing rapidly. Opportunities for misrepresentation and fraud are great, and the expense involved in a really accurate system of checking claims would be heavy. In 1930 thirteen states made no refund.[16] Several states, including Connecticut and Rhode Island, provide exemptions for gasoline purchased for purposes other than

[16] Florida, Georgia, Kentucky, Louisiana, Mississippi, Nebraska, New Mexico, Pennsylvania, Tennessee, Utah, Vermont, Virginia, and Wyoming.

highway transportation. Under this system no tax is paid and of course no refund is necessary. Cost of administration is less but evasion is probably increased. The subject deserves some intensive study, which might possibly lead to revision of the basis of refund and improvements in administration. In the meantime there seems to be no sufficient reason why refunds to road contractors should be continued.

ADMINISTRATION

There is great variation among the states as to the administrative office responsible for the collection of this tax. The efficiency of one collecting agency as compared with another cannot be determined; there appears to be no relation between the agency in charge in the several states and the cost of collection or the problem presented by exemption. Some states find, however, that the difficulties of administration are increased as a result of higher rates.

Since Minnesota already had an oil inspection law requiring that before it was unloaded all gasoline coming into the state be listed and sampled, for which processes a fee was collected, the legislature decided to leave the levying of the tax to the state oil inspector. Collection of the tax is easier and more economical in Minnesota than in most states because the tax is assessed on the in-shipments and must be paid monthly by the importing distributor. Aside from the office force required to make the statements and keep track of them until the receipts are certified to the state treasurer, no special tax collectors are required. To cover costs of collection in 1929 and 1930 the legislature appropriated $12,000 a year. The appropriation for 1931 was increased to $13,000. Out of these amounts had to come all expenses necessary for collection, including salaries of office personnel, printing costs, and postage, and all expenses connected with refund claims. Every distributor of gasoline must file a certificate according to the rules of the oil inspector. Every distributor and every person using gasoline in motor vehicles upon which a tax has not been paid must keep a prescribed record of transactions and of the use of gasoline in the state, to be examined by the oil inspector. The average cost of collecting the tax in Minnesota is slightly more than one-tenth of 1 per cent of the revenue. Few states have costs so low, and the administrative situation appears to be good.

NON-HIGHWAY USE OF THE PROCEEDS OF GASOLINE AND REGISTRATION TAXES

Since the gasoline tax was devised to meet the new and special highway demands created by the motor vehicle, it would seem only fair that the proceeds of the tax be devoted to improving roads, either by directly appropriating them to rural roads or city streets or by applying them in payment of the interest and principal of bonds and notes issued for road purposes. In general this policy has been followed, but there are a few notable exceptions. In 1931, $19,442,737, or 3.62 per cent of the total proceeds in all states, was used for "other than highway purposes," according to figures compiled by the Bureau of Public Roads.[17] Florida applied $3,000,000, or 20 per cent of its gasoline revenues, to educational purposes and the general fund. Georgia used $2,218,216, or 17 per cent, and Texas, $7,628,640, or 25 per cent, of these revenues for education.

There was much agitation in the state legislatures in 1931 to increase the tax and use the additional proceeds for general revenue purposes. While it may be true that some states have recently had difficulty in balancing their budgets and while modernized school systems have demanded greater financial support, diversions of revenue or increases in the tax rate for such purposes appear to be unjust and unwise, since large amounts from less appropriate taxes are used for highways. In virtually all states all the income from the gasoline tax is still needed if the highway and employment programs demanded are to be carried out. Some states, moreover, have issued highway bonds that are to be retired out of receipts from the gasoline tax. Then, too, the primary justification and popularity of the tax rests upon the use of the proceeds for road purposes. The inclusion of more mileage in the state highway systems and the diversion of the proceeds to local rural roads and city streets under state supervision are both to be preferred to diversion of the proceeds elsewhere. When the supply of road facilities is more favorably related to the demand for them than at the present, either reduction in gasoline tax rates or diversion of the proceeds elsewhere can and should be seriously considered.[18] The

[17] The proceeds of the gasoline tax in the entire United States in 1931 were $537,589,717 after deduction of refunds.

[18] Many would prefer, of course, that a smaller proportion of the people's resources be spent for highways, motor cars, and other purposes regarded as luxuries, in order that more funds might be devoted to education, health, and art. These persons feel it their duty to try to counteract the lobbying and advertising propa-

same may be said concerning the proceeds of the motor registration tax. Such diversions are much less common in the case of registration taxes than in that of gasoline taxes. In 1931 only $11,549,697, or 3.35 per cent of the total proceeds from registration taxes in all states, was used "for other purposes."[19] Most of this was used for refunds and for the state highway patrol, both of which are really related to roads. The most notable diversion from road purposes was $4,063,444 applied to the general fund in New York City. Thus it appears that the general sentiment favors the use of the proceeds on roads. Minnesota has not diverted any of its taxes on motor vehicles to non-road purposes; in fact, it may be said to have diverted the property tax on motor vehicles to highways by means of a relatively high registration tax.

CONSIDERATIONS CONCERNING RATES

Probably it must be admitted that there is no way of determining, a priori, the proper tax or the best tax per gallon of gasoline. Experience throws some light on the problem, however. A recent study of the relationship between gasoline taxes and consumption in forty states before and after increases in the tax rates from 1925 to 1929 indicates that increasing the tax tends to retard both the actual amount of increase in consumption of gasoline and the rate of increase. The higher the tax rate or the greater the increase in the tax rate, the more marked this tendency becomes.[20] With the funds put into more and better highways, the effect in the long run is, of course, another story. Officials who administer the tax generally maintain, moreover, that administrative difficulties increase with increased rates even though costs of collection do not. Attempts to evade the tax in several states by fraudulent consignments and in other ways have followed recent increases over the already substantial rates. The rate of tax is probably not so important a factor in this situation as the depression, however, nor as the weak tax administration in some states.

ganda of motor manufacturers, cement producers, and others by educating the people in the matter of relative values. But if despite their efforts the great majority still insist on highways and pass laws providing for highways that must be financed by one set of taxes or another, it seems unwise to divert funds from the most appropriate taxes so long as these funds are insufficient to pay the costs of highways.

[19] Proceeds from the motor vehicle registration tax in the United States were $344,337,654 in 1931.

[20] James W. Martin and Marshall Harris, "Increase in State Gasoline Taxes Retards Motor Fuel Consumption," *National Petroleum News*, December 17, 1930. pp. 83–87.

Rates in adjacent states should certainly be considered in determining the proper rate of tax in a given state. Absolute uniformity in rates among the several states is not necessary and probably is not desirable, in view of the different stages of development of their highway systems. But marked differences between adjacent states appear to encourage evasion. Wisconsin and South Dakota levy 4 cents; Iowa and North Dakota, 3 cents; and Manitoba and Ontario in Canada, 5 cents. Recent data on gasoline consumption are, of course, relevant in a consideration of rates. Table 11 gives these data for Minnesota.

TABLE 11.—MOTOR VEHICLE CONSUMPTION OF GASOLINE IN MINNESOTA, 1929–1931[a]

YEAR	REGISTRATION[b]	PERCENTAGE OF INCREASE	NET GALLONS TAXED	PERCENTAGE OF INCREASE	GALLONS USED PER VEHICLE REGISTERED	AVERAGE MILES TRAVELED PER VEHICLE[c]
1929........	727,082	...	338,631,771	..	429	6,435
1930........	733,012	.8	345,303,700	2.0	471	7,065
1931........	720,040[b]	...	369,014,000	6.9	512	7,680

[a] *Minnesota Highway News*, February 13, 1932.
[b] Trailers and motorcycles omitted. Registration to November 5, 1932, 703,238.
[c] It is assumed that the average motorist gets 15 miles to the gallon.

The decrease in registration in 1931 as indicated in Table 11 was the first recorded in the state since annual registration was begun. The number of heavier cars increased, however, so there was probably an increase in the total capacity of motor vehicles in the state. From 1921 to 1930 registration of motor vehicles in Minnesota increased 129 per cent. Gasoline consumption, however, was nearly three times as great in 1930 as in 1921. Traffic, therefore, has increased much more rapidly than registration. The trend in Minnesota has been toward more cars, heavier cars, greater speed, and the traveling of greater distances. In addition, the comparison of traffic counts with registration figures indicates that more and more vehicles are being driven throughout the year.

Of course, if an increase in the 3-cent gasoline tax is desirable, the extent of the increase should be governed in part by the readiness with which the additional funds can be used economically for highway purposes. If an analysis of traffic and the classification of highways disclose the need, the rate of this tax may be properly advanced to cover the costs of necessary expenditures. The degree of completeness of the state trunk system, the difficulty that the local units are meeting in caring for their highway and other needs almost entirely with the proceeds of property taxes, and the desirability of cutting down borrowing operations to a minimum, all call for diversion of additional mileage to the state trunk system or additional state highway aid to the counties, or both. The extent of each of these two changes is, of course, a matter of policy and law. The first is the more desirable.

In the light of the various factors mentioned above and also of those previously considered as bearing on the question of the rate of the gasoline tax, such as the proportion of highway expenditures being raised by motor vehicle taxes in Minnesota as compared with other states, the average tax load per vehicle in Minnesota as compared with other states, the growing tourist travel, the recent data on gasoline consumption and tax revenue, the administration of the gasoline tax, highway demands, and the need for relief from confiscatory taxes upon real estate, Minnesota should seriously consider increasing the gasoline tax to 4 cents a gallon. A 4-cent gasoline tax can be successfully administered and proceeds wisely used in this state. On the basis of net receipts in 1931, the additional cent would yield approximately $3,700,000. As provided in the constitutional amendment adopted in 1928, two-thirds of this would go to the trunk highway fund and one-third to the counties. It would really be best to improve the method of distribution and the supervision of expenditure before or at the time an increase in tax rates is made. The commissioner of highways recommended an increase of one cent in the gasoline tax in his biennial report to the legislature for 1929 and 1930.[21]

Motor Vehicle Registration Taxes

FACTORS TO BE CONSIDERED

The gasoline tax takes inadequate account of some previously mentioned factors that must be considered in a system of special taxation of motor vehicles.[22] The gasoline tax, moreover, is inadequate or ineffective in distributing highway taxes in certain other directions. For instance, highways are generally constructed on a scale sufficient to accommodate the peak traffic load during the summer and over week-ends. Many cars are operated on the high-

[21] Page 20.
[22] See page 382 above.

ways only during the peak periods and certainly escape their due share of taxes if they are taxed only on their gasoline consumption. Besides, many states cannot raise adequate revenue for highway purposes by means of the gasoline tax alone unless the rate is unduly high.

GROSS WEIGHT OF VEHICLE AND LOAD

A motor vehicle registration tax may be devised that will bear more relation than does gasoline consumption to the influence of the weight of the vehicle and load (gross weight), the distribution of load, and the type of tire upon wear and tear of the highway. Investigations in recent years by the Bureau of Public Roads and other authorities provide sufficient data upon which to construct a scientific plan of motor vehicle taxation based on the degree of wear and tear upon the road produced by various vehicles.[23]

The gross weight that can be carried is the chief consideration in the designing of new bridges and certain highways. Gross weight is, moreover, the only characteristic common to the several types of vehicles and at the same time more or less related to the use and consequent deterioration of the road. The registration tax ought therefore to be based on the weight of the vehicle and its capacity load. As pointed out previously, the gasoline tax reaches gross weight, but inadequately. A six-ton truck may be three times as destructive to the average highway as a three-ton truck, yet consume only from 25 to 50 per cent more gasoline.

DISTRIBUTION OF WHEEL PRESSURES

The relation between road destruction and gross weight is rather uncertain. Investigations of impact on pavement indicate that destruction as measured by impact increases at least as rapidly as gross weight.[24] So far as the paved highway and its design are concerned, the wheel load, not the gross load, is important. Tests made by the Bureau of Public Roads in the application of the wheel loads to the roads show that if the contact of one wheel is

[23] In investigations of impact the Bureau of Public Roads, by means of instruments attached to the vehicle, has measured the impact of the wheel operating over artificial obstructions which created the desired conditions of roughness on an otherwise smooth pavement. The impact or contact consists of a shock and a drop in moving over the obstruction. Load, type of tire, speed, and other factors were varied to ascertain their relations to impact.

[24] James A. Buchanan and E. B. Smith, "Report on Motor Truck Impact Studies," Proceedings of the Seventh Annual Meeting of the Highway Research Board, National Research Council, 1927, p. 94; and James A. Buchanan, "Impact Reactions Developed by a Modern Motor Bus," *Public Roads,* April, 1931, p. 27.

thirty-six inches ahead of the next wheel, there is no overlap of stresses in the road structure. The paved highways built with federal aid under the supervision of the Bureau of Public Roads, including the pavement on trunk highways in Minnesota with edges of nine inches and center of seven, are designed to carry a wheel load of 9,000 pounds on a pneumatic tire at thirty miles an hour. This wheel load is that of a loaded truck with a rated capacity of five tons and a gross weight of 23,000 pounds, 80 per cent of which is assumed to be on the rear axle (the worst condition in practice).[25] Obviously, such a design will take care of the buses. According to a study made by the bureau, a pavement designed for such a wheel load need be only 17.7 per cent thicker than the minimum thickness required to prevent destruction by sun and frost. This minimum thickness is sufficient for a wheel load of 5,600 pounds, or a truck with a rated capacity of not more than three tons, under the same conditions.[26] It makes no difference, moreover, according to the bureau, what portion of the traffic over a pavement with proper subgrade consists of vehicles having wheel loads equal to the maximum for that pavement. The wear on well-constructed pavements from pneumatic tires is negligible. Furthermore, a well-constructed paved road will stand up under an appreciable number of loads in excess of the maximum for which it is designed, if such loads are not very frequent. Of course, all this might be said to a less extent of surfaces of lower quality, but the facts given here certainly indicate that the relationship between various gross weights and road destruction depends on the type of highway surface. In a state like Connecticut, therefore, which has many heavy vehicles and a preponderance of high-grade pavement, a greater degree of tax differentiation between vehicles of various gross weights would be logical and equitable than in the opposite situation. In a state in which there are relatively few heavy vehicles the taxes on them would be prohibitive if they had to pay the construction and maintenance costs that they occasion, that is, the costs in excess of what would be adequate for light vehicles. This is true despite the fact that the additional costs have frequently been overrated. For instance, on well-constructed pavements the vehicle with a wheel load of 9,000

[25] With cushion and solid tires, the thickness required for various wheel loads is greater.

[26] National Automobile Chamber of Commerce, *Facts and Figures of the Automobile Industry* (1931 ed.), p. 39.

pounds or more is responsible for nearly all the thickness in excess of that which climatic conditions make necessary.[27] On surfaces of lower quality the wheel load limit is lower.

Pavements sufficiently strong and well built to stand the severe weather conditions of Minnesota are strong enough to carry most heavy vehicles in use, especially those with pneumatic tires and six wheels on three axles. But some of the highway surfaces are not adequate for all the vehicles that use them.

Whether the relatively few heavy vehicles should pay the entire additional costs that they occasion depends upon whether or not their use brings indirect net advantages to the public that offset all or part of such costs. Heavy trucks may mean fewer vehicles, lower freight costs to consumers, less use of road space, and possibly less traffic congestion; on the other hand, they may mean higher railroad rates, greater congestion, and more hazards to drivers of other cars. The balance of advantage to the public is uncertain, but it does not appear sufficient to exempt heavy vehicles from paying the extra costs that they occasion. If their services are not worth the costs, operators should be required to use lighter vehicles or vehicles that distribute load pressures with less damage to highways, or to keep off the roads. Costs must be met by somebody, why not by those who occasion them? Why should they be shifted to the public?[28]

As to the manner in which the load is distributed, the heavy vehicle fitted with six wheels on three axles is less destructive than one of the same weight provided with only four wheels on two axles. Evidence seems to indicate that the former is about half as destructive as the latter so far as the rear axle is concerned—

[27] According to road surveys made in several states in recent years, the percentages of loaded trucks on the state highway systems with a rated capacity of five tons and over ranged from .3 per cent in Maine to 9.8 per cent in Cook County, Illinois. See National Automobile Chamber of Commerce, *Truck Facts for 1927*, p. 20; and the testimony of Thomas H. MacDonald, chief of United States Bureau of Public Roads, before the Interstate Commerce Commission, March 5, 1931, Docket No. 23400, "Coordination of Motor Transportation," from the transcript of testimony furnished by the official reporter of the National Association of Bus Operators, page 2.

[28] In 1931 the legislature of Minnesota provided for new maximum load limits on highways. With axles eight feet or more apart, the maximum is 9,000 pounds per wheel or 18,000 pounds per axle; with axles less than eight feet apart, 6,000 pounds per wheel or 12,000 pounds per axle. These limits are for vehicles equipped with pneumatic tires. For vehicles with solid tires the maximums are 80 per cent of the weights specified for pneumatic tires. The length of vehicles and trailers is limited to 60 feet. See Mike Holm and C. M. Babcock, *The Uniform Traffic Act, 1931*, p. 17. Such restrictions will not restrict highway use uneconomically.

probably 60 per cent as destructive as a whole.[29] Obviously the gasoline tax does not take adequate account of this fact.[30] The available evidence does not seem to indicate any very significant difference in respect to highway damage between the single tire and the dual mounting on one end of the axle.[31]

TYPE OF TIRE

Solid tires are more destructive to roads than pneumatic tires. Of solid tires, metal tires are more destructive than solid rubber tires. Surely these facts should be considered in fixing the registration tax imposed on vehicles. The vehicle equipped with new solid rubber tires, the evidence indicates, is about three times as destructive as the same vehicle equipped with pneumatic tires.[32] Besides, it may be shown that cushion tires are twice as destructive as pneumatic tires, and badly worn solid rubber tires five times as destructive.[33] Metal tires seem to be at least six or seven times as destructive.[34] High-pressure pneumatic tires are more destructive than balloon tires, but these findings, it seems, are not significant in relation to the problem of taxation of motor vehicles. It hardly need be pointed out that the gasoline tax takes very inadequate account of tire equipment.[35]

These facts have led various authorities in recent years to suggest taxing motor vehicles on the basis of damage to highways.[36]

The registration tax should be based on gross weight, the rate of tax per unit of weight being graded upward as weight increases, since construction costs and wear and tear on the average highway increase proportionately faster than gross weight. The registration

[29] Buchanan and Smith, *op. cit.*, p. 94, and L. W. Teller, "The Six-Wheel Truck and the Pavement," *Public Roads*, October, 1925.

[30] Among the heavier vehicles there was a marked increase in 1931 in the production of six-wheeled units equipped with pneumatic tires.

[31] Buchanan, *op. cit.; Public Roads*, April, 1931, p. 26.

[32] E. B. Smith, "Motor Truck Impact Tests," *Public Roads*, March, 1921, p. 35.

[33] Buchanan and Smith, *op. cit.*, p. 93.

[34] E. B. Smith, "Present Status of Truck Tire Tests of the Bureau of Public Roads," *Public Roads*, August, 1925, p. 129.

[35] In 1931 only 3.3 per cent of the total number of trucks manufactured were fitted with solid or cushion tires. In 1921 the percentage was 29.8. The percentage on the highways is no doubt higher than the percentage of production.

[36] James W. Martin, "The Motor Vehicle Registration Tax," Bulletin of the National Tax Association, April, 1927, pp. 202–204; and "License Fee Properly Supplements Gasoline Tax," *Engineering News Record*, May 5, 1927, p. 722; Report of the Committee on Taxation of Motor Vehicle Transportation, Proceedings of the National Tax Association, 1930, pp. 156–160; and Charles F. Marvin, "A Technical Basis for Apportioning Motor Vehicle Taxes," *Public Roads*, May, 1930, pp. 41–50.

tax on a vehicle equipped with solid rubber tires should be at least three times as high as it would be if the same vehicle were equipped with pneumatic tires. If metal tires are permitted on the road at all, the registration tax on a vehicle equipped with such tires should be at least twice as much as on an identical vehicle equipped with solid rubber tires. The truck with six wheels on three axles should be subject to 60 per cent of the registration tax levied on a vehicle of the same gross weight equipped with four wheels.[37]

The use of gross weight as a base and discrimination on the basis of tire equipment and axle-wheel combination are comparatively recent developments for the most part, but the tendencies toward their adoption are quite clear.[38] In 1931 gross weight was used as a base, either alone or in a combination of bases, by nine states in the case of the private passenger car and by ten states in the case of the private truck. Twenty-four states discriminated against the truck fitted with solid tires. Maryland, Texas, and Wisconsin levied a lower tax on six-wheeled trucks.

TAXATION OF COMMERCIAL VEHICLES IN THE SEVERAL STATES

In recent years one state after another has differentiated the

[37] The following formula may be suggestive in applying such a registration tax; it takes into account gross weight but not tire equipment or axle-wheel combination:

$$\text{Registration tax} = a + b \text{ times (gross weight of vehicle in tons)}^2.$$

Here a is the constant charge for administrative and regulative purposes, while b is any selected multiple of the square of the gross weight. The larger this multiple the more steeply graduated is the total registration tax and the more revenue it will produce. Incidentally, b times the gross weight squared is a variable charge graduated according to gross weight as reflective of wear and tear on the highway. Data in the tabulation below indicate how the registration charges would run with such a formula. The constants in this particular case are not intended as recommendations for Minnesota. Probably smaller graduations than tons would be desirable in

REGISTRATION TAX PAYABLE UNDER THE FORMULA $4+2w^2$

Gross Weight of Vehicle in Tons	Registration Tax Payable	Gross Weight of Vehicle in Tons	Registration Tax Payable
1	$6	7	$102
2	12	8	132
3	22	9	166
4	36	10	204
5	54	11	246
6	76	12	292

the case of vehicles of relatively small gross weights. For administrative reasons the weight of the car and rated capacity load with some designated weight, 150 pounds per passenger, for instance, should be taken as the basis for the tax. Manufacturers' specifications will be satisfactory for standard vehicles. Other vehicles will have to be weighted.

[38] The tendencies are clearly revealed in Motor Vehicle Conference Committee, *Special Taxation for Motor Vehicles* (1931 ed.), pp. 8–35.

commercial car or car for hire from the private car by levying the registration tax on a different base or combination of bases. Different rates of tax are levied, moreover, and usually the tax, or in some cases the combination of taxes that constitutes the registration levy, is heavier than upon cars not operated for hire. This differentiation has gone further in the case of buses than of trucks and further for common carriers than for contract carriers.[39] The heavier tax on the commercial vehicle is brought about in a number of ways. Consider a few examples of bus taxation. In Rhode Island the levy is twice that on the private passenger car. Illinois adds to the "regular" levy, which applies to the private passenger car, a charge according to seating capacity and another on gross receipts, Iowa a charge on ton mileage, and Utah a charge on passenger mileage. Pennsylvania levies on different bases for private passenger cars and for buses — horsepower in the former case, seating capacity in the latter.

Comparative studies show that usually the registration tax is calculated in the several states on a vehicle having assumed specifications as to seats, horsepower, net weight, mileage, etc. According to one set of such calculations, the average registration tax on a certain 22-passenger bus in 1929 was $81.67 as a private car, $147.96 as a contract carrier, and $280.22 as an interurban common carrier. On a certain three-ton truck the average registration tax in 1929 was $60.10 as a private car, $77.20 as a contract carrier, and $177.16 as an interurban common carrier.[40] On another three-ton truck, according to data obtained in a traffic study of eleven western states conducted by the Bureau of Public Roads in cooperation with authorities in these states and completed in 1931, the average registration tax was $59.27 as a private car, $83.55 as a contract carrier, and $146.23 as a common carrier.[41]

[39] The common carrier operates over regular routes between fixed termini, and the operator is required to obtain a certificate of convenience from a state regulatory commission having power to regulate the service and rates. The contract carrier does not so operate and is not subject to such regulation, at least as far as rates are concerned.

[40] Calculated from tables in J. W. Martin, "Neglected Aspects of the Taxation of Commercial Motor Transportation," Proceedings of the National Tax Association, 1929, pp. 490, 506. In obtaining these averages no consideration was given to weighing the taxes in the various states according to the number of vehicles registered.

[41] Testimony of Thomas H. MacDonald, chief of the United States Bureau of Public Roads, before the Interstate Commerce Commission, March 5, 1931, Docket No. 23400, "Coordination of Motor Transportation," from the transcript of testimony furnished by the official reporter of the National Association of Bus Operators, p. 22.

JUSTIFICATION FOR SPECIAL TAXATION OF COMMERCIAL VEHICLES

Is there justification for heavier registration taxes on the private truck as compared with the private passenger car, still heavier taxes on the contract carrier, and even more burdensome taxes on the common carrier? There has been much discussion of this subject in recent years, but the whole matter is still too uncertain and controversial to permit of definite recommendations of unquestioned merit. Discussions in legislative assemblies and elsewhere reveal a number of theories in justification of such differentiation.

First, there is the "use of the highway" aspect. It is pointed out that the vehicle used in business operates over a greater mileage than the private pleasure car. Furthermore, its operations are more regular from day to day irrespective of road and weather conditions. Such operations are bound to result in greater wear and tear on the road and thus necessitate higher maintenance costs and more costly road construction. All this, it is said, applies to a greater extent to the common carrier, to a less extent to the non-common carrier commercial car, and to a still less extent to the private truck.

If we regard the registration tax as a special benefit tax, the factors heretofore considered as affecting its amount afford no justification for discrimination in this tax on the basis of the purpose for which a vehicle is used. Gross weight (of vehicle and capacity load), tire equipment, and distribution of load as to axles and wheels are the proper and the only necessary, logical, and equitable bases for discrimination. If it is true that certain classes of vehicles are used more continuously than private passenger cars, it is true also that they use more gasoline and are consequently more heavily taxed under the gasoline tax. The registration tax properly applied will take sufficient account of other factors in road use.

BUSINESS TAX THEORY

Then there is the "business" aspect, which has several phases. In the first place, the owner of a private truck uses the highway to transport his own products in connection with the operations of a profit-seeking business rather than for purposes of pleasure. The highway becomes an important element in business enterprise. Hence such use may be taxed more heavily than recreational use. In the second place, the owner of a commercial vehicle puts the bus or truck on the road not to transport himself or his family or even his products or goods but to transport other persons and the products of other businesses. The highway becomes an important element in a new business enterprise seeking profits directly from highway transportation. It is claimed that such use should be taxed still more heavily. In the third place, it is said, the operator of a commercial vehicle competes with other transportation agencies, especially the railroads, and a heavier charge should be levied up to the point where competitive costs are equalized. In the fourth place, it is claimed, the common carrier operator enjoys special privileges conferred by the state and not shared by the contract carrier. These include in certain states, though not in Minnesota, protection from unfair competition and certain highway privileges, such as the right to park on the pavement, special reserved spaces, etc. Hence a heavier tax than that on the contract carrier is justified.

The "business" theory of taxation is different from and perhaps more complicated than the cost of service, or cost of damage, theory. Legal uncertainties in connection with interstate commerce accentuate the difficulty. Of course a state may impose taxes for the privilege of using the highways, whether carriers are intrastate or interstate, provided such taxes represent a fair contribution to the cost of constructing and maintaining roads and regulating the traffic thereon. Furthermore, it appears to be unquestioned that those who use the highway as a place of business may justly be taxed more severely than those who make only private use of it.[42] If the matter rested here it would be logical to think of the taxation in excess of that imposed on non-commercial vehicles as a business tax very much like that imposed on railroads and other transportation agencies.[43] In such case it would not be necessary to isolate commercial carriers for separate business taxation because they would come under the general business laws of the state.

PAYING FOR GENERAL AND SPECIAL GOVERNMENT SERVICES

The model system of state and local taxation recommended by a committee to the National Tax Association in 1919 covers the situation. This plan calls for a tangible property tax, a personal net

[42] Clark v. Poor (1927), 274 U. S. 554; and Sprout v. South Bend (1928), 227 U. S. 163.

[43] It must be remembered that in legislation, and to a considerable extent in general discussions, the business element of the tax imposed on those who operate motor vehicles for profit has been regarded as a part of the special motor vehicle levies on gasoline and registration.

income tax, and a flat-rate business tax, of not less than a specified minimum amount, based upon net earnings from every business in the state. The owners of trucks used in business would pay this business tax. Their trucks could be considered part of their businesses. Of course different forms of business taxes may be desirable for different kinds of businesses. But whether the business tax is imposed in the form of a modified registration levy, a gross receipts tax, or a mileage tax, the rates should be as nearly as possible the equivalent of those on other transportation agencies. All taxes and exemptions applicable to motor vehicles and to their competitors, as well as those applicable to other businesses and property, should be taken into account.

If all motor vehicles everywhere were taxed "on a more onerous basis than other personal property," in the form of a registration levy in lieu of all other taxes on the vehicle (as in Minnesota),[44] and if the commercial carrier operator were paying property taxes on other property in the business office, garage, and station and on furnishings (as in Minnesota), and if other transportation agencies, such as the railroads, were paying a gross earnings tax of 5 per cent in lieu of all property taxes (as in Minnesota),[45] then there would seem to be no justification for a heavier tax on commercial carriers, provided the registration tax were sufficiently "onerous." In such case, it would seem also that the commercial carriers would meet their just share of the cost of the government by paying the gasoline tax and the "onerous" registration tax, whether or not the entire proceeds of these taxes were devoted to highways. The bus would pay much more, of course, than the lighter passenger car because of its greater mileage and size. If the registration tax were not more "onerous," however, or not sufficiently so to offset the property tax exemption, or if other businesses in the state paid extra taxes or special taxes, heavier taxes on commercial carriers would be justified. If the gasoline and registration taxes take proper account of weight, tire equipment, etc., the problem of special highway taxation as a factor affecting competition with

[44] The registration tax would then really contain two elements, one representing the tax levy on tangible personal property, the other, part of the share of the vehicle in highway costs. The former would be a general property tax.

[45] In recent years the gross earnings taxes paid by railroads in Minnesota at 5 per cent have amounted to substantially less than what would have been paid on an ad valorem basis at rates paid by owners of other property in the state so taxed. See Report of the Minnesota Tax Commission, 1930, pp. 158–161, and page 342 above.

other kinds of transportation need not arise, since in each case the different transportation agencies will provide their own facilities. Furthermore, a case could be made for placing the proceeds of this extra taxation (the difference between the taxes on the commercial and on the non-commercial vehicles) into the general fund; for this excess would not really be a special highway tax but a business tax.

The United States Supreme Court has decided otherwise, however, with respect to interstate commerce. In the recent Interstate Transit Case Mr. Justice Brandeis clearly pointed out that such extra tax or taxes on interstate commercial carriers must in some manner affirmatively set forth that the tax is actually imposed as a charge for the use of the highways. The Court explicitly approves that this be done by the form of tax imposed, that is, by making it bear a definite relationship to the use of the highway, or by a special allocation of the revenues to the construction, maintenance, or policing of highways.[46] Obviously, then, the legal situation makes it impracticable to tax interstate vehicle carriers directly on the basis of volume of business. Of course a state may tax the intrastate commercial vehicle in any way it sees fit and tax the interstate vehicle in a manner satisfactory to the Court, but this would complicate the administration. It seems advisable to tax intrastate and interstate commercial vehicles on the same basis. A mileage tax based on vehicle miles, passenger miles, or ton miles seems satisfactory as a measure of the use of the highway, and at the same time it will meet legal approval as a basis for the tax on interstate motor businesses. Passenger and ton mileage appear to be more refined measures of the use of highways than vehicle mileage.

SUGGESTIONS FOR SPECIAL TAXATION OF COMMERCIAL VEHICLES

The committee of the National Tax Association that reported in 1930 on the taxation of motor vehicle transportation gave further consideration to the problem of the commercial vehicle, and in its 1931 report to the association recommended an extra tax based upon passenger miles for commercial passenger cars and gross ton (vehicle and capacity load) miles for commercial trucks. If the state preferred, it might measure the contribution of the bus by gross ton miles with a specified weight for each passenger. The

[46] Interstate Transit Incorporated v. Lindsey (1931), 283 U. S. 183, 51 Sup. Ct. 380, 75 L. Ed. 953.

committee held the opinion that a tax based on vehicle miles might lead to the use of larger vehicles and to less frequent service.[47] It also expressed the opinion that as bases for calculating the tax, rated passenger and freight capacity instead of actual loads or estimated loads, and scheduled mileage instead of actual mileage, would simplify the administration of the tax and tend to encourage greater load-factor efficiency on the part of carriers below the average of their competitors. The committee considered this tax a business tax, even though the United States Supreme Court insists on its being called a highway tax, and suggested that the rates be set so that the amount of the tax on commercial motor vehicle carriers would require on the average substantially the same proportion of net income as the business tax payable by other classes of businesses, particularly other transportation agencies.[48] In states imposing a business income tax, the acceptance of the committee's proposal would mean equalizing taxation of motor vehicle businesses and other classes of enterprise. The committee's proposal, however, is intended to apply, at least for the present, only to common carriers. The problem of the contract carrier, to which it is more difficult to apply the proposed tax, is thus left unsolved.

At the present time the states are experiencing great difficulty in assessing such business use except possibly in the case of the bus. In the meantime it appears best that the heavier taxes on the contract carrier as compared with the non-commercial car take the form of a heavier levy, the same criteria, gross weight or other, being used as are used in the case of other cars, in order to avoid an inequitable tax discrimination against the common carrier.

The National Automobile Chamber of Commerce and certain other authorities oppose the levying of appreciably higher taxes on commercial vehicles. They maintain that distinction between the commercial and the non-commercial vehicle is not only difficult but to some extent arbitrary. Most private passenger cars are used for business as well as for pleasure. Of private trucks this is even more true. They point out also that heavier taxes on commercial cars tend to encourage users of commercial vehicles to provide their own cars. Regarding the private car, rather than the railroad, as the chief competitor of the commercial vehicle, they advocate taxing the commercial vehicle no more than is sufficient to measure its

[47] Such a tax was sustained by the United States Supreme Court in Interstate Buses Corporation v. Blodgett (1928), 276 U. S. 245.

[48] Proceedings of the National Tax Association, 1931, p. 362.

equitable share of highway costs. The public insists, however, that commercial vehicles pay more, and the problem then becomes one of selecting the most equitable method, whether or not such heavier taxation is to be justified as a business tax or as the equivalent of such a tax.

EQUALIZING MOTOR AND RAILROAD COMPETITION

Some persons argue that commercial vehicles should be so taxed that their costs of operation equal those of the railroads. It is proper to levy taxes on owners of motor vehicles, operators, and others for special benefits and also for the costs of general governmental services, but it is not good tax policy to go further and levy heavier taxes on the more efficient in order to equalize competitive conditions between them and the less efficient. This is a general principle which applies not only to transportation agencies but to others.[49] A tax system that attempted to handicap the "natural" advantages of one agency over those of another would hinder or prevent progress.

On the other hand, a tax system should not generally be used to subsidize any particular transportation agency. If it is so used, the results will be an uneconomical supply of the inefficient subsidized service and an inequitable distribution of the costs of that service. It is true that the commercial motor vehicle does not pay taxes on the road investment it uses, as the railroad does on its lines, but neither does the non-commercial motor vehicle, nor did the earlier horse-drawn vehicle. It has been shown that the state is more satisfactory than private agencies as a builder of highways, and the motor vehicle properly taxed in the form of gasoline and registration taxes will provide the funds. The costs of highways are, however, a part of the costs of motor transportation and, as suggested above, it would be proper to charge their costs, including cost of right of way, construction, and maintenance, against motor vehicles. This is done in large part at present, but it would be carried further if taxes on motor vehicles were increased to take over a larger part of the highway costs now paid out of general property taxes. Moreover, where motor vehicles are exempted from the general property tax, as in Minnesota, registration and other taxes levied on them should be sufficiently more "onerous" to

[49] We are discussing here tax policy, not regulation. If, however, the regulation policy results in special benefits to some, it may be perfectly legitimate to use these special benefits as bases for special taxes.

cover their fair share of general governmental costs also. When taxed thus, motor vehicles are put upon a virtual parity with railroads, provided railroads are properly taxed, without the use of taxes to offset the "natural" advantages of either agency.[50] But the view that commercial vehicles should be heavily taxed merely because they take business away from the railroads, or cause the yields of taxes on railroads to decline, or cause a decline in the employment of labor by railroads, deserves no consideration whatsoever. The sound tax policy would be one of no subsidy and no handicap. Let the entire transportation system be developed along the lines of "natural" advantage. Regulation may be required to bring this about, though one of the curses of regulation has been the building up and maintenance of "unnatural" economic conditions.

THE REGISTRATION TAX AND ITS OPERATION IN MINNESOTA

Minnesota began to provide for the registration of motor vehicles in 1903. Under the trunk highway amendment of 1920, motor vehicles may be taxed "on a more onerous basis than other personal property," but this tax must be in lieu of all other taxes except wheelage taxes, which may be imposed by cities or villages. At the first session of the legislature following the adoption of this amendment, some legislators advocated a nominal registration tax and a substantial gasoline tax. Since the registration tax was in lieu of the personal property tax, and since the legislature was authorized to tax motor vehicles on a "more onerous" basis than other property, it was felt that the registration tax must at least equal if not exceed the average personal property tax. The idea of a nominal tax was therefore abandoned. It was contended by some that if the registration tax were made less onerous than the personal property tax, it would become necessary to collect the personal property tax in addition to the registration tax. The constitutional provision and the fact that the registration tax was to be in lieu of the personal property tax made the legislature decide to base the tax on value.[51]

Passenger cars are taxed at 2.4 per cent of base value. The

[50] This disregards regulation, which cannot be discussed adequately here.

[51] The base value is the manufacturer's list price on October 1 preceding the year for which the tax is levied, minus depreciation. Ten per cent depreciation is allowed the second year; 20 per cent the third year; 30 per cent the fourth year, and so on up to 90 per cent the tenth year. After the tenth year the tax is not to exceed the minimum charge prescribed for a vehicle of that class.

minimum charge is $10 for vehicles of less than 2,000 pounds weight (Class A) and $12.50 for vehicles of 2,000 pounds and over (Class B). Buses and other passenger cars engaged in "commercial passenger transportation" (other than taxicabs and vehicles in the livery business) are taxed at 10 per cent of base value (Class C). The minimum charge is $350 when the seating capacity exceeds 15 and $250 when it is 15 or less. Commercial passenger transportation is defined as the carrying of passengers for hire between points not wholly within the limits of the same city, village, or borough, or between two or more contiguous cities.[52]

TABLE 12.—MOTOR VEHICLE REGISTRATION IN MINNESOTA, 1931[a]

CLASS OF VEHICLE	No.
"A" passenger cars (under 2,000 pounds)	151,573
"B" passenger cars (2,000 pounds and over)	460,118
Total, Classes "A" and "B"	611,691
"C" buses	275
"M" motor cycles	1,749
"T" trucks	26,425
"X" trucks	81,688
"Y" trucks	321
Total trucks	108,434
"Z" trailers	18,291
Total, all classes	740,440

[a] Data supplied by the secretary of state.

Trucks used for transporting agricultural, horticultural, dairy, and other farm products from their place of production to their destination (Class T) pay 2.4 per cent of base value. All trucks other than those in Class T and Class Y, defined below, pay 3.4 per cent of base value (Class X). Trucks operating as common carriers between fixed termini or over regular routes (Class Y) pay 10 per cent of base value. All trucks pay a minimum charge of $15 if the manufacturer's rated hauling capacity is one ton or less; $20, if over one ton and less than two; $30, if two and less than three; $60, if three and less than four; $85, if four and less than five; $125, if five and less than six; and $150, if six and over. Registration of motor vehicles in Minnesota in 1931 was as shown in Table 12.

[52] Thus, buses operating between Duluth and Superior pay a tax of 2.4 per cent of their base value.

It will be noted that the taxation of commercial vehicles in Minnesota involved only 275 buses and 321 trucks in 1931. The total number of vehicles registered and the revenue from the registration tax in Minnesota since 1921 are shown in Table 13.

From 1921 to 1930 the total registration of motor vehicles in Minnesota increased 129 per cent, but truck registration increased more than 300 per cent.[53] From 1925 to 1930 passenger car registration in Minnesota increased 19 per cent as compared with 32 per cent in all states. On the other hand, during the same period truck registration in Minnesota increased 141 per cent. In only one state, Maryland, was the increase of truck registration more rapid during this period.[54]

TABLE 13.—REGISTRATION AND TOTAL NET RECEIPTS OF THE REGISTRATION TAX IN MINNESOTA, 1921–1931 [a]

YEAR	NO. OF VEHICLES [b]	TOTAL NET RECEIPTS [c]
1921	332,652	$5,671,950
1922	384,398	6,536,383
1923	452,675	7,314,706
1924	507,892	8,580,810
1925	574,529	9,753,051
1926	635,502	9,957,405
1927	652,263	10,208,367
1928	679,590	10,094,067
1929	727,082	10,838,111
1930	744,271	11,074,654
1931	740,440	10,721,972

[a] Data supplied by the secretary of state.

[b] Includes all vehicles — passenger cars, trucks, trailers, and motor cycles. See also Table 11 and notes, page 389 above.

[c] Includes all registration taxes, penalties, and miscellaneous fees.

TAX BASIS DEFECTIVE

It is the truck of greater average weight than the passenger car, with an operator who wants to use the highways all the year around regardless of weather, and with a value that increases very slowly in proportion to gross weight (the best measure of highway destruction) as compared with the passenger car that is unfairly favored under Minnesota's ad valorem registration tax.

Gross weight is usually accepted as the best single basis on which to levy the registration tax. Minnesota and a few other

[53] Biennial Report of the Commissioner of Highways of Minnesota, 1929–1930, p. 19.

[54] *Minnesota Highway News*, September 12, 1931.

states use value or price as a base. There is obviously no direct relationship between the price of a vehicle and its use of the highway. There happens to be a remote relation between price and gross weight, but, as Figure 1 shows, this relation is evidently much too remote to provide an equitable measure of damage to highways.

FIGURE 1.—RELATION OF GROSS WEIGHT TO LIST PRICES OF TYPICAL VEHICLES[a]

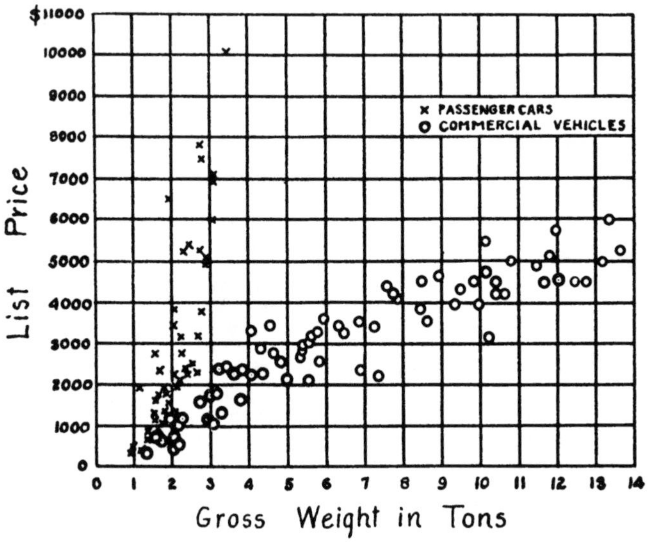

[a] *Public Roads,* May, 1930, p. 50.

The average price of passenger cars increases very rapidly with gross weight, whereas the average price of trucks increases very slowly. A single schedule of charges based on price would not, therefore, be applicable to both passenger cars and trucks; nor would the distribution among units of the same class be equitable, in view of the wide variation in the prices of passenger cars of approximately the same gross weight and of the great differences in the weights of trucks of approximately the same price. When a state levies a tax equal to a certain percentage of the price, there is, as Figure 1 shows, great discrimination in favor of the heavy trucks as compared with both private passenger cars and buses. The heavy trucks pound the road to pieces and with their trailers take up much road space, inconveniencing the motorists for whom the highways were primarily provided. The value of the vehicle with allowance for depreciation is even more illogical and unsuitable than price as a basis for taxing vehicles. It is hard to perceive any logic in charging a new truck in perfect mechanical condition and equipped with new solid tires more heavily than an old truck with tires worn down to near the legal limit of thickness, where such a limit exists, and in a mechanical condition that makes it a menace to public safety.[55]

The two preceding paragraphs consider the registration tax from the standpoint of benefits received by motorists or of the highway costs that they occasion. But inasmuch as part of Minnesota's registration tax is in lieu of a personal property tax, it is appropriate that this part should bear some relation to the value of the vehicle.

NEEDED CHANGES IN THE MINNESOTA REGISTRATION TAX

The gasoline tax is Minnesota's main benefit or privilege tax on motor vehicles. The so-called registration tax is really a combination of a property tax and a registration tax proper.[56] The latter is a kind of benefit or privilege tax.

Except for the very important administrative reasons mentioned below, it is of doubtful wisdom for Minnesota to exempt motor vehicles from the general property tax or to include a property tax in a "more onerous" registration tax. This combination of a lieu property tax with a privilege tax in one so-called registration tax leads to confusion in the establishment of a proper scale of rates for the registration tax and tends to distract the attention

[55] A comparison of the registration tax on certain standard vehicles paid in Minnesota and in other states is shown in *Highway Services and Costs* (1931), p. 50. See note 57 below. The amounts rest upon a diversity of bases and rates in the several states. It is difficult to compare the registration tax on a vehicle in Minnesota with that on the same vehicle in other states. In Minnesota the charge varies with time because of the deduction for depreciation from the value base or list price of the new vehicle. For comparative purposes the tax figure is too high on a new vehicle and too low at the prescribed minimum. The tax levied the third year is much better for comparative purposes. This year represents the midpoint in the average life of a bus on Minnesota highways, according to a prominent official of a bus transportation company. It will be noticed that the states are in much more accord in their charge on the light passenger vehicle and the light truck than on the heavy vehicles, especially the heavy truck and the bus. The third year tax on the heavy truck in Minnesota is substantially less than the tax on the same vehicle in many other states. It is important to note that most of the states (not including Minnesota) tax these vehicles as property.

[56] Minnesota's ad valorem registration tax has been held to be both a property tax and a privilege tax. See State v. Storaasli (1930), 180 Minn. 241. In the opinion of Mr. James E. Markham, deputy attorney-general, the legislature may change the base of this tax.

of the public from the obligation of automobile owners to pay their fair share of general governmental expenses in addition to the costs of special services in connection with highways.

The portion of this so-called registration tax that is a property tax, based as it now is upon the approximate value of the vehicle, conforms fairly well in the case of the private vehicle to the general tax on other property. If it were constitutional this tax might be graduated upward, particularly in the case of the more expensive private passenger cars, in recognition of their character as luxuries and the presumed ability of their owners to pay. The other part of the so-called registration tax, that is, the part designated above as the "registration tax proper," is probably too small. In fact, it almost or entirely disappears in some cases if proper allowance is made for the property tax. But the privilege tax, or the registration tax proper, should not be large, for gasoline consumption is, generally speaking, the best practical measure for a highway benefit or privilege tax. The registration tax should cover most special governmental service costs occasioned by automobiles that do not vary with use of highways, for example, most administrative costs of highway registration and tax departments. As explained earlier, this tax should be used also to correct the gasoline tax where the latter fails to take sufficient account of gross weight and other factors affecting the costs of government services to motor vehicles.

Minnesota's registration tax proper, hereafter for the sake of brevity designated simply registration tax, does not, however, furnish adequate correctives for the gasoline tax. As suggested earlier, gross weight (of vehicle and capacity load) should be the main basis of the registration tax. The separate T class for trucks in Minnesota is arbitrary and unjustified. These trucks should be treated like those in Class X. Graduation should begin with a gross weight of two tons, and rates should be stepped up more rapidly than the increase in gross weight. The tax on a vehicle equipped with solid rubber tires should be at least three times what it would be on the same vehicle equipped with pneumatic tires. The tax on a vehicle with six wheels on three axles should be about 40 per cent less than on the same vehicle equipped with four wheels on two axles, although it might be desirable to confine the latter discrimination to the heavier vehicles above a specified weight. All vehicles run by gasoline should be treated alike as to rates, gross weight basis, and discriminations as to tires and wheels.[57]

The present registration tax in Minnesota favors the contract carrier. If business use of the highway is to be taxed more heavily than other uses, Minnesota should levy an additional tax on the common carrier based on passenger miles in the case of buses and gross ton miles in that of trucks. For the time being at least, it would be best to tax the contract carrier more heavily than the non-commercial vehicle on the basis of gross weight — sufficiently more to make the burden as nearly as possible equal to that of the common carrier. The proceeds of the registration tax, including the entire levy on commercial cars, would, of course, continue to be used for highway purposes.

Certain information regarding the physical characteristics of vehicles in the state is necessary before suggestions may be made as to specific rates. In the registration of vehicles some of this information is not being recorded at present, and some that is recorded is not assembled in proper form for examination. The question of specific rates is a matter for further investigation and careful study. Rates should be set to maintain at least the present yield of the registration tax. Then with an increase in the gasoline tax, as already recommended, a relatively larger portion of the revenue from motor vehicle taxes will be obtained from the gasoline tax. As far as the registration tax in Minnesota is concerned, it is more important to change the basis of the tax and to eliminate inequalities among certain classes of vehicles than to obtain more revenue from that levy.

PROPERTY TAXATION AND MOTOR VEHICLES

Thirty-two states and the District of Columbia tax motor vehicles as personal property.[58] It may be argued that other property supports general governmental service and that motor vehicles ought to do the same. This is true; but it has already been pointed out that the present so-called registration tax is for the most part a property tax in fact. The disadvantages of thus combining the property tax with the registration tax proper have been cited

[57] A registration tax along these lines has recently been recommended by two investigating commissions for their states, New York and New Jersey. See Report of the New York State Commission for the Revision of the Tax Laws, Legislative Document No. 62 (submitted January 26, 1932), Part 1, pp. 20, 37–40; and Commission to Investigate County and Municipal Taxation and Expenditures (New Jersey), Report No. 5, *Highway Services and Costs* (1931), pp. 54–56.

[58] These states are designated in Table 8 on page 383.

above. On the other hand, it should be mentioned that there is one great advantage, namely, that administration is much simpler and more effective than when the property tax on motor vehicles depends upon assessment by local officials. For example, it was found in West Virginia that local assessors put unreasonably low valuations on automobiles and failed to discover half of them, although they were officially registered with the state highway department.[59] Wisconsin and other states have also reported poor administration under the local property tax assessment system. In fact, poor results are almost certain to accompany this system.

Distribution of the Proceeds of Gasoline and Registration Taxes

The question of the distribution of the proceeds of motor vehicle taxes is becoming an increasingly important one. Local governments, especially the cities, in recent years have been clamoring more and more loudly for a share in the proceeds. The need for local tax relief has been one of their chief arguments. In the cities the controversies have frequently been concerned with the portion of these taxes contributed by the urban car owners and the number of vehicles in the cities (taxicabs, etc.) that do not use the rural highways. According to figures compiled by the Bureau of Public Roads, $100,073,959, or 18.61 per cent, of the gasoline taxes, and $70,043,625, or 20.34 per cent, of the registration taxes in the several states were spent on local rural roads in 1931. If we consider both taxes together, we find that ten states allotted nothing and most of the rest allotted much less than half to local roads. The state shares its funds for the most part with the counties. The basis for distribution among the counties is usually amount of road mileage or number of cars registered in the case of the gasoline tax and amount of collections per county in the case of the registration tax. Furthermore, in certain states county bonds are being paid from these taxes. In some of these states, however, including Minnesota, the bonds were originally issued by counties in connection with local highways subsequently taken into the state system, the state assuming the debt.

PRACTICES IN OTHER STATES

According to figures compiled by the Bureau of Public Roads,

[59] Roy G. Blakey, *Report on Taxation in West Virginia*, 1930, p. 194. In 1931 the legislature of Wisconsin exempted motor vehicles from taxation as personal property.

$19,449,888, or 3.62 per cent, of the gasoline taxes collected in eight states and the District of Columbia was spent on city streets in 1931. This figure does not reflect accurately the extent to which city streets are being financed by gasoline and registration taxes. Cities are being aided to a large extent in at least twenty-two states. In most instances certain sums, derived for the most part from the gasoline tax, are being allocated on a mileage basis to state highways running through cities. A few examples, including Minnesota's neighbors, will be sufficient as illustrations. New Jersey distributes $5,000,000 of the receipts from its gasoline tax to municipalities, in proportion to the assessed value of taxable property. In Michigan, until recently, cities received $2,000 a mile for the maintenance of state roads within the city limits. In 1931 the legislature changed the method of state aid to cities. The state now participates in the cost of construction, reconstruction, and maintenance of state highways through cities to an extent varying inversely with the size of the city. In cities of 50,000 or more the state pays 50 per cent, in cities of 45,000 to 50,000, 55 per cent, and so on. The smaller the city the larger the portion paid by the state. In cities of less than 20,000 the entire cost is paid by the state. The work is supervised by the state. In Wisconsin, cities share in the gasoline and registration taxes. For each mile of state trunk highway within the cities they receive $400 for maintenance if it is a federal-aid highway, otherwise $300. For the improvement of streets not a part of the state or county trunk highway systems they receive from $25 to $200 a mile, the larger the city the larger the amount. In Iowa the state maintains the primary (state) routes through cities of less than 2,500 and pays cities with a larger population $200 a mile for maintaining these routes. In such cases the state sometimes, though not always, supervises the expenditure of its funds. In small cities, especially those of less than 2,500 population, the state frequently constructs and maintains the routes of the state system in order to assure continuous routes of uniform quality. It is significant to note that designating as parts of the state system routes through a city which the state improves or maintains, or pays the cities for improving or maintaining, is quite different from sharing the state tax proceeds with a local government that uses the funds on local roads not parts of the state system. The former method is the only one by which city streets are financed out of state funds in many states.

TREND TOWARD CENTRAL SUPERVISION

In recent years the percentage of the proceeds of gasoline and registration taxes distributed to the local units has decreased, although the amount of money so distributed has increased. Furthermore, the states are more and more designating the grants for road use and conditioning them upon state supervision of their expenditure and state approval of the contemplated project, the completed project, or both, by the state highway department.[60] Thus there is a fortunate tendency toward consideration of the highway problem as a state function and toward making it such.

The degree of improvement of the state system, the readiness to add new mileage to it, the importance and degree of improvement of local mileage, local tax burdens, the distribution of the population of the state between urban centers and rural areas, the extent to which rural highways are used by urban vehicles, attitudes toward local "self-government," and available revenue from motor vehicle taxes, all bear on this problem of the extent and methods of state aid. Of the alternatives — the inclusion of additional mileage in the state highway system and the sharing of revenue with the local units — the first appears to be the better. In the state highway department, administration, engineering skill, and perspective are all at their best, and uniform control and efficient operation are the result. If there must be sharing, then the funds should be designated for road use and spent under the supervision of the state highway department on those roads of greatest traffic importance, as best indicated by a traffic census. Since probably 80 per cent of the vehicles on rural highways are city-owned,[61] it appears that important rural mileage not now in the state highway systems has as strong a claim to state aid as have city streets. The case for the city is strongest with respect to streets connecting the routes of rural state highways.[62]

[60] Ruth Gillette Hutchinson, *State-Administered and Locally-Shared Taxes* (1931), pp. 39, 76–78, 85, 93–94.

[61] As indicated in the surveys of the state highway systems of Ohio, New Hampshire, and Vermont in recent years. Proceedings of the Ninth Annual Meeting of the Highway Research Board, National Research Council, 1929, p. 351.

[62] In several southern states, local governments are permitted to levy gasoline and registration taxes in addition to and independent of that collected by the state. Most cities in Alabama, for instance, are collecting gasoline taxes ranging from half a cent to 2 cents. In Mississippi, Hancock County collected 3 cents and Harrison County 2 cents in 1931. Such practice tends to make both local and state taxes unpopular. Besides, the local tax may be easily evaded or made ineffective by purchasing gasoline outside the city limits or across the county line. In 1928 fourteen states permitted municipalities to levy registration taxes on all classes of vehicles

DISTRIBUTION IN MINNESOTA

Minnesota levies a one-mill property tax, the proceeds of which go into the state road and bridge fund. The proceeds of the registration tax are placed in the trunk highway sinking fund, which is used to pay principal and interest on highway bonds issued by the state. The balance is transferred to the trunk highway fund, from which are met the costs of operating the highway department (not to exceed $150,000 a year), maintenance of state highways, interest and principal payments on assumed bonds originally issued by counties on routes now a part of the state system, and construction.

The proceeds of the gasoline tax are divided; one-third goes to the state road and bridge fund and two-thirds to the trunk highway fund. The money that goes into the state road and bridge fund (the one-mill tax and one-third of the gasoline tax) is distributed to the counties to aid them in maintaining and improving certain county roads. No county is to receive in any year more than 3 per cent or less than one-half of 1 per cent of the total amount distributed during that year. This is provided for in Article 16 (the trunk highway amendment) and Article 9 (the gasoline tax amendment) of the state constitution. Other details are provided for by statute. The allotments to the counties are made by a board consisting of the state auditor, state treasurer, and commissioner of highways.

Allotments of the one-mill tax proceeds are based largely upon assessed valuation in each county. Allotments of one-third of the proceeds of the gasoline tax are based upon mileage of county and town roads, area, traffic needs, and conditions in each county. The statutory minimum for any county is 1 per cent in the case of the former tax and three-fourths of 1 per cent in that of the latter. The maximum is 3 per cent in both cases. Special additional allotments are made occasionally to care for unusual needs, but only upon the request of the county board. The allotments from the proceeds of the one-mill tax must be spent on so-called state-aid roads under state supervision, as has been pointed out. The allotments from the gasoline tax must be spent on so-called county-aid roads without state supervision. The total allotments from the

and seven states permitted them to levy registration taxes on vehicles for hire. Where such a tax is levied it is generally a flat charge and lower than the state tax. Local registration taxation is also unfortunate and unwise. If there must be an alternative, distribution of a part of the proceeds of state motor vehicle taxes is better.

one-mill tax to counties in 1932 aggregate $1,897,000 as compared with $1,913,000 in 1931. The total allotments from the gasoline tax will aggregate $4,325,000 in 1932,[63] as compared with $3,200,000 in 1931.

Certain changes, some of which have been mentioned previously, are desirable.[64] The one-mill tax levy should be repealed. The basis of the distribution of this tax to the counties is not according to traffic needs. The gasoline tax should be increased to 4 cents. This would bring in about $3,700,000 additional, according to calculations based on the 1931 receipts. Under the gasoline tax amendment, about $1,200,000 of this would go to the counties to replace the one-mill tax. It is unfortunate that the constitution provides that one-third of the receipts of the gasoline tax shall go to the counties. If the portion were limited to 1 cent of the tax per gallon, the entire proceeds of any increase in the rate could be spent on a greater mileage in the state trunk highway system than is now possible even with an increase in the tax.

The distinction between the state-aid roads and county-aid roads should be eliminated. The allotments out of the gasoline tax proceeds should be spent under the supervision of the State Department of Highways, as are the allotments to the state-aid roads out of the one-mill tax. With the absorption of the township road system by the county, as previously recommended, there would be one comprehensive rural highway system in each county outside of state trunk highway mileage. The state highway department should, of course, use its supervisory powers to see that state funds are spent on the local roads according to their traffic importance.

As for the cities, the state should take over the streets in the three large cities that connect trunk highway routes or else pay these cities out of its receipts from motor vehicles taxes for maintaining or improving them, at least over a width equal to that of the trunk highway at the city limits. In the latter case the expenditures should be under the supervision of the State Department of Highways. These streets are really trunk highways. If revenues from motor vehicle taxes continue to increase, and if the urbanization of the population proceeds as it has in the past ten years, serious consideration should be given to the diversion of a share of the proceeds of gasoline and registration taxes to the cities. In

[63] Based on an estimated yield of this tax for 1932 and including $725,000 added as a result of an excess over the estimate in 1931. Data furnished by the State Department of Highways.

[64] See pages 374, 390, and 407.

any case, an increasing demand for such a diversion may be expected. The people in the city should realize, however, that the growing need for wider rural roads approaching the cities and semi-rural belt lines around the cities has been the result of urban growth. Moreover, the growth of motor vehicle and oil business in the cities has benefited these urban centers.

HIGHWAY BOND ISSUES

Several important studies in recent years have analyzed the results of the use of bonds in state highway finance.[65] These indicate that where there exists a large mileage of unimproved state trunk highway potentially of great general use, the use of bonds to obtain enlarged highway facilities without delay will return handsome dividends in reduced transportation costs. Under such conditions — as, for example, in North Carolina and Illinois some years ago — the proper use of credit is amply justified from an economic standpoint, though most states are too much inclined already to go into debt and need no urging.

There is lack of agreement on the proper length of term for highway bonds. Fifty-year bonds have been advocated when annual maintenance, to be paid out of current taxes, includes a pro rata share of the costs of reconstructing the road surface.[66] Terms of twenty, thirty, and even forty years are frequently defended on the ground that a large percentage of the original investment represents permanent value. For example, right of way, embankments, certain drainage features, surface foundation, and salvage value of surface and bridges are sometimes represented as constituting over half the investment.

The rapid development of the motor vehicle has, however, called for a correspondingly rapid development in road design. Many roads constructed according to the best standards of ten years ago are today inadequate. Heavier and speedier vehicles and shifts in population are the principal factors. Ten-year-old paved roads are too narrow, surfaces too rough, bridges too narrow, road crowns too high, curves too sharp, grades too steep, and routes too roundabout. In states that started their road programs early, many miles of pavement and numerous bridges must be completely re-

[65] A. J. Brosseau, *Highway Finance in the United States* (International Chamber of Commerce, Amsterdam, July, 1929), and Chas. H. Upham, "Highway Finance," Proceedings of the American Road Builders' Association, 1929, pp. 30–43.

[66] R. M. Haig, "A Challenge to Accepted Theories of Highway Finance," *Engineering News Record*, May 11, 1922, pp. 790–792.

TABLE 14.—RURAL HIGHWAY REVENUES OTHER THAN GENERAL TAXES AND BONDS COMPARED WITH TOTAL HIGHWAY EXPENDITURES IN THE UNITED STATES IN SELECTED YEARS[a]

Year	Total Expenditure	Federal Aid		Registration Tax Revenue		Gas Tax Revenue		Total Motor Tax Revenue	
		Amount	Percentage of Total Expenditure	Amount	Percentage of Total Expenditure	Amount	Percentage of Total Expenditure	Amount	Percentage of Total Expenditure
1904	$79,624,000	....	...	$50,000[b]	.1	....	...	$50,000	.1
1914	240,264,000	....	...	12,382,000	5.2	....	...	12,382,000	5.2
1921	1,001,588,000	$79,333,000	7.9	122,479,000	12.2	$5,302,000	.5	127,781,000	12.7
1926	1,187,596,000	79,163,000	6.7	288,282,000	24.3	187,603,000	15.8	475,885,000	40.1
1927	1,311,797,000	80,460,000	6.1	301,061,000	23.0	258,839,000	19.7	559,900,000	42.7
1928	1,423,870,000	80,798,000	5.7	322,630,000	22.7	304,872,000	21.4	627,502,000	44.1
1929	1,444,669,000	77,573,000	5.4	347,844,000	24.1	431,312,000	29.9	779,156,000	54.0
1930	1,680,493,000	92,463,000	5.5	355,705,000	21.1	493,865,000	29.4	849,570,000	50.5

[a] From data compiled by the United States Bureau of Public Roads.

[b] Estimated by the Committee of the National Tax Association on Taxation of Motor Vehicle Transportation on the basis of collections in New York and Massachusetts.

placed. Yet materials now in these highways that are capable of giving long service in their present form and location will have no salvage value if radical changes are made. Where are the "permanent" elements in these investments? They are very elusive. Further developments in the next ten years may make the highways of today as hopelessly out of date as many built during war times are now. The life of rural highway pavement is an unsettled question. In Minnesota, according to state highway officials, all the original pavement on state trunk highways is still in use except two short stretches around Winona where a route was changed in recent years. But on some of the paved stretches the old pavement is rough and the curves are very sharp for what would be considered ordinary speeds today. The state and local governments should therefore be very cautious in their use of credit for highway purposes. It should be used only in cases where its advantage is very clear after careful study. The length of term should not be more than twenty years (less for roads of low type), and the securities should be serial in form to assure their economical and prompt retirement.

On December 31, 1931, $15,497,561 was outstanding in Minnesota in assumed county bonds (issued on county highways subsequently taken into the state trunk system) and $19,000,000 in bonds issued by the state in 1930 and 1931, a total of $34,497,561 in state highway obligations. Another $10,000,000 will be issued in 1932.[67] The serial maturities of the state bonds are so arranged that along with the maturities of the assumed county bonds there will be a fairly even annual load of retirements running to 1948. The state highway commissioner believes that no additional bond issues will be asked for after 1932. The moderate use of credit in connection with the state trunk highways in Minnesota is to be commended.

On December 31, 1930, cities and villages had outstanding about $40,000,000 in road- and street-improvement bonds. Townships had about $1,500,000 outstanding and counties about $18,000,000.[68] Unfortunately the serial feature is not a requirement for certain bonds for local roads and bridges.

[67] Figures furnished by the State Department of Highways.
[68] Figures furnished by the Minnesota Tax Commission.

SUMMARY OF SUGGESTIONS FOR CONSIDERATION

The suggestions made in this chapter may be summarized as follows:

1. A comprehensive traffic census on the entire rural road mileage in the state as a guide to highway finance.
2. Absorption of the entire township road system by the counties. This move may be made in stages. It involves the elimination of the township as a road unit.
3. Abolition of the distinction between the so-called state-aid and county-aid road systems.
4. Extension of the supervision by the State Department of Highways over the expenditure of all state-aid funds distributed out of the receipts from the gasoline tax.
5. Making the appointment of county highway engineers subject to the approval of the State Department of Highways.
6. The absorption of additional mileage into the state trunk highway system. In the three large cities the streets connecting trunk highways should have preference in this respect over other highways.
7. The repeal of the state one-mill road tax, if accompanied by 8 below.
8. The increase of the gasoline tax to 4 cents a gallon, if proper provision is made first for allocation of proceeds and supervision of their expenditure.
9. Adoption of a gross weight registration tax on all motor vehicles; discrimination against vehicles equipped with solid tires and in favor of vehicles with six wheels on three axles.
10. If commercial motor vehicles are to be more heavily taxed than other vehicles, the adoption of an additional mileage tax on common carriers on the basis of passenger miles in the case of buses and gross ton miles in that of trucks; and extra heavy rates on contract carriers on the same basis used for all vehicles in order to equalize the tax burden on common and contract carriers.

CHAPTER 14

PUBLIC SCHOOL FINANCE[1]

The problems of taxation, school support, and school administration are all inextricably interwoven. A modification of the practices in any one of these fields is likely to demand some alteration in the other two, hence the financial issues of public education cannot be considered apart from its organization.

SCHOOL DISTRICT ORGANIZATION

One of the first school laws of Minnesota made "every township containing not less than five families" a corporate school district.[2] At that time, however, the people evidently thought the township was too large an area to be served by one school. The powers granted the county commissioners made it relatively easy to secure the division of townships into small school districts, with the result that by 1870 the township as a school division of the state had practically disappeared.

Since public education at first included only the work of the elementary or common school, the early divisions were called common school districts.[3] Through special legislation, however, beginning in 1856, the special chartered school districts made inroads on the common school district organization. These special districts include such cities as Albert Lea, Anoka, and at least twenty-nine other communities in the state.

The increased pressure of local communities for special legislation did not improve the educational facilities of the state as a whole. In fact, special legislation proved to be very unsatisfactory in many ways. To enable the more progressive school districts to develop an educational program more consistent with their needs, a new type, the "independent school district," was formed in 1865. The early law required that an independent school district include a part or the whole of a village, town, or city of not less than five hundred inhabitants. In subsequent years this restriction was modified.

[1] This chapter was prepared by Dr. Fred Engelhardt, professor of educational administration, University of Minnesota.

[2] Laws of Minnesota Territory, 1849, Ch. 7, pp. 41–43.

[3] It is of interest to note that Section 2 of Article VIII of the Constitution refers consistently to "schools within each township."

The three types of districts described above were in time extended to include a number of hybrid forms. In general the changes made resulted in a school district much like the independent type. The consolidated school districts, the "ten or more township" districts, the "unorganized territory" districts, and the one county school district were created to satisfy local needs and educational developments.

The Present Situation

The common school districts continue to be the most numerous, having increased from 5,128 to 7,258 during the forty-five years prior to 1931. The total number of Minnesota school districts in 1931 was 7,755, divided as follows: 7,258 common school districts, most of which maintain ungraded elementary schools in one-room buildings; 483 independent, consolidated, or special school districts that maintain graded elementary schools or a twelve-year public school program, including some in which the kindergarten is also maintained, and 7 in which a junior college is operated; 13 unorganized territory school systems maintaining both elementary and secondary schools; and 1 county school district.[4]

Provisions for Changing Boundaries

The individual freeholder has the legal right under certain prescribed conditions to petition the county commissioners to have his land transferred from one school district to an adjoining one. In recent years the number of approved transfers has decreased.[5] These requests to have a farm transferred from one district to another usually arise out of the interests of the individual landowner and frequently they are prejudicial to good school administration. School district boundaries in Minnesota (see Figure 1) now form most grotesque and heterogeneous figures.[6] Because of irregularities in boundaries and the system of highways many children residing in one district may be nearer the school of their neighbors, yet be compelled to attend the more distant school.

The division of the state into a large number of corporate educational units has hampered school administration throughout the state. The philosophy of self-determination that has permitted

[4] From mimeographed bulletin of the State Department of Education, St. Paul, 1932.

[5] *Law of Minnesota Relating to the Public School System*, Sec. 11, 1932.

[6] Adapted from mimeographed material of the State Department of Education, St. Paul, 1931.

school districts to be created with reference only to current local interests and without consideration of ultimate consequences has so intrenched the small common school district that obvious and desirable changes in school organization are made with the greatest apprehension on the part of the people. As conditions change from year to year, many of these districts have found themselves hard pressed for funds to maintain their schools. When aid is solicited of the state the faults of the system are not weighed nor challenged, and as a result new measures are enacted for distributing state money to certain local schools and the state as a

FIGURE 1.—GEOMETRIC FORMS OF SCHOOL DISTRICTS

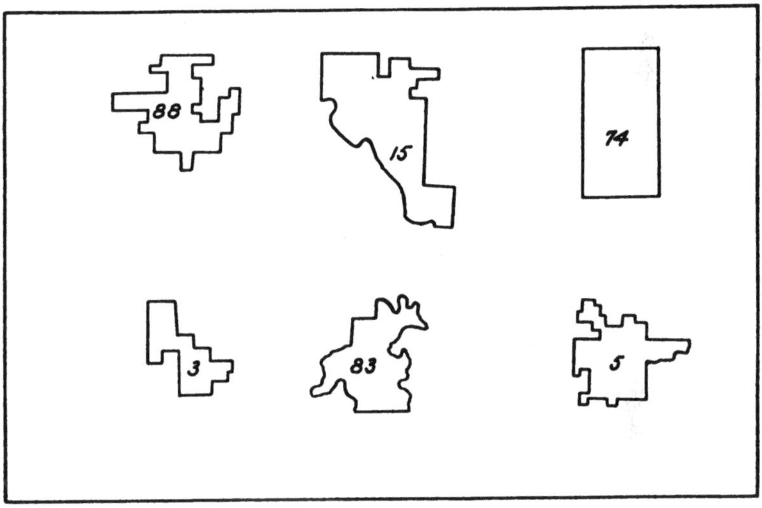

whole pays the bill. Thus state support under certain conditions tends to perpetuate that which was unsound in origin and which it is now unwise to continue.

School districts are created and perpetuated in which children have access to an ungraded school only. Children living on farms of comparable value but on different sides of a district line may not have direct access to the same type of school. Children may have their homes in school districts in which there are no public schools.

There are urban areas that maintain "graded schools" only and there are schools in the open country that operate twelve-year school systems. The common belief that inequalities in educational opportunities are almost solely between urban and rural children

FIGURE 2.—ILLUSTRATIONS OF SCHOOL DISTRICTS THAT COMPRISE CITIES AND FARMS

Left.—Austin School District. *Right.*—Ortonville School District.

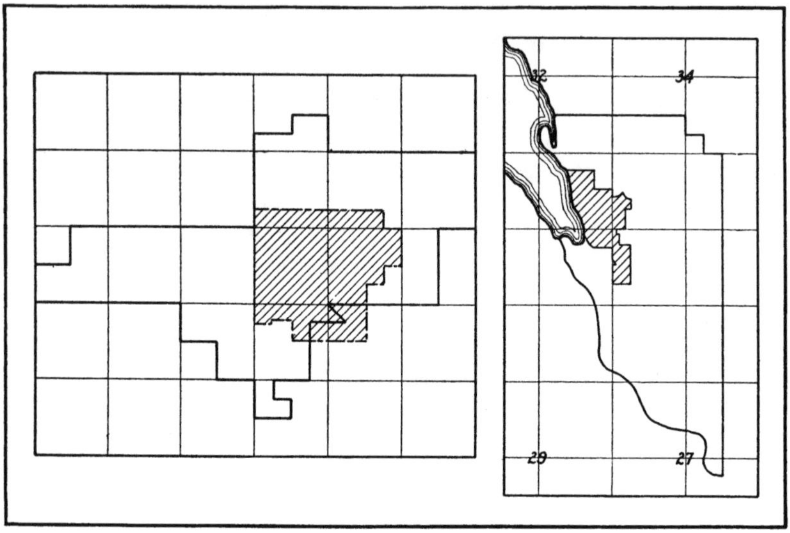

is far from true in Minnesota. These inequalities are even greater when school conditions in the various rural areas of the state are compared.

If the large cities are excluded, the material differences that should affect the educational program for the urban and the rural areas are few. In reality this state is largely rural. A condition that is peculiar to Minnesota is the extent to which one finds independent school districts composed of a city, a town, or a village combined with an extensive farm area. (See Figure 2.)[7] This condition forms an excellent foundation on which to build better schools and finer relationships between the town folk and those residing in the open country.

LOCAL AUTONOMY AND THE TAX BURDEN

The small school district has also been the cause for very disastrous educational financing. A small school district with low assessed valuation cannot afford to maintain a four-year high school, yet some districts have endeavored to do so and have resented it when the State Department of Education has discouraged them

[7] Adapted from reports by Fred Engelhardt of surveys of Austin and Ortonville (University of Minnesota Press, 1927).

from the attempt. The outcome has been excessive bonded indebtedness and high taxes in many small towns. As the tax load becomes unbearable, additional state funds are demanded. The very laws that are enacted to relieve many of the school districts with small resources foster opportunities for other districts to take unfair advantage of the measures created to equalize the cost burden. The net result in time is more inequality that in turn calls for further financial adjustment. There is no end to the cycle thus set in motion. The educational system of the state carries the brunt of the evil consequences of non-intelligent planning and false local pride. The results are a heavy drain on resources, economic loss, and poor high schools.

The annual tax bill presented to Minnesota taxpayers of comparable wealth and residing on land of like fertility is far from uniform. The following tabulation indicates some of the reasons for these differences in the tax burden:

There are school districts that maintain no public schools and hence levy no regular local school taxes. In the school year 1930–31 there were 78 school districts that levied no local school taxes. (The one-mill state tax levied within the county is the only school tax collected.)

There are a number of school districts that maintain no school and contract for a nominal fee with other districts for the education of their children.

There are 7,258 districts that maintain ungraded elementary schools only.

There are 390 districts that maintain twelve years of school, and 7 districts support junior colleges in addition to four-year high schools.

There are 412 districts that now levy less than a four-mill tax to support schools, and 13 districts that must levy a tax of 80 mills or more to maintain their schools.[8]

The size of district, the inequalities of assessment, and the variations in state support granted districts may cause some families to pay greater taxes for poorer educational facilities than those in a neighboring district — a peculiar paradox.

Attempts to Remedy Unsatisfactory Situations

The consequences of the small school district were recognized early by educational leaders in the state. In 1860 State Superin-

[8] Adapted from mimeographed bulletins of the State Department of Education.

tendent Edward D. Neill recommended the abandonment of the small districts.[9] In the same report he proposed that "each family in the state be allowed to send children to any public school that may be selected." This was a unique idea, predicated on the philosophy that education was a state function and hence school district boundaries should not be barriers to educational opportunity. It would be well to keep in mind the philosophy underlying the above recommendation when considering any proposed plan for the reorganization of the schools.

Although Neill's recommendation was not carried out, the legislature did endeavor to make it possible for every child to have free access to twelve years of schooling. To do this, free admission to any high school in the state was legally provided for children who were eligible residing in areas in which high schools were not maintained. In 1913 the school districts educating these nonresident children accepted them without any tuition payment. In many respects the legislation that made this practice mandatory established a very unusual precedent.[10] The law was evidently accepted by the people as fair and reasonable. But as the enrollment in high schools increased, the local tax burden in many districts became very heavy, and the state was forced to assume the greater share of cost for the tuition of nonresident high school pupils.[11]

The School District and Other Divisions of Government

In most districts school administration is practically independent of other local civil units, except that property assessments and tax collections are made by towns, municipalities, and counties. Except as limited by the state, the people of the district have almost complete control over tax levies, bond issues, and expenditures.

Although largely independent of control by other local units of government, school districts have various cooperative relations with them. In this connection mention may be made of the health service provided by the county nurse, the county library, and the county farm agent. Cities and school districts often cooperate in the maintenance of playgrounds and in the use of school audi-

[9] Annual Report of the Superintendent of Public Instruction, 1860, p. 15.

[10] General Statutes of Minnesota, 1913, Sec. 2799.

[11] Session Laws of Minnesota, 1919, Ch. 521. A tuition rate of seven dollars per pupil per month for not more than nine months is now paid by the state. In the case of districts that levy a tax of less than four mills the tuition is deducted from the state aid allocated to the district.

toriums. In some municipalities certain employees are appointed according to civil service regulations. In fact, the relations between school districts and civil divisions are usually those that arise out of mutual interests.

In contrast to the local civil units, the state has close and comprehensive control over school administration and finances. In theory, the state assumes full responsibility for educating its children and exercises this function through school districts as its agencies. It grants to the people of these districts such powers and aid as seem wise, but at all times watches over, aids, and directs them. To a large extent it directs educational policy, grants aid on certain conditions, fixes tax levies within certain limits, puts restrictions upon borrowing, and even takes responsibility for collecting principal and interest of bonds.

State Department of Education

The public examiner exercises some control through the examination of school accounts, but the chief organization provided by the legislature to protect the educational interests of the state is the State Board of Education. The executive officer acting for this board is the commissioner of education. The plan for creating the board and for securing the commissioner and his staff is consistent with the most modern practices in public school administration.

The State Department of Education has administrative, legislative, and supervisory control of the public schools. Although there are from time to time complaints regarding the restriction placed on local action by the state department, the administration of the laws has on the whole been motivated by the desire to conserve public funds and to promote the best interests of the schools. The mistakes that have been made have been due not to the organization but largely to individual errors or overzealousness. If the policies of the state had not been carried on as they have been during the past quarter of a century, the situation with respect to the common schools would have been virtually repeated in the field of secondary education, and the state would now be flooded with expensive, inefficient one-room, one-teacher, four-year high schools. An economical and efficient public school system cannot be fostered without leadership. The responsibility for such leadership must rest in the State Department of Education.

STATE SUBVENTIONS

The funds distributed to the local public schools may be classified as follows: (1) the funds allocated by the state as its share in the local educational costs; (2) moneys distributed to school districts to encourage educational development; (3) moneys paid to school districts that are unable, because of low property valuation, to maintain a minimum school organization with local tax receipts; and (4) moneys paid districts for rendering a service to other districts, the cost of which the state has agreed to assume. These classes are not mutually exclusive, for much of the money received by the local districts from the state actually serves two or more of the purposes mentioned. For example, the payment of nonresident high school tuition is virtually a state aid to the districts that do not maintain high schools. Many districts receiving this money could hardly maintain a satisfactory secondary school without it.

In 1931 the state distributed four million dollars, on the basis of $7.70 per pupil enrolled for at least forty days, to districts that operated schools for at least seven months. This money comes from (1) the income from the Permanent School Fund, (2) one-half the income received from the Swamp Land Fund, and (3) a portion of the one-mill state-wide property tax. About 70 per cent of this general state apportionment is derived from the income from the state school fund investments and from state lands.[12]

[12] Statements of the Permanent School Fund and the Swamp Land Fund as of June 30, 1931 (adapted from a mimeographed bulletin of the State Department of Education):

Permanent School Fund	
Sales of land, right of way	$15,491,135.19
Sales of timber	9,314,118.35
Mineral permits and leases	338,200.77
Royalty on iron ore	26,126,801.76
Occupation tax on iron ore	10,024,721.47
Profits on sale of bonds	365,672.64
Total	$61,660,660.18
Swamp Land Fund [a]	
Sales of land, right of way	$3,936,852.38
Sales of timber	5,154,829.68
Mineral permits and leases	87,937.00
Royalty on iron ore	2,259,208.67
Total	$11,438,827.73

[a] The law provides that one-half the income (interest) from the Swamp Land Fund shall be added to the current school (apportionment) fund. The other half is distributed to the University, the teachers' colleges, and the charitable institutions of the state.

The other state subventions paid to the school districts totaled $6,707,663 in 1931. This sum includes $179,581 received from the federal government for vocational education and other allied purposes. The distribution of this state and federal money was made for fourteen different purposes according to the following schedule:[13]

Nature of Aid	Amount
High schools and graded elementary schools	$634,233.60
Ungraded elementary districts	991,744.39
Total	$1,625,977.99
Supplemental aid	1,601,620.93
Special department aid	301,048.92
Aid to classes for defectives	400,725.78
Transportation aid	816,120.76
Building aid	14,583.66
Association aid	20,393.10
Tuition for nonresident high school pupils	1,382,406.00
Aid to teacher-training departments	187,482.00
Total	$6,347,630.80[a]
Federal aid under the Smith-Hughes and George-Reed laws	179,580.57
Aid to evening schools for adults	15,945.00
Gross earnings tax aid	133,998.96
Aid to public school libraries	30,507.20
Grand total	$6,707,662.53

[a] An adjustment of $2,728.34 has been deducted.

The funds distributed as outlined above (except the federal aid) are appropriated by the legislature from general state revenues.[14]

Distribution of State Aid Funds

In addition to the general state apportionment, school districts are entitled to receive state aid under the following legal provisions:

Regular aid. — Paid to a four-year high school, $810; high school department: $180 for one high school teacher, $350 for two, and $540 for three or more; junior high, $360; senior high, $540; graded elementary with eight school years of nine months, $450; with six school years of nine months, $360; ungraded elementary with eight-months term, $135 for each first grade teacher and $90 for each second grade teacher; to school with seven-months term, three-fourths of this sum. In no case to exceed $270 for an ungraded elementary school except a superior school, which may receive an additional sum of $112.50 annually.

Supplemental aid. — Paid to districts in which a 20-mill levy for maintenance does not yield $40 per pupil. The state pays the difference between the amount

[13] Adapted from a mimeographed bulletin of the State Department of Education.

[14] The state revenue for the year ending June 30, 1930, according to the state auditor's report, amounted to $20,378,591. Of this sum $3,650,062 was raised by a direct state property tax. The remaining $16,728,529 was collected from sources of which the following represent the larger items: gross earnings tax on railroads, insurance, telegraph and telephone, express, and freight line and sleeping car companies, $11,063,383; inheritance taxes, $1,539,635; occupation taxes on iron ore, $1,875,042; and iron ore royalty tax, $1,024,874.

raised and $40 per pupil, minus 10 per cent. Additional teacher aid is also granted under certain conditions to districts maintaining only ungraded elementary schools.

Aid for special departments. — Paid for the following departments: agriculture, $720; general industrial, home economics, and commercial training, $450 each.

Aid to classes for defectives. — Paid for classes of deaf, $225 for resident and $360 for nonresident; blind, $270 per pupil; subnormal, $90 per pupil; defective speech not to exceed $1,350 for each teacher; classes for crippled children, $225 per pupil.

Transportation aid. — Paid to consolidated school districts for transporting pupils not to exceed $4,000 annually for each school, minus 10 per cent. Also for transporting isolated pupils, not to exceed $50 annually for each pupil, minus 10 per cent.

Building aid. — Paid to consolidated school districts not to exceed $3,000 for each new building erected, minus 10 per cent.

Association aid. — Paid to a central school, $180 for each associated rural school and $45 to the rural school district.

Tuition aid. — Tuition payments for nonresident high school pupils coming from districts where no high school facilities are provided, $7 a month for each such pupil not to exceed ten months in any school year.

Aid to teacher-training departments in high schools. — Reimbursements made for salaries and other expenses in connection with such departments, the total not to exceed $225,000 annually.

Federal aid. — Distributed according to the Smith-Hughes Act for vocational education and for the preparation of teachers of agricultural, trade, industrial, and home economics subjects.

Evening school aid. — Reimbursements made to school districts of one-half the salary paid to teachers of evening schools for adults.

Gross earnings tax aid. — Paid to school districts wherein at least 20 per cent of the property is railroad property and therefore exempt from local taxation under the gross earnings tax laws.

Library aid. — Reimbursement made for library book purchases not to exceed $20 for each teacher nor $40 for each building.[15]

Relationship of State Aid to Local Tax Revenues

State aid approximates 30 per cent of the receipts from the one-mill tax plus the receipts from special local property taxes. (See Table 1.) In other words, for every dollar distributed annually by the state to the local school district (one-mill tax excluded), about $3.33 in taxes must be collected to meet all current obligations. During the three years 1929–1931 the ratio was approximately the same.

Irrespective of the manner in which local schools are organized, administered, and financed, the state will find it necessary to make more nearly equal the burden of support. For example, in 1929 the city of Hibbing on a 40-mill tax levy could have raised $810.44 per pupil; Minneapolis, $174.76; Albert Lea, $95.28; Faribault, $87.24; Mahnomen, $27.28, and Black Duck, $24.44. This wide range in

[15] Adapted from a mimeographed bulletin of the State Department of Education, 1929.

potential revenues from taxes on local resources indicates how unequally the wealth of the state is distributed among the various school districts. Obviously, if there is to be any semblance of equality in educational facilities for all the children of the state, some plan of distributing the burden equitably must be made acceptable to the people of the state.

TABLE 1.—REVENUES RECEIVED FROM LOCAL TAXES BY SCHOOL DISTRICTS AND AMOUNT RECEIVED FROM THE STATE, 1929–1931[a]

ITEM	1929	1930	1931
A. State and county apportionment....	$4,273,151	$4,329,988	$4,418,230
B. Special state aid..................	6,100,840	6,074,195	6,291,470
C. Total (A+B)	$10,373,991	$10,404,180	$10,709,700
D. One-mill tax	2,004,561	1,852,531	2,026,011
E. Local special taxes..............	33,211,863	33,451,620	34,213,922
F. Total (D+E)	$35,216,423	$35,304,151	$36,239,933
G. Ratio of C to F..................	29.5%	29.5%	29.6%

[a] Adapted from reports of the State Department of Education.

The fundamental weakness in the present methods of distributing state aid to equalize this burden lies in the school district system. In many districts receiving supplementary state aid the taxable resources per family are as great as in other localities where the burden is carried without additional state aid. The reason for such conditions is the varying size, wealth, and assessment of the taxable areas permitted to exist as corporate school systems. Everyone will grant that unequal educational opportunities in a state should be corrected, yet it is manifestly unfair to the people of the state to permit local whims to augment the inequalities that exist naturally and to expect the taxpayers of the state to come to the assistance of areas that could support local schools more effectively if the districts with small resources were abolished.

The converse of the above picture is likewise true. There are districts in the state that have ample resources to support schools by means of a very small property tax and yet their local revenue is supplemented by money received from the state. In many cases neighboring districts carry very different tax loads to support the same kind of schools. Thus the system of school districts creates economic inequalities that might be readily eliminated if the system were changed.

Some Deficiencies in the Present State-Aid System

In this discussion there is no thought of being critical of those who have struggled through the past years to bring about the present state public school system. It is fully realized that the problems have been many and complex. Educational leaders and legislators have always recognized these difficulties and have been forced to make compromises in bringing about improvements. The purpose of this discussion is primarily to indicate the problems that are now confronting the state and the necessity of attacking them because of present and future needs.

Recognizing the causes for the limitations in the present method of distributing state funds and the improvement in public education they have made possible, one must admit that a method that was adequate during the development period of the state may require adjustment from time to time. For schools are a dynamic institution and must be so treated if economy in their administration is to prevail continuously. To show more clearly how the methods of state support result in strange, unpredictable situations the following cases have been selected for presentation. These cases reveal the difficult tasks that are presented to state officials when planning legal measures that will equalize educational opportunity and at the same time distribute the burden of cost equitably throughout the state. In reading these pages one must not lose sight, however, of the many school systems that have been relieved through the very state aid that also causes the conditions portrayed here:

Case 1.—This is a suburban school district. The residents of this area are largely engaged in business in the adjoining city. They are as able to maintain twelve years of school work as the average district in the state. The pupils of the upper three years are sent to high schools outside of the district and the state pays the tuition.

Case 2.—This is likewise a suburban school district. Its municipal program was extended much faster than resources justified. This state of affairs was further complicated by bad politics. The district is in an unsatisfactory financial condition at the present time. Most of the citizens of the town earn their living in an adjoining city. Properties are not equally assessed. A school system extending from kindergarten through four years of high school is maintained. The tax levy is such that supplementary aid is received from the state. The state aid received on account of the low valuation is more than sufficient to pay for the operation of the kindergarten. Most school systems in the state of equal resources do not operate a kindergarten.

Case 3.—This is another suburban school district. The traveler passing through this district is unable to tell where the adjoining city boundaries run.

This district supports only an eight-year graded elementary school. Its neighbors maintain the high school and the state pays the tuition.

Case 4.—This situation involves two school districts of approximately the same size. One of these districts (of somewhat greater resources) maintains a high school while the other does not. The high school children of the second district attend the neighboring schools at state expense.

Case 5.—The school district in question operates a school bus line that passes through a neighboring district within a block or two of an excellent school.

Case 6.—This is a district that might readily be added to the adjoining city, yet it operates a twelve-year school system and is enabled to do so largely because nonresident pupils are brought in from an extensive surrounding area. The special state income accrues in proportion to the number of pupils in school. Every effort is made to stimulate enrollment and to increase state aid.

Case 7.—A school district projected a new school building much larger than local needs required with the understanding that high school pupils in a neighboring area would attend. The agreement failed to materialize and the school has some rooms that will never be used.

Case 8.—This case portrays a condition that is duplicated in many school districts. A farmer whose land lies in a school district that is composed in part of a city and in part of farms pays taxes to support the high school in that district. His neighbors whose lands lie in an ungraded school district contribute directly to the support of the one-room school only. When the children of the neighbors attend the high school the tuition is paid by the state.

APPORTIONMENT OF STATE MONEY ON BASIS OF NUMBER OF PUPILS UNSOUND

Probably most students of the problems connected with state subventions to schools are opposed to apportionment of state money to schools on the basis of the number of pupils enrolled.[16] Costs of school maintenance are directly proportional to teachers' salaries. In large districts with concentrated population elementary schools may be efficiently operated with an average enrollment of forty pupils per teacher. In sparsely settled areas it is difficult, particularly under the present school district organization, to bring together enough children to form a class of forty. A recent study made of the common school districts of the state shows that the average number of pupils per section of land is less than four, and in only a few of the common school districts does it exceed nine. The cost of instruction per pupil in the sparsely settled districts is necessarily much higher than in the larger districts.

The school district in the open country or in the small town (as a rule the district with the smaller taxable resources) will probably receive relatively less state aid than larger wealthier districts when funds are distributed on the basis of the number of pupils. One may question the desirability of granting any funds to

[16] Minnesota School Law, 1931, Sec. 247.

school districts that are able to maintain their local schools on a small local tax levy. And why apportion state money to a district on account of a pupil who has attended school for only forty days during the school year?

PROBLEMS INVOLVED IN STATE TUITION PAYMENT PLAN

In principle the policy followed by the state in paying the high school tuition of nonresident pupils is sound, and the results have been excellent in view of the type of school district organization that exists. On the other hand, the plan does tend to develop inequalities and to make it more difficult to consolidate school districts. Few districts that operate an ungraded school can be persuaded to consolidate with a district that maintains a high school so long as the state pays the high school tuition of children residing in areas that do not support secondary schools. The state tuition payment plan also tends to foster the continuance of a number of small high schools that could not otherwise be maintained. During 1928–29 the state paid the nonresident tuition of 20,780 pupils with a sum of $1,222,381. This sum was virtually a state subvention to the ungraded school districts. In 1931, it may be noted, 40 per cent or more of the enrollment in 49 per cent of the high schools was made up of nonresident pupils.

When the educational system of the state was being developed, there was some logic in encouraging school districts to maintain high schools and transform their ungraded schools into graded systems. Today such encouragement is no longer necessary. There are over seven thousand school districts in the state in which a graded school is neither economically possible nor educationally desirable. No one would encourage the establishment of a high school in these districts. Why, therefore, should cities and towns receive five hundred dollars from the state for maintaining a high school? There is little logic in a plan of apportioning state funds to school districts for maintaining a type of school that sound educational doctrine would dictate as essential to effective instruction.

POPULATION CHANGES IN MINNESOTA

Increasing Stabilization

During the decade prior to 1930 over half the counties of the state decreased in population or increased less than 1 per cent. Of the communities of one thousand inhabitants or less, 279 decreased in population; in only 107 out of 522 did the population increase 10 per cent or more. The more substantial increases were in cities of 2,500 or more.[17] These facts are reflected in the school enrollment. Practically every village comprises a school district, and with a stabilized population school enrollment decreases and the cost of education per pupil increases unless larger administrative units parallel population decreases.

During the eighty-year period from 1850 to 1930 the population in Minnesota increased from 6,077 to 2,563,953. The total population residing in unincorporated areas and in communities of less than 2,500 increased from 867,234 in 1890 to 1,306,337 in 1930. But, although the gross figures show an increase, there has been a decrease in the percentage of the total population residing in unincorporated places from 66 to 51, indicating a drift of population to the larger centers.

TABLE 2.—PERCENTAGE DISTRIBUTION OF TOTAL POPULATION OF MINNESOTA ACCORDING TO SPECIFIED AGE GROUPS, 1900–1930[a]

AGE GROUP	CENSUS YEAR			
	1930	1920	1910	1900
Under 1	1.8	2.1	2.2	2.7
1– 5	9.8	11.0	10.9	13.0
5–14	17.1	20.2	20.9	23.4
15–19	8.1	9.2	10.4	9.7
20–44	43.8	38.8	39.0	37.9
45 and over	21.4	20.8	18.5	15.8
Total of all groups over 1 year	100.2	100.0	99.7	99.8

[a] Data taken from *United States Census,* 1930.

Although the total population is one index of the changes that are taking place in school enrollment, there are other elements in the picture that are probably more important and that need consideration. In Minnesota the percentage of children under five years of age in the total population has decreased in thirty years from 13 per cent to 9.8 per cent, whereas the proportion of the population over forty-five years of age has increased from 15.8 to 21.4 per cent (Table 2). The percentage of the total population from five to fourteen years old has declined from 23.4 to about 17. These facts are very significant when they are related to future school growth.

[17] *United States Census, 1930: Population.*

Decline in Birth Rate

If the decline in birth rate is analyzed, the decrease in potential school population is more clearly portrayed. In 1915, according to the federal census, the birth rate per 1,000 population was 24.5 for Minnesota and in 1927 it was 19. In the rural areas the birth rate decreased during this period from 25.2 to 18 and in the urban areas from 23.3 to 20.1. On the basis of authoritative studies it is safe to predict that the decline will continue. As yet it has not had full effect upon school enrollments.

Figure 3.—Change in School Population in Ungraded School Districts Compared with Change in Other Types of School Districts, 1910–1930

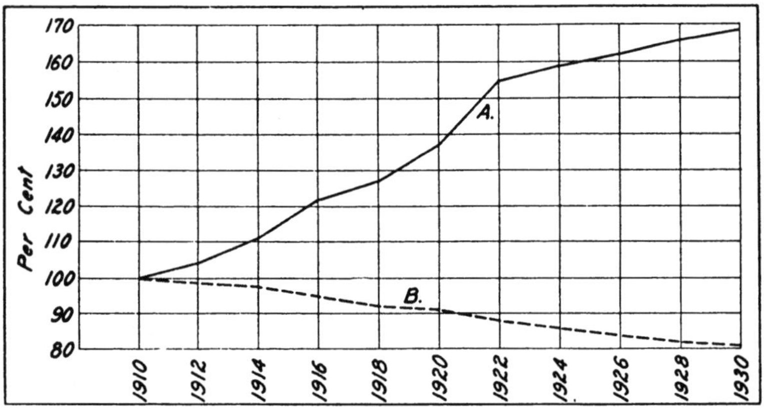

A.—Change in Enrollment in Graded and High School Districts. *B.*—Change in Enrollment in Ungraded School Districts.

Changes in School Population

The effect of the decrease in rural population is shown in the marked decrease in the number of pupils in the schools of ungraded school districts. During the twenty years prior to 1930 the decrease has been from 219,778 to 177,828. Part of this loss is due to the change in districts from one type to another. The contrast between this decrease and the increase in other school systems is more clearly shown in Figure 3.

ELEMENTARY SCHOOL POPULATION

If we compare the change in elementary school population in the public schools of the state for a period of years beginning with 1916 it will be noted that little increase has occurred since 1922. (See Figure 4.) The elementary school enrollments in the school districts outside the Twin Cities and Duluth have decreased slightly since 1922; in the three largest cities the decrease evidently began in 1928.

During the period from 1928 to 1931, 48 per cent of 361 districts maintaining graded and secondary schools reported no change in

FIGURE 4. — CHANGES IN TOTAL AND IN ELEMENTARY SCHOOL POPULATION OF MINNESOTA, 1916–1930

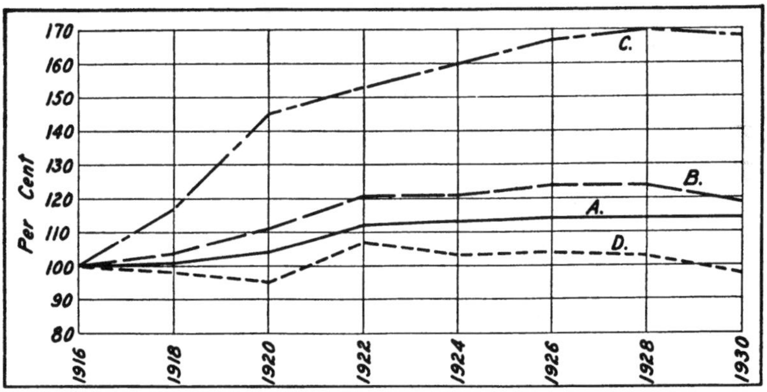

A. — Change in School Enrollment in All Public Schools. *B.* — Change in Elementary School Enrollment in Graded and High School Districts. *C.* — Change in Elementary School Enrollment in Duluth, Minneapolis, and St. Paul. *D.* — Change in Elementary School Enrollment in School Districts Outside Duluth, Minneapolis, and St. Paul.

elementary enrollments or reported decreases of 1 per cent or more. Only 68 districts reported increases of more than 20 per cent in enrollments in elementary schools.[18]

CHANGES IN THE HIGH SCHOOL POPULATION

The growth in high school enrollment following the war period has been very marked. (See Figure 5.) During the current economic depression an increasing number of pupils are continuing their schooling in high schools and many high school graduates are remaining in school for further study. It is believed, however, that the factors that have caused the elementary school population to decrease will soon show their influence on high school enrollments.

[18] Educational Directories, State Department of Education, 1928–1930.

Since 1917 the high school population has increased from 45,938 to 104,357. (See Table 3.) This rapid growth in secondary school enrollments has brought about an increase in the proportion of high school pupils in the total enrollment from 9.5 per cent in 1917 to 18.6 per cent in 1931.

The total public school enrollment in the three largest cities has grown since 1917 from 84,500 to 143,852. The percentage of the

FIGURE 5.—CHANGES IN TOTAL AND IN HIGH SCHOOL ENROLLMENT IN MINNESOTA, 1916–1930

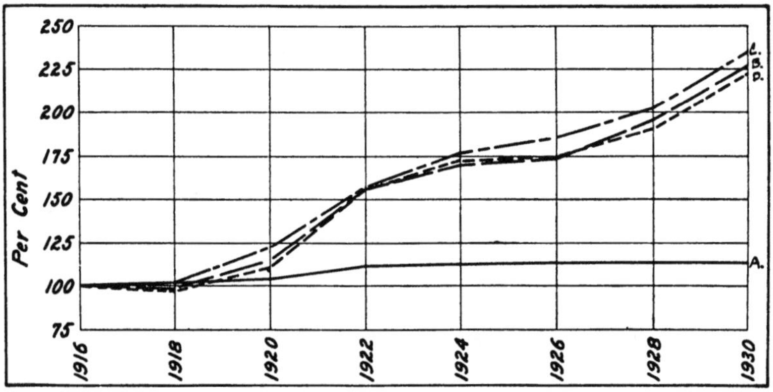

A.—Change in School Enrollment in all Public Schools. *B.*—Change in Enrollment in Public High Schools, Grades 9–12. *C.*—Change in High School Enrollment in Duluth, Minneapolis, and St. Paul. *D.*—Change in High School Enrollment Outside Duluth, Minneapolis, and St. Paul.

school population in the schools of the three largest cities has increased from 17.5 in 1917 to 25.7 in 1931. (See Table 4.) In contrast it is of interest to note that the percentage of the total high school population attending school in Duluth and the Twin Cities has increased only 1 per cent during this period. (See Table 3.)

COST OF EDUCATION IN MINNESOTA

TOTAL EXPENDITURES

The total current expenditures for public schools in Minnesota in the school year ending in 1931 were $45,629,084. During this year there was also a capital expenditure, largely for new buildings, of $5,000,410, and a disbursement of $3,985,907 for the payment of debt principal and interest. In considering the expenditures for debt service it must be recalled that the method fol-

TABLE 3. — COMPARISON OF HIGH SCHOOL ENROLLMENT WITH TOTAL PUBLIC SCHOOL ENROLLMENT, 1917–1931[a]

YEAR ENDING	TOTAL ENROLLMENT IN PUBLIC SCHOOLS OF STATE	HIGH SCHOOL ENROLLMENT		ENROLLMENT IN HIGH SCHOOLS OF MINNEAPOLIS, ST. PAUL, AND DULUTH	
		Total No.	Percentage of Total Enrollment	Total No.	Percentage of Total High School Enrollment
1917	484,586	45,938	9.5	14,738	32.3
1919	485,694	45,457	9.4	14,853	32.5
1921	505,681	52,788	10.4	18,058	34.5
1923	540,843	71,801	13.3	23,199	32.2
1925	545,956	80.195	14.7	26,107	32.7
1927	550,330	81,988	14.9	27,451	33.5
1929	553,336	90,533	16.4	30,835	34.0
1931	554,709	104,357	18.8	34,691	33.2

[a] Data obtained from the annual reports of the State Department of Education.

lowed by the state in collecting taxes for bonds sold by school districts to the state is such that the sums collected may or may not be included in the reports of school districts to the State Department of Education. The total disbursements in 1931 were thus $54,615,401. This item contains certain duplications and does not include the payments made from the cash income received during the year. The cash in the sinking funds for the same year was $1,380,000 and the money derived from the sale of bond issues was $3,563,025. A figure that represents the true cost of the public

TABLE 4. — COMPARISON OF SCHOOL ENROLLMENT IN THE TWIN CITIES AND DULUTH WITH TOTAL ENROLLMENT IN STATE[a]

YEAR ENDING	TOTAL ENROLLMENT IN STATE	ENROLLMENT IN TWIN CITIES AND DULUTH	
		Total No.	Percentage of Total State Enrollment
1917	484,586	84,500	17.4
1919	485,694	95,839	19.7
1921	505,681	119,268	23.6
1923	540,843	130,215	24.1
1925	545,956	137,890	25.3
1927	550,330	143,831	26.1
1929	553,336	143,441	25.9
1931	554,709	143,852	25.9

[a] Data obtained from the annual reports of the State Department of Education.

schools for a single year is not available, but for comparative purposes the total current expenditures have been used in Table 5.[19]

Though enrollment has increased slightly during the past three years, the cost per pupil has remained virtually the same — this in spite of the fact that the increase in school attendance has been caused primarily by additions to high school classes, which are much more expensive than the elementary schools.

Most of the districts maintaining high schools and graded schools are independent school districts. The common school districts with few exceptions operate ungraded schools. Table 6 presents a comparison of the current expenditures in 1931 in districts maintaining graded and high schools and districts maintaining ungraded schools.

TABLE 5. — OPERATING COST OF PUBLIC SCHOOLS, 1929–1931

	1929	1930	1931
General administration	$1,680,319	$1,711,234	$1,762,085
Salaries of professional staff	29,001,666	29,522,405	29,766,192
Books and instructional supplies	2,200,918	2,386,847	2,384,793
Cleaning, heating, lighting, and upkeep of buildings	8,605,965	8,564,257	8,421,374
Transportation of pupils	1,720,066	1,726,227	1,753,430
Other expenses	1,750,093	1,759,178	1,541,210
Total	$44,959,027	$45,670,148	$45,629,084
Total enrollment	553,336	551,741	554,943
Cost per pupil	$81	$83	$82

During the three years ending July, 1931, the costs per pupil in the districts maintaining graded elementary schools and high schools have decreased, whereas in the ungraded school systems the costs have increased slightly. The average annual cost per pupil is $58 in an ungraded school and $97 in districts that offer twelve years or more of instruction in a graded school system. If these figures are contrasted with those of any comparable state in the Union, it will be found that costs in Minnesota are not high. It is doubtful if parents in any part of the state could secure a comparable education for their children in private schools at the same cost.

Cost in relation to revenue received. — If the cost is distributed

[19] The school fiscal year begins on August 1. The term "current expenditures" covers only operating costs. It does not include capital expenditures or debt payments.

according to the sources of revenue, it is found that in the school districts that maintain graded schools and high schools the cost of public education to the local districts is 78 per cent of the total, or $73 per pupil, while in the ungraded districts the local burden represents 71 per cent of the total, or $42 per pupil.

Taxes as a Measure of Educational Costs

The average taxpayer usually regards educational costs as high or low not in relation to the measures usually applied in comparing school costs but in relation to the amount of his tax statement. Costs per pupil may decrease over a period of years when reliable

Table 6.—Comparison of School Costs in Districts Maintaining Graded Schools and Districts Maintaining Ungraded Schools, 1931

Expenditure	Districts Maintaining Graded and High Schools	Districts Maintaining Ungraded Schools
Current expenditures	$35,262,761	$10,366,323
Buildings and land	4,443,603	556,807
Bond payments	3,553,211	432,696
Enrollment	337,115	117,828
Cost per pupil	$97	$58

cost measures are used for comparison, yet the distribution of the burden among the taxpayers may result in increased taxes. The people who share the burden demand that lowered school costs be expressed in smaller tax payments and not solely in the improvement or extension of services at lower unit costs.

As shown in Chapters 3 and 4, unsatisfactory methods of assessment distribute the tax burden unfairly among the members of the local community; variations in assessing practices, unequal distribution of resources, and local power to determine the type of schools to be maintained create an unfair distribution of school costs among the different communities of the state. These injustices are not confined to any one area but are to be found among all types of school districts and in all sections. The system in operation makes it possible in certain school districts for one property holder to carry a fair and reasonable share of the school costs, while his neighbor residing in an adjoining district with equal re-

FIGURE 6.—MAINTENANCE TAX RATE IN 483 MINNESOTA SCHOOL DISTRICTS MAINTAINING GRADED ELEMENTARY AND HIGH SCHOOLS, 1931

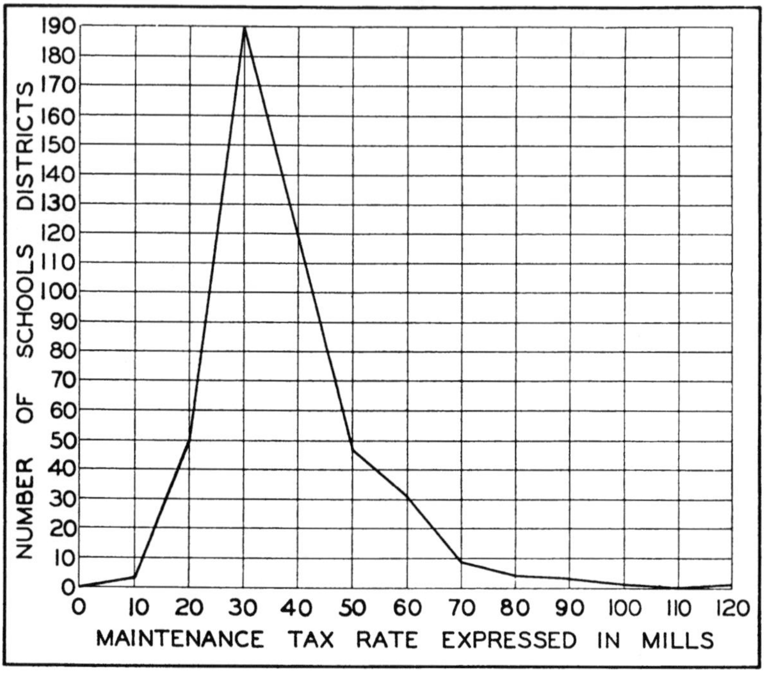

sources may be required to shoulder a heavier burden without receiving any greater educational advantages in return.

TAXES IN INDEPENDENT SCHOOL DISTRICTS

In 483 school districts in Minnesota (largely independent school districts) maintaining graded elementary schools and secondary schools the range in the school tax rate for 1931 was from 7 to 116 mills. The median tax rate was 32.9 mills in 1930 and 30.9 mills in 1931. These data do not include the local one-mill tax.[20] In 1931 there were 9 school districts that paid school taxes equivalent to $3.20 or more on every $100 of taxable real estate. On the other hand, in 53 districts property holders paid 80 cents or less in school taxes per $100 of property held.

TAXES IN COMMON SCHOOL DISTRICTS

In 7,257 school districts (largely common school districts) the tax rate ranged from zero to 102 mills in 1931. The median tax rate

[20] From mimeographed bulletin of the State Department of Education, 1931–32.

FIGURE 7.—MAINTENANCE TAX RATE IN 7,257 MINNESOTA SCHOOL DISTRICTS MAINTAINING UNGRADED SCHOOLS, 1931

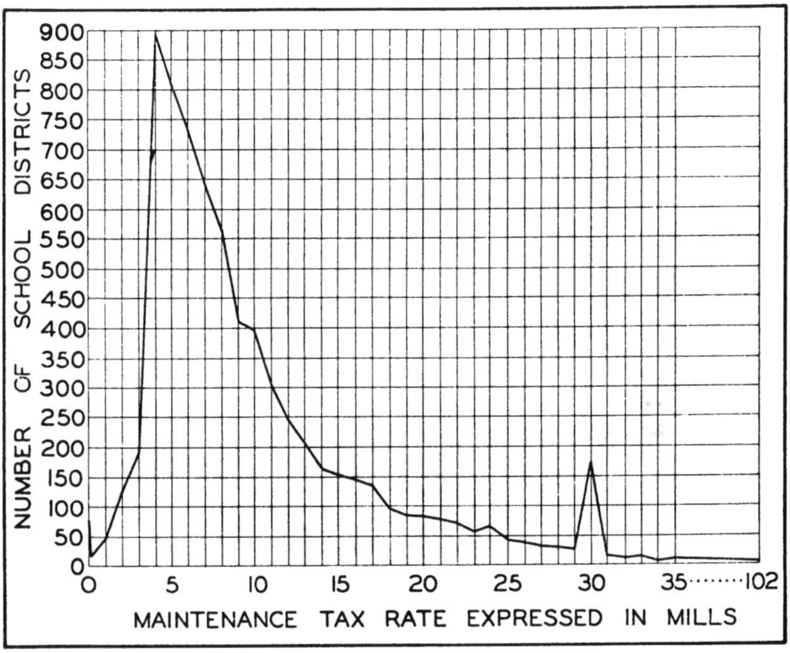

in these districts was 8.7 mills in 1930 and 8.2 mills in 1931. (See Figure 7.) Only 62 districts in this group levied a tax of $1.19 or more on each $100 of local farm property in 1932. On the other hand, there were 2,165 districts that collected only 16 cents or less on each $100 of taxables. As already pointed out, 78 districts collected no tax.

A study of the taxes collected in various school districts in the state shows clearly the wide range in taxes and school costs, and it also reveals many of the inequalities resulting from the plan of tax distribution.[21] The reader should observe particularly the variations in the tax burden on farms in independent and common school districts in the same counties. (See Tables 7 and 8.) Recall that most independent districts maintain high schools and that the state pays the high school tuition of the youth who reside in the common school districts and attend high schools in other districts. The cases portrayed in these tables were selected from among the best farms in the counties by the county auditors.

[21] O. R. Domian, "An Analysis of Local School Tax Payments in Minnesota," thesis on file in the University of Minnesota Library, 1928.

TABLE 7. — VARIATIONS IN TAXES ON HIGH-GRADE FARMS IN SCHOOL DISTRICTS MAINTAINING HIGH SCHOOLS, 1928

Case No.	County	No. of Children in School	Distance from School (in Miles)	No. of Acres in Farm	Valuation of Farm[a]	School Tax	Valuation per Acre	Tax per Acre
1	Aitkin	2	1	120	$1,540	$ 61	$13	$.50
2	Becker	2	1.5	150	2,600	133	17	.80
3	Blue Earth	1	1	80	2,438	68	30	.85
4	Big Stone	1	1	158	3,652	157	23	.99
5	Chisago	2	2	153	4,400	134	29	.87
6	Faribault	2	2	160	5,696	137	36	.85
7	Le Sueur	1	3	208	6,516	115	31	.55

[a] Data to nearest dollar.

TABLE 8. — VARIATIONS IN TAXES ON HIGH-GRADE FARMS IN SCHOOL DISTRICTS MAINTAINING UNGRADED SCHOOLS, 1928

Case No.	County	No. of Children in School	Distance from School (in Miles)	No. of Acres in Farm	Valuation of Farm[a]	School Tax	Valuation per Acre	Tax per Acre
1	Aitkin	2	10	80	$ 377	$ 6	$ 5	$.07
2	Becker	2	15	80	2,325	17	29	.21
3	Blue Earth	2	4	240	7,692	59	33	.24
4	Big Stone	1	9	160	2,792	26	18	.16
5	Chisago	1	3	139	3,490	34	25	.24
6	Faribault	3	3	242	8,988	180	37	.74
7	Le Sueur	2	4	163	5,485	33	34	.20

[a] Data to nearest dollar.

VARIATIONS IN TAX BURDEN WITHIN A COUNTY

In Table 9 are presented certain facts regarding the taxes paid by farmers in Carver County.[22] Some are in school districts that maintain high schools and others have properties in common school districts adjoining the districts that support high schools. Notice the high tax per acre paid for schools by the farmers in districts 78 and 32. One might well raise the question as to why all the farms should not be taxed for the maintenance of high schools if any farm is taxed and if high schools are to be supported at public expense.

TABLE 9.—VARIATIONS IN TAXES PAID BY FARMERS OF DIFFERENT SCHOOL DISTRICTS IN CARVER COUNTY, 1930

Farmer	District	School Tax Rate in Mills	Acres in Farm	Assessed Valuation of Farm	Total Tax	School Tax	School Tax per Acre
Farms Located in and near School District 78, Which Maintains a Four-Year High School							
A. H.	28	6	80	$4,400	$156	$26	$.33
A. and J. K...	58	5	80	4,600	159	23	.29
H. S.	41	3.5	80	4,300	151	15	.19
C. A. S.......	59	4.6	80	4,300	155	20	.25
J. R., Jr......	39	3	80	4,055	140	12	.15
J. K.	60	8	80	4,222	167	34	.42
J. H.	78	30	80	3,200	197	96	1.20
H. K.	78	30	80	4,745	292	142	1.78
Farms Located in and near School District 32, Which Maintains a High School Department							
C. A.	31	7	80	$4,033	$146	$28	$.35
O. B.	33	10.5	80	3,862	153	41	.51
W. H.	36	6	80	3,797	133	23	.26
C. M.	37	7	80	3,900	141	27	.34
M. H.	71	7	80	4,381	158	31	.38
C. C. J.......	32	30	80	3,467	205	104	1.30
H. M.	32	30	80	3,788	224	114	1.42

Table 10 presents data for selected school districts in each of three counties. Taxable resources (expressed in assessed valuations) and the tax collected per $1,000 of valuation are compared

[22] J. J. Halverson, "Education in Carver County, Minnesota, 1931," thesis on file in the University of Minnesota Library.

with the cost per pupil of operating ungraded schools.[23] Observe that common school district 15 ranks twenty-third among the 111 districts of Dakota County on the basis of taxable resources, seventy-ninth in respect to moneys collected for schools, and thirty-second in respect to local school costs. School district 17 ranks second in assessed valuation in Dodge County, seventieth with respect to the amount of tax collected per $1,000 valuation, and twenty-eighth with respect to the unit cost of the ungraded schools maintained. School district 55 in Dodge County, which ranks low in taxable valuation, ranks second among the districts of the county with respect to the annual school expenditure per pupil.

TABLE 10.—COMPARISON OF RESOURCES, TAX COLLECTED PER $1,000 OF VALUATION, AND COST PER PUPIL IN CERTAIN COMMON SCHOOL DISTRICTS IN DAKOTA, DODGE, AND STEELE COUNTIES, 1927

District	Assessed Valuation	Rank[a]	Tax Collected per Thousand Assessed Valuation	Rank[a]	Costs per Pupil	Rank[a]
Dakota County (111 districts)						
15	$131,000	23	$4.10	79	$80	32
23	119,000	32	3.40	83	129	6
6	41,000	85	24.00	5	59	69
8	79,000	72	11.10	17	48	78
28	55,000	81	14.00	10	131	5
30	84,000	67	8.30	24	109	10
Dodge County (84 districts)						
17	200,000	2	4.30	70	78	28
63	192,000	4	5.20	75	82	23
25	98,000	60	13.20	3	54	58
52	89,000	66	9.40	13	53	60
46	84,000	68	8.60	18	112	7
55	57,000	75	10.80	7	160	2
Steele County (97 districts)						
24	72,000	77	6.60	60	97	12
4	105,000	35	4.30	82	77	29
44	117,000	17	6.00	69	104	11
72	76,000	72	11.70	9	58	51
79	64,000	81	9.90	21	85	18
80	46,000	84	13.70	7	79	26

[a] Read thus: District 15 with a valuation of $131,000 ranks twenty-third among the 111 districts in Dakota County in respect to valuation, seventy-ninth in respect to tax collected per $1,000 assessed valuation, and thirty-second in respect to costs per pupil.

[23] F. R. Adams, "A Survey of School Costs in Dakota, Dodge, and Steele Counties," thesis on file in the University of Minnesota Library, 1929.

FIGURE 8.—VARIATION IN COST PER PUPIL IN AVERAGE DAILY ATTENDANCE IN ONE-ROOM SCHOOLS IN 968 COMMON SCHOOL DISTRICTS, 1930[a]

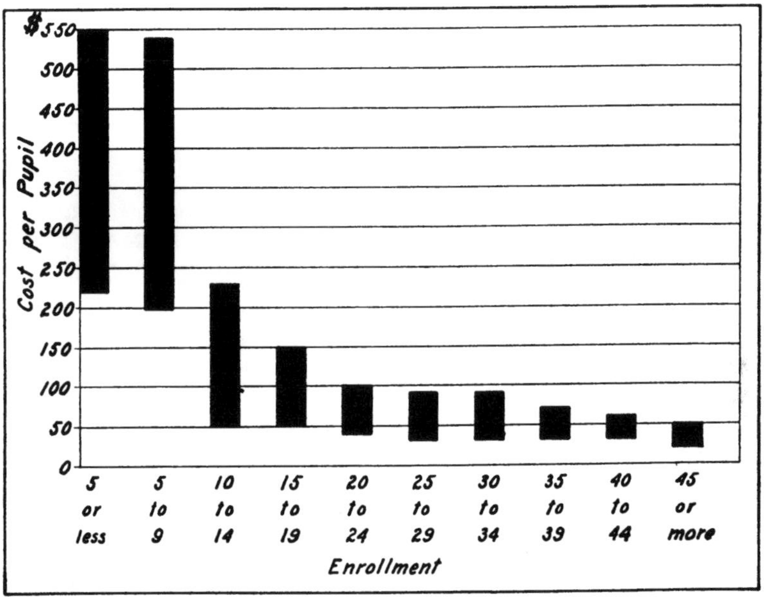

[a] T. J. Berning, *Study of One-Teacher Ungraded Elementary Schools*, State Department of Education, St. Paul, 1931, p. 38.

COST PER PUPIL

COMMON SCHOOL DISTRICTS

When the costs per pupil of operating schools in different districts are compared, an extremely wide range is evident. (See Figure 8.) Data not presented here show that the cost per pupil of maintaining ungraded schools in several counties varied from a minimum of $28 to a maximum of $259. When the counties were compared with respect to costs, the minimums ranged from $28 to $35 and the maximums from $160 to $259 per pupil.

The great variation in costs is also strikingly shown when the costs per pupil are arranged according to the number of pupils in each school. (See Table 11.) Note how rapidly the costs climb when a school is operated for less than forty pupils. Note likewise how the costs increase in a district in which from forty-five to sixty pupils are enrolled. A small school district must employ two teachers when the enrollment exceeds forty pupils and the cost in this case runs high.

Salary costs.—Teachers' salaries approximate 76 per cent of the total current cost of the common schools. Table 12 shows how wide the variation is in the proportion of the expenditures devoted to teachers' salaries in Steele, Dakota, and Dodge counties; variations of the same nature exist in each of the counties for which data are available. Obviously, to reduce the costs and taxes materially in small school districts it will be necessary either to reduce salaries or to abolish the small district.

TABLE 11.—COSTS PER PUPIL IN COMMON SCHOOL DISTRICTS IN DAKOTA COUNTY ARRANGED ACCORDING TO NUMBER OF PUPILS IN AVERAGE DAILY ATTENDANCE, 1927[a]

PUPILS IN AVERAGE DAILY ATTENDANCE	NO. OF SCHOOL DISTRICTS	COST PER PUPIL (TO THE NEAREST DOLLAR)
Less than 5	1	$361
5– 9.9	17	136
10–14.9	32	89
15–19.9	20	60
20–24.9	11	54
25–29.9	3	40
30–34.9	1	36
35–39.9	1	31
40–44.9	1	122
45–54.9	1	53
55–59.9	1	74

[a] Adapted from F. R. Adams, "Survey of Common Schools in Three Counties in Minnesota," 1929.

Salaries in the ungraded schools are low, too low to attract the best qualified teachers. In 1931 the median salaries paid in ungraded schools were between $700 and $900 a year for men and between $630 and $810 per year for women. Of the 8,346 teachers in ungraded schools less than 23 per cent are receiving salaries of more than $100 a month, and this amount is paid for only seven, eight, or nine months, according to the length of the school term.

Salaries in the common schools did not increase materially in the three-year period prior to 1929. In the three counties for which data are given in Table 12 the average median salary paid rural teachers was $735 in 1925, $746 in 1926, and $782 in 1927. Most of the teachers employed in these schools have had but one year of professional education beyond high school graduation. Reductions in the salaries paid will not induce better qualified teachers to seek positions in the ungraded rural schools.

INDEPENDENT SCHOOL DISTRICTS

If for convenience the districts maintaining graded schools and high schools may be classed as the independent school districts, variations as extreme as those found among the common districts will be noted. For example, the range in cost in 163 districts classed as high school departments is from $39 to $142 per pupil for the elementary schools and from $82 to $526 for the high

TABLE 12.—PERCENTAGE OF TOTAL CURRENT EXPENDITURES DEVOTED TO TEACHERS' SALARIES IN COMMON SCHOOL DISTRICTS OF STEELE, DAKOTA, AND DODGE COUNTIES[a]

(Average for three years, 1925–1927)

PERCENTAGE OF CURRENT EXPENDITURES DEVOTED TO TEACHERS' SALARIES	NO. OF DISTRICTS		
	STEELE COUNTY	DAKOTA COUNTY	DODGE COUNTY
45–49.9	..	4	..
50–54.9	..	2	1
55–59.9	1	2	1
60–64.9	4	3	5
65–69.9	9	11	13
70–74.9	18	18	28
75–79.9	23	24	16
80–84.9	18	16	6
85–89.9	5	3	..
90–94.9	1	..	..
Total number of districts	79	83	70
Median percentage of expenditures devoted to salaries	77%	75%	73%

[a] Adapted from Adams, *op. cit.*

schools. (See Figure 9.) Even in the largest school systems the elementary school costs range from $52 to $174 and the high school costs from $83 to $318 per pupil. The reader should note what proportions of the total costs are met out of local tax revenue.

In these independent districts the salaries of professional employees represent approximately 68 per cent of the total current expenditure. If the Twin Cities and Duluth are excluded, the median annual salary paid high school teachers is $1,427 and elementary teachers, $1,103.[24] There are few men teachers in the grade schools. Four years of professional education are required for teaching in the high school and two years of study beyond high

[24] "Teachers' Salaries," mimeographed bulletin of the State Department of Education, St. Paul, February 17, 1932.

FIGURE 9. — RANGE IN COST PER PUPIL OF MAINTAINING ELEMENTARY AND FOUR-YEAR HIGH SCHOOLS IN VARIOUS CLASSES OF SCHOOL DISTRICTS, 1929–1930 [a]

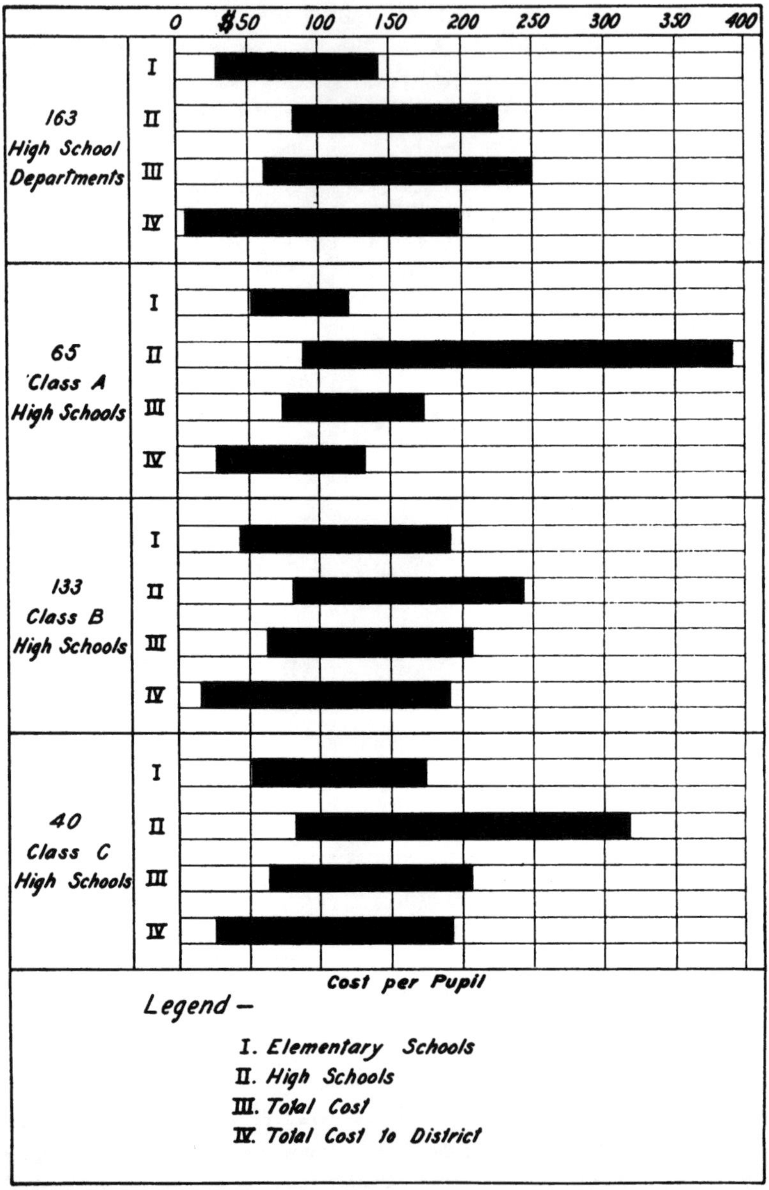

[a] Berning, *op. cit.*

school graduation must be secured by those who teach in the grades.

It will be noted that salaries paid teachers in the elementary and high schools of the state in 1932 are less than those paid in communities of corresponding size in the country as a whole in 1931. (See Figure 10.) Judging from the evidence received this spring (1932), it appears that teachers' salaries for 1933 are being reduced below those for 1932.

FIGURE 10.—SALARIES PAID HIGH SCHOOL AND ELEMENTARY SCHOOL TEACHERS IN COMMUNITIES OF VARIOUS SIZES IN THE UNITED STATES[a]

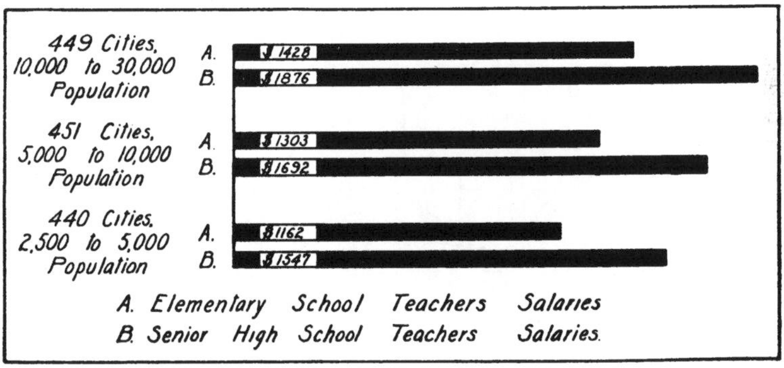

[a] *Salaries in City School Systems, 1930–1931* (Bulletin of National Education Association, Vol. 9, no. 3, May, 1931).

NUMBER OF TEACHERS EMPLOYED

The tendency toward stabilization in the public school enrollment pointed out earlier in this chapter (page 432) and the changes that are taking place in school organization are resulting in a decreased demand for regular classroom teachers. (See Figure 11.) In these graphs the percentage increase or decrease over 1910–11 is presented. Note the falling off of the teacher demand in the ungraded schools and the reduction in the number of teachers employed in the state at large.

In 1927 there were 22,099 school teachers in the public schools of the state; in 1931 there were 21,944. In 1928 there were 7,870 elementary school teachers; in 1931, 7,823. The number of elementary school teachers in the three largest cities has decreased from 5,180 in 1927 to 5,080 in 1931. The number of teachers in ungraded elementary schools has decreased from 8,319 in 1915 to 7,699 in 1931. Although the number of high school teachers in the three large cities has decreased since 1928, the number in the state as a whole has increased from 4,938 to 5,396 during the three years prior to 1931.

In 1930 there were 740 school districts in which there were fewer than ten pupils enrolled. (See Figure 12.) This type of district has nearly doubled in number during the past eighteen years. There are also 150 districts in which from ten to nineteen children were enrolled in school. If one assumes that it is uneconomical to operate a school with a load of less than thirty pupils per teacher, the annual loss to the state incurred through the perpetuation of the above districts is by no means small.

FIGURE 11. — CHANGES IN TOTAL NUMBER OF TEACHERS EMPLOYED IN 619 PUBLIC SCHOOLS IN MINNESOTA, 1910–1931

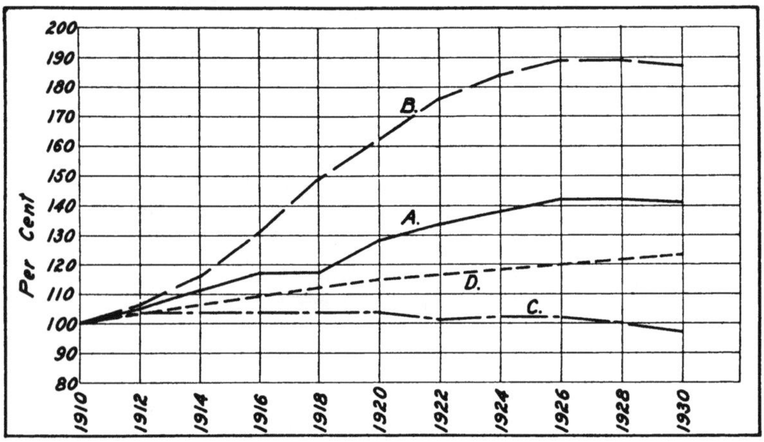

A. — Change in Total Number of Teachers Employed in Minnesota. *B.* — Change in Number of Teachers Employed in Graded Elementary and High School Districts. *C.* — Change in Number of Teachers Employed in Ungraded Elementary Districts. *D.* — Change in Population of Minnesota.

Of the elementary schools other than those in common school districts, 15 per cent operated with fewer than twenty-five pupils per teacher in 1930–31. There are 171 independent school districts in which there were thirty or more pupils per teacher in the elementary grades.

Another factor that contributes to excessive high school costs is the small enrollment in many of the high schools. Nearly half of the high schools of the state employ only four teachers or fewer. In over one-fourth of the secondary schools the enrollment is smaller than seventy-five, and to carry on an efficient school service the instructional cost will run very high. Although the State Department of Education has made every effort to reduce the number of small high schools, local pride continues to resist the abandonment of even the most expensive of them. If the number of

FIGURE 12.—CHANGE IN THE TOTAL NUMBER OF DISTRICTS IN THE STATE AND IN THE NUMBER OF DISTRICTS WITH SMALL SCHOOL ENROLLMENTS AS COMPARED WITH CONDITIONS IN 1916

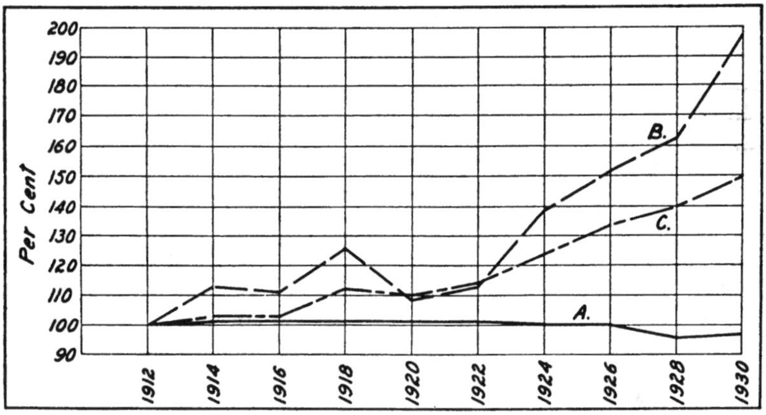

A.—Change in Number of School Districts. *B.*—Change in Number of School Districts Having an Enrollment of Less than Ten Pupils. *C.*—Change in Number of School Districts Having an Enrollment of from Ten to Nineteen Pupils.

pupils per teacher in the high school is considered, it will be noted that nearly half the schools have sixteen or fewer pupils per teacher.

INDEBTEDNESS FOR SCHOOL PURPOSES

In 1928 Minnesota ranked eighth among the states with respect to outstanding bonded debt for public schools. Michigan was sixth; Illinois, ninth; Wisconsin, twenty-fourth; and Iowa, twelfth. Minnesota's debt amounted to $135 per pupil enrolled.[25] For the most part the states with a smaller debt per pupil are those in which there are no very large cities.

In 1924 the school bonded debt in Minnesota was reported as about 15 per cent of the total state debt,[26] and in 1928 it was 21

[25] *Statistics of State School Systems,* Office of Education Bulletin No. 5, 1928.
[26] I. O. Friswold, "Public School Indebtedness in Minnesota," 1925, thesis on file in the University of Minnesota Library.

per cent. In 1928 the total school debt and the bonds outstanding amounted to $70,470,913 [27] and in 1929 it was $71,040,231. Of this amount only 6 per cent had been incurred for buildings in the ungraded school districts. Of the total, $42,338,923, or 61 per cent, represents outstanding obligations of the cities and large towns in Hennepin, Ramsey, and St. Louis counties.

The bonded debt in school districts outside the Twin Cities decreased from 73 per cent of the total in 1900 to 55 per cent in 1929. (See Table 13.) Obviously, as the two largest cities have grown, school building construction has kept pace with the demand for increased school facilities.

The increase in debt following the World War was due primarily to the rigid restrictions that had been placed on building by the federal government. Since 1924 there has been a decline in expenditures for school building and a decrease in the school bonded debt in districts outside Minneapolis and St. Paul from $47,139,168 in 1924 to $39,070,308 in 1929. (See Table 13.)

TABLE 13.—BONDED DEBT FOR PUBLIC SCHOOLS IN TWIN CITIES AND OTHER SCHOOL DISTRICTS OF THE STATE, 1900–1929 [a]

YEAR	BONDED DEBT FOR SCHOOLS				RATIO OF INDEBTEDNESS OUTSIDE TWIN CITIES TO STATE TOTAL
	In Minneapolis	In St. Paul	In Other School Districts	Total Debt	Per Cent
1900	$ 950,000	$ 744,000	$ 4,586,304	$ 6,280,304	73
1902	980,000	689,000	4,307,098	5,976,098	72
1904	1,180,000	839,000	4,778,911	6,797,911	70
1906	1,380,000	839,000	5,848,790	8,067,790	72
1908	1,821,000	964,000	6,459,219	9,244,219	70
1910	2,813,000	1,839,000	7,724,945	12,376,945	62
1912	4,429,700	2,058,000	11,897,120	18,384,820	65
1914	6,030,000	1,940,000	12,770,161	20,740,161	62
1916	7,994,500	1,840,000	14,701,614	24,536,614	60
1918	7,994,500	1,796,000	.........[b]	.........[b]	..
1920	12,213,500	2,146,000	.........[b]	.........[b]	..
1922	15,806,500	4,146,000	.........[b]	.........[b]	..
1924	17,454,000	7,546,000	47,139,168	72,139,168	65
1926	21,500,000	8,546,000	39,841,816	69,881,816	57
1927	20,478,210	9,546,000	40,390,153	70,414,363	57
1928	22,241,862	9,546,000	38,683,051	70,470,913	55
1929	22,423,923	9,546,000	39,070,308	71,040,231	55

[a] Data from the annual reports of the county superintendents.

[b] Data not included in the annual reports of county superintendents from 1917 to 1922, inclusive.

[27] C. G. Haugen, "The Trend in Public School Indebtedness in Minnesota," thesis on file in the University of Minnesota Library, 1931.

If the school population continues to change at its present rate and if bond obligations can be met when they fall due, the bonded debt for schools in places outside of the large cities should decrease at a much more rapid rate than during the past few years. The expenditures for land, buildings, and equipment for schools decreased from $5,078,604 in 1929 to $5,000,410 in 1931. It is to be noted that a large proportion of these expenditures were made from current revenue. Income from sale of bonds and accumulations in building funds amounted to $3,820,102 in 1929 and in 1931 to $3,563,025.

A detailed study of one hundred independent and special school districts taken at random shows that 27 per cent of them have a bonded debt of less than 1 per cent of the assessed valuation and that 8 per cent of them have a bonded debt of 21 per cent or more of the assessed valuation. Sixty-nine per cent of the school districts in the state have a bonded debt of less than 10 per cent of the assessed valuation. The relationship between the total assessed valuation in the state and the bonded debt for schools for the period 1900 to 1929 is shown in Table 14.

TABLE 14.—RATIO OF BONDED DEBT IN PUBLIC SCHOOLS IN MINNESOTA TO ASSESSED VALUATION, 1900–1929

Year	Assessed Valuation		Bonded Debt		Ratio of Bonded Debt to Assessed Valuation
	Amount[a]	Ratio to 1900 Valuation	Amount[b]	Ratio to 1900 Debt	
		Per Cent		Per Cent	Per Cent
1900	$ 588,016,668	100	$ 6,280,304	100	1.07
1902	761,760,274	130	5,976,098	95	.78
1904	845,897,111	144	6,797,911	108	.80
1906	917,017,413	156	8,067,790	128	.88
1908	1,065,101,201	181	9,244,219	147	.87
1910	1,194,962,312	203	12,376,945	197	1.04
1912	1,339,758,747	228	18,384,820	293	1.37
1914	1,475,999,608	251	20,740,161	330	1.41
1916	1,590,200,958	269	24,536,614	391	1.54
1918	1,750,180,951	298	No data	...	...
1920	2,084,286,979	354	No data	...	...
1922	1,952,017,240	332	No data	...	...
1924	1,976,549,257	336	72,139,168	1,149	3.65
1926	1,942,375,038	330	69,881,816	1,113	3.60
1927	1,942,921,185	330	70,414,363	1,121	3.62
1928	1,942,383,286	330	70,470,913	1,122	3.63
1929	1,947,713,489	331	71,040,231	1,131	3.65

[a] C. G. Haugen, "The Trend in Public School Indebtedness with Special Reference to Minnesota," thesis on file in University of Minnesota Library, 1931.
[b] Data from annual reports of county superintendents.

A school district that is required to carry a bonded debt burden in excess of 15 per cent of its assessed valuation finds the tax burden very heavy and as a rule encounters great difficulty in operating a school system of approved grade at the same time that the debt obligations are being met. Financial situations of this kind exist largely in those school districts with a small valuation that have endeavored to maintain twelve years of schooling.

Provision has been made in the law for the state to loan money under specific conditions to school districts for school buildings. By 1930 the sum of $27,239,985 had been loaned by the state to local subdivisions. It is estimated that approximately $15,000,000 of this amount has been borrowed by school districts of the state.

No data are available to indicate the extent of the outstanding interest payments made annually on overdue warrants issued by school districts. From contact with school situations and conferences with superintendents information has been received that leads one to believe that an increasing number of school districts have balanced their budgets and that a decreasing number are embarrassed by being forced to carry over from year to year unpaid current debts.

The provision in the law that makes it possible for the treasurer to endorse warrants on occasions when funds are lacking and thus to convert a warrant into a note does not promote sound business practice.[28] If the school business cannot be operated on a cash basis during a certain period in the year because tax incomes must be anticipated, then legal provision should be made whereby the board of education may create a working cash fund or borrow money. The amount to be borrowed, the interest to be paid, and the time of repayment of the principal may be easily regulated by law. The present practice of allowing unpaid warrants to become notes payable with interest leads to accounting difficulties and poor accounting control. The responsibility for the payment of obligations when cash is lacking should be placed on the board of education and not with the treasurer.

EFFECT OF SOCIAL AND ECONOMIC CHANGES ON THE SCHOOLS

Important population changes in the state have been discussed above. As a whole the large strategic centers have attracted more

[28] Minnesota School Law, Sec. 113, 1931.

people during recent years, whereas many of the small centers have become smaller. Developments in industrial methods, progress in agriculture, and advances in business methods have contributed their share to altering the status of the small city and town.

The small city today no longer serves the area in which it is located as it did twenty-five years ago. Today the improved highway and the automobile have destroyed the old popular concept of distance; what was a day's journey a few decades ago is but an hour's trip today. The custom of shopping in the near-by village has given way to doing business in the larger towns; communities such as Austin and Albert Lea, for instance, report the loss of certain classes of business to Minneapolis and St. Paul. Certain centers have gained in wealth as well as in population, whereas others not so advantageously located have lost tremendously.

These movements, of which we are all conscious and of which there appears to be no abatement, affect the merchant, the banker, the church, the school, and the social and recreational interests of the people. The forces that create a village, a city, or a town and the community interests that sustain its institutions are living and dynamic things. A change in the economy of a state may destroy the need for a town and may force the transfer of wealth and people to another locality. Artificial stimulation may retard a movement of this kind, but it probably will not alter the direction of the economic drift.

If people and wealth are constantly moving from one center to another within a state as it develops, can the state afford to maintain a system of schools in which a small unstable area is the unit of support and administration? Under such circumstances will there not always be school buildings in certain areas only partially occupied, while in other areas the people must sell bonds for new buildings to meet school population growth? In some communities of Minnesota that were once prosperous railroad centers the removal of certain shops and offices, as a result of economy in railroad management and other causes, has lowered taxable valuations and caused decreases in school enrollments. During the two years prior to 1931 the enrollment in the schools of the mining town of Aurora decreased from 744 to 625; in Biwabik from 560 to 442; in Chisholm from 3,516 to 3,228. These cases illustrate the effect on enrollment caused by improvement in management, industrial progress, and curtailment of production during the current depression. Although the decline in school attendance may be met by decreasing the number of teachers employed, nothing can be done to reclaim the capital expended on a school plant that can no longer be used to full capacity.

In other ways, too, the economic factor affects the schools, chiefly the local high school. Local merchants realize that an increase in the number of nonresident high school pupils will bring trade. Frequently a secondary school of very high cost will be built in a community largely because of the indirect effect the school is presumed to have on the business of the town. In many cases the true economy of the entire situation is overlooked.

Transportation of School Children

Only since 1920 have automobiles been used in sufficient numbers to affect seriously the economic life of communities, for only in recent years have the privately owned car and the truck become important vehicles for conducting business. During a period of about ten years prior to 1931 the surfaced roads in Minnesota increased from 16,905 to 37,317 miles. During the period from 1914 to 1931 highway mileage increased from 93,517 to 110,661. It is reported that in 1930–31 about 37,000 miles of road were kept open for traffic during the entire winter.[29] It is believed that the people have not yet taken full advantage of the state's splendid highway system for public school purposes. Often parents who are willing to have their children travel considerable distances for their social and recreational pleasures continue to be prejudiced against the transportation of children to school. The evidence indicates that children are much safer in a school bus than when they walk along the trunk highways on their way to and from school.

Complete and accurate data relative to the transportation of public school children are not available. The State Department of Education reports $1,753,430 as the amount expended for transportation of pupils in public school systems in 1931. During the period from 1912 to 1930 the number of children transported to consolidated schools increased from 932 to 36,226. The number of vehicles increased from 60 to 1,729, of which only 186 were horse-drawn. (See Table 15.)

[29] Mimeographed circular of the State Department of Highways, 1931.

TRANSPORTATION OF HIGH SCHOOL STUDENTS

A canvass recently made in a hundred small high schools in the state revealed some interesting facts regarding transportation. Of 6,212 pupils attending fifty-one different high schools in towns having a population of 2,500 or less, only 49 per cent reported that they walked to school regularly. In 30 per cent of the schools reporting, 40 per cent or fewer of the pupils stated that they walked. The others indicated that some means of transportation was provided them. Few children use the railroad in attending school, but the public bus, the school bus, and the private automobile convey a large percentage of those transported. The horse and the bicycle were reported as used by a considerable number of students.

TABLE 15.—TRANSPORTATION TO CONSOLIDATED SCHOOLS, 1911–1930[a]

School Year Ending	No. of Schools	No. of Transportation Vehicles				No. of Children Transported
		Wagons	Automobiles	Motor Buses	Total	
1912	30	60	...	...	60	932
1917	185	588	...	...	588	9,675
1922	312	1,089	...	204	1,293	24,515
1927	385	654	422	577	1,673	32,289
1930	410	186	616	927	1,729	36,226

[a] T. C. Engum, "Transportation in Minnesota," thesis on file in the University of Minnesota Library, 1932.

AREAS SERVED BY HIGH SCHOOLS

It is believed that the area served by the typical high school is not so extensive as many people think. A relatively small percentage of the pupils enrolled in the high schools in the larger towns are from out of town; a few report that they travel five miles or more daily to reach school. Although the small secondary schools have a much larger percentage of nonresident registration, the proportion of pupils who travel five miles or more is not great. In sixty-five high schools for which complete data were ascertainable, it was found that only 17 per cent of the pupils enrolled resided five miles or more from school. Less than 3 per cent of the nonresident pupils enrolled in the schools studied reside in town during the greater part of the school year.

If the distances between high schools in towns and cities are measured by railroad mileage, it will be found that half the schools outside large cities are twelve miles or less apart. Forty-seven high schools of various grades are within five miles of another high school. Seventy-nine high schools are twenty miles or more by railroad from the nearest neighboring high school.[30]

In reality the high schools in the state generally serve areas not much greater than can be included in a circle with a five-mile radius. It is believed that with a more general use of modern transportation facilities the high school can serve a larger area with economically as well as educationally advantageous results.

Recent Changes and Proposed Changes in School Organization

LAKE COUNTY SCHOOL DISTRICT

Two Harbors is the one city in Lake County. Since the rest of the county consists largely of undeveloped or farm land, the taxable wealth is hardly adequate to support schools. Under the leadership of the superintendent of schools of Two Harbors, the whole county was made into a corporate county school system by a more or less special act of the legislature.[31] When the county district was organized, in 1929, there were 24 school buildings and 70 teachers were employed. In 1932 there are 14 schools and 64 teachers. There are 1,641 school children enrolled in the schools, and about 90 per cent of the graduates of the eighth grade enter high school, a condition that does not exist in many counties of the state. All the elementary school teachers in the county are at least normal college graduates with two years of professional education.

The cost of operating the schools has decreased from $183,794 in 1929 to $164,377 in 1931, without salaries being reduced or the school program being cut. This cost is less than the total cost of operating the schools of the county under the old plan. The county has no school bonds outstanding and the balance on hand in the school treasury at the close of the school year 1931–32 was $68,082, or over one-third of the amount needed for annual current expenditures.

KOOCHICHING COUNTY REORGANIZATION

The State Department of Education has endeavored to assist in the solution of the difficult educational problems arising in the

[30] H. M. Lokken, "Availability of Secondary Schools in Minnesota," thesis in preparation, 1932.

[31] From correspondence received from Superintendent C. E. Campton, Lake County, Minnesota.

northern counties. For example, in 1931 staff members of the department undertook, on invitation of the local officials, an extensive survey of the schools of Koochiching County. On the basis of the facts brought out in this survey and with the assistance of the county superintendent an extensive reorganization plan was developed and put into operation. The reduction in school costs in the county was $75,000 the first year. The sum saved was made up somewhat as follows:[32]

Teachers' salaries	$36,000
Transportation and board of pupils	16,500
Operation and maintenance	15,000
Other expenditures	8,500

Below is shown what effect the modified organization has had on certain phases of the school situation in the county:[33]

	1931	1932
Number of schools in operation	39	20
Number of teachers in elementary schools	61	42
Number of teachers in high schools	19	18
Number of pupils transported	667	934
Transportation mileage	331	436
Average length of route in miles	5.3	9.5
Transportation cost of load per mile	$.38	$.22
Transportation cost per pupil per day	$.32	$.20

OTHER SURVEYS UNDER WAY

A similar survey of the unorganized territory in St. Louis County is resulting in a more economical administration of the schools in that area also. In the spring of 1932 the State Department of Education, at the request of the county superintendent of Aitkin County, made an intensive investigation of the school problems in the county and recommended that the entire area be converted into a county school district. If the plan proposed is put into operation, it is estimated that the net reduction in school costs to the taxpayers of the county will approximate $50,000 annually, though state aid will be over $38,000 greater. The distribution of the expenditures will be somewhat as follows:

Item	Under Present Organization	Under Proposed Plan
Expenditures in ungraded schools	$126,048	$72,149
Expenditures in graded and high schools	96,655	115,233
Transportation expenditures	33,743	57,500
Total expenditures	253,446	244,882
State aid	135,685	174,360
Net cost to the county	120,761	70,522

[32] C. P. Streeter, "Shall Some Schools Be Closed?" *The Farmer's Wife*, May, 1932, p. 9.

[33] T. C. Engum, "Study of School Organization of Aitkin County," a report to the county superintendent, dated April 14, 1932.

CONSOLIDATION OF SMALL SCHOOL DISTRICTS

A number of studies have been made that show very clearly that in many localities of the state small schools could be closed and the pupils of the district transported with a saving of expenditures. Some steps in this direction have been taken, but the number of schools with enrollments of less than twenty continues to be very large. In advocating a plan that will reduce the number of small schools it must always be kept in mind that although the step is exceedingly desirable and although economy in school operation will be accomplished thereby, the basic weaknesses of the present school district organization will not be corrected by this procedure.

WHAT OTHER STATES ARE DOING

Nearly every state in the Union is confronted with the demand for reducing local school taxes without curtailing public educational services, and many attempts have been made to comply with the demand. Some have sought solution through the extension of state subventions. In each case where this method has been applied it has been found that the cause of the greatest inequalities in tax burden lies primarily in the nature of the local school district unit.

Other states have attempted to find the solution to the problem of more economical school operation by creating corporate county school districts. North Carolina has resorted to a highly centralized state control of the public school and public school finances. The most progressive step has been taken in Arkansas, where school districts have been reorganized after a most intensive study of the local areas of the state, their resources, and their educational needs.

A study of reorganization in other states leads one to conclude that each state must solve its own problems in terms of local conditions and local requirements. The plan that may be applied effectively to improve schools in one section of the United States may not do at all in a state in another part of the country.

BASIC ISSUES IN SCHOOL FINANCE

It must be understood that difficult school finance problems exist not only in the small districts maintaining ungraded schools but are also abundant in many of the high school districts of the state. The small high school has always been a serious problem, and over 250 Minnesota high schools have 100 pupils or fewer.

The problems of school support will not be satisfactorily met unless the whole public school situation in the state is taken into consideration. Many of the undesirable conditions that exist today exist because in the past the "patchwork" policy was followed when adjustments were made to relieve financial pressures.

Out of tradition comes the belief held by many people that the small ungraded school provides the most satisfactory opportunities for bringing together those people in a neighborhood who have common interests. The facts do not support this contention. All investigations show the marked advantages of the larger school unit for keeping community interests alive as well as for school purposes. In fields other than education people have changed their manner of living to harmonize with new economic conditions. With the more modern means of travel there is no reason why the larger school unit should not provide in greater abundance and at no greater cost these things demanded by the people. It remains, however, for those interested in the schools to educate the people in order that prejudices may be destroyed.

The great error made in the earlier consolidations of schools was that a small number of small districts were united without regard to the financial burden the area would ultimately have to carry. The tax burden became exceedingly heavy in most of the unions where new buildings were constructed. It is believed that many larger units of school administration and support can be created in the state without the necessity of extensive capital expenditures.

The greatest care should be exercised to do nothing that will tend to perpetuate the assumed educational differences between rural and urban areas. The larger school administrative unit should contribute much to build a finer spirit of cooperation between town and country. The economic welfare of all the people in the state is so interdependent that all areas must work together. There is no institution that can bring together the people in the various sections as can the public schools. No sectional or factional differentiation should be tolerated when the educational program for the children of the state is being planned.

To bring about a wise reorganization in the school districts of the state demands the highest grade of statesmanship on the part of political and educational leaders. If schools are to be more economically and efficiently operated, attempts to make political capital of any development program should be laid aside. The general welfare of the state should dominate all plans, and action should follow the most intelligent consideration of all facts available.

Any change in school district organization will necessarily abolish certain positions of public trust and will take away a prestige that has been cherished by many who have sought membership in the local school boards. But schools are not presumed to be established for school board members, nor for the purpose of permitting certain people to make a living. Schools exist to educate children, and the aim of education is to provide the best schools possible with the money available. Schools are not created for individual profit, nor to bolster directly the economy of a community, nor to provide for the support of any of its adult citizens.

The public school system is a state enterprise carried on cooperatively by the people residing in the areas created as school districts. The history of the school district in the state shows that it was never assumed by the legislature that boundaries were to be fixed once for all time. There is ample evidence to show that the legislature has always acted on the theory that schools are dynamic institutions and that the divisions in which schools are to be administered and supported must be changed from time to time as the social and economic life of the people demands.

Home rule is a basic political issue involved in the problem of school district organization and school support. It is conceded by all students of education that local initiative and local pride in the schools should not be checked. It is likewise realized that unless there is a high grade of professional leadership one cannot expect to find good schools. Local pride and initiative are not of uniformly high caliber throughout any one state.

Few would openly advocate a principle that would permit groups of citizens to set themselves and their lands apart as a public school district. Such local freedom would find little support if these groups were able to petition the legislature for state aid when the local taxable resources were inadequate to maintain the schools established. Yet this is exactly what happens under the present school district organization. Can local autonomy be carried to the point where the people residing in any small area may reserve the right to operate their own schools and then, if they cannot support them, demand that other citizens of the state be compelled by law to help them financially? Consider the outcome if the citizens residing within any one city block in Minneapolis or St. Paul should have the power to create a school district in their block. Selfishness, partisanship, and local self-interest should not determine the divisions of the state for administration and support of schools.

Objections to changing school district organization are not insurmountable if political leaders are seriously interested in relieving the people of the inequalities in their burden for school support and if leadership is desirous of anticipating the consequences of that day when a more serious problem of school maintenance will arise because of the unsound practices now being perpetuated.

As the problems of school finance are analyzed, taxation issues arise. If property taxes are to remain the main source of income for school maintenance and if the farm lands are to be taxed along with village or city property for the support of schools, some further adjustment must be made to relieve the burden on the farm property. Many of the objections to the larger school districts would disappear if the main source of income for school support could be shifted from a property tax to some other form of taxation that could be spread more equitably with respect to the resources and wealth of the state.

There are many phases of public school finance and of related topics that should be treated in an analysis of this kind if there is to be a thorough understanding of the issues. Many of the topics left out in this review may appeal to the reader as more important than those treated. With the limited space available, it seemed best to treat in much detail the problem that always looms up in a crisis and that has its origin in the school district organization. If a foundation can be laid upon which the state can formulate a more satisfactory type of local school district, the problems of school finance may find a lasting solution. If the school districts are to remain in the form that exists today, the problems of school finance will continue to be increasingly baffling and difficult of solution.

If serious thought is to be given to modifying the school district plan in Minnesota, it will be well to keep certain basic principles in mind. To those who are attempting to solve the problem, help and encouragement should be given. Naturally every step that will reduce the number of districts contributes its mite to ultimate tax relief and to the probability that better schools will result. The process of evolution is slow and the resultant immediate tax relief is small, yet each step in advance that can be taken should be made.

The county school district unit may logically be the next step in school district organization. It may be the most expedient political move to create the corporate county school district. There is no doubt that an advanced step of this kind would bring about marked improvement in school organization and much tax relief in many sections of the state. If this step is taken, either in the form adopted in Lake County or by creating a school district of an entire county as a district of unorganized territory, the limitations of the county as a school district should be taken into consideration and recognized.

A county school system has many limitations. It cannot be universally applied to any state without creating other inequalities. The mere fact that counties were not created or laid out with any specific reference to their adaptability to school district organization is sufficient to make one skeptical of the county unit as the ultimate solution of the school problem. Glance at a map of Minnesota and note the outline of the counties and observe that many children whose homes are in one county live nearer the schools in neighboring counties. Review the wealth status of the counties and observe the marked variation in taxable resources available in the different sections of the state. The highways of Minnesota are so located that economy and efficiency in school administration may require the complete disregard of county boundaries in certain areas.

The solution of the school district problem is vital to the welfare of the schools of the state and no step should be taken that may lead in time to a backward movement. If considerable flexibility in the organization is made possible, then the most desirable ultimate plan might be produced through a factual demonstration. For example, for experimental purposes, provide for a number of county districts, permit other districts to operate as at present, combine the small districts in a third group of counties, and formulate a fourth group of school districts on the basis of a careful study of local resources and local needs, disregarding the county and municipal boundaries as necessary. Allow these various plans to operate over a period of years under intelligent observation and direction and then determine from the facts the kind of school district that does serve the children, the public at large, and the taxpayers most satisfactorily and economically. Such a project might readily be initiated and supported by the legislature and might be directed by a committee representing this body, the State Department of Education, and selected citizens of the state.

The following principles are suggested as worthy of consideration in any movement projected to improve the public schools. In recording these principles it is fully appreciated that it may not be possible or practicable to put each one into full operation because of existing conditions. Yet the more closely the following principles are approximated the more efficient will be the schools:

No school district should be created in which the minimum educational program accepted for the state cannot be economically operated. In other words the area included in a school district must have a school population sufficient to warrant the establishment of a complete and efficient school organization including four years of high school work.

No school district that does not warrant the employment of a full-time, properly qualified superintendent should be created.

A school district should have resources sufficient to support the minimum program of education without special assistance from the state other than that derived from state funds allowed for general state-wide equalization and for transportation.

School district boundaries should be flexible, in order that school districts may be readily expanded or modified to meet changing economic and educational conditions.

As long as small local school districts exist, some plan of equalizing the burden of support throughout the state must be maintained. The simplest plan to adopt when a satisfactory school district unit is created is to require all districts to tax themselves uniformly on some equal basis and to require these districts to maintain a minimum program of schooling. The most fortunate school districts as measured in taxable resources should receive no state money. The other districts should share directly in an equalization fund of the state to the extent that the local tax revenue falls short of the amount needed to support the minimum required program. Each district should be free to support wholly out of local revenues the part of the educational program that extends beyond the minimum requirements.

There are many public leaders interested in public schools who believe that the old order cannot be changed, and they are of the opinion that the forces that have perpetuated the present school district organization cannot be dislodged. It is true that prejudices that hold sway cannot be jolted loose unless an intelligent plan for public enlightenment is conducted for a time sufficient to produce public support for that which is desirable. It may take a decade or two to bring about the desired change in public attitude. If this be the case, why not begin planning now?

CHAPTER 15

THE STATE INCOME TAX

The Minnesota legislature of 1931 authorized a referendum upon a proposed income tax amendment to the state constitution at the general election of 1932.[1] On February 17, 1931, while the legislature was in session, Attorney-General Benson rendered an official opinion that a graduated progressive tax on incomes would be constitutional even without an amendment. Soon after, a bill to provide for such a tax at once was introduced in both houses of the legislature. It occasioned much discussion among the members of that body and throughout the state but did not get very far along the legislative path.

The bill to submit a constitutional amendment was passed, however. It was supported by those favoring the first bill as well as by some who questioned the correctness of the attorney-general's opinion. Possibly others favored submission in order to evade responsibility or to defeat or postpone such a tax, but some opposed the proposed amendment because it did not impose more restrictions upon the legislature.

At any rate, a state income tax is now and may continue to be one of the most prominent issues before the people of the state. If the amendment is adopted, the framing and passing of a law will be among the most important matters before the next legislature. Even if the amendment fails at the 1932 election, in which so many local, state, and national issues and personalities are involved, some income tax bill is likely to be before future legisla-

[1] Legal action was brought to restrain the secretary of state from putting the tax amendment on the ballot. It was claimed that this amendment covered three questions, whereas the Constitution permits the submission of only one question in a single amendment. *Minneapolis Tribune,* August 20, 1932, p. 1. The Minnesota Supreme Court dismissed this action. Winget v. Holm, September 23, 1932.

The proposed amendment reads as follows: "The legislature may enact any law required to make the taxation of national banking associations conform to the laws of the United States. Taxes may be imposed upon incomes and on franchises measured by income, including income, franchises and privileges of railroad companies, which may be classified, and which taxes may be graduated and progressive, and the legislature may prescribe reasonable exemptions, and such taxes may be in lieu, in whole or in part, of taxes on any class or classes of real or personal property as the legislature may determine. It shall not be necessary to submit to a vote of the people any law imposing a tax upon the income, franchises or privileges of railroad companies. Any and all provisions of the constitution of this state inconsistent herewith are hereby repealed."

tures until the question is definitely settled. It therefore behooves every citizen of the state to inform himself about such taxes in order that he may understand the issues in controversy and that Minnesota may profit by the experience of other states.

GROWTH OF THE INCOME TAX MOVEMENT

The gradual but continuous spread of the income tax, especially among the industrial states and nations, is one of the most significant developments of recent times. This is not a new form of tax. In fact, it has been employed in various parts of the world for centuries. In this country more or less use has been made of it for almost three hundred years. Our federal government first employed a comprehensive income tax during the Civil War. But during most of our history this method of taxation has been overshadowed, if not displaced, by other taxes in both national and state jurisdictions.

During the past two decades, however, there has been a great revival of income taxes in the United States, as there was in Europe about eighty-five years ago. Shortly before the late World War the federal government again resorted to the income tax and was able to raise far more revenue from this source than from all other taxes combined. The exceptional value of an income tax in an emergency as well as in normal times has also been forcibly demonstrated abroad. There it has become an accepted feature of national tax systems, as it has apparently with our own federal government.

Today half [2] the states in the Union have income taxes and the trend toward such taxes is unmistakable. The movement has gained unusual momentum during the past four years. At the beginning of 1929 only fifteen states had income taxes. During that year the legislatures of five more states passed income tax statutes, thus increasing the number of states having such laws by one-third. In no other single year has so large a number of states adopted this method of taxation. During the current biennium (1931–1932) five more states have adopted income taxes and seven others have extended the operation of existing laws.[2]

The modern state income tax movement in the United States was initiated by Wisconsin, where the tax was finally established

[2] Arkansas, California, Georgia, Oregon, and Washington adopted income taxes in 1929; Idaho, Ohio, Utah, and Vermont in 1931; and Illinois in 1932. The Washington law was declared unconstitutional in 1930 because its classifications were held violative of the equal-protection clause of the Fourteenth Amendment. The Illinois Supreme Court held the Illinois law unconstitutional just before this chapter went to press. See footnote to Table 3 on page 479.

FIGURE 1.—STATES HAVING INCOME TAXES

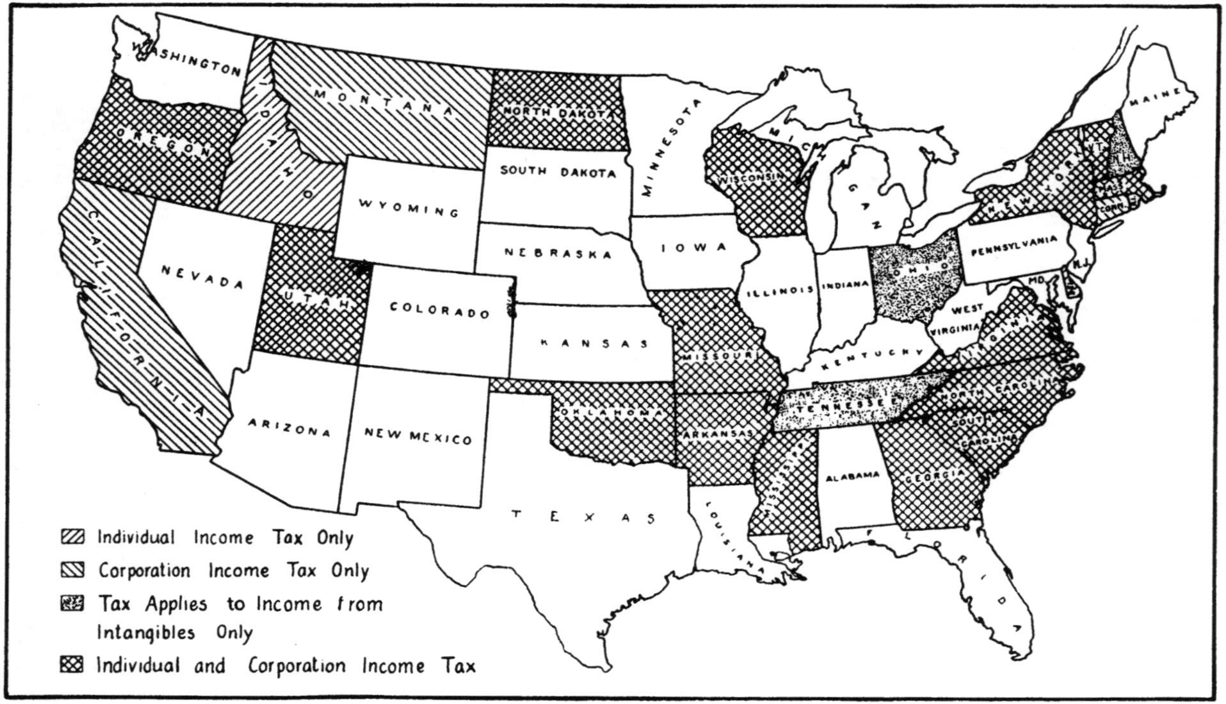

in 1911 after a decade of struggle. It is true that several states, notably Massachusetts, Virginia, and North Carolina, had had income taxes for many years prior to that date, but all these taxes had become relatively insignificant under faulty administration, and in most cases they had degenerated into almost or quite complete failures. Several other states had attempted to impose income taxes prior to 1911 but because of ineffective administration they were about as futile as are the intangible personal property taxes of various states today. It was only after Wisconsin showed what could be done with a modern, centralized, relatively nonpolitical administration that the revival of state income taxes really got under way.

The movement was rather slow at first. Naturally the experience in Wisconsin was watched closely for several years and with many doubts as to the outcome. Had not such taxes always failed before? Had not administrators and economists proved that such taxes could not succeed in America? But Wisconsin's convincing experience, together with the universal need for greater revenues, led other states to try the income tax. This stage of the movement reached its climax in 1917, when four states, Delaware, Massachusetts, Missouri, and Montana, established income taxes. New York and North Dakota followed in 1919.

In the decade following the war there was much agitation against the heavy federal income and excess profits taxes, and the movement for state income taxes was checked. It is true that in this period the Carolinas changed over from the old unsuccessful type to the more modern form and that New Hampshire adopted a very incomplete income tax. But in the five-year period from 1924 to 1929 not a single state was added to the number having income taxes.

With ten states adopting this type of tax from 1929 to 1932 and with various others considering it, it seems that the movement has again got under way. The recent extraordinary increases in federal tax rates will doubtless affect state legislation, but "it appears to be the consensus of opinion of students of taxation that taxation on the basis of net income will spread among the states as did the inheritance tax."[3] Figure 1 shows which states have income taxes at present.

The motives influencing state legislatures to adopt income taxes,

[3] National Industrial Conference Board, *State Income Taxes* (1930), 2:97.

as listed by the National Industrial Conference Board,[4] are as follows: (1) to tap a new source of revenue; (2) to equalize the burden between property-owning and non-property-owning classes having taxpaying ability; (3) to introduce a more accurate method of ascertaining taxpaying ability; (4) to reach incomes from intangibles escaping property taxes; (5) to introduce a convenient progressive element into the tax system; (6) to tax national banks in compliance with federal statutes; and (7) to reach income from property difficult to reach because of federal laws. Relief to owners of real estate has probably been uppermost in the minds of many advocates of the tax in Minnesota and elsewhere. The present plight of real estate following the extreme price deflation and mounting tax burden is known to all. This serious situation has been shown in some detail in preceding chapters, particularly in Chapters 3 to 7.

CHIEF FEATURES OF STATE INCOME TAXES

What Income is Taxed

In general the states follow the federal government's concept and definition of income, though there are many differences in details. Net income is usually arrived at by deducting expenses of production from gross income. Losses from bad debts, fires, and so forth, are usually deductible. Loss from estimated depreciation is usually an allowable deduction, though appreciation is not included as taxable income until "realized" by sale or otherwise, that is, capital net gains are usually considered as income when "realized" but not before. Rental values of houses occupied by owners and many other valuable usances and services are not included in taxable income, which is usually thought of as money income or its equivalent. Gifts and bequests are not usually included. Personal and other exemptions are commonly subtracted from net income to arrive at taxable income.

Of the twenty-four* income tax states, sixteen now tax both individual and corporate incomes. Five* — Delaware, Idaho, Illinois, New Hampshire, and Ohio — tax individuals only; and three — California, Connecticut, and Montana — corporations only. The income taxes of New Hampshire and Ohio are quite restricted, being applicable to the income from certain investments or intangibles only. Tennessee passed a new law in 1931 to make its tax apply to

[4] *Ibid.*, p. 171.

* One less since the Illinois decision. See note to Table 3 below.

incomes generally rather than to those from intangibles only, but the new law is now in the courts and is not being enforced.[5]

In Massachusetts the tax is levied only on certain kinds of income. It applies to income from annuities, professions, employments, trade, and business (rate, 1.5 per cent); to net gains from dealings in intangible personal property, such as stocks and bonds (rate, 3 per cent); and to interest and dividends (rate, 6 per cent). The theory in Massachusetts is that the income tax is a substitute or supplementary tax rather than an additional tax on the same base; that is, the aim has been to reach income that is not reached by the property tax or other taxes and to exempt from this tax much of the income that is reached by other taxes.

In Wisconsin the aim is to tax all income arising within the state, irrespective of the residence of the recipient and of whether property yielding income is already taxed under the property tax. In New York the attempt is to tax all the income of residents, regardless of whether it originates in that state or elsewhere and to tax also nonresidents on income derived from property and occupations within the state. Eight other states[6] follow the practice of New York, and four[7] tax residents on their entire income from within and without the state. The income from intangibles is generally presumed to follow the domicile of the owner.[8]

In New York corporate income is again taxed under the individual income tax when it is received in the form of dividends. The New York practice follows the recommendation of the National Tax Association "model" income tax in this respect. Most states that apply the income tax to corporations do not again tax the dividends of domestic corporations in the hands of individuals. A number of states exercise reciprocity with respect to the taxing of dividends of foreign corporations.[9]

[5] Since this chapter was written the *New York Times* (July 24, 1932) reports that the Tennessee Supreme Court "ruled that since the Tennessee Constitution specifically empowered the legislature to levy a tax on the income derived from stocks, and bonds 'not' taxed ad valorem, 'the necessary inference and logical deduction followed that no other income tax could be levied.' "

[6] Arkansas, Idaho, Illinois, Mississippi, Missouri, North Carolina, North Dakota, and Tennessee, but see the first note to Table 8 below.

[7] Delaware, Georgia, Utah, and Virginia.

[8] Henry Rottschaefer, "Power of the State to Tax Intangibles," *Minnesota Law Review*, 15:741 (June, 1931).

[9] For example, corporations chartered by state A may do business in A, B, and various other states. Likewise corporations chartered in B may do business in A, as well as in other states. A may agree that, when it calculates the income taxes due on incomes made in A by corporations from B, it will make allowance for income taxes assessed on the same corporations by B if B will do similarly when

In several states the taxes on corporations are technically excise or franchise taxes measured by income rather than income taxes, and they do not apply to the incomes of all corporations in every state. It is noteworthy that the difficulties of taxing national banks since the recent United States Supreme Court decisions had much to do with the adoption of the corporation franchise or income taxes in the three Pacific Coast states in 1929.

Rates of Taxation

INDIVIDUAL INCOMES

Nearly all states graduate the rates of taxes applying to the incomes of individuals but apply flat or ungraduated rates to incomes of corporations. The rates on individuals usually start at 1 per cent and rise by steps of 1 per cent or half of 1 per cent until they reach maximums of 4, 5, or 6 per cent. (See Table 3 on page 478 and Figure 2.)

For years Missouri was exceptional in having an ungraduated or flat rate of 1 per cent only, but in 1931 a graduated system was adopted with a 2 per cent minimum. New Hampshire and Ohio have flat rates, but their taxes apply to incomes from intangibles only; New Hampshire's rate is peculiar in that it is the same as the property tax rate; Ohio's rate is 5 per cent. Tennessee also had a flat rate of 5 per cent on intangibles only, prior to the adoption of a general income tax with graduated rates in 1931. The latter has been held unconstitutional and is not being enforced pending appeal to higher courts.[10] Oregon's new rate on income from intangibles is 8 per cent.

Though the most common minimum rate is 1 per cent, several states start with 2 per cent. The maximum is commonly 5 per cent, but five states now have maximums of 6 per cent and Wisconsin's is even higher. Wisconsin's rates were increased in 1931 so that the "normal" schedule reaches 7 per cent upon incomes in excess of $12,000. On incomes in excess of $3,000 there is, in addition, a surtax of one-sixth of the normal tax. The combined maximum is, therefore, 8⅙ per cent on incomes in excess of $12,000. Furthermore, a special session of the 1931 legislature enacted an emergency tax for unemployment relief applicable to the income of one year only. This emergency tax applies to the 1931 current incomes of

calculating income taxes that it collects on corporations from A when doing business in B.

[10] See note 5.

FIGURE 2.—COMPARISON OF MAXIMUM AND MINIMUM INCOME TAX RATES IN DIFFERENT STATES, 1932[a]

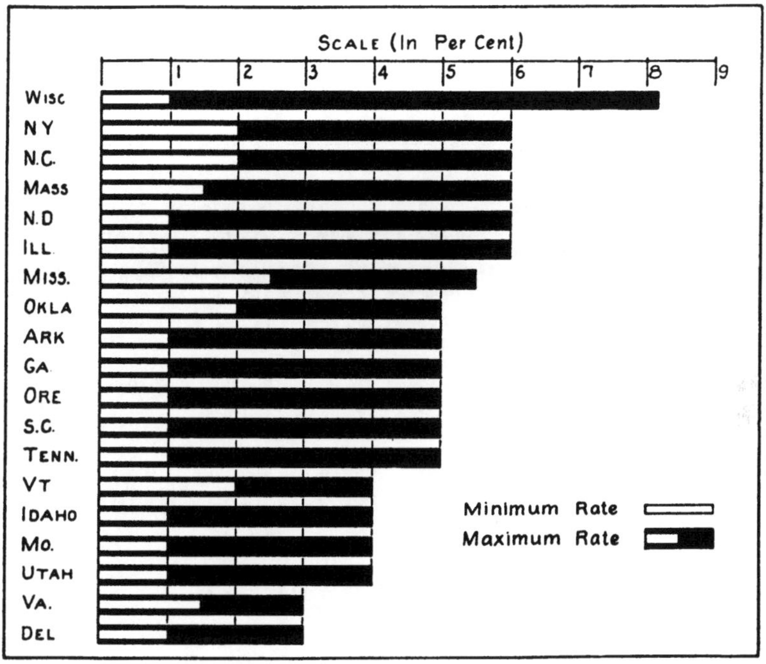

[a] Wisconsin's special unemployment relief surtax, in effect for one year only, is not included. See Tables 3 and 32 below.

individuals only, not to corporation incomes; dividends are included, but capital gains and losses are disregarded. This means that for one year the parts of individual incomes that are in excess of $12,000 are subject to a tax of 15⅙ per cent.

During the past winter New York doubled her income tax rates temporarily (for two years) to raise funds for unemployment relief. Many other states, as well as the federal government, raised their income tax rates in 1931 and 1932. They and the five new states adopting income taxes have doubtless been strongly influenced by the current depression. Wisconsin has levied surtaxes of different amounts on various occasions in the past when in need of additional revenues for special purposes, such as soldiers' bonuses and teachers' pensions. It has thus avoided borrowing when other states have not.

Income tax rates in Massachusetts are not graduated according to amount but are differentiated according to kinds of taxable in-

TABLE 1.—AMOUNT OF STATE INCOME TAX PAID BY SINGLE PERSONS ON INCOMES OF VARIOUS SIZES, 1932

STATE	AMOUNT OF NET INCOME BEFORE DEDUCTING PERSONAL EXEMPTIONS					
	$3,000	$5,000	$10,000	$25,000	$50,000	$100,000
Arkansas	$15.00	$40.00	$165.00	$740.00	$1,975.00	$4,475.00
Delaware	20.00	50.00	150.00	590.00	1,340.00	2,840.00
Georgia	15.00	35.00	120.00	675.00	1,925.00	4,425.00
Idaho	20.00	60.00	240.00	840.00	1,840.00	3,840.00
Illinois *	30.00	70.00	220.00	900.00	2,390.00	5,390.00
Mississippi	37.50	102.50	312.50	1,072.50	2,447.50	5,197.50
Missouri	25.00	70.00	225.00	825.00	1,825.00	3,825.00
New York [a]	10.00	50.00	150.00	700.00	1,700.00	4,650.00
North Carolina	40.00	100.00	335.00	1,230.00	2,730.00	5,730.00
North Dakota	20.00	60.00	250.00	1,140.00	2,640.00	5,640.00
Oklahoma	45.00	85.00	195.00	670.00	1,670.00	3,670.00
Oregon [b]	20.00	80.00	325.00	1,075.00	2,325.00	4,825.00
South Carolina	18.00	56.00	240.00	990.00	2,240.00	4,740.00
Tennessee [c]	15.00	40.00	137.50	775.00	2,025.00	4,525.00
Utah [d]	22.50	55.00	205.00	805.00	1,805.00	3,805.00
Vermont [b]	40.00	80.00	180.00	480.00	980.00	1,980.00
Virginia	26.25	63.75	207.50	657.50	1,407.50	2,907.50
Wisconsin [e]	29.50	80.67	314.00	1,509.83	3,551.50	7,634.83
	29.50	74.50	274.50	1,299.50	3,049.50	6,549.50

* See footnote to Table 3 below.

[a] Rates for 1931 and 1932 incomes. See page 473.

[b] Exclusive of the tax on intangibles.

[c] New part of Tennessee law not in operation, pending court decision. See page 471.

[d] Filing fee of $1.00 not included. See page 483.

[e] The first line is the regular income tax (normal and surtaxes); the second line gives the emergency tax for unemployment relief, authorized for one year only.

come, as indicated on page 471. This unique practice was imitated by Vermont in 1931, when it provided an ungraduated rate of 2 per cent upon income from business and one of 4 per cent upon income from intangibles.

The rates of taxes in the various states cannot be compared intelligently without considering exemptions and also the brackets to which the several rates apply. Moderate rates with small exemptions, especially if the tax is well administered, may raise as much revenue as a schedule with high maximum rates applicable only to very large incomes. It is the combination of all factors that counts. Tables 1 and 2 and Figures 3 and 4 have been prepared to show the comparative income tax burdens in the several states for a few incomes of different sizes. It will be observed that the Wisconsin tax, not including the one-year emergency surtax, is heavier than that of any other state for most incomes shown, although for single persons with incomes of $10,000 or less the tax of North

TABLE 2.—AMOUNT OF STATE INCOME TAX PAID BY A HUSBAND, WIFE, AND TWO DEPENDENTS ON INCOMES OF VARIOUS SIZES, 1932

STATE	AMOUNT OF NET INCOME BEFORE DEDUCTING PERSONAL EXEMPTIONS					
	$3,000	$5,000	$10,000	$25,000	$50,000	$100,000
Arkansas	..	$17.00	$111.00	$668.00	$1,885.00	$4,385.00
Delaware	$6	26.00	122.00	548.00	1,298.00	2,798.00
Georgia	..	7.00	64.00	535.00	1,785.00	4,285.00
Idaho	..	19.00	156.00	756.00	1,756.00	3,756.00
Illinois *	..	28.00	157.00	795.00	2,264.00	5,264.00
Mississippi	6	17.50	186.50	918.50	2,293.50	5,043.50
Missouri	6	37.00	176.00	769.00	1,769.00	3,769.00
New York [a]	..	4.00	104.00	608.00	1,608.00	4,512.00
North Carolina	12	58.00	260.00	1,146.00	2,646.00	5,646.00
North Dakota	4	28.00	176.00	1,044.00	2,544.00	5,544.00
Oklahoma	..	40.00	160.00	580.00	1,580.00	3,580.00
Oregon [b]	..	24.00	235.00	985.00	2,235.00	4,735.00
South Carolina	..	20.00	160.00	900.00	2,150.00	4,650.00
Tennessee [c]	..	19.00	100.50	695.00	1,945.00	4,445.00
Utah [d]	2	25.50	137.00	733.00	1,733.00	3,733.00
Vermont [b]	10	50.00	150.00	450.00	950.00	1,950.00
Virginia	..	21.00	137.00	587.00	1,337.00	2,837.00
Wisconsin [e]	12	60.25	293.59	1,489.42	3,531.09	7,614.42
	8	53.00	253.00	1,278.00	3,028.00	6,528.00

* See footnote to Table 3 below.

[a] Rates for 1931 and 1932 incomes. See page 473.

[b] Exclusive of the tax on intangibles.

[c] Tennessee law not in operation, pending court decision. See footnote 5 on page 471.

[d] Filing fee of $1.00 not included. See page 483.

[e] The first line is the regular income tax (normal and surtaxes); the second line gives the emergency tax for unemployment relief, authorized for one year only.

Carolina exceeds that of Wisconsin, and the taxes of Oregon and Mississippi exceed Wisconsin's for some incomes. With the emergency tax added, Wisconsin's income tax far exceeds that of any other state on all except the smallest taxable incomes.

CORPORATION INCOMES

In the case of taxes on corporation incomes, all states except Wisconsin and Mississippi had flat rates prior to 1931. In that year Oklahoma's revised law and Idaho's new law applied the same graduated rates to corporate as to individual incomes.

The flat rates of different states vary from 1 per cent in Montana to 6 per cent on certain kinds of income in Massachusetts, excluding the 8 per cent rate of Oregon, which applies to income from intangibles only. The graduated rates in Mississippi begin at 2.5 per cent and rise to 5.5 per cent; in Wisconsin they begin at 2 per cent and increase to 6 per cent on the excess above $6,000,

FIGURE 3. — COMPARISON OF TAXES PAYABLE ON INDIVIDUAL NET INCOMES OF $3,000 AND $5,000 IN DIFFERENT STATES, 1932

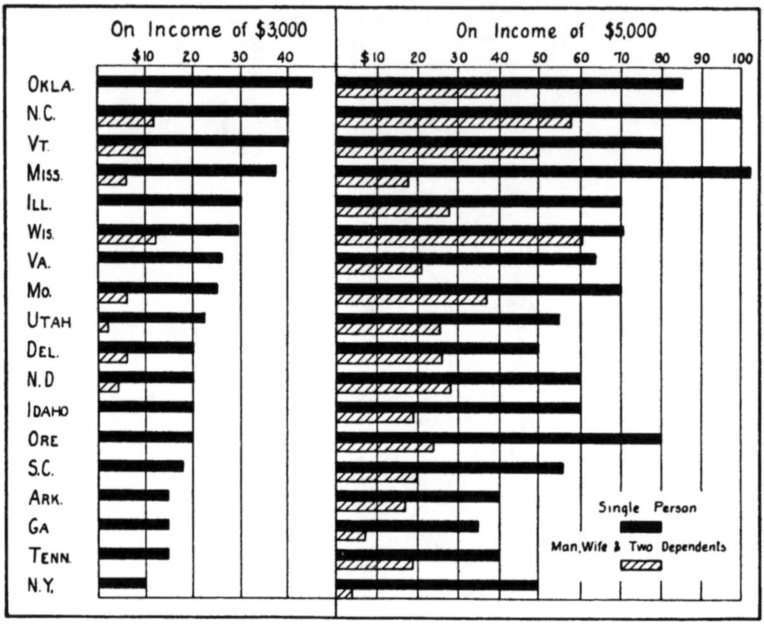

See Tables 3 and 32 of this chapter.

and in addition there is a surtax of one-sixth of the regular rates upon corporate incomes in excess of $3,000. This makes the maximum rate 7 per cent upon corporate incomes in excess of $6,000.

It is generally agreed that income tax rates are elastic or flexible; that is, they can be changed to meet changing needs for revenue perhaps as easily as rates of any kind of tax, and with as few bad effects. The experience of Great Britain and of our own national government in changing rates to meet varying needs is well known. The experience of Wisconsin, New York, North Carolina, and other states is also confirmatory of this elasticity. This feature of the income tax commends it to state officials who are concerned about adequate revenue; it may condemn the tax in the minds of taxpayers fearing higher levies.

PERSONAL EXEMPTIONS

The committee appointed by the National Tax Association in 1917 to prepare a plan for a model system of state and local taxation recommended that maximum personal exemptions should not exceed $600 for a single person, $1,200 for a husband and wife, and

FIGURE 4. — COMPARISON OF TAXES PAYABLE ON INDIVIDUAL NET INCOMES OF $25,000 AND $100,000 IN DIFFERENT STATES, 1932

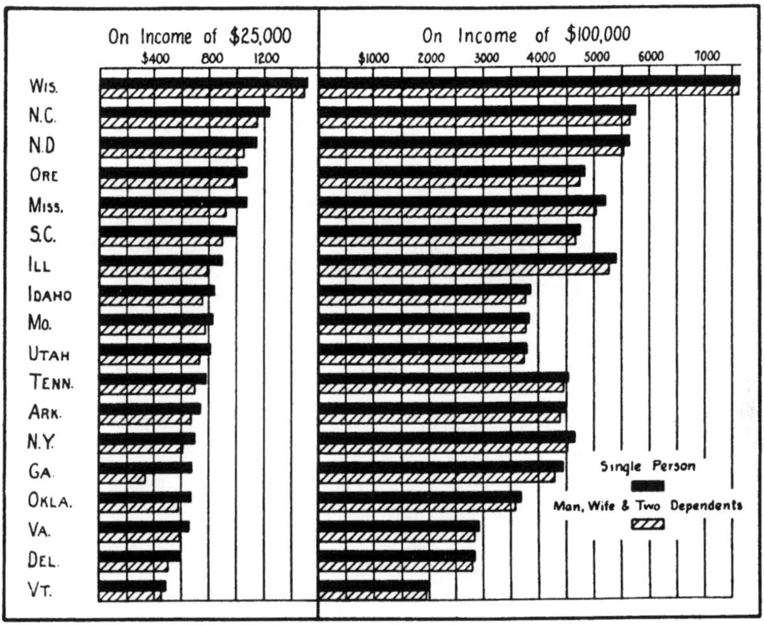

See Tables 3 and 32 of this chapter.

$200 for each dependent up to three. This meant a maximum of $1,800 for any family however large, and the committee suggested that some states might well have lower maximums than those named.[11] With the higher levels of prices and incomes following the war, these recommendations were changed in 1920 to $1,000, $2,000, and $200 for single person, husband and wife, and dependent, respectively.

Of twenty-one states* now taxing individual incomes, all but Ohio grant personal exemptions. This absence of exemption in Ohio and the small exemption in New Hampshire ($200) are to be ex-

[11] Proceedings of the National Tax Association, 1919, pp. 426–470; 1920, p. 277; 1922, p. 297; Bulletin, 6:105 (January, 1921). The National Tax Association and its committees have wielded the dominant influence in the improvement of American state and local taxation in the quarter of a century since it was founded. It holds annual conferences at which scholarly papers and reports of committees are given by well-qualified tax authorities and administrators. The proceedings of the Association are published annually, a bulletin is published monthly, and other important publications are issued from time to time. They may be obtained by writing the Association at 195 Broadway, New York City, or at Columbia, South Carolina. No other association in the tax field is comparable to this one; it is not a propaganda organization as are so many state and local associations.

* See footnote to Table 3 below.

TABLE 3.—EXEMPTIONS AND RATES OF STATE TAXES ON INDIVIDUAL INCOMES, 1932[a]

State	Tax Adopted	Personal Exemptions				Rates			
		Single Person	Head of Family	For Dependent	Fiduciary[b]	Minimum Tax Rate (Per Cent)	First Bracket of Income	Maximum Tax Rate (Per Cent)	Last Bracket of Income Begins at
Arkansas	1929	$1,500	$2,500	$400	$1,500	1	$3,000	5	$25,000
Delaware	1917	1,000	2,000	200	1,000	1	3,000	3	10,000
Georgia	1929	1,500	3,500	400	1,500	1	5,000	5	20,000
Idaho	1931	1,000	2,500	300	1,000	1	2,000	4	6,000
Illinois *	1932	1,000	2,500	300	1,000	1	1,000	6	25,000
Massachusetts[c]	1916	2,000	2,500	250	....	1.5	....	6	.....
Mississippi	1912	1,500	3,500	400	1,500	2.5	2,000	5.5	15,000
Missouri	1917	1,000	2,000	200	1,000	1	1,000	4	9,000
New Hampshire[d]	1923	200	200	...	200	..	....	..	.....
New York	1919	2,500	4,000	400	2,500	2	10,000	6	50,000
North Carolina	1921	1,000	2,000	200	1,000[e]	2	2,000	6	10,000
North Dakota	1919	1,000	2,000	300	1,000	1	2,000	6	10,000
Ohio[f]	1931	....	....	...	....	5	....	..	.....
Oklahoma	1915	750	1,500	750	No provision	2	10,000	5	100,000
Oregon	1930	1,500	2,500	400	1,500	1	1,000	5	4,000
South Carolina	1922	1,200	2,200	400	1,200	1	2,000	5	8,000
Tennessee[g]	1930	1,500	2,500	300	1,200	1	2,500	5	15,000
Utah	1931	1,000	2,000	400	1,000	1	1,000	4	8,000
Vermont[h]	1931	1,000	2,000	250	1,000	2[i]	....	4[j]	.....
Virginia	1843	1,250	2,800	400	1,250	1.5	3,000	3	5,000
Wisconsin[k]	1911	$8 of tax	$17.50 of tax	$4 of tax	....[l]	1	1,000	7	12,000

Footnotes to Table 3

[*] On October 22, 1932, just before this chapter went to press, the Illinois law providing for a graduated tax on the incomes of individuals was held unconstitutional (Bachrach v. Nelson, Illinois Supreme Court, No. 21470). The court held that income from property is also property and that the state constitution requires that all taxes on property must be levied according to valuation rather than "by graduation." *United States Daily,* October 26, 1932, p. 4. It is not feasible to revise all references to the Illinois tax in the text, tables, and illustrative charts throughout this study. This decision leaves 23 income tax states; 16 tax both individual and corporate income; 4 tax individual incomes only; and 3 tax corporate incomes only. See map, Figure 1.

[a] For fuller data see Table 32 on page 535.

[b] For the details as to kind of income taxable see *Federal and State Tax Systems, 1932,* p. 132, a study prepared under the direction of the New York State Tax Commission.

[c] On income from intangibles an exemption of $1,000 is allowed if the total income does not exceed $1,000 or if the income of husband and wife does not exceed $1,500. Exemptions here apply to earnings from trade, professions, and business. The 1.5 per cent rate applies to earnings; the 6 per cent to income from interest and dividends; the 3 per cent to profits from the sale of intangibles. There is no graduation of rates according to amount of income.

[d] Income from intangibles taxed at average property tax rate; no graduation; no personal exemption.

[e] Personal exemption and $1,000 to surviving spouse. *Federal and State Tax Systems, 1932,* p. 129.

[f] Applies to income from investments only. No exemptions allowed; no graduation of rates.

[g] Amendments of 1931 included herein held unconstitutional by state Supreme Court, July 23, 1932. See note 5.

[h] These are exemptions applicable to business income. In the case of a taxpayer having an income from intangibles only, a single person is allowed an exemption of $400 and the head of a family $800.

[i] Applies to income from business, trade, or professions.

[j] Applies to income from intangibles only.

[k] The normal maximum rate is 7 per cent. A surtax of 1/6 of normal rates applies to taxable incomes in excess of $3,000, making the rate 8 1/6 per cent on such excess. There is in addition an emergency unemployment relief surtax at normal rates on all taxable income for the year 1931. In other words, incomes in excess of $3,000 are subject to 8 1/6 per cent and, for the one year of 1931, to 7 per cent additional for special relief purposes (a total of 15 1/6 per cent on the excess over $3,000). On 1932 and later incomes the total of maximum rates returns to 8 1/6 per cent unless there is new legislation in the meantime. The emergency tax credit for dependents is $6.00 instead of $4.00.

[l] Taxable on net income received during income year by deceased resident individual, allowing first a personal exemption of the amount that would have been allowed deceased had he lived; and on entire net income of resident wards and insolvent or incompetent individuals where fiduciary has complete charge of such income, first allowing an exemption equal to that which beneficiary would have been entitled.

plained by the fact that the taxes in these two states are not general income taxes but apply to incomes from investments only. The exemption schedules of Massachusetts and Wisconsin are peculiar and not easily comparable with those of other states.[12] A large proportion of the remaining states conform approximately to the later recommendations of the National Tax Association committee, though there is a pronounced tendency on the part of more than half the group to exceed these standards. This is less noticeable with respect to exemptions for single persons than for others. (See Tables 3, 4, and 32 and Figure 5.)

TABLE 4.—PERSONAL EXEMPTIONS FROM STATE INCOME TAXES IN NINETEEN STATES, 1932[a]

Single Person		Husband and Wife, or Head of Family		For Each Dependent		Fiduciary	
Amount	No. of States	Amount	No. of States	Amount	No. of States	Amount	No. of States
$0	1	$0	1	$0	2	$0	2
200	1	200	1	200	3	200	1
750	1	1,500	1	250	1	1,000	8
1,000	8	2,000	6	300	4	1,200	2
1,200	1	2,200	1	400	8	1,250	1
1,250	1	2,500	5	750	1	1,500	4
1,500	5	2,800	1			2,500	1
2,500	1	3,500	2				
		4,000	1				

[a] Three states tax the incomes of corporations only. Two others, Massachusetts and Wisconsin, are not included in these tables because of peculiarities explained in the text, page 482. See Tables 3 and 32, including footnotes.

The most common exemption for a single person is $1,000 or $1,500; for a husband and wife or head of a family, $2,000 or $2,500; for a dependent, $400 or $300. Exemptions for guardians, trustees, and other fiduciaries are usually the same as for single persons, though there are more irregularities in all groups than can be shown in simple summary tables and charts.

Oklahoma's unusually high exemption for dependents is the result of radical changes enacted in 1931, though the net result is not so great a change for large families as might appear.[13] The present law provides for exemptions of $750, $1,500, and $750 for a single person, head of family, and dependent, respectively. In the preceding law the exemptions were $3,000, $4,000, and $300 for a single

[12] Explained on page 482.
[13] A referendum on other important changes is to be held this year.

FIGURE 5.—COMPARISON OF PERSONAL EXEMPTIONS ALLOWED INDIVIDUALS IN DIFFERENT STATES, 1932

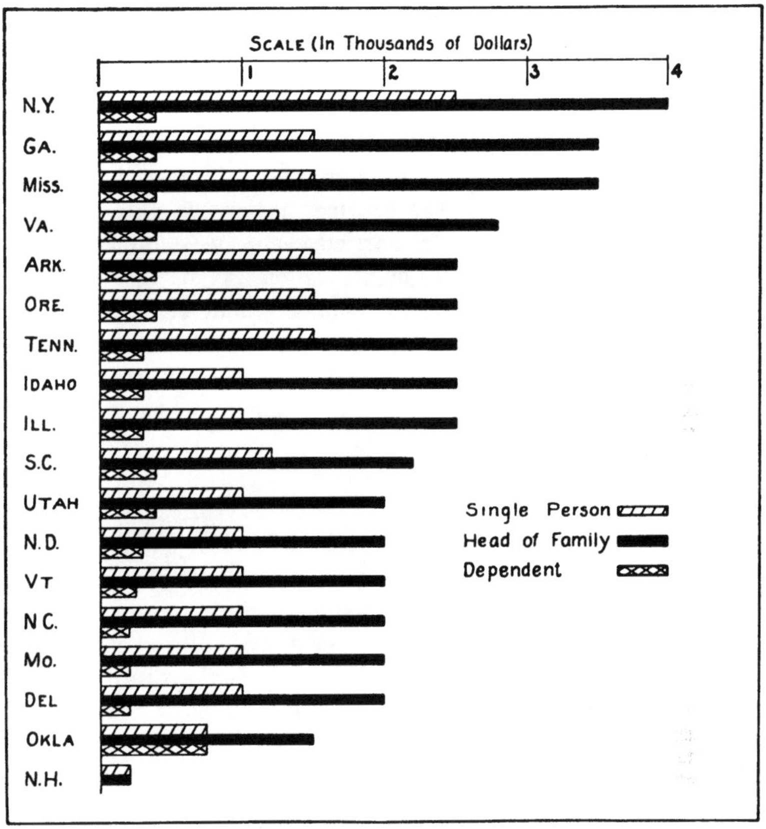

See Tables 3, 4, and 32, including footnotes.

person, head of family, and child under eighteen, respectively. For a dependent acquiring an education $500 was allowed; and $200 each was permitted for other dependents.

New York's exemptions are unusually large. For a number of years this state maintained the same personal exemptions as the federal government, changing them with each change in the federal statute. In 1929, however, the exemptions were increased to $2,500, $4,000, and $400, substantially above the federal figures of $1,500, $3,500, and $400.[14] In 1932 the New York State Commission for the Revision of Tax Laws recommended reduction to $1,500, $2,500,

[14] Under pressure of the fiscal emergency the federal exemptions were reduced in the law of June 6, 1932, to $1,000, $2,500, and $400 for a single person, head of family, and dependent, respectively.

and $200, and the imposition of a $2.00 filing fee for all persons with a gross income of $500 or more.

Massachusetts' exemptions are peculiar to its differentiated income tax system. Not everyone is allowed an exemption, and the amounts allowed depend upon the kind and amount of income. In the case of income derived from professions, employments, trade, or business $2,000 may be exempted; in the case of interest, dividends, or annuities $1,000 may be exempted if received by a person whose total income from all sources does not exceed $1,000, but this exemption does not apply to a married person if combined incomes of husband and wife exceed $1,500.

Vermont has a hybrid system, following that of Massachusetts in part and the usual system in part. Its main exemptions apply to business incomes only, but taxpayers having income from intangibles only are allowed $400 each ($800 for the head of a family).

In its first income tax law (1911) Wisconsin allowed an unmarried individual an exemption of $800 a year, a husband and wife $1,200, and dependents $200 each. But now Wisconsin allows "rebates" in terms of taxes rather than exemptions of income. The tax is computed on all taxable income without exemptions, and then $8.00 is deducted for a single person, $17.50 for a head of a family, and $4.00 for each dependent.[15] Thus the total deduction for a family with two dependents is $25.50. This is equivalent to permitting an exemption of $2,550 in terms of income if one's taxable income is such that the upper $2,550 of it falls in a bracket that is taxed at 1 per cent. But if one's income is of sufficient amount so that the upper $2,550 of it falls in a bracket that is taxed, say 6 per cent, the usual income exemption method employed by other states would permit a reduction in taxes of 6 per cent of $2,550, or $153, instead of only $25.50 as permitted under the Wisconsin method of rebates.[16] Under the usual income exemp-

[15] In the case of the special relief surtax for the one year, 1931, $6.00 is allowed for each dependent.

[16] In other words, if $2,550 in income is deducted from an individual's income before beginning to calculate the tax, that deduction reduces the amount taxable in the highest bracket to which the highest rate of tax applies. If the highest bracket is taxed 6 per cent, the taxpayer gets a reduction of 6 per cent of the amount falling in that bracket, but if his income is so small that the highest part of his income reaches only the bracket taxed at 2 per cent, he gets a reduction in taxes equal to 2 per cent upon the amount falling in that bracket. Under the Wisconsin method of exemption in terms of tax instead of in terms of income, the amount of the exemption is always the same regardless of the amount of the income, that is, if the total income tax is as much as the total amount of the exemption permitted.

tion method the largest income recipients get the largest tax reductions, if rates are progressive; under the Wisconsin method all recipients of incomes entitled to the full rebate get the same rebate regardless of the size of their incomes. Of course, one whose income tax does not equal the full amount of the possible rebate gets a reduction equal to his tax only. It is obvious that the Wisconsin system results in greater revenues to the state, particularly where there are many large incomes and the rates of tax are steeply graduated.

The main considerations in determining the proper amounts of personal exemptions are cost of living, revenue requirements, administrative expediency, and general public policy. Almost everyone would agree that a minimum of subsistence should be exempted. Many would leave untaxed a standard of living much higher than this minimum, how much higher depending upon the balancing of all considerations. Large exemptions obviously reduce revenue, but they greatly simplify administration. The expense of collecting taxes on the many small incomes at the base of the income pyramid is out of proportion to the revenue received. This is particularly true if a state is to build on a firm foundation by checking returns sufficiently well to prevent much evasion. It is much better never to let evasion develop on a big scale than to try to root it out after it has developed. It is especially important to pay attention to this fact when establishing a new income tax, that is, before the administrative staff has become experienced and before the machinery is in good working order.

The great objection to large exemptions, aside from the fact that they lessen public revenues, is that they make the income tax a class tax. Most income taxes are paid by a very small percentage of the voters. Moreover, the voting of heavy taxes upon very small minorities by large non-taxpaying majorities is not conducive to public economy.

Filing Fees

Partly in order to overcome some of the objections to exemptions, and partly in order to secure fuller information for administrative and other purposes, some states have required a filing fee from every person over twenty-one years of age.[17] The new income tax law of Utah provides for "universal" filing of returns and a fee of one dollar. From 1924 to 1927 Delaware had a $3.00 fee,

[17] There are some exceptions.

which is said to have been of administrative assistance. Returns are still required from every adult citizen and resident of Delaware, though only about 17,000 have taxable incomes. The New York recommendation for a filing fee has been mentioned. There is much to be said for such a fee if it is large enough to justify the expense of collection generally, and if the administration is sufficiently zealous. As in the case of most poll taxes, however, the cost of collection is likely to be unreasonably large and many whom it is designed to reach are likely to evade it.

The results of Utah's first returns (1932) are of interest in this connection:[18]

	No. of Returns	Revenue	
		Filing Fees	Tax
Nontaxable returns, filing fees paid	104,703	$104,703	....
Nontaxable returns, exemptions claimed	18,261	....	....
Taxable returns	11,393	11,298	$125,270
Total	134,357	$116,001	$125,270

Number of individuals failing to file, 35,000 (estimated).

Property Tax Offsets

Property tax offsets have been revived in recent discussion and legislation. The usual method is to credit certain property taxes of a taxpayer against his income tax. These offsets are thought of as exemptions or rebates that make the income tax a tax in lieu of property taxes instead of an additional tax. Inability to administer the general property tax on personalty, especially on intangibles, has occasioned much of the advocacy of the income tax as a lieu tax. Wisconsin, Mississippi, Montana, and North Dakota have all tried and abandoned the personal property tax offset. The three Pacific Coast states introduced this variety of offset in their laws of 1929. The 1931 law of Utah provides a credit for both personal and real property taxes not in excess of one-third of the income tax. The 1932 law of Illinois permits credits for taxes on income-producing property and also for taxes not in excess of $100 on an owner-occupied residence.* It will be noted that the Utah and Illinois offsets include more than personal property taxes.

[18] Letter of Commissioner George A. Critchlow, June 2, 1932. Apparently the returns are not quite complete for the entire year. See Table 20, page 521.

* The Illinois law has been declared unconstitutional; see footnote to Table 8.

It is argued in favor of a property tax offset that it aids in securing popular approval of the income tax; it safeguards the revenue as an untried substitute tax might not; and it appears equitable to those opposed to both income and property taxes on the same property. It is objected to by those favoring heavier taxes on funded incomes than on "earned" incomes and also on the ground that it reduces the yield without reducing the cost of administration. Furthermore, it interferes with the proper application of progressive rates. It may be noted also that it is contrary to the recommendations of the committee of the National Tax Association mentioned above.

INVESTIGATION OF OFFSET IN WISCONSIN

It has been contended often of late that the offset provision would afford material relief to real estate owners, particularly to farmers. In view of the lack of information on this subject it may be well to present a few extracts from a very intensive study recently made by Professor Herbert D. Simpson of Northwestern University. The variety of offset assumed in this particular study was not merely personal property tax, as tried in several states, or a fraction of property taxes, as in Utah, but all property taxes of each taxpayer, in so far as they did not exceed his income tax. The study covered the corporate incomes of the entire state of Wisconsin and individual incomes of one county (Dane) for 1928.[19] Of course the results would vary somewhat from year to year, from state to state, and with different rates of tax. (See Tables 5 and 6 and Figure 6, pages 487, 489, and 490.)

The income tax yield in Wisconsin was sufficient to permit the reduction of property taxes by about 15 per cent, assuming the same total revenue. If each taxpayer had been allowed to credit his property tax against his income tax, the yield of the latter would have been reduced by about half, that is, from 15 per cent to 7.5 per cent of the total. In other words, Wisconsin's income tax without offset made possible twice as much relief from the

[19] Herbert D. Simpson, "The Effects of a Property Tax Offset under an Income Tax" (MS, 1932). Citations have been made by special permission of the author. Since this chapter was prepared Professor Simpson's monograph has been published by the Institute for Economic Research, Northwestern University. See also Proceedings of the National Tax Association, 1931, pp. 126–150, and the President's Conference on Home Building and Home Ownership, *Home Finance and Taxation* (1932), pp. 208–217. Professor Simpson's study shows what the effects would have been *if* the assumed offset had been in use.

property tax as would have been possible if a full general property tax offset had been in effect.

Of course, in an offsetting process each taxpayer's relief differs from the average. He pays his property tax in any case; the offset is against the income tax only. One whose property tax just equals his income tax gets the largest proportionate relief; that is, he gets a full rebate of the income tax, or 50 per cent of the sum of the two taxes. One whose property tax is greater than his income tax is relieved of all income tax but of less than 50 per cent of the sum of the two. One who owns so little property that his property tax is less than his income tax has to pay the income tax to the extent that it exceeds his property tax and must therefore pay more than 50 per cent of the sum of the two.

For example, suppose that A is subject to a property tax of $100 before an income tax is adopted. If its adoption without offset raises 15 per cent as much as total property taxes, A's property tax will fall to $85 if the state raises the same total revenues as before. If, however, the yield of the income tax is reduced by half, that is to 7.5 per cent of former total property taxes through the allowance of property tax offsets against it, then A's property tax will be reduced to $92.50 by this type of income tax instead of to $85 as by the other type. But whether A has a total tax burden that is heavier or lighter than it was before the introduction of an income tax depends not only upon the amount of his property tax but upon the sum of his property and income taxes.

If his income is so small that exemptions let him out entirely, or if his income tax is less than the reduction in his property tax, he benefits by the income tax, but if his income tax exceeds the reduction in his property tax, his total burden is greater with the income and property taxes than with the property tax alone. If his income tax is less than 15 per cent of his property tax (Wisconsin experience), he will have the least burden with an income tax without offset, but if it is less than 7.5 per cent of his property tax he will have less burden under an income tax with offset for property tax than he would under a property tax alone.

Taxpayers having income taxes only, or property taxes only, obviously can offset nothing and hence are not benefited by the offset provision. In fact, such property taxpayers, as well as others with very small income taxes as compared with their property taxes, would be subject to larger aggregate taxes on account of the offset, because with the yield of the income tax cut in half by the offset, the property tax levies must be higher to make up the difference, assuming the same total revenue in all cases.

Effect of offset upon taxes of individuals.—In fact, it was found that in Wisconsin in the year studied, taxpayers, individual and corporate, could be classified as follows to show under what combination of property tax and income tax, with or without offset, the total tax burden for each would be at a minimum:

Class 1.—Where a person's income tax was less than 7.5 per cent of his property tax, he would have had a minimum tax burden (property tax plus income tax) if there had been no property tax offset.

Class 2.—Where his income tax was between 7.5 and 100 per cent of his property tax, he would have had a minimum tax burden if there had been a property tax offset against his income tax.

Class 3.—Where his income tax was more than 100 per cent of his property tax, he would have had a minimum tax burden under a property tax unaccompanied by an income tax.

The percentage of individuals in each occupational group falling in each of these three classes is shown in Table 5.

TABLE 5.—DISTRIBUTION OF OCCUPATIONAL GROUPS WITH REFERENCE TO PROPERTY TAX OFFSET IN DANE COUNTY, WISCONSIN, 1932[a]

Occupational Group	No. in Group	Income Tax of 0 to 7.5 Per Cent of Property Tax: Secure Minimum Tax Burden under Straight Income Tax[b]		Income Tax of 7.5 to 100 Per Cent of Property Tax: Secure Minimum Tax Burden under Income Tax with Property Tax Offset		Income Tax over 100 Per Cent of Property Tax: Secure Minimum Tax Burden under General Property Tax Alone	
		No.	Per Cent	No.	Per Cent	No.	Per Cent
Farmers	652	627	96.2	22	3.3	3	.5
Trades	833	479	57.5	108	12.9	246	29.6
Laborers	891	544	61.1	77	8.6	270	30.3
Clerical	659	202	30.7	55	8.3	402	61.0
Professional	516	139	26.9	106	20.5	271	52.6
Other salaried	758	304	40.1	149	19.6	305	40.3
Business	319	160	50.2	76	23.8	83	26.0
Unclassified	354	218	61.6	34	9.6	102	28.8
All groups	4,982	2,673	53.7	627	12.6	1,682	33.7

[a] Simpson, "Effects of a Property Tax Offset under an Income Tax" (MS. 1932), p. 18. See pages 485–488 for further explanations of this table.

[b] Property tax accompanied by income tax without offset provision.

It will be noted from this table that 96.2 per cent of the farmers, 61.1 per cent of the laborers, and 57.5 per cent of the skilled workers ("trades") had minimum tax burdens when the property tax was supplemented by an income tax without an offset. This is primarily because most persons in these occupational groups had incomes so small as to be exempt or nearly exempt from the income tax, hence could benefit little or not at all by an offset against the income tax. Most persons in these groups who paid any income tax at all formed part of Class 1 listed above.

On the other hand, most clerical and professional individuals would have fared best with a property tax unaccompanied by any income tax at all. That is, for most of them the income tax did not give enough relief from their relatively small property taxes to offset fully their income taxes. Most of these groups thus belonged in Class 3 listed above, though over a fourth of them belonged in Class 1.

About half the business group belonged in Class 1 and about one-fourth in each of the other two classes. This means that about half of the business group had income taxes of less than 7.5 per cent of their property taxes, hence the state income tax served to relieve their property taxes by amounts in excess of their income taxes. But 26 per cent of the business class had such large incomes or such small property holdings that their property taxes were not relieved by their income taxes to the full extent of their income taxes. Hence this 26 per cent of the business class would have preferred no income tax.

An analysis of taxpayers classified according to size of income is almost as instructive as the analysis by occupational groups. Professor Simpson's investigations included the incomes of 5,086 individuals, a random sample for the year and the area. Of these, 104 would not have been affected by the offset. Of the remaining 4,982, over half (2,619) had incomes of $2,000 or less. Of these, 83.1 per cent would have secured a minimum tax burden (sum of both taxes) with the property and income taxes as they stood, that is, without offset; .8 of 1 per cent would have had minimum tax burdens with the property tax offset; and 16.1 per cent of them would have had lowest taxes with a general property tax accompanied by no income tax. Of those with incomes above $2,000, a little over half (two-thirds in the $10,000–$20,000 income bracket) would have had minimum tax burdens under a general property tax only,

FIGURE 6.—DISTRIBUTION OF OFFSET BENEFICIARIES ACCORDING TO INCOME CLASSES, WISCONSIN, 1928 [a]

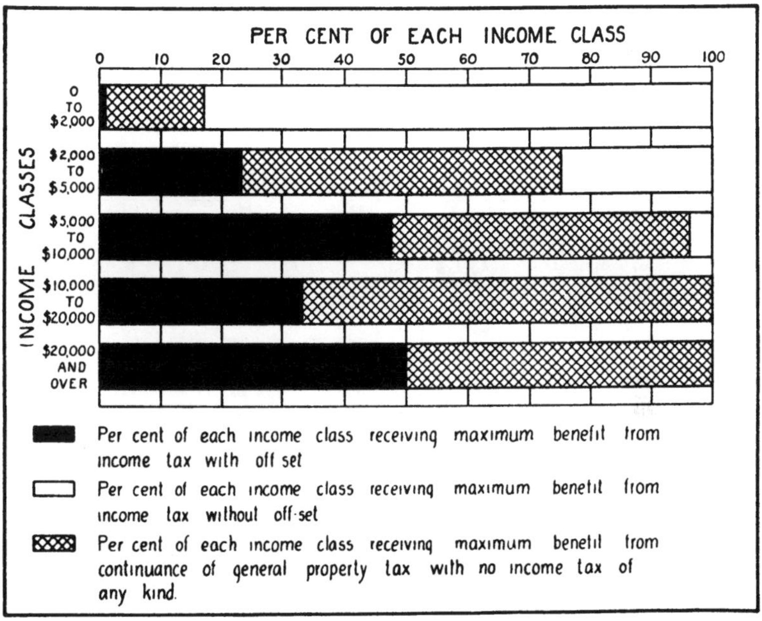

[a] Adapted from H. D. Simpson, *The Effects of a Property Tax Off-Set under an Income Tax*, p. 13 (Institute for Economic Research, Northwestern University, 1932).

while a little over one-fourth would have fared best with an offset income tax. Figure 6 shows these and additional data more graphically than does a word picture.

Effect of offset upon taxes of corporations.—The effect the offset would have had on the taxes of 13,104 corporations in Wisconsin is indicated in Table 6. In all cases the effect is determined not so much by the total amount of taxes payable by a corporation or an individual as by the ratio between the two taxes as explained above. (See page 486.) Because personal exemptions permit most small individual incomes to escape the income tax whether there is an offset or not and because property owners, individuals and corporations, with relatively large incomes usually have the most favorable ratios [20] between income and property taxes, the latter group would profit most by an offset provision under the conditions just discussed.

[20] As explained on page 487. See especially Class 1.

TABLE 6.—DISTRIBUTION OF OFFSET BENEFITS AMONG 13,104 CORPORATIONS IN WISCONSIN, 1928[a]

GROUP	TOTAL TAX ACTUALLY PAID PER CORPORATION	EFFECT OFFSET PROVISION WOULD HAVE HAD			
		On Property Tax	On Income Tax	Net	
				Amount	Per Cent
Agricultural	$ 481	$+ 41	$− 25	$+ 16	+ 3.3
Real estate	1,699	+141	− 93	+ 48	+ 2.8
Mining and quarrying	1,489	+108	−157	− 49	− 3.3
Manufacturing	3,824	+213	−738	−525	−13.7
Commercial	1,420	+103	−236	−133	− 9.4
Wholesale	1,786	+124	−333	−209	−11.7
Retail	1,315	+ 96	−208	−112	− 8.5
Banks	1,119	+ 68	−275	−207	−18.5
State	797	+ 48	−190	−142	−17.8
National	2,880	+176	−743	−567	−19.7
Brokerage and investment	807	+ 42	− 57	− 15	− 1.9
Public utilities	6,622	+509	−880	−371	− 5.6
Water transportation	4,977	+420	−323	+ 97	+ 1.9
Local transportation	838	+ 64	− 88	− 25	− 1.0
Service	1,954	+170	− 53	+117	+ 6.0
Holding companies	2,156	+ 16	0	+ 16	+ .7
Miscellaneous	626	+ 42	− 89	− 47	− 7.5
All corporations	$2,111	$+136	$−377	$−201	− 9.5

[a] Simpson, "Effects of a Property Tax Offset under an Income Tax" (MS, 1932), p. 49.

Of the Wisconsin corporations, banking, manufacturing, and wholesale companies would have received the largest percentages of benefit from the assumed offset provision. (See Table 6.) The ratio of income to property holdings was larger for these corporations than for the majority, hence they could get more benefit relatively by reducing their income taxes through property tax offsets. On the other hand, agricultural, real estate, and water transportation corporations would not have been benefited by the offset provision because it would not have reduced their income taxes by as much as it would have raised their property taxes, assuming always that the state and localities raised the same total of revenues under the different tax arrangements. It will be observed that the offset provision would have reduced average corporate taxes by 9.5 per cent, a percentage worth considering, perhaps worth fighting for by the beneficiaries of such reduction.

ADMINISTRATION

Good administration is a primary requirement for the success of any tax. In no case is it more important than in connection with

TABLE 7.—COMPARISON OF FEDERAL AND STATE INCOME TAX COLLECTIONS[a]

(Taxes payable in 1931 on income of 1930)

STATE	FEDERAL			STATE	
	Individual	Corporate	Total	Total	Per Cent of Federal
Arkansas	$617,189	$1,199,466	$1,816,655	$559,315	30.79
California	43,705,312	49,887,842	93,593,154	6,952,563	7.43
Connecticut	18,708,144	16,287,040	34,995,184	3,534,787	10.10
Delaware	9,743,127	23,134,000	32,877,128	635,760	19.34
Georgia	2,703,637	3,707,962	6,411,599	1,382,066	21.56
Idaho	200,736	484,111	684,847	....	....
Massachusetts ..	45,592,834	37,840,827	83,433,661	25,189,286	30.19
Mississippi	517,882	985,206	1,503,088	1,015,815	67.58
Missouri	15,245,679	25,663,332	40,909,012	3,420,464	8.36
Montana	910,113	780,133	1,690,247	168,156	9.95
New Hampshire.	1,600,002	1,173,610	2,773,612	641,663	23.13
New York......	306,633,690	308,343,744	614,977,434	99,474,000	16.17
North Carolina..	3,481,362	10,239,452	13,720,814	5,914,396	43.11
North Dakota...	113,255	238,377	351,632	303,122	86.20
Oklahoma	5,145,726	9,511,829	14,657,555	356,219	2.43
Oregon	1,719,410	2,391,325	4,110,736	2,521,968	61.35
South Carolina..	509,575	1,300,849	1,810,424	1,726,482	95.36
Tennessee	3,761,423	5,523,291	9,284,714	....	....
Utah	718,433	1,649,584	2,368,017	....	....
Vermont	858,101	842,158	1,700,259	....	....
Virginia	3,049,481	16,157,273	19,206,754	4,113,157	21.42
Wisconsin	8,981,111	17.604,559	26,585,670	18,452,928	69.41

[a] Computed from information furnished by tax officials and from the *New York Times* of July 9, 1931.

general taxes on net income. Modern business often involves large amounts of capital and is not confined within state or even national boundaries. The determination of net income, its allocation to particular areas, the proper checking and auditing of returns, and other problems of administration are often very complex matters, far too complex for the usual type of untrained, locally elected assessors.

Wisconsin has been the leader in the modern state income tax movement, and her success has been due largely to her centralized administration. The main reason for the failure of such taxes in other states in earlier years was that the administration was nearly always put in the hands of poorly qualified local officials and was without proper state supervision. Other states adopting income taxes have been successful largely in proportion to the degree to which they have followed the lessons to be learned from successful centralized administrative experience. The yields in Massachusetts and New York have been most conspicuous, while those of Missouri, Oklahoma,[21] and other states maintaining the old decentralized systems of administration have been much below what could be collected if better methods were followed.

It should not be forgotten, however, that strictly agricultural states having comparatively few and unimportant centers of industry, commerce, and finance, cannot expect large yields from an income tax, even though it may be well administered. For example, a well-supervised administration in North Dakota cannot secure large amounts from an income tax with ordinary rates and exemptions, though it can secure about as much as is collected by the federal government. (See Table 7 and Figure 7.)

Administrative Organizations of Typical States

WISCONSIN

The proper administration of the income tax is so important that it seems worth while to make clearer the character of the organizations in some of the more successful states. From the first Wisconsin provided that her income tax should be administered under the supervision of the state tax commission, which was itself an appointive body. The tax commission was authorized to divide the state into districts and to appoint supervisors over each district. The commission divided the state into forty[22] districts and appointed an assessor of income over each district. The assessors of income were put under civil service and their compensation and tenure were put in the hands of the tax commission. They and their assistants supervised the assessment of individual incomes, the assessment of corporate incomes being kept in the hands of the tax commission itself at its central office. Everything possible was done to avoid friction, to secure competent assessors and auditors, to make all appointments and tenures depend upon merit, and to reduce political influence in administration to a minimum. This general policy has been maintained throughout, though the organization has been improved as experience has been gained.

Today Wisconsin employs seven auditors in the central office to assess current corporation returns and to supervise audits made by

[21] In 1931 Oklahoma set up a tax commission to administer its income and other state taxes, besides making radical changes in the various provisions of its income tax. Collections in 1932 to date have been far below expectations, but it should be remembered that it takes time to bring about thoroughgoing administrative reform and, furthermore, that the depression has wiped out a large part of the tax base.

[22] Now reduced to twenty-two.

FIGURE 7.—COMPARISON OF STATE AND FEDERAL INCOME TAX COLLECTIONS IN VARIOUS STATES, 1929–1931

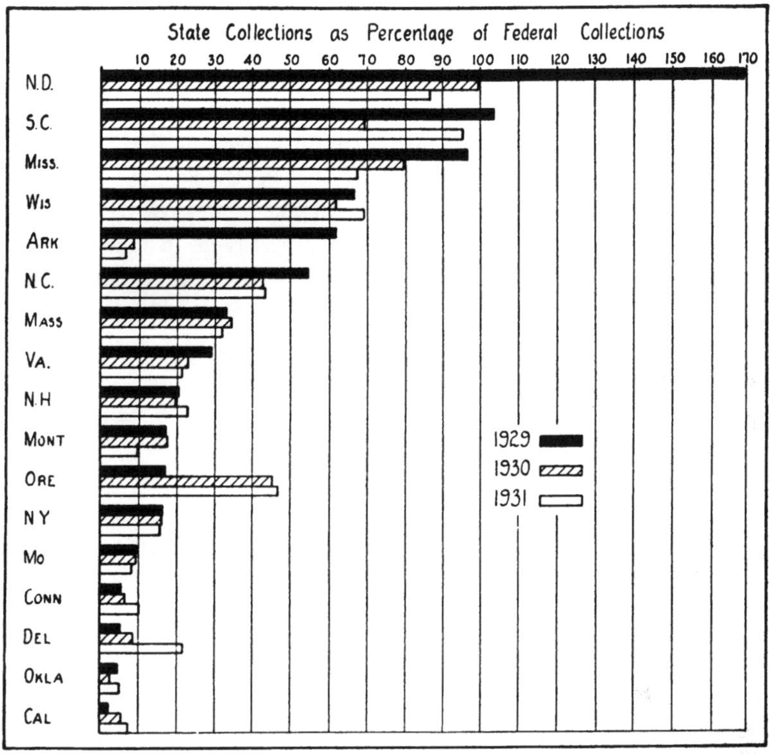

field auditors. Twenty-nine field auditors are employed on corporation audits, and thirty audit the returns of individuals, partnerships, and fiduciaries. Eighteen of the latter do office auditing only. The income tax assessors in Wisconsin spend from one-third to about one-half their time supervising local property tax assessors. The National Tax Association committee on the model plan of state and local taxation, in calling attention to Wisconsin's successful income tax, lays no small stress on the work of the district assessors, who are "bringing the administration of the law home to the people of the several districts." This committee commended Wisconsin, too, for utilizing the district income tax assessors as supervisors of local property tax assessors within their districts.[23] These district assessors, it should be kept in mind, are appointed

[23] Proceedings of the National Tax Association, 1919, pp. 465–466, quoted in National Industrial Conference Board, *State Income Taxes,* 2:134.

by a central state authority and are responsible to that authority; their tenure is not dependent on the voters of their districts. They may be moved from one district to another, however, if it seems desirable, though this is not done frequently.

Experience in Wisconsin has taught the desirability of separating the income and property tax work of the assessors of income (supervisors) wherever possible, assigning a specialized personnel to each tax. Complete separation of the work relating to the two taxes has been provided for in four districts and partial separation prevails in several others. Commissioner Groves, in charge of the income tax, looks forward to a division of the state into districts each of which will have sufficient business to justify one well-qualified full-time assessor or supervisor and one resident field auditor, both of whom will specialize on income taxes and nothing else.[24] This would mean a reduction to ten or twelve districts, each with a fairly populous city.

MASSACHUSETTS AND NEW YORK

In Massachusetts the district income tax offices are administrative agencies of the central state office and entirely under the direction and supervision of the commissioner of corporations and taxation. The state income tax unit prepares tax forms to be sent out, and from data received on them concerning taxpayers' incomes it assesses the income tax, bills the taxpayer, collects the taxes, and distributes them back to the localities. The collection section is used also for other tax collections. The income tax unit has a "mobile force" of from sixty to eighty persons who aid people in filling out returns at the beginning of the year. Then the same crew is put at assessing the tax, sending out bills, receiving collections, and gathering statistics as these functions become necessary.

New York has two bureaus under the state tax commission engaged in income tax work, one for the personal income tax and the other for the corporation tax. The state is divided into seven districts, each under a district director appointed by the commissioner of taxation and finance. All employees in New York are appointed under civil service rules from lists of persons who have qualified by competitive examination.

In each of these three states where the income tax has been best administered and where yields have been greatest, employees are

[24] Letter of June 9, 1932.

selected on a basis of merit and fitness. They are trained in accounting and understand the law. In each of the three states there is also a field auditing force. The staff is coordinated throughout the state and supervised by a central state tax administrative unit.

In Massachusetts the tax officials calculate the tax from information that each taxpayer submits under oath regarding his own income. The other states follow the practice of the federal government in allowing the taxpayer to calculate his own tax. The latter method eliminates a great deal of detailed work, but it necessitates careful auditing. The cost of administration in Massachusetts is now appreciably higher in proportion to the tax collected than that of New York, probably in part because officials compute the tax instead of requiring the taxpayer to do this and in part because costs are spread over a smaller total yield than in New York.

In New York the income tax is collected from nonresidents at the source of income. Wisconsin compels corporations to report income paid to others in order to permit them to deduct such amounts as expense in their own returns, and this provision furnishes a check on the individual's report of his income. Massachusetts requires all payments of interest, dividends, and wages to be reported. Other states have followed the system of obtaining information at the source of a taxpayer's income as a check on his return. The best results are secured where income tax assessors appointed by the tax commission maintain thorough supervision over districts that are not too large. These assessors or supervisors are able to keep in closer touch with the individuals in their respective localities than could a centralized staff alone, and at the same time their positions are not dependent on the taxpayers of the district as is the case in Missouri and Virginia.

Cost of Administration

The cost of administration of the income tax varies greatly in different states and in different years. (See Table 8.) It is difficult to get accurate comparable figures for many states. Perhaps the most usual cost is between 2 and 3 per cent. New York reports costs ranging from 3.4 to .7 per cent; North Dakota from 6.34 to 1.73 per cent; Oklahoma from 3.5 to 1 per cent; North Carolina about 1 per cent; Wisconsin from 2.6 to 1.3 per cent in recent years, the average for the period from 1911 to 1929 being 1.75 per cent.

TABLE 8.—COST OF ADMINISTRATION OF THE STATE INCOME TAX (INDIVIDUAL AND CORPORATION), 1925–1931[a]

State	Cost in Percentage of Tax Collected						
	1925	1926	1927	1928	1929	1930	1931
Connecticut[b] (average)	.19	.19	.19	.19	.19	.19	.19
Delaware[c]	...	4.54	3.52	2.68	2.28	1.59	1.88
Georgia (estimated)	...	...	...	...	...	3.00	3.00[d]
Massachusetts[e]	2.20	1.82	1.92	1.72	1.47	1.33	1.98
Mississippi	3.10	2.49	2.38	2.37	...	...	...
Missouri[b] (average)	3.00	3.00	3.00	3.00	3.00	...	...
Montana[f]	1.75	1.75	1.75	1.75	1.75	1.75	1.75
New Hampshire[b]	1.5	2.0	2.0	1.6	1.90	...	...
New York[g] (individual)	2.47	1.90	1.44	1.16	.79	.70	...[g]
North Carolina							
Individual	...	1.12	.87	.99	1.13	1.59	.93[h]
Corporation	...	.62	.65	.66	.44	.45	.24[h]
North Dakota[i]	2.65	2.07	2.50	2.32	2.04	2.39	4.12
South Carolina	3.82	3.94	3.58	2.70	2.89	3.20	3.53
Virginia[j] (individual)	6.0	6.0	6.0	6.0	6.0	6.0	6.0
Wisconsin[k]	2.58[b]	1.69[b]	1.30[b]	2.08[b]	1.86	1.78	1.80

[a] Compiled from data received from state officials. Incompleteness of the table is due to the fact that states do not always allocate expenses. In addition to the states mentioned, California reports a cost of .65 per cent for 1929; Oklahoma, 3.5 per cent for 1930; and Oregon, 1.4 per cent for 1931.

[b] Blakey, *Taxation in West Virginia* (1931), p. 263.

[c] This is the cost of administration of all taxes collected by the state tax department, of which income taxes comprise 40 per cent.

[d] About $70,000 a year.

[e] Computed on an estimated annual cost of $500,000.

[f] Average for entire period since tax has been collected, or since 1917.

[g] The cost of administering the corporation income tax has varied from .21 per cent to .26 per cent. For 1931 the cost of collecting taxes on personal incomes and banks was 1.39 per cent; taxes on corporations, .25 per cent.

[h] Period from July 1, 1931, to April 1, 1932.

[i] Computed on an estimated annual cost of $12,500.

[j] Average for the period. The cost of administering the corporation income tax has been about $12,000 annually; in 1931 this was .625 per cent of collections.

[k] Computed on an estimate that administration costs $375,000 per year. The Wisconsin Tax Commission has estimated that the cost of administering the income tax from 1911 to 1929 was 1.75 per cent for the entire period.

The cost of administering the tax upon corporations is usually much less than that for the tax on individuals. For example, since 1924 New York reports costs of 2.47 to .70 per cent for individual income taxes, and from .26 to .21 per cent for corporation taxes, the higher figures being for the earlier years. It seems that percentage costs usually decrease as collections increase in amount, though this may not always be the case. Sometimes more thorough auditing increases collections sufficiently to justify the additional expense, though the percentage cost of collection may be raised thereby. In general, costs show a tendency to decline as experience is gained and administration improved.

Distribution of Proceeds

When Wisconsin first enacted its income tax, 90 per cent of the collections went to the local units of government and only 10 per cent to the state. It was expected that a large part of the state's fraction would be needed for defraying the cost of administration. It was found in this state, however, as well as in New York and elsewhere, that some small cities with important industries sometimes had more revenue than they knew what to do with, whereas other sections were badly in need of funds. In more recent years Wisconsin has amended its law to allow the state 40 per cent, the county of origin 10 per cent, and the local units of origin 50 per cent of the income tax, though no local unit can retain as its share more than .7 per cent of its assessed value of property. This provision is made to prevent so-called "income tax colonies." [25]

New York first deducts $250,000 for refunds. Of the remainder, 50 per cent goes to the general fund of the state and 50 per cent to the counties in proportion to the assessed valuation of real property in each. This allocation was made to encourage full valuation of property by local assessors, but it has not been very successful in this respect. In Delaware all the net proceeds go to the school districts. In Massachusetts part goes to the local units under the Education Act and the remainder to the cities and towns in proportion to their contributions to the state tax.

In Oklahoma 25 per cent goes to the state and 75 per cent to the counties, cities, and towns for the support of schools. In Illinois all goes to the public school fund.* In Utah the filing fees and 25 per cent of the remainder go to the state; the rest, except what is required for refunds, goes to the state district school fund. In Mississippi all goes to the cities, towns, and villages except what is needed for refunds and expenses. In most states, however, all or nearly all of the income tax goes to the state.

[25] Before this limitation was set, a few rich persons or a large manufacturer could incorporate a small municipality in a suburb or in the country and support it out of the local share of the income taxes they paid, without resort to any property tax. Had they remained in Milwaukee, the local share of their income taxes would have been spread thinly over the entire city and they would have been subject in addition to heavy local property taxes.

* See footnote to Table 3 above.

FIGURE 8.—INCOME TAX COLLECTIONS IN VARIOUS STATES, 1929–1931

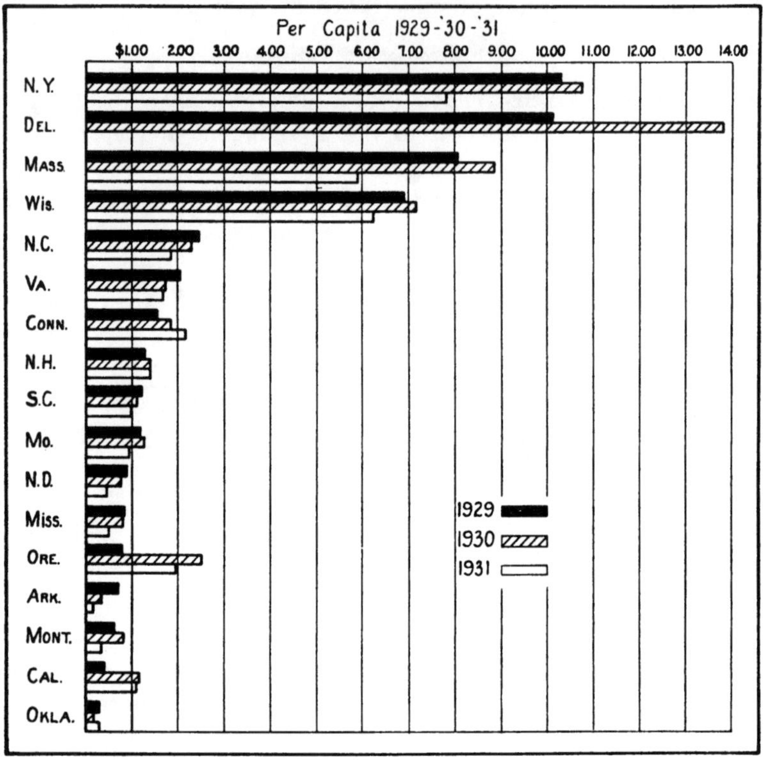

OPERATIONS AND EFFECTS OF INCOME TAXES

The chief features of state income taxes and also some characteristics of the better administrative organizations have been presented above. Some of the effects of income taxes, particularly those about which controversy now centers in Minnesota, will be discussed next.

Experience with such taxes in the United States has now been sufficiently extensive to justify some fairly definite and practical conclusions, though with respect to some questions there is still much difference of opinion. Such taxes can be administered fairly well under good centralized supervision reasonably free from political pressure. Under decentralized administration similar to that by which property taxes are usually administered, the income tax

TABLE 9.—STATE INCOME TAX COLLECTIONS (INDIVIDUAL AND CORPORATION COMBINED), 1925–1932[a]

(000 omitted)

STATE	1925	1926	1927	1928	1929	1930	1931	1932[b]
Arkansas	....	....	....	....	....	$1,333	$559	$306
California	....	....	....	....	....	6,838	6,953	$4,627
Connecticut	....	$1,996	$2,587	$2,623	2,471	2,984	3,535	1,381
Delaware	$676	1,052	1,474	1,842	2,399	3,300	636	579
Georgia	....	....	....	....	....	630[c]	1,382	1,144[d]
Massachusetts	22,730	27,412	26,083	29,113	33,923	37,650	25,189	3,456[e]
Mississippi	643	1,789	1,864	1,454	1,669	1,719[f]	660[f]	400[g]
Missouri	3,606	4,336	4,030	3,698	4,252	4,609	3,420	3,129
Montana	239	291	281	249	340	441	168	115
New Hampshire	434	453	502	563	595	638	641	....
New York	71,668	76,738	98,865	108,263	127,880	135,861	99,474	109,436
North Carolina	3,752	6,083	6,340	8,196	7,686	7,291	5,914	7,048
North Dakota[h]	473	604	501	538	614	522	303	200
Oklahoma	318	336	362	1,089	721	458	356[i]	937
Oregon	....	....	....	....	738	2,431	2,522	....
South Carolina	1,846	1,559	1,762	2,263	2,104	1,936	1,726	858[d]
Tennessee	....	....	....	....	....	572	....	606[j]
Utah	....	....	....	....	....	....	....	416
Virginia	1,688	1,692	3,453	3,796	4,949	4,253	4,113	2,834
Wisconsin	9,185	13,820	18,775	18,036	20,184	21,093	18,453	18,259

[a] Compiled from data received from state officials.
[b] Fiscal year ended on June 30, 1932.
[c] For four months only.
[d] For six months only.
[e] For seven months only. The fiscal year ends on November 30, and income taxes are due on October 15.
[f] Receipts for calendar years. Figures for other years are for fiscal years ending on September 30.
[g] Estimated by the tax commission.
[h] Includes penalties and interest not allocated in Table 20.
[i] From *Federal and State Tax Systems, 1932,* p. 143.
[j] For individuals only; corporation returns incomplete.

is almost certain to be very inequitable and to yield only a fraction of what it should.

Some states have derived a large part of their revenues for state purposes from the income tax, thus leaving the property tax wholly, or almost wholly, for local purposes. These states and some others have been enabled also to give much greater aid to education, especially to financially weak districts, out of state funds swelled by income taxes.[26] Among other uses, Wisconsin has employed its state income tax to provide soldiers' bonuses, teachers' pensions, and funds for unemployment relief. It has thus established an enviable record of keeping its indebtedness to a minimum.

[26] For comparative yields, see Tables 9, 20, 21, and 22.

TABLE 10.—PER CAPITA PROPERTY TAX LEVIES (STATE AND LOCAL), 1930[a]

(Income tax states in boldface)[b]

BELOW MEDIAN		ABOVE MEDIAN	
Alabama	$12.43	Illinois	$42.92
Arkansas	14.09	Ohio	43.98
Georgia	**14.34**	Iowa	44.34
South Carolina	**15.67**	Indiana	44.96
Tennessee	18.19	Connecticut	45.43
Virginia	**18.77**	**North Dakota**	**46.23**
North Carolina	**19.43**	**Wisconsin**	**46.31**
Delaware	**21.62**	Idaho	46.51
Kentucky	21.63	Wyoming	46.74
Mississippi	**22.65**	Florida	47.26
New Mexico	24.26	Kansas	47.45
Texas	25.61	Colorado	47.82
Oklahoma	**26.26**	MINNESOTA	48.85
Louisiana	27.09	**Massachusetts**	**49.07**
Missouri	**30.54**	Montana	49.84
West Virginia	31.13	South Dakota	50.74
Vermont	31.48	Arizona	51.13
Maryland	35.03	Oregon	51.63
Pennsylvania	36.04	Washington	52.17
Maine	36.64	California	56.34
Rhode Island	39.42	Michigan	57.25
New Hampshire	41.24	**New York**	**60.62**
Utah	41.67	Nevada	66.11
Nebraska	41.72	New Jersey	70.77

Median: $42.32.
Below the median: 8 income tax states and 16 others.
Above the median: 4 income tax states and 20 others.

[a] *Financial Statistics of States*, 1930; population estimates of the United States Bureau of the Census; National Industrial Conference Board, *The Cost of Government in the United States, 1929–1930*, pp. 114–115.

[b] "Income tax states" in this group of tables refers to those that have had substantial income taxes over a period of years.

REPLACEMENT OR ADDITIONAL TAX?

It is said, however, that an income tax will not reduce other taxes, but rather will lead to increased expenditures and thus add another tax to those already carried by the overburdened taxpayer. The extent to which income taxes lighten property and other taxes and the extent to which they occasion additional expenditures cannot be measured accurately or satisfactorily. There are too many inseparable factors involved. Moreover, it is impossible to secure complete and comparable data for all states and their subdivisions over a sufficient period of time to permit of general conclusions. The United States Bureau of the Census publishes annually data for the states and for cities of 30,000 and over, but not for the

TABLE 11. — INCREASES IN PER CAPITA PROPERTY TAX LEVIES (STATE AND LOCAL), 1922–1930 [a]

(Income tax states in boldface)

BELOW MEDIAN		ABOVE MEDIAN	
New Mexico	$—1.14 [b]	**Missouri**	**$9.00**
Arizona	1.50	Maine	9.13
Delaware	**2.48**	Indiana	10.20
Nebraska	2.61	Rhode Island	10.29
Georgia	**2.90**	Ohio	10.76
Alabama	3.53	**Massachusetts**	**10.77**
Tennessee	3.91	Iowa	11.38
South Carolina	**4.73**	Maryland	11.40
South Dakota	4.87	MINNESOTA	11.40
Virginia	**5.11**	Idaho	11.43
Louisiana	5.44	Pennsylvania	11.52
Kentucky	5.85	Utah	13.23
Vermont	5.95	Kansas	13.44
Oklahoma	**6.21**	Montana	13.86
Texas	6.64	Connecticut	14.00
Colorado	6.66	Illinois	14.07
North Dakota	**6.68**	Wyoming	14.57
North Carolina	**6.90**	Washington	15.72
Mississippi	**7.01**	Michigan	18.78
Arkansas	7.13	Oregon	18.79
Wisconsin	**8.43**	California	19.51
Nevada	8.51	**New York**	**19.69**
New Hampshire	8.65	Florida	21.24
West Virginia	8.99	New Jersey	32.11

Median: $8.995.
Below the median: 9 income tax states and 15 others.
Above the median: 3 income tax states and 21 others.

[a] See footnotes a and b in Table 10. [b] Decrease.

smaller cities, villages, counties, townships, and other units. The decennial reports on wealth, debt, and taxation do not fill all the gaps satisfactorily. Even if the data were complete, no one could tell certainly what various states would have spent if their tax systems had been other than they were, that is, if they had included or had not included income taxes.

Tables 10–13 give a few samples of many attempts to answer the questions raised above. The twelve states that have had income taxes for some time (referred to as the income tax states in this section) are compared with the other thirty-six states; the states are arranged in order of amount or increase of taxes, the income tax states being shown in boldface type.

Table 10 shows that in two-thirds of the income tax states per capita property taxes, state and local, are much below the median or middle point of the forty-eight states. Table 11 shows that in

TABLE 12.—INCREASES IN PER CAPITA PROPERTY TAXES (STATE AND LOCAL) IN PERCENTAGES, 1922–1930 [a]

(Income tax states in boldface)

BELOW MEDIAN	Per Cent	ABOVE MEDIAN	Per Cent
New Mexico	—4.49 [b]	Kentucky	37.07
Arizona	3.02	**Virginia**	**37.41**
Nebraska	6.67	Montana	38.52
South Dakota	10.62	Kansas	39.52
Delaware	**12.96**	Alabama	39.66
Nevada	14.77	West Virginia	40.61
Colorado	16.18	**Missouri**	**41.78**
North Dakota	**16.89**	Washington	43.13
Wisconsin	**22.25**	**South Carolina**	**43.24**
Vermont	23.31	Connecticut	44.54
Louisiana	25.13	**Mississippi**	**44.82**
Georgia	**25.35**	Wyoming	45.29
New Hampshire	26.54	Utah	46.52
Tennessee	27.38	Pennsylvania	46.98
Massachusetts	**28.12**	**New York**	**48.11**
Indiana	29.34	Maryland	48.24
MINNESOTA	30.44	Illinois	48.77
Oklahoma	**30.97**	Michigan	48.82
Ohio	32.39	California	52.97
Idaho	32.58	**North Carolina**	**55.07**
Maine	33.19	Oregon	57.22
Iowa	34.53	Florida	81.63
Texas	35.00	New Jersey	83.06
Rhode Island	35.32	Arkansas	102.44

Median: 36.20 per cent.
Below the median: 6 income tax states and 18 others.
Above the median: 6 income tax states and 18 others.

[a] See footnotes a and b in Table 10. [b] Decrease.

three-fourths of the income tax states the increase in per capita property taxes, in dollars, from 1922 to 1930 was less than the median. If the comparison is made in percentages of increase instead of in dollars only half the income tax states fall below the median (Table 12). In a comparison of the increase in mill levy on estimated true value of property from 1922 to 1930, eight income tax states fall below the median and four above it (Table 13).

It may be urged that the period from 1922 to 1930 is not typical but rather one of unusual expansion and that further experience with the income tax is necessary before valid conclusions can be drawn. This caution applies to what is said in the paragraphs immediately following as well as to what is in those above.

From these data, however, it appears that property taxes, state and local, tend to be lower in income tax states than in others, but the increase from 1922 to 1930 has been at about the same

TABLE 13.—INCREASES IN PROPERTY TAX LEVIES (STATE AND LOCAL) ON ESTIMATED ACTUAL WEALTH, IN TERMS OF MILLS, 1922–1930[a]

(Income tax states in boldface)

BELOW MEDIAN		ABOVE MEDIAN	
	Mills		Mills
New Mexico	0.8	West Virginia	3.9
Nebraska	0.8	Pennsylvania	4.0
Delaware	**1.0**	Kansas	4.3
South Dakota	1.4	Rhode Island	4.3
Georgia	**1.6**	Indiana	4.3
Montana	2.0	Ohio	4.5
North Dakota	**2.0**	Louisiana	4.6
Virginia	**2.3**	Utah	4.6
Arizona	2.3	Connecticut	4.7
Vermont	2.4	Kentucky	4.7
Idaho	2.4	**Oklahoma**	**4.8**
Iowa	2.6	Maryland	5.1
Colorado	2.6	Arkansas	5.1
Nevada	2.8	Texas	5.5
Tennessee	2.8	Washington	5.5
New Hampshire	2.9	**North Carolina**	**5.7**
South Carolina	**3.1**	Illinois	5.7
Missouri	**3.4**	Oregon	6.2
Wyoming	3.5	**Mississippi**	**7.5**
MINNESOTA	3.5	**New York**	**8.4**
Maine	3.5	Michigan	10.4
Alabama	3.6	California	11.7
Wisconsin	**3.8**	New Jersey	12.7
Massachusetts	**3.8**	Florida	16.6

Median: 3.85 mills.
Below the median: 8 income tax states and 16 others.
Above the median: 4 income tax states and 20 others.

[a] See footnotes a and b in Table 10.

rate in the two groups of states. This would seem to indicate that income taxes tend to replace property taxes, in part at least, but that the adoption of a state income tax does not usually mean that property taxes will remain stationary thereafter. Perhaps the most that can be hoped for is that the income tax will keep property taxes from increasing as fast as they would if there were no income tax.

The comparisons made above are made between income and property taxes. If instead of property taxes we substitute all taxes, property and other, except gasoline and motor vehicle taxes, we get somewhat less favorable showings for the income tax states. (See Tables 14–16.) On this basis seven of twelve states are still in the group with lowest per capita taxes and also in the group with the smallest increase in dollars from 1922 to 1930, but nine of the income tax states are in the group showing greatest percentage

TABLE 14. — TOTAL TAXES PER CAPITA IN EACH STATE, 1930 [a]
(Except Gasoline Taxes and Motor Vehicle Registration Fees)
(Income tax states in boldface)

BELOW MEDIAN		ABOVE MEDIAN	
Arkansas	$19.76	Ohio	$52.04
Alabama	19.79	Utah	52.45
Georgia	**20.10**	New Hampshire	53.80
South Carolina	**23.90**	Kansas	55.41
Tennessee	25.26	Idaho	56.06
Kentucky	26.76	Colorado	56.31
Mississippi	**27.79**	Rhode Island	57.30
North Carolina	**28.68**	**Wisconsin**	**60.30**
Virginia	**29.65**	Arizona	60.83
New Mexico	31.47	**North Dakota**	**60.91**
Louisiana	33.60	MINNESOTA	61.40
Texas	33.95	Washington	61.64
Oklahoma	**36.08**	Connecticut	62.10
West Virginia	37.77	Oregon	62.58
Missouri	**39.36**	Michigan	65.65
Nebraska	45.93	South Dakota	65.96
Maryland	46.30	Montana	66.03
Illinois	47.59	California	72.10
Pennsylvania	48.04	Wyoming	72.42
Maine	48.25	**Massachusetts**	**73.36**
Vermont	48.92	**Delaware**	**78.25**
Indiana	50.41	New Jersey	82.35
Iowa	50.98	**New York**	**85.43**
Florida	51.99	Nevada	91.86

Median: $52.02.
Below the median: 7 income tax states and 17 others.
Above the median: 5 income tax states and 19 others.

[a] Information furnished by the United States Bureau of Public Roads; *Financial Statistics of States*, 1930; National Industrial Conference Board, *The Cost of Government in the U. S., 1929–1930*, pp. 114–115; *Wealth, Debt, and Taxation*, 1922; population estimates of the United States Bureau of the Census. See also the footnotes to Table 10.

increases. These increases lend some color to the claim that income taxes result in additional taxes. It would be more accurate, however, to say that income taxes are sometimes accompanied by increasing taxes than to state that these increases are caused by income taxes. The causal connection is uncertain. Several states present exceptions, and even in the other states the increases may have been due to other causes. For instance, if a state had decided upon important increases in expenditures for school or other purposes, what was more natural than to adopt an income tax to help pay the increases rather than add them to already high property taxes, even though they might have been so added if the income tax had not been adopted?

The discussion of replacement up to this point may be sum-

TABLE 15.—INCREASE IN TOTAL TAXES PER CAPITA, 1922–1930[a]
(Except Gasoline Taxes and Motor Vehicle Registration Fees)
(Income tax states in boldface)

Below Median		Above Median	
New Mexico	$3.14	MINNESOTA	$14.20
Nebraska	4.16	Idaho	14.91
Georgia	**6.66**	Washington	15.78
Arizona	7.05	**Wisconsin**	**15.88**
Louisiana	7.59	Pennsylvania	16.24
Tennessee	8.09	Vermont	17.10
Alabama	8.24	Utah	17.28
Iowa	8.25	**North Dakota**	**17.41**
Kentucky	8.93	Kansas	17.55
Arkansas	8.94	Maryland	17.82
Mississippi	**9.22**	Oregon	17.83
Colorado	10.28	South Dakota	18.70
Virginia	**10.76**	Michigan	20.57
South Carolina	**10.99**	Rhode Island	20.70
Indiana	11.03	Connecticut	20.93
Ohio	11.35	**Massachusetts**	**21.85**
West Virginia	11.37	California	22.05
Illinois	11.95	Florida	22.54
Oklahoma	**12.31**	Nevada	23.20
Texas	12.78	Montana	23.21
Missouri	**12.90**	Wyoming	31.96
North Carolina	**12.94**	**New York**	**32.04**
New Hampshire	13.41	New Jersey	37.97
Maine	14.06	**Delaware**	**44.83**

Median: $14.13.
Below the median: 7 income tax states and 17 others.
Above the median: 5 income tax states and 19 others.

[a] See footnote to Table 14.

marized somewhat as follows. By picking out certain income tax states and comparing them with certain others not having such taxes, one may draw the conclusion that the income tax has afforded substantial relief from property taxes. By choosing other states for comparison one may purport to show that the income tax has meant easy money for additional expenditure. Partisans are likely to choose the examples that serve their respective purposes. An unbiased examination of the expenditures of all the states and a general knowledge of the situation, however, gives one the impression that both results have been brought about in part. In some cases the introduction of the income tax has occasioned directly and permanently the lowering or abolition of the state levy on property. Although the sum total of property and other taxes, exclusive of the income tax, has seldom declined for any length of time, in some cases it appears to have risen more

TABLE 16.—PERCENTAGE INCREASE IN TOTAL TAXES PER CAPITA, 1922–1930 [a]

(Except Gasoline Taxes and Motor Vehicle Registration Fees)
(Income tax states in boldface)

Below Median	Per Cent	Above Median	Per Cent
Nebraska	9.96	Tennessee	47.12
New Mexico	11.08	**Missouri**	**48.75**
Arizona	13.11	Utah	49.13
Iowa	19.31	**Georgia**	**49.55**
Colorado	22.33	**Mississippi**	**49.65**
Ohio	27.89	Kentucky	50.08
Indiana	28.01	Connecticut	50.84
Louisiana	29.18	Pennsylvania	51.07
MINNESOTA	30.08	**Oklahoma**	**51.79**
New Hampshire	33.20	Vermont	53.74
Illinois	33.53	Montana	54.20
Nevada	33.79	Rhode Island	56.56
Washington	34.41	**Virginia**	**56.96**
Wisconsin	**35.75**	**New York**	**60.01**
Idaho	36.23	Texas	60.37
South Dakota	39.57	Maryland	62.57
Oregon	39.84	Alabama	71.34
North Dakota	**40.02**	Florida	76.54
Maine	41.12	Wyoming	78.99
West Virginia	43.07	**North Carolina**	**82.21**
Massachusetts	**43.42**	Arkansas	82.62
California	44.06	**South Carolina**	**85.13**
Michigan	45.63	New Jersey	85.56
Kansas	46.35	**Delaware**	**134.14**

Median: 46.73 per cent.
Below the median: 3 income tax states and 21 others.
Above the median: 9 income tax states and 15 others.

[a] See footnote to Table 14.

slowly than it would have done had there been no income tax. But practically all individuals, in both public and private capacities, spend more when they have more, so it stands to reason that a tax that taps a new or more lucrative source of revenue almost inevitably makes probable some increase in expenditure. The question then is not one of the income tax but of the social justification for the increased expenditures.

Shall one, therefore, argue that a state or a city should not adopt an income tax but rather should adopt the taxes most difficult to raise and most unjust to its citizens in order that it may thus cut down its expenditures to a minimum? In such case it might adopt a poll tax as the sole source of revenue and require the same amount from everyone, regardless of his income or family needs; or, better still, it might adopt a regressive (reversed) income tax, taking the most from those who have least and vice versa. Such a suggestion seems absurd to the citizen of a modern state.

The essence of the matter is that the total amount of the money raised by taxation is determined by two things: (1) by how much the legislative authorities deem it advisable to spend for services and (2) by the revenue-yielding possibilities of the tax system. It is, of course, true that certain kinds of taxes can be imposed that will be so obnoxious to the public at large, or so impossible of collection, that public expenditures will perforce be held to very—even destructively—low levels. For example, a state that relied entirely upon a uniform poll tax for its revenue would not, in the nature of things, be able to collect more than enough revenue to finance the most necessary governmental services. Similarly, if the reverse of a progressive income tax were employed as the sole source of revenue, its obvious inequitableness alone would prevent the raising of considerable sums of revenue.

The advisability of an income tax as a supplement to the existing revenue system of any state cannot be logically determined by answering the question (if it could be answered) whether its adoption would be accompanied by larger public expenditures. The income tax should stand or fall on its merits as a tax, that is, as a source of revenue, and not on the policy of expenditure pursued by states that may have adopted it. One might as well argue that a new food should be prohibited by law because a number of persons will surely consume it gluttonously as to argue that a new tax will increase expenditures. To be sure, those who have pecuniary interests in the production of old foods might easily be persuaded that the introduction of new foodstuffs would be dangerous to the public health. Whether expenditures are to be large or small is a question for the duly constituted authorities to determine; the question here involved is the choice of taxes or a system of taxes that will raise adequate revenue and *at the same time* distribute the burden of the cost of governmental services most equitably among the people of the state who receive the benefits of the services provided by the state.

Does an Income Tax Drive Out Industry?

It has been charged that an income tax is bad for business and drives industries from a state. Such assertions are made much oftener than they are substantiated. Most investigations of the

TABLE 17.—COMPARISON OF TAX BURDENS IN WISCONSIN AND COMPETING STATES[a]

State	Per Capita State and Local Collections, All Taxes, 1930	Per Capita General Property Taxes, 1930	Percentage Increase in per Capita Total Tax Collections, 1925–1930[b]	Percentage Increase in General Property Tax Collections, 1925–1930[b]	Per Cent of Income Taken by Total State and Local Taxes, 1928–1930	Percentage Increase in Ratio of State and Local Tax Collections to State Income, 1925–1930[b]
Wisconsin	$62.65	$41.60	21.1	16.5	7.5	.0
Minnesota	63.66	48.39	10.5	9.0	10.5	15.4
Michigan	71.10	54.65	38.5	48.4	8.2	32.3
Illinois	63.94	54.83	29.7	35.9	6.4	16.4
New York	91.12	64.49	41.7	47.0	9.6	33.3
Ohio	57.23	45.62	28.3	26.7	7.0	27.8
Indiana	53.16	44.65	17.6	14.4	7.4	13.8
Average	71.10	54.11	32.3	34.7	8.1	26.7

[a] Adapted from Leffler and Groves, *Wisconsin Industry and the Wisconsin Tax System*, pp. 63, 65, 71, 73, 77, 79.

[b] Based on three-year moving averages.

cases cited in proof of such charges indicate that other factors were more influential in causing business shifts than was the income tax. The most extensive study of this subject has been made by Professors Leffler and Groves of the University of Wisconsin.[27] This study compares the tax burdens (income and property taxes) and the development of industry in Wisconsin and competing states for different series of years up to and including 1930. Tables 17 and 18 are made up of extracts from this study.

Among the pertinent findings of this study are the following: The present total per capita tax, state and local, is slightly less in Wisconsin than in Minnesota and distinctly less in Wisconsin than the average of the seven states compared. Wisconsin's per capita of general property taxes, state and local, is much less than the average. During the period from 1925 to 1930 Wisconsin's per capita of all tax collections increased twice as fast as Minnesota's but only two-thirds as fast as the average, whereas her property

[27] George L. Leffler and Harold M. Groves, *Wisconsin Industry and the Wisconsin Tax System* (Bureau of Business and Economic Research, University of Wisconsin, Bulletin 3, 2d ed., 1931). Dr. Groves is now a member of the Wisconsin Tax Commission.

taxes increased less than twice as fast as Minnesota's and less than half as fast as the average. In the three years from 1928 to 1930 Wisconsin's total taxes, state and local, took only two-thirds as large a percentage of the income of the people of the state as did Minnesota's taxes; this percentage for Wisconsin did not increase at all in the five-year period from 1925 to 1930, whereas it increased by 15.4 per cent in the case of Minnesota taxes and by 26.7 per cent, on the average, for the states compared. While these figures indicate that taxes in Wisconsin (an income tax state) have been increasing faster than in Minnesota (a non-income tax state), they show the increase in Wisconsin to have been less rapid than in every other non-income tax state compared except Indiana, though the greatest increase has been in New York, an income tax state.

It will be noted that total state and local taxes take a larger percentage of the profits of Wisconsin manufacturing corporations than of Minnesota manufacturing corporations, but if the profits of all corporations (manufacturing and others) are considered, total state and local taxes absorb a much larger percentage of the profits in Minnesota than in Wisconsin. (See Table 18.)

TABLE 18.—TAX BURDENS AND THE DEVELOPMENT OF INDUSTRY IN WISCONSIN AND COMPETING STATES [a]

State	Percentage Increase in					Ratio of	
	Income of the People of the State, 1925–1930	Federal Income Tax Collections, 1925–1930	Per Capita Wealth, 1922–1929	Net Income of All Corporations, 1923–1928	Net Income of Manufacturing Corporations, 1923–1928	Taxes [b] to Net Profit of All Corporations, 1926–1928	Taxes [b] to Net Profit of Manufacturing Corporations, 1926–1928
Wisconsin	29.7	45.9	6.4	47.3	56.3	17.1	14.4
Minnesota	— 0.7	19.7	8.4	47.6	12.9	25.3	12.6
Michigan	20.8	34.9	—3.6	34.1	24.6	12.7	8.8
Illinois	19.7	32.6	—2.1	46.5	26.2	15.6	8.2
New York	18.3	52.1	—4.7	62.5	34.7	16.3	10.9
Ohio	13.0	29.7	6.6	20.7	31.6	18.1	13.3
Indiana	8.1	— 8.4	4.8	— 4.8	— 6.8	19.3	12.7
United States as a whole	13.9	30.6	2.0	33.7	14.9	17.4	12.1

[a] Adapted from Leffler and Groves, *Wisconsin Industry and the Wisconsin Tax System*, pp. 15, 17, 19, 25, 38, 91, 117.
[b] State and local taxes collected from corporations.

Table 18 indicates that Wisconsin has not lagged behind industrially because of her taxes. According to these data, part of which are necessarily estimates, Wisconsin has increased its per capita wealth three times as fast as the United States as a whole, though somewhat more slowly than has Minnesota (1922–1929); the income of her people has increased much faster than that of any other state in the group (1925–1930); the increase in the net income of all her corporations has been about the same as the increase for Minnesota corporations but nearly half again as great as for the United States as a whole (1923–1928); and the increase in net income of her manufacturing corporations has been nearly four times that of the United States as a whole and more than four times that of Minnesota (1923–1928). Following the logic of some, it might be argued that, inasmuch as Wisconsin's income tax has been accompanied by phenomenal prosperity of industry, therefore this tax has been the cause of this prosperity. It might be sounder, however, merely to maintain that the charge that the income tax has driven an unusual number of industries from Wisconsin does not appear to be well founded. New York, the only other state in the group that has had an income tax during the years compared, has been second only to Wisconsin in rapidity of industrial development.

Though the data for the various other states are less reliable, comprehensive, and clear-cut than is desirable, a careful examination of what are available leads to the conclusion that the charge that the income tax is bad for business and drives industries from a state is not convincing, except to those who want to be convinced. Other factors than taxes are often more important in determining the location or removal of industries. Furthermore, if a state must raise a certain amount of revenue, an industry might just as well pay part of its share in income taxes as to pay equal or greater aggregates in the form of heavier property or franchise taxes. Net income taxes, rather than property taxes, should be particularly attractive to new industries. While they are getting on their feet they will have little or no income tax to pay; when they later become prosperous, the wherewithal to pay these taxes will be available. Such taxes are quite different from property and gross sales taxes, which have to be paid in years of heavy losses as well as in years of profits.

Various Objections and Other Considerations

Income taxes have their weak as well as their strong points. It has been said that they penalize the efficient and let the inefficient go free. This is true of most taxes. No Solomon has yet arisen to show how to get much public revenue from the have-nots and the ne'er-do-wells. Moreover, a government that depended on the ne'er-do-wells for its main support would be such a poor government that the people, particularly the efficient, could not afford it at any price. Rather than suffer its inadequate and inefficient services it would pay them to support a good government at much greater cost to themselves. In fact, poor government is one of the most expensive of luxuries. Therefore, fair taxes paid for the support of good government should not be thought of as *penalties* but rather as *contributions* to our cooperative organization. This organization, government, makes possible the creation of capital, the ownership of property, the carrying on of business; in fact, it safeguards our very lives and makes possible what we call civilization. Those who have most ability and are most efficient and consequently most able to pay taxes usually have also most at stake in good government. From this point of view the income tax accords admirably with both the benefit and ability-to-pay criteria of apportioning tax contributions; i.e., it falls upon those who get the most from maintaining stable and efficient government and are best able to pay for what they get.

It should be remembered also that the income tax is but one tax in the whole tax system. The property tax is usually the heaviest of all and falls upon the inefficient as well as the efficient, upon those who lose as well as upon those who gain. So long as this is true it cannot be argued that inefficient business enterprises contribute nothing for the benefits they receive from government.

Securing good administration is another difficulty that income taxes share with property and other taxes. It has already been said that proper administration is an especially important requirement for a successful income tax. Unquestionably it would be better to have no income tax in Minnesota than to have one with as decentralized an administration as that of the existing property tax.

The income tax was formerly objected to on the ground that it is difficult to ascertain net income, that such income is capable of manipulation by devious accounting methods, and therefore that evasion is easy. There was more point to this criticism twenty years ago, before the establishment of the federal income tax. But the experience of the people with the federal tax, the general installation of approved accounting systems, the provisions of the federal law permitting state officials to examine corporate income returns, and improvements in state administrations have obviated most of the serious obstacles of this sort. It is true that if the administration is decentralized and weak, as it is in some states, results will not be satisfactory. But progressive states have shown that state income taxes can be administered efficiently and economically with proper supervision. This is especially true of the part of the tax applying to corporations.

A consideration that should not be overlooked is that the collateral effects of a good income tax may be worth as much as the direct results. It has been claimed that the by-products of the Wisconsin tax in the way of improvements in the administration of the general property tax have been worth as much as the revenue yielded. When the new tax was about to be established there were no vested interests connected with the tax in the form of jobs, tradition, or "home rule," and political pressure had not yet handicapped the tax commission or the legislature. So the lawmaking body felt free to give the commission extensive powers to set up a really efficient, centralized, nonpolitical administrative organization. After the tax was established, during the seasons of the year when this organization was least busy administering the income tax, it helped with the property tax throughout the state. The supervision of the property tax administration was thus gradually improved and in time was brought to a point of efficiency that otherwise would have been very difficult if not impossible to attain.

Theoretically it would have been possible for the legislature to have set up a thoroughgoing system of centralized state supervision of local assessments of property without the adoption of an income tax. But there were too many obstacles in the way to make such a radical and sudden change politically expedient. It was easier to achieve the same end by setting up an efficient administration for a new general tax and then gradually extending the effective supervision over the other taxes of the state, particularly over the general property tax, the most important of all

Minnesota might well consider this possible administrative by-product of a general income tax.

Perhaps the greatest weakness of the income tax is its instability of yield. Property values, gross sales, and gross income are more stable bases than net income. Obviously it would be unwise to depend upon the income tax for a major part of the public revenue unless an adequate system of reserves were maintained. A recent New York committee recommended reserve systems for income, inheritance, and some other taxes.[28] The simplest reserve system that this committee recommended provides for the determination of a conservative average yield of the tax, allowing for trend over a long series of years; then for the diversion of excesses above this average to reserve. The reserve would be invested in state bonds that would be sold to meet deficiencies of poor years. A still simpler way to meet the situation would be to pay off all public debts rapidly when times are good and thus provide ample margins for borrowing in periods of depression. It is much easier to make plans, however, than it is to carry them out. Financial history is replete with cases of extravagance and mismanagement arising from the inability of legislators and others to resist the temptations offered by surpluses, sinking funds, trust funds, and reserves.

A few years ago Wisconsin changed the income tax base from the income of a single year to the average of the last three years. This was a modification of a former British practice and helped to smooth out the fluctuations in revenue. The averaging method is also much more equitable to taxpayers whose incomes vary greatly from year to year. Unfortunately, however, Wisconsin's averaging system is to be abandoned after 1932. The Wisconsin supreme court "held that only one current assessment of the three-year average could be made after the closing of the estate of a deceased person, which decision has the effect of exempting from income taxation two-thirds of one year's income of the deceased, and one-third of another year's income." It was thought that this rule might be applied to nonresidents discontinuing business in Wisconsin, to residents moving out of the state, and to corporations dissolving or reorganizing. Furthermore, the three-year average works hardships in a depression period by requiring taxes from people who have little or no current income. Another objection was

[28] Report of the New York State Commission for the Revision of the Tax Laws, 1932, Memorandum No. 11.

that many individual taxpayers had difficulty in understanding the average provision, and some thought erroneously that it made their taxes higher.[29]

Another way to meet the difficulty of fluctuating yields is to vary the rate of the income tax, much as the property tax rate is varied from year to year to adjust revenue to needs. This would cause highest rates in years of lowest incomes. In the worst years the higher rates would be heavy and also very disturbing psychologically and politically, as well as financially. Either the reserve or the debt-reduction plan mentioned above could prevent much of this difficulty.

As a matter of fact, under the present property tax, during poor years the tax rates actually take a large percentage of income. In some cases they take more than 100 per cent of the net income for the year. This causes much complaint and even agitation against high taxes. Even more dissatisfaction and agitation might be caused by income tax rates sufficiently high to bring in the same amount of revenue. If property normally brings in 6 per cent net, then a property tax of 1 per cent is equivalent to a net income tax of 16⅔ per cent. But most people who would think little of a property tax rate of 1 per cent would not be psychologically prepared to uphold a net income tax with rates as high as 16⅔ per cent, although on the average it is the exact equivalent of the 1 per cent property tax under the conditions assumed, and besides it distributes the burden of expenditures much more equitably among different taxpayers.

IF MINNESOTA ADOPTS AN INCOME TAX

Probable Yield

With a good system of administration there is no reason why Minnesota could not achieve results comparable to those achieved with income taxes in other states similarly situated. It is not reasonable to expect to secure at once as large yields as the richer

[29] The Wisconsin provision for the averaging of the incomes for three years was passed the same year as the provision for giving personal exemptions in terms of tax instead of in terms of income. (See page 482.) This lowering of exemptions made taxes higher upon all except the smaller incomes; but it is said that many taxpayers erroneously attributed this increase in taxes to the averaging system and consequently they continually tried to repeal this provision of the law. As a matter of fact, the averaging system reduces taxes, especially for those having fluctuating incomes that are large in some years. The great advantages of the averaging system to the state government are that it tends to stabilize the yield from year to year and makes it more easily calculable in advance.

industrial states. Most farmers and, in fact, the great mass of people would pay very small income taxes or none at all. The great bulk of the yield would come from businesses, especially from corporations, and from the wealthy owners of business enterprises. Substantial amounts also would come from retired owners of capital.

Professor Warren C. Waite of the University of Minnesota has made especially for this study the following calculations of the probable yield of an income tax in this state. Assuming the present rates, exemptions, and administration of Wisconsin,[30] the estimated yield for Minnesota on 1929 income would have been as follows:

Total normal tax, individuals	$12,294,031
Less allowance for exemptions	1,892,211
Net normal tax to state	$10,401,820
Surtax on incomes over $3,000	1,549,934
Total normal and surtax, individuals	$11,951,754
Income tax on corporations	8,472,000
Total, individual and corporation taxes	$20,423,754

As has been pointed out previously, for most incomes Wisconsin has the heaviest tax of any state in the Union.[31] More nearly normal were the rates and exemptions of the income tax bill introduced into the last session of the Minnesota legislature.[32] In Table 19 are shown estimates of yields that would have been received by Minnesota had this bill been law for the years indicated, again assuming as good administration as in Wisconsin.

Increasing the rates on individual incomes to 5.5 per cent on the eleventh thousand and 6 per cent on the remainder would have increased the estimated yield for 1929 by $796,831.

The years from 1927 to 1929 were unusually prosperous for most corporations and individuals who pay income taxes. Yields for average years would be considerably lower and for depression years like those of the present very much lower. Detailed federal income data for the last two years are not available as yet, but 1921 may be taken as fairly typical of a depression year; 1924, as a normal year; and 1929, as a boom year. It will be noted that the estimated yield for 1929 is more than twice that for 1921 and nearly once

[30] See pages 532 and 541 and Appendix A for Wisconsin provisions and further explanations of calculations. The one-year emergency tax for unemployment relief is not included in making these estimates.

[31] See pages 472 to 479 above.

[32] House File 973, Senate File 864, 47th Session, 1931.

TABLE 19.—ESTIMATED YIELDS OF AN INCOME TAX IN MINNESOTA [a]

INCOME OF	TAXES FROM INDIVIDUALS	TAXES FROM CORPORATIONS [b]	TOTAL
1921	$3,109,577	$2,631,117	$5,740,694
1924	4,109,809	5,061,982	9,171,791
1927	5,663,866	5,190,400	10,854,266
1928	7,559,413	6,957,384	14,516,797
1929	7,226,480	6,365,567	13,592,047

[a] See Table 31 on page 534. Rates and exemptions in House File 973 were as follows:

RATES FOR INDIVIDUALS

1 per cent on the first $1,000
1.25 per cent on the second $1,000
1.5 per cent on the third $1,000
1.75 per cent on the fourth $1,000
2 per cent on the fifth $1,000
2.5 per cent on the sixth $1,000
3 per cent on the seventh $1,000
3.5 per cent on the eighth $1,000
4 per cent on the ninth $1,000
4.5 per cent on the tenth $1,000
5 per cent on the remainder

RATES FOR CORPORATIONS

5 per cent

PERSONAL EXEMPTIONS

Dependent	$300
Head of family	2,000
Single person	1,000

[b] Omitting mining and banking corporations. These two classes of corporations and insurance companies were omitted from the provisions of the income tax of the Minnesota bill. Professor Waite was unable to separate insurance companies from "financial corporations" in making his estimates, hence insurance companies have not been omitted in the above calculations.

Estimated income tax yields under the 5 per cent rate of the Minnesota bill, for all corporations, and for all corporations minus certain classes, are as follows:

INCOME OF	YIELD OF 5 PER CENT TAX ON NET INCOME FROM: ALL CORPORATIONS	ALL CORPORATIONS EXCEPT MINING	ALL CORPORATIONS EXCEPT MINING AND PUBLIC UTILITIES	ALL CORPORATIONS EXCEPT MINING AND FINANCIAL
1921	....	....	....	$2,437,734
1924	....	....	....	4,878,932
1926	$6,509,400	$6,381,600	$4,386,650	5,732,450
1927	5,858,000	5,696,000	4,537,100	4,937,600
1928	7,780,850	7,590,850	5,456,800	6,640,650
1929	7,332,500	7,047,800	5,477,450	6,024,450

and a half that for 1924. The present depression is much more severe than that of 1921, hence income tax yields would probably be much less now than for that year.

In estimating tax yields it should be remembered, also, that no tax approaches its normal yield until it has been in operation for a few years. Furthermore, good administration is extremely important. Wisconsin's yields have been unusually good, partly because of her rates and exemptions, but largely because of her administration, which has been among the best, if not the best, in the United

States. But other income tax states also have shown income tax revenues gradually increasing with improving administration and with growing industry.

Simplifying Administration

When any state establishes an income tax great care should be taken in framing the law and in developing thorough administration from the beginning. These points cannot be stressed too emphatically. When the financial plight of taxpayers on the one hand and the needs of governments on the other are as extreme as they are today, there is great danger of wrecking an income tax at the start by making the rates too high and the various provisions too complicated before administrative organization and experience have been developed. Unfortunately, farmers and others expect more of an income tax than it will yield under existing depressed conditions. Professor Waite's estimates and other information available indicate, for example, that Minnesota could expect under present conditions not more than $5,000,000 annually, and probably less, from an income tax with reasonable rates and other reasonable provisions.

If any state makes the rates too high and other provisions too complicated at first, there is great danger of overloading administration and of developing evasion and perhaps such reaction that much of the future benefit that should be got from such a tax will never be obtained. Greatest progress in the long run will be made by starting with a relatively simple law with moderate rates and exemptions and with relatively few exceptional and complicated provisions. Later, as experience is gained, the tax can be developed. Due consideration should be given to the experience of other states as well as to the particular circumstances of Minnesota. Many of the important matters to consider in establishing and administering an income tax have been noted in preceding pages and throughout this report. Of the numerous issues that will come up in the framing of a law when this stage is reached (as it almost certainly will be sooner or later), there is space here to mention only a few and those very briefly.

In line with the suggestions made above, it would seem simplest and best, all things considered, to apply the income tax to corporations generally and to make exceptions only where necessary for legal or other important reasons. The difficulties connected with the taxation of banks are discussed in Chapter 10 and need not be repeated here. Inasmuch as the gross earnings taxes on railroad, telephone, and certain other public utility corporations are in lieu of property taxes and, furthermore, because most of these lieu taxes appear to be less burdensome than general property taxes,[33] it would seem proper to apply the income tax to these gross-earnings-taxed corporations as well as to those to which the general property tax applies. The mining companies are in a different situation because, besides being subjected to our heaviest class of property taxes, they already have to pay in addition special occupation and royalty taxes that are higher than the corporation income taxes of any state. One's opinion of the equity of the above suggestions is strengthened by an examination of the relative tax burdens of various classes or corporations shown in Table 2 of Chapter 10 on bank taxation.

Allocation of Income

The proper allocation of net income in the case of corporations doing an interstate business is a knotty problem various solutions of which have been offered by different states. Some allocate income according to the proportion of physical property in the state to total physical property everywhere; some use amount of business done, or expense of business carried on, or some other criterion, or a combination of several criteria. A composite base is probably generally more equitable and more likely to produce results meeting the judicial test of reasonableness than any single criterion, though the courts recognize that no base can be better than an approximation and are inclined to uphold a statute unless it can be shown to be quite unreasonable.[34]

Distribution of Proceeds

If the income tax is adopted, the hardest contest is likely to be over the distribution of the proceeds. The practices in other states are shown on pages 497 and 535 to 541. In Minnesota the greatest

[33] See Chapters 11 and 12.

[34] See Henry Rottschaefer, "State Jurisdiction of Income for Tax Purposes," *Harvard Law Review*, 44:1075 (1931); Roswell Magill, "Allocation of Income by Corporate Contract," *Harvard Law Review*, 44:935 (1931); E. M. Perkins, "Constitutionality of Income Allocation Formulae as Applied to Corporations," *North Carolina Law Review*, 9:470–474 (1931); and Ogden Mills, "Financial Relations of Federal and State Governments," Bulletin of the National Tax Association, 17:224 (1932).

demand has been for relief to owners of real estate, and much has been said of making sure that the income tax is a replacement instead of an additional tax. The proposal of the bill in the 1931 legislature (see page 466) was to substitute the income tax for the general property tax levy for state purposes, except the one-mill levy for the Road and Bridge Fund. It was stated at the time that this levy had yielded an average of over $10,000,000 annually during the past six years.

Later Governor Olson recommended the reduction of taxes on homesteads, rural and urban, and the using of the income tax to make up for the loss in taxes on such property. His suggestion was to reclassify homesteads by reducing the taxable valuation one-third. In estimating the effects upon revenue the Tax Commission took as the basis for levies 20 per cent of full valuations for rural homesteads and 25 per cent for urban (instead of the present 33⅓ per cent and 40 per cent, respectively) and calculated that such decreases would result in a reduction of $13,708,290 in property taxes.[35]

It does not seem probable that an income tax would raise the suggested amount of revenue for the first year or two, certainly not on 1932 income, though it might well do so in time. There would appear to be some difficulty also in working out a convenient method of distributing the income tax proceeds in such a way as to make it an exact replacement of the property tax on homesteads in every community, but a practical and approximate method would not be so difficult to devise.

Another suggestion is that all income tax collections be used to reduce public debts. This is closely related to the suggestions on page 513 regarding the building up of reserves and the paying off of debts in prosperous times.

The distribution of income taxes on the basis of school population, or as a part of a general or special state aid fund, is a common suggestion and not an unusual practice. All these methods mean a shifting of income from the richer to the poorer sections of the state. All of them would bring property tax relief to all sections, particularly to the poorer sections, if expenditures are not increased, but none would prevent the localities from increasing local property taxes to the extent of state relief received unless there were rigid state limitation of home rule. It is difficult to think of any

[35] The Tax Commission commented favorably upon the governor's proposal.

other sure guaranty of complete replacement short of such limitations.

The crux of the issue over distribution of proceeds will probably be the extent to which urban income taxes shall be returned to the localities where levied and the extent to which they shall be diverted to rural areas where small amounts of such taxes or none at all will be raised. Exemptions, especially high exemptions, and graduated rates make most income taxes narrow class taxes, levies that apply to a very small percentage only of those who vote them. Nearly all income taxes are paid by city and suburban dwellers. In view of the modern development of industry and communication and in view of the changed situation of agriculture, it seems desirable that the urban gatherers of large incomes should pay a larger proportion of the necessary public expenditures. On the other hand, it seems possible to go too far, in fact, in some cases we have already gone too far, in diverting urban-paid taxes to the support of uneconomic rural schools, roads, and farms. What is needed is a policy that takes due consideration of the welfare of all sections and classes in the state and of the commonwealth as a whole, one that avoids extremes by steering a happy middle course that harmonizes all interests, or comes as near to this goal as is possible.

The wise solution of modern economic problems puts democracy to a severe test. The survival and progress of civilization as we know it rests upon the ability of leaders (and followers) to work out such knotty problems as those presented by income and other taxes. If the great majority of nonpayers impose unduly upon the few payers, or if the able leaders disregard the welfare of the great majority, they will topple the structure on the heads of all. Never in the memory of the present generation has this truth been driven home so forcibly as now.

Table 20.—State Income Tax Collections (Individual and Corporation), 1925–1932[a]

(000 omitted)

State	1925	1926	1927	1928	1929	1930	1931	1932[b]
				INDIVIDUAL INCOMES				
Delaware	$676	$1,052	$1,474	$1,842	$2,399	$3,300	$636	$579
Massachusetts	17,682	21,872	21,020	24,061	28,868	32,176	22,008	2,420[c]
Mississippi	713	628	645	637	676[d]	626	240	....
Missouri	1,911	2,211	2,297	2,366	2,637	2,811	2,009	....
New Hampshire....	434	453	502	563	595	638	641	....
New York.........	33,767	41,179	53,952	63,607	83,019	80,271	39,717	29,948
North Carolina	978	1,734	1,703	2,354	2,477	1,700	1,006	1,324
North Dakota[e]	221	302	252	269	307	238	152	106
Oklahoma	318	336	362	1,089	721	458	227[f]	654
Oregon	....	....	....	....	....	1,875	1,526	....
South Carolina.....	485	480	343	399	437	434	364	216[g]
Tennessee	....	....	....	....	....	....	....	606
Utah	....	....	....	....	....	....	....	246
Virginia	....	....	1,581	1,776	2,055	2,289	2,048	1,251
Wisconsin	3,261	5,252	6,290	7,725	8,954	9,064	7,941	7,861[h]
				CORPORATION INCOMES				
California	....	....	....	....	....	$6,838	$6,593	$4,627
Connecticut	....	$1,996	$2,587	$2,623	$2,471	2,984	3,535	1,381
Massachusetts	$5,048	5,540	5,063	5,052	5,055	5,474	3,181	1,036[c]
Mississippi	936	1,108	983	991	993	993[i]	419[i]	....
Missouri	1,695	2,125	1,733	1,331	1,616	1,797	1,411	....
Montana	239	291	281	249	340	441	168	115
New York.........	37,901	35,560	44,912	44,656	44,861	55,590	59,767	79,488
North Carolina.....	2,774	4,349	4,637	5,842	5,210	5,591	4,909	5,723
North Dakota[e]	221	302	252	269	307	257	134	94
Oklahoma	....	....	....	....	....	....	....	283[j]
Oregon	....	....	....	....	738	556	400	....
South Carolina.....	1,361	1,078	1,419	1,864	1,666	1,502	1,362	642[g]
Tennessee	....	....	....	....	....	....	523	....
Utah	....	....	....	....	....	....	....	170
Virginia	....	....	1,872	2,019	2,894	1,964	2,065	1,583
Wisconsin	5,925	8,569	12,485	10,311	11,230	12,028	10,512	10,398[h]

[a] Compiled from data received from state officials.

[b] Fiscal year ended on June 30, 1932.

[c] For seven months only. The fiscal year ends on November 30, and income taxes are due on October 15.

[d] Total income tax less corporation tax.

[e] Prior to 1930, returns were not separated, hence the commission assumed that half the total was from individuals and half from corporations.

[f] From *Federal and State Tax Systems*, 1932, p. 143.

[g] For six months only.

[h] Allocated on the percentage that corporation and individual collections were to the total collections in 1930 and 1931.

[i] Receipts for calendar years. Figures for other years are for fiscal years ending on September 30.

[j] First year of corporation tax.

TABLE 21.—STATE INCOME TAX COLLECTIONS PER CAPITA (INDIVIDUAL AND CORPORATION COMBINED), 1925–1932 [a]

STATE	1925	1926	1927	1928	1929	1930	1931	1932
Arkansas	...	...	...	...	...	$ .44	$ .46	$ .16
California	...	...	...	...	$ .42	1.19	1.13	.78
Connecticut	...	$1.31	$1.67	$1.67	1.55	1.85	2.18	.85
Delaware	$2.92	4.52	6.29	7.82	10.11	13.81	2.65	2.41
Georgia	...	...	...	...	...	.22 [b]	.48	.39 [c]
Massachusetts	5.59	6.68	6.30	6.96	8.04	8.84	5.89	...
Mississippi	.34	.93	.96	.74	.84	.85	.33	.20
Missouri	1.02	1.22	1.13	1.03	1.18	1.27	.94	.86
Montana	.44	.54	.52	.46	.63	.82	.31	.21
New Hampshire	.95	.99	1.09	1.22	1.28	1.37	1.37	...
New York	6.20	6.51	8.24	8.87	10.29	10.75	7.80	8.52
North Carolina	1.30	2.06	2.11	2.67	2.46	2.29	1.84	2.17
North Dakota	.71	.90	.75	.80	.90	.77	.44	.29
Oklahoma	.14	.15	.16	.47	.30	.19	.09	.38
Oregon	...	...	...	...	.78	2.54	1.99	...
South Carolina	1.08	.91	1.02	1.31	1.21	1.11	.99	.49
Tennessee	...	...	...	...	...	...	.48	.23
Utah	...	...	...	...	...	...	...	.81
Virginia	...	...	1.44	1.58	2.06	1.75	1.69	1.16
Wisconsin	3.28	4.89	6.57	6.25	6.92	7.16	6.23	6.14

[a] Based on Tables 9 and 20. [b] For four months only. [c] For six months only.

TABLE 22.—STATE INCOME TAX COLLECTIONS PER CAPITA (INDIVIDUAL AND CORPORATION SEPARATELY), 1925–1932 [a]

STATE	1925	1926	1927	1928	1929	1930	1931	1932
INDIVIDUAL INCOMES								
Delaware	$2.92	$4.52	$6.29	$7.82	$10.11	$13.81	$2.65	$2.41
Massachusetts	4.35	5.33	5.07	5.75	6.84	7.55	5.14	...
Mississippi	.37	.33	.33	.32	.34	.31	.12	...
Missouri	.54	.62	.64	.66	.73	.77	.55	...
New Hampshire	.95	.99	1.09	1.22	1.28	1.37	1.37	...
New York	2.92	3.50	4.50	5.21	6.68	6.35	3.11	2.33
North Carolina	.34	.59	.57	.77	.79	.53	.31	.41
North Dakota [b]	.33	.45	.38	.40	.45	.35	.22	.15
Oklahoma	.14	.15	.16	.47	.30	.19	.09	.27
Oregon	...	...	...	...	...	1.96	1.58	...
South Carolina	.28	.28	.20	.23	.25	.25	.21	...
Tennessee	...	...	...	...	...	...	.28	.23
Utah	...	...	...	...	...	...	...	.48
Virginia	...	...	.66	.74	.85	.94	.84	.51
Wisconsin	1.17	1.86	2.20	2.68	3.07	3.08	2.68	2.64
CORPORATION INCOMES								
California	...	...	...	...	$ .42	$1.19	$1.13	$ .78
Connecticut	...	$1.31	$1.67	$1.67	1.55	1.85	2.18	.85
Massachusetts	$1.24	1.35	1.22	1.21	1.20	1.29	.74	...
Mississippi	...	...	...	...	.50	.49	.21	...
Missouri	.48	.60	.49	.37	.45	.49	.39	...
Montana	.44	.54	.52	.46	.63	.82	.31	.21
New York	3.28	3.02	3.74	3.66	3.61	4.40	4.68	6.18
North Carolina	.96	1.48	1.54	1.91	1.67	1.76	1.53	1.76
North Dakota [b]	.33	.45	.38	.40	.45	.38	.20	.14
Oklahoma	...	...	...	...	...	...	...	.12
Oregon	...	...	...	...	.78	.58	.41	...
South Carolina	.79	.63	.82	1.08	.96	.86	.78	...
Tennessee	...	...	...	...	...	...	.20	...
Utah	...	...	...	...	...	...	...	.33
Virginia	...	...	.78	.84	1.20	.81	.85	.65
Wisconsin	2.12	3.03	4.37	3.57	3.85	4.08	3.55	3.49

[a] Based on Tables 9 and 20.
[b] See Table 9, footnote h.

TABLE 23.—FEDERAL INCOME TAX COLLECTIONS (INDIVIDUAL AND CORPORATION COMBINED), 1921–1932[a]

(In millions of dollars)

STATE	1921	1922	1923	1924	1925	1926	1927	1928	1929	1930	1931	1932
Arkansas	$3.15	$4.26	$4.41	$3.32	$3.95	$3.60	$3.15	$2.45	$2.16	$3.04	$1.82	$ .98
California	68.97	79.24	82.99	82.04	87.66	100.56	102.57	125.75	98.32	125.89	93.59	61.57
Connecticut	18.14	23.66	24.36	24.44	28.42	29.40	32.95	42.67	44.47	45.46	35.00	19.06
Delaware	2.23	4.11	5.38	7.14	10.44	15.92	23.52	32.66	43.95	39.10	32.88	15.23
Georgia	8.30	10.76	10.79	8.94	11.23	10.45	11.93	10.70	8.89	12.15	6.41	4.17
Idaho	.70	.94	1.39	.94	1.15	1.02	.83	.82	.69	.83	.68	.47
Illinois	129.88	153.08	145.56	149.05	170.48	180.77	181.30	225.88	201.96	223.37	173.69	91.49
Massachusetts	93.47	105.59	95.68	81.65	90.32	85.62	93.12	105.66	102.48	109.68	83.43	45.08
Minnesota	17.17	20.52	19.69	19.42	21.92	22.63	21.61	29.02	24.50	28.60	20.80	12.99
Mississippi	1.69	2.94	3.41	2.49	2.65	2.08	2.06	1.83	1.73	2.05	1.50	.78
Missouri	34.28	39.10	38.87	38.41	47.59	47.44	44.02	46.86	43.20	50.54	40.91	25.48
Montana	1.62	1.92	1.60	1.57	1.78	2.08	2.23	2.55	1.96	2.53	1.69	.75
New Hampshire	3.39	3.27	3.05	2.31	2.39	2.27	3.07	3.16	2.85	3.29	2.77	1.47
New York	379.25	474.56	440.42	482.88	575.14	603.57	629.78	819.34	779.80	830.09	614.98	348.60
North Carolina	16.76	16.37	17.27	13.50	16.00	16.42	18.67	16.82	14.15	16.99	13.72	11.46
North Dakota	.82	.79	.49	.71	.71	.60	.59	.53	.36	.52	.35	.23
Ohio	72.46	84.02	90.50	83.19	99.50	99.38	99.01	120.17	115.03	126.16	96.01	47.53
Oklahoma	6.72	10.34	6.61	7.76	14.92	18.46	12.60	14.57	15.82	17.87	14.66	10.01
Oregon	7.32	7.27	6.52	5.13	4.94	5.17	4.41	5.12	4.26	5.38	4.11	2.38
South Carolina	3.16	4.29	4.93	2.10	2.34	2.11	3.25	2.52	2.03	2.80	1.81	1.50
Tennessee	9.11	11.17	10.18	9.21	10.92	11.83	11.44	12.66	9.49	12.30	9.28	5.46
Utah	1.86	2.43	2.56	2.70	3.09	2.81	2.80	3.10	2.70	3.12	2.37	1.43
Vermont	1.94	2.55	2.59	1.99	2.14	2.05	2.01	2.09	1.98	2.15	1.70	.86
Virginia	6.40	9.53	14.50	12.71	16.39	20.78	15.38	17.57	17.00	18.59	19.21	13.32
Wisconsin	20.00	23.33	25.41	22.46	27.12	31.61	33.74	32.58	30.22	34.13	26.59	15.16

[a] Including states having an income tax and Minnesota. Compiled from United States Bureau of Internal Revenue, *Statistics of Income* for 1921–1930 and 1932; and from the *New York Times* of July 9, 1931, for the year 1931.

TABLE 24.—FEDERAL INCOME TAX COLLECTIONS (INDIVIDUAL), 1921–1932[a]

(In millions of dollars)

STATE	1921	1922	1923	1924	1925	1926	1927	1928	1929	1930	1931	1932
Arkansas	$1.87	$2.31	$2.05	$1.46	$1.43	$1.48	$1.34	$ .88	$ .71	$1.15	$ .62	$ .28
California	36.44	43.78	39.96	37.88	37.13	46.24	46.04	63.71	45.36	61.53	43.71	27.59
Connecticut	10.63	13.13	11.20	12.59	13.53	13.75	16.12	23.10	23.69	24.46	18.71	10.10
Delaware	12.84	18.34	1.40	2.43	2.78	5.10	7.97	10.59	14.52	13.12	9.74	3.52
Georgia	3.89	4.56	3.77	3.40	3.53	2.89	3.61	3.81	2.79	3.62	2.70	1.71
Idaho	.49	.48	.43	.26	.17	.18	.25	.28	.18	.24	.20	.10
Illinois	68.57	77.20	62.88	66.58	64.79	64.21	73.80	110.66	86.83	100.82	71.88	36.80
Massachusetts	46.53	57.78	42.53	40.86	41.05	37.12	43.95	59.74	57.86	61.63	45.59	21.59
Minnesota	8.71	9.42	7.08	6.72	6.13	6.48	7.38	11.93	9.80	11.77	8.02	4.37
Mississippi	1.07	1.80	1.69	1.16	.99	.64	.82	.76	.60	.75	.52	.26
Missouri	14.66	15.97	13.09	12.37	14.25	13.50	13.74	18.91	16.42	19.81	15.25	8.57
Montana	1.05	1.03	.72	.73	.58	.56	.87	1.30	1.02	1.37	.91	.38
New Hampshire	1.76	2.13	1.64	1.38	1.22	1.20	1.82	1.99	1.73	1.90	1.60	.84
New York	210.77	273.96	192.31	236.77	252.16	247.16	305.21	451.61	396.69	447.94	306.63	143.18
North Carolina	3.76	4.91	4.77	3.78	3.18	3.40	4.52	6.05	3.28	5.36	3.48	2.45
North Dakota	.49	.45	.28	.27	.16	.18	.19	.21	.11	.18	.11	.13
Ohio	33.57	39.31	33.06	32.06	30.32	32.84	35.52	55.39	43.63	48.98	35.84	18.70
Oklahoma	4.21	6.41	3.91	3.79	6.90	8.13	6.23	6.45	6.02	7.18	5.15	2.69
Oregon	4.95	4.24	2.89	2.03	1.79	2.18	1.92	2.39	1.66	2.32	1.72	.90
South Carolina	1.25	1.27	1.56	.73	.43	.42	.55	.72	.57	.74	.51	.33
Tennessee	3.98	4.90	4.28	3.42	3.13	3.65	4.04	5.62	3.75	5.08	3.76	2.07
Utah	.84	.96	.73	.60	.66	.63	.85	1.10	.88	.99	.72	.36
Vermont	1.16	1.57	1.33	.98	.92	.82	.85	1.06	1.02	1.10	.86	.48
Virginia	4.16	4.92	3.67	3.31	2.98	3.50	3.61	4.41	3.20	4.23	3.05	1.99
Wisconsin	8.97	9.13	9.02	7.34	6.80	8.42	10.62	12.46	10.29	12.06	8.98	4.72

[a] Including states having an income tax and Minnesota. Compiled from United States Bureau of Internal Revenue, *Statistics of Income;* and from the *New York Times* of July 9, 1931, for the year 1931.

TABLE 25.—FEDERAL INCOME TAX COLLECTIONS (CORPORATION), 1921–1932[a]

(In millions of dollars)

STATE	1921	1922	1923	1924	1925	1926	1927	1928	1929	1930	1931	1932
Arkansas	$1.29	$1.95	$2.36	$1.86	$2.52	$2.12	$1.81	$1.57	$1.45	$1.89	$1.20	$ .70
California	32.53	35.47	43.03	44.16	50.53	54.32	56.53	62.04	52.96	64.35	44.89	33.98
Connecticut	7.51	10.53	13.18	11.85	14.89	15.65	16.83	19.57	20.78	21.00	16.29	8.96
Delaware	.94	2.28	3.98	4.70	7.66	10.82	15.55	22.07	29.42	25.98	23.13	11.71
Georgia	4.41	6.20	7.02	5.54	7.70	7.56	8.32	6.89	6.10	8.54	3.71	2.46
Idaho	.20	.46	.97	.68	.98	.84	.59	.54	.51	.59	.48	.37
Illinois	61.31	75.88	82.68	82.47	105.69	116.56	107.50	115.22	115.13	122.56	101.81	54.70
Massachusetts	46.94	47.81	53.15	40.80	49.27	48.50	49.17	45.92	44.62	48.06	37.84	23.48
Minnesota	8.48	11.10	12.60	12.70	15.80	16.16	14.23	17.09	14.70	16.83	12.79	8.62
Mississippi	.62	1.14	1.72	1.33	1.66	1.44	1.24	1.07	1.13	1.30	.99	.52
Missouri	19.62	23.13	25.78	26.04	33.35	33.95	30.28	27.95	26.79	30.73	25.66	16.90
Montana	.57	.89	.88	.84	1.20	1.52	1.36	1.25	.94	1.17	.78	.36
New Hampshire	1.63	1.14	1.40	.93	1.17	1.06	1.24	1.17	1.12	1.39	1.17	.63
New York	168.48	200.60	248.11	246.11	322.98	356.41	324.57	367.73	383.11	382.14	308.34	205.42
North Carolina	13.00	11.47	12.50	9.73	12.82	13.02	14.15	10.77	10.86	11.63	10.24	9.02
North Dakota	.34	.34	.22	.44	.55	.42	.40	.32	.25	.35	.24	.12
Ohio	38.88	44.71	57.44	51.13	69.18	66.54	63.49	64.78	71.39	77.19	60.17	28.82
Oklahoma	2.51	3.92	2.70	3.97	8.03	10.33	6.37	8.12	9.79	10.69	9.51	7.32
Oregon	2.37	3.03	3.63	3.11	3.15	2.99	2.49	2.74	2.60	3.06	2.39	1.48
South Carolina	1.92	3.02	3.37	1.37	1.91	1.69	2.69	1.80	1.46	2.07	1.30	1.17
Tennessee	5.13	6.27	5.90	5.79	7.79	8.18	7.40	7.04	5.74	7.22	5.52	3.39
Utah	1.02	1.47	1.83	2.10	2.43	2.18	1.95	2.00	1.81	2.13	1.65	1.07
Vermont	.78	.97	1.26	1.01	1.22	1.23	1.16	1.04	.96	1.05	.84	.37
Virginia	6.40	9.53	10.84	9.39	13.41	17.28	15.77	13.17	13.79	14.36	16.16	11.34
Wisconsin	11.03	14.20	16.39	15.11	20.33	23.19	23.12	20.12	19.93	22.07	17.60	10.44

[a] Including states having an income tax and Minnesota. Compiled from United States Bureau of Internal Revenue, *Statistics of Income;* and from the *New York Times* of July 9, 1931, for the year 1931.

TABLE 26. — FEDERAL INCOME COLLECTIONS PER CAPITA (INDIVIDUAL AND CORPORATION COMBINED), 1921–1932 [a]

STATE	1921 [b]	1922 [b]	1923	1924	1925	1926	1927	1928	1929	1930	1931	1932
Arkansas	$1.78	$2.40	$2.47	$1.85	$2.19	$1.98	$1.72	$1.33	$1.17	$1.64	$ .97	$ .52
California	18.36	19.93	19.28	18.58	18.92	20.72	20.22	23.76	17.78	21.96	16.00	10.35
Connecticut	12.83	16.48	16.71	16.52	18.92	19.29	21.31	27.21	27.97	28.20	21.55	11.66
Delaware	9.89	18.14	23.56	31.06	45.17	68.38	100.39	138.54	185.24	163.61	136.99	63.46
Georgia	2.87	3.71	3.72	3.08	3.87	3.60	4.11	3.68	3.06	4.18	2.20	1.43
Idaho	1.61	2.16	3.19	2.15	2.61	2.32	1.89	1.85	1.56	1.86	1.54	1.05
Illinois	19.52	22.63	21.17	21.33	24.01	25.07	24.76	30.38	26.76	29.16	22.50	11.78
Massachusetts	23.90	26.74	23.99	20.28	22.22	20.86	22.48	25.27	24.28	25.75	19.49	10.49
Minnesota	7.12	8.44	8.04	7.88	8.83	9.05	8.59	11.45	9.60	11.14	8.07	5.03
Mississippi	.92	1.59	1.83	1.32	1.39	1.08	1.06	.93	.87	1.01	.74	.38
Missouri	9.98	11.30	11.17	10.97	13.50	13.38	12.33	13.05	12.11	13.90	11.22	6.97
Montana	2.96	3.52	2.93	2.89	3.27	3.84	4.12	4.72	3.64	4.71	3.14	1.39
New Hampshire	7.58	7.30	6.76	5.09	5.25	4.96	6.67	6.85	6.15	7.05	5.94	3.14
New York	35.42	43.45	39.54	42.54	49.72	51.23	52.49	67.10	62.75	65.66	48.21	27.12
North Carolina	6.33	6.05	6.24	4.78	5.54	5.57	6.21	5.49	4.53	5.33	4.27	3.53
North Dakota	1.26	1.21	.75	1.08	1.07	.90	.87	.79	.53	.77	.52	.34
Ohio	12.30	14.06	14.93	13.53	15.96	15.72	15.45	18.50	17.48	18.92	14.30	7.04
Oklahoma	3.23	4.88	3.07	3.55	6.70	8.16	5.48	6.24	6.68	7.43	6.05	4.10
Oregon	9.06	8.81	7.75	5.98	5.65	5.80	4.86	5.54	4.53	5.61	4.25	2.44
South Carolina	1.87	2.53	2.89	1.23	1.37	1.23	1.88	1.46	1.17	1.61	1.04	.86
Tennessee	3.83	4.64	4.19	3.74	4.39	4.70	4.50	4.93	3.66	4.67	3.52	2.06
Utah	4.07	5.24	5.45	5.68	6.43	5.78	5.69	6.22	5.35	6.14	4.62	2.78
Vermont	5.49	7.18	7.31	5.60	6.00	5.75	5.62	5.84	5.52	5.96	4.72	2.39
Virginia	4.54	6.19	6.18	5.39	6.92	8.73	6.43	7.32	7.04	7.67	7.90	5.47
Wisconsin	7.47	8.62	9.28	8.12	9.70	11.18	11.81	11.29	10.36	11.59	8.97	5.09

[a] Including states having an income tax and Minnesota. Compiled from United States Bureau of Internal Revenue, *Statistics of Income;* and from United States Bureau of the Census estimates of population.

[b] Includes war profits and excess profits tax.

Table 27.—Federal Income Tax Returns of Minnesota Corporations for the Year Ending December 31, 1929 [a]

Group	Total No. of Returns	Corporations Reporting Net Income				Corporations Reporting No Net Income			No. of Returns of Inactive Corporations [c]
		No. of Returns	Gross Income [b]	Net Income	Tax	No. of Returns	Gross Income	Deficit	
Agriculture and related industries	311	129	$4,585,535	$501,284	$34,470	118	$2,487,961	$647,802	64
Mining and quarrying	317	119	22,722,519	5,694,086	537,911	89	3,350,564	783,585	109
Total manufacturing	1,931	1,182	966,001,937	53,628,317	5,666,666	598	116,834,249	6,710,072	151
Food products, beverages, and tobacco	503	336	574,720,559	19,898,255	2,172,825	141	28,773,235	1,135,910	26
Textiles and textile products	145	82	43,345,211	3,191,385	332,858	57	10,691,944	717,078	6
Leather and leather products	21	9	4,161,312 [d]	138,827 [d]	12,569	11	8,581,192	338,928	1
Rubber and related products	1	1	....	....	....	..	....	....	..
Lumber and wood products	150	81	59,662,236	3,917,791	389.640	53	12,102,292	1,259,102	16
Paper, pulp, and products	35	20	17,142,091	1,112,147	113,996	14	31,410,374	333,635	1
Printing and publishing	295	206	44,579,462	5,206,432	542,214	72	5,411,604	625,782	17
Chemicals and allied substances	112	62	83,779,759	5,265,639	556,909	41	2,291,423	340,508	9
Stone, clay, and glass products	100	61	16,036,544	2,273,960	236,925	34	2,041,072	256,083	5
Metal and metal products	379	228	96,437,127	10,620,064	1,111,650	113	8,684,801	1,247,752	38
Not elsewhere classified	190	96	26,133,086	2,003,777	197,080	62	6,846,312	455,294	32
Construction	356	190	35,427,366	3,298,577	283,322	118	8,920,663	658,426	48
Transportation and other public utilities	506	314	437,221,865	31,406,769	3,366,181	135	53,888,422	2,395,505	57
Trade	3,158	2,080	862,275,365	28,665,243	2,674,524	961	213,797,835	7,378,404	117
Service (professional, amusement, hotel, etc.)	685	386	36,307,599	2,989,339	256,856	221	11,889,955	935,248	78
Finance (banking, insurance, real estate, holding companies, stockbrokers, etc.)	3,630	1,890	137,989,545	20,467,174	1,877,354	1,268	66,012,454	13,124,917	472
Nature of business not given	588	26	456,778	17,991	....	55	136,319	98,312	507

[a] Compiled from *Statistics of Income for 1929*, United States Treasury Department, Bureau of Internal Revenue; 1929 is the last year for which these statistics are available. See also Table 2 in Chapter 10.
[b] Gross income corresponds to total income as reported on the face of the return plus the cost of goods sold.
[c] No income data reported.
[d] States grouped to conceal identity of taxpayer.

TABLE 28.—BROOKMIRE ESTIMATES OF PER CAPITA INCOME AND PER FAMILY INCOME BY STATES AND GROUPS OF STATES[a]

Section and State	Per Capita Income 1929	Per Capita Income 1930	Per Capita Income 1931	Per Family Income, 1931	
United States[b]	$715	$577	$425	$1,745	100
New England	810	651	545	2,248	129
Connecticut	987	788	598	2,483	142
Maine	605	486	386	1,553	89
Massachusetts	801	642	557	2,313	133
New Hampshire	660	548	488	1,900	109
Rhode Island	859	665	597	2,494	143
Vermont	699	611	503	2,034	117
Eastern manufacturing	845	692	537	2,232	128
Delaware	772	693	567	2,267	130
Maryland	745	586	481	2,039	117
New Jersey	916	723	560	2,305	132
New York	904	737	596	2,382	137
Pennsylvania	818	687	498	2,148	123
West Virginia	513	422	314	1,464	84
Central manufacturing	869	671	486	1,933	111
Illinois	950	729	534	2,114	121
Indiana	771	617	464	1,784	102
Michigan	865	605	410	1,855	106
Ohio	861	685	492	1,928	110
Wisconsin	796	654	494	2,036	117
West-central agricultural	663	566	437	1,752	100
Iowa	758	666	516	2,006	115
Kansas	671	581	454	1,747	100
Minnesota	647	553	433	1,834	105
Missouri	595	497	356	1,376	79
Nebraska	758	676	528	2,119	121
North Dakota	563	407	264	1,233	71
South Dakota	621	521	395	1,698	97
Southeast agricultural	315	250	191	856	49
Alabama	277	210	154	695	40
Florida	398	371	305	1,211	69
Georgia	287	236	177	786	45
Kentucky	308	246	197	846	48
Mississippi	257	156	109	465	27
North Carolina	355	291	222	1,105	63
South Carolina	237	193	162	770	44
Tennessee	323	251	180	788	45
Virginia	389	306	233	1,066	61
Southwest agricultural	421	318	238	1,013	58
Arkansas	285	164	137	581	33
Louisiana	380	283	236	1,027	59
Oklahoma	486	364	231	991	57
Texas	453	360	273	1,154	66
Rocky Mountain	737	561	427	1,712	98
Arizona	902	585	397	1,615	93
Colorado	671	591	477	1,827	105
Idaho	734	591	435	1,780	102
Montana	892	632	455	1,788	102
Nevada	1,033	791	620	2,111	121
New Mexico	501	324	270	1,140	65
Utah	673	488	373	1,619	93
Wyoming	825	664	522	2,052	118
Pacific Coast	840	678	494	1,764	101
California	876	706	517	1,830	105
Oregon	731	584	424	1,519	87
Washington	777	633	452	1,662	95

[a] Special Report, June 7, 1932. This table contains some adjustments from 1927 to 1930 not contained in earlier estimates upon which some data in other tables of this chapter are based. See Table 29, footnote a.

[b] Totals for the United States were computed separately and do not exactly equal footed totals of states.

TABLE 29. — BROOKMIRE ESTIMATES OF TOTAL INCOME BY STATES AND GROUPS OF STATES, 1920–1931 [a]

(000,000 omitted)

SECTION AND STATE	1920	1921	1922	1923	1924	1925	1926	1927	1928	1929	1930	1931
United States [b]	$74,599	$59,618	$60,195	$68,279	$66,750	$73,243	$77,497	$77,286	$82,364	$86,836	$70,814	$52,703
New England	6,858	5,026	5,089	6,084	5,267	5,876	6,095	6,092	6,309	6,572	5,313	4,485
Connecticut	1,387	912	963	1,260	1,168	1,241	1,321	1,349	1,478	1,570	1,267	971
Maine	539	441	401	437	399	444	470	414	386	481	387	309
Massachusetts	3,768	2,787	2,840	3,326	2,755	3,201	3,270	3,280	3,372	3,379	3,727	2,382
New Hampshire	334	237	239	282	254	274	283	283	306	306	255	228
Rhode Island	568	442	449	551	469	502	525	540	539	585	457	414
Vermont	262	207	197	228	222	214	226	226	228	251	220	181
Eastern manufacturing	22,197	17,069	17,268	21,137	20,170	21,351	23,178	23,418	24,038	24,970	20,661	16,211
Delaware	168	108	106	139	130	132	143	156	164	183	165	136
Maryland	909	678	669	796	765	859	927	983	1,011	1,205	957	791
New Jersey	2,913	2,241	2,285	2,711	2,519	2,874	3,064	3,129	3,391	3,643	2,922	2,303
New York	9,267	7,653	7,822	9,233	8,995	9,828	10,577	10,941	11,214	11,229	9,276	7,598
Pennsylvania	7,896	5,710	5,657	7,364	7,033	6,849	7,535	7,382	7,426	7,833	6,612	4,834
West Virginia	1,044	679	729	894	728	809	932	827	832	877	729	549
Central manufacturing	18,896	13,488	13,959	17,359	16.285	18,737	19,954	19,337	20,563	21,750	16,965	12,422
Illinois	6,035	4,614	4,760	5,541	5,443	6,187	6,501	6,439	6,983	7,167	5,560	4,123
Indiana	2,303	1,640	1,707	2,085	1,911	2,121	2,254	2,149	2,279	2,481	1,998	1,515
Michigan	3,390	2,335	2,388	3,262	2,960	3,632	4,010	3,727	3,984	4,115	2,930	2,020
Ohio	5,174	3,470	3,679	4,763	4,339	4,937	5,214	4,966	5,183	5,665	4,555	3,302
Wisconsin	1,994	1,429	1,425	1,708	1,632	1,860	1,975	2,056	2,134	2,322	1,922	1,462
West-central agricultural	9,207	6,649	6,585	7,403	7,720	8,324	8,251	8,140	8,480	8,777	7,530	5,837
Iowa	2,076	1,482	1,466	1,655	1,675	1,778	1,835	1,674	1,803	1,869	1,646	1,278
Kansas	1,560	1,117	976	990	1,134	1,202	1,230	1,157	1,317	1,256	1,092	858
Minnesota	1,663	1,224	1,255	1,509	1.437	1,574	1,560	1,444	1,490	1,651	1,418	1,117
Missouri	2,024	1,494	1,561	1,800	1,772	1,993	2,037	1,971	2,072	2,151	1,805	1,298
Nebraska	1,035	744	709	798	869	904	879	994	955	1,040	931	731
North Dakota	406	285	308	289	429	464	359	464	442	382	277	180
South Dakota	443	303	310	362	404	409	351	436	401	428	361	275

Section and State	1920	1921	1922	1923	1924	1925	1926	1927	1928	1929	1930	1931
Southeast agricultural	6,763	4,631	4,919	5,914	5,828	6,588	6,658	6,554	6,596	6,744	5,399	4,159
Alabama	648	430	497	642	642	708	713	726	706	726	555	412
Florida	454	372	377	484	508	808	812	614	589	570	545	460
Georgia	888	528	568	653	713	760	771	790	776	836	686	514
Kentucky	950	669	719	799	727	808	826	780	814	801	644	517
Mississippi	404	265	334	355	384	502	453	462	458	512	314	220
North Carolina	1,205	716	794	1,032	955	1,040	1,086	1,142	1,139	1,110	924	714
South Carolina	631	364	320	444	442	425	412	432	411	412	335	282
Tennessee	808	601	623	718	709	754	767	732	776	838	656	475
Virginia	955	686	687	787	748	783	818	876	927	939	740	565
Southwest agricultural	5,032	3,264	3,559	4,344	4,686	4,830	4,798	4,854	5,100	5,067	3,867	2,930
Arkansas	530	355	377	418	471	535	494	455	495	527	304	255
Louisiana	791	532	554	645	632	725	711	674	698	789	595	502
Oklahoma	1,171	710	778	851	1,009	1,132	1,137	1,138	1,196	1,151	872	561
Texas	2,540	1,667	1,850	2,430	2,574	2,438	2,456	2,587	2,711	2,600	2,096	1,612
Rocky Mountain	2,296	1,663	1,760	2,132	2,175	2,268	2,322	2,360	2,548	2,708	2,077	1.592
Arizona	248	133	150	226	232	254	259	284	346	386	255	176
Colorado	726	572	541	608	650	645	656	628	644	690	612	497
Idaho	268	203	203	248	247	290	299	304	298	326	263	194
Montana	358	253	324	402	407	409	411	451	482	480	340	245
Nevada	70	50	62	74	70	72	80	81	99	93	72	57
New Mexico	156	111	116	128	132	142	154	175	193	210	137	114
Utah	272	195	214	269	265	184	286	273	303	339	248	191
Wyoming	198	146	150	177	172	172	177	164	183	184	150	119
Pacific Coast	5,051	4,226	4,430	5,281	4,990	5,465	5,801	5,881	6,122	6,720	5,552	4,145
California	3,380	3,018	3,168	3,732	3,499	3,872	4,099	4,211	4,367	4,829	4,006	3,022
Oregon	578	437	453	561	548	596	620	619	646	688	557	410
Washington	1,093	771	809	988	943	997	1,082	1,051	1,109	1,203	989	713

[a] These estimates do not refer to government revenues but to the incomes of the people of the several states. *Income of the American People*, Brookmire Economic Service, Inc., Special Report, June 7, 1932. This table contains some adjustments from 1927 to 1930 not contained in earlier estimates upon which some data in other tables of this chapter are based. For Professor Waite's estimate of Minnesota incomes see Appendix A, pages 543–555 below.

[b] Totals for the United States were computed separately and do not exactly equal footed totals of states.

Table 30.—Estimate of Amount of Income in Each

Income Class	No. of Returns[b]	Total Net Income Reported	Amount of Net Income Falling within the Range of $0–$1,000	$1,000–$2,000	$2,000–$3,000	$3,000–$4,000	$4,000–$5,000	$5,000–$6,000
$0–$1,000[c]	6,652	$ 4,038,816	$ 4,038,816	....	....	....	....	....
0– 1,000	416	224,153	224,153	....	....	....	....	....
1,000– 2,000[c]	21,407	33,598,543	21,407,000	$12,191,543	....	....	....	....
1,000– 2,000	27,174	46,920,681	27,174,000	19,746,681	....	....	....	....
2,000– 3,000[c]	17,619	43,689,786	17,619,000	17,619,000	$8,451,786	....	....	....
2,000– 3,000	22,273	53,269,908	22,273,000	22,273,000	8,723,908	....	....	....
3,000– 4,000[c]	8,620	30,128,620	8,620,000	8,620,000	8,620,000	$4,268,620	....	....
3,000– 4,000	3,683	13,144,300	3,683,000	3,683,000	3,683,000	2,095,300	....	....
4,000– 5,000[c]	2,997	13,087,375	2,997,000	2,997,000	2,997,000	2,997,000	$1,099,375	....
4,000– 5,000	4,349	19,517,250	4,349,000	4,349,000	4,349,000	4,349,000	2,121,250	....
5,000– 6,000[c]	402	2,156,660	402,000	402,000	402,000	402,000	402,000	$ 146,660
5,000– 6,000	3,277	17,940,973	3,277,000	3,277,000	3,277,000	3,277,000	3,277,000	1,555,973
6,000– 7,000[c]	160	1,026,247	160,000	160,000	160,000	160,000	160,000	160,000
6,000– 7,000	2,260	14,580,002	2,260,000	2,260,000	2,260,000	2,260,000	2,260,000	2,260,000
7,000– 8,000[c]	108	807,540	108,000	108,000	108,000	108,000	108,000	108,000
7,000– 8,000	1,614	12,059,611	1,614,000	1,614,000	1,614,000	1,614,000	1,614,000	1,614,000
8,000– 9,000[c]	79	672,020	79,000	79,000	79,000	79,000	79,000	79,000
8,000– 9,000	1,202	10,181,267	1,202,000	1,202,000	1,202,000	1,202,000	1,202,000	1,202,000
9,000–10,000[c]	61	579,134	61,000	61,000	61,000	61,000	61,000	61,000
9,000–10,000	945	8,972,708	945,000	945,000	945,000	945,000	945,000	945,000
10,000–11,000	702	7,347,491	702,000	702,000	702,000	702,000	702,000	702,000
11,000–12,000	544	6,255,839	544,000	544,000	544,000	544,000	544,000	544,000
12,000–13,000	458	5,710,528	458,000	458,000	458,000	458,000	458,000	458,000
13,000–14,000	408	5,510,686	408,000	408,000	408,000	408,000	408,000	408,000
14,000–15,000	308	4,462,597	308,000	308,000	308,000	308,000	308,000	308,000
15,000–20,000	1,003	17,242,945	1,003,000	1,003,000	1,003,000	1,003,000	1,003,000	1,003,000
20,000–25,000	569	12,701,106	569,000	569,000	569,000	569,000	569,000	569,000
25,000–30,000	326	8,935,769	326,000	326,000	326,000	326,000	326,000	326,000
30,000–40,000	409	14,104,759	409,000	409,000	409,000	409,000	409,000	409,000
40,000–50,000	220	9,813,034	220,000	220,000	220,000	220,000	220,000	220,000
Over 50,000	513	57,226,579	513,000	513,000	513,000	513,000	513,000	513,000
Total	130,758	$475,906,927	$127,952,969	$107,047,224	$52,392,694	$29,277,920	$18,788,625	$13,591,633

[a] The computations in this table were made by Miss Adena Erickson of the Division of Agricultural Economics under the direction

[b] The number of returns are those reported by the United States Bureau of Internal Revenue for 1929, plus an addition in the lower

[c] This group consists of nontaxable returns under the federal income tax. Specific exemptions from normal tax exceed net income.

INDIVIDUAL INCOME BRACKET IN MINNESOTA, 1929[a]

AMOUNT OF NET INCOME FALLING WITHIN THE RANGE OF									
$6,000–$7,000	$7,000–$8,000	$8,000–$9,000	$9,000–$10,000	$10,000–$11,000	$11,000–$12,000	$12,000–$13,000	$13,000–$14,000	$14,000–$15,000	OVER $15,000
....	....	....	....	....	....	....	....	....	....
....	....	....	....	....	....	....	....	....	....
....	....	....	....	....	....	....	....	....	....
....	....	....	....	....	....	....	....	....	....
....	....	....	....	....	....	....	....	....	....
....	....	....	....	....	....	....	....	....	....
....	....	....	....	....	....	....	....	....	....
....	....	....	....	....	....	....	....	....	....
....	....	....	....	....	....	....	....	....	....
....	....	....	....	....	....	....	....	....	....
....	....	....	....	....	....	....	....	....	....
....	....	....	....	....	....	....	....	....	....
$ 66,247	....	....	....	....	....	....	....	....	....
1,020,002	....	....	....	....	....	....	....	....	....
108,000	$ 51,540	....	....	....	....	....	....	....	....
1,614,000	761,611	....	....	....	....	....	....	....	....
79,000	79,000	$ 40,020	....	....	....	....	....	....	....
1,202,000	1,202,000	565,267	....	....	....	....	....	....	....
61,000	61,000	61,000	$ 30,134	....	....	....	....	....	....
945,000	945,000	945,000	467,708	....	....	....	....	....	....
702,000	702,000	702,000	702,000	$ 327,491	....	....	....	....	....
544,000	544,000	544,000	544,000	544,000	$ 271,839	....	....	....	....
458,000	458,000	458,000	458,000	458,000	458,000	$ 214,528	....	....	....
408,000	408,000	408,000	408,000	408,000	408,000	408,000	$ 206,686	....	....
308,000	308,000	308,000	308,000	308,000	308,000	308,000	308,000	$ 150,597	....
1,003,000	1,003,000	1,003,000	1,003,000	1,003,000	1,003,000	1,003,000	1,003,000	1,003,000	$2,197,945
569,000	569,000	569,000	569,000	569,000	569,000	569,000	569,000	569,000	4,166,106
326,000	326,000	326,000	326,000	326,000	326,000	326,000	326,000	326,000	4,045,769
409,000	409,000	409,000	409,000	409,000	409,000	409,000	409,000	409,000	7,969,759
220,000	220,000	220,000	220,000	220,000	220,000	220,000	220,000	220,000	6,513,034
513,000	513,000	513,000	513,000	513,000	513,000	513,000	513,000	513,000	49,531,579
$10,555,249	$8,560,151	$7,071,287	$5,957,842	$5,085,491	$4,485,839	$3,970,528	$3,554,686	$3,190,597	$74,424,192

of Professor Warren C. Waite. See tbe explanations and qualifications in the text, pages 466, 515, 516, and 543–555.
income brackets based upon the ratio of federal to state income tax returns in corresponding brackets in Wisconsin.

Table 31. — Estimated Yields of a Tax on Individual Incomes in Minnesota, 1929[a]

(With proposed tax rates and exemptions of House File 973, Senate File 864, 47th Session of the Minnesota Legislature, 1931)

Income Class	No. of Returns[b]	Total Net Income Reported	Amount of Income Tax Paid on Portions of Income Falling within the Range of													Total Tax
			$1,000–$2,000	$2,000–$3,000	$3,000–$4,000	$4,000–$5,000	$5,000–$6,000	$6,000–$7,000	$7,000–$8,000	$8,000–$9,000	$9,000–$10,000	$10,000–$11,000	$11,000–$12,000	$12,000–$13,000	Over $13,000	
$0–$1,000[c]	6,652	$4,038,816	...	...	...	...	...	...	...	...	...	...	...	...	...	...
0– 1,000	416	224,153	...	...	...	...	...	...	...	...	...	...	...	...	...	...
1,000– 2,000[c]	21,407	33,598,543	$48,766	...	...	...	...	...	...	...	...	...	...	...	...	$48,766
1,000– 2,000	27,174	46,920,681	78,987	...	...	...	...	...	...	...	...	...	...	...	...	78,987
2,000– 3,000[c]	17,619	43,689,786	70,476	$62,543	...	...	...	...	...	...	...	...	...	...	...	133,019
2,000– 3,000	22,273	53,269,908	89,092	64,557	...	...	...	...	...	...	...	...	...	...	...	153,649
3,000– 4,000[c]	8,620	30,128,620	34,480	63,788	$53,785	...	...	...	...	...	...	...	...	...	...	152,053
3,000– 4,000	3,683	13,144,300	14,732	27,254	26,401	...	...	...	...	...	...	...	...	...	...	68,387
4,000– 5,000[c]	2,997	13,087,375	11,988	22,178	37,762	$16,601	...	...	...	...	...	...	...	...	...	88,529
4,000– 5,000	4,349	19,517,250	17,396	32,183	54,797	32,031	...	...	...	...	...	...	...	...	...	136,407
5,000– 6,000[c]	402	2,156,660	1,608	2,975	5,065	6,070	$2,581	...	...	...	...	...	...	...	...	18,299
5,000– 6,000	3,277	17,940,973	13,108	24,250	41,290	49,483	27,385	...	...	...	...	...	...	...	...	155,516
6,000– 7,000[c]	160	1,026,247	640	1,184	2,016	2,416	2,816	$1,398	...	...	...	...	...	...	...	10,470
6,000– 7,000	2,260	14,580,002	9,040	16,724	28,476	34,126	39,776	21,522	...	...	...	...	...	...	...	149,664
7,000– 8,000[c]	108	807,540	432	799	1,361	1,631	1,901	2,279	$1,299	...	...	...	...	...	...	9,702
7,000– 8,000	1,614	12,059,611	6,456	11,944	20,336	24,371	28,406	34,055	19,193	...	...	...	...	...	...	144,761
8,000– 9,000[c]	79	672,020	316	585	995	1,193	1,390	1,667	1,991	$1,209	...	...	...	...	...	9,346
8,000– 9,000	1,202	10,181,267	4,808	8,895	15,145	18,150	21,155	25,362	30,290	17,071	...	...	...	...	...	140,876
9,000–10,000[c]	61	579,134	244	451	769	921	1,074	1,287	1,537	1,842	$1,061	...	...	...	...	9,186
9,000–10,000	945	8,972,708	3,780	6,993	11,907	14,270	16,632	19,940	23,814	28,539	16,463	...	...	...	...	142,338
10,000–11,000	702	7,347,491	2,808	5,195	8,845	10,600	12,355	14,812	17,690	21,200	24,710	$13,165	...	...	...	131,380
11,000–12,000	544	6,255,839	2,176	4,026	6,854	8,214	9,574	11,478	13,709	16,429	19,149	21,869	$12,287	...	...	125,765
12,000–13,000	458	5,710,528	1,832	3,389	5,771	6,916	8,061	9,664	11,542	13,832	16,122	18,412	20,702	$10,340	...	126,583
13,000–14,000	408	5,510,686	1,632	3,019	5,141	6,161	7,181	8,609	10,282	12,322	14,362	16,402	18,442	19,666	$10,334	133,553
14,000–15,000	308	4,462,597	1,232	2,279	3,881	4,651	5,421	6,499	7,762	9,302	10,842	12,382	13,922	14,846	22,930	115,949
15,000–20,000	1,003	17,242,945	4,012	7,422	12,638	15,145	17,653	21,163	25,276	30,291	35,306	40,321	45,336	48,345	210,197	513,105
20,000–25,000	569	12,701,106	2,276	4,211	7,169	8,592	10,014	12,006	14,339	17,184	20,029	22,874	25,719	27,426	265,205	437,044
25,000–30,000	326	8,935,769	1,304	2,412	4,108	4,923	5,738	6,879	8,215	9,845	11,475	13,105	14,735	15,713	234,888	333,340
30,000–40,000	409	14,104,759	1,636	3,027	5,153	6,176	7,198	8,630	10,307	12,352	14,397	16,442	18,487	19,714	439,388	562,907
40,000–50,000	220	9,813,034	880	1,628	2,772	3,322	3,872	4,642	5,544	6,644	7,744	8,844	9,944	10,604	347,652	414,092
Over 50,000...	513	57,226,579	2,052	3,796	6,464	7,746	9,029	10,824	12,928	15,493	18,058	20,623	23,188	24,727	2,527,879	2,682,807
Total...	130,758	$475,906,927	$428,189	$387,707	$368,901	$283,709	$239,212	$222,716	$215,718	$213,555	$209,718	$204,439	$202,762	$191,381	$4,058,473	$7,226,480

[a] The computations in this table, which are based on Table 30, were made by Miss Adena Erickson of the Division of Agricultural Economics under the direction of Professor Warren C. Waite. See the explanations and qualifications in the text, pages 466, 515, 516, and 543–555.

[b] This group consists of nontaxable returns under the federal income tax. Specific exemptions from normal tax exceed net income.

[c] The number of returns are those reported by the United States Bureau of Internal Revenue for 1929, plus an addition in the lower income brackets based upon the ratio of federal to state income tax returns in corresponding brackets in Wisconsin.

TABLE 32.—SUMMARY OF STATE INCOME TAX LAWS (INDIVIDUAL AND CORPORATION), 1932 [a]

STATE	PERSONAL EXEMPTIONS	RATES FOR INDIVIDUALS ON AMOUNTS ABOVE EXEMPTIONS	RATES FOR CORPORATIONS	METHOD OF COLLECTION AND DISTRIBUTION OF PROCEEDS
Arkansas	Single person........$1,500 Husband and wife, or head of family..... 2,500 Dependent 400	1 per cent on first $3,000 2 per cent on next $3,000 3 per cent on next $5,000 4 per cent on next $14,000 5 per cent on remainder	2 per cent	State tax commissioner. First $500,000 go to charity fund; next $750,000 to common school equalization fund; remainder to special fund to reduce state taxation on property.
California		None	4 per cent [b]	Franchise tax commissioner. Proceeds go to state.
Connecticut		None	2 per cent [c]	State tax commissioner. Proceeds go to state.
Delaware	Single person........$1,000 Husband and wife, or head of family..... 2,000 Dependent 200	1 per cent on first $3,000 2 per cent on next $7,000 3 per cent on remainder	None	State tax commissioner. Proceeds go to state school department.
Georgia [d]	Single person........$1,500 Husband and wife, or head of family..... 3,500 Dependent 400	1 per cent on first $5,000 2 per cent on next $5,000 3 per cent on next $5,000 4 per cent on next $5,000 5 per cent on remainder	4 per cent	State tax commissioner. Proceeds go to state.

[a] From Prentice-Hall, *Tax Diary and Manual, 1932;* Tax Research Foundation, *Federal and State Tax Systems,* 1932; and letters and questionnaires from state officials.

[b] Offset is allowed for 10 per cent of local real estate taxes and all local personal property taxes up to 75 per cent of the 4 per cent of net income. The minimum tax is $25.

[c] Minimum tax, $10.

[d] "Residents with business or property in another state may deduct income tax if any imposed by the other state on incomes from such business or property but the credit shall not exceed the tax which would be payable to Georgia upon a like amount of taxable income." Taxpayers may offset in 1931 the amount of sales tax paid to Georgia in the same year. Credit allowed residents for income taxes paid to other states granting a reciprocal privilege.

TABLE 32. — *Continued*

STATE	PERSONAL EXEMPTIONS	RATES FOR INDIVIDUALS ON AMOUNTS ABOVE EXEMPTIONS	RATES FOR CORPORATIONS	METHOD OF COLLECTION AND DISTRIBUTION OF PROCEEDS
Idaho [e]	Single person........$1,000 Husband and wife, or head of family.... 2,500 Dependent 300	1 per cent on first $2,000 2 per cent on next $2,000 3 per cent on next $2,000 4 per cent on remainder	Same as for individuals	Tax Commission. Proceeds go to state.
Illinois [f] (law held unconstitutional; see note on page 479.)	Single person........$1,000 Husband and wife or head of family..... 2,500 Dependent 300	1 per cent on first $1,000 2 per cent on next $3,000 3 per cent on next $5,000 4 per cent on next $7,000 5 per cent on next $9,000 6 per cent on remainder	None	State Department of Finance. Proceeds go to state school fund.
Massachusetts	On income from professions, employment, trade, or business: Single person......$2,000 Husband and wife, or head of family 2,500 Dependent .... 250 For income from intangibles .... 1,000 [g]	1.5 per cent on income from professions, trade, or business 3 per cent on gains from dealings in intangible personal property 6 per cent on interest and dividends	Same as for individuals Minimum of 1/20 of 1 per cent of fair value of capital stock	Commissioner of corporations and taxation. Proceeds go first to state administration fund; next, to education fund; remainder to localities in proportion to assessment.
Mississippi	Single person........$1,500 Husband and wife, or head of family..... 3,500 Dependent 400	2.5 per cent on first $2,000 3.5 per cent on next $3,000 4.5 per cent on next $10,000 5.5 per cent on remainder	2.5 per cent on first $2,000; $50 plus 3.5 per cent on next $3,000; $155 plus 4.5 per cent on next $10,000; $605 plus 5.5 per cent on remainder	Commissioner of income tax. Proceeds go to state.

[e] Taxpayers may deduct taxes paid within the year except the taxes assessed by the United States, a tax on capital stock assessed by the state of Idaho, or taxes assessed against local benefit.

[f] Any tax on income-producing property imposed by the state of Illinois or any of its subdivisions may be used as an offset against the income tax, but the income tax "shall not be decreased by such credit in any greater proportion than his net income derived solely from property . . . bears to his total net income. . . ." Credit is allowed nonresidents for income taxes paid to other states granting a reciprocal privilege.

[g] The exemption from intangibles may be $1,000 if the taxpayer's total income from all sources does not exceed $1,000, but the exemption shall not be given to any married person if the combined income of husband and wife does not exceed $1,500.

State	Personal Exemptions	Rates for Individuals on Amounts above Exemptions	Rates for Corporations	Method of Collection and Distribution of Proceeds
Missouri [h]	Single person........$1,000 Husband and wife, or head of family..... 2,000 Dependent 200	1 per cent on first $1,000 1.5 per cent on next $1,000 2 per cent on next $1,000 2.5 per cent on next $2,000 3 per cent on next $2,000 3.5 per cent on next $2,000 4 per cent on remainder	2 per cent	State auditor. Proceeds go to state.
Montana		None	1 per cent on net income over $2,500	State Board of Equalization. Proceeds go to state.
New Hampshire	Single person........$ 200 Husband and wife, or head of family.... 200	Average rate upon other property in the state except polls, savings bank deposits, and property specially taxed for the year in which the income is assessed. (2.9 per cent for 1932)	None	State Tax Commission. 2 per cent to state for administration. Balance to localities.
New York [i]	Single person........$2,500 Husband and wife, or head of family.... 4,000 Dependent 400	2 per cent on first $10,000 [j] 4 per cent on next $40,000 6 per cent on remainder	Whichever of the following amounts is greatest: (a) 4.5 per cent of net income; (b) 1 mill of every dollar of par stock issued; (c) 4.5 per cent of net income plus salaries paid to officers and stockholders owning over 5 per cent of stock, less $5,000 and net loss; (d) $25	State Tax Commission. Proceeds of individual income tax: 75 per cent to state; 25 per cent to counties on basis of assessed valuation. Proceeds of corporation tax: ⅔ to state; ⅓ to counties on basis of location of tangible property.

[h] If the state income tax does not equal the amount that may hereafter be permitted to be deducted by the federal tax from the federal income tax "there shall be levied . . . a tax equal to the amount of such deduction in lieu of all other taxes on said income." Laws of 1931, H. B. 183.

[i] Credit is allowed nonresidents for income taxes paid to other states granting a reciprocal privilege.

[j] The rates for individuals are for 1932–33 only. "The object of such increase [100 per cent] is for the support of the government, for the relief of unemployed persons and alleviation of distress occasioned by the present economic depression." Credit is allowed nonresidents for income tax paid to other states granting a reciprocal privilege.

TABLE 32. — *Continued*

STATE	PERSONAL EXEMPTIONS	RATES FOR INDIVIDUALS ON AMOUNTS ABOVE EXEMPTIONS	RATES FOR CORPORATIONS	METHOD OF COLLECTION AND DISTRIBUTION OF PROCEEDS
North Carolina [k]	Single person........$1,000 Husband and wife, or head of family.... 2,000 Dependent 200	2 per cent on first $2,000 3 per cent on next $2,000 4 per cent on next $2,000 5 per cent on next $2,000 5.5 per cent on next $2,000 6 per cent on remainder	5.5 per cent	Commissioner of revenue. Proceeds go to state.
North Dakota	Single person........$1,000 Husband and wife, or head of family..... 2,000 Dependent 300	1 per cent on first $2,000 2 per cent on next $2,000 3 per cent on next $2,000 4 per cent on next $2,000 5 per cent on next $2,000 6 per cent on remainder	3 per cent	State Tax Commission. Proceeds go to state.
Ohio	None	5 per cent on income yielding investments	None	State Tax Commission. 1 per cent to state; remainder to municipality, school districts and library boards in proportion to previous share of classified property tax.
Oklahoma [l]	Single person........$ 750 Husband and wife, or head of family.... 1,500 Dependent 750	2 per cent on first $10,000 3 per cent on next $10,000 4 per cent on next $80,000 5 per cent on remainder	Same as for individuals	Tax Commission. 25 per cent to general state fund; 75 per cent to public schools on a scholastic enumeration per capita basis.

[k] In addition to the income tax on general income, the law of 1931 imposed a tax of 6 per cent upon residents of North Carolina who received dividends of stock of foreign corporations, as a condition of exemption of such shares of stock from the ad valorem tax. Credit is allowed nonresidents for income taxes paid to other states granting a reciprocal privilege.

[l] A referendum petition is being circulated throughout the state for an income tax measure that would impose normal rates lower than those now in force but would levy surtaxes.

State	Personal Exemptions	Rates for Individuals on Amounts above Exemptions	Rates for Corporations	Method of Collection and Distribution of Proceeds
Oregon [m]	On income from sources other than interest and dividends: Single person......$1,500 Husband and wife, or head of family. 2,500 Dependent 400	1 per cent on first $1,000 2 per cent on next $1,000 3 per cent on next $1,000 4 per cent on next $1,000 5 per cent on remainder	8 per cent	State Tax Commission. Proceeds go to state.
	On income from interest and dividends: Single person (maximum) .... $500 Husband and wife, or head of family 800 [n]	8 per cent	8 per cent	
South Carolina [t]	Single person ....$1,200 Husband and wife, or head of family.... 2,200 Dependent 400	1 per cent on first $2,000 2 per cent on next $2,000 3 per cent on next $2,000 4 per cent on next $2,000 5 per cent on remainder	4.5 per cent	Tax Commission. Proceeds go to state.
Tennessee [o]	On income other than dividends from stock and interest on bonds: Single person......$1,500 Husband and wife, or head of family 2,500 Dependent 300	1 per cent on first $2,500 1.5 per cent on next $2,500 2 per cent on next $2,500 2.5 per cent on next $2,500 3 per cent on next $2,500 4 per cent on next $2,500 5 per cent on remainder	4 per cent	All proceeds go to state.

[m] An individual may deduct taxes paid during the year imposed by the state of Oregon or any of its subdivisions, and a corporation may deduct personal property taxes paid, up to 90 per cent of the excise tax. The minimum corporation tax is $10.

[n] The exemption for a single person is found by subtracting the amount of total net income from $1,500, but it cannot exceed $500; the exemption for a married person or head of a family is found by subtracting the total net income from $2,500, but it cannot exceed $800. There is no exemption for either if the total net income exceeds $1,500 and $2,500, respectively.

[o] The constitutionality of this law is being tested in the courts, hence the law is not being enforced. See page 471, note 5.

TABLE 32. — *Continued*

STATE	PERSONAL EXEMPTIONS	RATES FOR INDIVIDUALS ON AMOUNTS ABOVE EXEMPTIONS	RATES FOR CORPORATIONS	METHOD OF COLLECTION AND DISTRIBUTION OF PROCEEDS
	On income from dividends from stock and interest on bonds ....None	5 per cent	5 per cent	55 per cent to state. 45 per cent to localities.
Utah [p]	Single person........$1,000 Husband and wife, or head of family.... 2,000 Dependent 400	1 per cent on first $1,000 1.25 per cent on next $1,000 1.5 per cent on next $1,000 1.75 per cent on next $1,000 2 per cent on next $1,000 2.5 per cent on next $1,000 3 per cent on next $1,000 3.5 per cent on next $1,000 4 per cent on remainder	3 per cent	State Tax Commission. 25 per cent to state; 75 per cent to school districts.
Vermont [q]	On income from business: Single person......$1,000 Husband and wife, or head of family 2,000 Dependent 250	2 per cent	2 per cent	State tax commissioner. Proceeds of individual income tax: $150,000 to towns and villages on basis of road mileage; $300,000 to consolidated school fund; remainder to state. All proceeds of corporation tax go to state.
	On income from intangibles: [r] Single person...... $400 Husband and wife, or head of family 800	4 per cent		

[p] The taxpayer may offset against the income tax the amount of real and personal property taxes paid in Utah, but not over one-third of the tax. Every resident of the state over 21 years must file an income tax return and pay a filing fee of $1.00. The minimum tax for corporations is 1/20 of 1 per cent of the fair value of tangible property in Utah but not less than $10.00.

[q] Credit is allowed residents for income tax paid to other states granting a reciprocal privilege.

[r] The personal exemptions of $400 and $800 are allowable only in case the income is entirely from intangibles.

State	Personal Exemptions	Rates for Individuals on Amounts above Exemptions	Rates for Corporations	Method of Collection and Distribution of Proceeds
Virginia [4]	Single person........$1,250 Husband and wife or head of family.... 2,800 Dependent 400	1.5 per cent on first $3,000 2.5 per cent on next $2,000 3 per cent on remainder	3 per cent	Department of Taxation. Proceeds go to state.
Wisconsin [5]	For normal tax: Single person, $8 of tax Husband and wife, or head of family, $17.50 of tax Dependent, $4 of tax	Normal tax rates: 1 per cent on first $1,000 1.25 per cent on next $1,000 1.5 per cent on next $1,000 2 per cent on next $1,000 2.5 per cent on next $1,000 3 per cent on next $1,000 3.5 per cent on next $1,000 4 per cent on next $1,000 4.5 per cent on next $1,000 5 per cent on next $1,000 5.5 per cent on next $1,000 6 per cent on next $1,000 7 per cent on remainder	2 per cent on first $1,000 2.5 per cent on next $1,000 3 per cent on next $1,000 3.5 per cent on next $1,000 4 per cent on next $1,000 5 per cent on next $1,000 6 per cent on remainder	State Tax Commission. 40 per cent to state; 10 per cent to counties; 50 per cent to localities.
		Surtax: 1/6 of normal tax rates on incomes over $3,000	Same as for individuals	Teachers' retirement fund.
	For one-year emergency surtax: Same as above except $6 for dependent	Emergency surtax: same as normal tax rates	None	State relief purposes.

[5] Laws of Special Session, 1931, Ch. 29. "Beginning January 1, 1933 the tax will be computed on the net income of the preceding year, the tax on 1931 income, payable in 1932 being the last to be computed by the three-year-average method." For 1932 there is an alternative method; "(a) only on 1932 income, or (b) one-third 1930 income plus two-thirds 1931 income, whichever method yields the higher amount." See page 472.

APPENDIX A

ESTIMATES OF MINNESOTA INCOME[1]

The income of a geographical area, such as Minnesota, may be considered either from the viewpoint of income produced within the borders of the state or of income received by individuals residing in the state. The totals of the two accounts would probably differ, since a part of the income produced within the state may go to persons residing outside, either because they own property rights in Minnesota or because they perform services for Minnesota residents. Similarly, persons residing in Minnesota may receive incomes from sources outside the state.

Two Methods of Procedure

The methods which suggest themselves as most convenient for estimating the income of the people of the state are, first, a summation of the values of all goods and services produced and sold by persons and enterprises in the state, care being taken to avoid double counting; and, second, a summation of the incomes of all individuals in the state. An estimate covering a series of years on a comparable basis is at present possible only by following the first method. The data must be drawn from a wide variety of sources, such as the federal census, reports of the Minnesota Tax Commission and other state bureaus, commercial publications, and so on. The estimate of individual incomes must depend primarily upon the reports made to the Bureau of Internal Revenue for the higher income groups. Estimates for the lower income groups must be made in other ways. We have utilized the Census of Occupations to make a single estimate for the year 1929.

Proper procedure would yield identical estimates from the two methods outlined above; moreover, we could make estimates of either the income produced or the income received within the state. Such a procedure would take some such form as given on page 544. Limitation of data prevents any such complete accounting. In the first type of estimate it has been possible to arrive at only item 1, the value of goods and services produced in Minnesota. It

[1] Prepared by Professor Warren C. Waite of the Division of Agricultural Economics, University of Minnesota Agricultural Experiment Station.

METHODS OF ESTIMATING INCOME IN MINNESOTA

METHOD I: INCOME ESTIMATED FROM VALUE OF GOODS AND SERVICES	METHOD II: INCOME ESTIMATED FROM INCOMES OF FINAL INCOME RECEIVERS
(1) Value of goods and services produced in Minnesota less (a) depletion of capital and material resources plus (2) Income due from outside the state (income from investments) less (3) Payments made outside the state (a) To holders of property in Minnesota (b) For services rendered elsewhere	(4) Payments for personal services to residents of Minnesota plus (5) Earnings from property in Minnesota less (a) depletion of capital and natural resources and (b) payments to property holders outside the state plus (6) Income due from outside the state (income from investments)

has not been possible to make deductions for 1a, the depletion of capital and natural resources, or to estimate items 2 and 3. The second type of estimate, made for 1929, of the individual income receivers includes item 4, payments for personal services to Minnesota residents, and portions of items 5, earnings from property, and 6, income from outside the state. No deduction is made for item 5a, depletion of capital and natural resources, but 5b, payments to property owners outside the state, is eliminated by the method of computation.

METHOD I: ESTIMATE OF INCOME FROM THE VALUE OF GOODS AND SERVICES PRODUCED IN MINNESOTA

This is an estimate of the money value of goods and services sold in the market. Such things as the contribution of the farm to the farmer's living and the services performed by a man for himself or his family are omitted. Care has been exercised to avoid double counting. It would be improper, for example, to include both the value of the wheat sold from Minnesota farms and the flour produced in Minnesota flour mills. We have made the estimate in steps to avoid this difficulty as far as possible. These steps include (1) an estimate of the value of primary production, which includes the value of agricultural products sold, the value of ore at the mouth of the mine, and the value of timber cut; (2) an estimate of the value of processing industries, which includes the value added by manufacturing and the value of new construction, less cost of materials; and (3) an estimate of the value of service industries, among the important groups of which are the services of mercantile establishments, transportation and public utilities, pro-

TABLE 1.—ESTIMATES OF THE VALUE OF GOODS AND SERVICES PRODUCED IN MINNESOTA, 1919–1931[a]
(In millions of dollars)

YEAR	VALUE OF PRIMARY PRODUCTION	VALUE ADDED BY PROCESSING INDUSTRIES	VALUE OF SERVICE INDUSTRIES	TOTAL
1919........	$585.1	$378.3	.....	.....
1920........	493.5	334.1	.....	.....
1921........	310.3	307.6	.....	.....
1922........	369.9	351.2	.....	.....
1923........	465.0	391.9	.....	.....
1924........	447.3	376.4	.....	.....
1925........	492.7	392.6	$727.9	$1,613.2
1926........	504.0	377.2	661.9	1,543.1
1927........	455.2	378.5	675.7	1,509.5
1928........	460.1	400.1	676.8	1,537.0
1929........	508.1	436.1	679.2	1,623.4
1930........	421.2	316.9	605.3	1,343.4
1931........	276.4	220.2	532.0	1,028.6

[a] For Brookmire's estimates of Minnesota income see pages 529 and 530.

fessional services (medical, legal, etc.), and banks and financial institutions. Estimates for these groups by years from 1910 to 1931 are given in Table 1.

VALUE OF PRIMARY PRODUCTION

The estimated value of the goods included in primary production ranged from 585.1 million dollars in 1919 to 276.4 million dollars in 1931. In this group the sale of agricultural products is the most important item, constituting nearly 75 per cent of the total in 1929. (See Table 2.)

The data for agriculture are estimates of the gross cash income received by Minnesota farmers from the sale of the sixteen principal agricultural commodities of the state. These estimates were made by the Division of Agricultural Economics of the University of Minnesota.[2]

The data for mining are the values of ore at the mouth of the mine as reported to the Minnesota Tax Commission for the period from 1921 to 1930.[3] The figure for 1919 is that of the federal census, and that for 1920 is a straight interpolation between 1919 and 1921.

[2] A. G. Black and D. D. Kittredge, *Minnesota Agricultural Indexes of Prices, Quantities, and Cash Incomes, 1910–1927* (University of Minnesota Agricultural Experiment Station Technical Bulletin No. 72, 1931); W. C. Waite, "Farmers' Income in Minnesota," *Minnesota Farm Business Notes,* No. 108, publication of the University of Minnesota Agricultural Experiment Station.

[3] Report of the Minnesota Tax Commission, 1930, p. 97.

TABLE 2.—VALUE OF PRODUCTS OF AGRICULTURE, MINING, AND FORESTRY IN MINNESOTA, 1909–1931
(In millions of dollars)

YEAR	AGRICULTURE	MINING	LUMBER	TOTAL
	Cash Sales of 16 Important Products	Value of Ore at Mouth of Mine	Cost of Materials for "Lumber and Timber Products Not Elsewhere Classified"	
1909	.....	$58.7	$20.8	....
1910	$165.9	....	....	....
1911	144.1	....	....	....
1912	162.6	....	....	....
1913	182.4	....	....	....
1914	184.4	....	....	....
1915	201.4	....	....	....
1916	227.7	....	....	....
1917	308.3	....	....	....
1918	450.9	....	....	....
1919	437.6	130.4	17.2	$585.1
1920	379.2	97.6	16.7	493.5
1921	229.3	64.8	16.3	310.3
1922	256.4	98.4	15.2	369.9
1923	286.6	164.4	14.0	465.0
1924	342.0	90.7	14.5	447.3
1925	395.2	82.6	14.9	492.7
1926	397.6	93.8	12.6	504.0
1927	365.8	79.1	10.3	455.2
1928	367.1	84.4	8.5	460.1
1929	383.7	117.7	6.7	508.1
1930	331.5	84.7	5.0	421.2
1931	230.0	42.4	4.0	276.4

The data for lumbering are the values of raw materials reported in the *Census of Manufactures* for the item "lumber not elsewhere classified."[4] It is possible that the value of lumber should properly be the item "value of products, lumber not elsewhere classified" rather than the smaller item "value of raw materials." The choice does not affect our estimate of total income in the state, but simply the allocation between value of lumber and value of manufactured products. The data have been interpolated between census years. The value of the individual items by years is given in Table 2.

It will be observed that certain small items have been omitted in these estimates—for example, minor crops, such as truck crops, clover seed, and fruits, in the case of agriculture; the value of the products of quarries in the case of mining; and sales of firewood and of individual small operators in the case of lumber.

[4] *Biennial Census of Manufactures,* 1919, 1921, 1923, 1925, 1927, 1929.

TABLE 3.—ESTIMATED GROSS AND NET CASH INCOME FROM THE SALE OF AGRICULTURAL PRODUCTS FOR THE STATE AND FOR THE AVERAGE FARM, 1910–1931

Year	Gross Cash Income from Sale of Agricultural Products[a]	Average Gross Cash Income per Farm[b]	Purchasing Power of Average Gross Farm Income[c]	Preliminary Estimate of Average Operating Expense per Farm[d]	Preliminary Estimate of Net Cash Income per Farm[e]	Purchasing Power of Net Farm Income[c]
	Million dollars					
1910	$165.9	$1,063	$1,085	$462	$601	$613
1911	144.1	911	902	471	440	440
1912	162.6	1,013	1,013	504	509	504
1913	182.4	1,120	1,120	538	582	582
1914	184.4	1,118	1,107	557	561	550
1915	201.4	1,204	1,136	598	606	566
1916	227.7	1,343	1,092	645	698	558
1917	308.3	1,794	1,196	779	1,015	686
1918	450.9	2,593	1,457	949	1,644	913
1919	437.6	2,482	1,211	1,071	1,411	659
1920	379.2	2,125	1,032	1,233	892	393
1921	229.3	1,271	815	1,030	241	146
1922	256.4	1,406	925	941	465	291
1923	286.6	1,556	1,017	1,017	539	335
1924	342.0	1,837	1,193	1,000	837	517
1925	395.2	2,100	1,321	1,028	1,072	650
1926	397.6	2,118	1,358	1,005	1,113	679
1927	365.8	1,956	1,270	1,029	927	576
1928	367.1	1,970	1,263	1,026	944	583
1929	383.7	2,065	1,332	1,025	1,000	625
1930	331.5	1,789	1,225	916	873	578
1931	230.0 (est.)	1,245	965	836	409	317

[a] Estimate by the Division of Agricultural Economics of the cash sales of the sixteen principal agricultural products of Minnesota. Certain minor crops are omitted. The data do not include value of produce used on the farm for household consumption.

[b] Column 2 divided by the number of Minnesota farms reported in the census. The number of farms in intercensal years has been interpolated by a straight-line method.

[c] Purchasing power of income in terms of things that the farmer buys. Based on the Department of Agriculture Index of Prices of things purchased by the farmers. This index may not be entirely representative of conditions in Minnesota, but it is the best available.

[d] Preliminary estimate of cash expenses for Minnesota agriculture. There are a number of omissions, and these figures may be too low. Computations were made by Mr. Mark Regan of the Division of Agricultural Economics of the University of Minnesota.

[e] Out of this the farmer must pay for food, clothing, fuel, and transportation expenses and accumulate savings.

Since agriculture is the most important single source of income in the state, contributing nearly 25 per cent of our estimated total income, some further analysis is desirable. This is given in Table 3.

VALUE ADDED IN PROCESSING INDUSTRIES

The values added by manufacturing and by new construction have been considered the value added in processing industries.

TABLE 4.—VALUE ADDED BY MANUFACTURE AND BY NEW CONSTRUCTION IN PROCESSING INDUSTRIES IN MINNESOTA, 1919–1931
(In millions of dollars)

YEAR	VALUE ADDED BY MANUFACTURE	VALUE ADDED BY NEW CONSTRUCTION	TOTAL VALUE OF PROCESSING INDUSTRIES
1919	$335.0	$43.2	$378.3
1920	300.0	34.1	334.1
1921	265.0	42.6	307.6
1922	290.2	61.0	351.2
1923	315.5	76.4	391.9
1924	323.2	53.2	376.4
1925	330.9	61.7	392.6
1926	334.2	43.0	377.2
1927	340.3	38.1	378.5
1928	364.2	35.9	400.1
1929	402.2	33.9	436.1
1930	289.6	27.3	316.9
1931	204.0	16.2	220.2

The data for manufacturing are the values added by manufacture as reported in the *Census of Manufactures,* with interpolations for intervening years. The value added by manufacturing represents the total value of the product less the value of raw materials used in manufacture. The total value of manufactured products has not been used, since this would include the value of raw materials, previously estimated under the primary production group. It is necessary to estimate intercensal years. The estimates for 1926, 1928, and 1930 have been made by computing the percentage change from the preceding year in the gross income of manufacturing corporations in Minnesota, as reported to the United States Bureau of Internal Revenue for corporation tax purposes, and applying the same percentage change to the value added by manufacture as reported in the census. The estimates for 1920, 1922, and 1924 are averages of the years next preceding and following.

The value added by new construction has been estimated on

the basis of building operations reported in the five cities of Minneapolis, St. Paul, Duluth, Winona, and St. Cloud.[5] The per capita value of building operations in these five cities has been computed for individual years. The value of building operations throughout the remainder of the state has been estimated on the basis of population and at half the per capita value of the five cities. The total reported value of building operations in the five cities plus the estimated value in the remainder of the state is the total estimated value of building operations in the state as a whole. A considerable amount of this total represents the cost of materials, which have already been accounted for if they come from Minnesota, or which were purchased outside the state. These have been roughly estimated at 50 per cent. The estimated value used in the analysis of income is thus half the computed value of building operations in the state as a whole.

VALUE OF PRODUCTS OF THE SERVICE INDUSTRIES

In this group are included transportation, public utilities, trade, and personal service enterprises. These produce for the most part intangible products difficult to allocate specifically to particular units of product. There are three principal parts to the total estimate: first, an estimate of the value added by trade, taken as the margin on sales; second, an estimate of the value of transportation and public utility services; and third, miscellaneous items, such as personal service and the services of financial institutions. The aggregate of these estimates is given in Table 5.

The estimate of value added by trade is computed by applying average margins to the sales of specific lines in Minnesota as reported in the *Census of Distribution,* 1929. (See Table 6.)[6] Average margins in particular businesses were obtained from averages found in studies made in Minnesota and elsewhere. The retail margins were as follows: food, 18 per cent; country general stores, 30 per cent; general merchandise, 30 per cent; automotive, 25 per cent; apparel, 32 per cent; furniture, 40 per cent; restaurants, 50 per cent; lumber and building, 20 per cent; all others, 30 per cent; wholesale margins, 10 per cent. Subsequent years have been interpolated on the basis of volume of trade reported in different sections of the state.[7] The years from 1925 to 1928 have been estimated on the

[5] *Commercial and Financial Chronicle,* January 30, 1932.

[6] Professor R. S. Vaile of the School of Business Administration has made the estimates of value added by trade.

[7] R. S. Vaile, "Summary of Minnesota Retail Trade, 1929–31," *Minnesota Business Review,* Vol. 1, no. 2, p. 11.

TABLE 5.—VALUE OF THE PRODUCTS OF SERVICE INDUSTRIES IN MINNESOTA, 1919–1931
(In millions of dollars)

YEAR	TRADE, GROSS MARGIN	PUBLIC UTILITY AND TRANSPORTATION	PERSONAL SERVICE AND FINANCE	TOTAL
1919	.....	$203.5	....	....
1920	.....	233.1	....	....
1921	.....	201.7	....	....
1922	.....	212.5	$38.9	....
1923	.....	231.1	39.1	....
1924	.....	220.7	40.2	....
1925	$458.6	227.7	41.6	$727.9
1926	394.6	223.9	43.4	661.9
1927	403.2	227.9	44.6	675.7
1928	407.1	223.9	45.8	676.8
1929	393.4	238.7	47.1	679.2
1930	344.4	212.9	48.0	605.3
1931	292.0	(200) (est.)	40.0	532.0

basis of the 1929 estimate, the assumption being that the margin varied in the same proportion as the gross income of the Minnesota corporations engaged in trade reported to the Bureau of Internal Revenue.

The estimate of the value of services from public utilities and transportation is the sum of individual estimates for steam railroads, telephones, urban and suburban electric railways, and elec-

TABLE 6.—VOLUME OF TRADE AND GROSS MARGINS IN MINNESOTA, 1929

	VOLUME (000 omitted)	MARGIN IN PERCENTAGE	MARGIN IN DOLLARS (000 omitted)
Retail			
Food	$ 202,380	18	$ 36,500
Country general store	57,230	30	17,200
General merchandise	191,910	30	57,300
Automotive	216,470	25	54,000
Apparel	78,400	32	25,100
Furniture	37,150	40	14,830
Restaurants	36,300	50	18,150
Lumber and building	63,930	20	12,800
All other	179,750	30	53,800
Total retail	$1,063,520	..	$289,680
Total wholesale	1,036,839	10	103,684
Total wholesale and retail margins			$393,364

TABLE 7.—VALUE OF SERVICES OF TRANSPORTATION AND PUBLIC UTILITIES IN MINNESOTA, 1919–1931
(In millions of dollars)

YEAR	TELE-PHONE, GROSS EARN-INGS	STEAM RAILROADS, TOTAL RAILWAY OPERATING REVENUE	SUBURBAN ELECTRIC RAILWAY, GROSS OPERATING REVENUE	URBAN ELECTRIC RAILWAY, GROSS OPERATING REVENUE	ELECTRIC POWER AND LIGHT	TOTAL
1919........	14.6	154.4	1.2	11.4	21.9	203.5
1920........	15.3	179.5	1.2	13.5	23.6	233.1
1921........	15.9	145.9	1.2	15.0	23.7	201.7
1922........	16.6	153.4	1.1	15.7	25.7	212.5
1923........	17.2	171.2	1.0	15.6	26.1	231.1
1924........	17.4	156.9	.8	15.4	30.2	220.7
1925........	18.5	163.7	.8	14.5	30.2	227.7
1926........	19.1	159.6	.7	14.3	30.2	223.9
1927........	19.7	160.3	.5	15.9	31.5	227.9
1928........	20.4	165.9	.4	15.4	31.9	233.9
1929........	21.1	166.2	.4	14.9	36.1	238.7
1930........	20.0 (est.)	137.8 (est.)	.4	15.3	39.3	212.9
1931........	...	99.7 (est.)	.4	...	...	(200.0) (est.)

tric light and power companies. (See Table 7.) The data for steam railways are the total railway operating revenue in the state of Minnesota reported to the Minnesota Tax Commission for purposes of taxation. Similar data are reported for the suburban electric railways. The data for the urban street railways are the sums of the total operating revenue of the street railway systems of Minneapolis, St. Paul, and Duluth as published in the annual reports of the respective companies. The value of electric power is the production of kilowatt hours in central station plants in Minnesota reported by the Geological Survey, to which an estimated rate has been applied. The telephone data consist of an estimate of gross earnings on the basis of the amount paid by the companies under the state earnings tax.

The estimate for miscellaneous service is the total of separate estimates of the value of the services of barbers, ministers, doctors, lawyers, and dentists, together with those of banks and financial institutions. (See Table 5, column 4.) The estimate for the individual occupations was made by interpolating from the Census of Occupations the probable number in each class each year and estimating the probable earnings of individuals in that class. The estimate of $5,250 as the average income of physicians in general practice made by R. G. Leland from a survey of 6,163 physicians in various parts of the United States was taken as the base for 1929.[8] The earnings of lawyers and dentists were estimated on the basis of the ratio of earnings of lawyers and dentists to the earnings of physicians as reported in the survey of the land-grant colleges.[9] Estimates of earnings in other years than 1929 were based on the assumption that these earnings fluctuated in the same proportion as the average annual earnings of those employed in the manufacturing industries. The rates for barbers are based on the average annual earnings of persons employed in manufacturing as reported by the census.[10] The rates for ministers are based on the average salaries of Methodist and Congregational ministers from 1910 to 1926 as reported by Paul Douglas; the 1926 salary is assumed to continue during the following years.[11] The estimate of the income of banking and financial institutions is the net income reported by banking and financial corporations in the state in federal income tax reports.

INCOME OF CORPORATIONS

Additional information is available on the gross and net incomes of corporations reporting to the Bureau of Internal Revenue for income tax purposes. The gross incomes reported are larger than the computation of the state income because of sales of goods and

TABLE 8.—GROSS INCOME OF MINNESOTA CORPORATIONS, REPORTED FOR INCOME TAX PURPOSES, 1925–1929
(000 omitted)

ITEM	1925	1926	1927	1928	1929
Agriculture and related industries	$ 6,537	$ 7,445	$ 11,433	$ 7,295	$ 7,074
Mining and quarrying	17,685	20,165	20,830	20,152	26,074
Total manufacturing	945,942	957,450	966,568	1,037,418	1,082,836
Construction	27,126	40,511	41,375	44,436	44,347
Transportation and public utilities	345,966	450,363	463,275	477,080	491,110
Trade	1,165,303	1,050,794	1,086,026	1,126,787	1,076,073
Service, professional, etc.	35,043	42,174	43,509	46,496	48,198
Finance, banking, etc.	148,122	193,147	206,666	203,702	204,002
Total	$2,691,724	$2,762,049	$2,839,682	$2,963,366	$2,979,714

[8] R. G. Leland, "Income from Medical Practice," *Journal of the American Medical Association,* 96:1, 683 (May 16, 1931).

[9] P. O. Johnson, *The Survey of Former Students of Land-Grant Institutions,* (Educational Research Bulletin No. 3, College of Education, University of Minnesota, 1932).

[10] The total wages reported divided by the average number of wage earners.

[11] Paul Douglas, *Real Wages in the United States,* p. 386.

services between corporations. In our estimates of state totals, we cannot accurately separate the value of goods from the value of services produced. Examination of the classifications discloses, however, that the value of goods and services produced by corporations must constitute 50 per cent or more of the estimated income of the state.

The gross incomes reported are given in Table 8. Manufacturing and trade, each with a gross income of a billion dollars in 1929, are the largest items; public utilities and transportation appear to have had gross incomes of close to 500 million dollars. Net income, which for many purposes is the more significant item, is shown in Table 9 on the next page.

Method II: Incomes of Individuals in Minnesota

The principal source of information on the distribution of income received by individuals in Minnesota is the report of the United States Bureau of Internal Revenue. The number of individuals reported in the several income groups is given by years for the period from 1920 to 1929 in Table 10.

For 1929 an estimate has been made of the incomes of the entire group of income receivers in the state. This was done in two steps: first, an estimate was made of the number of incomes that would have been reported if the requirements of 1924 had been maintained; and second, an estimate, based on the Census of Occupations, was made of the incomes of those who would not have reported under the 1924 requirements.

Those having *gross* incomes of over $5,000, whatever their *net* incomes, have been required to report incomes since 1921. In 1925 an important increase was made in the net income for which a report was required. In 1925 single persons with net incomes of $1,500 and married persons with net incomes of $3,500 were required to report, whereas in 1924 reports were required of single persons receiving $1,000 and of married persons receiving $2,500. The data for 1925 thus omit persons in the net income group of $2,500 to $3,500 in the married class and those in the net income group of $1,000 to $1,500 in the single class, which groups were included in the data for 1924. We have assumed that the difference between the number of income receivers in these classes in 1924 and 1925 was due to the change in requirements as to who must make returns. As a matter of fact, the groups probably would have been somewhat larger, since 1925 was a somewhat more pros·

TABLE 9.—NET INCOME LESS DEFICIT OF MINNESOTA CORPORATIONS, REPORTED FOR INCOME TAX PURPOSES
(000 omitted)

ITEM	1921	1922	1923	1924	1925	1926	1927	1928	1929
Agriculture and related industries	—$1,098	—$274	—$1,548	—$461	—$716	—$50	—$1,319	$242	—$147
Mining and quarrying	— 662	2,014	3,538	925	1,228	1,255	1,759	2,356	4,910
Total manufacturing	— 5,102	30,498	40,568	34,783	40,477	37,995	35,115	47,210	46,918
Construction	266	935	1,083	2,334	1,155	2,487	1,412	3,384	2,640
Transportation and public utilities	3,230	4,939	21,773	21,588	28,351	36,466	20,337	38,809	29,011
Trade	— 8,243	16,881	16,163	15,216	24,335	15,103	17,331	21,549	21,287
Service, professional, etc.	500	917	966	969	1,375	1,870	1,937	3,083	2,054
Finance, banking, etc.	4,084	2,503	—3,328	4,663	3,707	4,129	4,285	10,838	7,342
Total	—$6,935	$58,413	$79,215	$80,017	$99,912	$99,255	$80,857	$127,471	$114,016

TABLE 10.—NUMBER OF INCOMES IN SPECIFIED CLASSES REPORTED TO THE BUREAU OF INTERNAL REVENUE, 1920–1929 [a]

INCOME	1920	1921	1922	1923	1924	1925	1926	1927	1928	1929
Over $15,000	1,955	1,445	1,517	1,566	1,655	2,036	2,325	2,435	2,834	2,990
$10,000–$15,000	1,869	1,231	1,384	1,381	1,163	1,485	2,093	2,092	2,291	2,420
9,000– 10,000	725	494	515	460	490	568	805	802	974	1,006
8,000– 9,000	967	654	657	658	648	766	999	1,019	1,217	1,281
7,000– 8,000	1,515	987	1,009	929	876	1,166	1,625	1,487	1,537	1,722
6,000– 7,000	2,043	1,406	1,423	1,330	1,363	1,658	1,942	1,961	2,126	2,420
5,000– 6,000	3,251	2,048	2,171	1,968	2,305	2,440	2,893	2,837	3,452	3,679
4,000– 5,000	6,005	4,426	5,540	8,539	8,986	11,956	7,601	7,037	7,007	7,346
3,000– 4,000	15,765	13,706	14,415	17,644	17,866	13,233	11,628	10,279	10,104	9,320
2,000– 3,000	57,975	43,002	38,996	30,127	35,242	15,058	12,345	11,646	11,602	11,563
1,000– 2,000	62,048	51,140	49,647	64.980	51,188	18,758	17,626	17,730	15,644	15,087
Under $1,000	.....	4,009	4,611	4,778	6,455	2,167	2,445	2,114	1,966	1,817

[a] Individuals having amounts of income indicated below, or more, were required to report them.

	1920	1921–1923	1924	1925–1930
Married and living with husband or wife				
Net income	$2,000	$2,000	$2,500	$3,500
Gross income regardless of net income	.....	5,000	5,000	5,000
Single, or married and not living with husband or wife				
Net income	1,000	1,000	1,000	1,500
Gross income regardless of net income	.....	5,000	5,000	5,000

TABLE 11.—ESTIMATE OF NUMBER OF INDIVIDUAL INCOME RECEIVERS IN SPECIFIED CLASSES IN MINNESOTA, 1929

Income	No. Making Federal Income Tax Returns	No. Not Making Federal Income Tax Returns: Farmers	No. Not Making Federal Income Tax Returns: Selected Trades and Occupations	Total No. of Income Receivers	Total Amount of Net Income Received
Over $15,000	2,990	......	......	2,990	$120,000,000
$10,000–$15,000	2,420	......	......	2,420	29,286,000
9,000– 10,000	1,006	......	......	1,006	9,552,000
8,000– 9,000	1,281	......	......	1,281	10,853,000
7,000– 8,000	1,722	......	......	1,722	12,867,000
6,000– 7,000	2,420	......	......	2,420	15,606,000
5,000– 6,000	3,679	......	......	3,679	20,098,000
4,000– 5,000	7,349	9,263	......	16,612	74,754,000
3,000– 4,000	12,473	18,525	23,937	54,935	192,272,000
2,000– 3,000	27,164	37,051	88,370	152,585	381,462,000
1,000– 2,000	40,182	55,576	195,960	291,718	437,577,000
Under $1,000	1,817	64,840	374,333	440,990	220,495,000
Total	104,503	185,255	682,600	972,358	$1,524,822,000

perous year than 1924. It has also been assumed that changes in the number of returns would have been proportional to the changes that actually occurred in the reporting groups if these had included married persons with net incomes of from $2,500 to $3,500 and single persons with net incomes between $1,000 and $1,500. Thus we are able to estimate the number of returns that would have been reported under the 1924 requirements.

We may assume that the incomes reported for income tax purposes are almost entirely incomes of property holders, managers and proprietors of businesses, and professional persons. The remaining income receivers are assumed to be laborers of different kinds, small entrepreneurs, persons rendering personal services, and farmers. The number of persons reported in the Census of Occupations is used to indicate the probable number of income receivers in each class or branch of trade or occupation. An estimate is then made of the income receivers in each group who fall within the specified income class, miscellaneous sources of information being used to determine the income of that group. The agricultural group, the largest single class, has been distributed according to a recent survey of 764 Minnesota farms. Estimates are shown in Table 11.

APPENDIX B

INHERITANCE AND ESTATE TAXES[1]

Death taxes form part of the revenue system of every state in the Union except Nevada. There is, however, great variation in the rates in force in the several states and in the importance of the tax from the standpoint of revenue. Alabama and Florida, for example, have only an estate tax to absorb the credit allowed by the federal estate tax. In Pennsylvania, Delaware, and New York the tax is counted one of the substantial sources of state revenue. In Minnesota the tax produced slightly more than 1 per cent of the total state and local revenues in 1931. Table 1 shows the total collections in each state from this source during the past seven years. Table 2 shows the percentage of total state and local revenues represented by the inheritance tax in 1929 and 1930.

The cost of administering the tax is small, as shown in Table 3, though it is impossible to get complete data because many states do not separate the cost of collecting this tax from other costs. In Minnesota, for example, the administration of the tax is one of many duties of the state attorney-general.

Tables 4 and 5 show that Minnesota could materially increase revenues from this source by reducing exemptions and by raising the rates of tax. Table 4 shows comparative rates in a few states. The best way to appreciate the net effect of different rates and exemptions is to compare the amounts of tax due in each state from estates of the same size. Such comparisons for estates of $50,000, $200,000, and $1,000,000 are shown in Table 5. It will be noted that in the first case the tax in Minnesota is less than one-fifth of that in Utah; in the second case, slightly over half the Utah tax; and in the third case, approximately half the Wisconsin tax.

For years leaders in tax reform movements have tried to secure reciprocity among the states in taxing estates of nonresidents. By 1931 this had been accomplished in twenty-nine states. Apparently the desired end has now been achieved for the entire United States as the result of decisions of the United States Supreme Court which

[1] Prepared by Gladys C. Blakey.

hold that certain intangibles, as well as tangibles, may be taxed only in the state where the decedent had residence.[2]

Following these decisions the Minnesota Supreme Court ruled against the state in the case of Estate of Kennedy v. Minnesota, May 20, 1932.[3] This judgment resulted in a loss to the state of $250,000. The general effect, however, will be greater equity and uniformity of inheritance tax administration throughout the country because of the abolition of multiple taxation. A financial benefit will accrue to such states as New York, where large owners of corporation stocks and bonds have their residences. The loss to states in which the debtor corporations are located may be compensated for in other ways, as by franchise or income taxes, greater freedom of investment, and lower interest rates.[4]

In 1931 the legislature adopted an estate tax[5] to take full advantage of the 80 per cent credit permitted by the Federal Estate Tax Law of 1926. This tax took effect April 24, 1931, and, in the first nineteen months of its operation (to November 18, 1932), it yielded $687,824. It is expected that it will produce nearly as much more from three other estates now in process of settlement. During the fiscal year ending June 30, 1932, it yielded only $44,585. All the rest ($643,239) has been received between July 1 and November 18, 1932. This new tax imposes no burden on Minnesota citizens over and above that already imposed by the federal law, and it was not expected to yield very much additional revenue. The proceeds to date have exceeded expectations, partly on account of the retroactive provision. It is evident that yields are likely to be very unstable from year to year. They may, however, offset much of the loss caused by the Supreme Court decisions mentioned above.

[2] Farmers Loan and Trust Co. v. Minnesota (1930), 280 U.S. 204; Baldwin v. Missouri (1930), 281 U.S. 586; Beidler v. South Carolina (1930), 282 U.S. 1; First National Bank v. Maine (1932), 52 Sup. Ct. Rep. 174; Henry Rottschaefer, "Power of the States to Tax Intangibles," *Minnesota Law Review*, 15:741 (June, 1931).

[3] 242 N.W. 697. In preparing the brief for this case in January, 1932, the attorney-general computed that in the preceding two years inheritance taxes had been paid upon stock of Minnesota corporations to the value of $252,517, of which 95 per cent was held by nonresidents.

[4] J. A. Craine, "Some Recent Inheritance Tax Decisions," *Southern California Law Review*, 4:263 (April, 1931).

[5] Session Laws of Minnesota, 1931, Ch. 332.

Table 1. — State Inheritance and Estate Tax Collections, 1925–1931 [a]

State	1925	1926	1927	1928	1929	1930	1931
Alabama [b]	....	....	....	....	......	....	....
Arizona	....	....	....	$40,105	$80,197	....	$79,844
Arkansas	....	....	$443,000	234,194	312,217	$281,790	253,859
California	$6,423,134	$7,424,174	8,461,549	10,963,174	13,180,226	11,647,010	13,735,791
Colorado	911,210	876,008	....	1,544,093 [c]	919,984	908,328	225,001 [d]
Connecticut	2,872,813	2,506,930	2,601,557	3,018,665	3,604,074	3,619,744	4,827,397
Delaware	86,032	140,785	190,574	621,706	2,576,275	1,811,979	1,770,924 [f]
Florida [b]	....	....	....	....	....	....	....
Georgia	....	....	194,000	602,714	697,181	359,424	....
Idaho	15,292	22,229	12,701	30,937	31,201	35,330	32,040
Illinois	....	14,345,392 [c]	....	29,903,998 [c]	....	26,561,678 [c]	....
Indiana	952,771	1,047,238	1,108,947	1,171,523	1,213,183	1,450,555	1,985,133
Iowa	1,073,040	1,121,533	1,128,208	1,221,083	1,129,939	1,259,012	....
Kansas	328,550	396,742	441,115	697,557	630,647	617,766	617,478
Kentucky	387,503	689,549	667,393	734,311	1,012,629	1,034,891	1,075,142 [f]
Louisiana	466,694	606,768	627,899	676,279	698,232	621,264	....
Maine	1,372,655	687,898	799,556	1,693,269	924,926	1,013,190	2,656,514
Maryland	741,842	701,083	591,152	746,870	882,276	1,508,606	2,269,710
Massachusetts	5,920,307	6,511,302	10,751,882	10,337,738	11,586,072	14,117,402	11,943,450
Michigan	2,507,860	2,159,984	1,952,068	2,324,017	3,337,567	5,423,010	5,997,048
Minnesota	1,116,196	1,022,112	1,278,413	1,389,580	1,686,159	1,690,588	2,362,340
Mississippi	237,121	218,261	169,596	161,247	65,068	36,292	30,146
Missouri	1,165,500	1,901,305	1,960,553	3,056,262	2,729,738	3,840,011	2,753,601
Montana	193,891	1,029,070	535,951	654,369	161,505	229,802	66,659
Nebraska	....	....	....	....	....	....	72,621 [e]
New Hampshire	278,587	334,031	353,274	419,273	384,934	480,076	423,918
New Jersey	6,519,716	7,199,549	11,407,663	11,394,556	7,617,868	16,003,036	10,561,113
New Mexico	41,110	19,556	23,505	25,698	57,457	33,456	18,891

New York	23,584,767	22,222,748	24,479,953	35,566,274	47,164,582	50,395,171	52,587,632
North Carolina	765,862	856,115	814,540	710,446	1,022,927	1,385,525	1,006,074
North Dakota	46,843	36,320	63,376	69,167	74,649	60,006	40,345
Ohio	5,392,020	5,698,138	6,488,777	6,343,759	7,038,906	8,054,096	6,306,383
Oklahoma	96,176	293,493	159,952	332,099	414,128	182,979	226,652 [f]
Oregon	500,670	616,902	440,337	700,212	1,000,311	970,050	....
Pennsylvania	13,419,895	16,511,253	18,494,344	15,788,148	25,187,959	36,970,993	39,406,199
Rhode Island	435,458	421,515	718,006	566,319	1,668,830	979,586	893,498
South Carolina	461,817	292,915	227,095	146,192	360,682	265,507	200,894
South Dakota	201,163	170,463	146,300	268,117	209,931	209,454	185,404
Tennessee	299,704	624,458	516,046	425,375	520,120	442,806	......
Texas	587,546	1,013,645	1,561,926	1,029,201	1,247,093	663,702	901,333
Utah	368,477	174,296	387,558	268,332	343,890	369,198	......
Vermont	328,478	228,740	434,357	362,511	502,436	509,209	267,386 [f]
Virginia	620,281	769,873	841,731	768,932	941,440	1,117,271	1,099,253
Washington	443,398	533,063	662,797	697,855	655,178	839,784	941,382
West Virginia	875,743	802,731	1,027,733	667,456	1,233,501	752,070	1,076,306
Wisconsin	3,181,989	2,199,330	2,439,056	3,706,934	2,942,400	2,650,000	2,599,450
Wyoming	44,880	45,817	23,758	139,518	34,626	22,416	66,659

[a] Compiled from data received from state officials; from Tax Research Foundation, *Federal and State Tax Systems, 1932*, pp. 118, 142; and from National Industrial Conference Board, *Cost of Government*, 1928–29, 1929–30.

[b] An estate tax at 80 per cent of the federal estate tax was enacted in 1931.

[c] Two years' yield.

[d] A half year only.

[e] Total receipts of the estate tax only since the law was enacted in 1929. The inheritance tax is collected by the counties and the proceeds go to the counties, so total proceeds are unknown.

[f] Fiscal year ending July 1, 1931. Vermont collections for 1931–32 were $434,000.

TABLE 2.—STATE INHERITANCE AND ESTATE TAX COLLECTIONS COMPARED WITH TOTAL STATE AND LOCAL TAXES, 1929 AND 1930[a]

(000 omitted)

State	1929			1930		
	Total State and Local Taxes	Inheritance and Estate Taxes		Total State and Local Taxes	Inheritance and Estate Taxes	
		Amount	Percentage of Total Taxes		Amount	Percentage of Total Taxes
Arizona	$25,171	$80	.32%	$30,048	...	....
Arkansas	41,877	312	.75	47,409	$281	.59%
California	418,314	13,180	3.15	431,662	11,647	2.70
Colorado	57,907	919	1.59	66,494	908	1.37
Connecticut	100,295	3,604	3.59	104,589	3,619	3.46
Delaware	18,158	2,576	14.19	17,980	1,811	10.07
Georgia	65,465	697	1.06	76,346	359	.47
Idaho	24,653	31	.13	26,894	35	.13
Illinois	367,664	9,820	2.67	410,373	16,741	4.08
Indiana	165,139	1,213	.73	172,891	1,450	.84
Iowa	158,607	1,129	.71	142,136	1,259	.89
Kansas	106,906	630	.59	111,032	617	.56
Kentucky	72,537	1,012	1.40	84,927	1,034	1.22
Louisiana	75,520	698	.92	83,022	621	.75
Maine	39,428	924	2.34	44,471	1,013	2.28
Maryland	75,887	882	1.16	86,177	1,508	1.75
Massachusetts	372,727	11,586	3.11	392,437	14,117	3.60
Michigan	323,998	3,337	1.03	344,704	5,423	1.57
Minnesota	158,607	1,686	1.06	161,304	1,690	1.05
Mississippi	62,971	65	.10	27,396	36	.13
Missouri	145,225	2,729	1.88	130,523	3,840	2.94
Montana	31,013	161	.52	40,023	229	.57
New Hampshire	26,360	384	1.46	27,056	480	1.77
New Jersey	314,841	7,617	2.42	346,628	16,003	4.62
New Mexico	13,966	57	.41	17,372	33	.19
New York	1,023,792	47,164	4.61	1,140,986	50,395	4.42
North Carolina	97,299	1,022	1.05	102,131	1,385	1.36
North Dakota	35,866	74	.21	35,462	60	.17
Ohio	366,261	7,038	1.92	397,357	8,054	2.03
Oklahoma	87,782	414	.47	105,402	182	.17
Oregon	65,466	1,000	1.53	65,980	970	1.47
Pennsylvania	476,539	25,187	5.29	471,393	36,970	7.84
Rhode Island	38,423	1,668	4.34	36,819	979	2.66
South Carolina	45,282	360	.80	38,335	265	.69
South Dakota	43,199	209	.48	52,240	209	.40
Tennessee	66,490	520	.78	81,740	442	.54
Texas	200,271	1,247	.62	242,172	663	.27
Utah	24,199	343	1.42	26,219	369	1.41
Vermont	17,700	502	2.84	21,883	509	2.33
Virginia	80,786	941	1.16	80,347	1,117	1.39
Washington	95,319	655	.69	94,130	839	.89
West Virginia	69,788	1,233	1.77	75,636	752	.99
Wisconsin	183,023	2,942	1.61	194,414	2,650	1.36
Wyoming	13,726	34	.25	18,506	22	.12

[a] Compiled from the data in Table 1. In view of the varied sources from which these data were procured, it is probable that a number of the figures are inexact.

Table 3. — Cost of Administration of State Inheritance and Estate Taxes, 1925–1931 [a]

(Percentages of collections)

State	1925	1926	1927	1928	1929	1930	1931
California [b]	.93	.89	.93	.64	...	...	...
Colorado	2.8	2.8	3.2	3.2	2.2	2.2	...
Indiana [c]	...	...	...	3.5	3.3	3.2	2.04
Kansas	5% deducted by county treasurers for costs						
Kentucky	3.4	2.	2.	2.	1.5	1.5	...
Louisiana	Covered by a fee payable in addition to the tax						
Maine	.37	.79	.8	.39	.72	.69	.0022
Maryland [d]	...	...	...	...	...	...	...
Massachusetts	1.16	1.07	.66	.69	.59	...	.5 to .6
Michigan	.45	.52	.60	.48	.34	.22	...
Minnesota [e]	From about .5 of 1% to 1% a year						
Mississippi	5.	5.75	7.	5.75	24.	8.	...
Montana	4.	8.	1.5	1.2	5.2	4.	5.25
New Hampshire	Average for the entire period 2%						
New Jersey	2.	1.94	1.16	1.18	1.89	1.05	...
New Mexico [f]	...	...	...	1.18	1.89	1.05	...
New York	2.83	2.38	2.2	1.72	1.33	1.26	...
North Carolina	...	4.38	3.75	4.18	3.04	2.44	3.23
North Dakota	...	...	...	...	...	...	5.[g]
Oklahoma [h]	Approximately 1.7						
Rhode Island	...	...	...	...	...	...	1.5
South Carolina	1.73	2.73	3.52	4.95	3.01	4.09	5.41
South Dakota [i]	...	...	...	...	1.56	1.71	1.89
Tennessee	5% deducted by county court clerk for costs						
Virginia	.69	.55	.50	.55	.46	.56	...
Washington	4.37	5.33	3.78	3.82	4.55	3.65	3.38
West Virginia	...	.8	.68	1.04	.56	.9	...
Wisconsin	...	...	2.1	1.05	1.8	2.04	...
Wyoming [j]	13.37	13.09	26.36	4.30	17.33	26.77	5.03

[a] Compiled from the data in Table 1.

[b] Each county treasurer may retain in addition to his salary or fees 3 per cent of the first $50,000 of inheritance tax paid to the state, 1½ per cent of the next $50,000, and 1 per cent on all additional sums within certain limits, depending on the size of the county.

[c] Approximately $40,000.

[d] The cost of operating the offices of the registers of wills, the officials who collect the inheritance taxes, is approximately $223,000.

[e] $10,000 to $12,000 a year.

[f] $3,800 to $4,000 a year.

[g] $2,000 a year.

[h] $3,000 a year.

[i] $3,500 a year.

[j] $6,000 a year.

TABLE 4.—RATES OF INHERITANCE TAX ON DIRECT AND REMOTE HEIRS

STATE	EXEMPTION	RATES ON FIRST $15,000	$15,000–$30,000	$30,000–$50,000	$50,000–$100,000	OVER $100,000
CLASS A (MOST DIRECT HEIRS)						
Arkansas	$6,000[a] 4,000	1–3%	3–4%	4%	5–6%	7–10%
California	50,000	0	0	0	4	6–8
Illinois	20,000	2	2	2	4	4–14
Minnesota	10,000[a] 3,000	1	2	2½	3	4
Pennsylvania	500	2	2	2	2	2
Utah	10,000[b]	3	3–5	5	5	5
Wisconsin	15,000 2,000	2	2–4	4	6	8–10
CLASS D (MOST REMOTE HEIRS)						
Arkansas	None	4–12	12–16	16	20–24	28–40
California	500	5	10	10	12	12
Illinois	100	10	12	16	16	20–30
Minnesota	100	5	10	12½	15	20
Pennsylvania	None	10	10	10	10	10
Utah	10,000[b]	3	3–5	5	5	5
Wisconsin	100	8	8–16	16	24	32–40

[a] Widow. [b] Entire estate.

TABLE 5.—AMOUNTS OF STATE INHERITANCE AND ESTATE TAXES DUE ON ESTATES OF SPECIFIED AMOUNTS AFTER ALL DEDUCTIONS EXCEPT PERSONAL EXEMPTIONS

STATE	ESTATE OF $50,000 [a]	ESTATE OF $200,000 [a]	ESTATE OF $1,000,000 [b]
Alabama	....	$1,200	$33,200
Arizona	$380	4,380	36,380
Arkansas	900	8,100	70,060
California	10	4,510	67,650
Colorado	400	5,000	63,750
Connecticut	650	4,650	36,650
Delaware	270	2,970	33,200
Florida	....	1,200	33,200
Georgia	....	1,200	33,200
Idaho	150	1,950	27,970
Illinois	200	4,400	68,000
Indiana	300	4,300	38,330
Iowa	100	4,100	58,900
Kansas	100	1,925	33,200
Kentucky	200	4,200	41,250
Louisiana	900	5,400	29,400
Maine	450	2,700	33,200
Maryland	....	1,200	33,200
Massachusetts	500	5,500	42,500
Michigan	200	2,650	33,200
Minnesota	300	4,700	36,700
Mississippi	....	1,200	33,200
Missouri	200	2,533	33,200
Montana	305	4,305	36,305
Nebraska	150	1,200	33,200
New Hampshire	....	1,200	33,200
New Jersey	400	2,900	43,900
New Mexico	400	1,900	9,900
Nevada	....	....	.....
New York	200	1,800	33,800
North Carolina	350	3,100	33,200
North Dakota	250	3,500	33,800
Ohio	400	3,400	33,415
Oklahoma	250	4,250	36,250
Oregon	525	4,525	55,525
Pennsylvania	990	3,990	33,200
Rhode Island	400	3,150	44,950
South Carolina	325	4,500	47,300
South Dakota	500	4,500	36,500
Tennessee	525	4,525	38.525
Texas	....	2,500	32,500
Utah	1,700	9,200	49,200
Vermont	300	5,300	42,300
Virginia	300	2,800	33,200
Washington	350	2,700	39,250
West Virginia	200	6,200	46,200
Wisconsin	660	8,660	72,660
Wyoming	600	3,600	19,600

[a] Divided equally between widow and minor child.
[b] Divided equally between widow and adult child.

APPENDIX C

SALES TAXES [1]

Since about 1920 thirty states have adopted some form of sales or excise tax upon commodities or services in an effort to increase revenues without increasing property taxes, especially the property taxes of the farmer.[2] Such taxes may take the form of a general tax upon sales of manufacturers, producers, wholesalers, jobbers, or retailers;[3] or they may be selective and be applied to only a few articles, such as tobacco products, cosmetics, and soft drinks.

General Sales Taxes

West Virginia has had as complete a general sales tax over a period of years as any state. The tax is applicable to annual sales in excess of $10,000. The rates vary from .42 per cent of the gross proceeds of coal producers to 1.85 per cent of the gross sales of gas. Wholesalers and jobbers pay .05 per cent of gross proceeds, whereas retailers pay .20 per cent. The yield during the past five years has been as follows: 1928, $3,805,078.02; 1929, $3,656,632.31; 1930, $3,704,730.75; 1931, $3,065,010.21; 1932, $2,327,710.81.[4]

Mississippi has recently passed a general sales tax with rates in many cases twice as high as obtained under a previous law and much higher than those of any other state. Some of the rates are as follows:

Retailers	2.0	per cent of gross receipts
Producers of oil, glass, and sand	2.5	per cent of gross receipts
Manufacturers of soft drinks	1.0	per cent of gross receipts
Wholesalers and jobbers	.125	per cent of gross receipts
Ice manufacturers	.25	per cent of gross receipts

The amount of exemption is reduced from $5,000 to $1,200. A similar law with rates comparable to those of West Virginia but with an exemption of $30,000 to each taxpayer was in effect in Georgia for two years, from 1929 to 1931.

[1] Prepared by Gladys C. Blakey.

[2] See Table 4 on page 570 for a list of taxes, revenues, and costs of administration.

[3] The gasoline tax is the most widely known example of this kind of a tax in the United States, since it has been adopted by every state in the Union. Being closely linked with highway finance, it is fully considered in Chapter 13 and will not be further referred to here.

[4] From Roy G. Blakey, *Taxation in West Virginia,* p. 441, and information obtained from W. B. Calder of the Sales Tax Division of the West Virginia tax commissioner's office. The periods cover fiscal years ending June 30.

Taxes on merchants, both wholesale and retail, are imposed by Connecticut, North Carolina, Kentucky, Delaware, Pennsylvania, and Virginia, in addition to the two states mentioned above. Kentucky imposes taxes on retailers only. This is really a tax on chain stores, inasmuch as the rate increases in proportion to the amount of sales. The tax in Connecticut is levied upon unincorporated businesses in order to equalize the tax burden between such companies and incorporated concerns, which pay a tax on net income.

TABLE 1.—RECEIPTS FROM TAXES ON TOBACCO IN SEVEN STATES, 1927–1931 [a]

STATE	1927	1928	1929	1930	1931
Alabama	......	$912,254	$1,278,680	$1,262,664	$954,106
Arkansas [b]	$470,891	745,732	1,093,417	1,333,021	1,042,509
Georgia	877,221	737,751	797,064	1,051,377	1,580,874
Iowa	998,164	1,183,033	1,325,914	1,401,436	1,335,144
South Carolina [c]	......	1,812,140	1,975,371	1,907,826	1,751,368
South Dakota	......	398,019	522,394	467,616	418,672
Tennessee [d]	......	......	1,259,776	2,302,768	2,056,956

[a] Based on data used in compiling Table 4 below and the table on page 442 of *Taxation in West Virginia.*

[b] Fiscal years ending June 30. Receipts for 1931–32 were $906,630.

[c] Includes taxes on candy, ammunition, playing cards, and malt.

[d] $1,088,471 for the first six months of 1932.

CONSUMPTION TAXES

TOBACCO

The most common excise tax is that upon the sale of tobacco and its products. Such a tax is levied in thirteen states, of which six tax cigarettes only. The rates of tax are sometimes based upon size or weight of the product, sometimes upon price, number, or package; hence it is difficult to make valid comparisons. According to available data, the largest yield from tobacco taxes in 1931 was $2,056,956, collected in Tennessee; the smallest, $150,251, collected in Utah. The income from this source over a series of years is shown for a few states in Table 1.

Because many states do not separate their accounts, it is impossible to give complete statements of the cost of collecting taxes on tobacco sales, but in the states where such accounting is made, the costs are from 2.5 per cent to 7 per cent of the yield. It is generally agreed that if the tax is to be enforced effectively, it is necessary to have an adequate staff for collection in order to prevent illegal sales. The tax is not simple to administer and requires more careful supervision than most taxes. In this connection it may be interesting to note the following statement made before the Association of the Bar of the City of New York by the secretary of the treasury, Ogden L. Mills.[5]

> A study recently made of the administration of state taxes on cigarettes shows that, whereas in 1930 the per capita consumption of cigarettes in the entire country averaged 975, the five states which in that year levied a tax solely on cigarettes collected, on the average, taxes on only 431 cigarettes per capita. While we may not assume that the average actual consumption in these five states was the same as the average for the country, yet the figures indicate that many a cigarette was smoked in these states on which the state tax had not been paid.

SOFT DRINKS

Next to tobacco, soft drinks and malt are the consumption goods most commonly taxed. Eight states levy taxes on the sales of bottled drinks, syrup, carbonated water, or malt, but, as shown in Table 4 (pages 570–575), the revenue is small. South Carolina has had more experience with such taxes than any other state. It

TABLE 2.—SALES TAX RECEIPTS IN SOUTH CAROLINA, 1928–1931

SOURCE	1928[a]	1929[a]	1930[b]	1931[a]
Business license[c]	$1,812,140	$1,975,371	$1,907,826	$1,751,367
Documentary[d]	342,771	314,464	274,099	....
Admissions (10 per cent)	273,891	302,382	283,730	261,570
Soft drinks at fountains (syrups, $.76 per gallon)	204,425	194,459	207,665	180,214
Bottled drinks (20 per cent)	985,836	1,046,245	869,275	789,455
Pool rooms ($25 per table)	8,250	8,974	10,400	15,675
Contractors (annual, $100; single, graduated)	74,000	60,350	79,340	53,200
Chain stores and miscellaneous	26,353	2,252	......	......
Total	$3,727,666	$3,904,497	$3,632,335	$3,051,481

[a] Statement of receipts by the South Carolina Tax Commission.
[b] Memorandum of the Subcommittee on Research to the [Ohio] Governor's Taxation Committee, March 10, 1931, Table 11.
[c] Includes sales taxes on tobacco, candy, playing cards, and ammunition.
[d] The rate varies according to the value of the document.

taxes theater admissions, tobacco products, ammunition, sporting goods, soft drinks, playing cards, and candy above a certain price. Receipts from these taxes in the past four years are shown in Table 2. In 1930 the state adopted a tax on chain stores and in 1931 it imposed a tax of half a mill on each kilowatt of electric power generated or sold.

[5] Bulletin of the National Tax Association, 17:228 (May, 1932).

TABLE 3.—POSSIBLE YIELDS FROM SALES TAXES IN MINNESOTA

COMMODITY	SALES		RATE OF TAX	ESTIMATED REVENUE	
	1929 [a]	1932 [a]		1929 [a]	1932 [a]
Cosmetics [b]	$3,000,000	$2,225,000	5%	$150,000	$112,000
Cigarettes [c]	105,528,026 pkgs.	85,000,000 pkgs.	1c per pkg.	1,055,000	850,000
Soft drinks and ice cream	$4,000,000 / 8,000,000	$15,000,000	5%	600,000	750,000 [d]
Furs [e]	12,000,000	6,000,000	5%	600,000	300,000
Barber shops and beauty parlors [f]	30,000,000	25,000,000	5%	1,500,000	1,250,000
Jewelry [g]	1,700,000	800,000	5%	85,000	40,000

[a] Fiscal year ending July 1. [b] Data from reports of the St. Paul office of the Bureau of Internal Revenue.
[c] 2 per cent of total manufactured and consumed in the United States.
[d] Probably an overestimate.
[e] Data from Bureau of Foreign and Domestic Commerce and from large dealers.
[f] Computed from licenses. [g] Data from the commissioner of internal revenue.

The past few years have seen a rapid increase in the adoption of two new sales taxes, one on chain stores and the other on oleomargarine. The tax on the latter varies from 5 to 15 cents a pound, the lower rate being the more common. In two states the rate is doubled if the product is colored. These measures are obviously for regulative or other purposes rather than for revenue.

Possible Yields in Minnesota

The estimates in Table 3 have been made for this survey by Professor R. S. Vaile of the University of Minnesota. They show the probable yields from taxes on certain articles of consumption provided sales would not be reduced as a result of the tax.

As to the effect on business, Professor Vaile says, "People in the trade believed in 1928–29 that these taxes would not materially limit sales. In 1932, cigarette dealers, ice cream manufacturers, and beauty shop proprietors all estimated further reductions in sales if taxes were imposed now—probably by 10 to 15 per cent."

Effects of a General Sales Tax

Those in favor of a sales tax maintain that it is desirable because it is a successful device for procuring revenue, that it is elastic, that it is easy to compute, that it secures some support of government from those who would not pay a net income tax.

On the other hand, those who oppose such a tax point out several difficulties. The first consideration is the effect on business. Although the tendency is to shift the tax to the consumer, this cannot always be done immediately, and even if it is accomplished the seller cannot escape certain other difficulties. Marginal firms that cannot operate with the additional burden of the tax will be forced out of business. Merchants in a state imposing a sales tax whose businesses are located near the border of a state without such a tax are handicapped in comparison with merchants in the interior of the state, since consumers will try to do as much business as possible in the neighboring state. If the tax is on some articles only, there will be some falling off of purchases in these lines. Thus some kinds of business will suffer more than others. In any case, the tax necessitates general readjustments. The tendency is to discourage industries with large turnovers sold at small margins of profit. As compared with an income tax, a sales tax is more likely to discourage new industries from starting, because they would have to pay taxes before they made any profits. Ease of administration has been overemphasized by the advocates of the tax.

From the point of view of the consumer, the tax may be favored by some because it is paid in such small amounts and usually at times when it is not a serious burden. It is maintained that when the tax is on articles other than necessities the consumer may refrain from purchasing such goods if he objects to paying the tax. On the other hand, inasmuch as the general effect is to tax according to consumption, a general sales tax is regressive in its effects and thus tends to lower the standard of living of the poorer classes.

Table 4.—Taxes Imposed on Commodities and Services According to States, 1931 [a]

State	Commodity or Service	Rate of Tax	Yield, 1931	Cost of Administration
Alabama	Cigars and cigarettes	15% of wholesale price	$954,106	5.7% [b]
	Carbonic acid gas	2c on each pound used in soft drinks	$14,628	
	Chain stores, except those selling petroleum products	Graduated from $1 for 1 store to $75 each for over 20 stores	$5,708 [b]	
Arizona	Chain stores	Graduated, 1 store, $3; 2 to 5 stores, $5 each; over 20 stores, $25 each		
Arkansas	Cigars	10% of retail price	$1,042,509, fiscal year 1930–31 (cigars and cigarettes)	.... [c]
	Cigarettes	$3.00 per thousand	$906,630, fiscal year 1931–32 (cigars and cigarettes)	
	Malt	10% of selling price	$26,866, fiscal year 1930–31 $23,356, fiscal year 1931–32	
Colorado	Oleomargarine	5c per pound	First year in effect	
Connecticut	Theaters, including motion picture houses	Graduated, according to seating capacity, from 50c to $12 per day	$139,036.50	2.9% [d]
	Boxing matches	5%	$21,889	
	Unincorporated business tax [d]	$1.00 per thousand, retailers .25 per thousand, wholesalers	$617,770	
Delaware	Branch stores	$10 plus .1% of aggregate cost value of goods over $5,000	$160,755 [e] (branch stores and licenses)	
	Manufacturers' and merchants' licenses	$5 plus percentage of goods sold		

[a] Compiled from Memorandum Submitted to the Governor's Taxation Committee, Columbus, Ohio, March, 1931; Tax Research Foundation, *Federal and State Tax Systems,* 1932; *Report of the New York State Tax Commission for the Revision of the Tax Laws,* 1932; and data from state officials.

[b] "It is left to agreement among the dealers as to who shall pay the tax. . . . In practice, about 90 per cent is collected from wholesale dealers, who are allowed 10 per cent of the tax collected as a compensation for their services." *Report of the New York Tax Commission for the Revision of the Tax Laws,* Memorandum No. 6, p. 15. Receipts from chain stores are for a period of six months.

[c] Each wholesale and retail dealer must pay a license tax. The Department of Revenues collects income, inheritance, motor vehicle, slot machine, and severance taxes in addition to those on tobacco and malt. The cost of administration ranged from 1.69 per cent to 2.11 per cent per fiscal year up to 1930.

[d] The tax was imposed to equalize the burdens on unincorporated and incorporated businesses, since the latter pay a tax on net income. The cost of collecting the tax on admissions is estimated to be about $4,000 a year.

[e] All-business license as reported in *Federal and State Tax Systems* (1932), p. 141. The rate varies for retailers, wholesalers, manufacturers, and wholesalers of grain, fruits, and vegetables.

Florida	Chain stores except gas filling stations	$5 to $50[f]	First year in effect	
Georgia	Carbonic acid gas or substitute	4c per pound	$32,046.52	2% (Carbonic acid gas through Malt extracts)
	Soft drink syrups and carbonated water	½% of gross receipts	$9,913.53	
	Malt extracts and products	1% of gross receipts	$642.29	
	Cigars	10% of retail price	$1,580,874 (Cigars and Cigarettes)	5%
	Cigarettes	20% of retail price[g]		
	Milk powder	5c per pound	First year in effect	
	Chain stores	$50 each store over five		
	Admissions	3 mills per $1	$957,577[h] (Admissions through All other businesses)	2%
	Manufacturers	½ mill per $1 of gross receipts		
	Wholesale brokers	1 mill per $1 of gross receipts		
	Certain public utilities	3 mills per $1 of gross receipts		
	All other businesses	2 mills per $1 of gross receipts		
Idaho	Electric power	½ mill per kw. hr.	First year in effect	
	Oleomargarine	5c per pound; 10c if colored	First year in effect	

[f] On the following basis:

No. of Stores	In One County	In Different Counties
1	$5	
2–15	$10 for each additional store	$15 for each additional store
15–30	$15 for each additional store	$20 for each additional store
30–50	$20 for each additional store	$30 for each additional store
50–75	$30 for each additional store	$40 for each additional store
Over 75	$40 for each additional store	$50 for each additional store

For each $1,000 worth of stock carried in each store $3 additional is levied.

Each county and each municipality may levy a license tax of 25 per cent of the state tax, provided such taxes are graduated according to the number of stores located therein.

[g] After April 1, 1933, the rate will be reduced to 10 per cent, the same as it was before April 1, 1931. Dealers must have a license.

[h] The gross receipts tax granted an exemption of $30,000 to each taxpayer. The law was passed in 1929 and expired on December 31, 1931, in accordance with the provision made at the time of enactment. The tax was an alternative to the net income tax.

TABLE 4. — *Continued*

STATE	COMMODITY OR SERVICE	RATE OF TAX	YIELD, 1931	COST OF ADMINISTRATION
Illinois	Athletic exhibitions	10% of gross receipts		
	Horse races	20c per paid admission		....[i]
Indiana	Store license fee	Graduated from $3 for one store to $25 for each store over twenty		
Iowa	Cigarettes	1–2 mills per cigarette, depending upon weight	$1,335,144	4.5%[j]
	Oleomargarine	5c per pound	First year in effect	
Kansas	Cigarettes	2c per package of 20	$682,250 (Cigarettes and Cigarette papers)	6 to 7%
	Cigarette papers	1c per 50		
Kentucky	Gross retail sales			
	Minimum	1/20% on $400,000 or less[k]	$83,560 (Jan. 1 to Nov. 1, 1931) (Minimum and Maximum)	
	Maximum	1% on excess over $1,000,000		
Louisiana	Malt extracts	3c for each pound or fraction	$95,019	32.1%[l]
Massachusetts	Boxing matches	5% of gross receipts		None
Michigan	Malt	Wort, liquid malt, 5c per gallon; syrup and extract, 5c per pound	$660,469	9.8%
	Boxing matches	10% gross proceeds	$46,289	8.1%
Minnesota	Boxing or sparring matches	10% of gross proceeds	$16,381	None
Mississippi	Theaters, public amusements, etc.	Admission fee, 1c on each 10c or fraction over 30c	$84,242	5% (Theaters, public amusements, etc. and Cigars and cigarettes)
	Cigars and cigarettes	20% of usual selling price	$662,517	
	Soft drinks	1% of gross sales		

[i] In 1930 the tax on athletic exhibitions produced $145,737; the tax on admissions to horse races produced $664,567.
[j] Approximately $60,000.
[k] This is in effect a tax on chain stores.
[l] The expense of administration is limited by statute to $36,000. In 1931 it was $30,500.

Mississippi (*Continued*)	Gross sales [m]	Manufacturers, ¼% to 1% Jobbers and wholesalers, ⅛% Producers of oil, glass, and sand, 2½% Retailers, 2% Chain stores, ¼ of 1% additional if more than five stores are operated	$192,981	6% [n]
Missouri	Manufacturers and merchants (Kansas City and St. Louis only)	.1%		
New Jersey	Commercial feeding stuff	8c per net ton	$27,400	
	Fertilizer	15c per net ton	$22,647	
North Carolina	Gross sales	Wholesale, graduated, $12.50 to $400 Retail, graduated, $5 to $500, plus $250 for each $250,000 over $500,000	First year in effect	
	Chain stores	$50 for each store in excess of one	First year in effect	
North Dakota	Cigarettes	1½ mills to 2 mills each, depending upon weight	$325,529	8% [o]
	Cigarette papers	½c per 50 papers or major fraction thereof		
	Cigarette tubes	1c for each 50 tubes or major fraction thereof		
	Snuff	2c on each 1¼ ounce		

[m] The rates shown here are for 1932 and are much higher than those previously in force. Receipts for 1932–33 are estimated at $3,300,000.

[n] In addition, retailers are allowed a 10 per cent commission on the sale of stamps.

[o] Approximately $27,000. Each dealer must pay a license tax of $12.50.

TABLE 4. — *Continued*

STATE	COMMODITY OR SERVICE	RATE OF TAX	YIELD, 1931	COST OF ADMINISTRATION
Ohio	Cigarettes	1c on each 10 or fraction thereof	First year in effect	
Pennsylvania	Mercantile license	Wholesalers, $3 plus ½ mill Retailers, $2 plus 1 mill Dealers at exchanges, ¼ mill	.......[p]	7.8%
	Boxing and wrestling matches		.......[p]	
South Carolina	Admissions	1c for each 10c charged	$261,570	
	Soft drinks, bottled	1c for each 5c retail price	$789,455	
	Fountain syrups	76c per gallon	$180,214	
	Chain stores	Graduated, $5 for one store to $150 each store over thirty		
	Electric power tax	½ mill on each kilowatt of energy generated or sold	$750,000 (estimated)	
	Cigars	$1 to $10 per M		
	Cigarettes and smoking tobacco	20% of retail price	$1,751,367[q]	2.6%
	Snuff and chewing tobacco	1c for each 3 ounces or fraction		
	Malt extracts or substitutes	2c per pound		
South Dakota	Malt extracts and syrups	10% of retail price		
	Cigarettes	1½ to 4 mills each, depending upon weight	$418,672	1.79%[r]
	Cigarette papers	½c for each 50		
	Cigarette tubes	1c for each 50 or fraction		
	Butter substitutes	10c per pound	First year in effect	
	Lard substitutes	5c per pound		

[p] In 1930 the mercantile license tax produced $4,274,090; the tax on boxing and wrestling matches produced $82,311.
[q] Includes also proceeds from sales of candy, ammunition, and playing cards.
[r] $7,500.

Tennessee	Cigarettes	20% of retail price	$2,056,956	Not to exceed 4%[e]
	Cigars, manufactured tobacco, and snuff	10% of retail price		
	Malt	5c per pound	$98,948	Not to exceed 4%[e]
	Carbonic acid gas	5c per pound		
	Oleomargarine	5c per pound	$41,553	
Texas	Cigarettes	$1.50 per M weighing not more than 3 pounds; $3.60 if weighing more than 3 pounds	First year in effect	
	Feeding stuff	10c per ton	First year in effect	
	Commercial fertilizer	25c per ton		
Utah	Cigarettes	1 to 2 mills each, depending upon weight	$167,206[f]	8%
	Cigarette papers	1c for each 50 papers		
	Cigarette tubes	1c for each 50 tubes		
	Oleomargarine	5c to 10c per pound	$5,752.95	
Virginia	Merchants' licenses	Graduated, $10 to $20 plus 10c on each $100 on all gross purchases in excess of $100,000	$1,325,518	3%[g]
Washington	Butter substitutes	15c per pound	First year in effect	
West Virginia	Business and occupation	Varies according to business, .42% to 1.85%	$3,065,010.21	1.42%[h]
	Theater admissions	1% of gross income		
Wisconsin	Boxing matches	5% of gross receipts	$15,921	
	Emergency chain store licenses	Graduated from $10 for one store to $50 for each store over twenty	First year in effect	
	Oleomargarine	6c per pound plus dealer's fee	First year in effect	
Wyoming	Oleomargarine	10c per pound	First year in effect	

[e] Amount allowed by law for the operating expenses of the Sales Tax Division.

[f] $16,955 of this is from licenses required of dealers.

[g] Estimated. "The law is administered primarily by local commissioners of the revenue and local treasurers under the supervision of the Virginia State Department of Taxation. The Department of Taxation has full supervisory powers and itself engages in checking up the returns." Letter of July 8, 1932.

[h] $43,612. The collections for the fiscal year ending June 30, 1932, were $2,327,711.

APPENDIX D

SUMMARIES OF MINNESOTA TAX DATA

THE MINNESOTA TAX SYSTEM

PROPERTY TAXES[1]

Classified General Property Tax

Imposed on all property not exempt by law and not subject to gross earnings or other tax imposed in lieu of the property tax. Rates are determined by state and local officials as authorized by law. The total rate is made up of a rate for state purposes plus a rate for each of the local units. These rates vary from year to year and from unit to unit with varying needs for revenue. The state rate is a relatively small part of the total rate.

Classification for assessment.—The tax rate is applied not to full value of property but to certain *percentages* of full and true value, as indicated below:

Class 1.—Iron ore, mined or unmined, 50 per cent of full and true value. (See also special taxes below.)

Class 2.—Household goods, jewelry, wearing apparel, etc., 25 per cent.

Class 3.—Livestock, poultry, merchandise, manufactured articles, tools, implements and machinery, bank stock, unplatted real estate (agricultural land and improvements), 33⅓ per cent.

Class 3a.—Agricultural machinery used by owner and agricultural products in hands of producer and not for sale, 10 per cent.

Class 4.—Platted real estate (urban land and improvements) and personal property not included in other classes, 40 per cent.

Telegraph Companies

Ad valorem tax on 40 per cent of full value, assessed as a unit by the Tax Commission.

[1] Gross earnings taxes are property taxes by legal fiction. They, the motor registration tax, the vessel tonnage tax, and most of the property taxes other than the classified general property tax, are in lieu of the general property tax and are commonly spoken of as "lieu taxes." The premiums tax on insurance companies is similar to a gross earnings tax, but they are in addition to rather than in lieu of

Rate not over average of the general property tax rate.
Proceeds go to the state.

MONEY AND CREDITS

Does not include money and credits belonging to incorporated banks nor indebtedness on which mortgage registry tax has been paid. Includes currency, bank notes, promissory notes, secured and unsecured debts, book accounts, stocks, bonds, and other intangibles, though many intangibles among those mentioned are excepted.
Rate: 3 mills on the dollar.
Proceeds: 1/6 to the state; 1/6 to the county; 1/3 to the city, village, or town; 1/3 to the school district.

MORTGAGE REGISTRY

Rate: 15 cents on each $100 if the mortgage is due not more than 5 years and 60 days after date; otherwise, 25 cents on each $100.
Proceeds distributed like the money and credits tax.

JOINT STOCK LAND BANKS

Rate: 5 mills on each dollar of fair cash value of stock.
Proceeds distributed like the money and credits tax.

GROSS EARNING TAXES [2]

Levied on the following corporations in lieu of all other taxes.

Rates:

Railroads: 5 per cent of gross earnings of business within the state and a proportion of earnings of interstate business passing through the state, based on the ratio of mileage within the state to the entire mileage over which business is done.
Sleeping car companies: 5 per cent of gross earnings. Same basis as railroads.
Express companies: 8 per cent of gross earnings of business done in Minnesota.
Freight line companies: 6 per cent of gross earnings. Same basis as railroads.
Telephone companies: 4 per cent of gross earnings of business done in Minnesota.
Trust companies not doing a banking business: 5 per cent of gross earnings.

the general property tax on the physical property of insurance companies. The mining occupation and royalty taxes approximate net income taxes.

[2] See page 325 and Table 3, page 352, for fuller explanation of the taxation of public utilities. See also Note 1 above.

Proceeds go to the state, except that taxes paid by trust companies and trolley lines are apportioned like the general property tax.

SPECIAL TAXES

Insurance Companies

Rate: all companies, 2 per cent of gross premiums written within the state. (Certain small and mutual companies are exempt.)

Proceeds go to the state, but every city having an organized fire department receives an amount equal to the 2 per cent tax paid by fire insurance companies, to be used for firemen's relief. Fire insurance companies pay in addition 3/8 of 1 per cent of gross premiums for maintenance of the state fire marshal and 2½ per cent of gross premiums on policies written on property in cities having salvage corps. Proceeds go for maintenance of salvage corps.

Mining Industry (special taxes in addition to the property tax)

Occupation Tax

Rate: 6 per cent of valuation of all ore mined (after deduction of most expenses of production).

Proceeds: 50 per cent to the state, 40 per cent to the permanent school fund, 10 per cent to the permanent University fund.

Royalty Tax

Rate, 6 per cent upon all royalty received for permission to explore or mine ore.

Proceeds go to the state.

Motor Vehicles

Registration Tax

Rates on various classes of vehicles:

Passenger cars: 2.4 per cent of value; minimum, $10.

Trucks, 2.4 and 3.4 per cent, depending upon use; minimum, $15.

Buses: 10 per cent of value; minimum, $250.

Value is based on manufacturer's price minus 10 per cent the second year, 20 per cent the third year, etc.

Proceeds go to the state for the trunk highway fund.

Gasoline Tax

Rate: 3 cents per gallon.

Proceeds: 2/3 to the state, 1/3 to the counties for highways.

GRAIN IN ELEVATORS

Rates: wheat and flax, ½ mill per bushel; all other grain, ¼ mill per bushel.

Proceeds go to the state.

VESSEL TONNAGE (vessels plying international waters)

Rate: 5 cents per ton.

Proceeds: 50 per cent to the state, 50 per cent to the county.

INHERITANCE TAX

Person, Association, or Corporation to Whom Transfer Is Made	Exemption	Excess over Exemption But Not Over $15,000	$15,000–$30,000	$30,000–$50,000	$50,000–$100,000	Over $100,000
Wife or lineal issue of decedent.....	$10,000	1%	2%	2½%	3%	4%
Husband, adopted child of lineal issue of adopted child of decedent..	10,000	1½	3	3¾	4½	6
Lineal ancestor of decedent........	3,000	1½	3	3¾	4½	6
Brother, sister, descendant of brother or sister; wife or widow of a son, or husband of a daughter of decedent	1,000	3	6	7½	9	12
Brother or sister of father or mother, or descendant of either	250	4	8	10	12	16
All others	100	5	10	12½	15	20
Charitable, public, scientific, educational, and similar bequests.......	All					

Proceeds: 90 per cent to the state, 10 per cent to the county.

ESTATE TAX

Amount by which 80 per cent of the federal estate tax exceeds the state inheritance tax.

Proceeds: 90 per cent to the state, 10 per cent to the county.

POLL TAXES

In villages organized under general laws, every male inhabitant may be assessed from one to four days' road labor, which may be commuted at the rate of $1.50 a day.

Tables 1–4, pages 580 to 582, show the yield of these taxes for the years indicated and give an idea of their comparative importance.

STATE AND LOCAL REVENUES FROM TAXES AND OTHER SOURCES

TABLE 1. — MINNESOTA STATE AND LOCAL REVENUES DERIVED FROM TAXES OF ALL KINDS, BY FIVE-YEAR PERIODS, 1900–1930 [a]

Tax	1900	1905	1910	1915	1920	1925	1930
General property	$14,708,886	$21,208,303	$30,697,124	$49,378,168	$109,272,571	$116,667,205	$122,186,244
Money and credits	....	....	....	639,249	1,329,365	1,251,980	1,336,645
Mortgage registry	....	....	509,542	292,191	702,156	492,956	320,000
Bushel tax	....	....	35,820	45,613	67,924	120,947	72,691
Gross earnings:							
Railroads	1,439,349	2,865,415	3,933,310	5,436,573	9,062,652	8,028,095	6,848,853
Telephones	....	75,947	155,708	251,205	423,012	740,294	867,854
Express	8,460	31,924	37,290	51,820	129,613	65,752	45,174
Sleeping cars	371	1,186	9,372	24,279	82,061	63,308	51,311
Freight lines	2,114	2,662	4,058	19,677	21,975	67,687	104,232
Inheritance	....	159,455	459,406	672,814	1,074,039	1,022,112	2,362,340
Insurance	201,328	326,672	411,751	508,823	1,075,845	1,482,332	1,899.227
Telegraph	27,191	41,523	125,222	19,116	33,119	43,435	42,405
Vessel tonnage	9,106	15,990	19,572	17,171	5,903	27,019	27,343
Fire marshal	....	....	....	29,566	54,938	56,013	51,027
Motor vehicle	....	....	....	....	....	9,751,028	11,009,002
Gasoline	....	....	....	....	....	3,129,872	10,359,111
Occupation [b]	....	....	....	....	....	2,316,432	2,782,361
Royalty	....	....	....	....	....	825,800	921,167
Trust companies	....	....	....	....	....	....	17,954
Liquor license	....	....	54,615	43,533	....	....	....
Total, all taxes	$16,396,805	$24,729,077	$36,452,790	$57,429,798	$123,335,173	$146,152,267	$161,304,941

[a] Prepared by the Minnesota Tax Commission.
[b] One-half of tax is apportioned to permanent school funds. [c] Estimated.

TABLE 2. — MINNESOTA STATE AND LOCAL REVENUES DERIVED FROM TAXES FOR THE YEAR 1931, PAYABLE IN 1932 [a]

Tax	For the State	For All Minor Political Subdivisions	Total Taxes
General property	$14,777,168	$104,266,894	$119,044,062
Money and credits	209,811	1,049,454	1,259,265
Mortgage registry	50,000	225,000	275,000 [b]
Bushel tax	80,066	......	80,066
Gross earnings			
Railroads	4,828,353	10,000	4,838,353
Telephones	865,288	......	865,288
Express	38,778	......	38,778
Sleeping cars	38,270	......	38,270
Freight lines	98,452	......	98,452
Inheritance	1,637,642	181,960	1,819,602
Insurance	1,893,787	......	1,893,787
Telegraph	42,405	......	42,405
Vessel tonnage	12,444	12,444	24,888
Fire marshal	47,206	......	47,206
Motor vehicle	10,721,972	......	10,721,972
Gasoline tax	7,380,282	3,690,141	11,070,423
Occupation tax	1,383,145	......	1,383,145
Royalty tax	649,804	......	649,804
Trust companies	500	4,855	5,355
Total	$44,755,373	$109,440,748	$154,196,121

[a] Prepared by the Minnesota Tax Commission. [b] Estimated.

TABLE 3.—MINNESOTA STATE AND LOCAL GENERAL PROPERTY TAX LEVIES, 1930 AND 1931

A Comparison of Rural and Urban Taxes[a]

	1930	1931	INCREASE (+) DECREASE (—)
State taxes levied in			
Townships	$4,675,975.10	$6,373,385.11	$1,697,410.01+
Cities and villages	6,121,509.55	8,403,782.55	2,282,273.00+
Total	$10,797,484.65	$14,777,167.66	$3,979,683.01+
County taxes levied in			
Townships	$11,806,912.92	$10,395,169.51	$1,411,743.41—
Cities and villages	12,863,041.63	12,523,166.61	339,875.02—
Total	$24,669,954.55	$22,918,336.12	$1,751,618.43—
Local taxes levied in			
Townships	$8,978,102.77	$7,450,015.63	$1,528,087.14—
Cities and villages	34,574,732.55	33,452,488.56	1,122,243.99—
Total	$43,552,835.32	$40,902,504.19	$2,650,331.13—
School taxes levied in			
Townships	$13,244,885.38	$12,348,192.19	$896,693.19—
Cities and villages	29,682,480.91	27,824,005.39	1,858,475.52—
Total	$42,927,366.29	$40,172,197.58	$2,755,168.71—
Total general property tax levied in			
Townships	$38,705,876.17	$36,566,762.44	$2,139,113.73—
Cities and villages	83,241,764.64	82,203,443.11	1,038,321.53—
Total	$121,947,640.81	$118,770,205.55	$3,177,435.26—

[a] Prepared by the Minnesota Tax Commission.

TABLE 4.—PRINCIPAL SOURCES OF STATE RECEIPTS FOR THE YEAR ENDING JUNE 30, 1932[a]

SOURCE	AMOUNT
State taxes from counties	$11,662,719.27
Gross earnings taxes	7,822,149.97
Inheritance taxes	1,819,601.55
Motor vehicle taxes	10,292,934.75
Gasoline taxes	11,707,321.83
Royalty tax on iron ore (6 per cent)	632,767.09
Occupation tax on iron ore	1,383,145.36
Other taxes	235,508.88
Departmental earnings, fees, fines, etc.	2,799,710.90
State institutions, receipts, including federal aid to the University and the Soldiers' Home	5,333,394.15
Redemption of bonds	6,377,795.03
Interest on bonds	1,989,276.48
Interest on bank deposits	463,599.79
Mineral leases	1,877.47
Sand, gravel, etc.	19,401.51
Principal on invested funds	2,523,500.99
Interest on invested funds	1,179,296.48
Principal and interest on land contracts	134,382.61
Sale of timber on state lands, etc.	84,371.82
Federal aid for construction of roads	5,050,781.39
Sale of trunk highway bonds	20,000,000.00
Sale of rural credit bonds	3,230,000.00
Sale of State Board of Relief bonds	327,600.00
Sale of Red Lake Game Preserve bonds	426,360.00
Sale of Moorhead Teachers College bonds	500,000.00
Sale of Spanish war veterans bonds	900,000.00
Sale of military camp construction bonds	250,000.00
Sale of state office building bonds	700,000.00
Sale of Teachers' Retirement Association bonds	50,000.00
Sale of reforestation and flood control bonds	283,350.00
Royalty on iron ore	1,103,553.51
Teachers' insurance and retirement fund receipts	111,044.44
Rural credit receipts and refundments	2,825,154.61
Grain inspection fees	570,583.22
Sale of twine and farm machinery at prison	2,844,520.39
Teachers' retirement receipts	230,134.53
Public Employees' Retirement Association receipts	105,191.43
State Employees' Retirement Association receipts	384,222.70
Miscellaneous receipts and refundments	648,086.10
Total	$107,003,338.25

[a] As reported by the state auditor. This table includes state receipts but not local receipts, though much of what is received by the state is later distributed to the local units of government. It should be noted also that these receipts include proceeds from sales of bonds and numerous other items besides taxes. The data in this table are, therefore, not wholly comparable with those in the three preceding tables.

The state budget commissioner, Mrs. Jean W. Wittich, divides the above "payments into the state treasury" into the following percentages of the total: taxes, 42.6; federal aid, 5.4; departmental earnings, etc., 13.6; income from bonds and certificates of indebtedness, 24.9; redemption of bonds, interest and principal, 11.8; royalty on iron ore, 1.0; and miscellaneous, .7.

STATE AND LOCAL EXPENDITURES

STATE EXPENDITURES[1]

The accompanying tables show the services paid for by the state and the changes that have taken place in their relative importance during the past twenty years. The outstanding fact is the large increase in expenditures. Part of this increase is accounted for by capital outlays, especially for highways. For example, in 1926, out of a total capital outlay of $14,164,858, $11,188,900 was spent for highways. Another large increase, both in total amount and in percentage of increase, is due to the interest charges on bond issues. In 1921 the state issued $10,231,002 in certificates of indebtedness in order to pay the soldiers' bonus. In 1924 and 1925 approximately $37,000,000 in rural credit bonds were issued. By January 1, 1932, outstanding indebtedness on this account was over $61,000,000. It was assumed that interest paid by farmers on loans would cover the expenses of operation as well as the interest on these bonds, but this has not proved to be the case. On the contrary, in 1930 the state issued $1,000,000 worth of bonds to pay interest due on the rural credit bonds, and in the fiscal year 1931 the Rural Credits Bureau paid $3,327,926 interest. Furthermore, the state has come into possession of nearly three thousand farms through default of the loans. Bonds have also been issued for highway construction. Since 1929, $19,000,000[2] has been authorized for this purpose, and the state has assumed over $16,000,000 worth of county highway bonds. Additional data on public indebtedness are found on pages 601 to 606.

Increases in the cost of state health work and education are also significant. Expenses for charities and corrections remain more nearly constant than any others.

It will be noticed in Table 2 that the state is becoming more and more a collector of taxes for local units. Inasmuch as local units of government do not report their expenditures to any central office, it is impossible to give accurate totals or per capitas for all of them. Information has been obtained concerning a number of cities, villages, counties, and townships, however, and summaries are shown in Tables 4 to 15, pages 588-600.

[1] Prepared by Gladys C. Blakey and Violet Johnson
[2] Besides $10,000,000 for 1932.

TABLE 1.—STATE DISBURSEMENTS, 1911 AND 1931 [a]

	1911	1931
General government		
Legislative	$337,713.78	$441,523.48
Executive	145,300.34	557,490.75
Judicial	269,605.73	441,146.21
Public examiner	32,516.66	112,298.28
New and old capitols	88,599.04	216,959.77
Boards and commissions	32,016.03	1,339,310.03
Motor vehicle licenses	....	351,691.56
Miscellaneous	140,505.84	....
Total	$1,046,317.42	$3,460,420.08
Protection of persons and property		
Military	$119,102.48	$267,708.34
Banking department	78,792.14	147,948.19
Examining boards	121,810.59	113,861.31
Oil inspection	40,494.08	190,453.28
Grain inspection	282,205.83	874,162.49
Sheriff and fire marshal	21,587.43	....
Total	$663,992.55	$1,594,133.61
Health		
Board of health	$160,591.46	$256,449.90
Livestock sanitary board	46,360.53	454,264.21
Total	$206,951.99	$710,714.11
Conservation of natural resources		
Agriculture, dairy and food	$316,517.36	$350,541.25
Game and fish	99,635.22	780,691.35
Forestry	133,906.18	348,061.54
State agricultural society	....	159,441.87
Total	$550,058.76	$1,638,763.01
Highways (including reimbursement bonds and interest)	$31,001.50	$35,967,390.80
Charities and corrections		
Institutions	$3,004,993.34	$5,238,694.99
Soldiers' home	111,257.97	251,845.05
Prison (including industries)	191,989.53	2,988,050.34
Soldiers' relief fund	112,582.74	157,532.75
Total	$3,420,823.58	$8,636,123.13
Education		
Department of education	$120,974.12	$417,922.18
University	1,909,424.21	2,408,388.09
General University fund	....	6,981,469.96
University building fund	....	211,809.22
State teachers' colleges	395,524.21	1,092,592.33
Library	12,147.68	23,082.20
Historical Society	19,703.67	.... [b]
Total	$2,457,773.89	$11,135,263.98

[a] From the reports of the state auditor. Because of changes in classification it has not always been possible to allocate expenditures in exactly comparable groups. See footnote to Table 2 below.

[b] $52,582.86 included elsewhere, probably under "Societies and associations."

TABLE 1.— *Continued*

	1911	1931
Recreation		
Parks and game reserves	$22,299.62	$957,769.15
Miscellaneous		
Societies and associations	$54,209.77	$69,281.64
Indian war pensions	60,290.29	15,241.20
Teachers' insurance and retirement fund	....	361,559.74
State employees' retirement fund	....	270,109.02
Miscellaneous	11,604.50	1,906,161.09
Total	$126,104.56	$2,622,352.69
Rural Credits Department		
Loans and expense	....	$8,474,900.22
State aid		
Wolf bounties	$29,350.50	$58,957.50
County sanatoria	....	414,026.67
County agricultural societies	34,000.00	186,741.20
Schools (general revenue fund)	2,813,968.00	6,286,714.94
Schools (apportioned from general school fund)	....	4,000,300.16
Common school land aid	....	50,247.93
Road and bridge fund	78,337.10	5,044,686.13
National guard	9,250.00	47,851.25
Fire companies	127,982.69	....
Tree bounties	13,186.87	....
Horse thief bounties	1,799.99	....
Miscellaneous	13,681.64	....
Total	$3,121,556.79	$16,089,525.78
Revolving fund (prison)	$1,105,893.00	....
Interest and debt payments	$1,153,521.00	....
Grand total state disbursements	$13,906,294.66[d]	$91,287,329.56

[c] Included for the most part under "Highways" and "Rural Credits Department." In 1930 the state spent $18,648,491 for interest and debt payments.

[d] Investments and some minor items would have to be added to this total to bring it up to the total shown in Table 2.

TABLE 2.— COMPARISON OF MINNESOTA STATE DISBURSEMENTS IN 1911 AND 1930[a]

EXPENDITURE	1911	1930	PERCENTAGE INCREASE
State governmental services			
Salaries	$3,335,757	$15,133,503	353.68
Supplies, expense, etc.	5,909,365	27,766,999	369.88
Not separable into salaries or supplies	312,607	1,123,636	259.44
Total state activities	$9,557,729	$44,024,138	360.61
Aids, subventions, grants, etc.	3,107,875	13,595,987	337.47
Current state governmental expenditures	$12,666,604	$57,620,124	354.94
Custodial funds	68,011	574,464	744.66
Taxes collected by state, paid to localities	14,166	3,365,594	23,658.25
Debt and interest payments	1,153,521	18,648,491	638.19
Investments	2,526,228	10,773,229	833.90
Grand total	$16,427,520	$90,981,902	453.84

[a] These figures are derived from the state auditor's biennial reports for 1911–1912 and 1929–1930 and from the Biennial Budget of 1930. They represent all disbursements from the state treasury, not merely costs of state government, but they do not include costs of local units of government other than what is taken from the state treasury to pay such costs.

TABLE 3.— MINNESOTA STATE DISBURSEMENTS FOR THE YEAR ENDING JUNE 30, 1932[a]

Revenue fund disbursements	
Executive, judicial, and legislative	$916,597.11
State boards and commissions	1,243,421.15
Educational	417,994.53
Charitable institutions	7,057,634.04
State teachers' colleges	1,600,751.56
State University	1,747,956.60
State aid to schools	6,530,763.61
Sundry departments and miscellaneous	5,704,107.71
Other disbursements	
Relief of old soldiers and families	239,822.07
State road and bridge fund	4,942,140.06
State University buildings	415,197.74
Apportioned school	3,898,134.50
Grain inspection	712,027.23
Teachers' insurance and retirement	741,744.70
Trunk highways	32,515,996.03
Highway reimbursement	3,716,104.93
Rural credit funds	6,155,273.99
Invested trust funds	11,689,654.41
University maintenance	7,029,273.88
Prison twine plant	2,231,714.86
State employees' retirement	360,006.29
Public employees' retirement	105,008.16
Red Lake Game Preserve	853,857.87
Special aid	818,229.19
State office building	728,622.16
Spanish war veterans	848,462.63
Military camp construction	275,396.09
Miscellaneous	567,746.65
Total	$104,063,639.75

[a] As reported by the state auditor. See the footnotes to Tables 1 and 2. These data were received in this form and too late to put into a form exactly comparable with that in Table 1 or Table 2.

COUNTY EXPENDITURES[3]

The accompanying tables were derived from the reports of the public examiner's audits of county books. The report of the audit of Hennepin County was not available, so data on expenditures are based on reports covering only eighty-six counties in Minnesota. Per capita expenditures are figured on current costs. These expenditures include capital outlays for highways, because such outlays are regularly recurring costs, but they do not include other permanent improvements, such as new courthouses, nor do they include payment of interest or debts.

It appears from available information on county expenditures that the least populous counties have the highest per capita costs of county government. In Cook County, the population of which (2,421) is the smallest of any county in the state, the per capita cost of county government is $64.50, ten times as great as Kanabec, the least expensive county. Of the thirteen counties in which per capita costs for county government exceed $15.00, nearly half, or six out of the thirteen, have populations of less than 10,000, though in only 16 per cent of the counties of the state is the population as small as that.

County expenditures in 1911 were $2.33 per capita for current expenses, 33 cents per capita for interest, and 49 cents per capita for permanent improvements. The great increase in county expenditures is due in part to increasing expenditures for highways. Counties have taken over roads formerly maintained by localities, and highway standards have improved. The increase in the county property tax levy for roads and bridges was 466.4 per cent from 1911 to 1931, whereas the increase in total county taxes was 322.4 per cent. The gasoline tax in itself accounted for an increase of 57.4 per cent over the total taxes in 1911, and it is spent for highways only. This gasoline tax, added to the county road and bridge levy and the increase in state road and bridge aid, makes it apparent that highways account for much of the increase in county expenditures.

[3] These data were compiled by Violet Johnson.

TABLE 4. — COUNTY GOVERNMENT COSTS[a]

County	Total County Expenditures	Current Costs[b]	
		Total	Per Capita
Grant	$77,064	$63,827	$6.67
Lake of the Woods	93,495	84,734	20.28
Mahnomen	108,294	76,411	12.42
Red Lake	119,130	82,595	12.00
Kanabec	127,541	99,579	11.50
Big Stone	128,980	108,814	11.07
Wadena	131,360	115,216	10.48
Sherburne	135,541	121,374	12.50
Benton	140,846	119,212	7.92
Isanti	142,727	129,664	10.73
Traverse	143,295	124,118	15.63
Pennington	149,483	111,111	10.57
Clearwater	151,236	134,907	14.14
Nicollet	156,579	142,303	8.59
Hubbard	159,893	139,639	14.45
Roseau	166,886	163,108	12.87
Kittson	170,071	155,858	16.08
Lincoln	170,478	153,827	13.62
Pipestone	173,794	156,258	12.74
Kandiyohi	177,370	146,846	6.24
Sibley	180,898	148,026	9.35
Rock	185,299	108,040	9.86
Swift	186,303	159,181	10.82
Chippewa	190,505	161,867	10.18
Carlton	191,691	153,154	7.21
Cook	192,371	156,146	64.50
Lake	192,478	144,841	20.58
McLeod	196,837	171,373	8.37
Pine	196,948	162,759	8.84
Mille Lacs	198,599	135,280	11.50
Cottonwood	199,546	165,934	11.23
Murray	200,554	162,587	11.71
Martin	201,793	173,002	7.76
Houston	206,658	174,127	12.58
Meeker	208,510	174,632	9.76
Anoka	213,512	152,452	8.32
Watonwan	215,858	178,866	13.98
Chisago	220,892	181,959	13.80
Waseca	225,347	183,144	12.71
Jackson	225,967	203,000	12.81
Steele	228,392	208,942	11.30

[a] For sources and explanations see text, page 587, and footnote to Table 6.

[b] Total county costs minus fixed charges and capital outlay for all permanent improvements except highway construction equal current costs shown in this column. The amounts per capita are based on this column.

TABLE 4. — *Continued*

County	Total County Expenditures	Current Costs[a] Total	Current Costs[a] Per Capita
Dodge	229,419	131,873	10.87
Marshall	215,991	178,163	10.48
Norman	236,119	216,623	15.40
Carver	247,873	224,651	13.27
Wilkin	249,894	150,312	15.33
Becker	249,947	224,732	10.00
Morrison	256,688	221,187	8.70
Washington	267,114	244,302	9.88
Lac Qui Parle	268,609	186,143	12.10
Clay	271,790	251,274	10.87
Pope	272,593	116,222	8.88
Redwood	273,965	248,898	12.08
Yellow Medicine	280,296	259,908	15.68
Douglas	283,680	202,467	10.77
Le Sueur	284,603	181,500	10.09
Scott	296,478	254,489	18.08
Brown	308,590	280,954	12.00
Cass	316,959	195,457	12.55
Koochiching	320,949	190,027	13.56
Wright	321,198	297,357	10.97
Wabasha	332,332	309,118	17.55
Fillmore	350,318	312,664	12.44
Olmsted	353,427	297,257	8.48
Freeborn	359,532	283,492	9.86
Dakota	360,931	303,024	8.76
Renville	363,515	299,817	12.58
Beltrami	363,987	313,620	12.41
Todd	366,870	350,057	13.35
Blue Earth	367,177	346,293	10.23
Lyon	372,360	271,030	14.03
Goodhue	387,070	336,508	10.88
Winona	413,960	356,470	10.14
Stevens	417,866	147,327	14.45
Mower	419,944	291,767	10.40
Aitkin	461,861	240,716	16.36
Nobles	469,321	238,672	12.82
Faribault	493,423	239,589	11.12
Polk	502,488	474,589	13.18
Crow Wing	522,884	360,931	10.95
Otter Tail	546,931	479,878	9.41
Stearns	549,693	446,286	7.11
Rice	641,480	398,827	13.32
Itasca	836,499	551,736	20.45
Ramsey	4,110,409	3,555,843	12.43
St. Louis	5,070,846	4,429,044	21.64

TABLE 5.—COUNTIES IN WHICH THE CURRENT COST OF COUNTY GOVERNMENT IS MORE THAN $15 PER CAPITA [a]

FUNCTION	PER CAPITA COST OF MORE THAN	AIT-KIN	COOK	ITAS-CA	KITT-SON	LAKE	LAKE OF THE WOODS	NOR-MAN	ST. LOUIS	SCOTT	TRA-VERSE	WABA-SHA	WIL-KINS	YEL-LOW MEDI-CINE
Administration	$1.00	x	x	x	x	x	x	x	x	..	x	x	x	x
Judicial	1.15	x	x	x	..	x	x	..	x	x	x	..	..	..
Education	.20	x	..	..	x	..	x	..	..	..	x	..	x	..
Health	.40	..	..	x	x	..	..	x	..	..	..	x	..	x
Natural resource	.20	x	x	x	x	x	x	..	x	x	x	x	x	..
Charities and corrections.	1.15	x	x	x	x	x	x	x	x	x	..	x	x	x
Highway	7.50	x	x	x	x	x	x	x	x	x	x	x	x	x
Overhead	.60	x	x	x	x	x	x	x	..	..	x	..	x	..
Operation and maintenance	.30	..	x	x	..	x	..	..	..	..	x	x	x	..
Construction of highways	4.00	x	x	..	x	x	x	x	x	x	x	x	x	x
Maintenance of highways	2.50	x	x	x	x	x	x	..	x	x	..	..	..	..

[a] The x's show which counties have the relatively high costs indicated in the first column. It will be seen that in these most expensive counties the cost per capita of almost every function is high. Notable exceptions are health and education. For these the most expensive counties do not have extraordinarily high per capita costs.

TABLE 6.—PER CAPITA COSTS OF COUNTY GOVERNMENT [a]

EXPENDITURE	MEAN	MEDIAN (AVERAGE)	RANGE	INTERQUARTILE RANGE [b]	STANDARD DEVIATION
Total current costs	$12.72	$11.80	$6.24–$64.50	$10.12–$14.00	$6.25
Administration	1.00	.97	.55– 5.91	.80– 1.17	.63
Judicial	1.11	1.04	.71– 2.98	.92– 1.17	.34
Operation and maintenance	.29	.26	.09– 1.36	.21– .33	.16
Overhead	.57	.50	.24– 2.64	.42– .63	.16
Education	.19	.18	.03– .43	.14– .23	.06
Charities and corrections	1.15	1.23	.31– 5.33	.88– 1.64	.87
Conservation of natural resources	.18	.17	.00– .54	.09– .26	.12
Health and sanitation	.38	.30	.01– 2.24	.07– .56	.39
Highways	7.40	6.70	3.00– 45.91	5.32– 8.59	4.80
Highways (construction only)	3.59	2.87	.16– 35.98	1.89– 4.83	3.90

[a] This table was derived from information in the public examiner's reports of audits of county expenditures. No recent report on the Hennepin County audit was available. The reports of the latest audits were used; in most cases they covered expenditures for the year 1929.

[b] For an explanation of interquartile range see page 197, note 5, and page 595, note 6.

TABLE 7.—COUNTY REVENUES IN 1929 [a]

SOURCE OF REVENUE	AMOUNT RECEIVED	PER CENT OF TOTAL
Property taxes	$27,095,000	65.87
Other taxes	1,532,000	3.72
Aids, grants, and subsidies	6,677,000	16.23
Special assessments and liens	1,527,000	3.71
Earnings, fees, fines. and licenses	1,526,000	3.71
Loans, interest, investments, and miscellaneous	2,781,000	6.78
Total	$41,137,000	100.00

[a] Derived from material in League of Minnesota Municipalities, Proceedings of Conference on Governmental Relationships, 1930.

TOWNSHIP EXPENDITURES [4]

In Minnesota there is no uniform system of township accounting and no central agency at which township accounts are available; hence the available data on townships are limited. When taxes are levied, the funds into which they are to go are specified, and the amount that may be levied for each of several funds is limited by law. But Tables 9 and 10 show that they are not always spent according to the stated purpose of levy. Table 9 shows that

[4] Compiled by Miss Violet Johnson.

Table 8.—Percentage of Total Township Expenditures from Each Fund, 1921–1931[a]

No. of Township Audits, 1927–1931	1931	1930	1929	1928	1927	1926	1925	1924	1923	1922	1921
	15	26	40	40	41	32	25	12	7	2	1
Fund	Percentage of Expenditures from Each Fund										
Revenue	16.04	11.24	16.26	14.26	16.50	10.34	19.01	20.83	19.81	30.16	48.72
Road and bridge	61.00	70.34	72.96	71.29	67.42	80.44	66.60	60.57	59.21	60.77	2.34
Dray	5.19	7.21	5.36	4.62	4.77	3.57	5.29	2.32	3.92	3.96	....
Poor	.04	.19	.35	.05	.24	.15	.09	.07	.19	....	....
Fire	2.76	2.21	1.48	2.19	3.18	3.04	2.50	7.54	2.19	5.11	48.93
Town hall	12.50	1.82	.19	.32	1.25	1.09	1.92	1.46	.01	...	....
Cemetery	.01	.11	.08	.60	.81	.56	1.65	3.55	.40	...	....
Sinking fund	.66	4.70	...	2.05	3.89	.04	...	...	...	...	....
Emergency	1.81	.21	.04	.01	...	...	...	...	...	...	....
Need	...	.01	...	...	...	...	...	...	...	...	....
Telephone	...	.18	.05	.79	.71	.44	.40	.38	...	...	....
Debt and interest	...	1.76	3.23	2.80	.87	.34	2.46	3.28	11.74	...	....
Special	...	...	...	1.02	.02	...	.08	...	2.52	...	....
Contingent	...	...	...	...	.33	...	...	...	...	...	....
Total	100.01	99.98	100.00	100.00	100.00	100.01	100.00	100.00	99.99	100.00	99.99

[a] These data are from the state public examiners' audits of townships. Such audits are relatively few, hence the sample is not large, the number of township audits for each year being indicated above. See explanations in text.

in Oronoco Township, Olmsted County, for instance, 31.93 per cent of the total expenditures over a period of six years was made from moneys transferred to funds other than the one for which they were levied. During this period $2,971 was transferred from other funds to the general fund, $4,217 from other funds to a grading fund, and $3,420 from other funds to a gravel fund. There were no compensating transfers from the general fund, grading fund, or gravel fund to the funds from which money was taken. Total expenditures were $32,235, and the aggregate transfers were $10,613.

Table 10 shows that in Lawrence Township, Itasca County, only 24.78 per cent of the expenditures from the revenue fund over a period of nine years was composed of receipts of the taxes levied for that fund. When less than a fourth of the amount spent from a fund in nine years properly belongs to that fund, it is evident that money levied for other purposes has been used. Part of the reason for these transfers and for the disparity between the purposes for which township taxes are levied and those for which they are spent may be found in the fact referred to above that townships are limited as to the amounts that they may levy for each of several functions. If the assessed valuation of the township is less than $100,000, the tax levy for the general revenue fund may be as high as 5 mills per dollar of assessed valuation. If the assessed valuation of the township is greater than $100,000, the general revenue fund levy may not exceed 2 mills. The levy for the relief and support of the poor may not exceed 5 mills. The general limitation for the road and bridge levy is 15 mills, but an additional 5 mills may be levied for emergency road and bridge purposes and another mill for dragging roads. Still another levy, not to exceed 10 mills, may be made for draining roads. There is a blanket limitation of 17 mills, which includes levies for "all general or special purposes, including payment of indebtedness or bonds."

The accompanying tables were obtained from the audits of township accounts by the state public examiner. These audits are not numerous and may not be representative, though in the opinion of the examiner the proportions and amounts of expenditures of the transfers from fund to fund are not unusual.

Table 9. — Transfers between Funds Compared with Total Expenditures in Specified Townships [a]

Township	County	No. of Years Covered by Audits	Transfers in Percentage of Expenditures
Oronoco	Olmsted	6	31.93%
Sago	Itasca	3	25.66
Koochiching	Koochiching	3	20.39
Camden	Carver	1 (1928) 1 (1929)	19.54 10.02
Cramer	Lake	2	19.57
Wabedo	Cass	3	16.56
Wirt	Itasca	5	15.47
Carpenter	Itasca	3	11.30
Linden Grove	St. Louis	4	9.78
Lutsen	Cook	3	8.26
Eden	Brown	6	7.92
Moose Park	Itasca	2	7.67
Folden	Otter Tail	6	6.27
St. Mathias	Crow Wing	5	5.01
Rice Lake	St. Louis	4	4.92
Thomson	Carlton	1	4.10
Frohn	Beltrami	3	2.49
Horland	Cook	1	1.93
Trout Lake	Itasca	6	1.26

[a] These are not compensating transfers, such as occur when money is temporarily borrowed from a fund and then repaid.

Table 10. — Disparity between Specified Purpose of Tax Levy and Purpose for Which Expenditures Were Actually Made

Township	County	No. of Years Covered by Audits	Ratio of Receipts to Disbursements [a] from Revenue Fund
French	St. Louis	3	23.00%
Lawrence	Itasca	9	24.78
Hebron	Aitkin	3	36.74
Arbo	Itasca	3	38.62
Balsam	Itasca	6	41.05
Sago	Itasca	3	43.02
Island Lake	Mahnomen	7	45.21
Windemere	Pine	3	59.74
Rogers	Cass	5	60.21
Wrenshall	Carlton	3	60.24
Leiding	St. Louis	5	65.13
Trout Lake	Itasca	6	67.30
Pulaski	Morrison	6	69.02
Wirt	Itasca	5	69.50
East Gull Lake	Cass	3	70.47
Moose Park	Itasca	2	71.05
Kimberley	Aitkin	3	75.29
Sundown	Redwood	6	75.61
Two Harbors	Lake	5	83.26
Morgan	Redwood	3	86.47

[a] Receipts include recorded transfers into the revenue fund from other funds, and disbursements include recorded transfers from the revenue fund to other funds. Evidently some receipts or transfers were not recorded as such.

MUNICIPAL EXPENDITURES[5]

Most of the material in the accompanying tables was derived from information furnished in response to a questionnaire by the clerks of 421 cities and villages — 58 per cent of all cities and villages in the state. All debt and interest payments and all capital outlays were segregated so that the data on maintenance costs of municipal government in a single year, 1930, might be on a comparable basis. Since school districts in Minnesota are usually organized independently of the municipal government, school costs are not included. We cannot get a complete picture of municipal costs if we ignore debt charges and capital expenditures, but only by deducting these irregular and less prevalent costs can we obtain comparable data by which to judge whether small or large municipalities are more expensive in proportion to population, or how much greater relative costs are in iron-range municipalities than in others. The figures refer for the most part to the fiscal year ending in 1930, and they cover payments for direct municipal services only. They do not include such semi-commercial activities as municipal utilities. The data give some idea of the central tendencies of costs in each population group and of deviations within the group. They show also the relative proportions of expenditures for various governmental purposes. The per capita expenditures of half the municipalities in the group will be found between the first and third quartile limits.[6] The range shows the greatest and least expenditures in the group.

[5] Compiled by Miss Violet Johnson.

[6] If the costs of all the municipalities in a group are arrayed from the lowest to the highest, the "range" is shown by the first and the last (highest and lowest); the "median" cost is that of the city in the middle; the first quartile cost is that of the city a quarter of the distance from the lowest, i.e., halfway between the lowest and the median; the third quartile is halfway between the median and the highest. The "interquartile range" is the difference between the first and third quartile; it is normally much less than the (extreme) range from lowest to highest (called "range" above).

For example, in Table 13, in the group of 25 municipalities with populations of from 2,500 to 5,000, a little less than $.89 was the smallest per capita cost for streets and sidewalks while $14.95 was the highest cost for this purpose in any of them. The per capita cost for the middle city in this array was $2.12, that is, this was the cost for the thirteenth city, the one halfway between the first and the last. The first quartile cost of $1.52 was the cost of streets and sidewalks for the seventh city, the one halfway between the first and the median; the third quartile cost, $2.77, was that of the nineteenth city, the one halfway between the median and the highest cost city. The interquartile range is $1.25, the difference between $1.52 and $2.77.

The "standard deviation" is a statistical measure of the variations from the average of all cases in the group. It is the square root of the sum of the squares of all deviations from the average. If every city has the same cost, this cost will be the average, the median, the first quartile, and the third quartile, all at the

The 1911 figures are taken from the report of the Tax Commission for 1911–1912. They are maintenance figures only and do not include school costs, so they are comparable with the 1930 data.

same time, and the "standard deviation" will be zero; but if the difference between the lowest and the highest is great the "range" will be great, and the "standard deviation" will be large, particularly if many cities deviate greatly from the average.

These various statistical measures have been devised to make up for the shortcomings of an "average" (or "mean"), which shows nothing of the deviation or scatter about the average. For example, the average height of a four-foot man and a seven-foot man is five and a half feet, the same as the average of a five-foot man and a six-foot man. The "average" alone does not give us nearly so good an idea of a group as do the "average," the "median," the first and third "quartiles," the "range" and the "standard deviation" when considered in combination. The ratio of the "standard deviation" to the "average" is quite significant; if all samples in a group are nearly alike the standard deviation will be small; the greater the number and the extent of dissimilarities the larger will be the "standard deviation" in relation to the "average." These explanations should make clear the data in Tables 6 and 13, pages 591, 598, and 599.

TABLE 11.—AVERAGE CURRENT PER CAPITA COSTS OF MUNICIPAL GOVERNMENT, 1911

	Total Current Cost	General Administration	Police and Fire Protection	Health and Sanitation[a]	Streets, Sidewalks, Street Lights	Charities	Recreation
Average for cities of 5,000–25,000	$7.06	$1.93	$2.48	$.55	$1.35	$.15	$.08
Average for first class cities	8.98	.81	4.38	1.34	1.11	.40	.54

[a] Including sewers.

TABLE 12.—AVERAGE CURRENT PER CAPITA COSTS OF MUNICIPAL GOVERNMENT, 1930[a]

Cities Classified According to Population	No. of Cities in Each Class	Total Current Cost	General Administration	Police	Fire	Health	Streets	Street Lighting	Poor Relief	Recreation	Sewage
Less than 500	241	$6.21	$1.90	$.60	$.29	$.04	$1.38	$1.80	$.46	$.08	$.01
500– 1,000	78	8.33	1.78	1.04	.97	.09	2.19	1.86	.15	.25	.11
1,000– 2,500	52	11.02	2.20	1.40	.71	.39	3.20	1.14	.59	.36	.16
2,500– 5,000	25	9.46	1.81	.81	.42	.38	2.70	.91	.59	.60	.17
5,000–10,000	13	20.27	2.79	2.07	2.70	.96	4.36	1.38	1.09	2.09	.86
10,000–25,000	9	18.12	3.14	2.35	2.70	.92	4.03	1.08	.62	1.66	1.10
First class cities	3	19.22	2.21	2.84	3.51	.66	3.02	.99	1.33	1.52	.82

[a] 421 municipalities in Minnesota; see explanations in text.

TABLE 13.— CURRENT PER CAPITA COSTS OF MUNICIPAL GOVERNMENT

	Total Current Cost	General Administration	Police Protection	Fire Protection	Health	Streets and Sidewalks	Street Lighting	Poor Relief Welfare [a]	Recreation	Sewage Disposal
241 MUNICIPALITIES WITH POPULATIONS OF LESS THAN 500										
Average	$6.21	$1.90	$.60	$.29	$.04	$1.38	$1.80	$.46	$.08	$.01
Median	5.50	1.18	.08	.14	.00	.76	1.72	.32	.00	.00
1st quartile	3.82	.74	.00	.00	.00	.21	1.10	.15	.00	.00
3rd quartile	7.36	1.94	.90	.47	.07	1.60	2.44	.59	.21	.00
Range	.77–53.33	.13–53.33	.00–20.00	.00–2.52	.00–3.22	.00–15.87	.00–5.69	.01–2.03	.00–3.57	.00–3.62
Standard deviation	5.21	1.13	1.50	.51	.22	1.68	1.10	.49	.35	.34
78 MUNICIPALITIES WITH POPULATIONS OF FROM 500 TO 1,000										
Average	$8.33	$1.78	$1.04	$.97	$.09	$2.19	$1.86	$.15	$.25	$.11
Median	6.62	1.00	1.06	.32	.06	1.11	1.33	.33	.07	.00
1st quartile	4.85	.62	.27	.11	.03	.54	1.16	.16	.00	.00
3rd quartile	9.36	1.93	1.93	.60	.11	1.99	2.38	.50	.32	.05
Range	1.86–89.11	.17–9.12	.00–5.42	.00–5.00	.00–.83	.00–64.40	.00–5.47	.01–1.39	.00–1.49	.00–3.87
Standard deviation	9.16	1.88	.87	.84	.14	7.02	.99	.32	.27	.61
52 MUNICIPALITIES WITH POPULATIONS OF FROM 1,000 TO 2,500										
Average	$11.02	$2.20	$1.40	$.71	$.39	$3.20	$1.14	$.59	$.36	$.16
Median	7.00	1.51	1.04	.39	.07	1.79	1.25	.33	.23	.00
1st quartile	5.87	.84	.93	.17	.03	1.26	.46	.22	.00	.00
3rd quartile	9.87	2.27	1.55	.81	.16	2.92	1.83	.75	.55	.15
Range	1.34–68.89	.22–9.27	.00–8.23	.00–7.83	.00–9.34	.00–27.26	.00–3.66	.01–2.34	.00–3.45	.00–3.27
Standard deviation	11.91	2.16	1.38	1.24	1.32	4.80	.92	.52	.59	.52

[a] Since the county rather than the municipality is charged with poor relief in about two-thirds of the state, only municipalities listing some expenditures for this purpose are here considered. Terms are explained on page *595*, note 6, and page 197, note *5*.

Table 13. — *Continued*

	Total Current Cost	General Adminis-tration	Police Protec-tion	Fire Protec-tion	Health	Streets and Side-walks	Street Light-ing	Poor Re-lief Welfare [a]	Recrea-tion	Sewage Disposal
25 municipalities with populations of from 2,500 to 5,000										
Average	$9.46	$1.81	$.81	$.42	$.38	$2.70	$.91	$.59	$.60	$.17
Median	8.75	1.62	1.06	.49	.11	2.12	1.04	.27	.55	.00
1st quartile	5.25	.95	.82	.33	.08	1.52	.12	.14	.11	.00
3rd quartile	9.90	2.34	1.22	.90	.30	2.77	1.56	1.12	.79	.27
Range	2.96– 37.38	.58– 7.71	.00– 4.14	.00– 2.94	.00– 1.90	.89– 14.95	.00– 2.02	.01– 1.81	.00– 1.92	.00– 1.30
Standard deviation	6.46	1.21	.72	.56	.40	2.63	.60	.59	.57	.36
13 municipalities with populations of from 5,000 to 10,000										
Average	$20.27	$2.79	$2.07	$2.70	$.96	$4.36	$1.38	$1.09	$2.09	$.86
Median	13.50	2.08	1.54	2.12	.37	3.25	1.44	.75	.95	.35
1st quartile	11.25	1.72	1.03	1.78	.16	1.03	1.06	.50	.65	.02
3rd quartile	16.75	3.87	1.96	3.19	.79	6.38	1.96	1.75	1.95	.87
Range	5.70– 70.34	.98– 6.24	.64– 6.69	.29– 8.91	.00– 4.12	.01– 14.45	.20– 2.91	.08– 2.33	.44– 11.36	.04– 4.68
Standard deviation	16.71	1.59	1.67	2.04	.37	3.75	.79	1.25	2.95	1.29
9 municipalities with populations of from 10,000 to 25,000										
Average	$18.12	$3.14	$2.35	$2.70	$.92	$4.03	$1.08	$.62	$1.66	$1.10
Median	11.50	2.25	1.62	1.82	.52	2.25	1.25	.62	.55	....
1st quartile	9.61	1.62	1.31	1.31	.26	1.68	.58	.33	.12	....
3rd quartile	26.47	5.19	2.47	2.19	1.47	2.87	1.66	.75	.99	....
Range	7.00– 15.32	1.12– 6.39	.79– 7.55	.93– 7.55	.14– 2.97	.78– 8.72	.00– 2.55	.45– 1.11	.08– 8.35	....
Standard deviation	13.81	1.84	1.95	2.05	.46	3.68	.91	1.42	2.62	....
3 municipalities with populations of over 100,000										
Minneapolis	$21.18	$1.94	$2.81	$2.85	$.40	$3.55	$.99	$2.22	$1.76	$.91
St. Paul	18.40	2.09	2.80	3.54	.54	2.41	1.16	1.37	1.50	1.18
Duluth	18.09	2.60	2.93	4.14	1.04	3.10	.91	.41	1.29	.37

TABLE 14. — MEDIAN CURRENT PER CAPITA COSTS OF MUNICIPAL GOVERNMENT, 1930[a]

Cities Classified According to Population	No. of Cities in Each Class	Total Current Cost	General Administration	Police	Fire	Health	Streets	Street Lighting	Poor Relief	Recreation	Sewage
Less than 500	241	$5.50	$1.18	$.08	$.14	$.00	$.76	$1.72	$.32	$.00	$.00
500– 1,000	78	6.62	1.00	1.06	.32	.06	1.11	1.33	.33	.07	.00
1,000– 2,500	52	7.00	1.51	1.04	.39	.07	1.79	1.25	.33	.23	.00
2,500– 5,000	25	8.75	1.62	1.06	.49	.11	2.12	1.04	.27	.55	.00
5,000–10,000	13	13.50	2.08	1.54	2.12	.37	3.25	1.44	.75	.95	.35
10,000–25,000	9	11.50	2.25	1.62	1.82	.52	2.25	1.25	.62	.55	..
Over 100,000	3										
Minneapolis		21.18	1.94	2.81	2.85	.40	3.55	.99	2.22	1.76	.91
St. Paul		18.40	2.09	2.80	3.54	.54	2.41	1.16	1.37	1.50	1.18
Duluth		18.09	2.60	2.93	4.14	1.04	3.10	.91	.41	1.29	.37

[a] 421 municipalities in Minnesota; see explanations in text.

TABLE 15. — COMPARISON OF EXPENDITURES OF IRON RANGE MUNICIPALITIES WITH THOSE OF OTHER CITIES OF THE STATE, 1930[a]

Cities Classified According to Population	Range Municipalities		Non-Range Municipalities		All Municipalities[b]	
	No.	Average Current Cost per Capita	No.	Average Current Cost per Capita	No.	Average Current Cost per Capita
Under 500	4	$28.41	237	$5.84	241	$6.21
500– 999	1	89.11	77	7.35	78	8.33
1,000– 2,499	6	38.02	46	7.50	52	11.02
2,500– 4,999	1	37.38	24	8.30	25	9.46
5,000– 9,999	3	46.18	10	12.58	13	20.27
10,000–25,000	2	41.85	7	10.58	9	18.12
Total	17		401		418	

[a] Average per capita for current costs, excluding expenditures for schools and capital outlays.
[b] Except the three first class cities.

STATE AND LOCAL DEBTS[1]

The purposes for which the state and the local units have incurred debts, the tremendous increase in total amounts, in per capita amounts, and in percentages are given in Tables 1 to 4 below.

An analysis of the data shows that in 1931 the total state and local debt — that is, bonds and warrants — was about eight times that of 1902. On a per capita basis it was almost six times as large. The most rapid increase took place between 1912 and 1922, particularly in the years immediately following the war. The peak was reached in 1927. There was a slow decline from that time until 1930, but in 1931 a small rise occurred, so the per capita amount in that year was somewhat higher than in 1929.

The state highway program is largely the cause of this recent increase. In 1929 the legislature authorized bonds of $9,000,000 for this purpose and in 1931, $10,000,000, to be amortized by taxes on motor vehicles.[2] In addition, the state has assumed county highway bonds amounting to $16,257,643. Rural credit bonds amounting to more than $62,000,000 are theoretically obligations of individual farmers, but so far interest payments are in arrears and many borrowers have defaulted. Since 1922 the state has retired over $18,000,000 in bonds issued for soldiers' bonuses.

Counties and local units have also gone heavily into debt for road-building. For example, of the total bonded indebtedness of the counties, 27 per cent is for roads and bridges, 24 per cent for highway reimbursement; of the indebtedness of the townships, 78 per cent is for roads and bridges; of cities, 35 per cent is for streets. Of the total indebtedness incurred for highways by all units, 57 per cent consists of the obligations of cities and villages, 27 per cent of county, 15 per cent of state, and 1 per cent of township debts.

Building bonds and certificates are the second largest group, composing 27 per cent of the total bonded indebtedness of all units, state and local. There was an increase of 1 per cent in 1931 over 1930. School districts have incurred 81 per cent of this amount and cities and villages 13 per cent. The sudden increase in the building of schools is due partly to the fact that there was a moratorium on such construction during the war.

[1] Compiled by Mr. Harold Groven, graduate student in public finance at the University of Minnesota. Later data relative to state indebtedness are shown in Table 2, page 604, which became available after this section was sent to press.

[2] In addition, $10,000,000 was authorized for 1932.

TABLE 1. — TOTAL STATE AND LOCAL NET INDEBTEDNESS IN MINNESOTA, 1902–1931[a]

(Total, per capita, and percentage)

	1902	1912	1922	1927	1928	1929	1930	1931
Net indebtedness[b] (000 omitted)								
County	$6,137	$14,013	$81,262	$92,573	$91,128	$86,564	$73,931	$67,926
Township	19	7	4,445	4,307	4,381	4,171	4,029	3,497
City and village	28,466	46,461	103,834	112,365	109,600	110,175	101,841	97,961
School	4,307	8,537	59,759	72,695	69,727	66,987	74,409	75,547
Total local	$38,929	$69,018	$249,300	281,940	$274,836	$267,897	$254,210	$244,931
State	1,755	1,345	20,308	54,320	54,932	55,510	68,130	82,971
Grand total	$40,684	$70,363	$269,608	$336,260	$329,768	$323,407	$322,340	$327,902
Percentage of total indebtedness								
County	15.1	20.0	30.2	28.0	28.5	27.4	23.0	20.7
Township			1.6	1.3	1.3	1.3	1.2	1.1
City and village	70.0	66.0	22.2	33.9	34.3	34.9	31.6	29.9
School	10.6	12.1	38.5	22.0	21.9	21.2	23.1	23.0
Total local	95.7	98.1	92.5	85.2	86.0	84.8	78.9	74.7
State	4.3	1.9	7.5	14.8	14.0	15.2	21.1	25.3
Grand total	100.0	100.0	100.0	100.0	100.0	100.0	100.0	100.0
Per capita indebtedness								
County	$3.38	$6.43	$33.15	$36.78	$35.96	$33.93	$28.84	$26.36
Township	.01	.01	1.41	1.71	1.73	1.63	1.57	1.36
City and village	15.68	3.90	24.59	44.64	43.25	43.19	39.74	38.01
School	2.37	21.30	42.36	28.88	27.52	26.26	29.03	29.32
Total local	$21.44	$31.64	$101.71	$112.01	$108.46	$105.01	$99.18	$95.05
State	.97	.62	8.29	21.58	21.68	21.76	26.58	32.19
Grand total	$22.41	$32.26	$110.00	$133.59	$130.14	$126.77	$125.76	$127.24

[a] The basic figures for the last five years were obtained from the reports of the Minnesota Tax Commission. Figures for the first three columns are from Bureau of the Census, *Public Debt*, 1922. The township and school figures were combined in the census report. In order to separate these the school figures as reported by the State Department of Education were used. By subtracting these from the sum of the two, the township figures were obtained. As the State Department of Education and the Bureau of the Census have different fiscal years, the township figures, since they are usually relatively small, contain most of the inaccuracy involved in this somewhat faulty but necessary procedure.

[b] Bonded debt plus outstanding warrants and certificates of indebtedness minus sinking funds.

Increase or decrease over previous column (000 omitted)								
County		$7,876	$67,249	$11,310	—$1,444	—$4,564	—$12,633	—$6,004
Township		—12	4,438	—138	74	—210	—142	—532
City and village		17,995	57,373	8,531	—2,766	575	—8,333	—3,880
School		4,230	51,222	12,935	—2,967	—2,741	7,422	1,138
Total local		$30,089	$180,282	$32,640	—$7,103	—$6,940	—$13,686	—$9,279
State		—410	18,963	34,012	611	579	12,619	14,841
Grand total		$29,679	$199,245	$66,652	—$6,492	—$6,361	—$1,067	$5,562
Percentage of increase or decrease over previous column								
County		128	480	14	—2	—5	—15	—8
Township		—63	63,400	—3	2	—5	—3	—13
City and village		98	123	8	—3	1	—8	—4
School		63	600	32	—4	—4	11	2
Total local		77	261	14	—3	—3	—5	—4
State		—23	1,310	167	1	1	23	22
Grand total		73	283	25	—2	—2	—.3	2
Per capita increase or decrease over previous column								
County		$3.61	$27.67	$4.49	—$.57	—$1.79	—$4.93	—$2.35
Township		—.01	1.82	—.05	.03	—.08	—.06	—.21
City and village		8.25	23.61	3.39	—1.09	.23	—3.25	—1.50
School		1.94	21.08	5.14	—1.17	—1.08	2.89	.44
Total local		$13.79	$74.19	$12.97	—$2.80	—$2.72	—$5.35	—$3.60
State		.18	7.80	13.51	.24	.22	4.92	5.76
Grand total		$13.61	$81.99	$26.48	—$2.56	—$2.50	—$.43	$2.16
Percentage ratio of net indebtedness to assessed valuation of real estate and personal property								
County	.8	.9	4.2	4.7	4.8	4.1	3.9	3.6
Township	..	..	.5	.5	.5	.5	.5	.4
City and village	.6	.6	10.5	10.5	9.4	10.1	9.4	9.1
School	.2	.1	3.1	3.7	3.9	3.4	3.9	4.0
State	3.7	3.1	1.0	2.8	2.9	2.8	3.6	4.4

The largest county obligation is that for ditch bonds, which amount to over $26,000,000 and constitute 39 per cent of the total indebtedness. These are loans to individuals secured by liens on adjoining property. The main items in city and village indebtedness are for street improvements (35 per cent), water bonds (17 per cent), sewer bonds (14 per cent), and building bonds (11 per cent). Of the school indebtedness, building bonds make up 99 per cent.

There has been a tendency for all governmental units to overstep the legal limits of indebtedness through the issuance of outstanding warrants. This condition has improved somewhat during the last few years with the decrease of warrants and increase in sinking funds. The change in this respect from 1927 to 1931 is as follows:

	1927	1931
Outstanding warrants (local units)	$19,000,093	$12,697,810
Sinking funds (state and local)	15,622,362	20,142,370

TABLE 2.—OUTSTANDING INDEBTEDNESS OF THE STATE OF MINNESOTA[a]

	June 30, 1932	September 1, 1932
Reforestation and flood control	$ 283,350.00	$ 375,250.00
Executive council	529,600.00	561,600.00
Red Lake Game Preserve	726,360.00	428,860.00
University buildings	300,000.00	300,000.00
National Guard armories	572,000.00	570,000.00
State office building	775,000.00	975,000.00
Moorhead Teachers College building	700,000.00	700,000.00
Spanish war veterans	1,050,000.00	1,050,000.00
Military camp construction	300,000.00	300,000.00
Trunk highway	29,000,000.00	29,000,000.00
Rural credits	62,045,000.00	63,162,500.00
Teachers' retirement	50,000.00	....
County highway reimbursement	14,442,083.00	14,032,176.51
Total	$110,773,393.00	$111,455,386.51

[a] Data were supplied by Mr. M. J. Desmond, deputy state auditor, after the rest of this section had been sent to the University Press. These data of "outstanding indebtedness" are somewhat different from those of "net indebtedness" shown in Table 1, page 602. See note b to that table.

Table 3.—Percentage Distribution of Bonded Indebtedness of Different Units by Purposes, 1927–1931

	1927	1928	1929	1930	1931
County					
Buildings	5%	4%	5%	6%	7%
Road and bridges	19	19	20	26	27
Highway reimbursement	36	37	36	26	24
Ditches	38	38	37	40	39
Refunding	2	2	2	2	3
Township					
Buildings	3	3	4	4	5
Road and bridge	79	81	79	76	78
Refunding	17	12	13	17	13
Telephone	1	4	4	3	4
City and village					
Buildings	11	7	9	7	11
Street improvement	42	45	43	38	35
Sewer	10	10	11	13	14
Water	18	18	17	18	17
Light and heat	3	3	2	2	2
Refunding	8	7	10	12	10
Miscellaneous	8	10	8	10	11
School district					
Buildings	99	99	99	99	99
Refunding	1	1	1	1	1
Total local					
Buildings	31	29	29	33	35
Streets and highways	49	59	50	46	44
Ditches	13	13	12	11	10
Refunding	4	4	5	6	6
Miscellaneous	3	4	4	4	5
State					
Buildings	2	2	2	1	1
Highways	..	..	..	13	23
Education	3	3	2	2	..
Rural credit	84	89	93	82	73
Miscellaneous	11	6	3	2	3
Grand total					
Buildings	26	25	25	26	27
Streets and highway	40	41	41	39	38
Ditches	11	10	10	9	8
Education (state)	1	.4	1	.4	1
Refunding	4	3	4	5	4
Loans (rural credit)	14	15	3	17	18
Miscellaneous	4	5	16	4	4

Table 4.—Percentage Distribution of Bonded Indebtedness for Different Purposes by Units, 1927–1931

	1927	1928	1929	1930	1931
Building bonds and certificates					
County	5%	5%	4%	5%	5%
Township	.1	.1	.1	.1	.1
City and village	14	10	13[a]	9[a]	13
School	79	84	82[a]	85[a]	81
Total local	98	99	99	99	99
State	2	1	1	1	1
Grand total	100	100	100	100	100
Highways and streets					
County	38	37	37	30	27
Township	1	1	1	1	1
City and village	61	62	62	62	57
Total local	100	100	100	93	85
State	...	...	...	7	15
Grand total	...	...	...	100	100
Ditches					
County	100	100	100	100	100
Refunding					
County	19	15	12	10	15
Township	3	2	2	2	2
City and village	71	73	81	82	76
School	1	10	5	6	7
Education					
State	100	100	100	100	100
Loans					
State rural credit	100	100	100	100	100
Miscellaneous					
Township	1	1	1	1	1
City and village	59	74	83	87	81
State	40	25	16	11	18

[a] The disproportionate increase in school indebtedness with the corresponding decrease in city and village indebtedness in 1930 is due to the transfer by the city comptroller in Minneapolis of $7,617,923 from the permanent improvement fund to the school debt.

MINNESOTA ASSESSORS[1]

The accompanying tables present findings obtained from a questionnaire sent to all assessors in the state. The object was to ascertain the training, experience, and other qualifications of assessors and the cost of assessment. Replies of 1,482 of the 2,800 assessors yielded the data given below.

Several assessors sent enlightening comments upon their work, and some suggestions were made for improving the assessment procedure. Lack of space makes it impossible to present this material properly, but two phases of the assessors' work were mentioned so frequently that they deserve mention. One was the difficulty in the assessment of money and credits, which was mentioned by 117 assessors. One assessor suggested that a detailed list of all stocks and bonds should be required instead of the lump-sum assessment. Two assessors proposed that any interest or principal on any interest-bearing instrument should be non-collectible unless the instrument bore a stamp showing that it had been listed for taxation. Another assessor suggested that a record of all sales of intangibles be required. One assessor proposed that bank examiners assess money and credits. Forty-four assessors thought their work would be improved if they had access to records of bank deposits. Two recommended exemptions of checking accounts not drawing interest and two others recommended exemption of money and credits up to $500 per person. Seven assessors thought the low rate on intangibles should be increased.

The other matter mentioned most frequently by assessors was the action of the boards of equalization and local boards of review. Two assessors stated that the assessments they had made with regard to true property values were raised 100 per cent. The elimination of local boards of review and submission of equalization between persons to the county board was one improvement advocated. Other suggestions were that the assessors be required to attend meetings of the county board of equalization or that the county boards be present at the assessors' meetings held before assessment. Other assessors suggested establishment of larger assessment districts — the county commissioner's district or the county—which would automatically eliminate petty boards of review. In contrast to this sentiment for more centralized assessment, several assessors insisted on more local autonomy. Boards that equalize assessments are responsible for final valuations. Despite the complaints of assessors, their changes in assessments are not necessarily for the worse, though they may be in some cases.

[1] Compiled by Miss Violet Johnson.

TABLE 1.—OCCUPATIONS OF 1,482 MINNESOTA ASSESSORS, 1931

Occupation	Number
(1) Agricultural	
Farmers	958
Retired farmers	26
Threshers	10
Chicken or truck farmers	22
Farm labor	3
Forestry	2
Total	1,021
(2) Commercial	
Retail business men	8
Secretary of Commerce Club	1
Merchants	45
Oil station	5
Restaurant and pool hall	2
Resort owners	3
Clerks in stores	7
Salesmen	12
Lumber yard managers	4
Theater manager	1
Sawmill operators	9
Pickle factory owners	2
Bus builder	2
Total	101
(3) Dealers in produce, etc.	
Livestock and produce buyers	17
Creamery or cream station managers	5
Millers and grain buyers	18
Total	40
(4) Banking, insurance, real estate	
Insurance	35
Real estate	14
Bankers	7
Auctioneer	2
Surveyor	1
Field man, Rural Credits Bureau	1
Investment securities	1
Farm loans	2
Collection agencies	2
Total	65
(5) Contracting and building	
Contractors	13
Carpenters	36
Cement and stone	5
Electrician	2
Plumber	1
Decorator	2
Total	59
(6) Skilled labor (other than building)	
Skilled labor (not otherwise designated)	1
Tinsmith	1
Blacksmiths	2
Garage mechanics	5
Barbers	6
Undertaker's assistant	1
Well drillers	3
Stationary engineers	3
Total	22
(7) Unskilled labor	
Woodmen	9
Watchman	1
Janitor	4
Odd jobs	3
Road patrol	8
Labor (not designated)	24
Total	49
(8) Clerical	
Switchboard operator	1
Accounting	2
Auditing and bookkeeping	1
City clerk	2
Abstractor	1
Town clerk	1
United States mail service	13
Clerical	2
Total	23
(9) Professional	
Lawyer	1
Minister	1
Teachers	9
Total	11
(10) Public utilities	
Managers of telephone company	4
Railroad service	3
Manager of light plant	1
Total	8
(11) Housewives	12
(12) Miscellaneous	
Commercial fishing	1
Trapper	1
Game warden	1
Superintendent golf course	1
Students	2
Justice of the peace	4
Commissioner of the poor	1
Trucking and dragging	7
Weighmaster	1
Total	19
(13) Not reporting	45
(14) Full-time assessors	7
Grand total (all groups answering inquiry)	1,482

TABLE 2. — FREQUENCY TABLE OF MINNESOTA ASSESSORS' PREVIOUS EXPERIENCE IN ASSESSING, 1931 [a]

YEARS OF EXPERIENCE	NO. OF ASSESSORS	YEARS OF EXPERIENCE	NO. OF ASSESSORS
0	164	25	7
1	100	26	1
2	81	27	2
3	161	28	4
4	76	29	1
5	107	30	5
6	71	31	1
7	80	32	2
8	71	33	1
9	51	34	2
10	53	35	1
11	10	36	..
12	50	37	..
13	27	38	..
14	22	39	..
15	40	40	1
16	24	41	1
17	22	42	..
18	11	43	..
19	9	44	1
20	33	45	..
21	9	46	..
22	12	47	..
23	4	48	..
24	14	49	1
0–9	962	40–49	4
10–19	268		
20–29	87	Total reporting experience	1,333
30–39	12		

Average (mean) experience=7.53 years.
Experience of five years or more in assessing: 751 assessors, 56.34 per cent.
Median experience=5.79 years.

[a] Includes experience as assessor and assistant assessor.

TABLE 3. — FREQUENCY OF VARIOUS AGES AMONG MINNESOTA ASSESSORS

AGE IN YEARS [a]	NO. OF ASSESSORS	AGE IN YEARS [a]	NO. OF ASSESSORS
20	2	60	172
25	32	65	127
30	97	70	65
35	148	75	38
40	154	80	10
45	178		
50	166	Total reporting age	1,364
55	175		

Average (mean) age=49.7 years.
Median age=52 years.

[a] Each year given in this column represents the midpoint of a five-year age group; for example, those reporting ages from 78 to 82 are classed here as 80; those reporting ages from 73 to 77 are listed as 75; and so on.

Relation between property assessed and occupation of assessor.—Tables 4 and 5 present the results of an inquiry as to whether assessors are required to assess property with which they are not familiar. Of 1,195 assessors listing tillable land as one type of property assessed, 956 were engaged in agriculture, 41 in commercial occupations, 12 in clerical work. (See Table 4.) In Table 5 the same facts are presented in another way. It is seen that 80 per cent of the assessors listing tillable land were themselves engaged in agricultural enterprises, whereas only 41.61 per cent of the assessors listing factories were farmers.

TABLE 4.—NUMERICAL DISTRIBUTION OF 1,482 ASSESSORS ACCORDING TO OCCUPATIONS AND KINDS OF PROPERTY ASSESSED BY THEM

Type of Property Assessed	No. of Assessors in Each Occupation														Total Number Reporting Items Named
	Agriculture	Commercial	Livestock, Grain, or Produce Dealers	Banking, Insurance, Real Estate	Contracting and Building	Skilled Labor (Other than Building)	Unskilled Labor	Clerical	Professional	Public Utilities	Housewives	Miscellaneous	Unknown	Full Time	
Tillable land	956	41	22	22	37	8	37	12	7	6	7	9	28	3	1,195
Pasture land	895	39	16	22	36	9	27	12	7	5	8	9	28	3	1,116
Timber land	539	20	5	6	16	4	19	7	6	..	2	7	14	2	647
Cut-over land	422	14	1	2	12	7	15	7	2	2	5	5	7	2	503
Mineral land	4	1	..	1	2	..	..	..	..	..	2	..	1	2	13
Urban lots	180	48	26	32	36	6	16	11	7	8	9	8	27	7	421
Commercial buildings	138	47	27	31	29	3	16	14	6	4	6	8	25	7	361
Factories	67	15	11	16	15	1	5	5	3	3	2	5	7	6	161
Farm buildings	61	4	..	1	..	..	2	1	..	..	..	12	1	..	82

Other buildings	11	3	6	..	5	..	..	..	..	2	1	..	..	..	28
Buildings on railroad right of way	3	4	3	..	1	1	1	2	..	..	1	..	..	..	16
Elevators	32	11	8	5	4	4	3	1	1	1	1	2	4	..	77
Summer homes	13	2	..	..	1	..	2	1	..	..	1	1	2	1	24
Machinery	974	51	29	36	49	10	37	17	6	7	11	12	33	6	1,278
Household goods	954	67	33	45	58	11	42	21	8	10	12	15	41	6	1,323
Livestock	806	23	11	13	23	2	30	8	4	5	4	5	14	1	949
Boats	37	1	1	..	2	..	..	1	..	..	..	1	3	..	46
Signboards	12	3	1	1	3	..	..	..	..	..	1	1	3	..	25
Quarries	6	2	..	..	2	..	..	1	..	..	..	..	..	..	11
Mine machinery	1	..	..	..	..	..	..	..	..	..	..	..	..	1	2
Power plants	15	7	2	..	7	..	1	2	2	1	..	2	4	..	43
Brickyards	..	..	..	..	1	..	..	..	..	..	..	..	..	..	1
Sawmills	15	..	..	..	..	..	..	1	..	..	..	..	..	..	16
Pipe lines	3	..	..	..	..	..	..	..	..	..	..	1	..	..	4
Logs and wood products.......	60	1	1	1	4	1	7	..	2	..	1	2	3	..	83
Farm produce	150	..	2	1	3	..	3	..	..	..	1	2	1	..	163
Banks	9	1	1	..	1	..	1	2	..	..	..	..	1	..	16
Money and credits............	38	4	5	6	..	1	..	..	3	2	..	1	4	2	66
Fur farms	14	2	..	..	2	..	..	2	..	..	..	1	..	..	21
Bees	7	..	..	1	..	..	..	..	..	..	..	..	..	..	8
Iron ore	..	..	..	..	..	..	..	..	..	..	..	..	..	3	3
Firearms	10	..	..	..	..	..	..	..	..	..	..	..	..	..	10
Musical instruments	22	..	..	1	..	..	1	..	..	1	..	..	1	..	26
Merchandise	312	61	32	40	53	9	31	16	7	9	10	12	37	6	635
Total assessors reporting....	1,021	101	40	65	59	22	49	23	11	8	12	19	45	7	1,482
Number of assessment districts containing a city or village	132	51	28	38	35	7	21	12	8	6	7	11	24	7	387

Obviously, many assessors failed to report all the kinds of property assessed, and 45 failed to report their occupations when not engaged in assessing.

Table 5.—Percentage Distribution According to Occupation of Assessors of Various Kinds of Property [a]

Type of Property Assessed	Percentage of Assessors in Each Occupation														Total
	Agriculture	Commercial	Livestock, Grain, or Produce Dealers	Banking, Insurance, Real Estate	Contracting and Building	Skilled Labor (Other Than Building)	Unskilled Labor	Clerical	Professional	Public Utilities	Housewives	Miscellaneous	Unknown	Full Time	
Tillable land	80.00	3.43	1.84	1.84	3.10	.67	3.10	1.00	.59	.50	.59	.75	2.34	.25	100
Pasture land	80.20	3.49	1.43	1.97	3.23	.81	2.42	1.08	.63	.45	.72	.81	2.51	.27	100
Timber land	83.31	3.09	.77	.93	2.47	.62	2.94	1.08	.93	...	.31	1.08	2.16	.31	100
Cut-over land	83.90	2.78	.20	.40	2.39	1.39	2.98	1.39	.40	.40	.99	.99	1.39	.40	100
Mineral land	30.77	7.69	...	7.69	15.38	...	...	...	...	...	15.38	...	7.69	15.38	100
Urban lots	42.76	11.40	6.18	7.60	8.55	1.43	3.80	2.61	1.66	1.90	2.14	1.90	6.41	1.66	100
Commercial buildings	38.12	12.98	7.46	8.56	8.01	.83	4.42	3.87	1.66	1.10	1.66	2.21	6.91	2.21	100
Factories	41.61	9.32	6.83	9.94	9.32	.62	3.11	3.11	1.86	1.86	1.24	3.11	4.35	3.73	100
Farm buildings	74.39	4.88	....	1.22	....	...	2.44	1.22	...	...	...	14.63	1.22	...	100
Other buildings	39.29	10.71	21.43	....	17.86	...	...	...	...	7.14	3.57	...	...	...	100
Buildings on railroad right of way	18.75	25.00	18.75	...	6.25	6.25	6.25	12.50	...	...	6.25	...	...	...	100
Elevators	41.56	14.29	10.39	6.49	5.19	5.19	3.90	1.30	1.30	1.30	1.30	2.60	5.19	...	100
Summer homes	54.17	8.33	...	...	4.17	...	8.33	4.17	...	...	4.17	4.17	8.33	4.17	100

Machinery	76.21	3.99	2.27	2.82	3.83	.78	2.90	1.33	.47	.55	.86	.94	2.58	.47	100
Household goods	72.11	5.06	2.49	3.40	4.38	.83	3.17	1.59	.60	.76	.91	1.13	3.10	.45	100
Livestock	84.93	2.42	1.16	1.37	2.42	.21	3.16	.84	.42	.53	.42	.53	1.48	.11	100
Boats	80.43	2.17	2.17	...	4.35	...	...	2.17	...	...	...	2.17	6.52	...	100
Signboards	48.00	12.00	4.00	4.00	12.00	...	...	...	...	...	4.00	4.00	12.00	...	100
Quarries	54.55	18.18	...	...	18.18	...	...	9.09	...	...	...	...	...	...	100
Mine machinery	50.00	....	...	...	....	...	...	...	...	...	...	...	...	50.00	100
Power plants	34.88	16.28	4.65	...	16.28	...	2.33	4.65	4.65	2.33	...	4.65	9.30	...	100
Brickyard	....	...	...	...	100.00[b]	...	...	...	...	...	...	...	...	...	100
Sawmills	93.75	...	...	...	...	...	...	6.25	...	...	...	...	...	...	100
Pipe lines	75.00	...	...	...	...	...	...	...	...	...	...	25.00	...	...	100
Logs and wood products	72.29	1.20	1.20	1.20	4.82	1.20	8.43	...	2.41	...	1.20	2.41	3.61	...	100
Farm produce	92.02	...	1.23	.61	1.84	...	1.84	...	...	...	.61	1.23	.61	...	100
Banks	56.25	6.25	6.25	...	6.25	...	6.25	12.50	...	...	...	...	6.25	...	100
Money and credits	57.58	6.06	7.58	9.09	...	1.52	...	...	4.55	3.03	...	1.52	6.06	3.03	100
Fur farms	66.67	9.52	...	...	9.52	...	...	9.52	...	...	...	4.76	...	...	100
Bees	87.50	...	...	12.50	...	...	...	...	...	...	...	...	...	...	100
Iron ore	....	...	...	...	...	...	...	...	...	...	...	...	...	100.00	100
Firearms	100.00	...	...	...	...	...	...	...	...	...	...	...	...	...	100
Musical instruments	84.62	...	...	3.85	...	...	3.85	...	...	3.85	...	...	3.85	...	100
Merchandise	49.13	9.61	5.04	6.30	8.35	1.42	4.88	2.52	1.10	1.42	1.57	1.89	5.83	.94	100
Percentage of assessors reporting	68.89	6.82	2.70	4.39	3.98	1.48	3.31	1.69	.74	.67	.81	1.28	2.77	.47	100
Percentage of assessment districts containing a city or village	34.11	13.18	7.24	9.82	9.04	1.81	5.43	3.10	2.07	1.55	1.81	2.84	6.20	1.81	100

[a] See the footnote to the preceding table. [b] Only one.

TABLE 6.—RELATION BETWEEN COST OF ASSESSMENT AND ASSESSED VALUATION OF DISTRICT [a]

Ratio of Cost of Assessment to Total Valuation	No. of Districts with Costs Indicated	Ratio of Cost of Assessment to Total Valuation	No. of Districts with Costs Indicated
Mills		Mills	
.000– .249	149	2.500–2.749	3
.250– .499	213	2.750–2.999	2
.500– .749	90	3.000–3.249	1
.750– .999	31	3.250–3.499	..
1.000–1.249	18	3.500–3.749	..
1.250–1.499	15	3.750–3.999	..
1.500–1.749	7	4.000–4.249	1
1.750–1.999	5		
2.000–2.249	2	Total	540
2.250–2.499	3		

[a] Data on costs are not available for most assessment districts. It will be noted in all these tables that not all assessors answered all questions. The tabulation in each case is based on the number supplying the information tabulated.

In 24 assessment districts the ratio of the assessment cost to the total valuation is greater than 1.5 mills. The valuation in each of these districts is far below the median valuation. The district in which the ratio of assessment cost to valuation is highest has the lowest valuation of all districts. The median valuation is $382,000.

TABLE 7.—VALUATIONS OF HIGH-COST ASSESSMENT DISTRICTS

District	Valuation	District	Valuation
Beltrami County		Koochiching County	
Moose Lake	$54,456	Evergreen	$41,830
Turtle River	8,633	Lake County	
Nebish	84,129	Beaver Bay	163,956
Solway	23,004	Lake of the Woods County	
Alaska	63,579	Unorganized No. 1	37,635
Sugar Bush	44,341	Rock County	
Carlton County		Jasper	63,615
Perch Lake	58,795	St. Louis County	
Cass County		Clinton	94,236
Woodrow	92,338	Lake Vermillion	43,445
Hackensack	39,187	Calvin	60,629
Boy River Township	65,471	Floodwood	74,602
Rogers	43,395	Stoney Brook	39,235
Itasca County		Swift County	
Wirt	30,233	DeGraff	57,104
Pomroy	23,585		
Unorganized No. 5	112,057		

Table 8.—Relation between Cost of Assessment and Valuation of District

Valuation of Districts and Number in Each Group

Cost of Assessment in Mills	Under $100,000	$100,000–$200,000	$200,000–$300,000	$300,000–$400,000	$400,000–$500,000	$500,000–$600,000	$600,000–$700,000	$700,000–$800,000	$800,000–$900,000	$900,000–$1,000,000	$1,000,000–$1,100,000	$1,100,000–$1,200,000	Over $1,200,000	No. of Districts
.00– .249	1	3	2	4	11	9	21	25	37	9	2	4	21	149
.25– .499	9	30	31	36	35	19	17	14	5	2	3	2	10	213
.50– .749	18	41	16	9	3	..	..	..	..	1	..	1	..	89
.75– .999	16	13	1	1	..	..	..	..	..	..	..	..	..	31
1.00–1.249	10	7	1	..	..	..	..	..	..	..	..	..	..	18
1.25–1.499	13	1	1	..	..	..	..	..	..	..	..	..	..	15
1.50–1.749	4	3	..	..	..	..	..	..	..	..	..	..	..	7
1.75–1.999	5	1	..	..	..	..	..	..	..	..	..	..	..	6
2.00–2.249	2	..	..	..	..	..	..	..	..	..	..	..	..	2
2.25–2.499	3	..	..	..	..	..	..	..	..	..	..	..	..	3
2.50–2.749	3	..	..	..	..	..	..	..	..	..	..	..	..	3
2.75–2.999	1	1	..	..	..	..	..	..	..	..	..	..	..	2
3.00–3.249	1	..	..	..	..	..	..	..	..	..	..	..	..	1
4.00	1	..	..	..	..	..	..	..	..	..	..	..	..	1
Total	87	100	52	50	49	28	38	39	42	12	5	7	31	540
Average assessment cost in mills	1.17	.67	.48	.41	.41	.29	.24	.21	.16	.21	.17	.27	.21	

INDEX

Made in the USA
Las Vegas, NV
26 October 2025

33075840R00352